MW00806792

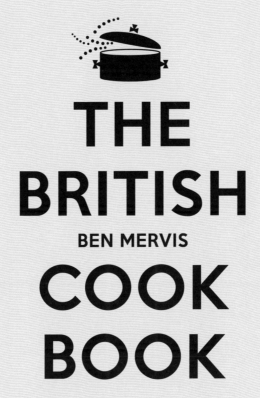

THE

BRITISH

BEN MERVIS

COOK

BOOK

THE
BRITISH

BEN MERVIS

COOK
BOOK

PHOTOGRAPHY BY SAM A HARRIS

VEGETARIAN

ONE-POT

VEGAN

5 INGREDIENTS OR LESS

GLUTEN-FREE

30 MINUTES OR LESS

NUT-FREE

DAIRY-FREE

MAP
OF
THE UK

To the right, you'll find a map of the United Kingdom and constituent countries labelled with cities, (numbered) counties and (official) major regions. As you read through the recipes in this book, you'll find that each lists an associated region or locality. With so many recipes included, it's easy to get lost in unfamiliar place names, and so this map will help you find your bearings.

SCOTLAND

1 Western Isles
2 Orkney
3 Shetland
4 Highland
5 Moray
6 Aberdeenshire
7 Aberdeen City
8 Angus
9 Dundee City
10 Perth & Kinross
11 Fife
12 Clackmannanshire
13 Stirling
14 Argyll & Bute
15 West Dunbartonshire
16 East Dunbartonshire
17 Inverclyde
18 Renfrewshire
19 East Renfrewshire
20 North Ayrshire
21 South Ayrshire
22 East Ayrshire
23 South Lanarkshire
24 Glasgow City
25 North Lanarkshire
26 Falkirk
27 West Lothian
28 City of Edinburgh
29 Midlothian
30 East Lothian
31 Borders
32 Dumfries & Galloway

ENGLAND

33 Northumberland
34 Cumbria
35 Tyne & Wear
36 Durham
37 North Yorkshire
38 Lancashire
39 Merseyside
40 Greater Manchester
41 West Yorkshire
42 East Riding of Yorkshire
43 South Yorkshire
44 Cheshire
45 Derbyshire
46 Nottinghamshire
47 Lincolnshire
48 Rutland
49 Leicestershire
50 Staffordshire
51 Shropshire
52 Herefordshire
53 Worcestershire
54 West Midlands
55 Warwickshire
56 Northamptonshire
57 Cambridgeshire
58 Norfolk
59 Suffolk
60 Essex
61 Hertfordshire
62 Bedfordshire
63 Buckinghamshire
64 Oxfordshire
65 Gloucestershire
66 Bristol
67 Wiltshire
68 Berkshire
69 Greater London
70 City of London
71 Kent
72 East Sussex
73 West Sussex
74 Surrey
75 Hampshire
76 Isle of Wight
77 Dorset
78 Somerset
79 Devon
80 Cornwall

WALES

81 Isle of Anglesey
82 Gwynedd
83 Conwy
84 Denbighshire
85 Flintshire
86 Wrexham
87 Powys
88 Ceredigion
89 Pembrokeshire
90 Carmarthenshire
91 Swansea
92 Neath Port Talbot
93 Bridgend
94 Vale of Glamorgan
95 Rhondda Cynon Taff
96 Merthyr Tydfil
97 Caerphilly
98 Cardiff
99 Newport
100 Torfaen
101 Blaenau Gwent
102 Monmouthshire

NORTHERN IRELAND

103 Antrim
104 Down
105 Armagh
106 Fermanagh
107 Tyrone
108 Londonderry

FOREWORD

There has been a book written on British cooking for each new generation for centuries. These are books written by people with wonderful voices and a sound understanding of the job in hand – to encourage cookery. There are voices from the middle of the nineteenth century and beyond, such as Eliza Acton and Mrs Beeton; Mrs Leyel and Constance Spry; Elizabeth David, Jane Grigson and Arabella Boxer; onto Jennifer Paterson and Clarissa Dickson Wright. Ladies who have flown the flag for butter and dipping a finger – with nail painted a racing-car red – into a pot of cream.

These are but a few who have written large of the subject and pleased mightily doing so. Ben Mervis joins this distinguished crew, picking up the torch for British cooking in this beautifully researched book.

When considering what is best about British cooking – or indeed any cooking – I always conclude that good ingredients, as fresh as can be, simply prepared, served at the height of their season, make for estimable eating.

I return often to the memory of a lunch enjoyed on a summer's day at a table laid in the sunshine. On the table sits a pot of melted butter. And on its way over, in the hands of a cook, is a dish of asparagus picked only minutes before from a bed in view of the diners. It has been rinsed lightly and popped into a waiting pan of boiling water. Once cooked, only a plate, a little sea salt and the aforementioned butter is required.

There were many dishes at that delightful gathering, each as good as the previous one served. I particularly recall a joyous pile of sun-ripened strawberries, just picked, dipped in a bowl of Jersey cream dusted lightly with sugar.

Such dishes are as appealing as they are near endless, thanks to the abundance of ingredients with which these islands abound. Langoustines from the Hebrides are served with mayonnaise; smoked fish and potted foods on an extraordinary array of sourdough breads from established and new bakeries that appear with uncurbed enthusiasm. There are crabs and cuttlefish of every size the length of the coast. Farmhouse cheeses to gooseberries to pumpkins to pears to cobnuts. Such produce delights in the seasons, biding its time until the calendar strikes at the allotted hour.

And with such produce, there is cooking too, of course. Wonderful pies and puddings, roasts and game, hams, bacon and sausages, braises and pot roasts, all manner of soups, and salads too. Trifles, tarts, crumbles, custards and creams, and so many other lovely things. When cherished by the home cook, this cuisine can flourish, where so often it is reduced to a shadow of its true self in the clutches of industry and mass production.

All too often has simplicity been swept aside in the wild adventures of modernity and whatever is 'le cooking de nos jours'. Whichever age or generation the cook might consider, one thing is certain: it is rarely, if ever, the magnificence of fanciful creation that lasts through time. Rather, it is the memory of an apple pie or strawberry tart that proves rare and elusive beyond the domain of the home kitchen.

This book celebrates all that is good in the rich traditions of regional and seasonal cooking in the British Isles, which, brilliantly, is as relevant today as it ever was.

Jeremy Lee
Chef Proprietor, Quo Vadis

WHAT IS 'BRITISH FOOD'?

What I find so weird and wonderful about British food is that it is simultaneously adored and derided.

Imagine for a moment that you're sitting down to your dream meal: something of real comfort, tinged with nostalgia. A steak pie with gravy and buttery mash. A hearty stew with dumplings. A roast chicken with greens. A trolley of puddings with custard, or even something warm and cheesy like a Welsh rarebit. Of course, these are all hallmarks of the British kitchen, but I imagine many people conjuring up this dream meal would also deny to the death that British food could be among their favourites. Besides me, of course. I have no trouble acknowledging that this sort of food gives me a pleasure unlike any other.

It was this love for British cooking that motivated me to write and compile this book. British food has long faced undue derision and a lack of celebration in the mainstream press. This book is an attempt to address some of those issues by understanding and contextualizing what Jane Grigson calls the 'inheritance' of British cooking through its diverse regionality. The distinct, sometimes obscure, yet often beloved recipes that characterize British regional cooking are often left out of a compendium such as this. This book presents a broad selection of recipes that cut across time, class and culture. Each is enticing in its own way.

British food is defined by its natural larder and the abundances and limitations of its landscape. Foundational differences in traditional culinary diversity are for the most part defined by the grain(s) that grew best in the ground, the types of animals that trod the earth, and the regional climatic conditions. This is why you'll see so much overlap between the food cultures of northern England, Wales and Scotland. These regions are characterized by wet upland terrain that's best suited to growing oats and barley and cooking breads and cakes on a griddle. In stark contrast, wheat is much easier to grow in southern England, with more arable land and a warmer, drier climate. Northern Ireland sits with a foot in both camps.

Although the label 'British food' is useful, it's important to understand that this is not a neatly unified cuisine. There are many similarities in the culinary legacies of the UK's composite countries (England, Scotland, Wales and Northern Ireland), but an equal (if not greater) number of ways in which they differ. Even the regions within each country vary in terms of tastes, traditions and techniques – many of which have been obscured by both time and trend.

A common thread drawn through much of European peasant-led cooking is the embrace of whole foods. In the case of British cooking that means three things especially. First, the whole animal; literally the use of all parts, from nose to tail. Second, the whole grain, either cooked in stews or milled as flour, with every bit of meal extracted from the chaff. And finally, a robust dairy tradition, using the milk and cream for a multitude of purposes, at various stages throughout the year, for everything from butter ('sweet', salted, whey or clotted cream) to fresh and hard cheeses made from full-fat (whole) or skimmed milk. These elements have been true to Britain for centuries, if not millennia, and with respect to the natural larder of the landscape, provide the foundation of traditional British food.

Today, farmers can overcome obstacles that once shackled their ancestors to growing certain crops. You can find excellent fruit and vegetables grown all across the UK, from Yorkshire's forced rhubarb and West Country apples to Shetland kale and Lincolnshire's yellow peas.

To rave about British produce is to extol the virtues of its superlative fish and shellfish, the many excellent heritage breeds – which, like Tamworth pigs or Aberdeen-Angus cattle, take their name from their locality – as well as the equally numerous and diverse varieties of dairy products and cheese; the peerless selection and quality of wild game and game birds; the bountiful foraged mushrooms and nuts, farmed and wild soft and stone (pit) fruit. And yes, it's true, root vegetables, pulses (beans) and legumes, which are near-essential and, thankfully, in great abundance.

This is an area that was wonderfully captured in *Traditional Foods of Britain: A Regional Inventory* (Laura Mason with Catherine Brown, 1999), financed by the Euro-Terroirs, a project of the European Union in the mid-1990s. *Traditional Foods* is incredibly thorough and details much of the best heritage foods grown (and animals bred) here in the UK.

The chapters of *The British Cookbook* are built around the classic dishes and produce that demonstrate the natural strengths of British cuisine. It follows then that chapters on fish, meat, hearty soups and stews, and all manner of baked pastries and puddings are all especially fulsome. It is for the same reason that the book is threadbare on salads and, you might notice, recipes involving mushrooms – a rather curious thing, since some of the most amazing wild mushrooms are found in the UK. Despite understanding the wealth of wild foods on their doorsteps, these ingredients rarely made it into home recipes.

HISTORY & LARDER

The heart of this island nation's food culture has been largely shaped from the outside. The foods and animals often considered 'native' were predominantly brought here by someone – migrants or invaders.

The earliest roots of Britain's culinary tradition can be traced to the arrival of Neolithic settlers several thousand years ago. Crossing a now-long-gone land-bridge between southeast England and the Benelux region, they brought domesticated animals and a knowledge of cultivating grain. As these people settled and cleared land to grow the first of Britain's cereals, such as emmer wheat and barley, they also created open land for their cattle – and especially sheep – to thrive. They hunted and trapped on land, and in summer they waded out into the water and caught both fresh fish and shellfish. Throughout the seasons they foraged wild plants and seaweeds, berries such as bilberries and brambles, and collected hazelnuts. We can see a glimmer of them in ourselves.

Some 3,000 years ago, the Celts began to settle in Britain. They had already developed a rich tradition of making and preserving butter with salt, and used the application of salt for preserving meat and fish, as well. To Britain they brought species of domesticated fowl – ducks and geese, especially – and could also preserve these meats, as well as those of their cattle or wild game, through salting. Their interest in dairy products led them to make fresh cheeses by separating the curds and whey of naturally soured milk. In time, either through accident or osmosis, they also learned that rennet – a set of enzymes found in the stomach bag of calves – could develop solid cheeses that were both long-lasting and flavourful. They continued to harvest grains such as wheat and barley, although oats and rye had likely arrived in Britain by this point as well.

The Roman conquest, and the subsequent three centuries of governance, introduced a trove of new vegetables – literally dozens of new foods and plants, including onions, garlic, turnips, apples, pears, celery, carrots, asparagus, leeks, peas, plums, chestnuts and lettuce, and plenty of kitchen herbs such as rosemary and bay leaves. The Romans also used a fermented fish sauce, called garum, to flavour dishes. While the Roman garum died out in Britain, the modern Worcestershire sauce – itself a fermented fish (anchovy) sauce – serves a similar purpose in today's kitchen.

After the fall of Rome, the Anglo-Saxons brought milk puddings and mead. Two hundred years later, the Danes began to raid large swaths of eastern England, ruling it for nearly a century and imparting some of their own traditions. One such food, the havercake, has lasted to this day. Far to the north, Scotland's most remote islands were settled by the Norse, and ruled by them for several hundred years. Their cultural presence was felt even more deeply, and a form of Old Norse, called Norn, was spoken into the mid-1800s. Many words in the local Shetland and Orkney dialects come from Norn and Norse influence.

In England, the eleventh-century Norman invasion established the elites of society as great lovers of meat. But their contributions to food culture were more significant in sociolinguistic terms: the words for meat from butchered cows, pigs, sheep and deer – beef, pork, mutton and venison – all come from Old French; our names for the animals themselves from Old English.

A century later, the Crusades, trade links and travel established a desire for spices and dried fruits and nuts from the east. The finest kitchens made liberal use of ginger, black pepper, nutmeg and mace, caraway, cinnamon, cloves, cumin, galangal (a cousin to ginger), mustard and grains of paradise (related to cardamom). The many variations of British gingerbread, and the Eccles cake's sweet-spiced filling, descend from the traditions of this era.

The lavishness and spectacle of royal court dining culture was a stark contrast to the diet of many Britons, who, if they were lucky enough, ate a form of pottage – a thick stew made with whatever grain, meat and vegetables were in season – along with wheaten bread, barley bread or oatcakes and butter. Those lower down might be forced to regularly sup on thin uncooked gruel or a 'soup' made from stale bread. There is little to glamorize about such diets.

From the early seventeenth century, Britain started to accumulate economic and territorial footholds in the Americas, the Caribbean and India through conquest and colonization.

Throughout the eighteenth and nineteenth centuries, territorial expansion, fuelled in major part by trade and commercial interests, rapidly ramped up. The empire sprawled and profited massively. Sugar, tea, liquor, wheat flour and spices became widely available to the average Briton. Yet these rich rewards came at the cost of mass-exploitation and slave labour, if not outright warfare and death. The inhumane conditions of the sugar plantations of the West Indies resulted in a seven-year life expectancy for those forced to work there. Even the Slavery Abolition Act in 1833 didn't stop Britain from profiting from systems of slavery through trade or finance. At the height of its power, the British Empire ruled over nearly a quarter of the world's population, and an equal percentage of its land area. Neither the end of slavery nor the end of imperialism meant the end of white supremacy within the new British Commonwealth.

Over the course of the late eighteenth and early nineteenth centuries a series of rapid technological advancements saw the kitchen set-up evolve from the open hearth to a closed oven and stove range. By the early twentieth century, most homes – especially in cities and towns – were fitted with an oven range and stovetop which made the cooking of most of the recipes in this book much easier and certainly more straightforward. Some skilled cooks bemoaned the consolidation of kitchen equipment, however, with Dorothy Hartley, author of *Food in England* (1954), describing the modern stove as a 'comprehensive ghost-house of accumulated experience'; no doubt it required less knowledge and expertise from the home cook.

The overlapping agricultural and industrial revolutions of the late eighteenth and nineteenth centuries transformed the British landscape (both literally and figuratively) and kitchen. Many of the recipes set out in this book were invented over the same period of time, as access to certain foods (once luxuries) bolstered the domestic pantry. Innovations of the agricultural revolution – chief among them the advent of winter feed for cattle and the implementation of crop rotation – meant that herds of cattle could be kept through the winter, and that the growing potential of wheat was improved – thus giving access to wheat flour for bread and pastry. But the agricultural revolution also exacerbated the seizure of communal grazing lands through enclosure acts, which transferred the public lands into private hands. The Inclosure (sic) Act of 1773 made agrarian lifestyles much more difficult to sustain and thousands left farms and villages in favour of working in factories in big cities, where poverty and poor diet were rampant problems.

The invention of the steam engine, and subsequent construction of national railway lines, meant greater accessibility of fresh meat and dairy all over the country, but especially in big cities. For centuries drovers had marched cattle hundreds of miles to slaughter at markets. Now they could butcher the meat locally, when the animals were fatter, meaning more meat and more profit.

At much the same time, all across the Scottish Highlands, clan chiefs and wealthy landowners cleared thousands of tenants off their lands, erasing centuries of tradition and culture to give more room to grazing sheep. The Highlands were brutally de-settled in favour of the few, and many customs were lost as thousands died destitute or fell into abject poverty. Many moved to the fishing villages of the east coast, large cities down south, or emigrated overseas to the US, Canada, Australia and New Zealand.

Foreigners had settled in the UK for centuries, but the nineteenth century brought successive larger waves of immigration. From the mid-nineteenth century, Italians arrived, hailing from poverty-stricken regions in the mountainous north of the country. Those numbers increased after Italian unification in 1861, and by the outbreak of World War I there were sizable Italian communities in England and Scotland – with much of the latter's population employed in ice cream or fish and chip shops. It took over a century for Italian food to be embraced in a way we would understand today. Although mentioned in passing by Mrs Beeton in 1861, olive oil was popularized in the UK through a recommendation by celebrated food writer Elizabeth

David in 1950. But readers wouldn't find olive oil while doing their food shopping; they'd need to make a separate trek to a chemist (pharmacy). Pizza and pasta were popularized roughly a decade later, the former thanks in large part to the Pizza Express chain set up in Soho, London, in 1965.

Rationing prompted by the UK's 1939 entry into World War II had a significant impact on its food culture. Rationing measures lasted, in some part, until 1954. This means that only a small percentage of Britain's retirement-age population will remember growing up without restrictions on what they ate. All Britons lived and cooked with much the same limitations for a decade and a half. These restrictions were on popular foods like bacon, sugar, tea, meat, cheese and all manner of cooking fats (as low as 60 g/ 2¼ oz/ ½ stick of butter per week). Despite the strains on home kitchens, wartime recipes gave rise to a style of cooking less reliant on butter and sugar: the most famous example being the humble apple crumble.

After the war, the UK's immigration policies opened up. The year 1948 was a watershed for entry into the UK as the country enacted legislation that allowed citizens of the British Commonwealth (former empire) to migrate to Britain, thus spurring mass immigration from Commonwealth countries around the world. However, little more than a decade later, in 1962, the British government tightened its immigration policies once again with the Commonwealth Immigrants Act.

Many new immigrants who made it to the UK settled in large cities and found jobs in hospitality, offering Britain a taste of something new. The food they cooked was just as much defined by the tastes of home as it was by the British consumer's palate and the ingredients that were available to them. As a result, many recipes traditional to other cuisines were significantly adapted to life in the UK. Plenty of these dishes have become new favourites of the British canon: from India, Pakistan and Bangladesh came the tikka masala and the balti. The Windrush generation, named after the ship Empire Windrush, which

carried much-needed workers from the Caribbean to England in 1948, brought Caribbean cuisines – roti, curried goat and patties – which already bore the hallmarks of Britain's cross-continental empire. Meanwhile, the ethnic Chinese from Malaysia (Nyonya) and immigrants from Hong Kong began to open restaurants, adapting new recognizably British dishes such as prawn (shrimp) toast and salt and chilli chicken. In the last few decades, the British public has sought to know – and taste – more of the incredible cuisines that have overlapped here in the UK, offering us an exciting glimpse at the multicultural future of British food.

HOW THIS BOOK CAME TOGETHER

I have spent the formative years of my life living as an outsider in the UK. Arriving first as an impressionable international student, I became enamoured with the freshness of British culture, and took to it quickly. I didn't understand the significance until much later, but my first feelings of cultural immersion came from that period. On so many Sunday mornings, after very late nights, I'd make my way – bleary-eyed – to a local café and order what I craved most. Unpacking the brown paper bag, I'd drag out a crisp buttered roll filled with griddled back bacon and finished with a few liberal squirts of ketchup. I'd bring a milky tea – a touch too sweet – to my mouth. This was my salvation, and my Proustian moment.

As a student of British history, I fell for traditional elements of culture and lamented the fact that they were often taken for granted. In my personal life, I simultaneously developed a passion for food, which took me from London to Copenhagen, Sydney to Seoul, and Istanbul to Tbilisi. Later, settling in the UK as a professional food writer and researcher, I developed my focus on traditional British foods as the natural convergence of my personal, professional and academic interests. It meant that dinner – and pudding, naturally – became a truly complete experience.

There was ritual-like calm to slowly making my way through a sausage roll, spreading English mustard over each bite. An unrestrained joy at serving up packed plates at a Sunday roast, as if Christmas came every week. I anointed Welsh rarebit with Worcestershire sauce. There were hot cross buns lathered with butter and marmalade… and with the leftover buns: the best of bread-and-butter puddings. Dining loch-side, I ate my weight in fresh fish, oysters and langoustines. And to close out each meal, pudding: from steamed syrup sponge to the cool red fruit of a summer pudding, and the gentle wobble of a custard tart. I took great comfort in the simple pleasures of British food.

Readers flicking through this book will recognize recipes, but many will be foreign to them. In some cases, the dish itself is familiar but its history – or even its Britishness – is not. There are cases where the recipe travelled across cultures, and is shared by many nations: this includes plenty of dishes, from scouse to pancakes, and skate wings with black butter to numerous puddings and pickles. An equal number of recipes in this book were created in former British-ruled regions, such as India, only to find new life when they were replicated in the seventeenth and eighteenth centuries by returning Britons. Long before battered fish and chips, Brits whipped up their own versions of kedgeree and cooked fruity curries from left-over roasts. The overlapping of culinary traditions is nothing new. Moreover, tradition is neither static nor unchanging – British food has been shaped for millennia by trade, religion, migration, conquest and plenty more besides.

I spent several years researching this book, reading, travelling and eating the length and breadth of the UK. A work like this is an inherently ambitious undertaking, but it is by no means the first of its kind. In the last forty years or so several publications have offered a similar purview, giving a comprehensive overview of British cooking through a sort of inventory of recipes. Although they all took different routes, each is a resource of staggering depth in its own right: *British Cooking* (Caroline Conran, 1978), *British Cookery* (edited by Lizzie Boyd, 1979), *Farmhouse Cookery* (Readers Digest, 1980), *The Observer Guide to British Cookery* (Jane Grigson,

1984), *Traditional Foods of Britain* (Laura Mason & Catherine Brown, 1999) and *British Regional Food* (Mark Hix, 2006), to name just a few. Many more books have tackled individual regions: the cooking of England, Scotland and Wales in particular, and to a lesser extent Northern Ireland. Some of the best books in this grouping include regional recipe books from the many local branches of the Women's Institute (in England, Wales and Northern Ireland) and the Scottish Rural Women's Institute: *Good Things in England* (Florence White, 1932), *English Food* (Jane Grigson, 1974), *The Scots Kitchen* (F. Marian McNeill, 1929), *Scottish Cookery* (Catherine Brown, 1985), *Food in England* (Dorothy Hartley, 1954), *Welsh Fare* (S. Minwell Tibbott, 1976), *First Catch Your Peacock* (Bobby Freeman, 1980). Dozens more excellent volumes have concerned themselves with singular aspects of British cookery, such as *English Bread and Yeast Cookery* (Elizabeth David, 1977), *Classic Game Cookery* (Julia Drysdale, 1975), *English Seafood Cookery* (Rick Stein, 1988) or *Oats in the North, Wheat from the South* (Regula Ysewijn, 2020). Finally, popular cookbooks from more contemporary chefs (and TV chefs) such as Gary Rhodes, Delia Smith, Tom Kerridge and Hugh Fearnley-Whittingstall, and restaurants including St. JOHN, The Sportsman and The Quality Chop House, have expanded the genre of British cookery books, and offer the chef's twist on familiar recipes.

Deep down a rabbit hole of traditional British cookbooks that spanned four centuries, insightful social histories, and food writing from the last several decades, I made a preliminary list of around 1,500 recipes that represented recipes of distinction from every determinable region of the UK. I consulted with food historians, writers and chefs from England, Scotland, Wales and Northern Ireland on the recipes that best represented local traditions. With help from these regional experts, the lists were refined and balanced.

Most of the recipes in this book were cooked over several generations, and are found in numerous sources across centuries. Others underscore interesting cultural and historical insights, long-running and well-loved traditions, or unique ingredients

or techniques. Plenty more were originally created abroad and then adapted to local tastes and adopted into the canon of British cooking across a generation or two. The recipes themselves came from dozens of generous contributors – food writers, chefs, bakers and home cooks. Chief among those contributors was Dr Neil Buttery, British food historian and cook, without whom this undertaking would simply not have been possible. Dr Buttery and I worked on creating or compiling many of the recipes in this book.

I have introduced each of the recipes with as much of its historical and cultural significance, and tips on serving, as space permits. In my humble opinion, that context is one of the strong points of this book and makes it a worthy reference point for recipes and histories alike. If a dish has any strong regional associations (or clear points of origin), that will be clearly marked at the start of the recipe – if not, it will simply state 'United Kingdom'. Determining association was not always a straightforward process, and many dishes originated in one region but have since become popular elsewhere. For that reason, try not to see this as what region the dish 'belongs' to, but where it's most likely to be found.

My ultimate wish for this book is that it serves as the first port of call for those individuals, both chefs and home cooks, who are looking to explore British food – whether they use this book for inspiration, recipe reference and cooking, or to learn the origin and history of particular dishes.

As you read, consider this book to be just a snapshot of a moment in time: tradition is really just slow-reeled innovation.

Whenever you're ready, dig in and enjoy.

Ben Mervis

Glasgow, March 2022

WITH THANKS

This book was made possible through the hard work, generosity and guidance of so many talented and highly knowledgeable individuals.

I am indebted to Sam Harris for the incredible energy and imagery he's created for this book, as well as to Rosie Mackean and Florence Blair for the cooking and styling, which helped bring the dishes to life so vividly. Thank you as well to Jeremy Lee for the wonderful foreword, which so brilliantly sets the scene for the book.

All the recipes in this book were contributed by others: by cooks, bakers, food writers and enthusiasts from across the country. This is as much their book as anyone else's. A very special thanks goes first to Dr Neil Buttery, a cook and scholar of boundless knowledge and enthusiasm, whose own body of recipes form a significant chunk of this book. Neil, this couldn't have been done without you.

Further thanks to Monisha Bharadwaj, Gilli Davies, Nichola Fletcher, Elisabeth Luard, Keshia Sakarah and Sumayya Usmani, who all advised and consulted on recipes and the balance of dishes. In many cases, they also contributed their own recipes, which helped to provide depth and balance to this book.

I am very grateful for the significant recipe contributions from Marian Armitage (with thanks to *The Shetland Times* for allowing us to include recipes from her book *Shetland Food and Cooking*), Leonora Belcher, Pamela Brunton, Erchen Chang, Justin Cherry, Shing Tat Chung, Michael Craig, James Ferguson, Karl Goward, Kate Hamblin, Blair Hammond, Calvin Holohan, Matthew Hook, Sarah Lemanski, Julie Lin, Andrew Lowkes, Anna Luntley, Sam Luntley, Peter McKenna, Joris Minne, James Murray, Alex Nietsvouri, Mirko Pelosi, Richard Phillips, Grant Reekie, Scott Smith, Gareth Storey, Will Verdino and Andrew Whitley. Catherine Brown, Tom Harris, Diana Henry and Laura Mason have also been a wonderful help in understanding and unpacking the legacy of British food. Laura sadly passed away during the course of writing this book, and I would love for this book to commemorate and honour someone who wrote so many excellent books on British food.

The writing and research behind this book took me several years from start to finish, and I have gotten here thanks to the support of my family and friends. Special thanks to Karin Brims, Josh Evans, Howie Kahn, Kate Lewin, Esther McLaughlin, May Rosenthal Sloan and Kanyakrit Vongkiatkajorn.

I'd also like to thank my editor, Rachel Malig, and the whole team at Phaidon, including Ellie Smith and creative director Julia Hasting for sharing my vision of the book, as well as Emilia Terragni for taking a chance on this enthusiastic ex-pat.

Finally, most importantly, to you the reader for picking this book up. I hope that we can one day share a meal together!

All the best,

Ben Mervis

> BY AND LARGE, THE BEST ACCOMPANIMENTS OF EGGS,
> HOWEVER YOU COOK THEM, ARE SEA SALT, FRESHLY
> GROUND BLACK PEPPER, GOOD SALTY BUTTER, CREAM AND
> GOOD BREAD – OR TOAST MADE FROM GOOD BREAD.
>
> JANE GRIGSON, ENGLISH FOOD, 1974

The heart and soul of British cooking. You'd be hard pressed to imagine a more complementary combination than eggs and dairy. From the frying pan or skillet to the pudding basin (bowl), a ready supply of fresh eggs and a pantry well stocked with milk, cream and cheese, you're well on your way to a very fine meal. While elsewhere in this book these ingredients play the role of essential supporting cast, here they act as the main star.

DAIRY

Our great love of dairy begins with a seemingly simple but highly technical act: milking. It seems too obvious to state, but the process gives us everything we need: first there is rich, fatty milk, imparted with its own flavour from the animal's feed (a strange but impactful effect) and time of year. Then from the milk: cream and cheese and butter, with residual ingredients such as whey (separated from the cheese curds) and buttermilk (from the butter, naturally). To the traditional home kitchen these are each special ingredients to be fully understood and utilized.

In rural cottage kitchens, cheeses were made from skimmed or unskimmed milk. The cheeses were then set with rennet (or later, an acidic mixture) and mixed with butter or cream and eaten fresh at the farmhouse, or matured into the sort of hard cheeses that have become emblematic of the British dairy. In recent years there has been a real reawakening and revitalization of British cheesemaking: now you'll find crowds of shoppers looking for everything from Cornish yarg, Montgomery Cheddar and Tunworth (itself a 'new' version of the famous French Camembert). In that time, as well, there has been a return to sheep's milk cheeses.

Cream can, and often should, be served as is, rich and thick (with a high fat content), or, blessedly, made even more indulgent through slow cooking, as in the famous clotted creams of England's southwest.

For butter, beyond the typical salted, semi- and unsalted variants, there are also clotted cream and whey butter, made with their respective ingredients – the latter being more tangy and almost cheesy. When possible, opt for something local and organic, but don't shy away from the salted stuff. Salted butter is a perfect partner to a good many spiced buns or fruited cakes.

EGGS

For much of British history, eggs would have been included in kind as part of the rent due to landowners, and were thus uncommon to everyday cooking. Now, perhaps, we take them for granted. But how many foods can rival the egg in as many excellent and varied preparations? In this chapter we count the ways: a soft-boiled egg with a sprinkling of sea salt is something simple but divine. Fried in butter or bacon fat until the edges are brown and crispy. Hard-boiled, coarsely chopped and mixed through with mayonnaise, mustard and cress to become a winning sandwich. Soft and richly scrambled piled onto buttered toast. Poached with greens and doused with hollandaise. Or prepared as a luxurious omelette Arnold Bennett, replete with flaked hot-smoked haddock.

THE GRAND FINALE

Perhaps the greatest marriage of eggs and dairy, however (in the British tradition at least), is custard – made to the cook's preferred thickness, and the natural partner to all manner of pies and puddings. This is something we will revisit (with excitement, naturally) over the latter half of this book. Custard, and especially milk puddings, are something ancient, very British, and very special.

EGGS

AND

DAIRY

UNITED KINGDOM
*

EGGS
AND
SOLDIERS

There's no reason why this dish, however cute and child-like, can't be for adults as well. After all, the 'soldiers' of toast are perfectly suited to savouring the runny yolk of the soft-boiled egg.

Serves: 4
Prep time: 5 minutes
Cook time: 10 minutes
{♥}{✎}{▲}{✕}

- 4 eggs
- 4 slices bread of choice
- butter, for spreading
- salt and pepper

* Bring a medium saucepan of water to the boil. Once boiling, carefully put the eggs into the water and cook for 5½ minutes. You will soft-boil the egg and keep its runny yolk.
* Remove the pan from the heat and drain the eggs. Put the eggs into a bowl of cold water for a moment to stop the cooking.
* While the eggs are cooling, toast the bread and butter it. Cut it into strips narrow enough to fit inside the egg once its top has been removed.
* Serve the egg in an egg cup, with the toast 'soldiers' alongside. Remove the top of the egg by tapping it with a knife or spoon to crack the shell, then slicing off the top of the egg. Season the exposed egg with salt and pepper and dip a soldier in.

UNITED KINGDOM
*

SCRAMBLED EGGS
BUTTERED EGGS

Scrambled eggs, made with butter – and sometimes a little milk or cream – were popular at least as far back as the 1600s, however the earliest references are for 'buttered eggs'. It's unsurprising how they got their name: recipes in early English cookbooks such as Mary Eaton's 1822 *The Cook and Housekeeper's Dictionary* called for a large piece of butter (about 25 g/1 oz/2 tablespoons) per egg.

Serves 3–4
Prep time: 5 minutes
Cook time: 10 minutes
{♥}{♨}{✎}{▲}{✕}

- 8 eggs
- 60 ml/2 fl oz (¼ cup) full-fat (whole) milk
or single (light) cream (optional)
- 60 g/2¼ oz (½ stick) butter
- salt and pepper

* Crack the eggs into a medium bowl and whisk until combined, then stir through the milk or cream (if using).
* Melt the butter in a medium saucepan over a low heat, add the eggs and cook, stirring frequently, for 2 minutes, or until they start to form solids. Stirring frequently will help the mixture keep a creamy texture throughout. Regularly scrape the bottom and edges of the pan to prevent any burning or overcooking.
* Cook the scrambled eggs for another 2 minutes, or until they are just slightly softer than your preferred texture, as they will continue to cook when removed from the heat. Remove from the heat and serve, seasoning to taste.

ENGLAND: LONDON
*

OMELETTE
ARNOLD BENNETT

This open-faced omelette is made with smoked haddock and topped with a creamy cheese sauce. This dish was created at the Savoy Hotel in the 1920s and named in honour of English novelist Arnold Bennett, who was a regular there. While this dish might be indulgent hotel cooking, it's replicated easily enough at home.

Serves: 4
Prep time: 30 minutes
Cook time: 30 minutes
{✎}

- For the fish:
- 300 ml/10 fl oz (1¼ cups) full-fat (whole) milk
- 1 small onion, halved
- 1 bay leaf
- 250 g/9 oz piece smoked haddock
- 15 g/½ oz (1 tablespoon) butter

- For the sauce:
- 15 g/½ oz (1 tablespoon) butter
- 15 g/½ oz (1¾ tablespoons) plain (all-purpose) flour
- 90 ml/3¼ fl oz (6 tablespoons) double (heavy) cream
- 2 teaspoons English mustard
- 100 g/3½ oz Cheddar cheese, grated
- 2 egg yolks
- salt and pepper

- For the omelette:
- 12 eggs
- 60 g/2¼ oz (½ stick) butter, for frying
- salt and pepper

* For the fish, put the milk, onion and bay leaf into a large saucepan and bring to a simmer over a medium-low heat. Cover with a lid and cook over a low heat for 10 minutes. Carefully strain the milk through a sieve into a bowl and then pour back into the saucepan and return to a simmer.
* Return the smoked haddock to the pan with the butter, cover with a lid and cook for 3 minutes. Remove from the heat and leave the fish to poach for another 5–8 minutes until it is just beginning to flake easily with a fork. Remove the fish, flake it into a bowl and set aside. Set the infused milk aside as well.

* For the sauce, melt the butter in a large saucepan over a medium-low heat for 2 minutes, or until foaming. Stir in the flour and cook for 2 minutes, stirring constantly, before slowly whisking in a third of the reserved infused milk. Once well combined, add another third and whisk again. Repeat until the milk is used up, then simmer for 10 minutes, stirring frequently.
* Remove the pan from the heat and beat in the mustard and cheese. Season to taste, then beat in the egg yolks.
* Preheat the grill (broiler) to its highest setting.
* To make the omelettes, beat 3 eggs with a little salt and pepper in a small bowl. Melt a piece of butter in an ovenproof frying pan or skillet over a medium-low heat for 2 minutes, or until foaming. Add the beaten eggs and stir to make a loose scrambled mixture, tipping the pan as you go and filling in any gaps with liquid egg. Carefully place a quarter of the flaked fish over the egg mixture – when still quite loose – as well as a quarter of the sauce.
* Quickly flash under the grill (broiler) for 2–3 minutes and serve immediately. Repeat with each omelette. Alternatively, keep them all warm in an oven preheated to 80°C/176°F/lowest Gas Mark and serve together.

WALES: ANGLESEY
*

ANGLESEY EGGS
WYAU YNYS MÔN

This Welsh breakfast casserole is a great 'kitchen sink' recipe: mashed potatoes, finely sliced leeks and hard-boiled eggs baked beneath a creamy cheese sauce.
Serve with good bread or toast and a mug of tea.

Serves 6
Prep time: 30 minutes
Cook time: 1½ hours
{🌶}{✎}

- 250 ml/8 fl oz (1 cup) full-fat (whole) milk
- 1 small onion, quartered
- 1 bay leaf
- 2 cloves
- ¼ nutmeg or ½ blade mace
- 6 black peppercorns, lightly crushed
- 45 g/1½ oz (3 tablespoons) butter
- 20 g/¾ oz (2⅓ tablespoons) plain (all-purpose) flour
- 50 ml/1¾ fl oz (3½ tablespoons) cream or extra milk
- 1 teaspoon English mustard
- 60 g/2¼ oz Caerphilly or Cheddar cheese, grated
- 1 tablespoon grated Parmesan cheese
- 1 egg yolk (optional)
- 4 leeks, sliced
- ½ quantity Mashed Potatoes (page 80)
- 6 eggs
- salt and pepper
- good-quality bread or toast, to serve

* Preheat the oven to 200°C/400°F/Gas Mark 6.
* Put the milk, onion, bay leaf, cloves, nutmeg or mace and peppercorns into a saucepan and bring to a simmer over a medium-low heat. Cover with a lid and simmer for 10 minutes, then strain through a sieve (discard the flavourings) into a jug (pitcher) and set aside.

* Melt 30 g/1 oz (2 tablespoons) of the butter in the pan over a medium-low heat for 2 minutes, or until foaming. Stir in the flour and cook for 2–3 minutes, stirring frequently to prevent lumps and without colouring. Slowly whisk in the reserved infused milk, a quarter at a time, making sure it is fully combined before you add more. Reduce the heat to very low and cook for 15 minutes, stirring occasionally.
* Add the cream and mustard, then remove from the heat and add half the cheeses and the egg yolk (if using), mixing until smooth. Season to taste.
* Melt the remaining butter in another saucepan over a medium-low heat. Add the leeks and cook for 20 minutes, or until they have softened. Add them to the Mashed Potato and mix thoroughly.
* Spoon the mixture into an ovenproof dish, creating 6 small wells in the middle to fit the eggs. Crack the eggs into the wells, making sure not to break the yolks. Pour over the sauce, sprinkle with the remaining cheeses and bake in the oven for 30–40 minutes until golden brown. Serve with bread or toast.

WALES
*

COCKLES
AND
EGGS

This breakfast dish is common to the Welsh coastline, where cockle gathering was once an important part of daily life. The cockles are briefly fried in bacon fat, before being scrambled in a creamy egg mixture. In days long past, this combination would be considered an aphrodisiac. Eat with buttered brown bread.

Serves: 4
Prep time: 5 minutes
Cook time: 10 minutes
{✎}{🌶}

- 8 eggs
- 15 g/½ oz (1 tablespoon) butter
- 25 g/1 oz bacon fat
- 100 g/3½ oz cooked cockles
- 2 tablespoons double (heavy) cream (optional)
- salt and pepper
- buttered brown bread, to serve

* Put the eggs, butter and a little salt and pepper into a large bowl and whisk well.
* Set a large frying pan or skillet over a medium heat, add the bacon fat and heat for 2–3 minutes to render the fat. Add the cockles and fry them well in the fat for 2 minutes until coated.
* Reduce the heat to low, pour the whisked egg mixture around the cockles and stir until very softly set, 2–3 minutes. At this point, remove the pan from the heat and stir through the cream (if using). This will enrich the mixture and stop any further cooking. Serve immediately with buttered brown (whole wheat) bread.

UNITED KINGDOM

*

FRIED EGGS
AND
BACON

It is strange to consider the origins of a dish so basic and universal as a plate of fried eggs and bacon, however many British food writers consider it to be – if nothing else – a foundational pairing of British cooking. Recipes for eggs and bacon stretch back well into the 1600s, although such a pastoral combination will, no doubt, have much earlier roots. Thin slices of bacon should be cooked in a hot pan and if the rashers (slices) are fatty enough, the rendered fat will be enough to crisp the bacon and later fry and baste the eggs. Serve with a plate of well-buttered toast.

Serves: 4
Prep time: 5 minutes
Cook time: 12 minutes
{ᵔ} {🍲} {✗}

- 1 tablespoon vegetable oil,
plus extra oil or butter, if needed
- 12 rashers (slices) bacon
- 8 eggs
- salt and pepper
- buttered toast, to serve

* Preheat the oven to 80°C/176°F/lowest Gas Mark.
* Heat the 1 tablespoon oil in a large frying pan or skillet over a low-medium heat. Add the bacon and fry for 10 minutes, or until crispy, turning once halfway through to ensure even cooking. Do this in batches, keeping the cooked bacon on an ovenproof plate in the oven.
* If there is enough bacon fat left in the pan, you may choose to fry the eggs in it. Either way, it is worth reserving the fat for cooking – strain it into a bowl, cover with clingfilm (plastic wrap), chill and use another time.
* If using butter or oil to fry the eggs, wipe the pan clean and melt over a low-medium heat before carefully adding the eggs. Cook for as long as it takes the egg whites to turn opaque, usually no more than 1–2 minutes. Season with salt and pepper.
* When the eggs are ready, remove the bacon from the oven and serve with buttered toast.

UNITED KINGDOM

*

FULL BREAKFAST

A full breakfast is a hefty meal, with just enough grease and carbohydrates to mend a sore head and send you back to bed. The composition of the quintessential big British breakfast, however, is an understandably contentious issue. Composed of up to a dozen elements, and varying widely from region to region, this is much more personal preference than textbook definition. Most would agree that essentials include eggs, bacon, sausage and toast, as well as fried mushrooms and grilled (broiled) tomatoes. Beyond that, however, it's the domain of either cook or diner. Some regional variations, recommendations and additions:

In Scotland: Haggis (page 192), White Pudding (page 176), Square Sausage (page 187), Potato Scones (page 90); in Northern Ireland (Ulster Fry): Soda Farls (page 256), Potato Bread (page 90), Vegetable Roll (page 187); in Wales: Laverbread (page 78), Lavercakes (page 78); in England: Bubble and Squeak (page 80); in southwest England: Hog's Pudding (page 177); in West Yorkshire: Dock Pudding (page 77); in the West Midlands: Staffordshire Oatcakes (page 261).

Serves: 4
Prep time: 10 minutes
Cook time: 35 minutes
{ᵔ}

- butter or vegetable oil, for greasing
- 4 sausages (Cumberland, page 164)
- 8 rashers (slices) bacon
- 12 cm/4½ inch thick slices of Black Pudding
(blood sausage) (page 168)
- 4 plum tomatoes, halved lengthways
- 400 g/14 oz button or chestnut
(cremini) mushrooms
- 4 slices bread (for toast or fried bread)
- 4 large eggs
- 400 g/14 oz can baked beans
- salt and pepper

- To serve:
- Tomato Ketchup (page 425) and Brown Sauce (page 426)
- tea, coffee and fruit juice

* Preheat the oven to 80°C/176°F/lowest Gas Mark and put a large roasting pan inside to warm.
* Lightly grease a frying pan, skillet or grill plate with butter or oil and heat over a low heat. Add the sausages and cook for 15–20 minutes, turning occasionally to ensure that they are cooked through and golden all over.
* Halfway through cooking the sausages, increase the heat to medium and add the bacon – being careful not to overcrowd the pan. Cook on each side for at least 4–5 minutes, then transfer the bacon and sausages to the roasting pan and keep warm in the oven.
* Add the Black Pudding (blood sausage) to the frying pan and fry for a few minutes on each side. Black pudding is already cooked, so this is just a matter of heating through and achieving a texture you like – ideally you want it to crisp slightly on both sides.
* Season the tomatoes and clean and cut the mushrooms to your desired thickness. If the pan has dried, add more butter or oil before frying the tomatoes, flat-side down, heating through to achieve a deep golden colour, then transfer to the warmed roasting pan and add the mushrooms to the frying pan. Flip the mushrooms over after 2 minutes and cook for another 2 minutes.
* Begin to toast and butter the slices of bread, stacking buttered sides inwards towards each other. If you are opting for fried bread, add the buttered slices of toast to the pan directly and fry on each side for 2 minutes.
* Finally, reduce the heat to low-medium, add more butter or oil if needed, and crack the eggs into the pan. Cook for as long as it takes the egg whites to turn completely opaque, usually no more than 1–2 minutes.
* While the eggs are cooking, heat the baked beans in a saucepan for a few minutes. Remove the warmed roasting pan from the oven and assemble all the components on 4 large serving plates. Serve with Tomato Ketchup, Brown Sauce and mugs of tea or coffee and fruit juice.

Full breakfast

WALES

GLAMORGAN SAUSAGES

These meatless sausages are made up of an all-Welsh pairing of finely chopped leeks and Caerphilly cheese. Breaded and fried until golden and crispy, they should be served with a tomato or tart (e.g. rhubarb or damson) ketchup. Glamorgan sausages were originally made with a hard, crumbly cheese made from the milk of Glamorgan cattle, a breed that is now nearly extinct. Caerphilly is the most similar cheese commercially available today.

Serves: 8
Prep time: 30 minutes
Cook time: 20 minutes
{ⓥ}{✿}

- For the 'sausages':
- 200 g/7 oz Caerphilly cheese, grated
- 200 g/7 oz (4 cups) fresh breadcrumbs
- 2 tablespoons chopped leek or spring onion (scallion)
- 1 tablespoon chopped flat-leaf parsley
- ¼ teaspoon chopped thyme
- 2 egg yolks
- 1½ teaspoons mustard powder

- For frying:
- 2 egg whites
- 5 tablespoons plain (all-purpose) flour
- about 50 g/2 oz (1 cup) fresh breadcrumbs
- lard or sunflower oil
- salt and pepper
- tart relish, ketchup or preserve, to serve

* Put all the ingredients for the 'sausages' into a food processor and pulse briefly. Alternatively, mix the ingredients together in a large bowl until combined. You want the sausages to have plenty of texture, so avoid overmixing. Divide the mixture into about 16 even-sized balls. Flatten each and roll them into sausage shapes about 5–6 cm/2–2½ inches long.
* Beat the egg whites in a small bowl until frothy, then pour into a shallow bowl. Put the flour into another shallow bowl and season with 1¼ teaspoons each of salt and pepper, then put the breadcrumbs into a third bowl. Dip each sausage into the flour, then into the egg whites, before rolling them in the breadcrumbs until coated.
* Fill a large, heavy saucepan with fat or oil for frying to a depth of about 5 mm/¼ inch and heat over a medium heat. Add the sausages and fry for 3–4 minutes on each side until golden and crispy. Drain on paper towels.
* Serve with a tart relish, ketchup or preserve.

UNITED KINGDOM

EGG-IN-A-HOLE
CURATE'S EYE

A curate's eye (or ox eye) is made by cutting out circles of toast fried with butter or beef dripping and then frying an egg in the hole until set. Today, it is known by the more literally descriptive name 'egg in a hole'.

Serves: 4
Prep time: 10 minutes
Cook time: 10 minutes
{🍲}{🥄}{🍴}

- 4 slices stale bread
- about 120 g/4 oz (8 tablespoons) butter or beef dripping
- 4 eggs

* Cut a circle about 6 cm/2½ inches in diameter from the centre of each slice of bread. Melt half the butter in a large frying pan or skillet with a lid over a medium-low heat for 2 minutes, or until foaming. Add the bread and fry for 1–2 minutes until just lightly golden brown.
* Turn the bread over and brown the other side for 1–2 minutes, adding more butter if needed. Add a small piece of butter to each hole, then crack in an egg. Cover and cook for 3–4 minutes until the eggs are just set. Serve.

ENGLAND

SCOTCH WOODCOCK

To the confusion of many, this dish is not Scottish, nor has it anything to do with the famous game bird. Instead, this pungent breakfast dish, a favourite of Victorian times, is composed of creamy scrambled eggs and anchovies spread on buttered toast. The anchovies may be served whole and draped over the eggs, or be replaced with Anchovy Butter (page 440), which is spread over the toast.

Serves: 4
Prep time: 5 minutes
Cook time: 20 minutes
{✿}

- 250 ml/8 fl oz (1 cup) single (light) cream
- 6 egg yolks
- 4 slices bread of choice
- 4 tablespoons softened butter
- 4 tablespoons Anchovy Butter (page 440)
or 12 anchovy fillets
- salt and pepper
- Worcestershire or Brown Sauce (page 426), to serve

* Preheat the grill (broiler) to medium-high.
* Set 2 tablespoons of the cream aside, then heat the rest in a small saucepan over a medium heat until scalding or 83°C/181°F on a thermometer.
* Whisk the egg yolks in a medium heatproof bowl. Once the cream is nearly boiling, slowly pour the warm cream over the egg yolks, beating constantly, then pour the mixture back into the pan and heat over a low-medium heat, stirring frequently, for 3–4 minutes until thickened and just starting to scramble.
* Meanwhile, toast the bread. Butter the toast and keep the slices warm, buttered-sides facing each other.
* Remove the egg mixture from the heat and stir in the remaining cream. Season with a little salt and pepper.
* Spread the buttered toast with Anchovy Butter (if using), then spoon the lightly scrambled egg mixture over the toast and grill (broil) for 30 seconds, or until they turn a pale golden brown. Top with anchovy fillets (if using) and serve with Worcestershire or Brown Sauce.

Glamorgan sausages

WELSH RAREBIT
WELSH RABBIT/CAWS POB

Thick buttered toast spread with a generous and sumptuous melting mixture of Cheddar, mustard, stout and Worcestershire sauce, the Welsh rarebit is a British treat par excellence. Serve at breakfast or lunch, or even as a post-dinner 'cheese course'. The rarebit's peculiar name has prompted much speculation about its origin, but most of the conversation has centred around the dish's English name. The earliest references to the dish, from the eighteenth century, call it 'rabbit' (and not rarebit), but it wasn't until Hannah Glasse's 1747 cookbook, *The Art of Cookery Made Plain and Easy*, that a recipe for the Welsh version (along with Scottish and English ones) was given. However, the name *caws pobi* ('roasted cheese'), dates back even further. In 1547, in his *The First Book of the Introduction of Knowledge*, writer and physician Andrew Boorde typifies the Welsh, saying 'I am a Welshman… I do loue cawse boby (sic), good rosted chese'.

Serves: 4
Prep time: 5 minutes
Cook time: 10–15 minutes
{❌}

- 120 ml/4 fl oz (½ cup) stout
- pinch of cayenne pepper
- 1 teaspoon English mustard powder or 1 tablespoon English mustard
- 175 g/6 oz Cheddar or any sharp, tangy hard cheese, grated
- good glug of Worcestershire sauce, plus extra to serve
- 1 egg yolk
- 4 thick slices white sandwich bread

* Preheat the grill (broiler) to its highest setting and line a large baking sheet with baking (parchment) paper.
* Bring the stout to the boil in a medium saucepan, then boil for another minute to reduce slightly. Add the cayenne pepper and mustard and whisk together to combine.
* Remove from the heat and slowly beat in the grated cheese. Add a good glug of Worcestershire sauce and mix well. Finally, beat in the egg yolk and leave to cool.
* Toast the sandwich bread slices before smearing them with generous portions of the cheesy paste. Arrange the bread on the prepared baking sheet and grill (broil) for 3–4 minutes, or until golden brown and bubbling. Serve with more Worcestershire sauce.

WELSH CHEESE PUDDING
PWDIN CAWS CYMREIG

Welsh food writer Bobby Freeman once hailed this savoury pudding as the 'final development' of a Welsh rarebit (*caws pobi*), which has been made since at least the late nineteenth century.
Serve in the same way as Welsh Rarebit (see left) on its own, or with a leafy green salad, but always with a bottle of Worcestershire sauce.

Serves: 6
Prep time: 20 minutes
Cook time: 1 hour

- about120 g/4 oz (1 stick) butter, plus extra for greasing
- 1 leek, very thinly sliced
- 6 slices white or brown (whole wheat) bread
- 200 g/7 oz Caerphilly or Cheddar cheese, grated
- 3 eggs
- 1½ teaspoons English mustard (optional)
- 400 ml/14 fl oz (1⅔ cups) full-fat (whole) milk
- pinch of cayenne pepper (optional)
- salt and pepper
- Worcestershire sauce, to serve

* Preheat the oven to 160°C/325°F/Gas Mark 3. Grease a baking dish with butter and set aside.
* Melt half the butter in a medium frying pan or skillet over a medium heat, add the leek and lightly cook for 7–8 minutes. Leave to cool.
* Butter the bread with the remaining butter on one side and make 3 'sandwiches' using all the leek and three-quarters of the grated cheese.
* Cut the sandwiches into quarters: triangles or squares, removing the crusts, if desired. This is to make them easier to fit together. When ready, arrange the layers, side by side, into the prepared baking dish.
* Put the eggs, mustard (if using) and milk into a large bowl and whisk together to combine. Season with cayenne pepper (if using), pepper and salt. Pour the egg mixture over the bread, sprinkle with the remaining cheese and bake in the oven for 50 minutes, or until the top has browned and the eggs have just set. Serve with Worcestershire sauce.

Welsh rarebit

UNITED KINGDOM
*

EGG MAYONNAISE
WITH
WATERCRESS

A favourite filling for sandwiches, a proper egg mayonnaise (bolstered by peppery watercress, a little mustard and even chopped capers) is pure pleasure – and not only at tea time.

Serves: 4
Prep time: 20 minutes
Cook time: 10 minutes
{ἄ} {ᴥ}

- 6 large eggs, at room temperature
- ½ quantity Mayonnaise (page 427)
- 1–2 teaspoons English mustard (optional)
- 2 tablespoons chopped watercress
- 1 tablespoon capers, chopped (optional)
- salt and pepper
- well-buttered brown (whole wheat) bread or Bridge Rolls (page 278), to serve

* Bring a medium saucepan of water to the boil. Carefully put the eggs into the boiling water with a wooden or slotted spoon and boil for exactly 7 minutes.
* Quickly drain the hot water and remove the eggs. Refill the saucepan with cold water, add the eggs and leave to cool for about 5 minutes. (You may need to refill the water once if the eggs warm it up.)
* When the eggs are cool to the touch, shell them and coarsely chop, then transfer to a small bowl. Add the Mayonnaise, mustard (if using), watercress and capers (if using) and mix together until combined. Season to taste with salt and pepper. Use as a sandwich filling between well-buttered brown (whole wheat) bread or between 2 halves of a Bridge Roll.

SCOTLAND
*

CROWDIE

Crowdie is a fresh cheese, soft and spreadable, traditional to Highland Scotland. It is made by setting warmed skimmed milk with rennet or an acidic liquid and then allowing the mixture to hang in a muslin (cheesecloth) or pudding cloth, and the whey to drip away. The fresh curds are then mixed through with cream and/or butter, and a little salt. Serve with oatcakes, or as any soft cheese. In Lowland Scotland the term 'crowdie' was given instead to an oatmeal-and-milk gruel commonly eaten for breakfast.

Makes: about 280 g/10 oz
Prep time: 15 minutes, plus several hours draining
Cook time: 20 minutes
{ἄ}{ᴁ}{ᴥ}{ᴁ}

- 1 litre/24 fl oz (4¼ cups) skimmed milk
- 1 tablespoon cider or white wine vinegar
- pinch of salt
- double (heavy) cream or softened butter, to taste

* Pour the milk into a large saucepan and slowly heat over a medium heat to scalding point or 83°C/181°F on a thermometer. Add the vinegar and stir it through, then remove from the heat and leave the milk to stand.
* Meanwhile, line a colander with a double layer of clean muslin (cheesecloth). When the curds have set, tip the contents of the pan into the cloth, then carefully gather up the ends of the cloth and tie them into a knot, so that the curds rest in the centre of the cloth bag. Hang the bag over a saucepan or large bowl so that the whey can drain out. It should take several hours.
* When the curds have stopped dripping, squeeze out any excess moisture and set aside the whey for use in another recipe (see Hattit Kit below for suggestions). Put the curds into a bowl with the salt and mix together with a whisk or wooden spoon. While mixing, gradually beat in a little cream or butter at a time, tasting as you add. Add more salt, if desired. Spoon into a small tub or a terrine and leave to chill until ready to use.

SCOTLAND: HIGHLANDS
*

HATTIT KIT

Traditionally, this is made by milking a cow into a pail of fresh buttermilk left from a previous milking. The acidity in the buttermilk curdles the fresh raw milk into a soft curd cheese, but this recipe has been adapted by Scottish chef Pamela Brunton to omit the cow. You can make your own buttermilk by adding a small amount of cultured buttermilk or cheese whey to fresh milk and leaving somewhere warm overnight, such as in a hay-banked byre in June; or you can buy it from a supermarket or a cheesemonger. Think of it as a light, fresh cheesecake.

Serves: 4
Prep time: 15 minutes, plus 12–14 hours standing
Cook time: 10 minutes
{ᴁ} {ᴥ}

- For the hat:
- 500 ml/17 fl oz (2 cups plus 1 tablespoon) good buttermilk
- 1.5 litres/50 fl oz (6¼ cups) full-fat (whole) fresh farm milk
- 2 g/½ teaspoon rennet (or according to packet instructions)

- For the hattit kit:
- 250 g/9 oz (1 cup plus 1 tablespoon) soft milk curds
- 50 g/2 oz (¼ cup) granulated sugar
- pinch of sea salt flakes
- 250 ml/8 fl oz (1 cup) whipping cream

- To serve:
- 250 g/9 oz fresh Scottish soft fruit, such as strawberries, raspberries or poached rhubarb, or jam of the same fruit
- shortbread biscuits (cookies)

* For the hat, put the buttermilk and milk into a large saucepan and heat slowly over a medium to low-medium heat until it reaches blood temperature or 37°C/98.6°F on a thermometer. Remove the pan from the heat and leave it to stand in a warm place, about 22–24°C/72–75°F.

* Measure the rennet into a small container and add 20 ml/¾ fl oz (4 teaspoons) cool water. Stir the rennet into the milk using a gentle up-and-down motion with the spoon. Incorporate evenly but don't overmix. Cover the pan with a cloth secured with an elastic band and leave undisturbed for 6–12 hours. The rennet should set the milk and separate it into soft curds and yellowish whey, while the buttermilk sours the fresh milk.
* Line a colander with muslin (cheesecloth) or a damp dish towel and gently spoon the curds into the cloth. Leave it to hang for a few hours in the fridge until the curds are just firm, like soft cheese. You should have about 1 kg/2¼ lb of soft curds and 1 litre/34 fl oz (4¼ cups) whey.
* At this stage you could add a little salt to the curds and eat them like Crowdie (page 32). Keep the whey to start a new batch of buttermilk, or to make Sour Skons (page 264), or maybe ferment further into Blaand or Frothy Oon. If you are Scottish you certainly don't throw it down the sink.
* For the hattit kit, put the curds into a large bowl, add the sugar and salt and whisk until smooth and loose. If they are too firm, add a little of the whey back in, a teaspoon at a time. In another bowl, whip the cream to soft peaks. Fold the cream gently and evenly into the curds until combined.
* Spoon the hattit kit into sundae glasses, then spoon over the fruit or jam and serve with biscuits (cookies).

ENGLAND
*

POTTED CHEESE

This English cheese spread was traditionally made with grated cheese (frequently Cheshire and Gloucester, mixed), spices and a dash of sweet wine or spirits. A great way to use up knobbly ends of cheese, potted cheese is especially lovely in winter, and should be spooned over oatcakes or crackers – perhaps with some fruit jam as well.

Serves: 6
Prep time: 20 minutes
{❂}{♨}{✗}

- 200 g/7 oz Stilton, or any other cheese, at room temperature
- 100 g/3½ oz (7 tablespoons) butter, softened
- 60 ml/2 fl oz (¼ cup) port, brandy or milk
- 1 tablespoon full-fat (whole) milk
- 80 g/3 oz (⅔ cup) chopped walnuts or dried cranberries, or a mixture (optional)
- pepper

* Put the cheese and butter into a food processor with the liquid/s and pepper to taste and blend until smooth. Fold in the chopped nuts and fruit (if using).
* Spoon the mixture into 6 ramekins or a small non-stick loaf pan, cover with clingfilm (plastic wrap) and refrigerate. It will keep for 7 days in the fridge. Remove from the fridge an hour before you want to serve it.

UNITED KINGDOM
*

CUSTARD

Many a British pudding is emphatically crowned with a liberal measure of custard. Traditionally made from a slowly heated egg-yolk-and-dairy mixture, and typically sweetened with sugar, custards themselves range in consistency from the thickest near-spreadable versions (used for setting trifles), to thin pouring custards served by the jug (pitcher) and doused over hot steamed pudding. This recipe is for something closer to the latter.
Heat your custard slowly to avoid cooking the egg. If you are still nervous, mix 1 teaspoon cornflour (cornstarch) into the egg yolks before whisking into the milk and cream mixture to stabilize. To create a thinner custard, use single (light) or whipping cream instead of the double (heavy) cream.

Serves: 2–4
Prep time: 5 minutes
Cook time: 20 minutes
{❂}{♨}{➛}{✗}

- 150 ml/5 fl oz (⅔ cup) full-fat (whole) milk
- 150 ml/5 fl oz (⅔ cup) double (heavy) cream
- ½ teaspoon vanilla extract or 1 vanilla pod (bean), split in half lengthways and seeds scraped out
- 4 egg yolks, or 3 egg yolks and 1 teaspoon cornflour (cornstarch)
- 40–50 g/1½–2 oz (3¼–4 tablespoons) caster (superfine) sugar

* Pour the milk, cream and vanilla pod (bean) and seeds (if using) into a medium saucepan and slowly heat over a medium heat until scalding or 83°C/181°F on a thermometer.
* Meanwhile, put the egg yolks, cornflour (cornstarch) (if using), sugar and vanilla extract (if using) into a large heatproof bowl and beat together with a whisk until smooth, making sure there are no lumps of cornflour. The paler you beat the mixture, the smoother the custard it will make.
* Gradually pour the hot milk and cream mixture over the eggs, whisking constantly. When thoroughly mixed, pour the custard back into the warm saucepan and stir with a wooden spoon until it thickens enough to coat the back of the spoon.
* Strain through a fine-mesh sieve into a jug (pitcher), ready to serve. Alternatively, sieve the custard into a container or bowl and cover the top with clingfilm (plastic wrap) to prevent a skin forming. It should last for 3 days in the fridge.

ENGLAND

*

CURDS
AND
WHEY

In England, a dish of curds and whey referred quite simply to milk set by rennet – the curds and whey would be eaten together and could be a snack for children or those too unwell to eat more solid foods.

For a thickened, sweetened version of this dish, try Junket (see right).

Makes: 500 ml/17 fl oz
Prep time: 5 minutes
Cook time: 10 minutes

{♨}{♨}{♨}{♨}{♨}

- 2 tablespoons lemon juice, cider vinegar or essence of rennet
- 500 ml/17 fl oz (2 cups plus 1 tablespoon) Jersey or full-fat (whole) milk
- jam, honey or other sweet syrup, to serve

* If using lemon juice or vinegar, slowly bring the milk to the boil in a medium saucepan. Once boiling, remove from the heat, add the lemon juice or vinegar and stir just once to incorporate it. Leave to stand undisturbed until completely cooled, when the curds will be set.
* If using essence of rennet, heat the milk in a medium saucepan until it is hand hot or 37°C/98.6°F on a thermometer. Pour into a dish and stir in the right amount of rennet; check the label for the appropriate dosage as it will change from one brand to another. Again, leave to stand undisturbed until completely cooled.
* Curds and whey are eaten as is with jam, honey or sweet syrup, or folded into the mixture for something sweet, such as a Yorkshire Curd Tart (page 384).

ENGLAND: DEVON AND CORNWALL

*

CLOTTED CREAM

A speciality of Devon and Cornwall, areas known for their rich dairy traditions, clotted cream is made by slowly cooking fresh cream into a thick, decadent spread. When cooked, the cream will form a nutty, golden 'crust' which has a more granular texture.

Some suggest that clotted cream was brought to the southwest of England by Phoenician traders sailing from the Middle East some 2,000 years ago. While clotted cream has a long history, there is no direct evidence for this theory, and no written records make mention of it before the sixteenth century.

The recipe below is a long but hands-off process. Prepare in advance as it will take at least 18 hours to get to the end result. Raw cream is preferable for this process but it's not always available – as long as it is not ultra pasteurized (UHT) cream or whipping cream, then any fresh high-fat (minimum 48%) double (heavy) cream will still work. Serve with jam on scones, use it to enrich the dough of the scones themselves, or churn into clotted cream butter.

Makes: 2 ramekins
Prep time: 5 minutes, plus 5–6 hours chilling
Cook time: 12 hours

{♨}{♨}{♨}{♨}{♨}

- 600 ml/20 fl oz (2½ cups) good-quality double (heavy) cream

* Preheat the oven to 80°C/176°F/lowest Gas Mark.
* Pour the cream into a large baking dish to a depth of 4 cm/1½ inches and put into the oven for 12 hours.
* The next day, remove the dish from the oven, cover with clingfilm (plastic wrap) and leave in the fridge for 5–6 hours to set completely. The top layer of the cream should be thick and set. This is the clotted cream – there will be some thinner cream beneath, which can be used in coffee or in another baking project.
* Use a large spoon to scoop the clotted cream into ramekins or small containers, cover and refrigerate until needed. Clotted cream will keep in the fridge for up to 5 days.

ENGLAND: DEVON AND CORNWALL

*

JUNKET

Junket is a simple milk pudding rooted in medieval origin. The modern junket is made by heating sweetened milk, flavouring it with rum or brandy and then setting it with rennet. The earliest versions of junket were much plainer, and closer to Curds and Whey (see left) – in fact the two names were used interchangeably until the eighteenth century. Serve with whipped or clotted cream, fresh or poached fruit, and a dusting of nutmeg.

Serves: 4
Prep time: 5 minutes,
plus 3–4 hours setting and chilling
Cook time: 10 minutes

{♨}{♨}{♨}

- 750 ml/25 fl oz (3 cups) full-fat (whole) milk
- 150 ml/5 fl oz (⅔ cup) double (heavy) cream
- 1½ tablespoons caster (superfine) sugar
- 1 vanilla pod (bean), split in half lengthways and seeds scraped out
- 2 teaspoons rennet (or according to packet instructions)

- To serve:
- lightly whipped cream
- grated nutmeg, for dusting
- soft summer fruit of your choice

* Pour the milk and cream into a saucepan and heat slowly over a low-medium to medium heat until it is hand hot or 37°C/98.6°F on a thermometer. Add the sugar and vanilla seeds and stir until the sugar has dissolved. Remove from the heat, add the rennet and stir through briefly. Leave to cool slightly, then pour into 4 serving dishes or glasses and leave to stand at room temperature until set.
* Once set, cover with clingfilm (plastic wrap) and refrigerate until chilled. To serve, top with lightly whipped cream, a dusting of nutmeg and soft summer fruits.

Junket

WHEN WE SAT DOWN, WITH ME IN MAMA'S LAP, MY FATHER WOULD
LADLE OUT OF THE CAULDRON THIN LEEK SOUP WITH A BIG
LUMP OF HAM IN IT, THAT SHOWED ITS RIND AS IT TURNED OVER
THROUGH THE STEAM WHEN THE LADLE CAME OUT BRIMMING OVER.
THERE WAS A SMELL WITH THAT SOUP. IT IS IN MY NOSTRILS NOW.
THERE WAS EVERYTHING IN IT THAT WAS GOOD, AND BECAUSE OF
THAT, THE SMELL ALONE WAS ENOUGH TO MAKE YOU FEEL SO WARM
AND COMFORTABLE IT WAS A PLEASURE TO BE SITTING THERE,
FOR YOU KNEW OF THE PLEASURE TO COME.

RICHARD LLEWELLYN, *HOW GREEN WAS MY VALLEY*, 1939

A sturdy black cauldron, bubbling away with a hearty soup or stew, is one of those enduring images we have of medieval life in Britain, the sort that we pick up from popular media. These ideas seem inextricable.

But cauldrons, a thing of the elite, were the steaming iron workhorse of the medieval kitchen – they were, as English food writer Dorothy Hartley wonderfully puts it, a '"complete cooker" and hot water system combined'. Indeed, once the desired heat was reached, earthenware jugs (pitchers), salted meats or bag puddings could be suspended into the cauldrons and cooked separately. Like the great granddaddy of today's double oven.

More of what we expect – a humble mishmash of ingredients, all dug up or snared from a modest kitchen garden or nearby wood – was to be found in smaller kitchens. There, the earliest ancestor of the British stew was pottage, a thick mixture of cereal, vegetables and sometimes meat, cooked slowly together. True,

it doesn't seem far off something like today's Scotch broth, but many such early medieval stews actually originated as a multi-course meal. 'Mouthful soups', as Scottish food writer Catherine Brown has dubbed them. The broth was created by slowly cooking a great chunk of meat (likely to have been salted). Once cooked, the meat was removed and sliced. The broth would be supped on its own, and the meat returned to the bowl to be eaten with the vegetables. Shetland's tattie soup with reestit mutton is a great living reminder of this cooking style.

British soups and stews are well-known by their many fantastic names: the likes of cock-a-leekie, bawd bree, scouse and groaty pudding seem as likely to get a belly filled with laughter as anything else. What differentiates many of these stews, and where you draw the line, however, is no laughing matter. The differences are important, but vary locally, often as much as from household to household. There is no proper, definitive answer to what you put into

a cawl, for instance. The recipes that follow should evoke the essence of the dish, but variations are out there, and there are plenty. Feel free to deviate a little based on what you have available in season where you are (hint: that's how these dishes came to be in the first place!).

Another feature of this chapter are recipes that will undoubtedly feel more recent – because, well, they are. Creamed or puréed soups feel (and are) the stuff of Victorian times, but never seem outdated. Similarly, the combination of curried parsnip and apple may date back a mere fifty years, but Jane Grigson (whose creation it was) conceived it from flavours we all know from elsewhere in the British kitchen.

These dishes, whether ancient or modern, all feel decidedly British. And if the great world of British soups can open up to new ingredients and new flavours, then shouldn't we hope for even more?

SOUPS

AND

STEWS

UNITED KINGDOM
*
BROCCOLI AND STILTON SOUP

Broccoli and Stilton may be a modern marriage of flavours, but creamy broccoli soups stretch back to the early 1900s at least; English food writer Florence B Jack's recipe (1914) looks much like this one, though with a little milk added last.

Serves: 4
Prep time: 15 minutes
Cook time: 35 minutes
{🝖}{🝖}{🝖}

- 30 g/1 oz (2 tablespoons) butter
- 1 onion, chopped
- 1 stalk celery, chopped
- 1 leek, chopped
- bouquet garni of 2 bay leaves, flat-leaf parsley stalks and 3 sprigs thyme tied together with kitchen string
- 2 potatoes, peeled and diced
- 2 litres/68 fl oz (8½ cups) vegetable or chicken stock
- 2 heads broccoli, about 750 g/1 lb 10 oz, diced
- 150 g/5 oz Stilton, grated
- salt and pepper

* Melt the butter in a large saucepan over a medium heat, add the vegetables and bouquet garni and fry for 10 minutes. Add the potatoes and cook for 5 minutes, then add the stock and simmer for another 10 minutes.
* Add the broccoli and simmer for another 10 minutes.
* Remove the bouquet garni and discard, turn off the heat and add the cheese. Using a hand-held blender, blend until smooth. Season with salt and pepper and serve.

UNITED KINGDOM
*
CARROT AND GINGER SOUP

This is a warming, lightly spiced carrot soup, lifted by the addition of freshly grated ginger.

Serves: 6
Prep time: 15 minutes
Cook time: 35 minutes
{🝖}{🝖}{🝖}

- 30 g/1 oz (2 tablespoons) butter or vegetable oil
- ½ teaspoon cumin seeds (optional)
- 1 onion, chopped
- 1 stalk celery, chopped
- 500 g/1 lb 2 oz carrots, chopped
- bouquet garni of 2 bay leaves, flat-leaf parsley stalks and 2 sprigs rosemary tied together with kitchen string
- 2 litres/68 fl oz (8½ cups) vegetable or chicken stock
- 50 g/2 oz piece fresh root ginger, peeled and grated
- salt and pepper

* Melt the butter in a large saucepan over a medium heat, add the cumin seeds (if using) and fry for 1 minute.
* Add the chopped vegetables and bouquet garni, season with salt and pepper and fry gently for 10–15 minutes until lightly golden. Add the stock and simmer for 10 minutes, then add the ginger and cook for another 10 minutes, or until the vegetables are very tender.
* Remove the bouquet garni and discard, then take off the heat and, using a hand-held blender, blend until smooth. Season to taste and serve.

UNITED KINGDOM
*
CURRIED PARSNIP AND APPLE SOUP

Lightly sweet and with a lick of spice, this soup is a marriage of familiar English flavours but does not come from historic cookery tomes. Curried parsnip soup was created by cookery writer Jane Grigson in the 1970s and was an instant success.

Serves: 4
Prep time: 15 minutes
Cook time: 45 minutes
{🝖}{🝖}{🝖}

- 60 g/2¼ oz (½ stick) butter
- 1 onion, chopped
- 2 cloves garlic, chopped
- 1 bay leaf
- 2 parsnips, peeled and chopped
- 1 apple, peeled, cored and diced
- 1 teaspoon mild/medium curry powder
- 1 litre/34 fl oz (4¼ cups) chicken or vegetable stock
- 150 ml/5 fl oz (⅔ cup) single (light) cream
- salt and pepper

* Melt the butter in a large saucepan over a medium heat, add the onion, garlic and bay leaf, then season and fry for 10–12 minutes until the onion is golden. Add the parsnips and apple and cook for another 10 minutes. Add the curry powder and cook for 2–3 minutes, then add the stock. Bring to the boil, then reduce the heat to medium and simmer for 20 minutes, or until the parsnip is tender.
* Remove from the heat, discard the bay leaf, and, using a hand-held blender, blend the soup until very smooth. Add the cream and check the seasoning. Serve.

ENGLAND
*
ENGLISH CELERY SOUP

Mrs Beeton was one of the first writers to give a recipe for this creamy celery soup in 1861. Since then, celery has earned an undue reputation as a rather bland vegetable, and the quality of this soup tends to vary based on the amount of cream added to enrich it. Made without dairy, however, you will soon find that fresh celery packs enough flavour to carry this soup all on its own.

Serves: 4
Prep time: 15 minutes
Cook time: 1 hour

{🏺}{🍴}{🍲}

- 60 g/ 2¼ oz (½ stick) butter or vegetable oil
- 1 bay leaf
- ¼ teaspoon ground allspice
- 8 stalks celery including the leaves, sliced
- 1 onion, chopped
- 1 potato, diced
- 700 ml/ 24 fl oz (2¾ cups plus 2 teaspoons) vegetable or chicken stock
- 60 ml/ 2 fl oz (¼ cup) whole milk (optional)
- 75 ml/ 2½ fl oz (⅓ cup) single (light) cream (optional)
- salt, preferably celery salt, and white pepper

* Melt the butter in a large saucepan over a medium heat. Add the bay leaf and allspice and fry for 30 seconds. Add the celery, onion and potato and mix well to coat the vegetables with the butter and spices, then season with a little salt. Reduce the heat to low and cover with a lid. Cook gently for 20 minutes, or until softened.
* Add the stock, bring to the boil, then reduce the heat and simmer gently for another 30 minutes.
* Remove from the heat and discard the bay leaf. Leave to cool a little, then, using a hand-held blender, blend until smooth. If you desire a particularly smooth texture, pass through a sieve, then pour it back into the saucepan.
* Return the pan to the heat, add the milk and season with white pepper and celery salt before stirring in the cream.

NORTHERN IRELAND
*

LEEK
AND
POTATO SOUP

This Irish soup is inspired by a recipe from County Armagh in Florence Irwin's *The Cookin' Woman: Irish Country Recipes* (1949). The soup is traditionally made rather thick, with the vegetables and potatoes all holding their shape, however today it's often blitzed to a creamy consistency before serving.

Serves: 6
Prep time: 10 minutes
Cook time: 45 minutes

{🏺}{🍴}{🍲}

- 30 g/ 1 oz (2 tablespoons) butter
- 1 onion, chopped
- 1 clove garlic, chopped
- 2 leeks, sliced, white part only
- 1 stalk celery
- 2 potatoes, peeled and diced
- 2 bay leaves
- 500 ml/ 17 fl oz (2 cups plus 1 tablespoon) full-fat (whole) milk (optional)
- 500 ml/ 17 fl oz (2 cups plus 1 tablespoon) chicken or vegetable stock or 1 litre/ 34 fl oz (4¼ cups) stock, if not using milk
- 75 ml/ 2½ fl oz (⅓ cup) single (light) cream
- salt and white pepper

* Melt the butter in a large saucepan over a medium heat, add the vegetables, including the potatoes, and bay leaves with some salt and pepper and cook for 10 minutes, without colouring.
* Add the milk (if using) and stock and simmer for 25 minutes, or until the vegetables are tender.
* Remove the bay leaves and discard, then take off the heat and, using a hand-held blender, blend to your desired consistency. For a very smooth soup, pass through a sieve into a clean pan. Return to a simmer, add the cream and season to taste with salt and pepper, then serve.

UNITED KINGDOM
*

JERUSALEM ARTICHOKE SOUP
PALESTINE SOUP

In British cooking, this rich and creamy soup is also known by the name 'Palestine soup', a reference to the historic region in which Jerusalem lies. There is, however, no relationship between these tubers and Jerusalem; instead it is a corruption of the Italian *girasole* (sunflower) – to which it is related. Over time this became confused with the Middle Eastern city.

Serves: 4–6
Prep time: 15 minutes
Cook time: 55 minutes

{🏺}{🍴}{🍲}

- 60 g/ 2¼ oz (½ stick) butter
- 100 g/ 3½ oz streaky (lean) bacon rashers, chopped (optional)
- 1 onion, chopped
- 3 cloves garlic, chopped
- 1 stalk celery, chopped
- 350 g/ 12 oz Jerusalem artichokes, peeled and chopped
- 1 potato, peeled and chopped
- 1 litre/ 34 fl oz (4¼ cups) chicken or vegetable stock
- 200 ml/ 7 fl oz (¾ cup plus 1 tablespoon) full-fat (whole) milk
- 75 ml/ 2½ fl oz (⅓ cup) double (heavy) cream
- 2 tablespoons chopped flat-leaf parsley
- salt and pepper

* Melt the butter in a large saucepan over a medium-high heat, add the bacon (if using) and fry for 7–8 minutes until it is slightly crispy. Add the onion, garlic and celery and fry for another 10 minutes until soft.
* Add the Jerusalem artichokes and potato and cook for another 10 minutes.
* Add the stock, reduce the heat to low-medium, and simmer for 25 minutes, or until tender. Add the milk, then remove the pan from the heat and, using a hand-held blender, blend the soup until smooth.
* Bring the soup back to a simmer, add the cream and season with salt and pepper. Stir the parsley through just before serving.

UNITED KINGDOM
*

WATERCRESS SOUP

Compared to other fresh greens such as sorrel, nettle or spinach, watercress has a strong pepperiness that translates well into creamy soups and gives them a kick that the others lack.

Serves: 4–6
Prep time: 10 minutes
Cook time: 30 minutes
{⚖}{☛}{🍲}

- 60 g/ 2¼ oz (½ stick) butter
- 1 onion, sliced
- 1 clove garlic, sliced
- 1 potato, peeled and cut into small dice
- 1 large bunch watercress, stems removed, plus 1 small handful, chopped, to garnish
- 250 ml/8 fl oz (1 cup) full-fat (whole) milk
- 750 ml/25 fl oz (3 cups) chicken or vegetable stock
- 75 ml/2 ½ fl oz (⅓ cup) single (light) cream
- ¼ nutmeg, grated
- salt and pepper

* Melt the butter in a large saucepan over a medium heat, add the onion and garlic and fry for 8 minutes, or until soft. Add the potato with some salt and pepper and cook for 5 minutes.
* Shred the watercress leaves, add to the pan and cook for another 5 minutes, or until wilted. Add the milk and stock, bring to the boil, then reduce the heat and simmer for 10 minutes, or until the potatoes are tender.
* Remove from the heat and, using a hand-held blender, blend the soup until smooth, then add the cream and nutmeg. Check the seasoning and add more salt and pepper, if necessary. Garnish with more chopped watercress or stir it through and serve.

SCOTLAND / WALES
*

NETTLE SOUP

When washing and preparing nettles, be sure to wear kitchen gloves so that your hands are protected. The nettles have an almost spinach-like flavour when cooked and could be swapped for an equal amount of spinach or sorrel, if desired.

Serves: 4–6
Prep time: 10 minutes
Cook time: 45 minutes
{⚖}{☛}

- 500 g/1 lb 2 oz young nettle leaves
- 35 g/1¼ oz (2 heaping tablespoons) butter
- 1 leek, sliced
- 250 g/9 oz potatoes, cut into 1 cm/½ inch wide slices
- 1 litre/34 fl oz (4¼ cups) chicken or vegetable stock
- 75 ml/2½ fl oz (⅓ cup) full-fat (whole) milk or double (heavy) cream
- salt and pepper

* Wash the nettles in salted water twice, then chop coarsely and set aside.
* Melt the butter in a large saucepan over a medium-low heat for 2 minutes, or until foaming. Add the nettles and leek and cook for 6–7 minutes until the mixture has gone quite dry. Add the potatoes and stock and bring to a simmer over a medium heat. Cook gently for 30 minutes, or until the potatoes are soft.
* Remove the pan from the heat and leave to cool a little, then transfer to a food processor and blend until smooth. Alternatively, use a hand-held blender. Add the milk or cream and season to taste with salt and pepper. Serve.

ENGLAND: CHESHIRE
*

CHEESY CHESHIRE SOUP

This is a cheesy harvest soup. Cheshire cheese is mild enough to balance (and not dominate) the other flavours. The ale used here is in place of adding further cream or milk, as found in some traditional recipes. Serve with good butter and crusty bread.

Serves: 4–6
Prep time: 15 minutes
Cook time: 40 minutes
{☛}{🍲}

- 30 g/1 oz (2 tablespoons) butter
- 2 carrots, diced
- 1 onion, diced
- 1 leek, diced
- 2 potatoes, peeled and diced
- 750 ml/25 fl oz (3 cups) chicken or vegetable stock
- 750 ml/25 fl oz (3 cups) good brown ale
- 50 g/2 oz (½ cup) porridge (steel-cut) oats
- 350 g/12 oz good-quality Cheshire cheese or similar cheese
- granulated sugar (optional)
- salt and pepper

- To serve:
- good-quality butter
- crusty bread

* Melt the butter in a large saucepan over a medium heat, add the vegetables and fry gently for 10 minutes until softened.
* Add the stock, ale and oats and bring to a simmer. Simmer for 20 minutes, or until the vegetables are very tender. Remove from the heat and, using a hand-held blender, blend the soup coarsely.
* Return the soup to a clean saucepan and heat over a very low heat, then add the cheese and stir until melted. Don't let the soup boil. Season with salt and pepper; if the ale was bitter, add a little sugar. Serve with good-quality butter and crusty bread.

Watercress soup

SCOTLAND
*

COCK-A-LEEKIE SOUP

This traditional Scottish soup is made from a chicken and leek broth, with shredded chicken, leek and prunes. Some recipes include other vegetables, and rice or barley, but these additions can have the effect of drowning out other more subtle flavours.

As food writers Alan Davidson and Catherine Brown have both noted, the earliest mentions of cock-a-leekie date to the eighteenth century, but the soup's peculiar inclusion of prunes suggests it was the product of medieval times, when sweet ingredients were commonly a part of savoury dishes. Traditionally, cock-a-leekie called for a 'boiling fowl' or an old bird, but today a left-over roast chicken works just as well.

Serves: 6
Prep time: 20 minutes
Cook time: 1¼ hours
{♨}{♨}{✷}

- 1 left-over roast chicken
- 1 onion, cut into large slices (optional)
- about 1.25 kg/2 lb 12 oz leeks, thinly sliced, white and green parts separated, ends (bottoms) reserved
- 4 sprigs thyme
- 2 sprigs rosemary
- 1 bay leaf
- 1–2 tablespoons rapeseed (canola) oil (optional)
- 175 g/6 oz (¾ cup) prunes, pitted, halved or quartered
- 15 g/1 oz (¼ cup) chopped flat-leaf parsley
- 1 teaspoon chopped thyme

* Using your fingers, separate the meat from the roast chicken carcass, leaving the skin and bones behind. Chop the meat into large bite-sized pieces and set the meat aside in a large bowl, covered with clingfilm (plastic wrap), in the fridge for later.
* Put the skin and bones into a stockpot, cover generously with about 3 litres/101 fl oz (12 cups) water and bring to the boil. Reduce the heat to a simmer, add the onion (if using), the ends (bottoms) of the leeks and the herbs and cook for at least 1 hour.
* Once cooked, skim the scum off the top with a slotted spoon, then strain the liquid into a large bowl or container. Leave to rest for a while before skimming off most of the fat, setting aside around 1 tablespoon.
* Put a large clean stockpot over a medium heat, add the reserved chicken fat or, if you prefer, use the rapeseed (canola) oil, then add the whites of the leeks and fry gently for about 5 minutes. Add the reserved chicken stock and as much of the reserved chicken meat as you desire. You will by no means need to use all the meat, but it's nice to get a little of the chicken in every spoonful. Add the green leeks, then simmer for 30 minutes. The green of the leeks should still be a vibrant colour at the time of serving. About 10–15 minutes before the soup is ready, add the prunes. Just before serving, add the parsley and thyme and stir through before spooning into bowls.

NORTHEAST OF SCOTLAND
*

CULLEN SKINK

This rich and creamy smoked haddock soup hails from the fishing village of Cullen in northeast Scotland. Over the course of the nineteenth century, this coastal region became famous for its smoked haddock industry and two particular preparations, Finnan Haddies (page 98) and Arbroath Smokies (page 98). These quickly became popular throughout the rest of the country.

Cullen skink was traditionally made by the wives of local fishermen, who preferred using the delicately cold-smoked finnan haddie when making this soup. Today, a lightly smoked haddock fillet makes a fine substitute.

The Scots word 'skink' refers to a cut of beef shin (the same as 'hough'), but over time came to mean a soup or stew made from the same, and used more broadly as a synonym for soup. Writer Alan Davidson suggests that Cullen skink is a seaside adaptation of this traditional beef shin stew.

Serves: 4
Prep time: 10 minutes
Cook time: 30 minutes
{♨}{✷}

- 60 g/2¼ oz (½ stick) butter
- 1 onion, finely chopped
- 2 potatoes, peeled and diced
- 750 ml/25 fl oz (3 cups) full-fat (whole) milk
- 1 bay leaf
- 4 cloves (optional)
- few sprigs of thyme (optional)
- 200 g/7 oz smoked haddock fillet (finnan haddies, if possible)
- 150 ml/5 fl oz (⅔ cup) double (heavy) cream
- juice of ½ lemon
- 1 tablespoon chopped flat-leaf parsley
- salt and pepper

* Melt the butter in a large saucepan over a medium heat, add the onion and cook for 8 minutes until softened. Add the diced potatoes and enough water to just cover them and cook for 25 minutes, or until tender.
* Meanwhile, bring the milk, bay leaf, cloves (if using) and thyme (if using) to the boil in a shallow pan. Reduce the heat to low, add the fish (whole or halved if the pan is not large enough) and poach very gently for 5 minutes.
* Remove the fish with a slotted spoon, flake with a fork and set aside. Strain the milk into a bowl and add to the soup together with the cream. Simmer for 10 minutes, adding the fish for the final few minutes, just to heat through, then season to taste with lemon juice, salt and pepper.
* Stir in the parsley just before serving.

Cock-a-leekie soup

UNITED KINGDOM
*

LENTIL
AND
BACON SOUP

This lightly spiced and warming soup is made with red
lentils, which will break down, colour and thicken this
soup. For a lentil soup with more texture, use the brown
or green varieties instead.

Serves: 4–6
Prep time: 15 minutes
Cook time: 1½ hours
{🥄}{🍴}{🍲}

- 30 g/1 oz (2 tablespoons) butter
- 175 g/6 oz dry-cured smoked bacon, chopped
- 2 cloves garlic, chopped
- 2 onions, chopped
- 2 stalks celery, sliced (optional)
- 1 large carrot, thinly sliced (optional)
- 200 g/7 oz (¾ cup plus 2 tablespoons) red lentils
- 1 teaspoon ground cumin (optional)
- 1.75 litres/60 fl oz (7½ cups) chicken stock
- 2 tablespoons chopped flat-leaf parsley
- 1 tablespoon chopped mint
- salt and pepper

* Melt the butter in a large saucepan over a medium heat,
  add the bacon and fry for 5–6 minutes until browned.
  Add the vegetables, stir through with the bacon and cook
  for 10–15 minutes until the vegetables have softened.
* Add the lentils and cumin (if using) and stir to coat them
  in the fried bacon and fat. Add the stock, then bring to
  a simmer and cook for 1 hour, or until the lentils have
  broken down completely.
* Add the herbs and season to taste with salt and pepper.

SCOTLAND
*

PARTAN BREE

Literally 'crab broth', partan bree is a creamy crab soup,
thickened with rice, traditional to Scotland. The earliest
recorded recipes simply reuse the boiling water from the
crabs as a base for the soup. Scottish chef Pamela Brunton
has adapted this recipe to include a crab stock painstakingly
made from the shells themselves. Serve for summer lunch
with good brown (whole wheat) bread and butter.

Serves: 4–6
Prep time: 30 minutes
Cook time: 3½–4 hours
{🥄}{🍴}

- 450 ml/15 fl oz (1⅔ cups plus 2 tablespoons)
  full-fat (whole) milk
- 35 g/1¼ oz (3 tablespoons) white rice,
  such as basmati or jasmine
- 2 large crabs, cooked (you need the shells and brown
  meat; white meat is optional)

- 100 ml/3½ fl oz (⅓ cup plus 1 tablespoon) crème
  fraîche and/or 50 g/2 oz (3½ tablespoons) brown butter
  (optional), plus extra crème fraîche, to serve (optional)
- citrus juice, from 1 lemon and ½ orange or
  50–75 ml/1¾–2½ fl oz (¼ cup minus 2 teaspoons–⅓ cup)
  sea buckthorn juice
- salt
- buttered brown (whole wheat) bread, to serve (optional)

- For the crab stock:
- shells of the 2 crabs
- about 50 ml/1¾ fl oz (3½ tablespoons) vegetable oil
- 50 g/2 oz (3½ tablespoons) butter, diced
- 2 carrots, diced into 1 cm/½ inch pieces
- 3 banana shallots, diced into 1 cm/½ inch pieces
- ½ teaspoon fennel seeds
- 1 star anise
- 6 green cardamom pods, crushed
- 6 black peppercorns

- To garnish (optional):
- grated lemon zest
- diced or shaved raw fennel bulb
- soft herbs such as chervil, bronze fennel and chive flowers
- fresh ripe gooseberries, whitecurrants and green
  strawberries

* For the crab stock, crush the crab shells well; you want
  all the pieces to be the size of small pieces of gravel.
  Heat 5 mm/¼ inch of the oil in a large wide saucepan
  over a medium heat for 2 minutes, or until shimmering.
  Add the crab shells to just cover the bottom of the pan,
  then add the butter. (If your pan is not big enough, roast
  the shells in 2 batches.) There should be insistent wild
  sizzling as soon as you add the shells. Roast the shells,
  stirring frequently, for 10–15 minutes until they are
  almost dry and the meat on them has caramelized. Add
  a splash of water to the pan and stir, scraping up all the
  tasty, gooey, sticky bits stuck on the bottom the pan. Stir
  the shells and repeat the process a couple more times,
  allowing the shells to dry out and roast again in between.
  Be very careful they don't scorch and burn, which will
  turn the stock bitter and unpleasant.
* When roasted, tip the shells into a colander set over a bowl
  to allow any excess oil to drip through (there should be no
  liquid dripping through, because the shells should be dry
  when you finish). Add a little fresh, clean water to the pan,
  then stir over a medium heat, using a wooden spoon to scrape
  up all the stuck-on bits one last time. Set this water aside.
* Warm a little of the crab oil back in the pan over a
  medium heat, add the carrots and cook, stirring frequently,
  for 5 minutes, or until just golden. Add the shallots and
  cook for another 5 minutes until they are translucent.
* Return the crab shells to the pan, add just enough water,
  including the reserved pan water, to cover the crab
  shells by 2 cm/¾ inch. Put all the spices into a paper
  teabag or scrap of fine cloth such as the toe of clean
  tights, tie with kitchen string and add to the pan. Bring
  to a brisk simmer over a medium heat, then reduce
  the heat to low and cook for 2½–3 hours, topping up
  (topping off) the water as needed to keep the level just
  above the crab shells. (Don't worry about skimming it;
  there's no fat in crab shells and any crab oil will infuse
  the stock and add flavour. Flavour matters more in the
  next step than perfect clarity.)
* Strain the liquid through a fine-mesh sieve or a normal
  sieve lined with muslin (cheesecloth) or a dish towel.

You need to get all the fragments of shell out. Taste it. You are probably going to want to reduce it a little to intensify the crab flavour. Pour it back into a clean saucepan and simmer over a low heat to evaporate and concentrate it. You should end up with around 450 ml/ 15 fl oz (1⅔ cups plus 2 tablespoons) stock.

* For the soup, put the crab stock and milk into a clean stockpot, add the rice and bring to a simmer over a medium heat. Cook for 15 minutes, or until the rice is very soft (exact timing will depend on what rice you use). Add the brown crab meat and return to a simmer. Cook for a few minutes, then ladle into a blender and blend until perfectly smooth. Alternatively, use a hand-held blender. Add the crème fraîche or butter (if using), plus citrus juices or sea buckthorn and blend briefly again to combine. Taste and add salt or more juice if necessary. (Brown crab meat may be quite salty, so adjust salt at the end rather than adding at the start.) Return the soup to a cleaned saucepan.

* To serve, heat the broth, butter some brown (whole wheat) bread and eat with an extra spoonful of crème fraîche. Or, dress the white crab meat with a little crème fraîche and drop it into 4–6 bowls. Garnish with grated lemon zest, diced or shaved raw fennel bulb and fresh soft herbs such as chervil, bronze fennel and chive flowers. Or, fresh ripe gooseberries, whitecurrants and green strawberries are also delicious additions in the early summer. Pour in the hot soup and serve.

SCOTLAND
*

MUSSEL BROSE

This creamy mussel soup is, like all traditional Scottish brose, thickened with a handful of finely ground oatmeal. The mussels should be cooked first then set aside to be added – and heated through – just before serving. Serve with good, thick slices of bread to sop up the brose.

Serves: 4
Prep time: 20 minutes
Cook time: 20 minutes
{🦪} {⌁}

- 1 kg/ 2¼ lb live mussels
- 750 ml/ 25 fl oz (3 cups) fish stock
- 150 ml/ 5 fl oz (⅔ cup) full-fat (whole) milk
- 60 g/ 2¼ oz (½ cup) fine oatmeal
- 150 ml/ 5 fl oz (⅔ cup) single (light) cream
- good thick slices bread, to serve

* Scrub the mussels under cold running water, removing any barnacles and pulling off any tendrils. Make sure the mussels are closed. If some are open, gently tap them on a work counter and if they still don't close, discard them.

* Put a large lidded saucepan over a medium-high heat, add the mussels and cook for 5 minutes, or until they open. Take the pan off the heat and remove the meat from the mussels. Discard any mussels that remain closed. Set the mussels aside. Pour the mussel cooking liquor through muslin (cheesecloth) into a jug (pitcher).

* Add the stock, milk and mussel liquor to the large saucepan and bring to a simmer. As the liquid simmers, put the oatmeal into a small dry frying pan or skillet and toast over a medium heat for 2–3 minutes.

* Put the toasted oatmeal into a heatproof bowl, add 2 ladles of the stock mixture and stir until smooth, then whisk back into the brose. Cook, stirring, for 3–4 minutes, waiting until just before serving to add the reserved mussels and the cream. Serve with thick slices of bread.

UNITED KINGDOM
*

MULLIGATAWNY SOUP

One of the earliest Anglo-Indian dishes, this spiced curry soup was created by Indian chefs in the late eighteenth century to suit the palate of the resident Brits. These chefs adapted a spiced broth-like dish called *milagu-tannir* (or 'pepper water'), which was traditionally served over rice, into a thicker dish more akin to British notions of 'soup'. By the early 1800s mulligatawny was already appearing in British cookbooks, and there it has stayed ever since. The recipe below is by no means definitive and is only meant as a starting point to find your own preferences. Many older mulligatawny recipes include sultanas (golden raisins) or diced apples – more modern recipes might riff on that sweetness by using butternut squash instead.

Serves: 6
Prep time: 15 minutes
Cook time: 1 hour 40 minutes
{🦪} {⌁} {⌁}

- 1 medium chicken, 1.5–2 kg/ 3¼–4½ lb
- 1.5 litres/ 50 fl oz (6¼ cups) light chicken stock or salted water
- 2 tablespoons ghee or groundnut (peanut) oil
- 1 teaspoon ground cumin
- 1 teaspoon ground coriander
- 2 teaspoons curry powder
- 4 cloves garlic, sliced
- 2 onions, chopped
- 50 g/ 2 oz (¼ cup) basmati rice
- 100 g/ 3½ oz (¾ cup) peas
- 4 tablespoons chopped coriander (cilantro) or flat-leaf parsley, or a mixture
- salt and pepper

* Put the chicken into a large stock pot or Dutch oven with 2 teaspoons of salt and the stock or water. Bring to the boil, then reduce the heat, cover with a lid and simmer for 45–60 minutes until the chicken is tender.

* Meanwhile, heat the ghee or oil in a large frying pan or skillet over a medium heat, add the spices and fry for 30 seconds. Add the garlic and onions and cook for 10–15 minutes until they turn golden brown.

* When the chicken has cooked, use a slotted spoon to remove it from the poaching liquid and set aside. Add the cooked onions, garlic and the rice to the pan and simmer for 20 minutes, then add the peas.

* Meanwhile, put the cooked chicken onto a chopping (cutting) board and separate the meat from the bones, making sure no chunks are overly large. Add the meat to the pan and heat it through for 5 minutes. Season to taste with salt and pepper.

* Serve in soup bowls sprinkled with the herbs.

ENGLAND: LONDON
*

PEA
AND
HAM SOUP
'LONDON PARTICULAR'

This thick pea and ham soup is made using a familiar English pairing of yellow split peas and ham. The soup, made using a stock from the simmered ham, is nicknamed 'London Particular', as a reference to the dangerous and dense London fogs of Victorian times. The thickest of these fogs were called 'pea soupers' and had a yellow-green hue.

Serves: 6
Prep time: 10 minutes, plus 8–12 hours soaking
Cook time: 2½ hours
{ 🧂 } { •• } { 🍲 }

- 500 g/ 1 lb 2 oz (2½ cups) yellow split peas
- 50 g/ 2 oz (3½ tablespoons) butter
- 1 large onion, chopped
- 1 large carrot, diced
- 1 ham hock
- Worcestershire sauce (optional)
- salt and pepper
- crusty bread, to serve

* Put the yellow split peas into a large bowl, cover with water and leave to soak overnight.
* The next day, drain the split peas and set aside. Melt the butter in a large saucepan or stockpot over a medium heat, add the onion and fry for 10–15 minutes until softened. Add the carrot and cook for another 10 minutes, then add the yellow split peas and ham. Pour in enough water to cover, about 2.5 litres/ 85 fl oz (10 cups) and slowly bring to a simmer over a low-medium heat. Cook for 2 hours, skimming off any scum that rises to the top with a slotted spoon until the ham is soft and can be pulled from the bone easily.
* Remove the ham from the pan using a slotted spoon, put it onto a chopping (cutting) board and leave to cool a little. When it has cooled enough to handle, strip it of its meat and return the meat to the pan. Season to taste with salt, pepper and Worcestershire sauce. Serve in bowls with crusty bread.

UNITED KINGDOM
*

OXTAIL SOUP

When making this rich soup, it is customary to add a small measure of red wine, port or even a little Mushroom Ketchup (page 426) at the end. If you have time, leave the soup to cool overnight, then skim off most of the fat before heating through and serving the following day.

Serves: 4–6
Prep time: 25 minutes
Cook time: 4½ hours
{ 🥩 } { •• }

- 4 tablespoons plain (all-purpose) flour
- 1 oxtail, trimmed of fat
- 50 g/2 oz (3½ tablespoons) lard or beef dripping
- 2 onions, chopped
- 2 carrots, chopped
- 1 leek, diced
- 2 stalks celery, chopped
- 2 cloves garlic, chopped (optional)
- 400 g/ 14 oz can plum tomatoes
- bouquet garni of 4–5 sprigs thyme, 3 bay leaves and a few flat-leaf parsley stalks tied together with kitchen string
- 300 ml/ 10 fl oz (1¼ cups) stout
- 1.5 litres/ 50 fl oz (6¼ cups) beef stock
- 50 ml/ 1¾ fl oz (3½ tablespoons) red wine or port, or a dash of Mushroom Ketchup (page 426)
- 1–2 tablespoons Worcestershire sauce
- 2 tablespoons chopped flat-leaf parsley (optional)
- salt and pepper

* Spread the flour out on a large plate and season with 1 teaspoon salt and 1 teaspoon of pepper, then dust the oxtail in the flour, shaking off any excess.
* Render the lard in a large frying pan or skillet over a medium-high heat, add the oxtail and fry for 5 minutes, or until browned all over. Transfer to a large saucepan and add the vegetables to the frying pan or skillet. Tip out some of the fat if there's a lot still left and fry the vegetables over a medium-high heat for 10 minutes, or until coloured. Add them to the large saucepan with the tomatoes and bouquet garni and heat over a medium heat.
* Pour a little of the stout into the frying pan or skillet and stir over a medium heat, scraping up all the crispy bits on the bottom of the pan, then pour into the saucepan. Add the remaining stout and the stock to the saucepan, stir well and cook over a low heat for 3–4 hours until the oxtail is tender and starting to fall away from the bone.
* At this point, remove the saucepan from the heat and put the oxtail onto a chopping (cutting) board. Pick off the meat with a fork – it should fall away easily – and return it to the saucepan. Remove the bouquet garni and discard, then stir through the wine, port or ketchup and season with Worcestershire sauce, salt and pepper. Stir in the parsley just before serving.

Pea and ham soup

UNITED KINGDOM

*

PHEASANT (OR GAME) SOUP
POACHER'S SOUP

This richly flavoured soup is best made at the height of autumn as a way of maximizing the use of game birds. This recipe uses pheasants, but partridge or wood pigeon would suit just as well.

Serves: 4–6
Prep time: 20 minutes
Cook time: 1½ hours

{🔥}{🍴}{🍲}

- about 60 g/2¼ oz (½ stick) butter
- 1–2 left-over pheasants, or mixed game birds
- 150 g/5 oz smoked ham, diced
- 1 small glass of port; about 120 ml
- 1.5 litres/50 fl oz (6¼ cups) game, beef or chicken stock
- 1 head celery, chopped
- 2 onions, chopped
- 2 carrots, chopped
- 2 parsnips, chopped
- pinch of ground mace or nutmeg
- 2 tablespoons finely chopped flat-leaf parsley
- salt and pepper

* Melt the butter in a large saucepan over a medium heat, add the game birds and cook for 5–6 minutes until browned all over. Remove from the pan and set aside, then add the ham and cook for 4–5 minutes until browned. Remove from the pan and set aside. Add the port to the pan and stir over a medium heat, scraping up all the crusty and browned bits on the bottom of the pan. Return the meat to the pan, add the stock and vegetables and simmer for 1 hour, or until the meat from the game birds is starting to come away from the bone. Remove the carcass from the pan, put it onto a chopping (cutting) board and leave to cool slightly.
* Once the meat is cool enough to handle, cut or pick the meat off the carcass, making sure that large chunks of meat are chopped to about 1 cm/½ inch. Return the meat to the pan without the carcass, and cook for 5 minutes. Season with salt, pepper and a little mace. Add the parsley just before serving.

SCOTLAND: SHETLAND

*

REESTIT MUTTON
TATTIE SOUP

A speciality of Shetland, reestit mutton is a salted cut of mutton dried above a smoky peat fire. The word 'reest' means to cure through drying or smoking and traditionally everything from hams to wild geese or fish could be 'reestit' as a means of preserving meat for winter.
These days, reestit mutton is still served at the end of the year. Slowly simmered, it creates a distinctly flavoured broth – an acquired taste for many – from which a potato soup is made.

Serves: 4–6
Prep time: 5 minutes
Cook time: 2½ hours

{🔥}{🔪}{🍴}{🍲}

- 1 kg/2¼ lb reestit mutton
- 2 large carrots, cut into large pieces
- ½ neep (swede/rutabaga), cut into large pieces
- 5 large potatoes, peeled and cut into large pieces
- 2 large onions, fairly finely chopped
- 2 tablespoons sunflower oil
- 1 small bunch of flat-leaf parsley
- salt and pepper
- Boiled New Potatoes (page 84), to serve (optional)

* Put the mutton into a large stockpot and generously cover with about 2 litres/68 fl oz (8 ½ cups) water. Bring to a simmer and cook for 2 hours, skimming off any scum that rises to the top with a slotted spoon.
* After 2 hours, remove the mutton from the pan using kitchen tongs, put it onto a chopping (cutting) board and leave to cool slightly. When the meat is cool enough to handle, cut the meat away from the bone, then shred or cut it into neat pieces. Set aside.
* Skim off any fat from the cooking liquor with a slotted spoon and add the vegetables. Bring the soup back to a simmer, cover with a lid and cook for 25 minutes, or until the vegetables are tender. Season to taste, and add as much of the mutton as you would like or set it aside to eat later alongside the soup with boiled potatoes.

ENGLAND: WEST MIDLANDS

*

GROATY PUDDING
GROATY DICK

This hearty Black Country stew is made with whole oat groats and almost resembles a rich meaty porridge (oatmeal). Traditionally cooked slowly through the night, if not nearly a whole day, it could be made so thick that it would be sliced up and taken to field workers. The good news is that it can be ready in no more than 6 or 7 hours today.

Serves: 6
Prep time: 10 minutes
Cook time: 6–16 hours

{🔪}{🍴}{🍲}

- 500 g/1 lb 2 oz diced beef shin (shank)
- 2 leeks, sliced
- 2 onions, sliced
- 100 g/3½ oz (¾ cup plus 2 teaspoons) oat groats
- about 750 ml/25 fl oz (3 cups) beef stock
- salt and pepper
- crusty bread, to serve

* Preheat the oven to 140°C/275°F/Gas Mark 1.
* Put the beef, leeks, onions and oat groats into a large bowl and mix together until combined. Transfer the mixture to an ovenproof casserole dish or Dutch oven, season well with salt and pepper and pour over the stock.
* Cover tightly with aluminium foil and the lid and bake for a minimum of 6 hours – or up to 16, if desired – until the beef and groats are tender. Serve with crusty bread.

ENGLAND
*

JUGGED HARE

The earliest recipes for this dark, rich hare stew date back
to the eighteenth century and suggest cooking the hare in
a large jug (pitcher), or as Dorothy Hartley suggests, a very
large pickle jar – although it's unlikely that she's referring
to one made from glass. These days a lidded casserole dish,
Dutch oven or large lidded stew pot will suit just fine.
The make-up of the stew varies, with Mrs Beeton's recipe
– cooked with beef gravy, port wine and served with
forcemeat balls – a timeless favourite. If you have caught
and butchered the hare yourself, or have a particularly
excellent relationship with your butcher, have the blood
reserved, then strain some into the stew with the port.

Serves: 6
Prep time: 30 minutes
Cook time: 3 hours 20 minutes
{•'}

- 4 tablespoons plain (all-purpose) flour
- 1 hare, cut into pieces
- 60 g/ 2¼ oz (½ stick) butter
- 100 g/ 3½ oz smoked bacon, chopped
- 400 ml/ 14 fl oz (1⅔ cups) red wine
- 400 ml/ 14 fl oz (1⅔ cups) beef stock
- 1 onion, diced
- bouquet garni of 3 bay leaves, celery leaves, 4 sprigs thyme
and 2 sprigs rosemary tied together with kitchen string
- 1 tablespoon anchovy sauce
- 2–3 tablespoons redcurrant jelly
- blood of the hare or 30 g/ 1 oz (3¾ tablespoons) plain
(all-purpose) flour and 30 g/ 1 oz (2 tablespoons) butter,
softened
- salt and pepper

* Spread the flour out on a large plate and season with
salt and pepper. Toss the pieces of hare in the seasoned
flour and set aside.
* Heat the butter in a large frying pan or skillet over a
medium heat, add the bacon and fry for 5 minutes, or
until crisp. Remove with a slotted spoon and put into a
large saucepan, then add the pieces of hare to the frying
pan or skillet and fry for several minutes until browned
all over. You may need to do this in batches. Add to
the pan with the bacon. Pour a little of the wine into
the frying pan or skillet and stir over a medium heat,
scraping up all the crispy bits on the bottom of the pan.
Pour into the saucepan with the hare, together with the
remaining wine, the stock, the onion, bouquet garni and
anchovy sauce. Bring to a slight simmer and cook very
gently for 2½–3 hours until the hare is tender. Remove
the pieces of hare with a slotted spoon and keep warm.
* Strain the cooking liquor through a sieve into a fresh
saucepan and cook over a medium heat until slightly
reduced. Add the jelly, then taste and season with salt
and pepper. Thicken either by beating in the blood off
the heat, or by mashing the butter and flour together in
a small bowl, then whisking it into the sauce in small
pieces. Pour some of the sauce over the hare, then serve
the rest in a jug (pitcher).

SCOTLAND
*

BAWD BREE

Much like the English Jugged Hare (see left), the Scottish
bawd bree ('hare soup'), is a deep, rich soup-stew that
utilizes the whole of the animal and dates back to some of
the earliest Scottish cookbooks, such as *The Household Book
of Lady Grisell Baillie* (1692–1733). The meat and offal are
removed and reserved from the carcass, which becomes the
stock base of the bree. Port wine, redcurrant or rowan jelly,
and again, the strained blood of the hare (if available) are
the recommended flavourings.

Serves: 6
Prep time: 30 minutes, plus 8–12 hours soaking
Cook time: 6 hours
{•'}

- 1 hare and its blood, if available
- 1 onion, diced
- 2 swedes (rutabagas), peeled and diced
- 2 carrots, diced
- 4 stalks celery, finely chopped
- 2 onions, quartered
- bouquet garni of flat-leaf parsley stalks, bay leaves, sprigs
thyme and rosemary tied together with kitchen string
- 1 teaspoon black peppercorns
- 2 tablespoons plain (all-purpose) flour
- 60 g/ 2¼ oz (½ stick) butter
- 100 ml/ 3½ fl oz (⅓ cup plus 1 tablespoon) port
- 3 tablespoons fine oatmeal
- salt and pepper

* Remove the meat from the hare – focusing on the legs
and saddle. Try to remove in large pieces, then slice them
into 1 cm/ ½ inch steaks. Cover with clingfilm (plastic
wrap) and set the meat aside in the fridge.
* Put the carcass into a large stockpot with 2 litres/
68 fl oz (8½ cups) water, cover with the lid and and
leave to soak overnight.
* The next day, bring the stockpot to a simmer over a medium
heat, skimming off the scum that rises to the top with a
slotted spoon.
* When there is no more scum, add the vegetables,
1 tablespoon salt, the bouquet garni and peppercorns,
then simmer gently for 3 hours. Strain, pushing the
vegetables through the sieve as much as possible into a
large, clean saucepan and bring the mixture back to a
gentle simmer.
* Meanwhile, spread the flour out on a large plate and
season with ½ teaspoon each of salt and pepper. Coat the
steaks in the flour, shaking off any excess.
* Melt the butter in a large frying pan or skillet over a high
heat, add the steaks and fry for several minutes, or until
browned. Put the steaks into the soup with the port and
simmer for 1½ hours, or until the meat is tender. Remove
the pan from the heat.
* Put the blood (if using) into a small heatproof bowl
with the oatmeal and mix together. Alternatively, mix
the oatmeal with enough water to form a paste. Add a
ladleful of hot soup to the mixture and stir through.
Return to the pan and cook for several minutes to allow
the liquid to thicken. Once thickened, season to taste
with salt and pepper and serve.

SCOTLAND
*

HAIRST BREE
HODGE PODGE/HOTCHPOTCH

The emphasis of this traditional harvest soup is on its medley of seasonal vegetables. Over time, the dish's name expanded to usage outside the kitchen, and 'hotchpotch' can be used to describe any jumbled mixture.

Serves: 4–6
Prep time: 15 minutes
Cook time: 2½ hours

{🜂}{🝙}{🝧}

- 2 lamb (or mutton) necks
- 6 small swedes (rutabaga), peeled and diced
- 12 small carrots, 400 g/ 14 oz (3 cups) fresh peas or broad (fava) beans, or a mixture of the two
- 1 bunch spring onions (scallions), chopped
- 1 small cauliflower, cut into florets
- 3 little gem lettuces, quartered
- 3 tablespoons chopped fresh flat-leaf parsley
- salt and pepper

* Put the necks into a large stockpot with 3 litres/ 101 fl oz (12 cups) water and 1 teaspoon of salt. Slowly bring to the boil, then reduce the heat to low and simmer for 1 hour, skimming off any scum that rises to the top with a slotted spoon.
* Add the swede (rutabaga), carrots, peas and spring onions (scallions) and season with pepper. Simmer for another 1½ hours.
* Meanwhile, put the cauliflower and lettuce into a large bowl, cover with salted water and leave to soak for 1–1½ hours to crisp up.
* About 15 minutes before the end of the cooking time, drain the cauliflower and lettuce and add them to the soup. Check for seasoning, then add the parsley just before serving.

SCOTLAND
*

SCOTCH BROTH
BARLEY BROTH

Scotland has a long, proud tradition of flavourful broth-based soups, which, cooked with pieces of meat and plenty of vegetables, were often eaten in two parts. Once cooked, the meat would be set aside and kept warm, and the broth and vegetables supped in bowls on their own. Later, the meat was carved up and could be eaten with buttered Oatcakes (pages 260 and 261). This is still the tradition with Shetland's Tattie Soup (page 50).

The core elements to this broth are lamb or mutton, peas and barley, but often also include whatever vegetables are in abundance. Scottish food writer Catherine Brown notes that the barley broth served in wealthier households would have placed more emphasis on the meat, the poorer ones an emphasis on the pulses (legumes) and cereals. Today, it's up to the cook's preference.

Serves: 6
Prep time: 15 minutes, plus 8–12 hours soaking
Cook time: 3¼ hrs

{🜂}{🝙}{🝧}{🝨}

- 60 g/ 2¼ oz (⅓ cup) dried peas
- 2 lamb or mutton necks
- 60 g/ 2¼ oz (⅓ cup) pearl barley
- 200 g/ 7 oz carrot, diced
- 200 g/ 7 oz neeps (swede/rutabaga), peeled and diced
- 2 onions, chopped
- 1 small white cabbage, thinly sliced
- 3–4 tablespoons chopped flat-leaf parsley
- salt and pepper

* Put the dried peas into a medium bowl, cover with water and leave to soak overnight.
* The next day, drain the peas and put into a large saucepan with the necks and pearl barley, cover generously with water and add 1 teaspoon salt. Slowly bring to a simmer over a medium heat and cook for 1 hour, skimming off the brown scum that rises to the top with a slotted spoon.
* Add the carrots, neeps (swede/rutabaga) and onions, cover with a lid, reduce the heat to low and simmer for 2 hours. You may need to top up with a little water during this time.
* Remove the necks from the pan and set aside. Add the cabbage and cook for 10–15 minutes until tender. Use a fork to pick the meat from the neck bones and return the meat to the pan. Season with pepper and more salt, then stir in the parsley just before serving.

WALES
*

LEEK BROTH

Once simmered, salty Welsh bacon makes for an excellent base or stock to a soup or stew. This leek broth was traditionally made from such a base; the bacon piece could be sliced up and added to it, or served on its own.

Serves: 6
Prep time: 15 minutes
Cook time: 1 hour 35 minutes

{🜂}{🝙}{🝧}{🝨}

- 6 leeks
- 2.5 litres/ 85 fl oz (10 cups) bacon, pork, chicken or vegetable stock or water
- 3 tablespoons pearl barley
- 3 bay leaves
- 2 onions, sliced
- 2 carrots, sliced
- 3 stalks celery, sliced
- 750 g/ 1 lb 10 oz potatoes, peeled and diced
- salt and pepper

* Split 3 of the leeks lengthways, rinse them well and tie them together with kitchen string, then put them into a large casserole dish or Dutch oven with the stock or water, pearl barley and bay leaves. Bring to a simmer over a medium-low heat and cook for 1 hour.
* Remove the leeks, add the onions, carrots, celery and potatoes to the pan and simmer for another 30 minutes.

* Meanwhile, finely slice the remaining leeks and add to the soup, simmering for 5 minutes. Season well and serve.

NORTHERN IRELAND / SCOTLAND
*

BOYNDIE BROTH
OATMEAL SOUP

Porridge (steel-cut) oats are used as both grain and thickener in this simple versatile soup, common to oat-growing regions of Northern Ireland, as well as Scotland.

Serves: 3–4
Prep time: 10 minutes
Cook time: 45 minutes
{🫙} {🥄} {🍲}

- 60 g / 2¼ oz (½ stick) butter
- 1 onion, sliced
- 1 carrot, diced
- 2 bay leaves
- 60 g / 2¼ oz (⅔ cup) porridge (steel-cut) oats
- ¼ teaspoon ground mace
- ¼ teaspoon ground nutmeg
- 750 ml / 25 fl oz (3 cups) chicken stock
- 250 ml / 8 fl oz (1 cup) full-fat (whole) milk
- 150 ml / 5 fl oz (⅔ cup) single (light) cream
- salt and pepper

* Melt the butter in a large saucepan over a medium heat, add the onion, carrot and bay leaves and fry for 10–15 minutes until the vegetables are soft and lightly golden. Add the oats, mace and nutmeg, then toss the oats and spices with the vegetables and fry for another 5 minutes.
* Add the stock and milk, season, then bring to a simmer over a medium-low heat and cook for 25–30 minutes until the oats have plumped up and become soft.
* Remove from the heat, remove the bay leaves, and, using a hand-held blender, blend until smooth. Add the cream and season to taste before serving.

SCOTLAND / WALES
*

SHEEP'S HEAD BROTH
POWSOWDIE

In rural Scotland and Wales, after a sheep's slaughter, the animal's head would be set aside for making broth. Held aloft over a fire, the head would be singed of its hairs, then split in half and prepared for the stockpot. In addition to a flavourful soup, the offal from the head could be used to make a sort of country terrine. While this recipe may seem several centuries out of date, it remained a common feature of most Scottish cookbooks well into the 1950s. Today, however, this is mainly one for reference.

Serves: 5–6
Prep time: 2–3 hours, plus 8–12 hours soaking
Cook time: 3–4 hours
{🫙} {🔪} {🥄} {🍲}

- 25 g / 1 oz (¼ cup minus 4 teaspoons) pearl barley
- 25 g / 1 oz (¼ cup minus 4 teaspoons) dried green peas
- 1 sheep's head
- vinegar, for soaking
- 1 small swede (rutabaga), peeled and diced
- 2 large carrots, diced
- 2 large leeks, thinly sliced, white and green parts separated
- 2 stalks celery, chopped
- 1 tablespoon chopped flat-leaf parsley
- salt and pepper

* Put the pearl barley and dried peas into a large bowl, cover with water and leave to soak overnight.
* The next day, drain the pearl barley and peas and set aside.
* Split the sheep's head in half and remove the tongue and brains. Wash the brains, then put them into a large bowl and cover with cold water and a little vinegar and leave to soak; the brains are not used in the broth.
* Wash the head thoroughly, removing the eyes and all the soft gristle from the nostrils and discard. Scrub and wash the tongue, then add the tongue and the head halves to a large stockpot, cover with cold water, stir in a pinch of salt and leave to stand for at least 1 hour.
* Drain the water from the stockpot and pour in enough fresh cold water to cover. Bring to the boil, then remove from the heat. Pour the water away and rinse the head, tongue and stockpot with fresh water.
* Put the head and tongue back into the stockpot with the barley, dried peas, salt and 3.5 litres / 118 fl oz (14 cups) cold water. Bring to the boil and skim well with a slotted spoon to remove any scum that rises to the top. Once boiling, add the swede (rutabaga) and carrots, the whites of the leeks and the celery, then reduce the heat to low and simmer slowly for 3 hours, or until the head and tongue are tender and cooked.
* Remove the head and tongue from the pot, then cut away the meat from the head and add a small handful of meat per person back into the pot. Just before serving, add the greens of the leeks, the parsley, and more salt and pepper, if necessary, and heat through for a few more minutes.
* It's important to skin the boiled tongue before serving. Peel away the skin, then cut the tongue into thin slices and eat cold with a green sauce and lentils or a Horseradish Sauce (page 415). The brain can be blanched in milk, mixed with flat-leaf parsley and breadcrumbs, then dipped in beaten egg and further breadcrumbs, fried in hot oil, and served with a mayonnaise dip.

WALES
*
CAWL

The traditional Welsh harvest stew, the cawl (simply 'broth' in Welsh) varied in substance from house to house, and indeed season to season, depending on what was in abundance. Typically, however, it was made using salted bacon or beef and leeks, cabbage and potatoes, along with the cook's choice of root vegetables. Today, tough cuts such as lamb neck or beef shin are preferred to bacon pieces. In many parts of Wales, it is still common to eat cawl in wooden bowls with wooden spoons, with a crusty bread and good cheese served alongside.

Serves: 6
Prep time: 15 minutes
Cook time: 2¼ hours
{♠}{♣}{♦}

- 30 g/ 1 oz (2 tablespoons) beef dripping or lard
- 1 kg/ 2¼ lb best end of lamb neck, on the bone, trimmed of fat
- 2 onions, sliced
- 2 carrots, sliced
- 2 leeks, sliced, white and green parts separated
- 1 parsnip, sliced
- 1 swede (rutabaga), peeled and diced
- 3 potatoes, cut into eighths
- bouquet garni of 4 sprigs thyme, 2 sprigs rosemary and 2 bay leaves tied together with kitchen string
- salt and pepper
- marigold flowers, to garnish (optional)
- crusty bread, to serve

* Heat the fat in a large stockpot over a medium heat, add the lamb and cook for 5 minutes, or until browned all over. Pour in 2.5 litres/ 85 fl oz (10 cups) water or enough to generously cover the lamb by about 2.5 cm/ 1 inch and bring slowly to a simmer for 30 minutes, skimming off any scum that rises to the top with a slotted spoon.
* Taste and season with salt and pepper, then add the onions, carrots, white part of the leeks, parsnip, swede (rutabaga), potatoes and herbs and simmer for 90 minutes.
* Using kitchen tongs, carefully remove the neck piece from the pan, put it onto a chopping (cutting) board and cut away the meat. Chop the meat into large pieces and return it to the pan with the green leeks. Cook for another 5 minutes, then remove the bouquet garni and season to taste. Garnish with marigold flowers (if using) and serve warm with good crusty bread.

UNITED KINGDOM
*
BEEF
AND
STOUT STEW

Beef stew is something of great pleasure: comforting, hearty and warming. Plenty of regional variations exist, but the star of the show is always a tough 'cheap' cut of beef, so tender and flavourful by the time it's served. Most Irish recipes also include a good glug of stout. If you have the time to spare, leave the stew to stand uncovered, and let the flavours mingle and saturate before serving.

Serves: 6–8
Prep time: 15 minutes, plus 1 hour standing
Cook time: 2–2½ hours
{♠}{♣}

- 50 ml/ 1¾ fl oz (3½ tablespoons) neutral oil
- 1 kg/ 2¼ lb cubed beef rib (short rib or 'Jacob's ladder')
- 2 onions, finely chopped
- 2 cloves garlic, finely chopped
- ½ teaspoon cornflour (cornstarch)
- 1 litre/ 34 fl oz (4¼ cups) beef stock
- about 285ml/ 10 fl oz (1 cup plus 2 tablespoons) stout
- 1 bay leaf
- ½ teaspoon black peppercorns
- 400 g/ 14 oz waxy potatoes (such as Charlotte), diced
- 2 carrots, diced
- 2 stalks celery, diced
- 1 sprig thyme
- 1 quantity Suet Dumplings (page 244), made with 1 tablespoon chopped flat-leaf parsley
- salt and pepper

* Heat half the oil in a large frying pan or skillet over a medium heat. Increase the heat to medium-high, add the beef and fry for 5 minutes, or until browned all over. Remove from the heat, transfer the meat to a deep lidded casserole dish or Dutch oven and wipe the pan clean with paper towels.
* Heat the remaining oil in the frying pan or skillet over a medium heat, add the onions and garlic and fry for 7–10 minutes. Remove from the heat.
* Put the cornflour (cornstarch) into a small bowl and stir in a little of the stock until a paste forms. Add it to the casserole dish or Dutch oven. Pour the stock and stout into the casserole dish or Dutch oven together with the bay leaf and peppercorns, and bring to the boil. Skim off any scum or fat with a slotted spoon, then reduce the heat, cover with a lid and simmer for 1 hour.
* Add the onions, garlic, potatoes, carrots, celery and thyme to the casserole and cook for another 50 minutes, skimming off any scum or fat when necessary. About 25 minutes before the stew has finished, add the dumplings (but don't overcrowd the pan), cover with the lid and cook. Once the meat and vegetables are tender and the liquid has thickened, remove from the heat and leave to stand, uncovered, for 1 hour.
* Alternatively, after cooking the vegetables for 50 minutes, preheat the oven to 200°C/400°F/Gas Mark 6.
* Add the dumplings to the top of the casserole dish or Dutch oven, then cook in the oven, uncovered, for 25–30 minutes until cooked through. Season to taste and serve.

Cawl

WALES / NORTHWEST OF ENGLAND
*

SCOUSE

Scouse (from 'lobscouse') is a thick lamb stew that is popular in Liverpool and areas of northwest England but rooted in shared northern European traditions. The stew was first popularized by travelling merchants and sailors and later became common to many port cities of the North and Baltic seas. Called *labskaus* in Germany and *lapskaus* in Norway, its recommended serving suggestion – pickled red cabbage – is a telling reminder of such roots. Scouse's popularity in the Liverpool area also led to the designation of its locals as 'Scousers', a term that has become commonplace over time.

Serves: 6
Prep time: 20 minutes
Cook time: 2¾ hours
{♨}{🔥}{🌶}

- 60 g/¼ oz (4 tablespoons) lard or beef dripping
- 750 g/1 lb 10 oz lamb neck or any stewing beef, such as beef shin, cut into large pieces
- 2 leeks, thickly sliced
- 2 onions, chopped
- 2 carrots, chopped
- bouquet garni of 2 sprigs rosemary, 4 sprigs thyme and 2 bay leaves tied together with kitchen string
- 1.5 litres/50 fl oz (6¼ cups) lamb or beef stock (to match the meat you have chosen)
- 1 kg/2¼ lb potatoes, peeled and chopped
- 100 g/3¼ oz (¾ cup) garden peas
- salt and pepper

- To serve:
- Pickled Red Cabbage (page 444)
- crusty bread

* Preheat the oven to 160°C/325°F/Gas Mark 3.
* Render the fat in a large saucepan over a medium heat, add the meat and fry for several minutes, or until well-browned. Using a slotted spoon, carefully transfer the meat to a deep casserole dish or Dutch oven, making sure to leave the fat behind in the saucepan to cook the vegetables in.
* Add the leeks, onions and carrots to the fat in the pan, season with salt and pepper and fry for 7–8 minutes until just turning golden. Put the vegetables into the casserole dish or Dutch oven with the remaining ingredients, except the peas. Cover tightly with the lid and cook in the oven for 2 hours.
* Add the peas, taste the stock and add more salt and pepper, if desired, then cook for another 30 minutes. Remove the bouquet garni, and serve with Pickled Red Cabbage and crusty bread.

NORTHERN IRELAND
*

IRISH STEW

This hearty stew is made from a very simple list of ingredients: mutton or lamb necks, potatoes, onions and sometimes carrots. In Northern Ireland, the prevalence of cattle-raising meant beef was sometimes used in place of lamb.

Serves: 4–6
Prep time: 20 minutes
Cook time: 2½ hours
{♨}{🔥}{🌶}

- 3 lamb, hogget or mutton necks, 1–1.2 kg/2¼–2½ lb in total, or the same weight in braising steak or beef shin, diced
- 2 bay leaves
- 3 sprigs thyme
- 2 cloves garlic
- 5 white peppercorns
- 2 onions, peeled
- 600 g/1 lb 5 oz carrots, peeled
- 1 tablespoon vegetable oil
- 400 g/14 oz floury (baking) potatoes (such as Maris Piper or Yukon Gold), peeled and coarsely diced
- 600 g/1 lb 5 oz waxy potatoes (such as Charlotte), peeled and diced
- salt and pepper

* To make the stock, remove the flesh from the bones on the necks then dice. Cut the bones (if possible), then put the bones and meat into a large stockpot with a pinch of salt. Generously cover with water and bring to the boil. Once boiling, skim off the scum that rises to the top with a slotted spoon, then reduce the heat to a simmer. Add 1 bay leaf, a sprig of thyme, a clove of garlic, 2 peppercorns, 1 onion and a carrot, cut in half, to the pot and cook for 1½ hours.
* For the stew, finely dice the remaining onion and garlic. Heat the oil in a large saucepan over a medium heat, add the onions and garlic and cook for 8 minutes, or until translucent but not coloured. Coarsely dice the remaining carrots and add them with the floury (baking) potatoes to the pan.
* Strain the stock into a heatproof bowl or jug (pitcher), setting the meat aside and discarding the bones. Pour the stock onto the vegetables in the saucepan and bring to the boil, skimming off the scum that rises to the top. Add the meat and remaining aromatics, reduce the heat and cook for 40 minutes. Add the waxy potatoes and cook for 20 minutes, or until tender. For best results, leave the stew to stand for at least 1 hour before serving. Season to taste.

Irish stew

THE HERBACEOUS PLANTS WHICH EXIST FIT FOR FOOD
FOR MAN, ARE MORE NUMEROUS THAN MAY BE IMAGINED,
AND WHEN WE REFLECT HOW MANY OF THESE, FOR WANT
OF KNOWLEDGE, ARE ALLOWED TO ROT AND DECOMPOSE
IN THE FIELDS AND GARDENS, WE OUGHT, WITHOUT LOSS
OF TIME, TO MAKE OURSELVES ACQUAINTED WITH THEIR
DIFFERENT NATURES AND FORMS, AND VARY OUR FOOD
AS THE SEASON CHANGES.

ALEXIS SOYER, SOYER'S SHILLING COOKERY, 1854

Any naysayers on the topic of British vegetables need only cast an eye to the role and reverence attributed to some of our traditional favourites: honey-glazed and roasted root vegetables, buttered and vibrant greens, or bowls of peas – slow-cooked and malty black peas, or fresh minted green ones – to understand that the nation's appreciation is appropriately deep-running and diverse.

Britain has few truly 'native' vegetables, and so this topic inevitably leads us back to the immigrants and invaders who, over thousands of years, brought with them vegetables native to the Mediterranean and even further east. The many Roman introductions, for instance, reads like a grocer's inventory. From late Roman and early medieval times, pulses (beans), legumes and root vegetables were the most widely eaten vegetables. And despite nearly two millennia, little has happened to change that. Peas, for instance, were so commonly available that they could be milled and used to supplement flour for bread in times of scarcity. And while sweet green peas are the most common type today, it is yellow split peas that were (and still are) traditionally used to make the iconic pease pudding; peasemeal, made from dried and roasted yellow peas, is still a familiar flavour to some

in Scotland. Carrots and parsnips are deep-rooted favourites of the British diet, with turnips and swedes (rutabagas) – and even the king of tubers, the potato – not reaching their level of ubiquity before the middle of the eighteenth century at the earliest.

The most fertile, arable lands could grow a wide variety of vegetables. The best lands were found in the south of England and here even the common folk had a much greater diversity to their diet than their northern counterparts. With that being said, pockets of good land could be found all across the country, and stark contrasts could exist within a single region: James VI of Scotland once dubbed the East Neuk 'the golden fringe' of a 'beggar's mantle' – the latter a reference to the rest of Fife, of which the East Neuk is part.

Conditions could be particularly bad in the north and upland areas, where cold, rocky soil and poor weather were ill-fated growing conditions for many plants. The hardiest of crops, such as winter cabbages, were understandably well-prized in these areas. Such was kale's importance to the diet in northern Scotland, for instance, that kitchen gardens were dubbed 'kailyards'. Cabbage, in a broad sense, was king. That appreciation

later extended to other members of the *Brassica oleracea* family: broccoli, cauliflower and Brussels sprouts, which became more widely available by the eighteenth and nineteenth centuries.

While most vegetables were grown, plenty were cultivated in the wild as well, with an abundance gathered from along coastlines and even beach fronts: edible seaweeds, like carrageen and laver, were hugely popular among coastal communities, and could be used for everything from savoury sauces and cakes to sweet puddings. Other sea vegetables, such as samphire or sea kale, are rather less versatile, but are wonderfully suited to pairing with seafood caught just metres away.

With a few exceptions – green peas or wild garlic, for example – most vegetables are traditionally well-cooked before eating. (It's true, the British are not great innovators of salad.) The autumn harvest of vegetables suits an array of basic preparations, from boiling to roasting, mashing and frying. The only uniform addition is that perhaps everything can be improved by a healthy dollop of butter or a good glug of cream. No bad thing.

VEGETABLES

UNITED KINGDOM
*

BEETROOT SALAD
WITH
GOAT'S CHEESE

This recipe is best made with a fairly strong and crumbly goat's cheese – something equal to the tartness of a pickled beetroot (beet) and zest of an orange. If desired, replace the oranges with 50 g / 2 oz (⅓ cup) crushed walnuts.

Serves 2
Prep time: 30 minutes
Cook time: 30–40 minutes
{♦}{♨}

- 6 baby beetroot (beets) or 2–3 large
- olive oil, for drizzling
- 2 oranges, such as navel, Valencia or blood
- 100 g / 3½ oz goat's cheese
- 1 large handful rocket (arugula)
- salt and pepper

* Preheat the oven to 160°C / 325°F / Gas Mark 3.
* Put the beetroot (beets) into the centre of a piece of aluminium foil large enough to wrap completely around them. Sprinkle a little salt and a glug of olive oil over them, then close the foil to make a package and put it onto an oven tray or baking sheet. Roast in the oven for 30–40 minutes until they are easily pierced with a fork. (If cooking larger ones, wrap them individually in the foil.)
* Meanwhile, peel and segment the oranges and crumble or slice the goat's cheese, depending on the type being used.
* When the beetroot are cooked, while still warm, carefully remove the skins using kitchen gloves, if necessary. The skins should be easy to remove with your fingers or a small knife. Leave them to cool, then cut them in half.
* Put the beetroot into a serving bowl, add the rocket (arugula), the orange and most of the goat's cheese and mix to combine. Add a little oil and toss, then season with salt and pepper and sprinkle the remaining cheese over the top. Serve.

UNITED KINGDOM
*

WATERCRESS SALAD
WITH
CAPERS

The English have been making watercress salads since the seventeeth century. Typically tossed with parsley and a root vegetable (parsnips or waxy potatoes), this adaptation draws inspiration from the iconic watercress salad served at St. JOHN restaurant in London. Serve with roast game birds.

Serves: 4
Prep time: 5 minutes
{♦}{♠}{♨}{♣}{♪}{♠}{♟}

- 2 teaspoons mustard
- 2 tablespoons cider vinegar
- 5 tablespoons rapeseed (canola) oil
- 500 g / 1 lb 2 oz watercress, thick woody stems removed
- 1 tablespoon capers, chopped
- 1 shallot, finely sliced
- 1 tablespoon chopped flat-leaf parsley
- salt and pepper

* To make the dressing, combine the mustard and vinegar in a small bowl, then gradually whisk in the oil until the dressing emulsifies. Season with salt and pepper.
* Put the watercress, capers, shallots and parsley into a large salad bowl, then drizzle over the dressing. Toss well and serve immediately.

UNITED KINGDOM
*

CELERIAC, SPELT
AND
SPENWOOD SALAD

This grain salad makes for an idyllic late autumn lunch – a flavourful balance of deep, rich and nutty flavours.

Serves: 2
Prep time: 15 minutes
Cook time: 1½ hours
{♦}

- 1 celeriac (celery root), peeled and halved
- splash of rapeseed (canola) oil, plus extra for oiling
- 150 g / 5 oz (1 cup) spelt
- splash of sherry or cider vinegar
- 1 handful toasted and chopped hazelnuts
- wedge of Spenwood cheese, for shaving
- salt and pepper

* Preheat the oven to 180°C / 350°F / Gas Mark 4.
* Rub the celeriac (celery root) halves with oil, season with salt and pepper and wrap in aluminium foil. Put the foil package on a baking sheet and bake in the oven for 1½ hours, or until the celeriac is soft and easily pierced.
* Meanwhile, bring a medium saucepan of salted water to the boil. Rinse the spelt thoroughly and add it to the pan. Cover with a lid, reduce the heat to low and cook for 40 minutes, or until soft but still with some bite. Drain and set aside.
* When the celeriac is ready, leave it to cool in the foil before slicing into wedges. Assemble the salad while both the spelt and celeriac are still slightly warm. Toss the spelt and celeriac wedges together with the oil and vinegar and season. Top with the chopped hazelnuts and shave over the cheese liberally.

Beetroot salad with goat's cheese

SUMMER SALAD

This bright, fresh salad features not only the best of British summertime but gets an added burst of colour from its edible flowers: blue from the borage, and the warm red and orange tones from the nasturtiums.

Serves: 4–6
Prep time: 15 minutes, plus 10 minutes steeping
Cook time: 5 minutes
{ⓥ}{◆}{▲}{▲}{↵}

- 2 shallots, thinly sliced
- 4 tablespoons cider vinegar
- 50 g/2 oz (⅓ cup) shelled peas
- 50 g/2 oz young broad (fava) beans, podded
- 1 large butterhead lettuce, shredded
- 6 cherry tomatoes, halved
- 2 tablespoons olive oil
- caster (superfine) sugar, to taste (optional)
- 6 nasturtium leaves, 4 nasturtium flowers
and 12 borage flowers
- salt and pepper

* Put the shallots and 2 tablespoons of the vinegar into a small bowl, mix together and leave to steep for 10 minutes. Drain well and set the shallots aside.
* Meanwhile, bring a small saucepan of water to the boil, add the peas and broad (fava) beans and blanch for 3 minutes, before draining and leaving to cool slightly.
* Put the shredded lettuce into a large salad bowl and add the drained shallots, beans, peas and tomatoes.
* Put the remaining 2 tablespoons of vinegar and the oil in another small bowl. Season to taste with salt, pepper and sugar (if using) and stir together. Pour the dressing over the salad and toss. Arrange the flowers on top and serve.

FRIED FIELD MUSHROOMS

Fried field mushrooms, golden brown and just a little crisp, are a crucial part of any Full Breakfast (page 26).

Serves: 2–3
Prep time: 5 minutes
Cook time: 10 minutes
{ⓥ}{▲}{↵}{▦}{▲}{Ⓧ}

- 250 g/9 oz Portobello mushrooms
- 25 g/1 oz (2 tablespoons) butter

* Clean the mushrooms thoroughly, then remove and discard their stalks. Slice into halves or quarters depending on their thickness and your own preference.
* Melt the butter in a large frying pan or skillet over a medium-low heat for 2 minutes, or until foaming. Add the mushrooms and fry for a few minutes until lightly golden brown. Serve hot.

GRILLED HISPI CABBAGE

This preparation of hispi (sweetheart) cabbage has become a new classic on British pub menus: grilled (broiled) until just lightly charred, then brushed with butter.

Serves: 4
Prep time: 5 minutes
Cook time: 20 minutes
{ⓥ}{▲}{↵}{▲}{Ⓧ}

- 1 hispi (sweetheart) cabbage, cut into quarters
- oil, for oiling
- melted butter, for brushing
- salt

* Bring a large saucepan of salted water to the boil. Add a cabbage quarter and blanch for 3 minutes, or until the core of the cabbage can be pierced with a fork. Remove with a slotted spoon and set aside to steam-dry. Repeat with the remaining quarters.
* Preheat the grill (broiler) to medium-high. Oil an oven tray or large baking sheet. Brush the quarters with a little melted butter, place on the prepared tray, rounded-side down, and grill (broil) for 5 minutes, or until the quarters start to char. Serve.

STILTON, PEAR
AND
WALNUT SALAD

This salad has a very pleasing meeting of flavours and textures, and all the composite ingredients can be found – of great quality – throughout the UK.

Serves: 4
Prep time: 10 minutes
{ⓥ}{▲}{Ⓧ}

- 100 g/3½ oz (¾ cup) walnuts
- 1–2 ripe pears
- 100 g/3½ oz salad leaves
- 150 g/5 oz Stilton cheese (or similar)
- Mustard Dressing (page 427)

* Preheat the oven to 160°C/325°F/Gas Mark 3 and line a baking sheet with baking (parchment) paper.
* Spread the walnuts out on the prepared baking sheet and cook in the oven for 8–10 minutes, or until just lightly toasted. Set aside to cool.
* Slice the pears very thinly before combining with the salad leaves in a large bowl. Crumble the cheese into the salad. Coarsely chop or crush the toasted walnuts before sprinkling them into the salad as well. Add a little of the Mustard Dressing and toss the salad until combined. Serve immediately.

Stilton, pear and walnut salad

WALES
*

CREAMED LEEKS

Sliced thin and sweated in butter and cream, these leeks make for a decadent side dish that pairs well with roasted meats, and in place of Creamed Spinach (below) or even Cauliflower Cheese (page 72).

Serves: 4
Prep time: 10 minutes
Cook time: 20 minutes
{🐟}{🔥}{🍴}{🍲}{🥄}

- 10 g/¼ oz (2 teaspoons) butter
- 6 leeks, thinly sliced
- 100 ml/3½ fl oz (⅓ cup plus 1 tablespoon) double (heavy) cream
- salt and pepper

* Melt the butter in a medium saucepan over a low heat, add the sliced leeks and turn to coat them in the butter. Cook for 10–15 minutes. Season with salt and pepper.
* Add the cream and simmer gently for another 2 minutes, or until the liquid has reduced slightly and the leeks are fully coated in the cream. Serve hot.

SCOTLAND
*

BUTTERED LEEKS

These leeks, slowly softened in butter, are an excellent alternative to the creamy or cheesy greens that often surround a Sunday roast chicken.

Serves: 4
Prep time: 5 minutes
Cook time: 15 minutes
{🐟}{🔥}{🍴}{🍲}{🥄}{🍽}

- 120 g/4 oz (1 stick) butter
- 6 leeks, cut into diagonal slices, about 2 cm/¾ inch wide
- salt and pepper

* Melt the butter in a medium saucepan over a low heat, add the leeks and stir them well to coat them in the melted butter. Cover with a lid and cook for 10–15 minutes until soft. Season to taste with salt and pepper and serve hot.

UNITED KINGDOM
*

CELERIAC PURÉE

This celeriac (celery root) purée is luxuriously creamy, with a slight nuttiness that makes it an excellent accompaniment to roasted red meats and wild birds. If you prefer, you can mash the cooked celeriac with butter instead of blending it.

Serves: 4
Prep time: 10 minutes
Cook time: 20–30 minutes
{🐟}{🔥}{🍴}{🍲}{🥄}

- 150 g/5 oz (1¼ sticks) butter
- 1 celeriac (celery root), peeled and diced
- salt and pepper

* Melt the butter in a medium saucepan over a medium heat, add the celeriac (celery root) and mix to coat in the butter. Add a little salt and pepper and fry the celeriac for 1–2 minutes. Reduce the heat to low, cover with a lid and cook, stirring occasionally, for 15–20 minutes, or until the celeriac has softened. If it starts to stick to the pan, add 1 tablespoon or so of water.
* When the celeriac has softened, uncover and cook for another minute, or until any excess water has reduced. While still warm, using a hand-held blender, blend the celeriac with the butter until smooth. Taste and season, if desired, then serve.

UNITED KINGDOM
*

CREAMED SPINACH

This classic side dish pairs well with Roast Chicken (page 136) or Roast Forerib of Beef (page 180) and should be served warm, alongside the typical roast accoutrements.

Serves: 4
Prep time: 10 minutes
Cook time: 15 minutes
{🐟}{🍴}{🍲}

- 500 g/1 lb 2 oz spinach
- 50 g/2 oz (3½ tablespoons) butter
- 1 white onion, diced
- 50 g/2 oz (½ cup minus 2 teaspoons) plain (all-purpose) flour
- 150 ml/5 fl oz (⅔ cup) full-fat (whole) milk
- 100 ml/3½ fl oz (⅓ cup plus 1 tablespoon) single (light) cream
- nutmeg, grated, to taste
- salt

* Bring a large saucepan of salted water to the boil, add the spinach and blanch for 3–5 minutes. Quickly drain and chop the spinach. Set aside.
* Melt the butter in a large frying pan or skillet over a medium heat, add the onion and fry for 8–10 minutes until soft and translucent. Add the flour and stir it into the onion. While stirring, slowly pour in the milk, then cook over a low-medium heat for 3–5 minutes, or until the mixture thickens slightly.
* Add the chopped spinach and cream and stir through. Bring the mixture to a simmer briefly, then remove from the heat. Season with grated nutmeg and salt and serve warm.

Buttered leeks

UNITED KINGDOM

*

BRAISED RED CABBAGE

This preparation of red cabbage is common to many countries across northern Europe. To make it, shredded red cabbage and onions are simmered with red wine, red wine vinegar and red apples until sticky, sweet and well-spiced. It makes a good friend to roast and cold meats of all sorts, but especially pork.

Serves: 6
Prep time: 10 minutes
Cook time: 1–2 hours
{👤}{⚱}{↩}{🍽}

- 1 red cabbage, shredded
- 1 red onion, thinly sliced
- 1 red apple, peeled and sliced
- 50 ml/1¼ fl oz (3½ tablespoons) red wine vinegar
- 100 ml/3½ fl oz (⅓ cup plus 1 tablespoon) red wine (or cider)
- 1 cinnamon stick
- 10 g/¼ oz (2 teaspoons) butter
- salt and pepper

* Put all the ingredients into a large saucepan, stir through, add a pinch of salt and pepper, cover with a lid and heat over a medium heat. Once bubbling, reduce the heat to low and simmer for at least 1 hour, stirring occasionally, until the cabbage is reduced, tender and sweet.
* Remove the cinnamon stick and serve hot.

ENGLAND

*

GREEN PEAS
MINTED PEAS

The English manner of preparing peas is to boil them briefly, then toss them with butter, some chopped mint leaves and perhaps the tiniest pinch of sugar. The natural flavour and sweetness of the peas should be lifted but not overwhelmed. These 'minted' peas make an ideal accompaniment to Braised Duck Legs (page 146), Faggots (page 177), liver and bacon, or savoury pies and mash.

Serves: 4
Prep time: 5 minutes
Cook time: 5 minutes
{👤}{⚱}{↩}{🍽}{⏳}

- 500 g/1 lb 2 oz (3¾ cups) fresh or frozen green peas
- 2 sprigs mint, leaves picked and chopped
- 20–30 g/¾–1 oz (1½–2 tablespoons) butter
- small pinch of caster (superfine) sugar (optional)
- salt

* Bring a large saucepan of salted water (enough to cover the peas) to the boil. Add the peas and cook for 2 minutes, or until the peas are just tender. Drain and return them to the pan. Add the chopped mint, butter and a small pinch of sugar (if using) and toss until the peas are coated. Serve.

ENGLAND: LANCASHIRE

*

MUSHY PEAS

Much-loved throughout the UK, this classic dish originates in the north of England and follows in the tradition of older Lancashire favourites like black peas and Pease Pudding (page 76). To make it, dried marrowfat peas are reconstituted and simmered until quite soft – mushy is an accurate if not enticing descriptor. They can be eaten plainly or lifted with a piece of butter and some finely chopped mint leaves or a lemon wedge.

Mushy peas make an ideal pairing for Fish and Chips (its classic accompaniment) (page 112) but work just as well with lamb and a little mint sauce, meat pies and gravy, or even fried on their own as fritters.

Serves: 3–4
Prep time: 15 minutes, plus 8–12 hours soaking
Cook time: 1–2 hours
{👤}{♠}{⚱}{🥄}{↩}

- 200 g/7 oz (1 cup plus 2 tablespoons) dried marrowfat peas
- 1 teaspoon bicarbonate of soda (baking soda)
- piece of butter (optional)
- 1 small handful chopped mint leaves (optional)
- salt and pepper

* Put the dried peas in a bowl and add 600 ml/20 fl oz (2½ cups) cold water to cover. Add the bicarbonate of soda (baking soda), cover with clingfilm (plastic wrap) and leave to soak in the fridge overnight.
* The next day, drain the peas and put them into a large saucepan with enough fresh water to cover. Bring to the boil, reduce the heat to low and simmer for 1–2 hours until the peas have soaked up the water and are soft. If the water evaporates before the peas have completely softened, then add a little more water to top it up. If desired, add the butter and some chopped mint leaves and toss well. Season and serve.

Green peas

UNITED KINGDOM
*

BRUSSELS SPROUTS
WITH
ROAST CHESTNUTS
AND BACON

A Christmas classic and fully deserving of its proud placement beside the roast turkey.

Serves: 6–8
Prep time: 10 minutes
Cook time: 25–45 minutes
{🍳}

- 1.25 kg/2¾ lb Brussels sprouts, trimmed
- 2 tablespoons rapeseed (canola) oil
- 250 g/9 oz bacon lardons (pieces) or 300 g/ 11 oz rashers (slices)
- 1 quantity Roast Chestnuts, shelled (page 71)
- salt and pepper

* Preheat the oven to 200°C/400°F/Gas Mark 6. Line a large baking sheet with baking (parchment) paper.
* Bring a large saucepan of water to the boil, add the Brussels sprouts and cook for 5 minutes. Drain and run under cold water before leaving to cool slightly.
* Heat 1 tablespoon of the oil in a large frying pan or skillet over a medium heat, add the bacon and fry for 10 minutes, or until crispy. If using rashers (slices), chop the bacon into thin slices, about 5 mm/¼ inch wide and 2 cm/ ¾ inch long.
* Meanwhile, quarter the Roast Chestnuts.
* At this point, you can either braise the sprouts with the chestnuts and bacon in a large saucepan, or choose to roast them together in the oven.
* If braising them in a pan, add the Brussels sprouts to the frying pan or skillet with 1 tablespoon of water, cover with a lid and cook over a medium heat for about 5 minutes. Uncover, add the remaining tablespoon of oil and turn until the sprouts are coated. Fry for a few minutes, then add the bacon and chestnuts and heat them through again before transferring to a serving dish. Season with salt and pepper and serve.
* If roasting, add the chestnuts, bacon, Brussels sprouts and oil to a large bowl and stir through with a large spoon until well mixed. Spread over the prepared baking sheet and roast in the oven for 30 minutes. Halfway through roasting, stir well so everything gets evenly browned. If the sprouts are browning too quickly, reduce the oven temperature to 180°C/350°F/Gas Mark 4 and continue cooking. Season with salt and pepper, leave to cool slightly and serve warm.

UNITED KINGDOM
*

TURNIP TOPS
WITH
BACON

If your turnips arrive farm fresh and whole, save the tops for cooking. This recipe is inspired by one from Florence B Jack's *Cookery for Every Household* (1914). Jack suggests boiling them before frying them briefly in butter (or beef dripping), with a little seasoning and dash of spice, if desired. Here, they are also fried with a little bacon and maybe a touch of cream. Serve with roast rabbit.

Serves: 4
Prep time: 10 minutes
Cook time: 20 minutes
{🍳}{🔪}{🍲}

- 45 g/1½ oz (3 tablespoons) butter
- 1 clove garlic, finely chopped
- 150 g/5 oz bacon lardons (pieces)
- tops of 6–8 turnips, cut into 5 cm/2 inch pieces
- 60 ml/2 fl oz (¼ cup) double (heavy) cream (optional)
- grated nutmeg (optional)
- salt and pepper

* Melt the butter in a large frying pan or skillet over a medium-low heat for 2 minutes, or until foaming. Add the garlic and bacon and cook for 8 minutes until the bacon is browned. Add the turnip tops and 1 tablespoon of water. Cover with a lid and simmer for 10 minutes, stirring occasionally. Season with salt and pepper and serve.
* To cream the turnip tops, omit the extra water, then add the double (heavy) cream in the last 2 minutes of cooking. A small pinch of grated nutmeg can be an additional seasoning.

SCOTLAND
*

STEWED WHITE ONIONS

A classic accompaniment to roast mutton, lamb or even pork, these sweet onions are cooked slowly, until very soft, before being served in a sauce made from their own cooking liquid.

Serves: 4
Prep time: 5 minutes
Cook time: 1 hour 10 minutes
{🍳}{🔪}{🍲}

- 1 kg/2¼ lb small white onions, peeled and left whole
- 750 ml/25 fl oz (3 cups) chicken or vegetable stock or full-fat (whole) milk
- 1 sage leaf (optional)
- piece of butter
- salt and pepper

* Put the peeled onions into a large saucepan and cover with the stock or milk, adding some water if needed to cover the onions. If serving the onion with pork, add the sage leaf. Cover with a lid and bring to the boil. Reduce

the heat to low and simmer for 1 hour, or until the onions are very tender.

* Using a slotted spoon, remove the cooked onions and set aside, then cook the remaining liquid for several minutes until is reduced and thickened. Add the butter, season to taste, then return the onions to the pan and cook for 5 minutes until they are warmed through. Serve hot.

UNITED KINGDOM
*

PURPLE SPROUTING BROCCOLI

Although varieties of broccoli have exploded in popularity over the last couple of decades there is mention of a 'purple broccoli' in Mrs Beeton's 1861 classic. However it's cooked, purple sprouting broccoli should be brushed with butter before serving alongside fish or meat dishes.

Serves: 2
Prep time: 5 minutes
Cook time: 5–20 minutes
{🌱}{◆}{🔥}{🍴}{✒}{🧂}{🗲}

- 400 g/14 oz purple sprouting broccoli
- salt
- melted butter, for brushing

* Using a knife, trim away the woody stems at the base of the broccoli. Halve or quarter lengthways any particularly large pieces so that all the broccoli is roughly the same size.
* **To blanch:** Bring a large saucepan of salted water to the boil over a high heat. When boiling, add the broccoli and cook for 2–3 minutes for large pieces, removing them quickly from the boiling water when just tender. If planning to use the broccoli cold, or to grill later on, put the broccoli into a large bowl of iced water to stop the cooking, then drain immediately when cooled.
* **To roast:** Once blanched and drained, let the broccoli dry out. Put the broccoli on a lined baking tray and roast at 200°C/400°F/Gas Mark 6 for 10–15 minutes, or until the pieces start to char, but still have some bite. Season and serve.
* However the broccoli is cooked, brush with a little melted butter before serving.

UNITED KINGDOM
*

ROASTED AND GLAZED PARSNIPS OR CARROTS

Glazed with honey, these parsnips or carrots make an ideal accompaniment to most roasted meats and game.

Serves: 4
Prep time: 5 minutes
Cook time: 30–45 minutes
{🌱}{🔥}{🍴}{✒}{🧂}

- 1 tablespoon runny honey
- 2 tablespoons rapeseed (canola) oil
- 500 g/1 lb 2 oz parsnips or carrots, halved or quartered lengthways
- salt and pepper

* Preheat the oven to 180°C/350°F/Gas Mark 4. Line a large oven tray or baking sheet with baking (parchment) paper.
* Put the honey, oil and a pinch of salt and pepper into a large bowl and mix together. Add the parsnips or carrots and toss them in the dressing. Arrange the parsnips or carrots on the prepared tray with a little space in between each one and roast in the oven for 30–45 minutes, turning occasionally, until they are tender and have caramelized a little. Serve immediately.

UNITED KINGDOM
*

ROAST CHESTNUTS

The image and aroma of roasting chestnuts is immutably linked with the changing of seasons, from autumn into winter, and all of the joys of a new festive season. Once shelled, serve the chestnuts on their own, or toss them with fried brussels sprouts.

Makes: 20 chestnuts
Prep time: 10 minutes
Cook time: 30 minutes
{🌱}{◆}{🔥}{🍴}{🧂}

- 20 chestnuts

* Preheat the oven to 200°C/400°F/Gas Mark 6.
* Use a small, very sharp kitchen knife to cut a cross in the pointed side of each chestnut. The cross will open up while cooking, so make the cross wide enough to make your job of peeling a bit easier.
* Arrange the chestnuts, cut-side facing up, on a large oven tray or baking sheet and roast in the oven for 30 minutes, or until the scored crosses have opened up and the skins are somewhat pulled back. The meat inside the nuts should have softened as well. Leave the nuts to cool slightly.
* Once they have cooled enough to hold, peel the chestnuts. Serve on their own or use to make stuffing.

UNITED KINGDOM
*

CAULIFLOWER CHEESE

A friend to roast dinners, this classic dish has evolved from simple creamy cauliflower, or cauliflower au gratin, of Victorian times into the much cheesier dish known today.

Serves: 6
Prep time: 30 minutes
Cook time: 50 minutes
{👤}{🌶}

- 500 ml/17 fl oz (2 cups plus 1 tablespoon) full-fat (whole) milk
- 1 bay leaf
- ½ onion, studded with 2 cloves
- 1 cauliflower, outer leaves removed
- 30 g/1 oz (2 tablespoons) butter
- 30 g/1 oz (3¾ tablespoons) plain (all-purpose) flour
- 200 g/7 oz (1⅔ cups) Cheddar cheese, grated
- 3 tablespoons grated Parmesan cheese
- 150 ml/5 fl oz (⅔ cup) double (heavy) cream
- pinch of cayenne pepper (optional)
- 1 tablespoon dried breadcrumbs
- pinch of grated nutmeg
- salt and pepper

* Preheat the oven to 180°C/350°F/Gas Mark 4.
* Put the milk, bay leaf and clove-studded onion into a large saucepan and slowly bring to a simmer over a medium-low heat for 10 minutes. Remove from the heat.
* Meanwhile, put the whole cauliflower into another large saucepan with a tight-fitting lid and pour in enough water to cover the cauliflower by about 2.5 cm/1 inch. Cover with the lid and bring the water to the boil. Reduce the heat to medium-low and simmer for 15 minutes, or until the cauliflower is tender. Carefully remove the cauliflower from the pan and set aside.
* Melt the butter in another saucepan over a medium-low heat for 2 minutes, or until foaming. Whisk in the flour and cook for 2–3 minutes, stirring frequently to prevent lumps and without colouring. Remove the bay leaf and onion from the hot milk and slowly whisk a third of the milk into the butter and flour mixture until smooth and the milk is fully combined. Keep adding the milk in this way until it is a smooth sauce, then reduce the heat to low and simmer gently for 10 minutes, stirring occasionally.
* Meanwhile, cut the cauliflower into florets and arrange in a large baking dish.
* Remove the sauce from the heat and stir in all the Cheddar and three-quarters of the Parmesan. When the cheeses are incorporated, add the cream, then season with the cayenne pepper (if using) and some salt and black pepper. Mix gently to combine, then pour over the cauliflower.
* Mix the remaining Parmesan with the breadcrumbs in a small bowl and sprinkle over the top of the cauliflower. Grate over a little of the nutmeg and bake in the oven for 30 minutes, or until golden brown. Serve.

UNITED KINGDOM
*

SAMPHIRE

Crisp marsh samphire needs a careful clean and wash before cooking, but only the simplest of preparations. Boil briefly until tender (and still a vibrant green), toss with butter and serve with fish of all kinds.

Serves: 4
Prep time: 10 minutes
Cook time: 5 minutes
{👤}{🍴}{🌶}{🍲}{🍲}{✗}

- 500 g/1 lb 2 oz marsh samphire
- 20 g/¾ oz (4 teaspoons) butter

* Wash the samphire. The samphire stems will have tough, woody parts at their base, so pinch them off and discard them. Remove any grit by washing the samphire thoroughly in cold water.
* Once thoroughly cleaned, bring a large saucepan of water to the boil. Add the samphire and boil for 5 minutes. The samphire should be salty enough as not to need seasoning. Drain the samphire, return to the pan and toss in the butter before serving.

UNITED KINGDOM
*

LANG KAIL

Kale, and other cabbages of the colewort family, were among the few vegetables that grew well across Scotland, to the extent that vegetable gardens were called 'kailyards'. This simple preparation is based on old accounts of farmhouse cooking and can be served with meat or, when cooked with good stock and 1–2 tablespoons of fine oatmeal, can form the base of a soup or stew.

Serves: 6
Prep time: 10 minutes
Cook time: 25 minutes
{🍲}{🍲}

- 1 large bunch curly kale, about 300 g/11 oz
- ham or beef stock (optional)
- 1–2 tablespoons fine oatmeal (optional)
- about 60 g/2¼ oz (½ stick) butter
- salt

* Strip the kale leaves from the stems and discard the latter. Shred the leaves. Bring a large saucepan of salted water to the boil, then reduce the heat to low and add the leaves. Cook for 10–15 minutes.
* Alternatively, bring a large saucepan of stock to the boil with the oatmeal, reduce the heat to low, add the leaves and cook for 10–15 minutes.
* Drain the kale thoroughly, put into a large bowl, add the butter and toss well, seasoning with more salt if desired.
* Notes: If desired, you can carefully chop the stems into small pieces and boil for 10 minutes before adding the leaves and boiling them together.

Cauliflower cheese

UNITED KINGDOM

SEA KALE
WITH
HOLLANDAISE
AND
POACHED EGGS

A favourite of eighteenth-century eaters, when it was farmed as a winter substitute for asparagus, sea kale was still a common feature of cookbooks by Victorian times, and was often cooked with a cream sauce. Sea kale is only now coming back into favour. In this recipe, it is used as a substitute for asparagus spears. Serve as a light lunch or late breakfast.

Serves: 2
Prep time: 5 minutes
Cook time: 20 minutes
{👤}{🧄}{✗}

- 4 large eggs (as fresh as possible)
- 1 bunch sea kale, washed
- ½ quantity Hollandaise Sauce (page 424)
- 10 g/¼ oz (2 teaspoons) butter, warmed
- salt

* Fill a medium saucepan halfway with water and bring to the boil. Reduce the heat to medium and keep to a simmer. One at time, crack an egg into a small teacup or ramekin, then, using a wooden spoon, stir the simmering water to create a vortex. In one motion, add the egg to the centre of the vortex and cook for 3–4 minutes depending on how set you like your egg. Repeat with the other eggs and keep warm.
* Meanwhile, fill another saucepan half to three-quarters full of water and bring to the boil. Add 2 pinches of salt, then carefully add the sea kale. Boil for 3–4 minutes until tender. As the sea kale cooks, warm through the Hollandaise (if it's not warm already).
* Drain the sea kale well and toss with a little warm butter and salt.
* Divide the sea kale between 2 serving plates, then add the poached eggs with the warm Hollandaise poured over the top and serve.
* **Notes:** The sea kale can be steamed instead of boiled, if desired.

UNITED KINGDOM

SALSIFY
AND
BREADCRUMBS

Salsify root tastes unmistakably like oyster and is often served with seafood. This is another classic serving, dredged in breadcrumbs, fried and then baked with a creamy sauce until browned and bubbling. Serve on its own or as a side dish to white fish with lemon slices to squeeze over the top.

Serves: 4
Prep time: 15 minutes
Cook time: 1 hour
{👤}{🌶}

- squeeze of lemon juice
- 700 g/1 lb 8½ oz salsify
- 500 ml/17 fl oz (2 cups plus 1 tablespoon) full-fat (whole) milk
- 2 bay leaves
- 120 g/4 oz (1 stick) butter
- 4 cloves garlic, chopped
- 60 g/2¼ oz (½ cup) plain (all-purpose) flour
- 2 teaspoons English mustard
- 90 g/3¼ oz Cheddar cheese, grated
- 100 g/3½ oz (2 cups) fresh breadcrumbs
- 1 tablespoon finely chopped flat-leaf parsley
- pepper

* Preheat the oven to 180°C/350°F/Gas Mark 4.
* Fill a large bowl with water and add the lemon juice. Peel the salsify, then cut it into lengths the size of your baking dish and put it into the lemon water. This will stop the salsify oxidizing.
* Heat the milk and bay leaves in a large saucepan over a medium heat to scalding point or 83°C/181°F on a thermometer. When it is about to boil, add the salsify and cook for 8 minutes, or until almost tender. Strain into a bowl or jug (pitcher), setting both the milk and salsify aside.
* Melt half the butter in the saucepan over a medium-low heat, add the garlic and cook for 2–3 minutes until softened. Stir in the flour and cook for 2–3 minutes, stirring frequently to prevent lumps and without colouring. Slowly whisk in the reserved milk, making sure it is fully combined before you add more. Add the mustard, season with pepper and simmer, stirring occasionally, for 6 minutes. Remove from the heat and stir in the cheese.
* Meanwhile, heat the remaining butter in a medium frying pan or skillet over a medium heat, add the breadcrumbs and stir to combine. Fry, stirring occasionally, for 5 minutes, or until a pale golden brown. Remove from the heat and stir in the parsley. Arrange the salsify in a baking dish, pour over the sauce, then top with the breadcrumb mixture. Bake in the oven for 20–25 minutes until bubbling and golden brown. Serve.

Sea kale with hollandaise and poached eggs

SCOTLAND
*

PEASE BROSE

Pease brose is a Scottish dish, once cooked during conditions of poverty or wartime rationing. The peasemeal is made from hulled, roasted and milled yellow peas, onto which boiling water is poured. The eater uses a spoon to stir vigorously, adding any butter, honey or sweetener they like. When left for several minutes the mixture will solidify, so it's best to eat quickly!

Serves: 1
Prep time: 5 minutes
Cook time: 10 minutes
{♨}{🔥}{•}{✕}

- 15 g/½ oz peasemeal
- up to 200 ml/7 fl oz (¾ cup) full-fat (whole) milk or water
- 15 g/½ oz (1 tablespoon) butter
- 1 small handful dried fruit (optional)
- 1 tablespoon heather honey, warmed

* Put the peasemeal into a small heatproof serving bowl. Bring the milk or water to a simmer in a small saucepan over a medium heat.
* Remove from the heat and quickly but carefully stir 150–200 ml/2–7 fl oz (⅔–¾ cup plus 1 tablespoon) of the milk or water into the peasemeal to your desired consistency. Add the butter, dried fruit (if using) and warm honey and stir through again with a spoon. Serve.

UNITED KINGDOM
*

CREAMED PEASEMEAL

This recipe treats peasemeal as if it were polenta: cooked into a rich, creamy accompaniment for pork or game.

Serves: 2
Prep time: 5 minutes
Cook time: 10–15 minutes
{🔥}{•}{🍲}{✕}

- 250–300 ml/8–10 fl oz (1–1¼ cups) full-fat (whole) milk for either a thick or thin, creamy, 'polenta'-like consistency
- large pinch of salt
- 20 ml/¾ fl oz (4 teaspoons) double (heavy) cream
- 10 g/¼ oz (2 teaspoons) butter, plus an extra piece to finish
- 25 g/1 oz peasemeal

* Heat the milk in a large saucepan over a medium heat and add the salt, cream and butter. Just before it's about to boil, sift the peasemeal over the surface and immediately begin whisking to fully incorporate it. Keep whisking until the mixture thickens and becomes smooth, 3–5 minutes, then check the taste – it should be smooth, not grainy, and well-seasoned. If the mixture dries out too much, add more milk and whisk in. Finish with a piece of butter and serve with pork or game.

NORTHEAST OF ENGLAND
*

PEASE PUDDING

Peas have been a staple of the British diet for at least 2,000 years, and were once a fixture of medieval pottages. In the seventeenth century, the pudding cloth allowed them to be cooked in a novel way: yellow split peas were packed into a ball, wrapped in the cloth and then boiled in water or ham stock. Once cooked, they were pulled apart and served with slices of gammon (ham) or bacon chops. In northeast England, they are still served in much the same way – although the pudding is now often broken up and blended with butter.

Serves: 6
Prep time: 5 minutes
Cook time: 2¼ hours
{♨}{🔥}{•}

- 500 g/1 lb 2 oz (2¾ cups) yellow split peas
- 1 large white onion, diced (optional)
- 75 g/2¾ oz (¾ stick) butter
- 1 egg, beaten
- salt and pepper
- boiled gammon (ham) or braised pork shanks, to serve

* Put the peas and onion (if using) into a saucepan and cover with water. Bring to the boil, then reduce the heat to low and simmer for 1 hour, or until the peas are soft.
* Grease a 1 litre/34 fl oz pudding basin (ovenproof bowl) with 25 g/1 oz (2 tablespoons) of the butter.
* When the peas have finished cooking, drain, return to the pan and stir the remaining butter through the hot peas, then leave long enough so that it can melt and mix in well. Season to taste with salt and pepper, then blend coarsely using a hand-held blender – you want to retain some of the texture. Add the beaten egg, stir through well, then tip the mixture into the prepared basin.
* Cover the basin with a double layer of greaseproof (wax) paper and aluminium foil, secure with kitchen string and steam for 1 hour. Turn out and serve in slices or break up and serve large spoonfuls of the pudding alongside boiled gammon (ham) or braised pork shanks.

ENGLAND: LANCASHIRE
*

BONFIRE NIGHT BLACK PEAS
PARCHED PEAS

This recipe is a speciality of Lancashire. It is often made in autumn and eaten on its own as a snack as part of Bonfire Night celebrations or as an accompaniment to fried fish or slices of cooked ham. When cooked, the peas should reach the thick viscosity of baked beans.

Serves: 6
Prep time: 5 minutes, plus 8–12 hours soaking
Cook time: 45–60 minutes
{♨}{❄}{🔥}{🔪}{•}{🍲}

- 250 g/9 oz (1⅓ cups) dried black peas/Carlin peas
- ½ teaspoon bicarbonate of soda (baking soda) (optional)
- 1 small carrot, chopped (optional)
- 1 stalk celery, chopped (optional)
- 1 small onion, chopped (optional)
- malt vinegar, to taste
- salt and white pepper

* Put the peas into a large heatproof bowl. If the peas are old, add the bicarbonate of soda (baking soda), then pour in enough boiling water to cover by 2.5 cm/1 inch. Leave to soak overnight in the fridge or at room temperature.
* The next day, drain the peas and put them into a large saucepan. Cover with fresh water, add the vegetables (if using) and bring to the boil. Reduce the heat to medium-low and simmer for 45–60 minutes until soft, but with still a little bite. Spoon into bowls and season to taste with salt, pepper and a few shakes of malt vinegar. Serve.

SCOTLAND
*
VEGGIE HAGGIS

Vegetarian haggis was first popularized by John MacSween, a butcher who helped to create it for the opening of the Scottish Poetry Library in January 1984. The success of that veggie haggis led Macsween to expand his business and open an entire factory dedicated to its production. Veggie haggis is now commonplace on many Scottish menus; meatless haggis mixtures swap out offal for seeds, beans, carrots, swede (rutabaga), mushrooms and lentils, although the spice mixture remains much the same. The heavily spiced minced (ground) vegetables keep the flavour and texture consistent with the meaty one, and just as tasty. Serve the same way as haggis, with Neeps and Tatties (page 192).

Serves: 6
Prep time: 30 minutes
Cook time: 4 hours
{ⓥ}{♨}{↝}

- 2 tablespoons yellow split peas
- 2 tablespoons pearl barley
- 750 ml/25 fl oz (3 cups) vegetable stock
- 50 g/2 oz (3¾ cups) dried mushrooms
- 60 g/2¼ oz (½ stick) butter
- 1 onion, finely chopped
- 1 carrot, finely chopped
- 100 g/3½ oz (1 cup) pinhead oats
- ½ teaspoon each salt and ground black pepper
- ¼ teaspoon ground mace
- ¼ teaspoon ground nutmeg
- ¼ teaspoon ground allspice
- salt

* Put the peas, pearl barley and stock into a large saucepan and cook over a medium heat for 45 minutes, or until tender. Strain, setting the liquid, peas and barley aside.
* Meanwhile, put the dried mushrooms into a medium heatproof bowl and cover with about 200 ml/7 fl oz (¾ cup plus 1 tablespoon) boiling water. Leave to steep while you cook the vegetables.
* Melt half the butter in another saucepan over a medium

heat, add the onion and carrot and fry for 20 minutes, or until the vegetables are soft and the onion is golden. Add the reserved stock, peas and barley, along with the oats, salt and spices. Strain the soaked mushrooms through a sieve into a bowl, then chop the dried mushrooms finely and add them with their soaking water to the pan. Mix well, then bring to a simmer over a medium-low heat and cook for 30 minutes, or until very thick.
* Use the remaining butter to generously grease a large 1 litre/34 fl oz pudding basin (ovenproof bowl). Carefully add the vegetable mixture to the basin. Pleat a double layer of greaseproof (wax) paper and aluminium foil cut to a square 3–4 cm/1¼–1½ inches wider than the basin, then lay the pleated layer over the top of the bowl, turn down the sides and secure it with kitchen string. Steam for 2½ hours, then turn out of the basin and serve.

ENGLAND: WEST YORKSHIRE
*
DOCK PUDDING

A speciality of the Calder Valley in West Yorkshire, dock pudding is made from dock-like leaves (*Persicaria bistorta*) which are cooked with oatmeal, nettles and onion. It can be formed into cakes or cut into slices and fried for breakfast alongside eggs and bacon.

Serves: 6
Prep time: 15 minutes, plus 8–12 hours cooling
Cook time: 50 minutes
{↝}

- 60 g/2¼ oz (½ stick) butter
- 1 large onion, chopped
- 500 g/1 lb 2 oz young dock leaves,
nettles or spinach, or a mixture, washed
- 75 g/2¾ oz (½ cup plus 1 tablespoon) medium oatmeal
- bacon fat, lard or beef dripping, for frying

- To serve:
- as part of a Full Breakfast (page 26)
- Fried Eggs and Bacon (page 26)
- buttered toast

* Line a small loaf pan with baking (parchment) paper and set aside.
* Melt the butter in a large frying pan or skillet over a medium heat, add the onion and fry for 10 minutes, or until it is soft and golden.
* Add the leaves to the pan and cook for 10–12 minutes until soft. They will let out a lot of water, but don't be tempted to boil it away or strain it. Add the oatmeal and cook for another 10 minutes, or until it looks like a very thick porridge (oatmeal). If the mixture becomes too thick to stir easily, add a little water.
* Tip the mixture into the prepared loaf pan and leave overnight at room temperature until completely cooled.
* Once the pudding is cold, remove from the pan and cut into 1.5 cm/⅝ inch thick slices. Heat the fat in a large frying pan or skillet over a medium heat, add the pudding and fry for 3–4 minutes, or until heated through and well browned on both sides.
* Serve in a Full Breakfast in place of bubble and squeak, or eat with Fried Eggs and Bacon and some buttered toast.

WALES
*

LAVERBREAD

Laver (or sloke, as it's called in Scotland) is a seaweed that can be gathered from many beaches across Britain. Well cleaned, and cooked down with vinegar, it turns an inky-black and reaches the consistency of porridge (oatmeal), while retaining the saline flavour. From this point, the resulting 'laverbread' can be used to make a sauce for Roast Rack of Lamb (page 192) or mixed with oats and fried as cakes.

Makes: 1.5 litres/50 fl oz (6¼ cups)
Prep time: 10 minutes
Cook time: 6–8 hours
{✿}{♦}{▲}{▮}{✎}{▦}{▲}

- 1 kg/2¼ lb fresh laver
- 100 ml/3½ fl oz (⅓ cup plus 1 tablespoon) cider vinegar

* Wash the laver well in a colander, making sure you remove any possible grit, sand or small crustaceans. Put the laver into a large saucepan and cover with about 1 litre/34 fl oz (4¼ cups) water. Add the vinegar. Cover the pan with a lid and bring to the boil. Reduce the heat to low and simmer very gently for 6–8 hours. If you like the laverbread finer, use a hand-held blender to pulse throughout for a few seconds.
* Drain away any excess water, then pour the laverbread into tubs to cool and refrigerate. It should keep for about 5 days in the fridge.

WALES
*

LAVERCAKES
AND
SALTY WELSH BACON

These simple cakes are formed from a mixture of Laverbread (see above) and oats and make for a hearty Welsh breakfast. If you can, try and use salty Welsh bacon with a nice ribbon of fat, so that the lavercakes can be fried in the rendered bacon fat.

Serves: 4
Prep time: 10 minutes
Cook time: 20 minutes
{▲}{▮}{✎}{✗}

- 125 g/4¼ oz Laverbread (see above), plus extra
- 250 g/9 oz (2 cups) medium-cut oats,
plus extra for rolling
- 30 g/1 oz (2 tablespoons) lard or rapeseed (canola) oil
(optional, if the bacon is very fatty)
- 8–12 rashers (slices) salty Welsh bacon
- Tomato Ketchup (page 425) or condiment of your choice,
to serve

* Put the laverbread and oats into a large bowl and mix together to form a thick paste that can hold its shape. You may not need all of the oats, so start by adding three-quarters of them.
* Spread the extra oats out on a large plate. Using wet hands, roll large tablespoons of the paste into balls on a work counter. Flatten each ball with your fingers, then toss the cakes in the extra oats so that each one is completely covered. Set aside.
* Heat the lard or oil (if using) in a large frying pan or skillet over a medium heat, add the bacon and fry for 8–10 minutes, or until crisp. Remove from the pan and keep warm.
* Add the lavercakes to the pan and fry over a medium heat for about 10 minutes, turning occasionally, until they turn a dark golden brown on both sides. Serve the lavercakes and bacon warm with Tomato Ketchup or the condiment of your choosing.

WALES
*

CREMPOG LAS

These are a traditional savoury cousin to Welsh pancakes (crempog) and were often cooked for breakfast alongside fried bacon. A similar green pancake (or dumpling) was also served in Scotland and made with any spring green – such as nettles or even wild garlic.

Serves: 3–4
Prep time: 10 minutes
Cook time: 10 minutes
{✎}{✗}

- 200 g/7 oz (1⅔ cups) plain (all-purpose) flour
- pinch of grated nutmeg
- 2 eggs, beaten
- 50 ml/1¾ fl oz (3½ tablespoons) full-fat (whole) milk
- 1 tablespoon finely chopped flat-leaf parsley
- 1 small shallot, very finely diced
- lard or rapeseed (canola) oil, for frying
- salt and pepper

* Preheat the oven to 80°C/176°F/lowest Gas Mark.
* Put the flour, nutmeg, and a pinch of salt and pepper into a large bowl and mix together. Make a well in the centre and use a fork to whisk in the eggs. Beat together to form a very thick batter, loosening with the milk, so it becomes the consistency of double (heavy) cream. Mix in the parsley and shallot.
* Melt the fat in a large frying pan or skillet over a medium heat. Add the batter, a ladleful at a time, and fry, keeping the pancakes thin by swirling the pan around while the batter is still liquid, for 2–3 minutes until golden brown. Remove and keep warm in the oven before serving.

Lavercakes and salty Welsh bacon

WALES
*

WELSH ONION CAKE
TEISEN NIONOD

This Welsh classic is actually a close adaptation of the French baked potato and onion dish, *pommes de terre à la boulangére*. The Irish food writer Theodora Fitzgibbon gives the added suggestion of alternating each layer of potato and onion with some grated Caerphilly cheese.

Serves: 6
Prep time: 30 minutes
Cook time: 1½ hours
{♨}{☛}

- 100 g / 3½ oz (7 tablespoons) butter, plus extra for greasing
- 1 kg / 2¼ lb potatoes, peeled
- 500 g / 1 lb 2 oz onions
- 50–100 ml / 1¾–3½ fl oz (3½– 7 tablespoons) beef stock (optional)
- salt and pepper

* Preheat the oven to 150°C/300°F/Gas Mark 2. Grease a large baking dish with plenty of butter and set aside.
* Using a mandoline or a very sharp knife, carefully slice the potatoes and onions as thinly as possible and set aside in separate bowls.
* Arrange a layer of potatoes in the bottom of the prepared baking dish, followed by a layer of onions. Season with salt and pepper and dot with some of the butter. Repeat this layering until you have used up all the ingredients, finishing with a neat layer of overlapping potatoes. Pour in the stock (if using), then dot with the remaining butter, cover tightly with aluminium foil and bake in the oven for 1½ hours, removing the foil in the final 30 minutes so the potatoes can crisp up. Serve.

UNITED KINGDOM
*

MASHED POTATOES

The best creamy mash is made by heating the milk and butter through together before mashing them into the potatoes. The most luxurious recipes call for nearly equal amounts of butter and potatoes – this recipe is in line with the amount used in English food writer Hannah Glasse's original 1747 recipe. For a further touch of decadence, make a well in the centre of the mashed potatoes and add a piece of butter; wait for it to begin to melt, then dip each spoonful of mash into a little bit of butter before eating.

Serves: 4
Prep time: 10 minutes
Cook time: 20 minutes
{♨}{♨}{☛}{♨}

- 1 kg / 2¼ lb floury (baking) potatoes, such as Maris Piper, Desirée or Yukon Gold, peeled
- 125 ml / 4¼ fl oz (½ cup) full-fat (whole) milk
- 125 g / 4¼ oz (9 tablespoons) butter
- salt

*

* Halve or quarter the potatoes, then cut into large chunks. Make sure all the pieces are about the same size.
* Bring a large saucepan of water to the boil. Once boiling, add the potatoes and cook for 15 minutes, or until tender. Check by piercing with a knife or fork.
* Heat the milk and butter together in a small saucepan over a medium heat for 3–4 minutes, or until the butter has melted and mixed into the milk well.
* Drain the potatoes, return them to the pan and leave them to steam-dry for 1–2 minutes, before adding the milk and butter and mashing thoroughly. Season to taste with salt. Serve.

ENGLAND
*

BUBBLE
AND
SQUEAK

The popularity of this greasy spoon classic actually predates that of the potato itself and originated in the eighteenth century as a simple fry of left-over chopped beef and cabbage. Decades later, potatoes became a crucial component and the meat much less so – if included at all. Nowadays, it is almost exclusively potatoes and greens: left-over kale or cabbage mixed through with mashed or smashed potatoes, formed into cakes and fried in fat until crisp and brown. Serve with sausages or rashers (slices) of bacon, as well as some fried eggs and buttered toast.

Serves: 6
Prep time: 15 minutes
Cook time: 35 minutes
{☛}

- about 300 g / 11 oz Mashed Potatoes, ideally left-overs, (see left)
- 30 g / 1 oz (2 tablespoons) butter
- 1 onion, chopped (optional)
- 200 g / 7 oz left-over steamed or boiled vegetables, coarsely chopped into chunks
- 25–50 g / 1–2oz (2–3½ tablespoons) lard or butter, for frying
- salt and pepper
- Full Breakfast (page 26), or fried eggs, sausages and well-buttered toast, to serve

* Put the Mashed Potatoes into a large bowl.
* Melt the butter in a small frying pan or skillet over a medium heat, add the onion (if using) and fry for 10–15 minutes until golden brown. Stir the onion into the Mashed Potatoes, then fold in the left-over vegetables. Season to taste with salt and pepper.
* Heat a heavy frying pan or skillet over a medium-low heat, add the lard and heat until rendered. Add the potato and vegetable mixture either in a single layer, or in large cakes or patties, about 10–12 cm/4–4½ inches wide. Fry for 10 minutes, or until the bottom is dark brown. Don't be tempted to move or break them up.
* If frying as one large pan-size cake, cut the bubble and squeak into wedges and, using a fish slice (spatula), turn over one at a time. If frying as smaller cakes, flip them over and fry the other side for 3–5 minutes until dark

brown and cooked through. Add more lard if the pan dries out.

* Serve in a Full Breakfast, or with fried eggs, sausages and well-buttered toast.

SCOTLAND
*

RUMBLEDETHUMPS

This breakfast casserole is Scotland's answer to the English Bubble and Squeak (see left) – potatoes coarsely mashed with cabbage and baked with a Cheddar cheese topping. Spoon out with Fried Eggs and Bacon (page 26) or serve as part of a full Scottish breakfast. If using left-overs, simply mash, season and skip to the last step of the recipe.

Serves: 6
Prep time: 15 minutes
Cook time: 1 hour 20 minutes
{👹}{🔥}{•}

- 1 kg/2¼ lb potatoes, peeled and cut into equal-sized pieces, about 4–5 cm/1½–2 inches thick
- 1 small cabbage, sliced
- 125 g/4¼ oz (9 tablespoons) butter
- 60 g/2¼ oz Cheddar cheese, grated
- salt and pepper

* Preheat the oven to 180°C/350°F/Gas Mark 4.
* Put the potatoes into a medium saucepan of lightly salted water and bring to the boil. Cook for 20–25 minutes until tender. Drain, then return the potatoes to the pan and cover with a lid while you cook the cabbage.
* Fill a large saucepan about halfway with water and bring to the boil. Add the cabbage slices (the cabbage should be covered by the water), and boil for about 10 minutes. Drain well, add to the potatoes with the butter and mash coarsely. Season to taste with salt and pepper.
* Spoon into a baking dish, fork the top and sprinkle over the cheese. Bake in the oven for 45 minutes, or until golden brown. Serve.

NORTHERN IRELAND / SCOTLAND
*

CHAMP
CHAPPIT TATTIES

Here, lush, fluffy mashed potatoes are made with finely chopped spring onions (scallions). The onions can be either fried, as in this recipe, or heated through with the milk before being mixed into the creamy mashed potatoes. Although champ is typically associated with Ireland, it is also common in parts of Scotland, where it is known by the Scots name chappit tatties.

Serves: 4
Prep time: 15 minutes
Cook time: 35 minutes
{👹}{🔥}{•}

- 750 g/1 lb 10 oz floury (baking) potatoes, such as Maris Piper or Yukon Gold, peeled and cut into large chunks about 2.5cm/1 inch thick
- 75 g/2¾ oz (¾ stick) butter
- 1 large bunch spring onions (scallions), both white and green parts finely chopped
- 100 ml/3½ fl oz (⅓ cup plus 1 tablespoon) double (heavy) cream
- salt and pepper

* Bring a large saucepan of lightly salted water to the boil, add the chopped potatoes and cook for 25–30 minutes until very tender.
* Meanwhile, melt half the butter in a small frying pan or skillet over a medium heat, add the spring onions (scallions) and fry for several minutes until they soften.
* When the potatoes are cooked, drain, setting the cooking liquid aside for soup or sauce stock, if desired, then return the potatoes to the pan and mash. Add the fried spring onions with the remaining butter and cream and beat well using a wooden spoon until everything is combined. Season to taste with salt and pepper and serve.

WALES
*

STWNSH
STWNSH RWDAN/STWNSH MORON/
STWNSH FFA/STWNSH PYS

Stwnsh is a common Welsh root mash, which is made from a mix of potatoes and other vegetables, often carrots, broad (fava) beans or even peas. Similar to Orcadian Clapshot (page 82), *stwnsh rwdan* is a mixed mash of potato and swede (rutabaga) – with a slightly higher proportion of the former.
Ponchmipe (or *punchnep*) is a similar Welsh dish made using white turnips instead of the yellow variety (swede/rutabaga). *Stwnsh moron* (carrot and potato mash), *stwnsh ffa* (broad/fava bean and potato mash) or *stwnsh pys* (peas and potato mash) are also traditional.

Serves: 4
Prep time: 15 minutes
Cook time: 30 minutes
{👹}{🔥}{•}{🍴}

- 600 g/1 lb 5 oz potatoes, peeled and cut into large chunks
- 400 g/14 oz swede (rutabaga), peeled and cut into bite-sized chunks, or 400 g/14 oz bite-sized chunks of carrots, broad (fava) beans or peas
- 50 g/2 oz (3½ tablespoons) butter or about 100 ml/ 3½ fl oz (⅓ cup plus 1 tablespoon) buttermilk
- salt and pepper

* Fill a large saucepan two-thirds full with water, add 1 teaspoon salt and bring to the boil before carefully adding the potatoes. Reduce the heat to medium and simmer for 5 minutes. Add the remaining vegetables and cook for another 20 minutes, or until tender. Drain very well, return to the pan and mash together with the butter or as much buttermilk as needed. Season to taste with more salt or pepper if needed. Serve.

NORTHERN IRELAND
*

COLCANNON

Similar to Champ (page 81), colcannon is made from a base of creamy mashed potatoes that have been stirred through with greens – typically cabbage or kale.

Serves: 4
Prep time: 15 minutes
Cook time: 30 minutes

{♥}{≛}{⤙•}

- 500 g/1 lb 2 oz floury (baking) potatoes, such as Maris Piper or Yukon Gold, peeled and cut into large chunks
- 500 g/1 lb 2 oz cabbage or curly kale, sliced
- 75 g/2¾ oz (¾ stick) butter
- 1 onion (encouraged, but optional)
- 100 ml/3½ fl oz (⅓ cup plus 1 tablespoon) double (heavy) cream (optional)
- ¼ teaspoon ground nutmeg or mace (optional)
- salt and pepper

* Put the potatoes into a large saucepan of salted water, bring to the boil, then reduce the heat to medium and cook for 25 minutes, or until very tender.
* Meanwhile, if your cabbage is not already cooked, fill a saucepan with about 2.5 cm/1 inch of water, bring to the boil and add the cabbage. Return to the boil, then reduce the heat to medium-low and cook for 20–25 minutes until the cabbage is tender, topping up with hot water if necessary. If using kale, reduce the cooking time by 5 minutes.
* If using the onion, melt half the butter in a small frying pan or skillet over a medium heat, add the onion and fry, stirring, for 10–12 minutes until golden brown. Set aside. (If you're not using onion, skip this step and stir all the butter into the cabbage with the cream (if using) in the next step.)
* Drain the potatoes, return to the pan and mash well using a potato masher. Stir in the cabbage, onion (if using), any remaining butter and the cream (if using). Season with salt and pepper and add the nutmeg or mace, if desired. Serve.

UNITED KINGDOM
*

MASHED SWEDE
BASHED NEEPS

Mashed or coarsely bashed neeps (swede/rutabaga) have a touch of sweetness and offer a nice contrast in flavour and texture to creamy, fluffy mashed potatoes. Serve with Haggis (page 192) and Mashed Potatoes (page 80), or indeed, most roasted red meats.

Serves: 4
Prep time: 5 minutes
Cook time: 20 minutes

{♥}{≛}{⤙•}{🍲}{🧴}{✗}

- 1 swede (rutabaga), about 600 g/1 lb 5 oz, peeled and cut into 2.5 cm/1 inch cubes
- 50 g/2 oz (3½ tablespoons) butter
- salt and pepper

* Bring a large saucepan of salted water to the boil. Once boiling, carefully add the swede (rutabaga) cubes and cook for 15–20 minutes until the swede is tender and can be easily pierced with a fork. Drain, return to the pan and leave to steam-dry for 1 minute. Add the butter and mash coarsely, so that there are still small chunks of swede throughout. Season to taste with salt and pepper and serve.

SCOTLAND: ORKNEY
*

CLAPSHOT

To make this Orcadian classic, mashed potato and swede (rutabaga) are cooked and mashed separately and then stirred together. Serve as you would mashed potatoes; this is especially good with Haggis (page 192).

Serves: 4–5
Prep time: 10 minutes
Cook time: 30 minutes

{♥}{≛}{⤙•}

- 500 g/1 lb 2 oz floury (baking) potatoes, such as Maris Piper or Yukon Gold, peeled and cut into large chunks
- 500 g/1 lb 2 oz swede (rutabaga), peeled and cut into large chunks
- 75 g/2¾ oz (¾ stick) butter
- 100 ml/3½ fl oz (⅓ cup plus 1 tablespoon) double (heavy) cream (optional)
- salt and white pepper

* Bring 2 separate large saucepans of water to the boil. Add the potatoes to one pan and the swede (rutabaga) to the other and cook for 25 minutes, or until both are tender. Drain each pan separately, then return the potato to its pan and the swede to its pan and mash each until smooth. Add the swede to the potatoes and mix them together, then beat in the butter and cream (if using). Season with salt and pepper.
* **Notes:** If making this in batches, keep the first batch covered and warm while you cook the second.

Colcannon

UNITED KINGDOM
*

BOILED NEW POTATOES
IN PARSLEY
AND
BUTTER

Ideally, all new potatoes should be cooked like this – until just tender, before being tossed, still warm, with butter and parsley and maybe a burst of lemon juice.
Serve with fish, meat, pies and savoury steamed puddings.

Serves: 2–3
Prep time: 5 minutes
Cook time: 20 minutes
{🍲}{🥄}{🔪}{🍳}{🧂}{🍽}

- 500 g/1 lb 2 oz new potatoes/Jersey Royals
- piece of butter
- 1 handful finely chopped flat-leaf parsley
- salt

* Bring a large saucepan of salted water to the boil. Add the potatoes and make sure they are all well covered by the water. If there are any particularly large potatoes, cut them so they are the same size as the others.
* Cook for 10–15 minutes until the potatoes give easily when prodded with a fork or knife.
* Drain the potatoes, return to the pan and leave to steam-dry for a moment. Add the butter and parsley and toss until the butter has melted and coated the potatoes evenly. Serve.

UNITED KINGDOM
*

BAKED POTATOES
JACKET POTATOES

Large floury (baking) baked potatoes, cooked in their skins until crisp and steamy, make for joyful little packages – a snack, a side dish or a meal all their own. Gently slice into them, mash the fluffy white interior with a piece of butter and enjoy.
In the old days, bacon rind (then a more commonplace ingredient) would be rubbed on the potatoes before they entered the oven and act as both its salt and fat.

Makes: 1 potato
Prep time: 5 minutes
Cook time: 1½ hours
{🍲}{🥄}{🔪}{🧂}

- 1 floury (baking) potato, such as Maris Piper or Desirée
- 10 ml/2 teaspoons rapeseed (canola) oil
or a piece of bacon rind
- 15 g/½ oz (1 tablespoon) butter
- sea salt and pepper

* Preheat the oven to 190°C/375°F/Gas Mark 5.
* Wash and clean the potato, then dry well. Coat the potato evenly with the oil or rub the bacon rind over and season generously with salt and pepper, then pierce its skin in a few places with a fork or knife to allow steam to escape when cooking.
* Bake in the oven for 1½ hours, or until the centre of the potato gives way when pierced. Cut down the middle and add the butter and some salt and pepper. Serve immediately to keep a crispy skin.

UNITED KINGDOM
*

CHIPS

The British chip (French fry) is defined by its thick finger-width cut and the contrast of its crisp outer shell and fluffy centre. Loved unequivocally across the nation, they are not for battered fish alone: a side of well-fried chips can join virtually any preparation of meat or fish, including savoury pies and puddings. And there is something just so satisfying about crispy fresh-fried chips in a buttered roll. For such a seemingly static item of food, the chip has changed a lot in the last hundred years. The first chip shops to spring up, in the mid-nineteenth century, had fryers that ran on either beef dripping or lard – both more flavourful alternatives to vegetable oil – and this was the norm well into the 1900s.
Later, triple-cooked chips, invented by Heston Blumenthal in the early 1990s, became a smash hit, and the new gold standard. That recipe calls for cooling or freezing of the chip in between three batches of frying, and somehow manages to exaggerate that balance between its distinctively crispy shell and soft insides.
The recipe below is a little more straightforward for the average home cook trying out deep-frying at home. Once cooked, remember to drain on paper towels before sprinkling with sea salt and malt vinegar.

Serves: 3–4
Prep time: 15 minutes
Cook time: 20 minutes
{🍲}{🔥}{🥄}{🧂}{🔪}{🍳}{🧂}

- rapeseed (canola) oil, for deep-frying
- 750 g/1 lb 10 oz floury (baking) potatoes,
such as King Edward, Maris Piper or Yukon Gold
- salt
- malt vinegar, to serve

* Fill a large, deep saucepan or deep fryer halfway with the oil and heat it slowly until it reaches 140°C/284°F on a thermometer.
* Cut the potatoes lengthways into chips (fries) somewhere between 1–2.5 cm/½–1 inch thick.
* Working in batches, deep-fry the chips for 8–9 minutes until they soften. Remove with a slotted spoon and drain well on paper towels.
* Heat the oil for frying again until it reaches 190°C/375°F on a thermometer, then re-fry the chips for 7 minutes, or until golden brown. Remove with a slotted spoon and drain on paper towels. Season with salt and malt vinegar to serve.

Chips

NORTH OF ENGLAND
*

POTATO PATTIES
HULL PATTIES

A popular feature of the chip shops of the northeast of England, Hull patties are a simple mix of mashed potato and some onions fried with sage. Like traditional Fish and Chips (page 112), they are best when fried in beef dripping until golden and crispy.

Serves: 4–6
Prep time: 15 minutes
Cook time: 40 minutes
{👁}{🍴}

- 60 g/ 2¼ oz (½ stick) butter
- 1 onion, diced
- ½ teaspoon dried sage
- 1 kg/ 2¼ lb cold Mashed Potatoes (page 80)
- sunflower oil, for frying
- 1 quantity yeast batter (page 112)
- 100 g/ 3½ oz (¾ cup plus 2 teaspoons) plain (all-purpose) flour
- salt and pepper

* Melt the butter in a medium frying pan or skillet over a medium heat, add the onion and sage and fry for 10–12 minutes until the onion has softened and turned golden.
* Put the Mashed Potatoes into a bowl, add the onion and sage and mix together. Season with salt and pepper.
* Fill a large, deep frying pan or skillet or deep fryer no more than one-third full with oil and heat until it reaches 180°C/350°F on a thermometer.
* Meanwhile, put the batter into a shallow bowl. Put the flour into another shallow bowl and season with 4 teaspoons each of salt and pepper. Scoop egg-sized pieces of the potato mixture and shape them into patties.
* Working in batches, toss each patty in the seasoned flour, tapping away any excess, then dip into the batter and carefully lower them into the hot oil. Deep-fry for 10 minutes, or until golden all over. Remove with a slotted spoon and leave to drain on paper towels. Serve.

UNITED KINGDOM
*

OVEN CHIPS

Oven chips (fries) are much less of a hassle than their deep-fried counterpart. Make sure the chips get enough time blanching in the pan, as this is crucial to getting the inside so soft. Flip the chips regularly as they bake, so that they colour nicely on all sides.

Serves: 4
Prep time: 20 minutes
Cook time: 50–60 minutes
{👁}{♠}{🍴}{🍴}{🍴}{🍱}{🍴}

- 1 kg/ 2¼ lb floury (baking) potatoes, such as King Edward, Maris Piper or Yukon Gold
- at least 2 tablespoons rapeseed (canola) oil
- sea salt

* Preheat the oven to 200°C/400°F/Gas Mark 6. Line a large baking sheet with baking (parchment) paper.
* Cut the potatoes into chip- (fry-) like shapes, about 1–1.5 cm/½–⅝ inch or the thickness of your finger. It's best to do this by cutting the potatoes into lengths about 1.5 cm/⅝ inch wide, then turning each slice onto its flat side and cutting it once more into slices 1.5 cm/ ⅝ inch wide.
* Bring a large saucepan of slightly salted water to the boil, add the chips and cook for 3 minutes, then drain well.
* Drizzle a little of the oil, about 1–2 teaspoons, across the prepared baking sheet and add the chips. Drizzle the remaining oil over the chips and season with sea salt.
* Bake in the oven for at least 45–50 minutes until the chips are an even golden brown colour and are still soft and slightly fluffy on the inside. Turn and flip the chips 2–3 times while baking to ensure they cook evenly, adding a little more oil if the baking sheet dries out, or the chips are not picking up colour. Serve.

UNITED KINGDOM
*

ROAST POTATOES
ROASTIES

The best roast potatoes are baked until they reach a deep golden brown – their insides pillowy soft, and their outer shell so crisp they crackle as they slide onto your plate. A critical component of any Sunday roast dinner, they are an absolute joy when served with any meat or fish course.

Serves: 4
Prep time: 10 minutes
Cook time: 1 hour
{🍱}{🍴}{🍴}{🍱}

- 1 kg/ 2¼ lb roasting potatoes, preferably Maris Piper or Yukon Gold, peeled and cut into chunks, about 2.5 cm/ 1 inch thick
- 100 g/ 3½ oz (7 tablespoons) beef fat or rapeseed (canola) oil
- 3–4 sprigs rosemary, finely chopped (optional)
- salt

* Preheat the oven to 200°C/400°F/Gas Mark 6.
* Put the potatoes into a large saucepan of well-salted water and bring to the boil. Reduce the heat to medium and simmer for about 5 minutes. When they are boiling, put the beef fat or oil into an oven tray or baking sheet, then put into the oven to heat – avoid leaving the tray in the oven for too long as the oil or fat will start to smoke.
* Drain the potatoes and shake them in the colander or sieve to fluff them and let them steam-dry for a few minutes. Add the rosemary (if using) and toss together.
* Very carefully remove the oven tray from the oven and, avoiding splashing hot fat or oil, spoon the potatoes into a single layer on the tray. Move them around to cover them in the fat, then roast in the oven for 15–20 minutes. Take them out again and turn them over, then roast for another 15–20 minutes. Turn the potatoes again and roast for another 10–20 minutes until they are crisp and tender inside when pierced with a fork. Remove from the oven and season to taste with salt. Serve immediately.

UNITED KINGDOM
*
PARSNIP CHIPS

These parsnip chips are cut like matchsticks and take nicely to the addition of some added heat or spice. Serve as for roast potatoes.

Serves: 4
Prep time: 15 minutes
Cook time: 15 minutes
{ö}{♠}{☷}{♠}{☞}{☷}{☷}

- about 1 litre/ 34 fl oz (4¼ cups) sunflower oil or any other flavourless cooking oil, for deep-frying
- 500 g/ 1 lb 2 oz parsnips
- 1–2 teaspoons spices of your preference, such as cayenne pepper, garlic powder, etc.
- salt

* Heat the oil for deep-frying in a large, deep saucepan or deep fryer until it reaches 180°C/ 350°F on a thermometer.
* Peel the parsnips and cut into very thin matchsticks, about 3 mm/ ⅛ inch in thickness. The best way to do this is to use the julienne attachment on a food processor or mandoline. Alternatively, use a very sharp knife.
* Pat the parsnips dry with paper towels. Working in 2–3 batches, carefully lower the parsnips into the hot oil and deep-fry for 5 minutes, or until golden brown. Remove with a slotted spoon and leave to drain on paper towels. Season with salt and spices and serve immediately.

UNITED KINGDOM
*
MOGO CHIPS

Faced with expulsion from East Africa in the late 1960s and early 1970s, many people of Indian heritage migrated to Britain and brought with them the foods they had grown to love in Africa, such as mogo (or cassava) chips. Mogo chips are found in Indian restaurants in the UK but are less popular in India. The thick brown cassava root is commonly found in Indian, Caribbean and African grocery shops, and available both fresh and frozen.

Serves: 4
Prep time: 15 minutes
Cook time: 40 minutes
{ö}{♠}{☷}{♠}{☞}

- 500 g/ 1 lb 2 oz cassava root, peeled and cut into thick even-sized chips (fries)
- 2 tablespoons vegetable oil
- 1–2 teaspoons hot chilli powder
- lemon juice, for drizzling
- salt
- few sprigs coriander (cilantro), leaves finely chopped, to serve

* Put the cassava chips (fries) into a large saucepan, cover with boiling water and bring to the boil. Reduce the heat and cook for 20 minutes, or until the chips are tender when pierced with a knife. Drain and set aside.

* Heat the oil in a large frying pan or skillet over a medium heat, add the chips in batches, taking care to stand back as they can splutter, and fry for a couple of minutes on each side until golden brown.
* Put the fried chips into a serving bowl and sprinkle in the chilli powder, a little salt and lemon juice. Mix gently until all the chips are coated, then serve hot with a sprinkle of coriander (cilantro).

UNITED KINGDOM
*
CREAMY SCALLOPED POTATOES

To 'scallop' something is an old culinary term that means to bake in a sauce. These creamy scalloped potatoes are quite similar to potato au gratin, with the exclusion of breadcrumbs and Parmesan. Bake until well bronzed and bubbling through the cracks.

Serves: 3–4
Prep time: 15 minutes
Cook time: 1–1½ hours
{ö}{☷}{☞}

- 500 g/ 1 lb 2 oz potatoes, peeled and sliced as thinly as possible
- 1 tablespoon chopped fresh thyme
- 250 ml/ 8 fl oz (1 cup) full-fat (whole) milk
- 100 ml/ 3½ fl oz (⅓ cup plus 1 tablespoon) double (heavy) cream
- 20 g/ ¾ oz (4 teaspoons) butter
- 50 g/ 2 oz Cheddar cheese, grated (optional)
- salt and pepper

* Preheat the oven to 160°C/ 325°F/ Gas Mark 3.
* Arrange the potatoes in layers in a deep casserole dish or Dutch oven, sprinkling with thyme and seasoning as you go.
* Heat the milk, cream and butter in a medium saucepan over a medium heat for 1–2 minutes, making sure the butter has melted. Add the cheese (if using) and stir through. Season to taste with salt and pepper.
* Pour the liquid over the potatoes and bake in the oven for 1–1½ hours until the top has browned and a knife can easily pierce all the way to the bottom. Serve.

GAME CHIPS

These thin, crispy chips more closely resemble the size and thickness of crisps (American 'chips') and often feature a distinctive cross-hatched pattern. Serve with grouse, pheasant or partridge.

Serves: 4–6
Prep time: 40 minutes
Cook time: 25 minutes
{ⵗ}{◉}{♨}{♨}{↲}{♨}

- rapeseed (canola) oil, for deep-frying
- 750 g/1 lb 10 oz floury (baking) potatoes, such as Maris Piper or Yukon Gold, peeled
- salt

* Preheat the oven to 80°C/176°F/lowest Gas Mark.
* Fill a large, deep frying pan or skillet or deep fryer with 2.5 cm/1 inch of oil and heat until it reaches 180°C/350°F on a thermometer.
* Have a large bowl of cold water ready. Finely slice the potatoes using the thinnest setting of a mandoline. Put the slices of potatoes into the cold water to rinse away any starch, then drain and dry the slices on paper towels.
* Working in small batches, carefully lower the chips into the hot oil and deep-fry for 3–4 minutes until they are golden brown and have stopped bubbling. Remove with a slotted spoon and leave to drain on paper towels. Keep the chips warm while you cook the rest. Season with salt just before serving.
* Notes: To create the cross-hatched pattern, finely slice the potatoes using the ridged attachment of the mandoline. After each slice, rotate the potato 90 degrees, so that successive slices form a lattice.

BOXTY BREAD

Boxty is a versatile Irish concept: made from left-over mashed and grated potatoes, mixed with flour and buttermilk, and prepared in a number of different ways. This bread is a well-risen loaf with a nicely browned top resembling soda bread. Boxty, however, is more flavourful, moist and chewy – on account of the potato. Slice and serve warm with butter or spread with jam or dipped into a hearty soup.

Serves: 6
Prep time: 45 minutes
Cook time: 40 minutes
{ⵗ}{↲}

- 200 g/7 oz Mashed Potatoes (page 80)
- 200 g/7 oz floury (baking) potatoes, such as Maris Piper or Yukon Gold, skins on
- 20 g/¾ fl oz (4 teaspoons) butter
- 300 g/11 oz (2½ cups) self-raising flour
- 5 g/⅛ oz (1 teaspoon) baking powder
- 50 ml/1¾ fl oz (3½ tablespoons) buttermilk
- salt

* In advance, boil and mash your potatoes following the directions on page 80 before spreading them out on a large baking sheet and leaving them to cool completely.
* Grate the remaining potatoes with the skins on, then put them into a sieve with a little salt and set the sieve over a bowl to catch the liquid. Leave for 10 minutes, then squeeze them to remove any excess liquid.
* Preheat the oven to 180°C/350°F/Gas Mark 4. Line a large baking sheet with baking (parchment) paper.
* Melt the butter in a saucepan over a medium-low heat.
* Put all the ingredients, including the potatoes and butter, into a large bowl. Add 10 g/¼ oz (2 teaspoons) salt and mix together until combined. Turn the dough out onto a floured work counter and, using your hands, mould into a circle. Cut a deep cross into the top of the dough, then put it onto the prepared baking sheet and bake in the oven for 30–40 minutes or until well risen.

BOXTY PANCAKES
POTATO PANCAKES

These potato pancakes follow the same formula as the Boxty Bread (see left), but use a higher proportion of buttermilk, as well as an egg to bind. The mixture should still be thick enough to spoon out into cakes on the griddle. Serve hot and buttered, with Fried Eggs and Bacon (page 26) or as a part of an Ulster Fry breakfast (page 26).

Serves: 4
Prep time: 45 minutes
Cook time: 20 minutes
{ⵗ}{↲}

- 150 g/5 oz Mashed Potatoes (page 80)
- 150 g/5 oz floury (baking) potatoes, such as Maris Piper or Yukon Gold, skins on
- 250 g/9 oz (2 cups) self-raising flour
- 5 g/⅛ oz (1 teaspoon) baking powder
- 300 ml/10 fl oz (1¼ cups) buttermilk
- 1 large egg, beaten
- 20 g/¾ fl oz (4 teaspoons) butter
- salt and pepper

* In advance, boil and mash your potatoes following the directions on page 80 before spreading them out on a large baking sheet and leaving them to cool completely.
* Grate the remaining potatoes with the skins on, then put them into a sieve with a little salt and set the sieve over a bowl to catch the liquid. Leave for 10 minutes, then squeeze them to remove any excess liquid.
* Put the flour and baking powder into a large bowl, then gradually whisk in the buttermilk to make a smooth paste. Add the beaten egg and incorporate before adding the potatoes, 5 g/⅛ oz (1 teaspoon) salt and a little pepper.
* Heat a little of the butter in a large frying pan or skillet over a medium heat. Working in batches, spoon circles of the mixture into the hot pan and cook for 3–4 minutes, or until the pancakes have puffed up and you can see holes appearing across the top. Using a fish slice (spatula), flip the pancakes over and cook the other side for 3 minutes, or until browned. Remove from the pan. Continue until all the batter is used up. Serve.

Game chips

NORTHERN IRELAND
*

BOXTY DUMPLINGS

These potato dumplings are made from a stiff boxty dough that's made without buttermilk. Cooked and bronzed on the top of stews and casseroles, they should be served much like the Suet Dumpling (page 244), but can also be pan-fried or served like potato gnocchi with a sauce.

Serves: 4
Prep time: 45 minutes
Cook time: 15 minutes
{👤}{🔥}

- 150 g/5 oz Mashed Potatoes (page 80)
- 150 g/5 oz floury (baking) potatoes, such as Maris Piper or Yukon Gold, skins on
- 150 g/5 oz (1¼ cups) self-raising flour
- 5 g/⅛ oz (1 teaspoon) baking powder
- 1½ tablespoons finely chopped chives
- salt

* In advance, boil and mash your potatoes following the directions on page 80 before spreading them out on a large baking sheet and leaving them to cool completely.
* Grate the remaining potatoes with the skins on, then put them into a sieve with a little salt and set the sieve over a bowl to catch the liquid. Leave for 10 minutes, then squeeze them to remove any excess liquid.
* Put all the ingredients, including the potatoes, into a large bowl, add 5 g/⅛ oz (1 teaspoon) salt and mix to form a stiff dough. Using your hands, shape the dough into equal-sized balls.
* Bring a large saucepan of salted water to the boil, then carefully drop in the dumplings. Wait until they all float then boil for 4–5 minutes until they have visibly puffed up and are looking shaggy. Drain and chill in the fridge until needed. Place on top of a stew or casserole 15–20 minutes before serving, or cook as desired.

NORTHERN IRELAND
*

PRATIE OATEN

These potato cakes follow the same basic idea behind Potato Scones (see right), but use oats instead of flour. Serve alongside eggs and sausages.

Makes: 6
Prep time: 10 minutes
Cook time: 20 minutes
{🍳}{🔥}

- 75 g/2¾ oz (¾ stick) butter
- 500 g/1 lb 2 oz cold Mashed Potatoes (page 80)
- 75 g/2¾ oz (¾ cup) medium-cut oats, plus extra for rolling
- 50 ml/1¾ fl oz (3½ tablespoons) full-fat (whole) milk
- lard or sunflower oil, for frying

* Melt the butter over a low heat in a saucepan. Pour into a bowl and add the potatoes and oats. Mix together, adding enough milk to make a loose but workable dough.

* Sprinkle the work counter with some extra oats and roll or press out the mixture into a circle about 2 cm/¾ inch thick, then cut into 6 equal-sized wedges or 'farls'.
* Heat the lard in a griddle or heavy frying pan or skillet over a medium heat, add the wedges and fry, without moving them, for 4–5 minutes on one side until they are deep golden brown. Quickly but carefully turn the wedges over with a fish slice (spatula) and cook the other side for another 4–5 minutes until golden brown. Serve.

NORTHERN IRELAND / SCOTLAND / ENGLAND
*

POTATO (TATTIE) SCONES
FADGE/POTATO BREAD

These potato cakes are – like Boxty (page 88 and left) – made from mashed potato, then cut into thin farls (wedges) and fried on a griddle. Once both sides are a rich golden brown, butter and serve as part of an Ulster Fry (page 26) or with Fried Eggs and Bacon (page 26). You can also eat these as an accompaniment to soups and broths.

Makes: 12
Prep time: 15 minutes
Cook time: 20 minutes
{🔥}

- 500 g/1 lb 2 oz floury (baking) potatoes, such as King Edward, Maris Piper or Yukon Gold, peeled and cut into equal-sized pieces
- 30 g/1 oz (2 tablespoons) butter
- 85 g/3 oz (¾ cup) plain (all-purpose) flour, sifted, plus extra for dusting
- ½ teaspoon baking powder
- lard or oil, for frying
- salt and pepper
- butter, jam, marmalade or cheese, to serve

* Put the potatoes into a medium saucepan of water, add 2 pinches of salt, bring to the boil over a high heat and cook for 15 minutes, or until tender enough to pierce with a fork. Drain and leave them to cool for 5 minutes.
* Meanwhile, melt the butter in a small saucepan over a medium-low heat. Set aside.
* Preheat a griddle, heavy frying pan or skillet over a medium heat. While they're still warm, put the potatoes into a large bowl and mash, then add the melted butter and salt and pepper to season and mix thoroughly. Using a rubber spatula, begin to stir in some of the flour and the baking powder. Continue to add the flour until a stiff but still soft dough is formed (extra flour may be needed).
* Preheat the oven to 80°C/176°F/lowest Gas Mark.
* Divide the dough into 3 equal-sized portions, then roll out each one on a lightly floured work counter into a circle, about 5 mm/¼ inch thick. Use a fork to prick the surface of the circles throughout, then cut each circle into 4 farls (triangular wedges).
* Heat a piece of lard or a drizzle of oil on the griddle or pan over a medium heat, wiping up any excess with a paper towel. Working in batches, add the scones and fry for 3–4 minutes on one side, then turn over and fry for 2–3 minutes on the other side until golden brown. Remove each batch and keep warm in the oven.
* Serve warm with butter, jam, marmalade or even cheese.

Potato (tattie) scones

SCOTLAND

*

STOVIES

This rather unglamorous dish is still a Scottish classic. Made slightly differently from household to household, the core ingredients are typically the left-overs from a roast; boiled potatoes, chunks of beef, sliced onion and gravy or stock. These days, a can of corned beef is typically supplemented for the left-over meat.

As the stovies cook, the floury (baking) potatoes break down and create a rather viscous mixture more casserole than stew. Serve with Oatcakes (pages 260 and 261).

Serves: 4
Prep time: 15 minutes
Cook time: 1 50 minutes hours
{å}{•}{☰}

- 60 g/2¼ oz (4 tablespoons) lard or butter
- 150 g/5 oz corned beef or left-over roast beef, diced, or minced (ground) beef
- 2 large onions, sliced
- 1 bay leaf
- ½ teaspoon thyme leaves (optional)
- 6 sage leaves, chopped (optional)
- 2 tablespoons finely chopped flat-leaf parsley (optional)
- 750 g/1 lb 10 oz floury (baking) potatoes or a 50/50 mix of floury (baking) and waxy potatoes
- 200 ml/7 fl oz (¾ cup plus 1 tablespoon) beef stock
- salt and pepper
- Oatcakes (pages 260 and 261), to serve

* Preheat the oven to 160°C/325°F/Gas Mark 3.
* Melt the lard or butter in a deep casserole dish or Dutch oven over a medium heat, add the corned beef or left-over meat and fry for 10 minutes, or until crisp. Remove from the pan with a slotted spoon and set aside.
* Add the onions, bay leaf, thyme (if using), sage (if using) and parsley (if using) to the fat in the pan and fry for 8–10 minutes until the onion is golden brown.
* Meanwhile, peel and cut the potatoes into large circles, about 2 cm/¾ inch thick.
* Return the meat and any juices to the casserole dish, then arrange the potatoes in a layer on top. Season. Pour over the stock, cover with the lid and cook in the oven for 1 hour. Increase the oven temperature to 200°C/400°F/Gas Mark 6, uncover and cook for another 30 minutes so that the potato becomes crisp at the edges. Serve with Oatcakes.

ENGLAND: NORTHUMBERLAND

*

PANACKELTY
PAN AGGIE

The panackelty is an economical casserole that originates in northern England and is made from left-over meat – often corned beef and/or bacon – and onions, which are simmered in stock beneath a neat layer of sliced potatoes. Given the nature of the dish, variations are common from house to house, but all follow the same basic principle and rely on a small number of core ingredients.

Serves: 4
Prep time: 20 minutes
Cook time: 2 hours
{å}{▮}{•}{☰}

- 1 kg/2¼ lb potatoes, peeled and thinly sliced into circles
- 2 onions, thinly sliced into rings
- 4 rashers (slices) dry-cured bacon or slices of corned beef
- about 400 ml/14 fl oz (1⅔ cups) beef stock or water
- salt and pepper

* Preheat the oven to 160°C/325°F/Gas Mark 3.
* Arrange layers of potatoes and onions in an ovenproof casserole dish or Dutch oven, adding the rashers (slices) of bacon as a single layer about halfway through. Lightly season with salt and pepper as you go.
* Pour over enough beef stock or water to almost cover, then bake in the oven for 2 hours, or until the potatoes are tender. If the potatoes begin to turn too dark, cover with a lid or aluminium foil.

SCOTLAND / NORTH OF ENGLAND

*

PAN HAGGERTY

Similar to the Panackelty (see left), the pan haggerty varies from family to family and is sometimes made with a little meat, stock or even cabbage. Made in its most common form, the pan haggerty is a potato casserole made with layers of butter-fried onions and grated cheese. When these ingredients are included, however, the distinction between this dish and its sister serving blurs considerably.

Serve alongside a leafy green salad, or as an alternative to Cauliflower Cheese (page 72).

Serves: 4
Prep time: 15 minutes
Cook time: 55 minutes
{å}{•}{☰}

- 75 g/2¾ oz (¾ stick) butter
- 250 g/9 oz onions, thinly sliced into rings
- 500 g/1 lb 2 oz potatoes, peeled and thinly sliced into circles
- 4 rashers (slices) bacon, finely chopped (optional)
- 125 g/4¼ oz Cheddar cheese, grated
- salt and pepper

* Preheat the oven to 180°C/350°F/Gas Mark 4.
* Melt half the butter in a large, deep ovenproof frying pan, skillet or sauté pan over a medium heat, add the onions and fry for 10 minutes, or until softened. Remove the onions with a slotted spoon and set aside.
* Leave the pan to cool, then arrange a thin layer of potatoes on the bottom, followed by one of onion and the bacon (if using), and some of the cheese. Season with a little salt and pepper. Continue layering up, making sure you finish with a layer of potatoes and grated cheese on the top. Finish with a little more pepper and dot the top with the remaining butter.
* Bake in the oven for 45 minutes, or until the potatoes are cooked through. Leave to stand for 5–10 minutes before turning out onto a serving plate.

UNITED KINGDOM

FRITTERS

In Britain, the term fritter refers to fruit, vegetables or meat that is battered and fried. Chip shop fritters made from potatoes or mushy peas are the most common today, but at home, thick slices of fruit are also fried and dusted with sugar – just swap out the courgette (zucchini) for your chosen fruit or vegetable and omit the cheese.

Makes: 16
Prep time: 10 minutes
Cook time: 25 minutes
{♥}{✒}{🍲}

- 500 g/1 lb 2 oz courgette (zucchini)
- 100 g/3½ oz Cheddar cheese, grated
- 2 medium eggs, beaten
- pinch of spice of your choice
- 200 g/7 oz (1⅔ cups) plain (all-purpose) flour
- vegetable oil, for shallow-frying
- salt and pepper

* Grate the courgette (zucchini) on a box grater, then put it into a clean dish towel, gather up the corners and squeeze out all the moisture, then pat dry.
* Put the courgette into a large bowl with the cheese and beaten eggs and mix to combine. Add salt, pepper and the spice of your choice, then mix in the flour, a little at a time, making sure everything is combined thoroughly.
* Heat enough oil for shallow-frying in a large frying pan or skillet over a low–medium heat. Working in batches, use a spoon to take a ball of the fritter mixture and weigh it out to about 50 g/2oz, then carefully lower it into the oil. It should sizzle. Press down slightly with the spoon to flatten it a little and fry for 2–3 minutes until golden.
* Flip the fritters over and fry for 2–3 minutes until golden and crisp. When cooking a few fritters at a time, leave space between them and don't overcrowd the pan. Using a slotted spoon, remove the cooked fritters from the pan and leave to drain on paper towels before serving.

UNITED KINGDOM

ONION BHAJIA

These onion fritters are called onion bhajia in India, but in Britain they have become popular as onion bhaji. The term 'bhaji' was originally a dry stir-fry with mushroom or okra, for instance. In Britain, bhaji are often round, doughy and dense. This recipe is a little lighter, closer to the original.

Serves: 4
Prep time: 10 minutes
Cook time: 10 minutes
{♥}{♦}{🌶}{🍖}{✒}{✗}

- ½ teaspoon chilli powder
- ½ teaspoon ground turmeric
- pinch of ajowan seeds (carom seeds)
- 4 tablespoons gram (chickpea) flour
- sunflower oil, for deep-frying

- 2 onions, very finely sliced
- salt

* Put the chilli powder, turmeric, a pinch of salt, ajowan seeds and gram flour into a large bowl and mix together until combined. Add water, a tablespoon at a time, and stir to make a thick batter, the consistency of double (heavy) cream. Set aside.
* Pour enough oil for deep-frying into a large, deep, heavy saucepan to a depth of about 5 cm/2 inches and heat until it reaches 180°C/350°F on a thermometer.
* Meanwhile, working with a batch at a time, fold the sliced onions into the gram (chickpea) flour mixture, evenly coating them with the batter. Test the oil by dipping a slice of onion into it. If it sizzles, the oil is ready. Carefully lower in spoonfuls of the mixture in batches and deep-fry for 2 minutes on each side, or until golden brown. Remove with a slotted spoon and leave to drain on paper towels before serving.

UNITED KINGDOM

BOMBAY ALOO

This dish gets its name from the coastal city of Bombay, now called by its precolonial name Mumbai. Recipes for potato curries are popular in Britain, but few people from Mumbai would recognize this recipe – which is frequently served as a side dish, rather than a main.

Serves: 4
Prep time: 15 minutes
Cook time: 25 minutes
{♥}{♦}{🌶}{🍖}{✒}{🍲}

- 2 tablespoons sunflower oil
- 1 teaspoon mustard seeds
- 2 fresh green chillies, very finely chopped, seeds and all
- 10 fresh curry leaves or 15 dried
- 1 teaspoon ground turmeric
- 3 large waxy potatoes,
peeled and cut into 1 cm/½ inch cubes
- 1 teaspoon caster (superfine) sugar
- 2 large tomatoes, finely chopped, seeds and all
- 1 handful coriander (cilantro) leaves, chopped
- salt

* Heat the oil in a large saucepan over a high heat, add the mustard seeds and fry for 1 minute, or until you hear them pop. Add the green chillies and curry leaves, then reduce the heat to medium, stir in the turmeric and add the potatoes.
* Increase the heat, season with salt, add the sugar and stir to blend. Add the tomatoes and 150 ml/5 fl oz (⅔ cup) water and bring to the boil.
* Reduce the heat to medium and cook for 10–15 minutes, or until the potatoes are done, adding a little more water if needed. The final dish should be fairly dry. Add the coriander (cilantro) leaves, mix lightly and serve.

THE HERRING LOVES THE MERRY MOON-LIGHT,
THE MACKEREL LOVES THE WIND, BUT THE OYSTER LOVES
THE DREDGING SONG, FOR THEY COME OF A GENTLE KIND.

THE DREDGING SONG, C. 1850

In many ways, Britain is defined by its coastline and the waters that lay beyond it. A love for seaborne foods stretches back in time: from shellfish middens left by mollusc-loving Neolithic inhabitants, to the Anglo-Saxon's 'kettle of fish', and countless clever methods of smoking and salting fish.

Preservation has always been an important part of preparing seafood in Britain. Despite the fact that in Britain you are never more than 70 miles from the sea – and usually far less, unless you live in the Midlands – fish spoils quickly, so fresh fish was a rarity for those who didn't live by the coast. This changed in Victorian times when the steam engine and new trainlines criss-crossed and connected the country. Even after this point, huge industries were devoted not only to fishing but also to smoking – both hot- and cold-smoking – herring, haddock, salmon and mackerel. Towns like Craster, Whitby and Arbroath are still famous for their unique methods and styles of preparing fish.

For those who lived by the sea, seafood and shellfish could be gathered fresh, and beach-combing for molluscs or seaweeds was common. No elaborate preparations were needed to enjoy their catch: seafood from British shores – from Cornwall to Shetland – ranks among the best in the world. Poached or grilled (broiled) fish, with squares of butter and a good squeeze of lemon, are sometimes all you need. And for the next day: fishcakes made from the left-over flaked meat.

This is not to say there wasn't a more extravagant approach as well. Mrs Beeton and her contemporaries had recipes for a host of more elaborate, expensive preparations that required a wealth of time or a full-time cook. Many involved rich sauces that were often made from oysters, lobster coral and shrimp, and suitable for pairing with white and flat fish. Some classic examples of these recipes are found within this chapter.

British seas are a treasure trove that deserve a bit of love and exploration. Your local fishmonger is your guide to the goods – and can help us branch outside of our comfort zones. When in (or without) doubt, opt for the day-boat catch, from smaller boats working closer to shore, for the freshest and best fish. Of course, there's the common haddock, cod and salmon, the familiar mackerel and herring, but there's still so much else besides – even historically important fish such as coalfish (also known as coley) or pollack, tusk, turbot or skate can be bought today from a good fishmonger. Of molluscs and crustaceans there are many fine options that are widely available: native oysters, hand-dived scallops, langoustines and remarkable razor clams – as well as the less common but equally important cockles, whelks or limpets. Waft through these pages, and when you find something that takes your fancy, get to the source and push the boat out.

FISH
AND
SHELLFISH

EAST OF SCOTLAND
*
GRILLED ARBROATH SMOKIES

Arbroath smokies are a popular preparation of hot-smoked haddock that originated in the small village of Auckmithie, just north of Arbroath on Scotland's east coast. The popularity of smokies took off in the early 1800s, when many of Auckmithie's fishermen resettled in Arbroath and a new industry was built around their production.
As the smokies are hot-smoked, they are already cooked through and are safe to eat, however they will taste much nicer when grilled (broiled) – low and slow so as not to dry them out!

Serves: 4
Prep time: 5 minutes
Cook time: 15 minutes

{⌁} {🕯} {✗}

- 4 Arbroath smokies

- To serve:
- 4–8 thick slices good-quality brown (whole wheat) bread
- about 60 g/ 2¼ oz (4 tablespoons) butter
- 1 lemon, quartered into wedges

* Preheat the grill (broiler) to a medium setting and line a large oven tray with baking (parchment) paper.
* Arrange the smokies on the tray and grill (broil) for 12–15 minutes, turning them at least once as they cook. Either peel away the skins or leave them on before serving with brown (whole wheat) bread, butter and lemon wedges.

NORTHEAST OF SCOTLAND
*
FINNAN HADDIES

This simple preparation was once a staple of breakfast tables in Scotland. The milk absorbs flavour from the fish and thickens slightly to become a light serving sauce. Serve with poached eggs and buttered bread.

Serves: 4
Prep time: 5 minutes
Cook time: 15 minutes

{⌁} {✗}

- smoked haddock fillet, about 700 g/ 1 lb 8½ oz
- 350 ml/ 12 fl oz (1½ cups) full-fat (whole) milk, plus a little extra
- ½ teaspoon ground black peppercorns
- 1½ teaspoons mustard powder (optional)
- 2 teaspoons cornflour (cornstarch) (optional)

- To serve:
- poached eggs
- buttered toast

* Slice the smoked haddock fillet into 4 equal servings and set aside.

* To make the sauce, pour the milk into a heavy saucepan, add the ground black peppercorns and mustard powder (if using), and bring to the boil. Once the milk is boiling, reduce the heat to medium-low and simmer for another 5 minutes, then remove from the heat. If you prefer a thick sauce to serve over the fish, whisk the cornflour (cornstarch) and a little extra milk together in a small bowl, then stir it into the hot milk mixture.
* Put the haddock into the milk mixture, skin-side down, and bring to a bare simmer. Cook for 5–6 minutes, before removing the pan from the heat. Using a slotted spoon, carefully transfer the fillets to a warmed serving dish and serve with poached eggs and buttered toast.

ISLE OF MAN / SCOTLAND /
ENGLAND: EAST ANGLIA, YORKSHIRE AND
NORTHUMBERLAND
*
GRILLED KIPPERS

Kippered herrings are split and butterflied, salt-brined and then cold-smoked. While great shoals of herring were once common to British waters – and an apparent draw for early Vikings – the kippering process (for herring at least) was only created in the 1840s. First invented by John Woodger of the Northumbrian fishing village Seahouses, there are still distinctive regional cures across the UK that vary in their use of smoke and salt, as well as colouring.
Kippers should be fried or cooked quickly under a hot grill (broiler) and then served hot with buttered toast, a lemon wedge and a sprinkling of chopped parsley. Eat for breakfast or an early lunch.

Serves: 4
Prep time: 2 minutes
Cook time: 5–6 minutes

{⌁} {✗}

- 40 g/ 1½ oz (3 tablespoons) butter
- 4 kippers

- To serve:
- 1 lemon, quartered
- pinch of chopped flat-leaf parsley
- buttered toast or thick brown (whole wheat) bread

* Preheat the grill (broiler) to a medium-high heat and line a baking sheet with baking (parchment) paper.
* Put half of the butter into a small saucepan and heat over a low heat for 2 minutes, or until melted, then set aside. Put the remaining butter into the fridge to chill.
* Using a sharp knife, score the skin of the kippers, then arrange them, skin-side up, on the lined baking sheet. Grill (broil) for 2–3 minutes before flipping them over. Carefully brush the belly of each kipper with 1 teaspoon of the melted butter and grill (broil) for another 2–3 minutes, or until the skin crisps.
* Serve hot with a small pat of the chilled butter, a lemon wedge, a sprinkle of chopped parsley and buttered toast or brown (whole wheat) bread.
* **Notes:** You can also follow this recipe for bloaters and buckling, which are respectively cold-smoked whole herring and hot-smoked whole herring, although they will benefit from an extra minute of cooking on both sides.

Grilled kippers

ENGLAND
*

SOUSED HERRING

Sousing is an old English phrase for pickling, and while the earliest references to sousing are applied to meat, these days the term is almost exclusively used to describe herring and mackerel. A similar weight of mackerel could be used here.

Serves: 2–4
Prep time: 10 minutes, plus 24 hours brining
Cook time: 8 minutes
{⚖}{🔪}{➴}

- 475 ml/6 fl oz (2 cups) apple cider vinegar
- 60 g/2¼ oz (¼ cup) salt
- 1 teaspoon mustard seeds
- 2 teaspoons whole allspice
- 2 teaspoons black peppercorns
- 500 g/1 lb 2 oz fresh herring fillets

* Fill a medium saucepan with about 1 litre/34 fl oz (4¼ cups) water and the vinegar and bring to the boil. Add the salt and stir until it has dissolved, then stir through the spices and remove the pan from the heat.
* Arrange the herring in a single layer in a glass or ceramic baking dish and pour over the pickling liquid. Cover and allow the herring to lightly pickle for 24 hours in the fridge before serving.

NORTHERN IRELAND / SCOTLAND / WALES
*

POTTED HERRING

Below is a classic Northern Irish preparation of pickled herring baked in a spiced vinegar mixture until their tops have crisped. Similar recipes for potted herring were also made in Scotland and Wales.
Serve with wheaten bread and butter.

Serves: 5
Prep time: 15 minutes
Cook time: 30 minutes
{⚖}{🔪}{➴}

- 200 ml/7 fl oz (¾ cup plus 1 tablespoon) malt vinegar
- 1 white onion, finely diced
- 2 bay leaves
- 1 teaspoon whole allspice
- 10 herring, butterflied and with heads and tails removed
- salt and pepper

* Preheat the oven to 180°C/350°F/Gas Mark 4.
* Put the vinegar, onion, bay leaves and allspice into a small saucepan and bring to the boil. When the mixture has reached boiling point, remove from the heat and set aside.
* Roll the herrings up and pack them tightly into a large glass or ceramic baking dish, then season with salt and pepper. Carefully remove the bay leaves from the vinegar mixture and discard, then pour the vinegar mixture over the rolled herrings. Cook in the oven for 30 minutes, or until golden on top. Serve either hot or chilled.

UNITED KINGDOM
*

SMOKED FISH PÂTÉ

Filleted smoked fish makes a pungent but delicious creamy pâté to be spread over good-quality bread.

Serves: 6
Prep time: 15 minutes
{➴}{🔪}

- 4 kippers, bloaters, buckling or other smoked fish
- 60 g/2¼ oz (4 tablespoons) unsalted butter, softened
- 2 pinches of cayenne pepper
- 2 pinches of ground mace or nutmeg
- 30 ml/1 fl oz (2 tablespoons) double (heavy) cream
- lemon juice, to taste
- salt

* Using a sharp knife, debone the fish. Pick or scrape the flesh clean from the skin and put it into a food processor.
* Add the butter, cayenne, mace or nutmeg and cream and process until it has a uniform texture and a pâté-like smoothness. Gradually add salt and lemon juice to taste, and when satisfied, spoon into 6 ramekins. Cover each of the ramekins with clingfilm (plastic wrap) and leave to cool in the fridge until ready to serve.

ENGLAND: LANCASHIRE
*

POTTED BROWN SHRIMP

The tradition of potting shrimp originates in Lancashire, in the area around Morecombe Bay, where the country's best brown shrimp is caught – and has been for several hundred years. The shrimp are cooked quickly in a pan with a little spiced butter then sealed in a small pot or ramekin with a layer of clarified butter on top. The butter originally served a very practical purpose – to preserve the shrimp – but these days a fridge will do that, so now it's more about the taste.

Serves 4–6
Prep time: 5 minutes, plus 15 minutes chilling
Cook time: 5 minutes
{➴}{🥘}

- 125 g/4¼ oz (½ cup) clarified butter
- pinch of ground mace
- pinch of cayenne pepper
- 250 g/9 oz cooked and peeled brown shrimp
- 1 teaspoon lemon juice
- pepper
- thinly cut warm toast or fresh crusty bread, to serve

* Melt the clarified butter in a medium saucepan over a medium-low heat. Set about 3 tablespoons of clarified butter aside, then add the dried spices to the pan and mix well. Reduce the heat to low, add the shrimp and coat them in the warm spiced butter. Add the lemon juice and seasoning to taste.
* Pack into your chosen pots and chill for 15 minutes before capping with a thin layer of the reserved melted clarified butter. Serve with warm toast or crusty bread.

Potted brown shrimp

UNITED KINGDOM
*

POTTED SALMON
(OR TROUT/CHAR)

The salmon meat should be flaked enough to become spreadable, but still maintain a good bit of texture. Eat with brown (whole wheat) or crusty bread and a lemon wedge.

Serves: 6–8
Prep time: 1 hour, plus 2 hours salting
Cook time: 15 minutes
{🗄}{🍴}

- 20 g/¾ oz (4 teaspoons) salt
- 1 kg/2¼ lb salmon fillet or an equal weight of left-over salmon meat
- 1 onion, halved
- 1 bay leaf (optional)
- 10 black peppercorns
- 500 ml/17 fl oz (2 cups plus 1 tablespoon) full-fat (whole) milk
- 100 ml/3½ fl oz (⅓ cup plus 1 tablespoon) white wine
- grated nutmeg, to taste
- generous pinch of chopped flat-leaf parsley, chives or chervil (optional)
- few pinches of cayenne pepper
- grated zest of 1 lemon
- 200 ml/7 fl oz (¾ cup plus 1 tablespoon) clarified butter

* Use half the salt to lightly coat the salmon, then cover or wrap the salmon in clingfilm (plastic wrap) and set aside for about 2 hours.
* To make the poaching liquid, put the onion, bay leaf (if using), and peppercorns into a wide-based saucepan and pour in the milk to cover, then add the remaining salt and the wine and stir until the salt has dissolved. Bring to the boil, then immediately reduce the heat to medium-low and simmer for 10 minutes.
* Uncover the salmon and rinse off any visible salt under cold running water, then carefully put the fish into the simmering stock and poach gently for 5–10 minutes, depending on the fish's thickness, until it is completely opaque and the flesh flakes easily with a fork. Carefully remove the fish using a slotted spoon and leave to cool for several minutes until it is at room temperature.
* Put the fish into a large bowl and flake it into pieces, then add the grated nutmeg, chopped parsley (if using), the cayenne and lemon zest and mix together until combined. Add more salt if necessary. Pour in a small splash of the clarified butter and mix until combined.
* Pack the salmon mixture tightly into sterilized jars (page 464), then pour the remaining clarified butter over the top of the mixture. Leave to cool, then cover and seal. When cool, the butter will form a preservative seal. Store in the fridge for up to 1 week or eat as soon as it has cooled.
* Notes: If you like, the salmon can be poached in fish stock (equal to the amount of milk), with the bay leaf and black peppercorns.

UNITED KINGDOM
*

PAN-FRIED COD
WITH
PARSLEY SAUCE

This classic British pairing is both easy to make and comforting. Traditionally, the fish is poached and the parsley sauce made rather simply, either with a milk base or one made with the starchy boiling water from the potatoes. However, the sauce can be spruced up with a splash of cream. A nice crusty skin on the pan-fried cod will go a long way towards breaking up the soft, mellow flavours.

Serves: 2
Prep time: 5 minutes
Cook time: 10 minutes
{🍴}{🔪}

- 2 x 150-g/5-oz cod fillets, skin on
- 1 quantity Parsley Sauce (page 420), warmed through
- 1 quantity Mashed Potatoes (page 80), warmed through
- 2 tablespoons rapeseed (canola) oil
- salt

* 30 minutes before cooking, sprinkle the cod fillets with salt and leave them to come to room temperature. (If your Parsley Sauce or Mashed Potatoes are not ready at this point, start them first and keep warm.)
* Heat a frying pan or skillet over a medium heat, add the oil and when the pan is hot, put the cod, skin-side down into the oil. Press the fish down with a fish slice (spatula) so that all of the skin is in contact with the pan. Cook for 4 minutes, or until the skin is visibly browned at the edges, then turn it over and cook for another 2–3 minutes until the fish is completely cooked through and the flesh has turned white and opaque. Remove the pan from the heat and leave the fish to rest for 1 minute.
* Serve the fish with the Parsley Sauce poured over the top and the Mashed Potatoes on the side.

SCOTLAND
*

BAKED COD
WITH
MUSTARD SAUCE

The combination of cod and mustard sauce is sometimes said to originate with the Nordic influence on Scotland's coastal communities, however it seems just as likely to have originated with the plethora of sauces for fish that were popularized by Victorian cooking.

Serves: 4
Prep time: 10 minutes
Cook time: 20 minutes
{🍴}

- 4 x 200-g/7-oz cod steaks, skin on
- 1 tablespoon rapeseed (canola) oil
- 60 g/2¼ oz (4 tablespoons) butter

- 1 quantity Melted Butter Sauce (page 420)
- 30 g/1 oz (3¾ tablespoons) plain (all-purpose) flour
- 1 tablespoon full-fat (whole) milk
- 1 tablespoon English mustard or a mix of wholegrain and English mustard
- 100 g/3½ oz mustard greens
- salt
- hot new potatoes or buttery mash, to serve

* 30 minutes before cooking, salt the cod steaks and leave them to come to room temperature.
* Preheat the oven to 200°C/400°F/Gas Mark 6.
* Heat the oil and 30 g/1 oz (2 tablespoons) of the butter in a large roasting pan over 2 rings on the hob (stovetop). Alternatively, use an ovenproof frying pan or skillet. Put the cod steaks, skin-side down, into the pan and fry for 3–4 minutes before turning them over and baking in the oven for another 8 minutes, or until the skin is golden brown and the flesh is firm and flaky.
* Meanwhile, make the Melted Butter Sauce in a large saucepan following the directions on page 420. Put the flour into a small bowl, add the milk and mix together until combined, then gradually stir the mixture and the mustard into the butter sauce.
* Heat a separate pan over a medium-high heat and add the remaining butter. Add the mustard greens and leave to wilt for 1 minute, then remove from the heat.
* Serve the cod immediately with the mustard sauce poured over the top and with the mustard greens on the side with hot new potatoes or a buttery mash.

UNITED KINGDOM
*

COLEY WITH SAMPHIRE
AND
HARICOT BEANS

Coley, or coalfish, are found in Britain's coldest waters, particularly around the northern isles of Scotland, where the fish has been a part of the local diet for centuries. The coley in this recipe is interchangeable with pollack or a similarly firm white fish.

Serves: 2
Prep time: 15 minutes, plus 12 hours soaking
Cook time: 10 minutes
{🖲}{🖝}

- 200 g/7 oz (1 cup plus 2 teaspoons) dried haricot beans
- 4 tablespoons cold-pressed rapeseed (canola) oil
- 1 onion, sliced
- 1 sprig thyme
- 1 sprig rosemary
- 1 sprig marjoram
- 2 bay leaves
- 45 g/1½ oz (3 tablespoons) butter, plus extra for frying
- 2 x 150-g/5-oz coley fillets, skin removed
- 200 g/7 oz samphire, washed
- salt and pepper

* Put the haricot beans into a large bowl of cold water and leave to soak for 12 hours. When ready to cook the beans, drain and put them into a heavy saucepan. Cover with

cold water, add the oil, onion, herbs and 15 g/½ oz (1 tablespoon) of the butter and bring to the boil. Reduce the heat to medium-low and cook for 12–15 minutes until soft but not mushy. Drain and set aside, reserving the cooking water.
* Pat the coley fillets dry with paper towels and season with salt and pepper. Heat a large frying pan or skillet over a high heat. Drop in a large knob of butter, then add the coley and fry for 2–3 minutes on each side, depending on the thickness of the fish and adjusting the heat so the butter doesn't burn. Transfer to a plate and keep warm.
* Add the samphire to the pan and cook for 1–2 minutes to warm through, but do not overcook. Set aside.
* Pour 150 ml/5 fl oz (⅔ cup) of the reserved bean cooking liquid into a large saucepan and bring to the boil. Add the cooked beans and stir frequently for 1 minute. Remove from the heat, add the remaining 30 g/1 oz (2 tablespoons) butter and stir until the beans are coated all over. The bean cooking liquid will act as a sauce for the dish.
* Serve the beans, samphire and coley immediately in bowls with the sauce spooned over the top.

ENGLAND
*

GRILLED MACKEREL
WITH
GOOSEBERRY SAUCE

A slightly tart gooseberry sauce does a wonderful job balancing out the oil-rich mackerel and makes for the perfect alfresco summer lunch. The mackerel would be just as nice poached or baked, but the flavour of the grill (broiler) adds that little bit extra. Serve with a dollop of English mustard and boiled new potatoes.

Serves: 2
Prep time: 5 minutes
Cook time: 7–15 minutes
{🖲}{🖝}{🗡}{🍴}

- 1 large or 2 small-medium whole mackerels, gutted
- 10 ml/2 teaspoons rapeseed (canola) oil
- salt

- To serve:
- Gooseberry Sauce (page 423)
- sharp English mustard

* Preheat the grill (broiler) to high and line a large baking sheet with baking (parchment) paper.
* Rub the mackerel all over with the oil, then season with salt. Arrange the mackerel on the lined baking sheet and grill (broil) for several minutes, or until the skin starts to crisp and colour. Flip over and cook for the same amount of time on the other side. The cooking time will vary depending on the size of the mackerel.
* When the mackerel has crisped up nicely on both sides, serve with a small bowl of Gooseberry Sauce and a little dollop of sharp English mustard.

UNITED KINGDOM
*

LEMON SOLE
WITH
CAPER BUTTER SAUCE

This is an English riff on the French *sole meunière*, an unelaborate but excellent preparation meant to accentuate and not mask the quality of the fish.

Serves: 2
Prep time: 5 minutes
Cook time: 15 minutes
{🍲}{🥄}{📷}{🍴}

- 4 lemon sole fillets, about 125 g/4¼ oz each
- 2 tablespoons rapeseed (canola) oil
- 40 g/1½ oz (3 tablespoons) butter
- 175 g/6 oz (1 cup) capers, drained, rinsed and crushed
- salt
- Boiled New Potatoes (page 84), to serve

* Pat the fish dry with paper towels and remove any pin bones you come across using tweezers. Sprinkle the fish with a little salt and set aside.
* Heat the oil and butter in a large frying pan or skillet over a medium heat. Once the butter has melted and begins to froth, put the fish into the pan and cook for 3 minutes on each side, or until the fish is opaque and cooked through.
* Remove the fillets from the pan with a fish slice (spatula) and set aside. Add the capers to the pan and warm over a medium heat, being careful not to burn the butter or capers. You are merely flavouring the butter and warming the capers.
* When the sauce is ready, serve the lemon sole on individual plates with the caper and butter sauce poured over the top. They will go quite well with hot Boiled New Potatoes.

ENGLAND
*

SOLE IN CREAM SAUCE

This recipe comes from Eliza Acton's *Modern Cookery for Private Families* (1845), but good simple cooking needs little adjustment. The sole is parboiled in water then simmered in cream until cooked through. While the fish rests, the cream is spiced with a little ground mace and cayenne pepper, as well as a squeeze of lemon juice. Serve with boiled Jersey Royal (new) potatoes and asparagus spears.

Serves: 4
Prep time: 15 minutes
Cook time: 10 minutes
{🍲}{🥄}{📷}

- 1 x 600 g (1 lb 5oz) sole, cleaned and gutted
- about 300 ml/10 fl oz (1¼ cups) double (heavy) cream
- pinch of ground mace (or nutmeg)
- pinch of cayenne pepper
- juice of ½ lemon
- salt

- To serve:
- cooked Jersey Royal potatoes
- steamed asparagus spears

* Prepare the sole by trimming off the fins and putting it into a pan just large enough to hold the fish. Pour boiling water around it so that the water almost covers the fish, then add a pinch of salt and simmer very gently over a low heat for 2 minutes. Carefully pour away the water, reserving a few tablespoons, and pour in the cream so that it comes halfway up the fish. Bring to a simmer over a medium-low heat and cook for 4–5 minutes, basting the fish with the hot cream until cooked through. If the cream thickens too much, add some of the reserved cooking liquid or water.
* Transfer the sole to a warmed serving dish and finish the cream sauce by adding some more salt, if desired, a little ground mace, cayenne pepper and a squeeze of lemon juice – you may not need all the juice.
* Pour the sauce over the fish and serve with Jersey Royal potatoes and some lightly steamed asparagus spears.

UNITED KINGDOM
*

HALIBUT
WITH
OYSTER SAUCE
AND
SEA KALE

This is a Victorian pairing that has aged very well indeed – it wouldn't look out of place on the menu of a good British restaurant today.

Serves: 2
Prep time: 10 minutes
Cook time: 10 minutes
{🥄}{🍴}

- 2 x 150-g/5-oz halibut fillets, skin on
- 1–2 tablespoons rapeseed (canola) oil
- 400 g/14 oz sea kale leaves, stems removed
- 150 ml/5 fl oz (⅔ cup) Oyster Sauce (page 422)
- sea salt flakes

* Remove the fish from the fridge 30 minutes before cooking. Pat dry with paper towels, grind a pinch of sea salt over them and leave them to come to room temperature.
* Heat a large frying pan or skillet with the oil over a medium heat. When hot, add the fish, skin-side down, and press the fish against the pan using a fish slice (spatula) to ensure that the skin is in contact with the pan. Cook for 4 minutes, or until the edges of the skin are visibly browning.
* Meanwhile, heat a medium saucepan over a medium heat, add the sea kale, a splash of water and the Oyster Sauce and heat through for 2–3 minutes, or until just hot.
* Flip the fish over and cook for another 4 minutes, or until the flesh has completely cooked through and is white and opaque.
* Serve the halibut immediately with the wilted sea kale and Oyster Sauce on top of the fish.

Lemon sole with caper butter sauce

UNITED KINGDOM
*

HALIBUT
WITH
MUSSELS AND SEA VEGETABLES

Sea vegetables, like sea purslane, are common to British coastlines, and today they are often foraged for use at restaurants, where they're typically cooked with fish or shellfish. This recipe is inspired by a serving from Scottish chef Pamela Brunton, who uses halibut sourced from Gigha, an island in the Inner Hebrides.

Serves: 2
Prep time: 10 minutes
Cook time: 10 minutes
{🐟}{🔪}{🌶}{🍴}

- 2 x 150-g/5-oz halibut fillets, skin on
- 200 g/7 oz mussels
- 1–2 tablespoons rapeseed (canola) oil
- 80 ml/2¾ fl oz (⅓ cup) cider or white wine
- 400 g/14 oz mixed sea greens, such as sea beet, sea kale and sea purslane
- sea salt flakes

* Remove the fish from the fridge 30 minutes before cooking. Pat the fillets dry with paper towels, grind a pinch of salt over them and leave them to come to room temperature. Scrub the mussels under cold running water, removing any barnacles and pulling off any tendrils. Make sure the mussels are closed. If some are open, gently tap them on a work counter and if they still don't close, discard them. Set the mussels aside.
* Heat a large frying pan or skillet with a little oil over a medium heat. When hot, add the fish, skin-side down, and press the fish against the pan using a fish slice (spatula) to ensure that the skin is in contact with the pan. Cook for 4 minutes, or until the edges of the skin are visibly browning. Flip the fish over and cook for another 4 minutes, or until the flesh has completely cooked through and it is white and opaque.
* If the halibut is finished cooking before you have started your mussels, transfer them to a plate and cover or put them into a low oven, about 80°C/176°F/lowest Gas Mark, to keep warm.
* To cook the mussels, set a large saucepan over a high heat and carefully drop in the mussels. Pour in the cider and add the sea greens. Immediately cover with a lid and let the mussels steam for a minute or so until they have opened and the greens have wilted. Discard any mussels that still remain closed.
* Serve the fish with the mussels and sea greens.

UNITED KINGDOM
*

WHOLE ROASTED BRILL
WITH
CRUSHED JERSEY ROYALS

Crispy crushed and fried potatoes make such a pleasing accompaniment to the soft, slightly sweet brill. A Caper Lemon Butter Sauce (page 422) would make a very fine accompaniment as well. This is no-frill, fresh-tasting comfort food.

Serves: 2
Prep time: 10 minutes
Cook time: 30 minutes
{🐟}{🔪}{🌶}

- 1 x 1–2-kg/2¼–4½-lb brill
- 125 ml/4¼ fl oz (½ cup) rapeseed (canola) oil
- 1 bunch rosemary
- 1 bunch lemon thyme
- 1 bunch marjoram
- 75 ml/2½ fl oz (⅓ cup) white wine or water
- juice of 1 lemon
- 500 g/1 lb 2 oz Jersey Royals (new potatoes)
- salt and pepper

* Preheat the oven to 200°C/400°F/Gas Mark 6.
* Cut the fins off the fish.
* Pour 40 ml/1¼ fl oz (2⅔ tablespoons) of the oil into an ovenproof baking dish large enough to fit the fish inside in a single layer. Arrange the herbs over the bottom of the dish and place the fish on top. Add the wine or water, then rub another 40 ml/1⅓ fl oz (2⅔ tablespoons) of the oil over the fish. Season with salt and lemon juice, leaving the cut lemon halves inside the dish as you cook to add extra flavour.
* Cook in the oven for 20 minutes, or until the flesh of the fish is coming away from the spine at the thickest part. If it needs more time, continue cooking, checking every 10 minutes.
* Meanwhile, bring a large saucepan about half or two-thirds full of salted water to the boil. When boiling, carefully add the potatoes using a slotted spoon and cook for 6–8 minutes until tender and easily pierced with a fork.
* Drain the potatoes and let them steam-dry, before putting a large frying pan or skillet over a medium heat with the remaining oil. When the oil is hot, add the potatoes and press them down with a fork until they are slightly squished. Fry them for 1–2 minutes until they turn a deep golden brown, then flip them over and fry the other side for another 1–2 minutes.
* Season the potatoes to taste with salt and pepper and serve alongside the roasted brill.

Whole roasted brill with crushed Jersey royals

UNITED KINGDOM
*
POACHED TURBOT
WITH
LOBSTER SAUCE

A rich lobster sauce provides extra oomph to this special fish. Oyster or shrimp sauce would also work well here – serve luxury with luxury, the adage goes.

Serves: 2
Prep time: 10 minutes
Cook time: 15 minutes

{ᴗ˙}{▮}

- 2 x 150-g/5-oz turbot fillets
- 400 g/14 oz mixed sea greens, such as sea beet
  or samphire, etc.
- 100 ml/3½ fl oz (⅓ cup plus 1 tablespoon) Lobster Sauce
  (page 421)

- For the poaching liquid:
- 1 onion, halved
- 1 bay leaf
- a few flat-leaf parsley stalks
- 10 peppercorns
- 100 ml/3½ fl oz (⅓ cup plus 1 tablespoon) white wine
- pinch of salt

* Pour 500 ml/17 fl oz (2 cups plus 1 tablespoon) water into a large saucepan, then add all the ingredients for the poaching liquid and bring to the boil. Reduce the heat to medium-low and simmer for 10 minutes.
* Carefully put the fish into the simmering poaching liquid. If they are not completely covered, add more water until they are submerged and gently simmer for 2–3 minutes. Turn off the heat and leave the fish in the pan for another 3–4 minutes until they are cooked through and the flesh is opaque.
* Put the sea greens into a medium saucepan with a little splash of water. They shouldn't need seasoning as they are already naturally salty. Cook over a medium heat for 3–4 minutes, or until wilted.
* Gently warm the Lobster Sauce in another saucepan over a low heat for 5 minutes, or until it is hot through. Serve the turbot fillets with the Lobster Sauce poured over the top with a side of sea greens.

WALES
*
POACHED SALMON
WITH
TEIFI SAUCE

In Wales, salmon was served with a piquant sauce, called Teifi sauce, made from a base of melted butter. To the butter, port, wine, mushroom ketchup and a boned anchovy (or anchovy essence) would be added. The salmon could then be served alongside a jug (pitcher) of the sauce, or baked whole with the sauce poured around it.

Serves: 4
Prep time: 10 minutes
Cook time: 30 minutes

{ᴗ˙}

- 4 x 175-g/6-oz pieces salmon fillet
- 12 asparagus spears
- 1 quantity Melted Butter Sauce (page 420)
- 125 ml/4¼ fl oz (½ cup) port
- 1 teaspoon Mushroom Ketchup (page 426)
- ½ teaspoon anchovy paste

- For the poaching liquid:
- 100 ml/3½ fl oz (⅓ cup plus 1 tablespoon) white wine
- dash of white wine vinegar
- 2 shallots or 1 small onion, sliced
- 6 cracked black peppercorns
- celery tops from 1 bunch
- 1 carrot, thinly sliced
- flat-leaf parsley stalks from ½ bunch
- ½ lemon, sliced
- 1½ teaspoons salt

* Preheat the oven to 80°C/176°F/lowest Gas Mark.
* Put all the poaching liquid ingredients with 400 ml/ 14 fl oz (1⅔ cups) water into a large saucepan and bring to a simmer over a medium-low heat. Cook at a bare simmer for 15 minutes, then reduce the heat to low and carefully add the salmon steaks, making sure they are only submerged in the water about halfway up. Poach for 5 minutes, turning them over halfway through, then remove the pan from the heat. Leave the salmon to stand in the hot poaching liquid for another 3–4 minutes, then carefully remove the fish and keep warm in the oven.
* Meanwhile, trim the asparagus and remove any woody ends. Put the asparagus into a steamer or bring a pan of water to the boil and steam or boil for 4–5 minutes.
* Warm the Melted Butter Sauce through in a medium saucepan. Stir in the port, Mushroom Ketchup and anchovy paste and simmer over a medium heat for several minutes until it has sufficiently reduced.
* Ladle the sauce over the salmon to serve, or bring to the table in a sauceboat and serve with the asparagus.

SCOTLAND: EDINBURGH
*
TWEED KETTLE

This salmon hash was especially common in Edinburgh, and is named after the River Tweed, famous for its salmon.

Serves: 4
Prep time: 10–15 minutes
Cook time: 20 minutes

{♨}{ᴗ˙}

- 1 kg/2¼ lb piece of salmon on the bone, skin on
- 50 g/2 oz (3½ tablespoons) butter
- 4 spring onions (scallions) or chives, finely sliced
- 125 g/4¼ oz chestnut (cremini) mushrooms, quartered
- 100 ml/3½ fl oz (⅓ cup plus 1 tablespoon) white wine
- ⅛ teaspoon ground nutmeg
- ⅛ teaspoon ground mace
- salt and pepper

- For the bouquet garni:
- 2 sprigs thyme, 1 bay leaf, 1 stalk flat-leaf parsley and
½ lemon rind

- boiled or fried potatoes, to serve

* Put all the ingredients for the bouquet garni into a small muslin (cheesecloth) square, gather up the corners and tie with kitchen string. Put the bouquet garni into a large saucepan together with 500 ml/17 fl oz (2 cups plus 1 tablespoon) water and bring to a simmer over a medium-low heat. Season with salt and pepper.
* Carefully put the salmon into the simmering poaching liquid, cover with a lid and simmer over a medium-low heat for 5 minutes. Remove from the heat and leave to stand for another 5 minutes.
* Meanwhile, melt the butter in a large frying pan or skillet over a medium-high heat until it begins to foam. Add the spring onions (scallions) and fry for 2 minutes. Add the mushrooms and wine and cook for another 5 minutes.
* Remove the salmon from the poaching liquid and flake into a bowl, being sure to remove the skin and bones. Season with salt and pepper, the nutmeg and mace, then add the flaked salmon to the pan and fold into the vegetables.
* Serve immediately with boiled or fried potatoes.

UNITED KINGDOM
*

SKATE WINGS
WITH
BLACK BUTTER SAUCE

Skate was once considered a food of poverty, but by Victorian times cooks were far more amenable to the large ray fish. It could be either baked, broken down for soups, or simply poached and brushed with butter. Today it's the skate's 'wings' that are its most popular cut, and they are typically fried in a *beurre noisette* with capers, in French fashion. It is very telling of the era that the translation in historic English cookbooks is 'black butter', rather than the far more common 'brown butter'.

Serves: 6
Prep time: 5 minutes
Cook time: 15 minutes
{ ♨ }

- 3 x 250 g/9 oz skate wings, cut in half
- 80 g/3 oz (⅔ cup) plain (all-purpose) flour
- 175 g/6 oz (1½ sticks) unsalted butter
- 50–75 ml/1¾–2½ fl oz (3½ tablespoons–⅓ cup) white wine vinegar
- 2 tablespoons capers, drained, rinsed and chopped if large
- 2 tablespoons finely chopped flat-leaf parsley leaves
- salt and pepper

* Remove the skate wings from the fridge 30 minutes before cooking. Coat them in the flour and season with salt and pepper.
* Heat 50 g/2 oz (3½ tablespoons) of the butter in a deep-rimmed frying pan or skillet over medium heat, add the skate wings and fry for 4 minutes on each side, then remove from the pan and leave to rest.
* Melt the remaining butter in the pan and cook gently

until it becomes a dark brown colour and smells nutty. Make sure it doesn't burn. Add the vinegar a tablespoon at a time, followed by the capers and parsley, stir and season.
* Spoon the sauce over the skate and serve.

UNITED KINGDOM
*

POACHED SEA TROUT
WITH
WATERCRESS SAUCE

This is a rather more luxurious watercress sauce, similar to a beurre blanc. For the more classic serving, see the Watercress Sauce on page 424.

Serves: 2
Prep time: 10 minutes
Cook time: 35 minutes
{ ♨ }{ ♨ }

- 100 ml/3½ fl oz (⅓ cup plus 1 tablespoon) white wine
- dash of white wine vinegar
- 4 sea trout fillets
- 2 shallots or 1 small onion, sliced
- 6 black peppercorns, cracked
- celery tops from 1 bunch
- 1 carrot, thinly sliced
- flat-leaf parsley stalks from ½ bunch
- ½ lemon, sliced
- 1½ teaspoons salt
- Mashed Potatoes (page 80), to serve

- For the watercress sauce:
- 1 tablespoon butter
- 2 shallots, finely diced
- 75 ml/2½ fl oz (⅓ cup) white wine
- 100 ml/3½ fl oz (⅓ cup plus 1 tablespoon) fish or vegetable stock
- 50 ml/1¾ fl oz (3½ tablespoons) double (heavy) cream
- 100 g/3½ oz (2 cups) watercress, picked and chopped
- salt

* For the watercress sauce, melt the butter in a saucepan over a medium-low heat, then add the shallots and a pinch of salt and gently fry for 8 minutes, or until soft and translucent. Add the wine and cook for another 5 minutes, or until reduced by half. Add the stock and cook for 5 minutes, or until reduced by half. Add the cream and simmer for just a minute. Add the chopped watercress and cook for 2 minutes, or until it has wilted. Remove from the heat and set aside.
* Pour 400 ml/14 fl oz (1⅔ cups) water into a large saucepan and add the wine and vinegar. Bring to the boil over a medium heat, then reduce the heat to medium-low and simmer for 10 minutes. Carefully add the fish and remaining ingredients and simmer for 5–6 minutes. Turn off the heat and leave the fish in the pan for a few more minutes depending on the thickness of the fillets.
* Take the fish out of the pan and serve with the sauce and Mashed Potatoes.

WALES
*

TROUT BAKED IN BACON
BRITHYLL A CHIG MOCH

In Wales, it is traditional to bake trout coated in oatmeal – in much the same way as the Scots treat herring (page 118). Larger sea trout (*sewin*) were frequently stuffed and baked whole.

Serves: 4
Prep time: 30 minutes
Cook time: 20–25 minutes

- butter, for greasing
- 4 fresh trout, about 200–250 g/7–9 oz each
- 1 quantity Herb Stuffing (page 242)
- 12 rashers (slices) smoked streaky (lean) bacon
- pepper

* Preheat the oven to 200°C/400°F/Gas Mark 6 and grease a large ovenproof baking dish with butter.
* Gut and clean the fish and snip the fins off with scissors.
* Divide the stuffing between the fish. Lay 3 bacon rashers on a work counter, then lay a fish over them, season with pepper and wrap up the fish. Repeat with the other trout.
* Arrange the trout in the prepared baking dish, leaving a 2 cm/¾ inch gap between the fish and bake in the oven for 20–25 minutes until cooked. To check if it's cooked, use a knife to pierce the thickest part of the fish, remove and check whether the flesh feels hot. Serve.

UNITED KINGDOM
*

WHOLE ROASTED PLAICE
AND
SHRIMP SAUCE

Plaice, roasted whole, makes an excellent and flavourful meal for two – or one, depending on the size of the fish and the diner! Serve with buttered, Boiled New Potatoes (page 84) tossed with chopped parsley.

Serves: 2
Prep time: 5 minutes
Cook time: 20 minutes
{�335}

- 1 large or 2 small plaice
- 80 ml/3 fl oz (⅓ cup) rapeseed (canola) oil
- 75 ml/2½ fl oz (⅓ cup) white wine or water
- juice of 1 lemon
- 150 g/5 oz (⅔ cup) Shrimp Sauce (page 421)
- salt

- To serve:
- Boiled New Potatoes, well buttered (page 84)
- finely chopped flat-leaf parsley, for sprinkling

* Preheat the oven to 200°C/400°F/Gas Mark 6.
* Dry the skin of the plaice with paper towels, then, using a sharp knife, score the top side of each fillet in 3 diagonal slashes.
* Pour half the oil into an ovenproof baking dish large enough to fit the fish inside in a single layer. Arrange the fish in the dish, add the wine and rub the rest of the oil over the fish. Season with salt and lemon juice, then leave the cut lemon halves inside the dish as you cook for more flavour.
* Cook in the oven for 20 minutes, or until the flesh of the fish is coming away from the spine at the thickest part. If it needs more time, continue cooking, checking every 5 minutes.
* Meanwhile, gently heat the Shrimp Sauce in a small saucepan over a medium-low heat for 5 minutes, or until heated through.
* Serve with the sauce poured over the length of the fish and a big bowl of buttered and boiled potatoes tossed with a little finely chopped parsley on the side.

ENGLAND
*

ELVERS
AND
BACON

Elvers, or baby eels, are silver candescent, but turn a pearly white when they hit a hot pan – much like an egg white, as food writer Dorothy Hartley notes. Although they are uncommon today, they were once a regular find in southwest England. Notably, they were live until they hit the pan, then cooked briefly in bacon fat, seasoned with salt and pepper, then eaten warm with bread and butter.

Serves: 4
Prep time: 40 minutes
Cook time: 20 minutes
{�335}{🍶}{🌶}

- 400 g/14 oz elvers
- 1 tablespoon bacon fat or lard
- 8 rashers (slices) dry-cured smoked bacon, cut into lardons
- 2 eggs, beaten
- salt and pepper

* Line a colander with a large square of muslin (cheesecloth) or a clean dish towel, then add the elvers and rinse under cold, running water. Sprinkle the elvers with a handful of salt and mix in by hand. Rinse and repeat 1–2 more times until they have lost their slime.
* Heat the fat in a frying pan or skillet over a medium-high heat, add the bacon and fry for 4 minutes, or until brown and crisp. Season the eggs with salt and pepper.
* Increase the heat to high, tip in the elvers and cook for 2 minutes, or until they are no longer transparent. Add the eggs and stir for 2 minutes, or until just cooked. As soon as the eggs are softly scrambled, tip into a warmed serving dish and serve.

UNITED KINGDOM
*

BREADED MONKFISH CHEEKS

Heaven forbid you try to toss away a monkfish without savouring these meaty morsels. In the late 1980s, jaunty British chef Keith Floyd followed this preparation of monkfish on a Somerset visit for his popular TV show *Floyd on Britain & Ireland*. The monkfish cheeks in this recipe can be swapped quite easily for skate knobs – which are also just cheeks.

Serves: 6
Prep time: 30 minutes
Cook time: 40 minutes
{ ❧ } { 🍲 }

- 12 monkfish cheeks
- 60 g / 2¼ oz (½ cup) plain (all-purpose) flour
- 2 eggs, well beaten
- 100 g / 3½ oz (1½ cups) dried breadcrumbs
- sunflower oil, for frying
- salt and pepper
- 1 quantity Tartare Sauce (page 423), to serve

* Place a cheek between two sheets of clingfilm (plastic wrap) and hit gently with a rolling pin to flatten and double its area. Repeat with the remaining cheeks.
* Put the flour into a shallow bowl and season with ½ tablespoon each of salt and pepper. Put the eggs into another shallow bowl and put the breadcrumbs into a third bowl. Coat each cheek in the seasoned flour, tapping away any excess, then dip into the egg, making sure they are well covered before rolling them in the breadcrumbs.
* Preheat the oven to 80°C / 176°F / lowest Gas Mark.
* Pour 5 mm / ¼ inch of oil for frying into a large frying pan or skillet and heat over a medium heat. When hot, add the cheeks in batches and fry, turning occasionally, for 8 minutes, or until golden brown. Remove from the pan and leave to drain on paper towels, then keep warm in the oven while cooking the remaining cheeks. Season with salt and serve with Tartare Sauce.

ENGLAND: LONDON
*

JELLIED EELS
AND
MASH

Eels, when stewed, produce a natural jelly within which they are sometimes set. Dorothy Hartley has suggested that they were once cooked in vinegar, like Soused Herring (page 100), and that the jellying occurred as a by-product of the process. In any case, beginning in the eighteenth century, jellied eels became a fixture of the menu at London's many pie and mash shops. Once numbering into the hundreds, there are now just a handful left in the city. Those craving the speciality – and there are plenty who seek it out – are probably more likely to buy it rather than cook it themselves.

Serves: 4
Prep time: 20 minutes, plus 4 hours chilling
Cook time: 20 minutes
{ 🐟 } { 🍴 } { ❧ }

- 1 kg / 2¼ lb skinned eels,
cut into 2.5–5 cm / 1–2 inch pieces
- 500 ml / 17 fl oz (2 cups plus 1 tablespoon) fish stock
- 1 small onion, halved
- 2 small carrots, cut into thin rounds (optional)
- 1–2 bay leaves
- 1 tablespoon black peppercorns
- juice of 1 lemon
- grated nutmeg
- salt

- To serve:
- malt or chilli vinegar
- pie and mash
- eel liquor

* Put the eel pieces into a large pot of lightly salted water and leave to soak for a few minutes.
* Meanwhile, put the fish stock and all the remaining ingredients, except the nutmeg and lemon juice, into another large saucepan and bring to the boil.
* When the poaching stock is boiling, carefully add the eel pieces and reduce the heat to medium-low. Cook for 20 minutes, then remove from the heat and add the lemon juice and a little grated nutmeg. Transfer the eels and liquid to a large airtight container. You can strain the liquid to remove the vegetables and spices or leave them in to develop flavour. Either way, cover with a lid and leave the eels to cool in the fridge for up to 4 hours. Eels are gelatinous due to the collagen in their skin, and the jelly will form naturally as it cools.
* Serve with malt or chilli vinegar and as a side to pie and mash and (eel) liquor.
* Notes: The 'liquor' offered as gravy at pie and mash shops was traditionally made from the reserved stewing liquid used to cook the eels.

UNITED KINGDOM
*

BATTERED FISH
AND
CHIPS

Britain's love affair with fish and chips dates back to the early 1860s, when the first proper chip shops opened in London. Many of these were established by Jewish immigrants who advertised 'fish fried in the Jewish fashion' – which is to say, in a simple flour and water batter. A recipe in Alexis Soyer's 1845 *A Shilling Cookery for the People* describes a 'fried fish, Jewish fashion' in the same manner, and it is often theorized that this form of fried fish found its way to Britain via *pescado frito*, a dish brought by Jews emigrating from Portugal.

The fish in question is always a white fish, usually cod or haddock, and fried in batter until light and crispy. No one wants a soggy batter. When made at home, or in restaurants, beer is often swapped for water in the batter, but you will never find that in a proper chippy. In fact, many of the old-school chippies, the ones staffed with white-haired workers, also fry both their fish and chips in beef dripping rather than vegetable oil – and this adds a more flavourful finish that many prefer.

Fish and chips are more than the dish itself, however, and it harkens back to a moment in time or even a mood. Salt and grease are part and parcel here.

Enjoy with an extra sprinkling of sea salt and malt vinegar and serve with lemon wedges and a side of Mushy Peas (page 68).

Serves: 4
Prep time: 1 hour, plus 2 hours standing
Cook time: 20 minutes
{ ✴ }

- rapeseed (canola) oil or beef dripping, for frying
- 4 tablespoons plain (all-purpose) flour
- 4 x 200-g/7-oz cod or haddock steaks, skin on
- salt and pepper

- For the batter:
- 300 ml/10 fl oz (1¼ cups) tepid beer, ale or water
- 1 teaspoon instant dried yeast
- 240 g/8½ oz (2 cups) plain (all-purpose) flour
- 1 teaspoon salt

- For the chips:
- 750 g/1 lb 10 oz floury (baking) potatoes, such as King Edward or Maris Piper, peeled or unpeeled and cut into finger-width strips, about 1–2 cm/½–¾ inch thick

- To serve:
- lemon wedges
- Mushy Peas (page 68)
- Tartare Sauce (page 423), optional
- Tomato Ketchup (page 425), optional
- Mayonnaise (page 427), optional
- Pickled Onions (page 445), optional

* For the batter, pour the tepid beer or water into a large bowl. Add the yeast and beat together with a whisk until combined. Sift the flour and a pinch of salt into a separate bowl before folding it into the yeasted liquid and mixing together to form a smooth batter. Cover the batter with a dish towel and leave to stand for 2 hours.
* Meanwhile, line a large plate with paper towels. Heat enough oil for deep-frying in a large, deep saucepan or deep fryer until it reaches 140°C/284°F on a thermometer. Preheat the oven to 80°C/176°F/lowest Gas Mark.
* Working in batches, carefully lower the chips into the hot oil and deep-fry for 8–9 minutes until soft. Remove with a slotted spoon and leave to drain on the lined plate. If you have time, let the chips firm up by chilling in the fridge for at least 1 hour.
* Increase the temperature of the oil to 190°C/375°F and deep-fry the chips again in batches, for another 4–5 minutes until they are nicely browned.
* Remove and leave to drain in an ovenproof dish or roasting tray.
* Keep the chips warm in the oven until the fish is ready. Reduce the temperature of the oil in the saucepan or deep fryer to 180°C/350°F.
* For the fish, season the flour with salt and pepper, then sprinkle the seasoned flour over a large plate and coat the fish in it, patting off any excess. Using tongs, completely immerse the fillets into the batter before carefully placing them into the hot oil, making sure they are well away from you, in case you splash yourself. Deep-fry for at least 5–7 minutes, depending on the thickness of the fish, until they are evenly golden brown and crispy. Remove and leave to drain on paper towels. You may need to do this in batches.
* Serve the fish with the chips, lemon wedges, Mushy Peas and any accompaniments including Tartare Sauce, Tomato Ketchup, Mayonnaise or Pickled Onions.

Battered fish and chips

FISHCAKES

Originally a means of using up left-over fish, the humble fishcake is now typically made with richer, creamier (sometimes even cheesy) fillings. Flaked salmon, smoked haddock or cod are most commonly used for this recipe.

Serves: 4
Prep time: 10 minutes
Cook time: 40 minutes
{⚬•}

- 350 g/12 oz floury (baking) potatoes,
  such as Maris Piper or Yukon Gold
- about 250 ml/8 fl oz (1 cup) full-fat (whole) milk
- 2 bay leaves
- ¼ teaspoon freshly grated nutmeg
- 500 g/1 lb 2 oz salmon or smoked haddock fillets
- 1 tablespoon chopped flat-leaf parsley
- 100 g plain (all-purpose) flour
- 2 eggs, beaten
- 100 g dried breadcrumbs
- vegetable oil, for frying
- salt

* Put the potatoes into a large saucepan, cover with cold water, add a pinch of salt and cook over a low heat for 20 minutes, or until soft. Drain, return to the pan and mash using a potato masher until smooth. Set aside.
* Meanwhile, heat a large saucepan over a medium heat, add the milk, bay leaves and nutmeg and bring to a bare simmer. Reduce the heat to low, carefully add the fish and poach for 7–8 minutes on each side until evenly cooked through. If you are using left-over fish, reheat the fish in the same mixture. Remove the fish with a fish slice (spatula) and reserve the cooking liquid.
* Flake the fish into a medium bowl and lightly stir in the mashed potato and parsley. Slowly pour in enough of the reserved cooking liquid to bind the mixture easily into cakes. Roll the mixture into 3–4-cm/1¼–1½-inch wide cakes, about 2.5 cm/1 inch thick.
* Put the flour, eggs and breadcrumbs into 3 shallow bowls. Dip each cake lightly in the flour, then dip into the beaten eggs and, finally, dip into the breadcrumbs until coated all over.
* Heat enough oil for frying in a heavy frying pan or skillet over a medium-high heat until it reaches 180°C/350°F on a thermometer. Carefully add the cakes and fry for 4 minutes, or until brown, then turn them over and cook on the other side for another 4 minutes, or until brown all over. Alternatively, use a deep fryer and fry the cakes for 4–5 minutes until evenly brown. Remove with a slotted spoon and drain on paper towels before serving.
* **Notes:** If you prefer a creamier texture, a basic béchamel or Foundation Sauce (page 416) can be folded into the mixture instead of the infused milk.

CEANN CROPAIG
CRAPPIT HEIDS/KRAPPIN

Ceann cropaig are cod heads cooked with a stuffing made from oats and fatty cod's liver. It is a traditional dish favourite to the isles of northern Scotland, where it is known by different names: the Gaelic (ceann cropaig), Scots (crappit heids) or Shetland dialect (krappin). Unfortunately, in recent years cod's liver has become very hard to find, so the dish has begun to fade out of the mainstream.
This recipe presumes access to cod's liver – but not head – so the mixture is made in a pudding basin (ovenproof bowl). If the heads (gutted) can be sourced too, then all the better!

Serves: 4
Prep time: 5 minutes, plus overnight soaking
Cook time: 30–35 minutes
{⚬•}

- 500 g/1 lb 2 oz livers (cod or ling)
- full-fat (whole) milk, to cover
- 175 g/6 oz (1½ cups) fine oatmeal
- 50 g/2 oz (½ cup minus 2 teaspoons) plain
  (all-purpose) flour
- ½ onion, finely diced (optional)
- 4 gutted heads (optional)
- salt and white pepper

- To serve:
- baked or boiled fish (typically the rest of the cod)
- hot, boiled potatoes

* Put the livers into a large bowl, add enough milk to cover and leave to soak overnight. The next day, drain off the milk, then put the livers into a large bowl and wash and clean them, removing the membranes surrounding them.
* Heat a large frying pan or skillet over a medium heat, add the livers and cook for a few minutes until the oil begins to run. Remove from the pan and put into a large bowl. Using a wooden spoon or potato masher, mash the livers, then gradually stir in the oatmeal, flour and onion (if using) until the mixture is soft and sticky. Season to taste.
* Spoon or use your hands to stuff the liver mixture into the gutted heads (if you can find them), or add the mixture to a 1 litre/34 fl oz greased pudding basin (ovenproof bowl). Cover with a double layer of baking (parchment) paper or aluminium foil.
* Bring some well-salted water to the boil in a large saucepan or stockpot and carefully place the covered basin into the pan so that the water comes two-thirds of the way up the bowl. Cover with a lid, reduce the heat and simmer for 25–30 minutes until cooked.
* Serve with baked or boiled fish (typically the rest of the cod), and hot boiled potatoes.

Ceann cropaig

UNITED KINGDOM
*

MUSSELS
WITH
BACON AND CREAM

This is a classic way of cooking and serving mussels in Britain. The recipe itself comes from the northeast, where it was served seasonally at an excellent pub called The Hadrian Hotel, now Restaurant Hjem, set in the rolling hills of Northumberland.

Serves: 2
Prep time: 5 minutes
Cook time: 15–20 minutes
{🍳}{🥄}{🍲}{🧂}

- 1 kg/2¼ lb mussels
- 50 ml/1¾ fl oz (3½ tablespoons) rapeseed (canola) oil
- 140 g/5 oz bacon, diced
- 2 shallots, finely sliced
- 2 cloves garlic, finely sliced
- 150 ml/5 fl oz (⅔ cup) cider
- 100 ml/3½ fl oz (⅓ cup plus 1 tablespoon) double (heavy) cream
- 15 g/½ oz (½ cup) finely chopped flat-leaf parsley, to garnish

* Scrub the mussels under cold running water, removing any barnacles and pulling off any tendrils. Make sure the mussels are closed. If some are open, gently tap them on a work counter and if they still don't close, discard them. Set the mussels aside.
* Heat the oil in a saucepan large enough to easily fit all the mussels over a medium heat. Add the bacon and fry for 4 minutes, turning occasionally until it starts to turn crisp. Add the shallots and garlic and cook for 1 minute, or until softened. Increase the heat to high, add the mussels, then pour over the cider. Cover with the lid, shake the pan well and cook for 5–7 minutes, shaking the pan occasionally, until all the mussels have opened. Discard any mussels that remain closed.
* Using a slotted spoon, scoop the mussels into serving bowls, then put the pan back over the heat, add the cream and bring the cream and juices to the boil to reduce. Pour the sauce over the mussels and garnish with parsley.

UNITED KINGDOM
*

SCALLOPS

The best hand-dived scallops are so naturally sweet and delicious that they don't require much cooking at all. Whether fried with butter and garlic or baked in their shells, with great-quality scallops, less is more.

Serves: 3–4
Prep time: 30 minutes
Cook time: 5–10 minutes
{🍳}{🥄}{🍲}{🧂}

- 12 hand-dived scallops in the shell
- 70 g/2¾ oz (⅔ stick) butter
- 4 cloves garlic, finely chopped (optional)
- salt

* You will need a shellfish knife or a flat-handled spoon. To remove the scallops from the shell, first locate the connecting abductor muscle, then gently slide a shellfish knife through it to cut the muscle from the upper shell.
* Once the shell springs open, cup your hand under the scallop to gently remove it from the bottom shell. Once removed, take off the roe (the orange tail) and skirt (the frilly lining) from the centre white meat. Discard the skirt and roe, or set the roe aside to add to soups and stocks for a boost of flavour. Inspect the scallop meat to find a small piece of connective muscle that is a bit harder than the rest of the scallop, then gently remove this to avoid tearing the precious scallop meat.
* Quickly rinse the scallops under cold running water to remove any remaining part of the skirt and dry immediately. Set aside.
* Put the raw, cleaned scallops between 2 paper towels and pat dry, then lightly season the scallops with salt. The salt will draw out excess moisture from the scallop and achieve a better crust when fried.
* Melt the butter in a large frying pan or skillet over a medium-low heat. If using, add the chopped garlic and fry for 1–2 minutes, then add the scallops. Be careful not to overcrowd the pan. Fry the scallops on one side for 1–2 minutes until they start to turn golden brown, basting with the melted butter. If the butter starts to burn, add another piece to cool it down. Using kitchen tongs, flip the scallops over and cook for another minute. Remove from the pan to avoid overcooking and serve immediately.

Mussels with bacon and cream

SCOTLAND / WALES
*
HERRINGS FRIED IN OATMEAL

Herring and mackerel were often freshly made for breakfast. First, they were gutted, butterflied (and sometimes filleted), then coated in finely ground oatmeal and fried in butter until a crisp golden brown. Fresh herrings were a common breakfast fry in many coastal areas of Britain, but the oatmeal coating is a decidedly Scottish twist.

Serves: 4
Prep time: 5 minutes
Cook time: 20 minutes

{♨}{🔥}{✏}{🍶}{🅧}

- 4–8 herrings (whole or fillets)
- 60 g / 2¼ oz (½ cup) fine oatmeal (or a 50/50 mix of fine and medium)
- 30–60 g / 1–2¼ oz (2–4 tablespoons) butter or rapeseed (canola) oil
- salt and pepper

* Rinse the herrings, then pat them dry with paper towels. Sprinkle the herrings with a pinch of salt and leave to rest for at least 5 minutes.
* Put the oatmeal into a shallow bowl and season well with salt and pepper. Dip the herrings into the seasoned oats until they are coated evenly on both sides.
* Heat a large frying pan or skillet over a medium heat. When hot, add a little of the butter (don't add it all at once – you will want to add a little more butter for every batch or two). As soon as the butter melts, add the herrings in batches. Cook whole herring for 5–6 minutes on both sides or cook fillets for 2–3 minutes on each side. Serve hot.

UNITED KINGDOM
*
MUSSELS with CIDER

This is a British riff on the classic French *moules marinière*, using the best of British pear cider, or perry. If desired, a thinly sliced leek or two could be added at the same time as the shallots.

Serves: 2
Prep time: 30 minutes
Cook time: 10 minutes

{🔥}{✏}{🍲}

- 1 kg / 2¼ lb mussels
- 25 g / 1 oz (2 tablespoons) butter
- 1 clove garlic, finely chopped
- 2 shallots, finely sliced
- 150 ml / 5 fl oz (⅔ cup) dry pear cider (perry)
- salt
- few picked thyme leaves or a little chopped flat-leaf parsley, to garnish

* Scrub the mussels under cold running water, removing any barnacles and pulling off any tendrils. Make sure the mussels are closed. If some are open, gently tap them on a work counter and if they still don't close, discard them. Set the mussels aside.
* Melt the butter in a large saucepan over a high heat. Add the garlic and shallots and fry for 3–4 minutes until just starting to soften. Add the mussels with the cider and quickly cover with a lid. The pot should sizzle if hot enough. Leave the mussels to steam with the lid on, shaking the pan occasionally for 3–5 minutes until all the mussels have opened. Discard any mussels that remain closed.
* Serve the mussels immediately garnished with a few thyme leaves or some chopped parsley and a spare bowl for discarding empty shells.

UNITED KINGDOM
*
MUSSEL POPCORN
BATTERED MUSSELS

Mussels, fried in a lightly crisp batter, make for excellent and moreish snacking. Serve with Tartare Sauce (page 423).

Serves: 2
Prep time: 20 minutes
Cook time: 10 minutes

{✏}

- 1 kg / 2¼ lb mussels
- 40 ml / 1⅓ fl oz (2⅔ tablespoons) white wine or cider
- 125 g / 4¼ oz (1 cup plus 1 teaspoon) strong white flour, plus extra for dusting
- pinch of baking powder
- vegetable oil, for deep-frying
- salt and pepper
- Tartare Sauce (page 423), to serve

* Scrub the mussels under cold running water, removing any barnacles and pulling off any tendrils. Make sure the mussels are closed. If some are open, gently tap them on a work counter and if they still don't close, discard them.
* Heat the wine in a large saucepan over a medium heat until very hot. Add the mussels, immediately cover with a lid and steam for around 3 minutes, until all the shells have opened. Drain the mussels, discarding any mussels that remain closed. Leave the mussels to cool, then remove them from the shells and set aside.
* Put the flour, baking powder and 140 ml / 4¾ fl oz (½ cup plus 4 teaspoons) cold water into a large bowl and mix together to form a batter. Put some extra flour for dusting into a shallow bowl.
* Heat enough oil for deep-frying in a large, deep saucepan until it reaches 180°C / 350°F on a thermometer. Dip the picked mussels into the extra flour to coat them, then drop them into the batter. Carefully drop a few of the battered mussels into the hot oil and deep-fry for 3–4 minutes until golden and crisp. Remove with a slotted spoon and leave to drain on a rack or paper towels.
* Season the mussels and serve with Tartare Sauce.
* **Notes:** You can use the same quantity of beer instead of water in the batter, if desired.

WALES
*

COCKLE CAKES
BATTERED COCKLES

In Wales, cockles are sometimes dipped into a thick batter and then fried in small spoonfuls – one or two cockles at a time. This preparation resembles the Mussel Popcorn (see left) and can be served similarly with quartered lemon wedges and Tartare Sauce (page 423).

Serves: 4
Prep time: 15 minutes
Cook time: 10 minutes
{♨}{🍲}

- about 750 ml/25 fl oz (3 cups) vegetable oil, for deep-frying
- 100 g/3½ oz (¾ cup plus 2 teaspoons) plain (all-purpose) flour
- 1 tablespoon sunflower oil
- 1 egg, separated
- 250 g/9 oz cooked cockles
- salt

- To serve:
- lemon wedges
- malt vinegar
- Tartare Sauce (page 423)

* Preheat the oven to 80°C/176°F/lowest Gas Mark.
* Heat the oil for deep-frying in a large, deep saucepan or deep fryer until it reaches 190°C/375°F on a thermometer.
* Put the flour, sunflower oil, egg yolk, 120 ml/4 fl oz (½ cup) water and a little salt into a large bowl and mix together until combined. Stir in the cockles. Whisk the egg whites in another bowl or in a stand mixer fitted with a whisk attachment until stiff peaks are formed, then gently fold them into the batter.
* Working in batches of 12, carefully drop dessertspoon-sized portions of the batter into the hot oil and deep-fry for 2 minutes, or until crisp. Turn the cakes halfway through frying. Remove using a slotted spoon and leave to drain on paper towels, then keep warm in the oven.
* Serve with lemon wedges, malt vinegar and some Tartare Sauce.

UNITED KINGDOM
*

LIMPETS

Limpets are occasionally eaten in Scotland and Wales. In the Scottish Hebrides, they were sometimes cooked in Stovies (page 92) in place of beef, with a fish stock. When cooked in Wales, they were often fried like cockles then scrambled with eggs, or as food writer Bobby Freeman suggests: boiled with nettle – to tenderize – and then tossed and fried with oatmeal.

When foraging, to release a limpet from its rock, hit it hard a few times on the side to detach it, then press the 'foot', the visible part of the limpet on the underside of the shell, against the shell and wiggle it to release it. There is a black sac at the top of the limpet behind the foot. Pull this off the foot and return the foot to the shell.

Prep time: 5 minutes
Cook time: 1 minute
{♨}{🍲}{🔥}

- limpets, butter, chopped garlic, lemon wedges

* **To grill:** Preheat the grill (broiler). Put a small piece of softened butter and some finely chopped garlic on the top of the limpets, then place the limpets, shell down, onto the hot grill (broiler) and cook for a minute – overcooking makes for a very chewy limpet. Serve immediately with lemon wedges.

UNITED KINGDOM
*

WHELKS

These sea snails are almost always boiled. Once cooked, its meat is picked out from the shell with a pick and doused with malt vinegar. They were often sold at street markets throughout Scotland and in the English Midlands. Today, a good garlicky mayonnaise would make an excellent condiment as well.

Serves: 4
Prep time: 5 minutes, plus 1–2 hours soaking
Cook time: 10–15 minutes
{🔥}{♨}{🍲}{🍴}

- 1 kg/2¼ lb whelks
- salt
- splash of vinegar or Mayonnaise (page 427), to serve

* Wash the whelks thoroughly under cold running water, before adding them to a large bowl or bucket of cold salty water (around 3 percent salinity: 30 g/1 oz salt per 1 litre/34 fl oz water). Leave them to soak for 1–2 hours, before washing them again.
* Bring a large saucepan of salted water (3 percent salinity again) to the boil. Add the whelks, reduce the heat to medium-low and simmer for 10–15 minutes. Overcooking will leave them rubbery.
* Use a small pick or fork to eat the whelks. Serve with a splash of malt vinegar or a little Mayonnaise for dipping.

UNITED KINGDOM
*

LANGOUSTINES
DUBLIN BAY PRAWNS

Langoustines were not commonly eaten in Britain until the 1950s, when the craze over 'scampi' began. The Irish took to the langoustine quicker and its availability at fish markets and with street vendors in Dublin gave rise to the name 'Dublin Bay prawn'. These days, the Scottish market for langoustines is huge, although unfortunately the majority of the catch is sold abroad.

In recent times, langoustines are often seen as being wasted when used for scampi, but they are excellent when simply boiled or split, grilled and brushed with butter. Don't ignore the head – the brains are one of the tastiest parts. When buying langoustines, check for fresh-looking shiny black eyes and undamaged shells, legs and antennae.

Prep time: 5 minutes
Cook time: 3–4 minutes
{🥄}{🍲}{🔥}

- langoustines, melted butter, lemon wedges

* **To boil:** Bring a large saucepan of well-salted water to the boil over a high heat. When at a rolling boil, drop the langoustines into the water and boil for 3–4 minutes. Be careful not to overcrowd the pan.
* If serving the meat chilled, remove the langoustines from the pan and drop them immediately into a large bowl of iced water to stop them overcooking.
* Halve them by first placing your knife at the base of the head and cutting down through it, then do the same along the body. Serve simply with lemon and melted butter.
* **To grill:** Halve the langoustines as above, making sure to start with the head. Once halved, brush with melted butter and grill, cut-side up, on a barbecue for a few minutes, or under a grill (broiler) in the same way.

SCOTLAND
*

PARTAN PIE

Partan pies are Scottish crab cakes topped with buttery breadcrumbs, then cooked in the shell of the crab until golden brown.

Serves: 2
Prep time: 15 minutes
Cook time: 15 minutes
{🥄}

- 2 large brown crabs
- 2 teaspoons wine vinegar
- 1 tablespoon Dijon mustard
- ¼ teaspoon ground nutmeg
- 100 g/3½ oz (2 cups) fresh breadcrumbs
- about 50 g/1¾ oz (3½ tablespoons) butter, cut into small pea-sized cubes
- salt and pepper

* Preheat the grill (broiler) to medium-high.
* Prepare the crabs according to the directions on page 122, mixing the brown and white meats together.
* Put a small saucepan over a medium-high heat, then pour in the vinegar and mustard. Whisk together and when combined and boiling, add the crab mixture and nutmeg and cook very briefly to warm through, then mix them together. Remove from the heat and season with a little salt and pepper.
* Spoon the mixture back into the main body shells of the crabs, sprinkle with the breadcrumbs and dot with the butter. Grill (broil) the crabs for about 10 minutes, or until the breadcrumbs are a deep golden brown. If the breadcrumbs are browned before the crab is fully heated through, transfer to an oven preheated to 160°C/325°F/ Gas Mark 3 to finish the cooking. Serve.

UNITED KINGDOM
*

FRIED SCAMPI

The name scampi comes from the Italian word for langoustine, *scampo*, and was inspired by an increase in British tourism to the Adriatic. To make this dish, the meat from the langoustine's tail is breaded or battered, fried, and served with lemon wedges and Tartare Sauce (page 423). These days, monkfish cheeks are also used in the same way.

Serves: 2
Prep time: 20 minutes
Cook time: 10 minutes
{🥄} {🍲}

- 20 langoustine tails or king prawns (jumbo shrimp)
- vegetable oil, for frying
- 1 large egg
- 80 g/3 oz (⅔ cup) plain (all-purpose) flour
- 100 g/3½ oz (1½ cups) dried breadcrumbs
- salt and pepper

- To serve:
- 2 lemons, cut into wedges
- Tartare Sauce (page 423)

* To prepare the langoustine tails, remove the head and legs of the langoustines, then use kitchen scissors to cut down the back and peel away the shell and rear fins. Using a sharp knife, scrape the black vein from the top of the tail. Set aside.
* Heat enough oil for deep-frying in a large, deep saucepan over a medium heat until it reaches 180°C/350°F on a thermometer. Once the oil is at the correct temperature, reduce the heat slightly to maintain the temperature.
* Beat the egg with 1 tablespoon water in a shallow bowl, then put the flour into another shallow bowl and the breadcrumbs into a third.
* Season the tails with salt and pepper, then dredge them in the flour. Dip them into the egg until completely covered, then roll them in the breadcrumbs. Working in 2–3 batches and using a slotted spoon, carefully drop the tails into the hot oil and fry for 2 minutes on each side until the outside is golden brown. Remove and leave to drain on paper towels. Season to taste.
* Serve with lemon wedges and Tartare Sauce for dipping.

Langoustines

ENGLAND
*

DRESSED CRAB

To 'dress' a crab quite simply means to prepare it for eating – i.e. to boil and painstakingly pick the meat from its shell. The tradition of British 'dressed crab' dates back to the start of the nineteenth century, if not earlier. The crab meat is picked from the shell, seasoned and whisked through with a little mayonnaise and finely chopped parsley before being carefully spooned back into the shell.
Serve the creamy crab mixture with good bread or toast, with a squeeze of lemon.

Serves: 4
Prep time: 30 minutes
Cook time: 6½ minutes
{♠}{♟}

- 2 brown crabs, weighing about 1.25 kg/2½ lb in total
- 2 large tablespoons Mayonnaise (page 427)
- 1 tablespoon chopped flat-leaf parsley

- To serve:
- lemon wedges
- slices brown (whole wheat) bread, buttered

* Bring a large stockpot of water to the boil. Add the crabs whole, cooking each crab for 1 minute for every 100 g/3½ oz – in this case 6½ minutes each. Once cooked, remove the crabs from the pot and leave to cool.
* Remove the legs and claws from the crabs, then turn the body upside-down to pull away the underside of the carapace. Remove the dead-man's fingers (the gills; it's very obvious what they are when you do this). Remove the brown meat from the sides of the shell, then, using a sharp pair of kitchen shears, cut the body of the crab in half and use a skewer and pointed knife to extract the meat into a bowl.
* Using the heel of a knife or nut crackers, crack open the legs and claws, scraping the flesh out of the leg with the skewer. Put this meat into the same bowl. Break up the leg meat with your fingers, making sure you remove the cartilage from the crab's larger claws.
* Prepare the shell by removing the stomach sac and head. Cut away the membranes holding in the brown meat and spoon the meat into a separate bowl. Tidy up the shell by trimming or snapping away any rough edges.
* Mix the white meat with the Mayonnaise, adding salt, pepper and the parsley. Either spoon the mixture back into the crab, reserving space for the brown meat mixture, or combine the two before spooning them together into the shell.
* Serve with lemon wedges and buttered brown (whole wheat) bread.

ENGLAND
*

DEVILLED CRAB ON TOAST

This spicy crab mixture can be cooked in its shell, or just spread over any good crispy toast – either way it is a thing of pure comfort. Given the brown crab's lengthy season, devilled crab is good at most times of year, either as a light lunch or an appetizer.

Serves: 4
Prep time: 30 minutes
Cook time: 25 minutes

- 100 g/3½ oz (7 tablespoons) butter
- 100 g/3½ oz (2 cups) fresh white breadcrumbs
- 2 dressed crabs, in their shells (see left)
- 1 small onion, finely chopped
- 50 ml/1¾ fl oz (3½ tablespoons) double (heavy) cream
- 2 teaspoons English mustard, or to taste
- 1 teaspoon Worcestershire sauce
- ½ teaspoon cayenne pepper, or more to taste
- 1 tablespoon finely chopped flat-leaf parsley
- 25 g/1 oz (⅓ cup) Parmesan cheese, grated (optional)
- salt and pepper
- good-quality bread, toasted, to serve

* Preheat the oven to 200°C/400°F/Gas Mark 6.
* Melt the butter in a medium saucepan over a medium-low heat.
* Put 75 g/2¾ oz (1½ cups) of the breadcrumbs into a large bowl with the melted butter, the meat from the dressed crabs, onion, cream, mustard, Worcestershire sauce, cayenne, parsley, salt and pepper and mix together to combine. Taste, then add extra cayenne pepper, mustard and any further salt and pepper, if desired.
* Spoon the spiced crab mixture back into the crab shells. Mix the remaining breadcrumbs and the cheese together in another bowl, then sprinkle it evenly over the top of the shells. Place the shells on a baking sheet and bake for 15–20 minutes until the topping has crisped.
* Serve with toast.

Dressed crab

SCOTLAND
*

RAZOR CLAMS
SPOOTS

Spoot is a Scots word for a razor-shell clam. This bivalve – shaped a wee bit like a single-blade razor – is gathered from sandy beaches on Scotland's northern islands. Spoots were traditionally boiled and eaten straight from the shell, sometimes with a little butter. They taste just as nice when thrown on the grill, briefly, then thinly sliced.

Prep time: 5 minutes
Cook time: 1 minute
{⚬•} {👹} {🐟}

- razor clams, cider or wine, lemon juice, butter, chopped parsley, garlic

* **To prepare:** Only select clams with unbroken shells. They are very brittle and will close or react when knocked against a surface if open. Clams with open shells that don't react are dead and should not be eaten. If not using straightaway, don't store them submerged in water; just keep them covered in a damp cloth. Wash them under plenty of cold running water to rinse them of any left-over grit or sand.
* **To boil or steam:** To boil, drop them into a large saucepan of boiling salted water and cook for just 1 minute. To steam in the same style as other clams or mussels (pages 116 and 118), drop them into a large hot saucepan with water, cider or wine, cover with a lid and steam for just 1 minute, or until they open.
* Before eating, check for any sand remaining in the shell and cut off and discard the black stomach of the clam.
* **To grill or barbecue:** Before grilling (broiling) or barbecuing, open up the shell by carefully running a knife along one side of the shell's opening, then pull the two halves of the shell apart. Release the clam meat from the shell using a sharp knife, then rinse off any sand and cut off and discard the black stomach.
* Preheat the grill/barbecue, then cook plain or brushed with butter or oil for no more than 1 minute. They are delicious with lemon juice, butter, parsley and garlic.

UNITED KINGDOM
*

OYSTERS

Once affordable and in great abundance, in the eighteenth and nineteenth centuries, oysters were guzzled down by the dozen in oyster taverns and bars in Edinburgh and London. They were also used quite liberally at home in soups, stews, puddings and pies. They were unsustainably fished, however, and over time became a rarity and a food associated with luxury. Today, the best British oysters are native oysters from southeast England and west-coast Scotland.
Choose oysters that are closed tightly and store them curved-side down to prevent them losing their juices. There are two varieties: rock and native. Rocks are commercially grown widely and so are much cheaper and easier to find. Serve raw, on the half shell, with a lemon wedge and a little Tabasco or grated horseradish.

Prep time: 15 minutes
{👹}{👹}{⚬•}{🐟}

- oysters, lemon juice, Tabasco, grated horseradish

* **To shuck:** You will need an oyster knife and a cloth. Wrap the curved 'opening' end of the oyster, flat-side up, in the cloth and hold it against a flat surface with your hand protected by the cloth. With your other hand, take the blade of the oyster knife and insert it into the oyster's 'hinge', the pointed part of the shell that connects the top and bottom shells of the oyster. Taking care, apply pressure into the hinge with the knife and wiggle the blade into the muscle that holds the two shells together to release the top shell from the bottom. You should feel a pop and hear the 'shucking' noise as it comes loose. To release the oyster meat from its shell, run the oyster knife blade under it and find the muscle holding onto the inside of the shell, then release with the knife.
* **To serve raw:** Put the oysters in their shells in a large bowl of ice, so that their curved shells are held upright, and their liquor isn't lost. Serve them with lemon juice, Tabasco or grated horseradish.

UNITED KINGDOM
*

OYSTER LOAVES

To prepare this recipe, bread rolls are hollowed out, baked, and then filled with a simple creamy mixture made from oyster liquor, cream and spices. While this recipe sounds decidedly on-trend with modern taste and preparations, it actually dates from the eighteenth century, appearing first in Elizabeth Moxon's *English Housewifry* in 1741.

Serves: 4
Prep time: 30 minutes
Cook time: 20 minutes
{⚬•}

- 100 g/3½ oz (7 tablespoons) butter
- 4 white bread rolls or 1 large Cottage Loaf (page 270)
- 12 oysters, shucked (see above), liquor reserved
- 150 ml/5 fl oz (⅔ cup) double (heavy) cream
- ¼ teaspoon cayenne pepper
- juice of ½ lemon
- salt and pepper

* Preheat the oven to 200°C/400°F/Gas Mark 6.
* Melt the butter in a medium saucepan over a medium-low heat, then set aside.
* Cut the tops off the rolls and scoop out much of the inside, so that only the crusts and a thin 'insulation' of bread remains. Brush the rolls inside and out with the melted butter, then put them onto a baking sheet and bake in the oven for 12–15 minutes until golden brown.
* Bring the reserved oyster liquor and the cream to a simmer over a medium-low heat in a large saucepan and reduce until thick, about 4 minutes. Add the cayenne pepper, salt and pepper and the lemon juice to taste, then add the oysters. Remove the pan from the heat and leave the oysters to heat through, 3–4 minutes. Divide the mixture between the rolls, replace their lids and serve.

Razor clams

ENGLAND
*

ANGELS ON HORSEBACK

This popular British appetizer first found fame in the late nineteenth century, then re-emerged into the mainstream as a favourite of dinner parties in the 1950s and 1960s. The 'angels' should be served skewered onto little sippets of buttered toast, which are cut to their size.

In Florence B Jack's *Cookery For Every Household* (1914), Jack provides a variation on the traditional recipe: the 'angels' are seasoned with lemon juice and cayenne pepper, dipped in batter, then fried until golden brown and crispy.

Serves: 4
Prep time: 5 minutes, plus 10 minutes soaking
Cook time: 10 minutes
{🖐}{👅}{🥄}{❄}

- 8 rashers (slices) streaky (lean) bacon
- 16 oysters, shucked (page 124)

- To serve:
- 4 slices toast, buttered
- 1 lemon, cut into wedges

* Soak 16 cocktail sticks in a large bowl of hot water for 10 minutes. This prevents them burning during cooking.
* Preheat the grill (broiler) to high.
* Cut each bacon rasher (slice) in half, then wrap a strip around each shucked oyster and secure with a soaked stick. Arrange the angels on a large baking sheet and grill (broil) for 5–6 minutes, turning once, until the oysters are plump and fully cooked and the bacon is crispy.
* Serve immediately on buttered toast with lemon wedges.

SOUTHEAST OF ENGLAND
*

FRIED WHITEBAIT

Whitebait are the small fry of herring or sprat (sometimes a mix of both), once used, as the name suggests, as bait for larger fish. A speciality of London and southeast England, they are lightly coated in seasoned flour and fried until crisp. A popular summer outing some 200 years ago in west London was a fish lunch along the Thames, with whitebait caught straight from the water and brought to the table in a matter of moments.

And whitebait is still served in exactly the same way today – with brown (whole wheat) bread, butter and lemon wedges. Dust over a little cayenne pepper if you like, but be sure to squeeze some of the lemon over the top.

Serves: 4–6
Prep time: 5 minutes
Cook time: 5–10 minutes
{👅}{❄}

- 500 g/1 lb 2 oz whitebait, defrosted if frozen
- 250–475 ml/8–16 fl oz (1–2 cups) rapeseed (canola) oil
- 50 g/2 oz (scant ½ cup) plain (all-purpose) flour
- 1 teaspoon salt
- ½ teaspoon cayenne pepper (optional)

To serve:
- lemon wedges
- Mayonnaise (page 427)

* Ensure that the whitebait is dry. If at all moist, pat dry with paper towels. Heat the oil in a large frying pan or skillet to 190°C/375°F. Preheat the oven to 80°C/176°F/ lowest Gas Mark.
* Mix the flour, salt and cayenne (if using) together in a large bowl, add the whitebait and toss them in the spiced flour mixture until coated, shaking off any excess flour.
* Working in batches, fry the whitebait in the oil for 1 minute, then remove using a slotted spoon and drain on paper towels. Keep them warm on a lined baking sheet in the oven.
* Serve the whitebait in a shallow bowl with lemon wedges and a generous amount of Mayonnaise.

UNITED KINGDOM
*

PRAWN JALFREZI

In Bengali, the word for spicy hot is *jhal* and in many takeaway restaurants outside of India, a jalfrezi suggests a spicy curry, usually with green peppers. Originally, a jhal was a way of utilizing the left-overs from a roast, and so is much better known in Britain than in India.

Serves: 4
Prep time: 15 minutes
Cook time: 25 minutes
{🖐}{❄}{👅}{🥄}

- 2 tablespoons vegetable oil
- 1 teaspoon cumin seeds
- 1 large onion, finely sliced
- 1 tablespoon ginger-garlic paste
- 1 teaspoon turmeric
- 1 teaspoon Kashmiri chilli powder
- 1 teaspoon ground coriander
- 1 large green pepper, seeded and sliced
- 300 g/11 oz raw king prawns (jumbo shrimp), shelled and deveined
- 2 ripe tomatoes, sliced
- salt
- coriander (cilantro) leaves, chopped, to garnish

* Heat the oil in a heavy saucepan over a high heat, add the cumin seeds and fry for 1 minute, or until slightly dark. Add the onion and fry, stirring, for 5 minutes, or until it starts to change colour.
* Reduce the heat to low and fry for another 2 minutes, then add the ginger-garlic paste and fry for 30 seconds. Sprinkle in the spices and a little salt and mix well. Add a splash of cold water and cook for 3 minutes, or until the water evaporates and the oil begins to separate.
* Add the peppers and cook for 6–7 minutes, then reduce the heat, cover the pan with a lid and cook for 8 minutes, or until they are nearly done but still hold their shape, adding 2 tablespoons of water if the mixture begins to stick. Add the prawns (shrimp) and mix well for 3 minutes, or until they become opaque. Add the tomatoes and cook for another 2 minutes, until soft but not mushy.
* Serve hot, garnished with coriander (cilantro) leaves.

Fried whitebait

UNITED KINGDOM
*
SESAME PRAWN TOAST

Prawn toast is ubiquitous in British-Chinese restaurants – and households. The following recipe comes from Glasgow-based chef, Julie Lin, who is of Nyonya (Chinese/Malaysian) heritage. For her, this moreish dish evokes the familiarity of fried bread at a greasy spoon café. Julie turns hers into a sort of sandwich before it's fried, to keep the prawns (shrimp) juicy and sweet inside, and to avoid overcooking in the deep fryer. The sesame seeds on the outside turn almost golden brown and buttery once they've hit the golden oil of the fryer

Serves: 4–5 as a snack
Prep time: 45–60 minutes, plus 30 minutes chilling
Cook time: 10–15 minutes

- 200 g/7 oz raw deveined prawns (shrimp)
- 1 egg, beaten
- 2 tablespoons minced ginger
- 2 tablespoons soy sauce
- ½ teaspoon chicken stock powder
- squeeze of lemon juice
- 2 tablespoons cornflour (cornstarch)
- 10 slices thick white supermarket-style bread
- vegetable oil, for deep-frying
- sesame seeds, for coating

- To serve:
- lemon wedges
- sweet chilli dipping sauce

* Using a sharp knife, very finely chop the prawns (shrimp) until they are almost paste-like. Put them into a medium bowl, add the beaten egg, ginger, soy sauce, chicken stock powder and a small squeeze of lemon juice and mix together. Add the cornflour (cornstarch) and mix in until it's smooth. The mixture shouldn't be too sloppy in texture; if it is, then add a little more cornflour. Cover and chill in the fridge for about 30 minutes to firm up a little.
* Slice the crusts off the bread. Spread about 1½ tablespoons of the prawn mixture evenly over one side of a bread slice. Put a second slice on top to form a sandwich and make sure it sticks. Repeat until all the bread and all the prawn mixture has been used. Cut all the sandwiches into 4 squares, halving the sandwich both ways using a sharp knife and ensuring the mixture doesn't fall out the side. Take some care doing this and make sure to cut gently.
* Pour the oil for deep-frying into a large deep saucepan or deep fryer until it comes two-thirds of the way up the sides and heat until it reaches 170°C/344°F on a thermometer.
* Sprinkle a layer of sesame seeds over a large plate, then dip the mini sandwiches in the seeds until coated all over.
* Working in batches, use a slotted spoon to carefully lower the sandwiches into the hot oil and deep-fry, turning as you go, for 3–4 minutes until golden, crispy and the prawn mixture is cooked through. Remove with a slotted spoon and drain on a metal rack.
* Serve immediately with lemon wedges and some sweet chilli dipping sauce.

UNITED KINGDOM
*
KEDGEREE

One of the earliest and best loved Anglo-Indian dishes, this breakfast staple has its origins in the late seventeeth century, when Britons returning from India attempted to recreate a spiced rice-and-lentil dish called khichri.
Eliza Acton was the first to add fish to the recipe in 1845, and although she doesn't mention haddock specifically, it was around this time that Scottish finnan haddies (page 98) had become hugely popular down south. The eggs in a kedgeree are typically hard-boiled and quartered, but on occasion they were poached instead – with the runny egg yolk stirred through the rice.
While kedgeree is most often associated with breakfast, it's not uncommon to see it on lunch or the occasional dinner menu as well.

Serves: 6
Prep time: 10 minutes
Cook time: 30–35 minutes
{🍲}{🌶}

- 450 ml/15 fl oz (1⅔ cups plus 2 tablespoons) full-fat (whole) milk
- 1 bay leaf
- 1 bunch flat-leaf parsley, leaves finely chopped, stalks set aside
- 500 g/1 lb 2 oz undyed smoked haddock fillets
- 75 g/2½ oz (⅓ cup) butter
- 1 large onion, finely chopped
- 2 tablespoons mild/medium curry powder
- 1 teaspoon turmeric
- 400 g/14 oz (2 cups) basmati rice
- 6 eggs, at room temperature
- 100 g/3½ oz (⅔ cup) peas, fresh or frozen
- 1 lemon, cut into 6 wedges, to serve (optional)

* Pour the milk into a large saucepan, add the bay leaf, parsley stalks and smoked haddock and bring to the boil. Once boiling, cook for 1 minute, then remove the fish from the pan using a slotted spoon. It should be completely cooked and opaque. Flake it into a bowl. (If not completely cooked, put it back into the saucepan and cook for another 1–2 minutes.) Strain the milk into a jug (pitcher) and set aside.
* Melt the butter in a medium saucepan over a medium-low heat, add the onion, curry powder and turmeric, then stir well and fry for 10 minutes, or until the onion is slightly crispy. Add the rice and stir to coat in the spices. Pour in enough water to the reserved milk mixture to reach 800 ml/27 fl oz (3¼ cups), stir through, then pour into the saucepan. Cover with a lid, reduce the heat to very low and cook for 12–15 minutes while the rice absorbs most of the liquid.
* Meanwhile, bring another medium pan of water to the boil. When boiling, carefully lower in the eggs and cook for 6 minutes. Drain the water and fill the pan, still with the eggs in it, with cold water until the eggs are submerged. Leave to cool for 3–4 minutes, then peel the eggs, cut them into quarters and set them aside.
* Add the peas to the rice and fold through with three-quarters of the chopped parsley and all the flaked smoked haddock. Put the lid back on and cook for another 2 minutes. Serve topped with the eggs, sprinkled with the remaining parsley and with lemon wedges, if desired.

Kedgeree

FOR ALL THIS GOOD FEASTING, YET ART THOU NOT
LOOSE / TILL PLOUGHMAN THOU GIVEST HIS HARVEST
HOME GOOSE / THOUGH GOOSE GO IN STUBBLE,
I PASSE NOT FOR THAT / LET GOOSE HAVE A GOOSE,
BE SHE LEANE, BE SHE FAT

THOMAS TUSSER, 'HARVEST HOME'
FROM *FIVE HUNDRED POINTES OF GOOD HUSBANDRIE, 1557*

THE TRADITIONAL

This chapter is devoted to traditional home recipes for all manner of domestic fowl – from chicken to duck, turkey and goose. These animals were reserved for the grandest of special occasions, like a Michaelmas roast goose or roast turkey at Christmas. Roasts were the most popular way to cook young birds (those with the most tender meat), and had – even back then – all the same pomp and circumstance of a great roast beef: roast potatoes, rich gravy, sprouts, cranberry sauce or bread sauce. The works. Of course, cookery books also devised ways of helping the home cook make the most of their left-overs by turning them into a fruity chicken or turkey curry, pâté or pie.

Older birds like the 'boiling fowl' (chicken) were stronger in flavour, with tougher flesh, and would go straight from the butcher to the pot for soups or stews. Think Cock-a-Leekie Soup (page 44). These household recipes were perhaps more realistic for the average Briton.

THE MODERN

The majority of this chapter's chicken recipes will be quite familiar, as they are modern classics. Just a couple of these recipes predate the twentieth century, and that's because chicken's ubiquity in the home kitchen is a modern phenomenon: something of the last 60–70 years.

Before World War II, chicken, much like other domestic fowl, was a luxury food, but in the 1950s and 60s, in the wake of the war, the UK followed the US in rolling out massive factory farms. In the intervening years, the white meat became popular enough to challenge the dominance of beef at the Sunday roast, and these factory farms – inhumane though they may be – made chicken the most affordable, equitable meat.

It's for this reason that this chapter's glut of chicken recipes suggests to us something deeper about the way British food has evolved in the last several decades. The chicken Parmo may speak to overindulgence, and chicken Balmoral to a sense of nationalism, but most of the others share something deeper. What they have in common is that they originated in immigrant communities from former British colonies, cooked by chefs who tailored ingredients and spices from their home to meet the modern British palate. For the dining public, especially the more conservative, maybe chicken offers a means of branching out without stepping entirely out of your comfort zone.

While some may question the 'authenticity' of a chicken tikka masala, for instance, few can debate the extent to which it has been embraced, and its stellar rise to outplace fish and chips as the country's top comfort dish is an indicator of how British food can continue to redefine itself. Now new generations are brought up on flavours and ingredients that seemed foreign to their elders. It is part of what promises to keep the British kitchen fresh and exciting, and continue to bring us all together.

POULTRY

CORONATION CHICKEN

Originally created by Constance Spry and Rosemary Hume for the coronation of Queen Elizabeth II in 1953, this cold chicken salad is made with a curried mayonnaise sauce and sweetened with mango chutney – or dried apricots, as in the original recipe. Coronation salad will work just fine on its own as a salad for a spring or summer lunch, but it works even better as a sandwich filling.

Serves: 4–6
Prep time: 10 minutes
Cook time: 10 minutes
{♨}{✿}

- about 2–2.2 kg/2¼ lb–4 lb 13 oz whole chicken, roasted or poached
- 1 tablespoon rapeseed (canola) oil
- 1 yellow onion, finely chopped
- 1 teaspoon curry powder
- 2 teaspoons tomato purée (paste)
- 125 ml/4¼ fl oz (½ cup) red wine
- juice of ½ lemon
- 500 g/1 lb 2 oz (2¼ cups) Mayonnaise (page 427)
- 2 tablespoons chopped dried apricots or mango chutney
- 4 tablespoons double (heavy) cream, lightly whipped
- salt and pepper
- caster (superfine) sugar, for seasoning

* Take the meat off the bones of the chicken and cut into neat pieces. Set aside.
* Heat the oil in a large saucepan over a medium heat, add the onion and fry for 6–7 minutes. Stir in the curry powder and tomato purée (paste) and fry for another minute, before adding the wine, 100 ml/3½ fl oz (⅓ cup plus 1 tablespoon) water and the lemon juice and simmer together, uncovered, for 10 minutes. Strain the curry through a sieve into a bowl and leave to cool.
* Once the curry is cool, use a wooden spoon to beat in a quarter of the Mayonnaise. Once it is incorporated, beat in another quarter, followed by the rest of the Mayonnaise and the apricots or mango chutney. Once fully incorporated, fold in the cream, then season to taste with the salt, pepper and sugar. Finally, add the chicken to the mixture and stir through to mix. Cover with clingfilm (plastic wrap) and chill in the fridge for at least 3 hours, or until completely cold.

FARMHOUSE PÂTÉ

Recipes for a rustic style farmhouse pâté will vary widely. This one is made from a rather coarse mixture of chicken liver, streaky (lean) bacon and minced (ground) pork – the splash of brandy gives it that extra kick. It is typically baked in a wrapping of bacon.

Serves: 6
Prep time: 20 minutes, plus 6–8 hours setting
Cook time: 1¾–2 hours
{♨}{❖}{✿}

- 500 g/1 lb 2 oz unsmoked streaky (lean) bacon rashers (slices)
- 300 g/11 oz (2½ cups) minced (ground) pork
- 250 g/9 oz chicken livers
- 2 tablespoons brandy
- ½ teaspoon chopped oregano or marjoram
- ½ teaspoon chopped thyme
- ¼ teaspoon cayenne pepper
- 1½ teaspoons salt
- ¼ teaspoon ground black pepper
- 300 g/11 oz rashers (slices) smoked streaky (lean) bacon

* Preheat the oven to 150°C/300°F/Gas Mark 2.
* Mince (grind) the unsmoked bacon or chop it very finely in a food processor. Transfer to a large bowl, add the minced (ground) pork and the chicken livers, breaking the livers up with your hands, and mix well. Add the brandy, herbs, cayenne pepper, salt and pepper and mix well until combined.
* Line a 900 g/2 lb loaf pan or 1.75 litre/60 fl oz terrine mould with the smoked bacon rashers (slices), overlapping them very slightly, and leaving enough overhang to line the top of the pan or mould. Spoon the mixture into the pan, level the top, then put the overhanging bacon across the top to cover.
* Put the loaf pan or mould into a large roasting pan half-filled with boiling water and cook in the oven for 1¾–2 hours. Remove from the oven and put the loaf pan on a wire rack to cool.
* Once cold, place weights on top to keep its shape (a couple of cans, scale weights, a brick wrapped in aluminium foil, etc.) and chill in the fridge for 6–8 hours until set. The pâté will keep in the fridge for up to a week.

Coronation chicken

UNITED KINGDOM

ROAST CHICKEN

Once considered a luxury meat for rare occasions, chicken has, in the course of the last several decades, become one of the most available meats, and a veritable classic of Sunday roast dinners; it is served with crispy Roast Potatoes (page 86), glazed vegetables, greens and sometimes something more decadent – Creamed Spinach (page 66), Cauliflower Cheese (page 72), or the like.

For crispy bronzed skin, start your bird at a higher temperature for the first 10–20 minutes and be vigilant with your basting so that it retains moisture throughout its cook time. It's recommended that you buy a bigger bird than needed, as left-over meat becomes pies, curries or salads, and the bones a rich stock for soups.

Serves: 4
Prep time: 10 minutes, plus 20–30 minutes resting
Cook time: around 1½ hours
{🏺}{☙}{🍽}

- 100 g/3½ oz (7 tablespoons) butter, softened
- 2 cloves garlic, very finely chopped, or ½ truffle thinly sliced, or 1 tablespoon finely chopped flat-leaf parsley and the grated zest of 1 lemon (optional)
- about 1.75 kg/3 lb 13 oz oven-ready chicken, trussed
- 250 g/9 oz stuffing of your choice (pages 242–243)

* Preheat the oven to 190°C/375°F/Gas Mark 5.
* Mash 75 g/2¾ oz (¾ stick) of the butter with any chosen flavourings in a small bowl, then use your fingers to push the butter under the skin of the chicken, massaging away any air pockets, and making sure the butter has been evenly spread across the bird. Smear the remaining butter over the legs, then loosely pack the stuffing into the cavity. Weigh the bird and calculate the roasting time, allowing 45 minutes per 1 kg/2¼ lb plus 15 minutes.
* Put the chicken into a large roasting pan, then cook in the oven, basting the chicken with the roasting juices at several intervals as it cooks. To check that the chicken is fully cooked, insert a skewer into the thickest part of the leg and if the juices run clear, it's done.
* Remove the chicken from the pan, cover with aluminium foil and leave to rest for 20–30 minutes. Roast chicken can be served simply with the pan juices, or use them to make Gravy (page 420). Serve.
* **Notes:** For crispy, bronzed skin, preheat the oven to 220°C/425°F/Gas Mark 7. Roast the chicken in the oven for 10–20 minutes before reducing the temperature to 190°C/375°F/Gas Mark 5 and continuing to cook the bird. Take 10–20 minutes off the total cook time, but be vigilant in basting and checking whether the bird is cooked as it will do so a little quicker than usual.

SCOTLAND

CHICKEN BALMORAL

This dish of chicken breast stuffed with haggis, wrapped in bacon and served with a whisky sauce seems a little too cute – a little too on-the-nose – to be a truly traditional Scottish dish. More likely it is the creation of Scottish hotel and restaurant kitchens drawing in tourists. Nevertheless, it has made its way into cookbooks and supermarket aisles and now home kitchens. Named after Queen Victoria's favourite Scottish estate, this dish might be fanciful in some sense, but that doesn't stop it from being delicious. Serve with creamy Mashed Potatoes (page 80) and an ounce of scepticism.

Serves: 6
Prep time: 20 minutes
Cook time: 20–25 minutes
{☙}

- 6 large boneless chicken breasts, about 175 g/6 oz each, skin on
- 1 small haggis, precooked, about 200 g/7 oz in weight
- 12 rashers (slices) streaky (lean) bacon or prosciutto
- 40 g/1½ oz (3 tablespoons) butter
- 1 quantity Whisky Cream Sauce (page 418), warmed through
- buttered seasonal vegetables, to serve

* Preheat the oven to 180°C/350°F/Gas Mark 4.
* Lay the chicken breasts on a chopping (cutting) board, skin-side up, and use a sharp knife to make a long, deep cut across the centre of the breast without piercing through the other side of the meat – you will use this incision for the stuffing.
* Remove the haggis from its skin. Spoon out 30–35 g/1–1¼ oz of the haggis, about a sixth, and stuff each breast with it. Wrap 2 bacon rashers (slices) around each breast. You may also opt to stick cocktail sticks or toothpicks through the breast as well, to keep the bacon carefully wrapped around it.
* Heat the butter in a large roasting pan or a large ovenproof saucepan over a medium-high heat. Add the chicken breasts and sear on one side for 2 minutes. Turn the breasts over and fry for another 2 minutes, then transfer the pan to the oven and roast for 20–25 minutes until cooked through. When ready, remove from the oven and leave to rest while you make the sauce according to the directions on page 418.
* Serve the stuffed chicken breasts with buttered seasonal vegetables and the whisky sauce.

Chicken Balmoral

NORTHEAST OF ENGLAND
*

CHICKEN PARMO

This Teesside chip shop staple originated in Middlesbrough in the 1950s, and is believed to be an adaptation of the chicken parmigiana or escalope parmigiana, which were newly popular among Italian communities of the American Northeast at the time. The dish was allegedly first served by a former American soldier, Nicos Harris, at The American Grill, in 1958. Unlike its American cousin, the Teesside chicken parmo is topped with a white sauce (or béchamel) and a lot of melted cheese. Serve, in Teesside takeaway (takeout) fashion, with a big bowl of Chips (page 84).

Serves: 2
Prep time: 25 minutes
Cook time: 15 minutes
{ ᴥ }

- 2 large skinless, boneless chicken breasts,
  about 150–175 g/5–6 oz each
- ½ teaspoon cayenne pepper (optional)
- ½ teaspoon salt
- ½ teaspoon ground black pepper
- 100 g/3 ½ oz (¾ cup plus 2 teaspoons) plain
  (all-purpose) flour
- 2 large eggs, beaten
- 150 g/5 oz (2⅓ cups) panko breadcrumbs
- 1 quantity White Sauce (page 416)
- vegetable oil, for frying
- 100 g/3½ oz Cheddar cheese or Red Leicester cheese,
  or a mix of the two, grated
- Chips (page 84) or small salad, to serve

* Lay out a piece of clingfilm (plastic wrap) on a chopping
  (cutting) board and put the chicken breasts onto it side
  by side. Cover the chicken with more clingfilm, then,
  using a meat mallet or rolling pin, flatten each breast
  until it is about 1 cm/½ inch thick. Set aside.
* Mix the spices and flour together in a large shallow bowl.
  Put the beaten eggs into another large shallow bowl, then
  put the panko breadcrumbs into a third.
* Make or reheat the White Sauce according to the directions
  on page 416 and keep warm.
* One at a time, dip the flattened chicken breasts into the
  flour until completely coated, then dip into the beaten
  eggs and finally, coat them in the breadcrumbs. Make sure
  that they have picked up enough of the breadcrumbs to
  form a good crust. Set aside on a plate.
* Pour the oil for frying into a large heavy frying pan or
  skillet until it is at a depth of 5 mm/¼ inch and heat until
  it reaches 180°C/350°F on a thermometer.
* Preheat the grill (broiler) to medium and line a grill tray
  with aluminium foil.
* Carefully add the chicken breasts to the pan, one at a
  time or both at once if the pan is large enough, and fry
  for 3 minutes on each side, until golden brown and crispy.
  Using a fish slice (spatula), transfer the chicken to a
  chopping board or counter and leave to drain.
* Put the chicken breasts onto the prepared grill tray, then
  pour enough of the White Sauce over the top so that it
  coats each piece. Sprinkle with the grated cheese, then
  grill for several minutes, until the cheese is melting and
  just beginning to colour. Serve with a side of Chips or a
  small salad.

UNITED KINGDOM
*

CHICKEN BALTI

Balti is named after the wok-style pan in which it's cooked, which literally means 'bucket'. Made popular in Pakistani-owned restaurants (mainly in Bradford and Birmingham), the cooking style is a fast stir-fry, with balti pans set over large stoves with vertical jet flames. This particular recipe is better suited to home kitchens rather than restaurant settings.

Serves: 4
Prep time: 15 minutes
Cook time: 30 minutes
{ ♨ } { ᴥ }

- 2 tablespoons vegetable oil
- 1 teaspoon cumin seeds
- 1 teaspoon garlic purée (or 1 clove garlic, crushed)
- 1 teaspoon grated ginger
- 200 g/7 oz chicken breast, cut into 5 cm/2 inch chunks
- 2 large tomatoes, finely chopped
- 1 tablespoon tomato purée (paste)
- 2 tablespoons plain yogurt
- ½ teaspoon chilli powder
- ½ teaspoon ground black pepper
- ¼ teaspoon ground turmeric
- 1 tablespoon fenugreek leaves
- 1 tablespoon unsalted butter
- salt

- To garnish:
- 5 cm/2 inch piece fresh root ginger,
  peeled and cut into very thin sticks
- 1 handful coriander (cilantro) leaves, chopped
- 2 green chillies, finely chopped
- 10 mint leaves, chopped
- ½ lemon

* Heat the oil in a wok-style pan over a medium heat, add
  the cumin and allow to splutter for 30 seconds. Add the
  garlic purée and grated ginger and fry for another 30
  seconds, or until the raw smell of garlic disappears. Add
  the chicken and fry for 3–4 minutes, or until sealed all
  over. Add the tomatoes and cook for 5–7 minutes until
  softened, then add the tomato purée (paste) and yogurt
  and cook for 8–10 minutes until the oil starts to separate.
* Add the chilli powder, black pepper, turmeric, fenugreek
  leaves and salt to taste, then cook for another 5–7 minutes
  until the chicken is cooked. Add the butter before turning
  off the heat and letting the butter melt.
* Before serving, add the fresh ginger, chopped coriander
  (cilantro), chillies and mint, then squeeze the lemon on
  top and stir through.

Chicken balti

CHICKEN MADRAS

Although you will not find a Chicken Madras in India, it has found a firm place on British menus. This is a recipe that takes in the ingredients and flavours of Tamil Nadu, the southern state of India, of which Madras, now known as Chennai, is the capital. Early iterations of this recipe used Madras curry powder from Sharwood's, the British food company, which was produced in Madras.

Serves: 4
Prep time: 10 minutes
Cook time: 25 minutes
{🎄}{🍴}{🌶}{🍲}

- 2 tablespoons vegetable oil, plus an extra splash
- 10 curry leaves
- 2 onions, finely chopped
- 2 teaspoons ginger-garlic paste
- 2 tomatoes, chopped
- 1 teaspoon ground turmeric
- 1 teaspoon Kashmiri chilli powder
- 600 g/ 1 lb 5 oz skinless, boneless chicken thighs or breast
- salt
- 1 handful coriander (cilantro) leaves, finely chopped, to garnish

- For the spice mix:
- 4 dried red chillies, broken in half
- ½ teaspoon black peppercorns, crushed
- 1 teaspoon aniseed
- 4 cloves
- 6 green cardamom pods, seeds removed and husks discarded
- 1 teaspoon ground cinnamon

* For the spice mix, heat a large frying pan or skillet over a high heat, add the dried chillies, crushed peppercorns, aniseed, cloves and cardamom seeds and dry-roast for 2–3 minutes, until they begin to darken and develop an aroma. Remove from the heat, put into a mortar and crush with a pestle to a powder. Alternatively, use a spice mill. Mix in the ground cinnamon and set aside.
* Heat the oil in the frying pan or skillet over a high heat, add the curry leaves and onions and stir-fry for 7–8 minutes until the onions are soft. Add the ginger-garlic paste and cook for 30 seconds. Add the tomatoes, season with salt and cook for another 3–4 minutes until well blended. Add the reserved ground spice mix, the turmeric and chilli powder and cook for a few seconds. Pour in 4–5 tablespoons cold water, bring to the boil and let the water evaporate, releasing the oil around the edges of the mixture.
* Move the mixture to one side of the pan, add a splash of oil then add the chicken. Cook, turning, for 3–4 minutes, or until it is sealed on all sides. Mix the chicken with the onion mixture in the pan, add a few tablespoons of water, cover with a lid and cook for 15 minutes, or until the chicken is white all the way through when you cut open a piece. Garnish with coriander (cilantro) leaves and serve hot.

CHICKEN TIKKA MASALA

Chicken breast marinated with yogurt and spices and cooked in a creamy tomato curry, chicken tikka masala is one of Britain's best-loved dishes and is said to have originated in either Glasgow or Birmingham. The story at Glasgow restaurant Shish Mahal is that it was invented by the restaurant's Pakistani head chef Ali Ahmed Aslam, who addressed a guest's complaint that their curry was 'too dry', by returning it to the kitchen and adding to it some of the tomato soup he was supping. In any case, the dish is now so ubiquitous that in recent years it has overtaken fish and chips in UK polls of the nation's favourite dish.

Serves: 4–6
Prep time: 5 minutes, plus 30 minutes–8 hours marinating
Cook time: 20 minutes
{🎄}

- 2 tablespoons ginger-garlic paste
- 1 teaspoon chilli powder
- 1 teaspoon ground turmeric
- 1 teaspoon ground cumin
- 1 teaspoon ground coriander
- 1 teaspoon garam masala
- 3 cardamom pods, seeds crushed and husks discarded
- 2 tablespoons plain full-fat (whole) yogurt
- 500 g/ 1 lb 2 oz skinless, boneless chicken breast, cubed
- 3 tablespoons vegetable oil
- 2 onions, sliced
- 1 tablespoon cashew nuts
- 2 tablespoons tomato purée (paste)
- salt

- To serve:
- 2 tablespoons chopped coriander (cilantro) leaves
- warm Naan (page 275) or boiled basmati rice

* For the tikka, put 1 tablespoon ginger-garlic paste, the ground spices, yogurt and a little salt into a bowl and mix together until combined. Add the chicken and turn until coated, then cover with clingfilm (plastic wrap) and leave to marinate for 30 minutes, or overnight in the fridge.
* When ready to cook, heat 2 tablespoons of the oil in a heavy saucepan over a high heat, add the onions and fry for 5 minutes, or until they start to turn brown. Reduce the heat to medium and cook for another 5–10 minutes, or until they become very soft. Add the remaining ginger-garlic paste and the cashew nuts and cook for 30 seconds. Stir in the tomato purée (paste) and fry for 1 minute. Remove from the heat and leave to cool slightly, then transfer to a blender or food processor, add enough water to cover the mixture and whizz until smooth.
* Heat the remaining oil in the pan over a high heat, add the chicken and fry for 3–4 minutes until the meat is sealed. Add 2 tablespoons cold water and cook for another 2 minutes until the water has mostly evaporated. Add the curry paste and rinse out the blender with about 100 ml/3½ fl oz (⅓ cup plus 1 tablespoon) water. Add to the curry, season with salt and mix well. Bring to the boil, then reduce the heat to low, cover and cook for 10 minutes, or until the chicken, when cut, is white all the way through. Serve topped with coriander (cilantro) leaves and warm Naan or boiled basmati rice.

Chicken tikka masala

UNITED KINGDOM

SALT
AND
CHILLI CHICKEN

The recipe for this British-Chinese classic comes from the Glasgow-based chef Julie Lin, whose mother Lang used to make it for her as a child. For Julie, it evokes the familiarity and fondness for chicken nuggets but with that extra punchy, smoky wok flavour. Although chicken is the most common serving for this salt and chilli dish, the same preparation can also be applied to tofu or even Chips (page 84)!

Serves: 2
Prep time: 15–20 minutes, plus 1–8 hours brining
Cook time: 10–15 minutes
{🔥}{🌶}{🍴}

- 4 tablespoons salt
- 500 g/1 lb 2 oz skinless, boneless chicken thighs, diced
- vegetable oil, for deep-frying, plus 2 tablespoons extra
- 1 onion, cut into large chunks
  about 3 cm/1¼ inches wide
- 1 green pepper, cut into large chunks
  about 3 cm/1¼ inches wide
- 1 long red chilli, halved and seeded,
  if you don't like it spicy
- 3 cloves garlic, finely chopped
- 4 dried red chillies, halved and seeded,
  if you don't like it spicy
- 3 spring onions (scallions), cut into sections, about
  3 cm/1¼ inches, white parts set aside
- pinch of fine salt (optional)

- For the coating:
- 6 tablespoons potato starch
- 3 tablespoons cornflour (cornstarch)
- 1 teaspoon salt

- For the salt and chilli spice mix:
- 1 tablespoon five spice powder
- 1 teaspoon ground ginger
- 1 teaspoon ground white pepper
- 1½ teaspoons chicken stock powder
- 1 teaspoon chilli (red pepper) flakes, plus extra for
  seasoning (optional)

* Begin by brining the chicken for at least 1 hour (this can be done overnight, but 1 hour will definitely make a noticeable difference as it will soften the chicken and ensure you have a tender bite inside). Pour 600 ml/20 fl oz (2½ cups) warm water into a large spacious wide bowl, add the salt and stir until dissolved, then add the chicken and set aside.
* Put all the ingredients for coating the chicken into a large bowl, mix together and set aside.
* Put all the ingredients for the salt and chilli mix in another bowl, mix together and set aside.
* Heat enough oil for deep-frying in a large, deep saucepan or deep fryer until it reaches 180°C/350°F on a thermometer.
* Remove the chicken from the brine and dip the chicken pieces into the coating mixture until they are completely covered, then carefully lower 3–4 pieces of chicken at a time into the hot oil and deep-fry for 3 minutes, or until crispy, golden brown and cooked through. Remove with a slotted spoon and leave to drain on a metal rack set over a tray while you cook the remaining chicken.
* Heat the 2 tablespoons of oil in a large wok over a medium-high heat, add the onion and fry for 3–5 minutes until soft. Add the pepper, chilli and garlic, then add the dried chillies and spring onions (scallions) and stir-fry for 3 minutes, or until smoky and fragrant. Add the chicken and let all the pieces mix in with the wok ingredients for 1–2 minutes. Add the salt and chilli mix and toss until everything is thoroughly coated. Add more salt and chilli (red pepper) flakes if you desire more heat. Serve immediately.

UNITED KINGDOM

DEVILLED CHICKEN
(OR TURKEY)

To 'devil' something is an old culinary term used to denote the addition of hot spices, typically cayenne. A variety of different 'devil sauces' could be made, the most enjoyable of which is a spicy, creamy 'white devil sauce', often used for cooking left-over meat – chicken in particular.

Serves: 2–4
Prep time: 10 minutes
Cook time: 35 minutes

- oil or butter, for greasing
- 8 chicken pieces or 1 turkey thigh and drumstick
  (precooked, ideally from a left-over roast)
- 80 g/3 oz (¾ stick) butter
- 45 g/1½ oz (⅓ cup plus 1 teaspoon) plain
  (all-purpose) flour
- 1 tablespoon English mustard powder or 3 tablespoons
  English mustard
- 1 teaspoon curry powder of your choice (optional)
- 1 tablespoon Worcestershire sauce
- 1–2 teaspoons cayenne pepper (to taste)
- 150 ml/5 fl oz (⅔ cup) double (heavy) cream
- 200 ml/7 fl oz (¾ cup plus 1 tablespoon) chicken gravy
- 1 tablespoon mango chutney (optional)
- salt

* Preheat the oven to 160°C/325°F/Gas Mark 3.
* Lightly grease a casserole dish or Dutch oven and evenly space the chicken joints within it.
* Gently melt the butter in a small saucepan over a medium-low heat. Stir in the flour and cook for 2 minutes, stirring constantly. Add the mustard and curry powder (if using), the Worcestershire sauce and cayenne pepper and stir well. Season to taste with salt and add more cayenne pepper or mustard, if desired.
* Spread a third of the sauce evenly over the chicken in the dish, then add the rest to a large heatproof bowl with the cream and gravy. Add the chutney (if using), making sure any chunks are broken down, then whisk well to create the sauce. Pour this into the pan all around the chicken pieces and cook in the oven for 25–30 minutes. If the chicken browns too much, cover with aluminium foil. If it doesn't brown enough, put it under a hot grill (broiler) for a few minutes until dark golden brown. Serve.

Devilled chicken

CHICKEN KIEV

The Chicken Kiev is originally a dish of French or Russian origin, but it has, over the last several decades, been firmly adopted into the canon of British cookery. It is a simple enough concept to embrace – chicken breast is stuffed with a garlicky butter sauce, then breaded and fried until a crispy golden brown.

The Kiev was also the UK's first 'ready-chilled' meal when it debuted in Marks & Spencer supermarkets in 1979. Although it remains there to this day, it is now also a fixture of more upmarket gastropub menus as well.

Serves: 6
Prep time: 20 minutes, plus at least 2 hours chilling
Cook time: 30–35 minutes
{✻}

- 150 g/5 oz (1¼ sticks) unsalted butter, softened
- at least 6 cloves garlic, crushed
- 2 tablespoons coarsely chopped flat-leaf parsley
- grated zest of ½ lemon (optional)
- 6 boneless chicken breasts, skin on
- 6 tablespoons plain (all-purpose) flour
- 2 eggs, beaten
- about 150 g/5 oz (2⅓ cups) dried breadcrumbs
- 3 tablespoons grated Parmesan cheese (optional)
- 2–4 tablespoons rapeseed (canola) oil
- salt and pepper

* Put the butter, garlic, parsley and lemon zest (if using) into a blender or food processor and process until combined. Alternatively, grate the garlic and mash into the butter with the parsley and lemon zest. Season well. Put the garlic butter onto a piece of clingfilm (plastic wrap) and roll up into a log shape, twisting the ends tightly. Refrigerate for at least 2 hours, or until hard.
* Preheat the oven to 180°C/350°F/Gas Mark 4.
* Lay the chicken breasts on a chopping (cutting) board, skin-side up, and use a sharp knife to make a long, deep cut across the centre of each breast without piercing the other side of the meat – you will use this incision for the stuffing.
* Remove the garlic butter from the clingfilm (plastic wrap), cut into 6 lengths and put one into each incision.
* Put the flour into a large shallow bowl and season with 1½ teaspoons each of salt and pepper. Add the beaten eggs to another bowl and spread out the breadcrumbs and grated Parmesan (if using) on a third. Season with salt and pepper.
* Dip a chicken breast into the flour until coated, tapping away any excess, then dip into the egg mixture, making sure it is completely covered. Remove any excess, then roll in the breadcrumbs. Repeat with all the breasts.
* Heat 2 tablespoons of the oil in a large frying pan or skillet over a medium-high heat. Add the chicken breasts and fry on each side for 2–3 minutes. You may need to do this in batches.
* Arrange the chicken breasts on a large baking sheet with a 2 cm/¾ inch gap between each one and bake in the oven for 20–25 minutes until the breasts are cooked through and a skewer inserted into the thickest part comes out hot. Alternatively, a meat thermometer inserted into the thickest part should read at least 72°C/162°F. Serve.

JERK CHICKEN

Britain and Jamaica have a long and integrated history. In 1655, the British took the island from Spanish rule. During warfare between the Spanish and British, many enslaved families escaped plantations and formed new communities in mountainous areas of the island. The cooking process of roasting meat (originally wild pig) over pimento wood introduced jerk to Jamaican food culture, where it has remained ever since. The warm climate in Jamaica means jerk is always made using a jerk pan or barbecue and served dry. Adapting this cooking process to British weather has meant the recipe has adopted more of a wet style, with the spices featured in a marinade-like sauce.

This recipe is from London-based chef Keshia Sakarah.

Serves: 4
Prep time: 15 minutes, plus 8 hours brining
Cook time: 50 minutes
{🔥}{✻}

- 4 chicken legs, thighs and drumsticks attached, skin on
- coleslaw and hard dough bread, to serve

- For the brine:
- 40 g/1½ oz (3 tablespoons) sugar
- 20 g/¾ oz (4 teaspoons) salt

- For the jerk paste:
- 1 bulb garlic
- 6 scotch bonnet chillies, about 45 g/1½ oz
- 3 spring onions (scallions)
- 2 onions, coarsely chopped
- 10 g/¼ oz thyme, leaves picked
- 40 g/1½ oz fresh root ginger
- 20 g/¾ oz (4 teaspoons) ground allspice (pimento)
- 10 g/¼ oz (2 teaspoons) ground cinnamon
- 10 g/¼ oz (2 teaspoons) ground nutmeg
- juice of 2 limes
- 150 ml/5 fl oz (⅔ cup) soy sauce
- 45 g/1½ oz (3 tablespoons) soft brown sugar
- 60 ml/2 fl oz (¼ cup) vegetable oil

* For the brine, fill a large bowl with 1 litre/34 fl oz (4¼ cups) boiling water and add the sugar and salt. Whisk until they have dissolved, then leave to cool. Once cooled, add the chicken pieces, cover with clingfilm (plastic wrap) and leave to brine in the fridge overnight.
* The next day, prepare the jerk paste. Peel each clove of garlic and put into a blender or food processor with the chillies and spring onions (scallions) and coarsely chop. Add the onions, thyme leaves, ginger, ground spices, lime juice, soy sauce, brown sugar and oil and blend again until the paste comes together evenly. Set aside.
* Preheat the oven to 170°C/325°F/Gas Mark 3. Remove the chicken from the brine, discarding the liquid, and pat dry with paper towels. Put the chicken onto a baking sheet, skin-side up, and score the skin with a knife.
* Rub the chicken with 8 tablespoons of the jerk paste, ensuring it covers the meat and gets inside the scores. Cover with foil and bake in the oven for 40 minutes. Uncover and bake for another 10 minutes to allow the skin to crisp and any excess moisture to evaporate. Serve with coleslaw and hard dough bread.

Jerk chicken

UNITED KINGDOM

BRAISED DUCK LEGS
WITH
MINTED PEAS AND GRAVY

Serving duck with minted green peas is a hallmark of English springtime. In this recipe, the duck legs are slowly braised until tender and giving, then served in a gravy made from their own braising liquid. Serve with a generously sized bowl of Minted Peas (page 68). Mashed Potatoes (page 80) are an excellent idea as well, as the perfect vehicle for soaking up all that sauce.

Serves: 6
Prep time: 10 minutes
Cook time: 1½ hours
{⌀}

- 30 g/1 oz (2 tablespoons) butter, plus 1 extra teaspoon
- 2 tablespoons rapeseed (canola) oil
- 2 cloves garlic, bashed
- 6 sprigs thyme
- 1 sprig rosemary
- 1 bay leaf
- 6 duck legs
- 100 ml/3½ fl oz (⅓ cup plus 1 tablespoon) chicken or duck stock
- 1 teaspoon plain (all-purpose) flour
- salt and pepper

- To serve:
- Mashed or Boiled Potatoes (pages 80 and 84)
- Minted Peas (page 68)

* Preheat the oven to 150°C/300°F/Gas Mark 2 if braising the duck in the oven.
* Heat the 30 g/1 oz (2 tablespoons) butter and the oil in a large, wide ovenproof saucepan over a medium heat, add the garlic, thyme, rosemary and bay leaf and fry for 4–5 minutes. Add the duck legs in a single layer, then pour in the stock and season with salt and pepper.
* When the stock has begun to simmer, cover the pan with a lid, reduce the heat to low and braise the legs for 1 hour. Alternatively, put into the oven for 1 hour.
* When the legs are tender, preheat the grill (broiler) to high and line a baking sheet or roasting tray with aluminium foil. Remove the duck legs from the stock and arrange them on the prepared sheet or tray. Grill (broil) for 6–8 minutes until the skin is crisp and golden brown.
* Meanwhile, mash the 1 teaspoon butter and the flour together in a small bowl until a paste forms. Strain the stock into a clean saucepan and bring it to a simmer over a medium-low heat, whisking in the butter and flour mixture to thicken the gravy. Pour into a jug (pitcher).
* Serve the duck legs with Mashed or Boiled Potatoes, Minted Peas and the duck gravy.

UNITED KINGDOM

ROAST DUCK
WITH A
RICH GIBLET GRAVY

Roast duck, its skin bronzed and crispy, makes for an exceptional alternative to the typical Sunday poultry.

Serves: 6–8
Prep time: 20 minutes
Cook time: 3–3½ hours
{⌀}

- about 1.8–2 kg/4–4½ lb duck, giblets set aside
- salt and pepper

- For the giblet gravy:
- 1 tablespoon vegetable oil
- neck and giblets of the duck, chopped
- 1 onion, unpeeled and coarsely chopped
- 1 garlic clove, unpeeled and lightly crushed
- 1 carrot, roughly chopped
- 1 stalk celery, roughly chopped
- 1 bay leaf and a few sprigs thyme
- about 6 black peppercorns
- 125 ml/4¼ fl oz (½ cup) red wine
- 15 g/½ oz (1 tablespoon) butter
- 15 g/½ oz (1¾ tablespoons) plain (all-purpose) flour
- 1 teaspoon redcurrant jelly or juice of ½ orange (optional)

* For the gravy, put a medium saucepan over a high heat and add the oil. When hot, add the giblets, followed by the vegetables and cook for 5 minutes, or until browned. Add the herbs and peppercorns, then pour in 500 ml/17 fl oz (2 cups plus 1 tablespoon) water, cover with a lid and bring to the boil. Reduce the heat to low and simmer gently for 2–3 hours until thickened and flavourful.
* Preheat the oven to 220°C/425°F/Gas Mark 7. Weigh the duck and calculate the roasting time, allowing 40 minutes per 1 kg/2¼ lb plus an extra 20 minutes.
* Using a fork, prick the fatty parts of the duck, i.e. the breast and the area where the legs meet the body. Season the duck with salt and pepper, then set it on a rack over a large roasting pan and put it into the oven. After 20 minutes, reduce the temperature to 180°C/350°F/Gas Mark 4, then baste the bird with its fat every 20 minutes.
* To test if the duck is done, insert a knife or skewer into the thickest part of the leg. If the juices run clear then the duck is done. When cooked, remove from the oven and leave to rest for at least 15 minutes before carving.
* Meanwhile, finish off the giblet gravy. Strain the stock through a sieve into a jug (pitcher). Pour away most of the fat from the roasting pan, adding the meat juices to the gravy. Heat the roasting pan on the stove over a medium heat. Add the wine and heat for 2–3 minutes, stirring with a wooden spoon to scrape up all the crispy and browned bits on the bottom of the pan. Tip into the gravy.
* Melt the butter in a small saucepan over a medium-low heat, stir in the flour and cook for 2 minutes, stirring constantly. Whisk this into the gravy, then return to a pan and simmer for about 15 minutes, before stirring in the redcurrant jelly or orange juice, if using. Season to taste with salt and pepper and serve with the duck.

WALES: BORDERS

*

WELSH SALT DUCK

This is the traditional Welsh way of cooking large fatty ducks, which author Bobby Freeman suggests originates along the Marches (the Welsh-English border). The duck is salted for a few days, then slowly braised in stock and cider or otherwise cooked in a bain-marie, as suggested originally by Lady Llanover's *Good Cookery from Wales* (1867). This recipe is for the former method. Serve with Onion Sauce (page 418) and Roast Potatoes (page 86).

Serves 6
Prep time: 10 minutes, plus 3 days chilling
Cook time: 2 hours
{🝳} {🝲} {🝱} {🝰}

- 250 g / 9 oz (1 cup) sea salt
- 2–2.2 kg / 2¼ lb–4 lb 13 oz duck
- 1 onion, sliced
- 600 ml / 20 fl oz (2½ cups) duck or giblet stock
- 600 ml / 20 fl oz (2½ cups) cider
- pepper

* Rub the salt all over the bird, then cover with aluminium foil and keep covered in the fridge for 3 days, turning the bird every day.
* When ready to cook, preheat the oven to 180°C / 350°F / Gas Mark 4.
* Rinse the duck thoroughly in cold running water to remove the salt and dry well using paper towels.
* Put the duck into a deep casserole dish or Dutch oven with the onion slices, then pour over the stock and cider. Season well with pepper, cover with a lid or aluminium foil and cook in the oven for 2 hours. Once cooked, uncover and leave to rest for 20 minutes before cutting into pieces and transferring to a deep serving dish together with the cooking stock to serve.

NORTHERN IRELAND
*

ROAST GOOSE
WITH
POTATO AND APPLE STUFFING

Roast goose is traditionally served for either Michaelmas, a Christian holiday celebrated around harvest time, or at Christmas dinner. In autumn, the bird would be leaner and 'green', having fed on grass and stubble from the harvest, whereas by Christmas time they would have fattened considerably. The harvest-time birds especially would have been served with this potato and apple stuffing – both foods having just come into season, but Sage and Onion Stuffing (page 243) is more common today. Serve with Apple Sauce (page 414).

Serves: 6
Prep time: 30 minutes, plus 40 minutes resting
Cook time: 4 hours
{🝳} {🝱}

- 5 kg / 11 lb goose
- 1 quantity Apple Sauce (page 414)
- salt and pepper

- For the potato and apple stuffing:
- 60 g / 2¼ oz (½ stick) butter
- 2 onions, diced
- 2 apples, about 350 g / 12 oz, peeled, cored and diced
- ½ tablespoon finely chopped sage
- ½ tablespoon finely chopped flat-leaf parsley
- ½ tablespoon finely chopped thyme
- about 650 g / 1 lb 7 oz Mashed Potatoes (page 80)

* Weigh the goose and calculate the roasting time, allowing 45 minutes per 1 kg / 2¼ lb. If the goose has come with its giblets then you can make a rich gravy from them, in the same way as you would make the Giblet Gravy for the roast duck (see left). If not, make the Gravy according to the directions on page 420.
* For the stuffing, melt the butter in a large frying pan or skillet over a medium heat, add the onions and cook for 10 minutes, or until soft and translucent. Add the apples and chopped herbs and cook for another 5 minutes, or until the apples soften and the mixture smooths out. Remove from the heat and stir through the Mashed Potatoes until it forms an evenly mixed and cohesive stuffing. Season with a little salt and pepper, then leave to cool a little.
* Preheat the oven to 190°C / 375°F / Gas Mark 5.
* When the stuffing is cool enough to handle, use it to fill the cavity of the goose. Prick the stuffed goose all over with a fork and rub all over with salt. Season with pepper and put it onto a roasting rack above a large roasting pan. Put the goose into the centre of the oven and cook, basting every 30–40 minutes. A cooked goose should be about 57–58°C / 135–136°F when a thermometer is inserted into the thickest part of the thigh.
* When the goose is cooked, remove from the oven and leave to rest for 40 minutes before carving and serving with the stuffing, Gravy and Apple Sauce.
* Notes: For crispy, bronzed skin, preheat the oven to 220°C / 425°F / Gas Mark 7. Spread 1 tablespoon of vegetable oil over the bird and roast it in the oven for 10–20 minutes before reducing the temperature to 190°C / 375°F / Gas Mark 5 and continuing to cook. Take 10–20 minutes off the total cook time, but be vigilant to check doneness, as the higher initial temperature may mean the bird cooks quicker than usual.

UNITED KINGDOM

ROAST TURKEY
ROASTIT BUBBLY JOCK

A well-bronzed turkey is the showstopper of many a Christmas feast. Perhaps the one event of the year when going 'all out' is the norm. Serve your roast turkey with Gravy (page 420), Chestnut Stuffing (page 242), Brussels Sprouts with Roast Chestnuts and Bacon (page 70), Roast Potatoes (page 86) and both Cranberry and Bread Sauces (pages 415 and 416).
The traditional Scottish name, 'bubbly jock' seems to derive as Victorian rhyming slang for 'turkey cock'.

Serves: 6–8 with left-overs
Prep time: 20 minutes, plus 30 minutes resting
Cook time: about 2½–3 hours

- 1 lemon
- 80 g/3 oz (¾ stick) butter, softened
- 1 medium turkey (4–5 kg/8 lb 13 oz–11 lb)
- 1 quantity Chestnut Stuffing, cooled (page 242)
- 12 rashers (slices) streaky (lean) bacon
- 4 sprigs thyme
- salt and pepper

* Preheat the oven to 190°C/375°F/Gas Mark 5. Line a large roasting tray with aluminium foil.
* Halve the lemon, then squeeze a little of one half into the butter, season to taste with salt and pepper and mix well.
* Put the turkey onto a work counter and untruss it (if trussed). Ease the breast skin away from the meat, using one hand to keep the skin taut as you use the other to separate it. Smear three-quarters of the butter mixture over the breast meat and underneath the skin and season with salt. Stuff the neck end of the bird loosely with the stuffing, then make sure to tuck in the skin, securing it with cocktail sticks or toothpicks if available. Drape the bacon rashers (slices) over the breast of the greased bird and smear the remaining butter over the legs. Insert the lemon halves into the cavity of the bird, along with the thyme sprigs.
* Weigh your stuffed bird and calculate the roasting time, allowing 30 minutes for each 1 kg/2¼ lb.
* Make a double layer of aluminium foil that fits comfortably over the turkey as it sits in the prepared roasting tray, then put the tray onto the centre shelf of the preheated oven. About 45 minutes before the bird has finished cooking, remove the foil lid and the bacon and baste the top with the roasting juices. Return the bird to the oven without the foil lid so that it browns for the remaining cook time. Baste once more before the bird is done. Check if the bird is ready by inserting a meat thermometer into the thickest part of the breast and the innermost part of the thigh: both should read at least 74°C/165°F and the juices should run clear.
* If the bird still needs cooking, then baste with more of the juices and return to the oven for another 20 minutes. If not, set aside to rest for at least 30 minutes, and use the juices to make a gravy as on page 146.
* If there is a substantial amount of stuffing left, then bake it while the turkey rests. Grease a 500 g/1 lb 2 oz loaf pan with butter or line it with the bacon, then fill it with the extra stuffing. Cook for 30 minutes, then serve with the turkey.

UNITED KINGDOM

ROAST TURKEY CURRY

Fruity curries, made from left-over roast turkey, are a Boxing Day classic. Sweetened with raisins, they have a decisively British touch, harkening back to the eras in which curry-making was more about impressions of India than authenticity.

Serves: 3–4
Prep time: 5 minutes
Cook time: 20 minutes

{🍴}{🥄}{🍲}{✕}

- about 450 g/1 lb left-over meat from a roast turkey or chicken, carved from the carcass
- 3 tablespoons groundnut (peanut) oil, vegetable oil or ghee
- 1 teaspoon cumin seeds
- 1 onion, thinly sliced
- 4 cloves garlic, sliced
- 1 tablespoon ground coriander
- 1–2 teaspoons curry powder
- 75 g/2¾ oz (⅔ cup) flaked (slivered) almonds (optional)
- 300 g/11 oz canned chopped tomatoes
- 300 ml/10 fl oz (1¼ cups) canned coconut milk
- 75 g/2¾ oz (½ cup) raisins or sultanas (golden raisins)
- coriander (cilantro) leaves, to garnish
- freshly boiled basmati rice or Naan (page 275), to serve

* Cut the turkey meat neatly into 2 cm/¾ inch pieces and set aside.
* Heat the oil or ghee in a large saucepan over a medium-high heat, add the cumin seeds and sizzle for about 15 seconds. Add the onion and garlic and fry for 2–3 minutes, then add the ground coriander, curry powder and almonds and fry for 2 minutes. Add the tomatoes and simmer for 5 minutes, or until they have reduced by half.
* Fold in the pieces of turkey and add the coconut milk and raisins. Simmer for another 10 minutes to heat through, then serve sprinkled with coriander (cilantro) leaves and boiled basmati rice or Naan.

Roast turkey

> HERE IS A BIRD (GROUSE) AS NOBLE IN THE EATING AS ANY
> THAT FLIES, IN WHICH, BEING INDIGENOUS TO OUR SHORES,
> WE HAVE A MONOPOLY; A REMARKABLE BIRD WHICH HAS
> CREATED A RAILWAY TRAFFIC OF ITS OWN, AND CONTAINS
> PARLIAMENT TO ADJOURN BEFORE THE TWELFTH OF
> AUGUST IN ORDER THAT MEMBERS MAY BE FREE TO SHOOT
> IT UNTRAMMELLED BY CARES OF STATE. WHO CAN THINK
> OF THE DELICATELY FLAKING, PEAT- AND LING-SCENTED
> BLACK FLESH OF A PLUMP GROUSE UNMOVED?
>
> P. MORTON SHAND, *A BOOK OF FOOD*, 1927

As the name 'game' suggests, the history of hunting wild mammals and birds is inextricably linked with sport – particularly that of the gentry and upper classes, and dates back well over a thousand years. For millennia before that, across Britain, wild animals were hunted in woodlands, upland moors and even grasslands by those of all classes. After the time of the Norman Conquest, however, forest laws enacted by William I of England and his successors preserved these lands (they were not all strictly forests, but hunting reserves) for the Crown. Scottish monarchs followed with similar, though less restrictive policies, over the next couple of centuries. The romance of poachers flouting royal laws and risking their lives can be traced back to a similar period as well. Along with the gradual deforestation of Britain, these wild animals have moved into more rugged, remote areas like the Highlands of Scotland and the Yorkshire moors.

Thankfully, after centuries of classist exclusion, these meats are once again more accessible. Venison, in particular, has emerged as a popular meat to be found in most supermarkets. This is much to do with the introduction of deer farming, which began in Fife in 1973 with John and Nichola Fletcher. Now there are some 400 deer farms in the UK, with demand for this lean meat increasing year on year.

Game birds are still more exclusive, but can be sourced in some speciality butchers, or ordered at high-end restaurants. A few upmarket supermarkets may also offer some of the most familiar game birds, such as pheasant or partridge.

The season for hunting (and eating) game birds begins annually on 12th August, a day that is known as the 'Glorious Twelfth'. The first birds to come into season are grouse and snipe, followed by partridge, wild ducks and moorhen a few weeks later on 1st September. Seasons for deer stalking vary based on sex, species and region, but like game birds, they, broadly speaking, also begin in autumn and last into late winter. Lastly, for rabbit and hare there are no closed seasons, although restrictions apply to when they can be sold (again, typically late summer into early winter).

All manner of British game have strong attachments to autumn. Not only the mental images, although they are special: grouse peeking above purple heather, stags strident on russet hilltops or pheasants scurrying into roadside hedges. But, more significantly the larder, which is the natural complement for these meats when cooked. Most game besides the smallest of game birds (to be eaten simply, roasted and well-larded) take to the best of seasonal produce such as root vegetables, soft and stone (pit) fruit or tart berries, nuts and mushrooms.

Once killed, game and game birds are also hung to tenderize the meat and deepen the flavour. After the animal was skinned and butchered, game was traditionally consumed in a manner not dissimilar to today: rabbits and hare could be roasted or stewed, venison might receive the same treatment or be minced (ground) for pasties and marinated for pies. The best cuts, of course, went to the elite, but those of lower standing – the gamekeeper especially – might have enjoyed 'lesser' cuts of meat as well. The origin of the phrase 'humble pie' is a reference to this: a savoury pie made from a deer's numbles (offal). The blood might also be utilized for stews, as in jugged hare or bawd bree. Game birds, although they differ massively in taste from poultry, could be cooked in broadly the same way: the young, early season birds roasted, and the older, tougher birds reserved for stews, casseroles and pies.

Of course, despite the resurgent interest in game, the range of wild birds and animals eaten today is a fraction of what was once available. Bears became extinct in Britain by the early medieval period, and wild boars by the start of the seventeeth century. Many game birds are no longer hunted – thanks to either conservation, or conscience. Sea birds were also commonly hunted, but never enjoyed the same class association as game birds. In the Hebrides and on the Northern Isles of Scotland, these animals were frequently eaten by common folk. While cormorant casserole or puffin porridge (oatmeal) may be in living memory for some, these birds are all protected now – with only a small population of guga (young gannet) hunted (and salted) each year on the Scottish isle of Sula Sgeir. If you make it that far, you are in for a special experience.

GAME

AND

GAME

BIRDS

UNITED KINGDOM
*

VENISON STEW
WITH
HERB DUMPLINGS

Diced venison shoulder is the cut of choice for this stew – a lighter alternative to the more typically rich and hearty stews of beef or lamb. This recipe comes from Nichola Fletcher, a Scottish food writer, who, along with her husband John, set up the UK's first deer farm and venison business in 1973. It is taken from Nichola's book *The Venison Bible* (2015).

Serves: 4
Prep time: 15 minutes
Cook time: 2–2½ hours
{🔪}{🍷}

- 650 g/1 lb 7 oz diced venison shoulder
- plain (all-purpose) flour, for coating (optional)
- 2 tablespoons vegetable oil
- 2 onions, chopped
- 4 carrots, cut into large pieces
- 2 stalks celery, chopped
- 2 large tomatoes
- salt and pepper

- For the dumplings:
- 50 g/2 oz (¼ cup) suet
- 120 g/4 oz (1 cup) plain (all-purpose) flour, plus extra for dusting
- ½ teaspoon baking powder
- 1 large handful mixed herbs, finely chopped

* Preheat the oven to 190°C/375°F/Gas Mark 5.
* If you like a slightly thickened gravy, roll the venison in the flour until coated. Heat the oil in a large frying pan or skillet over a medium-high heat, add the onions and venison and cook for 10–15 minutes, until browned. Transfer them to a deep ovenproof casserole dish or Dutch oven. Add the other vegetables and enough water to nearly cover the meat in the dish and bring to the boil. Once it's boiling, transfer to the oven and cook for 1½–2 hours until the venison is tender. When the meat is tender, add a little more water to thin the gravy (the meat should be just submerged), then season with salt and pepper and keep warm.
* For the dumplings, put the suet, flour, baking powder, a generous pinch of salt and some pepper into a large bowl and mix together until combined. Add the herbs and mix them in, then pour in enough cold water to form a soft dough. If it is too dry, they won't swell so much. Dust your hands with flour and form the mixture into balls, 3–4 cm/1¼–1½ inches in diameter.
* Bring the stew gently to the boil and stir to prevent it sticking on the bottom. Drop the dumplings into the stew and cover the pan with the lid. Cook for 3 minutes, then reduce the heat to low and simmer very gently for another 20 minutes, by which time they should have doubled in size. Serve immediately so the dumplings don't collapse, though it isn't a disaster if they do.

UNITED KINGDOM
*

ROAST HAUNCH
OF VENISON

A haunch of venison refers to a whole back leg of the animal, and thus varies wildly in weight depending on the species of deer, ranging from around 2–3 kg/4½–6½ lb for roe deer up to around five times the size for red deer. This recipe is for a haunch of roe deer, which makes for a prime roasting meat. Serve with gravy, made from the roasting juices, Mashed Potatoes (page 80) and Rowan or Redcurrant Jelly (page 434).

Serves: at least 6
Prep time: 15 minutes, plus 24 hours chilling
Cook time: 3 hours
{🍷}

- 2.5 kg/5½ lb haunch of venison (roe deer)
- 2 carrots, sliced
- 2 onions, chopped
- 2 stalks celery, chopped
- 12 sprigs thyme
- 6 bay leaves
- 6 sprigs rosemary
- 12 black peppercorns, crushed
- 12 juniper berries, crushed
- 120 ml/4 fl oz (½ cup) olive oil
- 100 ml/3½ fl oz (⅓ cup plus 1 tablespoon) wine or cider vinegar
- 600 ml/20 fl oz (2½ cups) red wine
- 1 sheet caul fat, large enough to wrap the meat, about 40 x 40 cm/16 x 16 inches (optional)
- a little white wine, vinegar and lemon juice, for soaking
- 100 g/3½ oz (7 tablespoons) butter, softened
- salt and pepper

- For the gravy (optional):
- about 500 ml/17 fl oz (2 cups plus 1 tablespoon) beef stock
- 1 tablespoon plain (all-purpose) flour
- 1 tablespoon butter, softened
- 1 tablespoon Redcurrant or Quince Jelly (page 434)

- To serve:
- Mashed Potatoes (page 80)
- Rowan or Redcurrant Jelly (page 434)

* Put the meat into a large close-fitting container, tuck in the vegetables, herbs, peppercorns and juniper berries, then pour over the oil, vinegar and wine. Cover with aluminium foil and leave to chill in the fridge for 24 hours.
* Meanwhile, put the caul fat (if using) into a large bowl, cover with water and leave to soak in the fridge for 45 minutes. Drain, rinse under running water, then soak again for 45 minutes with a little white wine vinegar and lemon juice, then drain and rinse again.
* When ready to cook, preheat the oven to 220°C/425°F/Gas Mark 7.
* Remove the meat from the fridge and pat dry with paper towels. Set the marinade aside. Spread the 100 g/3½ oz (7 tablespoons) butter all over the meat, season with salt and pepper, then wrap in the caul fat (if using). Pour the reserved marinade into a large roasting pan and sit the

meat on top. Calculate the roasting time: 30 minutes per 1 kg/ 2¼ lb for rare, or 35 minutes per 1 kg/ 2¼ lb for medium, and cook, basting every 30 minutes and reducing the oven temperature to 180°C/ 350°F/ Gas Mark 4 after 20 minutes.

* When the meat is cooked, transfer to a large dish, cover with aluminium foil and leave to rest. Strain the vegetables well, pressing them through a sieve to get all the flavour. These juices can be used as is or made into a gravy. For the gravy, pour the juices into a large saucepan, add the beef stock and bring to a simmer over a medium heat for 5–10 minutes until it coats the back of a spoon.
* Put the flour and butter into a small bowl and mash into a paste, then whisk the paste into the sauce, a little at a time to slightly thicken the sauce (it should be as thick as regular gravy). Add the jelly and check for seasoning. Serve with the meat alongside Mashed Potatoes and Rowan or Redcurrant Jelly.

UNITED KINGDOM
*

ROAST LOIN OF VENISON
WITH
RED WINE SAUCE

Venison loin is an excellent cut for whole roasting and makes a very easy substitute for the classic beef or pork. It is taken from *Nichola Fletcher*'s *Ultimate Venison Cookery* (2007).

Serves: 4
Prep time: about 30 minutes
Cook time: about 40 minutes
{🏛}{🔥}

- butter and vegetable oil, for browning
- 700 g/ 1 lb 8½ oz trimmed venison loin
- 1 heaped tablespoon Rowan Jelly (page 434)
- 12 juniper berries, crushed
- 200 ml/ 7 fl oz (¾ cup plus 1 tablespoon) dry red wine
- 150 ml/ 5 fl oz (⅔ cup) reduced venison stock
- salt and pepper

* Preheat the oven to 220°C/ 425°F/ Gas Mark 7.
* Heat a little butter and oil in a large frying pan or skillet over a medium-high heat until the butter is golden. Add the meat and cook for a couple of minutes each side, or until browned thoroughly all over.
* Transfer the meat to a small roasting pan and tip the hot fat over the top. Don't wash the pan. Roast the venison in the oven for 10–12 minutes, then remove it from the oven and leave to rest for 12–15 minutes. The meat will be quite pink – if you want it done more than this, then leave it to rest for another 10 minutes – the meat must not actually cook further, merely be kept warm so that the meat relaxes and ends up evenly pink throughout.
* Meanwhile, add the Rowan Jelly, crushed juniper berries and red wine to the frying pan or skillet and stir over a medium heat, scraping up all the stuck-on bits on the bottom of the pan. When the jelly has dissolved, add the stock, then cook for several minutes, until you have a small amount of exquisite ruby-coloured sauce. Remove from the heat and set aside until the meat is ready. Strain the sauce through a sieve into a small saucepan.

* When the meat has rested, add the juices that came out of the meat to the sauce and bring to the boil. Adjust the seasoning before straining the sauce into a serving jug (pitcher). Cut the meat into thick chunks or thin slices according to taste and serve with the sauce.

UNITED KINGDOM
*

ROAST SADDLE
OF RABBIT

Turnip Tops (page 70) would make for a fitting accompaniment to rabbit – given their penchant for them!

Serves: 6
Prep time: 30 minutes, plus 1 hour chilling
Cook time: 15–20 minutes
{🍲}

- 3 saddles of rabbit, boned (ask your butcher to do this as it is quite tricky)
- 1 quantity Herb Stuffing (page 242)
- 9 very thin rashers (slices) streaky (lean) bacon or pancetta
- 30 g/ 1 oz (2 tablespoons) bacon fat or butter
- salt and pepper
- Turnip Tops, to serve (page 70)

* Lay the saddles in front of you with the cut-side facing towards you and season with salt and pepper. Divide the stuffing mixture into 3 equal portions and form into sausage shapes long enough to fit along the backbone. For bread-based stuffings, try not to compress the stuffing too much as it will be stodgy when cooked.
* Lay 3 rashers (slices) of bacon overlapping each other sightly and sit a saddle along one edge, cut-side upwards still. Roll over and trim away any excess. You should have a wrapped saddle with the cut-side underneath. Tuck the edges underneath, then repeat with the other saddles. Leave to chill in the fridge for at least 1 hour to firm up.
* Preheat the oven to 200°C/ 400°F/ Gas Mark 6.
* Heat the fat in a large roasting pan over over a high heat. Add the saddles and cook for 5 minutes, or until browned on all sides. Transfer the roasting pan to the oven and cook for 10–12 minutes depending on size. Serve with Turnip Tops.

UNITED KINGDOM
*

ROAST GROUSE
WITH
ALL THE TRIMMINGS

Each year on 12th August (the 'Glorious Twelfth' as it's also known), grouse-shooting season opens, lasting well into December. Grouse, which live on moorland throughout Britain, are often regarded as the 'king of game birds'. Their hunting season, incidentally, is also the first of the year. Young early season grouse should be roasted simply – so their flavour is not masked – but later season birds tend to be older, tougher and gamier in flavour, making them better suited to pot roasts, stews or pies. Serve with Bread Sauce (page 416), Game Chips (page 88), Rowan Jelly (page 434) and Watercress Salad with Capers (page 62).

Serves: 1–2
Prep time: 1 hour, plus 5½–7½ hours chilling and resting
Cook time: 20–25 minutes
{⁂}

- 250–300 g/9–11 oz grouse (or use an oven-ready grouse and skip the first step)
- 1 tablespoon rapeseed (canola) oil
- 60 g/2¼ oz (½ stick) butter
- salt

- To serve:
- Game Chips (page 88)
- Bread Sauce (page 416)
- Rowan Jelly (page 434)
- Watercress Salad with Capers (page 62)

* Pluck off the excess feathers from the outside of the grouse, then, using a sharp knife, remove the neck, head and wings (keeping the wingtips attached). Leave the claws on the legs, but pluck all the feathers from the legs. Open up the legs and make an incision at the base of the crown, then use your hands to remove the guts. Keep the heart and liver, if desired, for another recipe, such as pâté. Use a cloth to clean out the insides thoroughly, then pat the bird dry with paper towels and leave to chill in the fridge, uncovered, for 4–6 hours to dry out the skin a little.
* An hour before cooking, remove the grouse from the fridge and let it come gently to room temperature. Season the bird all over with salt. Be liberal and season inside the cavity as well.
* Preheat the oven to 140°C/275°F/Gas Mark 1.
* Heat a large frying pan or skillet over a medium-high heat. When hot, add the oil, then add the bird and cook for several minutes, until it is browned all over and has a lovely caramelized and rendered skin. Reduce the heat to medium-high and add 30 g/1 oz (2 tablespoons) of the butter. This will foam and go nut brown very quickly, so add the remaining 30 g/1 oz (2 tablespoons) butter and remove from the heat. Baste the bird all over, including in the cavity, with the butter for another 1 minute.
* Put the bird onto a wire rack set above a large roasting pan to catch any drips and cooking juices and roast in the oven for 11–15 minutes. Check the thickest part of the breast with a meat thermometer. You want it to reach 52°C/126°F for a medium rare cook or 56°C/133°F for medium. Once the grouse is cooked, remove from

the oven and leave to rest somewhere warm, such as an oven preheated to 80°C/176°F/lowest Gas Mark, for 30 minutes before serving with Game Chips, Bread Sauce, Rowan Jelly and Watercress Salad with Capers.

UNITED KINGDOM
*

POTTED GROUSE
(OR PHEASANT/PARTRIDGE)

One excellent use for the shredded left-over meat from roast game birds is to turn it into a thick, rich spread. Sealed with a lid of clarified butter, this traditional preparation is analogous to the French *rillette*. Serve on good bread with pickles and chutney.

Makes: 4–6 ramekins
Prep time: 20 minutes, plus 2 hours chilling
Cook time: 1½–2 hours
{⁂}

- 4 grouse or equivalent in other game birds, or 200 g/ 7 oz left-over roast game, underdone
- 1 tablespoon salt
- 1 teaspoon ground black pepper
- 1 teaspoon cayenne pepper
- 1 teaspoon ground mace
- 250–300 ml/8–10 fl oz (1–1¼ cups) game or chicken stock
- 125 g/4¼ oz (9 tablespoons) butter
- 2 tablespoons port, brandy or Calvados (optional)
- 100 g/3½ oz (7 tablespoons) clarified butter

- To serve:
- crisp toast
- good-quality jelly or fruit chutney of choice

* Preheat the oven to 140°C/275°F/Gas Mark 1.
* Cut the grouse in half.
* Put the salt and spices into a small bowl and mix together, then rub the mixture over the grouse. Transfer the grouse to a large casserole dish or Dutch oven with the stock and braise in the oven for 1½–2 hours. If the grouse is already cooked, reduce the braising time by half. Remove the grouse from the dish and leave to cool. Set all the cooking juices aside.
* When the grouse are cool enough to handle, separate the meat from the bones, discarding the bones. Strain the juices and reduce them if you find the flavour is a little weak: heat them in a medium saucepan over a medium heat for 5 minutes until reduced to your taste.
* Put the meat and butter into a food processor and moisten with a little (at first) of the strained braising juices and the alcohol (if using) and process once before deciding how much more of the juices to add. You want the mixture to be somewhat coarse.
* When the mixture has reached a desirable consistency, pack it into 4–6 ramekins and level the tops with a spoon. Pour over the clarified butter, cover with aluminium foil and leave to chill in the fridge for at least 2 hours until the clarified butter is set. It should last for a week in the fridge.
* Serve with crisp toast and jelly or fruit chutney.

Roast grouse

UNITED KINGDOM
*
ROAST PHEASANT
WITH
ALL THE TRIMMINGS

Pheasant is an easy entry point into the world of game birds. Pheasants have only a very subtle gaminess and are often closer in taste to chicken than grouse. Of all game birds, pheasants are the ones you're most likely to find in British supermarkets.

Young pheasants should be roasted, but as they are a very lean bird, it is important to keep them well basted or larded with bacon. As with grouse, older birds are better suited for slow cooking, casseroles and pies, although in practice, pheasant is more interchangeable with many more chicken recipes.

Serve with Bread Sauce (page 416), Game Chips (page 88), Rowan Jelly (page 434) and Watercress Salad with Capers (page 62).

Serves: 2–3
Prep time: 1 hour, plus 5½–7½ hours chilling and resting
Cook time: 25–30 minutes
{ₒ•}

- 500 g/ 1 lb 2 oz oven-ready pheasant
- 2 tablespoons rapeseed (canola) oil
- 90 g/ 3¼ oz (6 tablespoons) butter
- salt

- To serve:
- Game Chips (page 88)
- Bread Sauce (page 416)
- Rowan Jelly (page 434)
- Watercress Salad with Capers (page 62)

* Prepare the pheasant in the same manner as the Roast Grouse on page 156.
* An hour before cooking, remove the pheasant from the fridge and let it come gently to room temperature. Season the bird all over with salt; be liberal and season inside the cavity as well.
* Preheat the oven to 140°C/ 275°F/ Gas Mark 1.
* Heat a large frying pan or skillet over a medium-high heat. When hot, add the oil, then add the bird and cook for several minutes, until it is browned all over and has a lovely caramelized and rendered skin. Reduce the heat to medium-high and add 45 g/ 1½ oz (3 tablespoons) of the butter. This will foam and go nut brown very quickly, so add the remaining 45 g/ 1½ oz (3 tablespoons) butter and remove from the heat. Baste the bird all over, including in the cavity, with the butter for another 1 minute.
* Put the bird onto a wire rack set above a large roasting pan to catch any drips and cooking juices and roast in the oven for 18–21 minutes. Once the pheasant is cooked, remove from the oven and leave to rest somewhere warm, such as an oven preheated to 80°C/ 176°F/ lowest Gas Mark, for 30 minutes before serving with Game Chips, Bread Sauce, Rowan Jelly and Watercress Salad with Capers.

UNITED KINGDOM
*
ROAST PARTRIDGE
(OR WOODCOCK/SNIPE)
WITH
TRAIL BUTTER TOAST

The meat of the partridge is fairly sweet and only mildly gamey; aside from the pheasant, it is the most common game bird found at speciality markets and butchers across the country.

Woodcock and snipe are both small game birds, with long narrow beaks and excellent but very gamey meat. The woodcock is of a similar size to a partridge, and can be cooked in much the same manner. The snipe, a much smaller bird, will not need as much time. Given their relatively small size, these birds should be cooked as precisely as possible or they will completely dry out.

One popular, and rather luxurious way of cooking the two smaller birds is to roast them ungutted – their liquified 'trails' should be mixed through with butter or whisked into a quick pâté to spread across the toast they are traditionally served with.

Serves: 4
Prep time: 1 hour, plus 5½–7½ hours chilling and resting
Cook time: 20 minutes
{ₒ•}

- 2 partridge, woodcock or snipe
- 2 tablespoons rapeseed (canola) oil
- 90 g/ 3¼ oz (6 tablespoons) butter
- 4 thick slices toast, buttered (optional)
- salt

* Prepare the birds in the same manner as the Roast Grouse on page 156, but if using woodcock or snipe, leave the guts intact.
* An hour before cooking, remove the birds from the fridge and let them come gently to room temperature. Season all over with salt; be liberal and season inside the cavities too.
* Preheat the oven to 140°C/ 275°F/ Gas Mark 1.
* Heat a large frying pan or skillet over a medium-high heat. When hot, add the oil, then add the birds and cook until they are browned all over and have a lovely caramelized and rendered skin. Reduce the heat to medium-high and add 45 g/ 1½ oz of the butter (30 g/ 1 oz for the snipe). This will foam and go nut brown very quickly, so add the remaining 45 g/ 1½ oz butter (30 g/ 1 oz for the snipe) and remove from the heat. Baste the birds all over, including the cavity, with the butter for another minute.
* Put the birds onto a wire rack set above a large roasting pan to catch any drips and cooking juices and roast in the oven for 14–16 minutes (7–10 minutes for the snipe), slipping the buttered toast under the woodcock or snipe for the last half of the roasting time.
* If using woodcock or snipe, take the bird off its toast and use a sharp knife to cut off the head, then use a chef's knife to cut its head in half lengthways. Some may find it a bit grotesque, but the brain makes for exceptional eating. Serve the roast woodcock and snipe with the head on a plate with a small teaspoon alongside so that the trails (the liquified innards) can be scooped out and spread upon the toast.

UNITED KINGDOM

POT-ROAST PARTRIDGE
WITH
PRUNES AND CABBAGE

This pot roast is best made at the height of autumn, when leaves are a russet amber, before winds turn from brisk to biting. Roasted and peeled chestnuts or root vegetables would also make a fine addition here.

Serves: 4
Prep time: 15 minutes
Cook time: 1¼ hours
{🦴}{🍷}

- 100 g/3½ oz (1 stick minus 1 tablespoon) butter
- 4 rashers (slices) dry-cured smoked streaky (lean) bacon, chopped
- 4 oven-ready partridges
- 1 onion, chopped
- 1 teaspoon chopped thyme leaves
- about 15 prunes, halved
- 125 ml/4¼ fl oz (½ cup) white wine
- about 250 ml/8 fl oz (1 cup) chicken or game stock
- ½ small Savoy cabbage, cut into 12 wedges, core intact

* Heat half the butter in a large casserole dish or Dutch oven over a medium heat, add the bacon and fry for 10–12 minutes until crisp. Remove and set aside.
* Add the partridges to the pan and, using a pair of kitchen tongs to turn them, cook the birds for 10 minutes, or until brown on all sides. Set aside to rest. If the pan is not large enough, then brown the birds in batches, adding 1–2 tablespoons butter to the pan after each batch.
* Add the onion and thyme leaves to the pan and cook for 12–15 minutes until golden. Spoon in the bacon and arrange the partridges inside. Sprinkle with the prunes, then pour over the wine and then the stock.
* Bring a large saucepan of water to the boil, add the cabbage and blanch for 5 minutes. Drain, then put into a large heatproof bowl and stir in the remaining butter. Tuck the buttery cabbage in between and around the partridges, cover with a lid and braise over a low heat for 30 minutes, or until the birds are cooked. Serve.

UNITED KINGDOM
*

ROAST WILD DUCK
(MALLARD)

Wild ducks are those that are hunted like game birds and not farmed for their meat. The latter, which don't fly, have a fattier meat and more familiar taste – the leaner, stronger taste of wild duck will more closely resemble other game birds. The trade-off is flavour for fat.

Serves: 2
Prep time: 15 minutes, plus 15 minutes resting
Cook time: 15–18 minutes
{🍷}

- 600–800 g/1 lb 5 oz–1¾ lb oven-ready wild mallard
- about 60 g/2¼ oz (½ stick) unsalted butter, softened
- stuffing of your choice, such as at least 1 large apple or orange peeled and sliced into wedges, or a small quantity of Herb Stuffing (page 242)
- salt

- To serve (optional):
- Orange Sauce (page 422) or Cumberland Sauce (page 415)
- Roast Potatoes (page 86) or Game Chips (page 88)

* Preheat the oven to 140°C/275°F/Gas Mark 1.
* Leave the duck to come to room temperature, then truss with kitchen string. Rub salt evenly into the bird all over, then spread the softened butter all over and stuff the cavity with your stuffing of choice.
* Put the bird onto a roasting tray and roast in the oven for 15–18 minutes, basting frequently. The bird should be cooked until a thermometer in the thickest part of the leg reads 54°C/129°F (rare) or 60°C/140°F (medium).
* Once the duck is cooked, remove from the oven and leave to rest for 15 minutes before serving as for roast duck or game birds, with Orange Sauce or Cumberland Sauce and Roast Potatoes or Game Chips.

UNITED KINGDOM
*

ROAST WOOD PIGEON

The wood pigeon is large enough to feed one person, and its gaminess is balanced nicely by the creamy, nutty celeriac (celery root), and sweetly tart cabbage.

Serves: 2
Prep time: 10 minutes, plus 10–15 minutes resting
Cook time: 20 minutes
{🦴}{🍷}

- 2 oven-ready wood pigeons, about 250 g/9 oz each
- 2 tablespoons rapeseed (canola) oil
- 70 g/2½ oz (⅔ stick) butter, plus 20 g/¾ oz (4 teaspoons) melted
- salt

- To serve:
- ½ quantity Celeriac Purée (page 66)
- ¼ quantity Braised Red Cabbage (page 444)

* Preheat the oven to 140°C/275°F/Gas Mark 1.
* Remove the birds from the fridge a little ahead of time to let them come up to room temperature. Using a cloth, remove any excess blood from the cavity, then rub them with the oil and season with salt inside and out.
* Heat a heavy saucepan over a medium heat. Add the butter, then put the pigeons, breast-side down, into the pan and brown the birds on both breasts, then all over, adding more butter, if necessary, for a total of 5 minutes.
* Transfer to a large roasting tray and roast in the oven for 14–16 minutes, brushing the birds with the melted butter at least twice as they roast.
* When the birds are cooked, remove from the oven and leave to rest somewhere warm for 10–15 minutes. Serve whole or carve the breasts and leg and plate with the Celeriac Purée and Braised Red Cabbage.

...BEEF, MUTTON, VEAL, PORK AND LAMB; YOU HAVE WHAT
QUANTITY YOU PLEASE CUT OFF, FAT, LEAN, MUCH
OR LITTLE DONE; WITH THIS, A LITTLE SALT AND MUSTARD
UPON THE SIDE OF YOUR PLATE, A BOTTLE OF BEER AND A ROLL;
AND THERE IS YOUR WHOLE FEAST.

– HENRI MISSON, M. MISSON'S MEMOIRS AND
OBSERVATIONS IN HIS TRAVELS OVER ENGLAND,
WITH SOME ACCOUNT OF SCOTLAND AND IRELAND, 1719

For centuries, British meat and meat-eating traditions have been a revelation for foreign visitors. Yet despite this reputation, for much of British history very few could afford to eat meat regularly, and even fewer kept animals for their meat alone. Britain's relationship with meat developed not out of an abundance, but out of scarcity and clever preparation.

Cattle and sheep were predominantly kept for dairy and for wool – their slaughter came at the end of the year, and not just to whet the appetite, but as a means of preventing food scarcity (for humans and animals alike) in winter. Once butchered, they would be processed and prepared for eating from nose to tail (quite literally). To prevent the meat from spoiling, the bulk would be salted, pickled, potted, or otherwise preserved. Offcuts and offal could also be turned into country classics: brawn or broth made from a cleaned and halved head, richly flavoured and well-seasoned offal puddings made with the organs, the blood, and the suet (hard kidney fat, a household staple). The finest cuts of meat may have gone to landowners, but the tougher cuts – beef shin or lamb neck for instance – would be treated with love and attention, slowly cooked in their own gravy or a stew of root vegetables until tender. These dishes may come from poverty and scarcity, but they have rightly earned their place as favourites.

The issue surrounding winter feed (and its scarcity) saw a breakthrough in the eighteenth century: it was discovered that certain root vegetables, such as turnips, could be grown throughout the coldest months and provide enough sustenance to keep herds of cattle alive. At the same time, breeders expanded their herds and began to focus on 'improving' them: creating bigger, bulkier beasts with much more meat on the bone. Some of these breeds, like the Aberdeen Angus or Hereford cattle, became a real mark of quality both within the UK and around the world.

Over the course of the nineteenth century, a few big factors – steam-powered trains, refrigeration, and trade with Australasia – combined to help change the diet of many Brits, increasing the availability of products previously deemed a great luxury. Mutton was quickly replaced by lamb in the larder and in cookbooks, and the prospect of eating fresh (i.e. unsalted) meat became a reality for many.

PORK/HAM/BACON
Pig-farming was most common in England, especially in the southwest and Midlands. There thrived heritage breeds like the British favourite, Tamworth – famous for its great hams and bacons.

The need to preserve meat was the impetus for the rich British traditions of curing bacon and ham – and not only in those areas with substantial pig-farming. Up and down the nation, dozens of regions specialized in smoked and unsmoked cuts of pork with a range of saltiness and occasionally the sweetness of brown sugar.

BEEF
Many of the heritage breeds of British beef cattle, including the South Devon, Dexter and Lincoln Red, have meat that is well-marbled with fat, giving it an excellent flavour that deepens considerably with ageing. The various breeds range massively in size, from the smallest Dexter beef cattle (just 300–350 kg/660–770 lb), to the red South Devon cattle – believed to have arrived with Norman conquerors – which weigh nearly up to four times as much.

LAMB/MUTTON
There are three main distinctions between the many British heritage sheep: the well-fattened sheep of the valley, the mountain sheep grazing on wild herbs and grasses, and sheep that live along salty marshland and feed on seaweeds. In each case, the foods and climate impact on the flavour of the meat and what it's served with: a thyme stuffing will bring out that flavour in mutton or lamb that grazed on it in mountain fields, and a sauce made of a seaweed called laver (or sloke) is commonly served with saltmarsh sheep – especially in Wales.

THE ROAST
The tradition of Sunday roasts began in England, probably by the end of the eighteenth century. At this point, very few home kitchens had their own oven, so joints of meat were originally taken to the local bakery to be cooked in the large oven – otherwise empty on a Sunday – while the family was at church.

Traditionally, home-cooked roasts were quite large and their left-overs would be used throughout the week. An old saying lays out the week's dinners in rotation: 'Hot on Sunday, cold on Monday, hashed on Tuesday, minced on Wednesday, curried on Thursday, broth on Friday, cottage pie Saturday'. Now, with most kinds and cuts of meat available, you can have cottage pie any day you like.

PORK, BEEF
AND
LAMB

ENGLAND: CUMBRIA
*

CUMBERLAND SAUSAGES

A favourite in the world of English sausages, this pork sausage is best known for its pepperiness – the dominant spicing. Serve these with Mashed Potatoes (see below).

Serves: 6
Prep time: 1½ hours, plus 4–5 hours soaking and chilling
Cook time: 40 minutes
{🔪} {🍴}

- about 1 m/ 3 ft natural pig's casing
- 500 g/ 1 lb 2 oz (2¼ cups) minced (ground) pork
- 100 g/ 3½ oz (½ cup minus 1 tablespoon) minced (ground) back fat
- 1 tablespoon fresh breadcrumbs
- 2 teaspoons salt
- ¼ teaspoon ground black pepper
- ¼ teaspoon ground white pepper
- ½ teaspoon ground nutmeg
- ½ teaspoon ground mace
- ¼ teaspoon dried marjoram or sage
- lard, for frying

* Put the casing into a bowl of water and soak for a minimum of 2 hours. Drain and set aside.
* Put all the ingredients, except the casing and lard, into a large bowl and mix very well with your hands. Tie a knot in one end of the casing, then take the untied end and place it over the nozzle of a sausage machine and pull the casing back until you reach the knot. Turn on the machine and feed the meat through, letting the skin fill with the meat, easing it into a coil shape. Alternatively, use a wide-mouthed funnel to fill the casings. Leave the sausage to firm up in the fridge for 2–3 hours.
* To cook, smear some lard thinly over a heavy frying pan or skillet, then put it over a medium-low heat and sit the sausage inside. As it heats, secure it by inserting a couple of skewers through it so that it keeps its shape when cooking. Reduce the heat to low and fry for 40 minutes, turning frequently, until browned all over. This will allow the sausage to stay moist and juicy.

ENGLAND
*

BANGERS AND MASH

A simple but unfailing combination of nicely browned sausages and creamy Mashed Potatoes (page 80) – both smothered in a rich Onion Gravy (page 420). Serve with Minted Peas (page 68) and a little English mustard.

Serves: 4
Prep time: 20 minutes
Cook time: 30 minutes
{🍴}

- 1 quantity Onion Gravy (page 420)
- 1 quantity Mashed Potatoes (page 80)
- 1 teaspoon vegetable oil or lard
- 8 good-quality sausages, bought or homemade
- 1 tablespoon wholegrain mustard

- To serve:
- Minted Peas (page 68)
- English mustard

* Make the Onion Gravy following the recipe on page 420. It may be easier to make the gravy in advance and simply keep warm or reheat when ready.
* Start to make the Mashed Potatoes following the recipe on page 80. When the potatoes have been boiling for 5–10 minutes, heat the oil or lard in a large, heavy saucepan over a low-medium heat, add the sausages, leaving space between each one – don't be tempted to prick them – and cook undisturbed for 5 minutes. Reduce the heat if they are getting too coloured.
* Turn the sausages over and cook for another 5 minutes. Keep turning and cooking for a total of about 20 minutes, until evenly browned and cooked through.
* Add the wholegrain mustard to the gravy, then serve the sausages with plenty of Mashed Potatoes, with everything smothered in the gravy, and Minted Peas and English mustard on the side.

ENGLAND: LINCOLNSHIRE
*

LINCOLNSHIRE SAUSAGES

This coarsely ground pork sausage is another one of England's favourites. It is typically classed as the 'herby' sausage, with sage the dominant herb used.

Makes: 8
Prep time: 45 minutes, plus 4–5 hours soaking and chilling
Cook time: 40 minutes
{🔪} {🍴}

- about 1 m/ 3 ft natural pig's casing
- 500 g/ 1 lb 2 oz (2¼ cups) minced (ground) pork
- 150 g/ 5 oz (⅔ cup) minced (ground) back fat
- 60 g/ 2¼ oz (1¼ cups) fresh breadcrumbs
- 2 teaspoons salt
- ¼ teaspoon ground black pepper
- ½ teaspoon dried sage
- lard, for frying

* Put the casing into a bowl of water and soak for a minimum of 2 hours. Drain and set aside.
* Put all the ingredients, except the casing and lard, into a large bowl and mix very well with your hands. Tie a knot in one end of the casing, then take the untied end and place it over the nozzle of a sausage machine and pull the casing back until you reach the knot. Turn on the machine and feed the meat through, letting the skin fill with the meat. Alternatively, use a wide-mouthed funnel to fill the casings. When all the meat is used up, tie the skin at the other end and twist the sausage into links of the desired lengths; 20 cm/ 8 inches is a good size. Put the sausages into the fridge to firm up for 2–3 hours.
* To cook, smear some lard thinly over a heavy frying pan or skillet, then put it over a medium-low heat and sit the sausages inside. Reduce the heat to low and gently fry for 40 minutes, turning frequently, until browned all over. This will allow the sausages to stay moist and juicy and keep the fattier ones from bursting. Serve.

Bangers and mash

SCOTLAND / ENGLAND
*

SCOTCH EGG

To make this beloved bar and picnic snack, soft-boiled eggs are wrapped in a layer of sausage meat and a dusting of breadcrumbs, then fried until golden and crispy. They should be sliced in half then either eaten on their own, or with English mustard and a little chutney. For something a little different, swap the sausage meat for an equal amount of Black Pudding (page 168) or even Haggis (page 192). There are several competing theories on where the Scotch Egg originates, and curiously the one thing agreed on most is that this dish is not Scottish in origin. That much is inconsequential now, though, as the name association alone has made it a proud part of Scottish cuisine.

Serves: 5
Prep time: 15 minutes, plus 8–12 hours chilling
Cook time: about 30 minutes
{ ✿ }

- 1 tablespoon rapeseed (canola) oil
- 100 g/3½ oz white onion, diced
- 2 g/¼ teaspoon chopped thyme
- 2 g/¼ teaspoon chopped rosemary
- 300 g/11 oz sausage meat
- 150 g/5 oz (⅔ cup) minced (ground) pork shoulder
- 10 g/¼ oz (2 teaspoons) wholegrain mustard
- 10 g/¼ oz (2 teaspoons) Dijon mustard
- 150 ml/5 fl oz (⅔ cup) apple cider
- 5 large eggs
- 2 egg yolks
- 2 tablespoons full-fat (whole) milk
- 75 g/2¾ oz (½ cup plus 1 tablespoon) plain (all-purpose) flour
- 200 g/7 oz (4 cups) fresh breadcrumbs
- vegetable oil, for deep-frying
- salt and pepper

* Heat the rapeseed (canola) oil in a large frying pan over a medium heat, add the diced onion, thyme and rosemary and cook for 7–10 minutes until softened. Transfer to a large bowl and leave to cool slightly, then add the sausage meat, minced (ground) pork shoulder, mustards and cider to the bowl. Season with a little salt and pepper and mix together. Cover with clingfilm (plastic wrap) and leave in the fridge overnight.
* The next day, weigh the sausage mix into 5 x 100 g/3½ oz balls and set them aside.
* Have a large bowl of iced water nearby. Fill a medium saucepan two-thirds full of water and bring to the boil. Carefully add the eggs and cook for 5½ minutes exactly, before putting them into the bowl of iced water to cool. Alternatively, cool them under cold running water. Peel the eggs, then form the sausage mix around the eggs, while maintaining its approximate shape.
* Put the egg yolks and milk into a shallow bowl and beat together, then put the flour into another shallow bowl, and the breadcrumbs into a third shallow bowl.
* Cover each 'egg' in the flour, followed by the egg wash and finally the breadcrumbs. Dip once more into the egg wash before covering with a second layer of the breadcrumbs. Set aside.
* Preheat the oven to 180°C/350°F/Gas Mark 4. Line a large baking sheet with baking (parchment) paper.

* Heat enough vegetable oil for deep-frying in a large, deep saucepan or deep fryer until it reaches 180°C/350°F on a thermometer. Working in batches, carefully lower the Scotch eggs into the hot oil and deep-fry for 3–5 minutes until golden brown. Remove with a slotted spoon and arrange them on the prepared baking sheet. Bake in the oven for 8 minutes. Eat warm or cold.

UNITED KINGDOM
*

PORK
AND
APPLE SAUSAGES

It's a classic British combination in pies and for Sunday roasts, so there are no prizes for deducing that minced (ground) pork and apple make a mighty fine sausage as well. Serve as Bangers and Mash (page 164). If you are wary about the fruitiness, try it with a mix of Lincolnshire or Cumberland Sausages (page 164) as well.

Makes: 8
Prep time: 45 minutes, plus 4–5 hours soaking and chilling
Cook time: 40 minutes
{ 🔪 } { ✿ }

- about 1 m/3 ft natural pig's casing
- 500 g/1 lb 2 oz (2¼ cups) minced (ground) pork
- 150 g/5 oz (⅔ cup) minced (ground) back fat
- 60 g/2¼ oz (1¼ cups) fresh breadcrumbs
- 1 small Bramley (cooking) apple, peeled, cored and grated
- 2 Cox's Orange Pippin apples (or similar tart eating apple), peeled, cored and grated
- 2 teaspoons salt
- 1 tablespoon honey
- 40 ml/1½ fl oz (2 tablespoons plus 2 teaspoons) cider (optional)
- ¼ teaspoon ground black pepper
- ½ teaspoon ground nutmeg
- 2 tablespoons finely chopped flat-leaf parsley
- lard, for frying

* Put the casing into a bowl of water and soak for a minimum of 2 hours. Drain and set aside.
* Put all the ingredients, except the casing and lard, into a large bowl and mix very well with your hands. Tie a knot in one end of the casing, then take the untied end and place it over the nozzle of a sausage machine and pull the casing back until you reach the knot. Turn on the machine and feed the meat through, letting the skin fill with the meat. Alternatively, use a wide-mouthed funnel to fill the casings. When all the meat is used up, tie the skin at the other end and twist the sausage into links of the desired lengths; 20 cm/8 inches is a good size. Put the sausages into the fridge to firm up for 2–3 hours.
* To cook, smear some lard thinly over a heavy frying pan or skillet, then put it over a medium-low heat and sit the sausages inside. Reduce the heat to low and gently fry for 40 minutes, turning frequently, until browned all over. This will allow the sausages to stay moist and juicy and keep the fattier ones from bursting. Serve.

Scotch egg

ENGLAND: OXFORD

*

OXFORD SAUSAGES

These herby pork and veal sausages were originally shaped and cooked without casings – as such, they are especially suited to making at home.

Makes: 12
Prep time: 10 minutes, plus 20–30 minutes soaking
Cook time: 15 minutes
{•}

- 150 g/5 oz bread, crusts removed or 150 g/5 oz (3 cups) fresh breadcrumbs
- 150 ml/5 fl oz (⅔ cup) full-fat (whole) milk
- 500 g/1 lb 2 oz (2¼ cups) minced (ground) pork
- 500 g/1 lb 2 oz (2¼ cups) minced (ground) veal
- 250 g/9 oz (1 cup plus 4 teaspoons) chopped or minced (ground) pork back fat or beef suet
- 2 teaspoons salt
- ½ teaspoon ground black pepper
- ½ teaspoon dried sage
- ½ teaspoon dried thyme
- natural casings (optional)
- lard or dripping, for frying

* If using fresh bread, put the crustless bread in a large bowl, pour in the milk to cover and leave to soak for 20–30 minutes. Remove the bread from the milk and gently squeeze out any excess. Tear up the bread into small pieces, then put into a large bowl with the remaining ingredients, except the casings. If using breadcrumbs, then add to the bowl with the rest of the ingredients, except the casings. Mix together until combined. The mixture can then be used to fill natural casings following the recipe on page 164, or formed into patties, about 1 cm/½ inch thick and weighing 175 g/6 oz, or rolled into 'skinless' sausages.

* To fry, heat a little lard or dripping in a large frying pan or skillet over a low-medium heat, add the sausages or patties and fry for 7–8 minutes until they are deep golden brown. Turn over and repeat on the other side. For the sausages, turn every few minutes to get an even colour throughout. Serve.

SCOTLAND / NORTH OF ENGLAND

*

BLACK PUDDING

These earthy, well-spiced blood puddings (blood sausages) are traditionally made with oats and the blood and fat of an animal, typically pigs but sometimes also cattle. The 'pudding' designation harkens back to the original meaning of the word pudding, an ancient term for mixtures of meat, fat and cereal that were cooked in an animal's stomach. In a black pudding, blood takes the place of meat, and serves as an effective and delicious method of preserving and utilizing every bit of the animal.

In mainland Britain, black puddings are frequently associated with the Midlands, north England (Bury in particular) and also Scotland, where it is a famous export of the Hebridean Isle of Lewis. Spices and flavourings range throughout the country, and recipe to recipe. Black puddings have a reddish tone to them until fried, when they darken to a deep black. Nowadays they are also served in artificial black casings, but traditionally the natural casing of the pudding was brushed with blood just before it was baked and would blacken in the oven.

Black puddings are most frequently served fried, either as part of a Full Breakfast (page 26), with fresh Scallops (page 116), or on a buttered Breakfast Roll (page 276). The best puddings, with deep rich flavours and a marbling of fat and whole groats, can be the star of any meal.

The following method of making black pudding comes from Scottish chef Michael Craig, who steams his puddings rather than poaching them.

Serves: 12
Prep time: 15 minutes, plus 8–12 hours cooling
Cook time: about 1 hour
{🂠}{🍴}{•}

- 600 g/1 lb 5 oz pork or beef fat
- 250 g/9 oz crushed oats
- 225 g/8 oz onions, finely diced
- 250 g/9 oz fresh pig's blood (see Notes)
- 12 g/½ oz salt
- 12 g/½ oz ground black pepper
- natural sausage casings (optional)
- oil, for frying
- sea salt flakes

* Put all the ingredients, except the sausage casings and oil, into a large bowl and mix into a porridge (oatmeal) where the blood is evenly distributed. You can either shape the mixture into a large sausage form (using the natural casings) or stuff into a 900 g/2 lb terrine mould, making sure there are no air pockets. Wrap the terrine or sausage in clingfilm (plastic wrap) or aluminium foil and steam in a steamer at 100°C/212°F for 45–60 minutes.

* Leave to cool in the fridge overnight, then slice to your desired thickness and fry in a small amount of oil in a frying pan or skillet over a medium-high heat for 3–4 minutes each side, until crispy on both sides. Remove with a slotted spoon and leave to drain on paper towels, then season generously with sea salt flakes.

* **Notes:** Fresh blood will be hard to find, but you can source dried blood, and follow the packet instructions for use.

ENGLAND: WILTSHIRE AND SOMERSET
*

BATH CHAPS

This fatty cut of cured pork cheek probably originated in the nineteenth century as a by-product of the then thriving Wiltshire bacon industry. It should be cooked slowly, then baked (as in the recipe below) or fried until crisp and golden. English food writer Dorothy Hartley recommends serving them similar to bacon chops – with broad (fava) beans or Pease Pudding (page 76) and Parsley Sauce (page 420).

Serves: 4
Prep time: 10 minutes
Cook time: 2¼ hours
{♦}{•}

- 4 Bath chaps, uncooked
- 1 onion, quartered
- 1 carrot, quartered
- 2 bay leaves
- 1 teaspoon black peppercorns
- 1 teaspoon allspice berries
- 4 tablespoons fresh breadcrumbs
- oil, for frying (optional)
- salt and pepper

- To serve:
- freshly cooked broad (fava) beans
- Pease Pudding (page 76), optional
- Parsley Sauce (page 420), optional

* Put the Bath chaps, vegetables, bay leaves and spices into a large saucepan and cover generously with water. Bring slowly to a simmer over a low-medium heat and cook for 2 hours, or until the meat is tender. Remove the Bath chaps from the water and leave them until they are cool enough to handle.
* Preheat the oven to 200°C/400°F/Gas Mark 6.
* Put the breadcrumbs into a small bowl, add a little salt and pepper and mix together, then spread them out on a large plate. Cut the fat away from the Bath chaps and press the cut-side down into the breadcrumbs to coat.
* Put them onto a large baking sheet and bake in the oven for 10–15 minutes until crisp. Alternatively, fry them in oil in a large frying pan or skillet over a medium heat for 7 minutes on each side until crisp. Serve with cooked broad (fava) beans or Pease Pudding and Parsley Sauce.

UNITED KINGDOM
*

GLAZED GAMMON

A classic Christmas ham with a sweetly spiced glaze; carve into slices and serve alongside the stuffing of your choice. Left-over gammon (ham) will keep for at least a few days after serving, which should give you plenty of time to fit in a number of good ham and mustard, or ham and Pease Pudding (page 76) sandwiches – a definite perk of making your gammon for Christmas.

Serves: 6 with plenty of left-overs
Prep time: 20 minutes, plus 30–45 minutes resting
Cook time: about 4½ hours
{♠}{♦}{•}

- 1 piece gammon, skin on, at least 3 kg/6½ lb
- bouquet garni of 6 bay leaves, 4 sprigs thyme, 1 bunch parsley stalks (use the parsley for Parsley Sauce, page 420), tied together with kitchen string
- 2 teaspoons black peppercorns
- 3 blades mace
- 2 carrots, chopped
- 2 onions, halved
- 4 stalks celery, chopped
- about 25 cloves

- For the glaze:
- 2 tablespoons English mustard or any smooth mustard
- 4 tablespoons soft brown sugar or honey, or Redcurrant or Quince Jelly (page 434), or marmalade, or even reduced pineapple juice from a can of pineapples
- 1 teaspoon mixed spice
- 4 tablespoons double (heavy) cream (optional)

* Put the gammon into a large saucepan and cover with cold water. Bring slowly to a bare simmer over a low-medium heat (it will take about 45 minutes). Skim away any scum with a ladle or slotted spoon, and when clear, add the bouquet garni, peppercorns, mace and vegetables. Cover with a lid and simmer on a very low heat for 1 hour per 1 kg/2¼ lb minus 30 minutes (3 kg/6½ lb would be 2½ hours). Leave in the pan for 30 minutes to cool slightly, then remove and set aside. Keep the stock for soup.
* Meanwhile, preheat the oven to 180°C/350°F/Gas Mark 4.
* To make the glaze, put all the glaze ingredients into a medium bowl and mix together. If using a jelly, melt it in a saucepan first over a low heat for 1–2 minutes.
* Remove the skin from the gammon, keeping on plenty of fat, then, using a sharp knife, carefully score a diamond pattern into the fat, being careful not to cut into the meat. Put a clove into the intersection between each diamond and liberally brush the glaze all over the gammon. Put the gammon onto a trivet in a large roasting pan and bake in the oven for 30 minutes, or until shiny and brown at the edges, basting once or twice during the roasting time. Remove from the oven, cover loosely with aluminium foil and leave to rest for 30–45 minutes before slicing (it remains piping hot for about 2 hours).

GAMMON STEAKS
WITH
FRIED EGGS AND CHIPS

Serve this pub classic with green peas and a few tomatoes halved and grilled (broiled). No extra marks for fancy presentation – this is all about simple satisfaction.

Serves: 4
Prep time: 15 minutes
Cook time: 15 minutes
{ఎ}

- 1 tablespoon bacon fat or lard, plus an extra 20 g/¾ oz (4 teaspoons) (optional), for frying
- 4 gammon (ham) steaks, cut about 1 cm/½ inch thick, about 125 g/4¼ oz each
- 4 eggs (optional)

- To serve:
- 1 quantity Chips (page 84)
- 1 quantity Parsley Sauce (page 420), optional

* Preheat the oven to 80°C/176°F/lowest Gas Mark.
* Melt the fat in a large frying pan or skillet over a medium-high heat, add the gammon (ham) steaks and fry for 10 minutes, or until golden brown and cooked through. Flip the steaks halfway through frying to ensure an even cook. Transfer to a baking sheet or ovenproof plate and keep warm in the oven.
* If eating with eggs, heat about 20 g/¾ oz (4 teaspoons) extra fat in the frying pan or skillet over a medium heat, add the eggs and fry, basting them constantly with the fat for 1 minute, or until the egg whites have lost their translucency. Sit an egg on top of the gammon steak and serve with the Chips and Parsley Sauce, if desired.

BACON CHOPS
WITH
PARSLEY SAUCE

Bacon chops – thick, fatty, crispy – work very well with fluffy Mashed Potatoes (page 80) and a gentle, creamy Parsley Sauce (page 420). A satisfying, soothing combination, which would also benefit from steamed or buttered cabbage.

Serves: 4
Prep time: 10 minutes
Cook time: 45 minutes
{ఎ}

- 1 quantity Parsley Sauce (page 420)
- 1 quantity Mashed Potatoes (page 80)
- 4 bacon chops with fat attached, about 2 cm/¾ inch thick
- 50 ml/1¾ fl oz (3½ tablespoons) cider or water

* Make the Parsley Sauce following the recipe on page 420. It may be easier to make the Parsley Sauce in advance and simply keep warm or reheat when ready.
* Start to make the Mashed Potatoes following the recipe on page 80.
* When the potatoes are two-thirds of the way through boiling, put a heavy frying pan or skillet over a medium heat.
* Put the chops into the pan with the ridge of fat against the pan and cook for several minutes to render the fat until it has become crispy – it should render enough fat to fry the chops. Turn the chops onto one side and cook for 3–4 minutes, before turning again and cooking the other side for the same time.
* When they are cooked, remove from the pan and set aside, then add the cider or water to the pan and stir over the heat, scraping up all the crispy bits that are stuck on the bottom of the pan. Tip it into the Parsley Sauce and pour into a jug (pitcher) or sauce boat. Serve the chops with the sauce and Mashed Potatoes on the side.

DEVILS ON HORSEBACK

The name of this classic British appetizer is a clear allusion to the more famous Angels on Horseback (page 126) and is made from stoned (pitted) and stuffed prunes wrapped in a layer of bacon. Whereas angels have a pearly white filling (oysters), the prunes in this recipe turn a deep, dark purple that's nearly black – and perhaps where the contrasting name comes from.

Serves: 4
Prep time: 10 minutes, plus 30 minutes soaking
Cook time: 10 minutes
{ 🦴 } { 🧂 } {ఎ}

- 16 stoned (pitted) prunes
- 200 ml/7 fl oz (¾ cup plus 1 tablespoon) strong brewed hot black tea
- 16 roasted almonds
- 8 rashers (slices) streaky (lean) bacon

* Put the prunes into a medium bowl, pour in the tea and leave to soak for 30 minutes until plump. Put 16 cocktail sticks or toothpicks into another bowl, cover with water and leave to soak for 15–30 minutes. This prevents them burning during cooking.
* Preheat the grill (broiler) to medium-high.
* Drain the soaked prunes and stuff each one with an almond.
* Cut the bacon rashers (slices) in half, then wrap each prune with each half strip and secure with a soaked cocktail stick or toothpick. Brush with water to prevent burning, then place onto a baking sheet and grill (broil) for 10 minutes, or until the bacon is crispy, turning once to ensure it has cooked evenly. Serve immediately.

Bacon chops with parsley sauce

NORTH OF WALES
*

TATWS PUM MUNUD
'A FIVE-MINUTE DISH'

This Welsh stew is actually made in a deep frying pan or skillet with thin layers of bacon, onion and potato cooked down in a rich gravy. Despite the name, it will take quite a bit longer than five minutes to cook!

Serves: 4
Prep time: 15 minutes
Cook time: 45 minutes
{🍳}{🌶}{🍲}

- 60 g/2¼ oz (4 tablespoons) lard or butter
- 100 g/3½ oz (½ cup) dry-cured bacon rashers (slices), chopped
- 2 onions, sliced
- 500 g/1 lb 2 oz potatoes, peeled and cut into 1 cm/ ½ inch thick slices
- 500 ml/17 fl oz (2 cups plus 1 tablespoon) beef stock
- 125 g/4¼ oz (1 cup minus 2 teaspoons) peas, fresh, or defrosted (optional)
- salt and pepper

* Melt the fat in a large sauté pan or deep frying pan or skillet over a medium heat, add the bacon and fry for 3–4 minutes, or until its fat has rendered. Add the onions and cook for another 10–12 minutes until golden and soft and the bacon is a little crispy.
* Remove the pan from the heat and arrange the potatoes in a single layer on top of the bacon and onion mixture. Season with salt and pepper and pour in the beef stock. Return to the heat, cover with a lid and bring to a simmer over a medium heat. Cook for 30 minutes, or until the potatoes are tender, stirring occasionally and breaking the potatoes slightly as you go. Add the peas (if using) about 5 minutes before serving.

ENGLAND: LINCOLNSHIRE
*

STUFFED CHINE OF PORK

A speciality of Lincolnshire, cured pork neck chine is scored and stuffed with finely chopped parsley, then slowly simmered. Once cooked, the chine is allowed to cool completely before it is served in thin slices. In addition to parsley, the chine was traditionally stuffed with a number of herbs and foraged plants, such as thyme, marjoram, sage and even nettles and blackcurrant leaves.

Serves: 6
Prep time: 30 minutes, plus 2–3 hours cooling
Cook time: 3 hours
{🍳}{🔪}{🌶}

- 1 x 2-kg/4½-lb piece cured pork chine
- 1 leek, sliced
- 1 bunch flat-leaf parsley, leaves chopped, stems removed
- 1 teaspoon thyme leaves
- 2 tablespoons chopped mint leaves (optional)
- 2 tablespoons chopped sage leaves (optional)

* Lay the pork in front of you with the fatty-side down. Using a very sharp knife, make deep cuts, about three-quarters of the way through, across the chine, spaced about 1.5 cm/⅝ inch apart. The cuts should be deep but stop at the fatty part, or about 2 cm/¾ inch away.
* Put the remaining ingredients into a food processor and blend until it becomes a fairly dry mixture, then spoon it into the cuts to fill. Wrap the meat securely in a large piece of muslin (cheesecloth) or a clean dish towel and put it into a large saucepan or stockpot. Cover with water and bring to a bare simmer over a low heat. Cook for 3 hours, or until tender.
* Remove the meat from the pan and leave to cool for 2–3 hours under a weight – a plate with a few cans on it should be enough. When cooled, slice thinly and serve.

UNITED KINGDOM
*

GRILLED PORK CHOPS
WITH
APPLE SAUCE

When serving pork chops, there will be no overpowering sauces or marinades to hide the inherent flavours of the meat, so buy the best quality possible and don't shy from a nice rib of fat. Grill (broil) until the meat is golden brown on both sides, but still soft and juicy in the middle. Serve with Mashed or Boiled New Potatoes (pages 80 and 84), together with English mustard and Apple Sauce (page 414).

Serves: 4
Prep time: 5 minutes, plus overnight brining
Cook time: 12 minutes
{🍳}{🔪}{🌶}{🍴}

- 40 g/1½ oz (2 tablespoons plus 2 teaspoons) salt
- 4 loin chops on the bone, 240–250 g/8–9 oz, about 2 cm/¾ inch thick
- olive oil, for rubbing
- salt and pepper

- To serve:
- Apple Sauce (page 414)
- Mashed Potatoes (page 80) or Boiled New Potatoes (page 84)
- English mustard

* Put the salt into 200 ml/7 fl oz (¾ cup plus 1 tablespoon) water in a large bowl and stir to dissolve. Add the pork chops, cover with clingfilm (plastic wrap) and leave in the fridge overnight.
* The next day, preheat the grill (broiler) to high. Remove the pork chops from the brine and pat dry with paper towels. Rub a little olive oil over the chops and then rub in salt and pepper.
* Arrange on a grill (broiler) tray and grill (broil) 6–7 cm/ 2½–2¾ inches below the heat source. Cook, turning the chops occasionally, for 12 minutes, or until golden brown and cooked all the way through. Test by inserting a skewer into the thickest part of a chop for a few seconds, then remove and check if it is hot. Leave to rest for a few minutes before serving with Apple Sauce, Mashed Potatoes or Boiled New Potatoes, and some English mustard.

Stuffed chine of pork

UNITED KINGDOM
*
ROAST SUCKLING PIG
ROAST SUCKING PIG

A whole roast suckling pig brings an element of spectacle and makes the perfect show and feast for any special occasion. The crackling skin and soft, giving meat bring a peerless primal joy. The pig is a belly-filling centrepiece, so there is less fanfare about what to serve alongside it, but Apple Sauce (page 414) and a good rich Gravy (page 420) will be very much appreciated. Save left-overs for breakfast the next morning (or early that night), to be served on fresh Breakfast Rolls (page 276).

Serves: 6
Prep time: 45 minutes, plus 30–40 minutes resting
Cook time: about 3 hours 20 minutes

{⌄•⌄}

- 60 g/2¼ oz (½ stick) butter
- 125 g/4¼ oz dry-cured streaky (lean) bacon, diced
- liver, heart and kidneys of the pig, sinews removed and chopped
- 1 onion, chopped
- 2 cloves garlic, chopped
- 6 sage leaves, chopped
- 500 g/1 lb 2 oz mushrooms, chopped
- 250 g/9 oz sausage meat
- 250 g/9 oz (5 cups) fresh breadcrumbs
- 2 eggs, lightly beaten
- 1 oven-ready suckling pig, about 4.5 kg/9 lb 15 oz
- 1–2 tablespoons olive oil
- salt and pepper

- To serve:
- Apple Sauce (page 414)
- Gravy (page 420)

* Preheat the oven to 240°C/475°F/Gas Mark 9, or as high as it will go. Heat the butter in a large frying pan or skillet over a medium heat, add the bacon and fry slowly for 15 minutes, or until crisp. Remove using a slotted spoon and set aside in a bowl. Increase the heat to high, add the pig's offal and fry for 5 minutes. Remove using a slotted spoon and set aside with the bacon.
* Reduce the heat to medium, add the onion, garlic and sage and fry for 12–15 minutes until golden and soft. Tip in the mushrooms, increase the heat to high and cook the mixture for 5 minutes, or until it is quite dry. Tip it into the bowl, then add the sausage meat and mix together, Add the breadcrumbs, a little salt and pepper, and the eggs and stir in lightly.
* Loosely fill the cavity of the pig with the stuffing, then stitch it closed using strong kitchen string. Cover the pig with the olive oil and rub in at least 1 tablespoon of salt, so that the pig is lightly covered all over. Weigh the pig to calculate its roasting time, allowing 35 minutes per 1 kg/2¼ lb. Put the pig into a large roasting pan and roast for 30 minutes, then reduce the oven temperature to 180°C/350°F/Gas Mark 4 and cook for the remainder of its cooking time. Leave the meat to rest for 30–40 minutes before carving. Serve with Apple Sauce and Gravy.

UNITED KINGDOM
*
ROAST LOIN OF PORK

A roast loin with crisp crackling skin – the prospect conjures such a pleasing image. It can be an art to get the skin crisp and crunchy without the meat getting too tough. There is less dogma around the serving of roast pork loin than with other roasts, but the traditional tracklements are no bad choice: a bowl of Apple Sauce (page 414), a loaf pan of Sage and Onion Stuffing (page 243), potatoes of your choosing and some sweet Braised Red Cabbage (page 68). In colder months, no one would fault you if you wanted to forgo all the other sides for a belly-filling Pease Pudding (page 76). In either case, a jar of English mustard is most welcome.

Serves: 6
Prep time: 10 minutes, plus 20 minutes resting
Cook time: 2 hours

{⌄•⌄}

- 1 pork loin, about 2 kg/4½ lb
- 1–2 teaspoons rapeseed (canola) oil
- 1 heaped teaspoon salt
- 1 onion, thickly sliced
- 2 bay leaves
- 200 ml/7 fl oz (¾ cup plus 1 tablespoon) chicken or beef stock
- 1 heaped teaspoon plain (all-purpose) flour
- 50 ml/1¾ fl oz (3½ tablespoons) cider
- pepper

- To serve:
- Apple Sauce (page 414)
- Sage and Onion Stuffing (page 243)
- potatoes of choice
- Braised Red Cabbage (page 68)

* Preheat the oven to 240°C/475°F/Gas Mark 9, or as high as it will go. Using a sharp knife, score the pork loin skin, then rub in the oil followed by the salt. Season with pepper. Arrange the onion slices in the centre of a large roasting pan, then add the bay leaves and sit the pork on top. Calculate the roasting time, allowing 40 minutes per 1 kg/2¼ lb plus 20 minutes. Put the pork into the oven and roast for 20 minutes. Reduce the oven temperature to 180°C/350°F/Gas Mark 4 for the remainder of its roasting time.
* Take the pan out of the oven, put the pork onto a chopping (cutting) board and leave to rest for around 20 minutes while you make the gravy.
* Heat the stock in a saucepan over a medium heat for 5 minutes, or until hot. Put the roasting pan on the stove over a medium heat and scrape the sides and bottom to catch any of the flavourful bits left in the pan, then pour the roasting juices into a small saucepan and heat over a medium heat. Whisk in the flour and cook for 2 minutes before whisking in the cider. When smooth, add half the hot stock, whisking until smooth, then add the remaining stock and stir again. Leave to bubble gently for 5 minutes before straining into a sauce boat or jug (pitcher). Serve the pork with the gravy, Apple Sauce, Sage and Onion Stuffing, potatoes and Braised Red Cabbage.

Roast loin of pork

UNITED KINGDOM
*

BRAWN
HEAD CHEESE

Brawn is a British terrine, typically made from pig's head, which has been a favourite of both court and country for several centuries. To make brawn, the pig's head is split, prepared and cooked down slowly with a mixture of herbs and spices before being set in its own naturally forming jelly. It is not uncommon to also find recipes for farmhouse brawns made from the white meat of rabbits, or even sheep's head – as a by-product of Powsowdie (page 53). Brawn should be eaten cold, in slices, with English mustard, pickles and good bread.

Serves: at least 6
Prep time: 40 minutes, plus 2–3 days brining
and 9–13 hours chilling
Cook time: 4 hours
{⚱}{🔪}{⭒}

- 1 split pig's head, brain removed
- 3 pig's trotters (feet), split
- 6 litres/203 fl oz (24 cups) Brine (page 189)
- 4 onions, quartered
- 8 cloves
- 4 large carrots, cut lengthways
- 6 stalks celery, cut into 10 cm/4 inch pieces
- 1 whole head garlic, cut in half across its width
- 1 lemon, halved
- 1 small bunch thyme
- 4 sprigs rosemary
- 4 bay leaves
- 2 tablespoons chopped flat-leaf parsley
  or chives or a mixture (optional)
- 2 blades mace
- ½ teaspoon black peppercorns, crushed
- 12 juniper berries, crushed
- 2 teaspoons salt
- 1 tablespoon cider vinegar

* If not already done, clean the head and remove any hairs with a razor or chef's torch. Cut off the ears from the head. Make the Brine following the recipe on page 189, then pour into a large container and add the ears and head. Cover with a lid and leave to brine in the fridge for 2–3 days.
* Remove the ears and head, discarding the brine, and rinse under cold running water. Put them into a large saucepan, cover with water and bring to the boil over a medium heat. Boil for 1 minute, then drain and put into a clean saucepan with the remaining ingredients, except the herbs, spices and vinegar, then add fresh water to cover. Bring slowly to a bare simmer over a low-medium heat and cook for 3 hours, removing the ears after 1½ hours. Remove the head and leave to cool slightly.
* Strain the stock into a clean saucepan. Put the pan over a medium heat and cook until the liquid has reduced by a third. Remove the meat from the head and cut into neat pieces. Arrange the meat in a large terrine dish and leave to cool in the fridge for around 1 hour.
* Add the fresh herbs, spices and vinegar to the liquor and season with more pepper and salt if desired, then pour the concentrated liquor over the terrine. Cover with aluminium foil and leave to chill in the fridge overnight.

SCOTLAND /
NORTH AND SOUTHWEST OF ENGLAND
*

WHITE PUDDING
MEALY PUDDING

White puddings are sausages made principally with cereal, animal fat, onions and spices. In England they were traditionally made from pigs, and occasionally included pork fat and even meat – as in the West Country Hog's Pudding (see right).

In the east coast of Scotland, both white and black puddings (blood sausages) were originally known as 'mealy puddings', made every autumn from the blood and suet of butchered cattle – this was before farmers had a means of keeping their herds alive through winter. Over time, the phrase mealy pudding came to refer to those puddings made without blood – the white puddings. Thus, Scottish white puddings are made with beef suet and not pork fat, as in the south.

Enjoy slices of white pudding fried until lightly crisp in a Full Breakfast (page 26) or broken up and used as stuffing (like Skirlie, page 243).

Serves: 4
Prep time: 30 minutes
Cook time: 45 minutes
{⚱}{🔪}{⭒}

- 500 g/1 lb 2 oz (4¼ cups minus 2 teaspoons) oatmeal
- 2 onions, finely chopped by hand or in a food processor
- 250 g/9 oz fresh beef suet, shredded,
  or pork back fat, chopped or minced (ground)
- 1 teaspoon ground white pepper
- natural hog casings
- fat, for frying
- salt

- To serve:
- as part of a Full Breakfast (page 26), optional
- Mashed Potatoes (page 80), optional
- meat of choice (optional)

* Heat a large, dry frying pan over a medium heat, add the oatmeal and toast for 2–3 minutes until it turns a few shades darker. Transfer the oatmeal to a large bowl, add the remaining ingredients, except the casings, and 2 teaspoons salt and mix together until combined.
* Tie the casings at one end, then, using a sausage stuffing attachment or a wide-mouthed funnel, fill the casings with the mixture, making sure there is plenty of room for the oats to expand. Tie into links or leave coiled, then tie the other end.
* Bring a large saucepan of salted water to a simmer over a medium-low heat. Poach the puddings very gently for 45 minutes, pricking the casing with a pin wherever air bubbles appear. Remove with a slotted spoon and leave to drain.
* To eat, cut the puddings into slices, then heat some fat in a large frying pan over a medium heat, add the white pudding and fry for 3–4 minutes each side, or until crisp. Serve for breakfast. You can also empty the puddings out from their casings and fry like Skirlie on page 243 and serve with Mashed Potatoes and a meat of your choosing.

ENGLAND: DEVON AND CORNWALL
*

HOG'S PUDDING
GROATS PUDDING

Similar to a white pudding, hog's pudding is a fatty and well-spiced pork sausage made with rusk or whole grains or oats, which is unique to the southwest of England. Sliced and fried until golden, it is often served as part of a Full Breakfast (page 26) – in place of either white or black pudding (blood sausage).

Notes: Some regional variations include a high proportion of offal and are likened to a West Country haggis, although these are quite rare.

Makes: 12
Prep time: 20 minutes, plus 8–12 hours soaking
Cook time: 1¼ hours
{ ✎ }

- 100 g / 3½ oz (1 cup) whole oat groats
- 1 kg / 2¼ lb (4½ cups) minced (ground) pork
- 500 g / 1 lb 2 oz (2¼ cups) minced (ground) pork back fat
- 2 teaspoons salt
- 2 teaspoons ground white pepper
- 1 teaspoon dried thyme
- 200 g / 7 oz (1⅓ cups) raisins (optional)
- 1.5 m / 5 ft natural hog casings
- salt
- Full Breakfast (page 26) or fried eggs and buttered toast, to serve (optional)

* Put the groats into a large bowl, cover with water and leave to soak overnight.
* The next day, drain the groats and put into a large saucepan. Cover with water and bring to a simmer over a low-medium heat. Cover with a lid and cook for 25 minutes, or until tender. Drain and leave the groats to cool slightly.
* Put the cooled groats into a food processor with the pork, back fat, salt, pepper and thyme and pulse until the mixture is smooth but still has a bit of texture. Mix in the dried fruit (if using) using a wooden spoon.
* To stuff the filling into the natural casings, tie the casings at one end, then, using a wide-mouthed funnel, stuff the mixture in to loosely fill the casings, removing as many air bubbles as possible. Tie loosely at the other end. You should have enough to make 12.
* Bring a large saucepan of salted water to a simmer over a medium-low heat. Poach the puddings very gently for 45 minutes, pricking the casing with a pin wherever air bubbles appear. Remove with a slotted spoon and leave to drain.
* Once the puddings are poached, they are ready to eat, but if desired, leave them to cool in the fridge and use later (they will keep for 3 days), or slice and fry them in lard or oil in a frying pan over a medium heat for 2 minutes on each side. Serve with a Full Breakfast (page 26) or with fried eggs and buttered toast.

WALES / ENGLAND: MIDLANDS
*

FAGGOTS
SAVOURY DUCKS

These rich and earthy offal meatballs are a favourite of the Midlands and across Wales, where they originated as a traditional method of utilizing the offcuts of a pig. They are typically made from a base mix of pig's liver and pork belly – to which herbs, spices, breadcrumbs and sometimes more meat are added. The meatballs are then wrapped in a webby intestinal fat called the caul and baked in a rich beef stock.

Many historical cookbooks praise faggots for being economical but they are rather luxurious and can be made with not only pork, but also beef, lamb and even venison. Provided that the meat used is well-sourced, they will far surpass the homespun meatball in deliciousness.

Serve faggots with an Onion Gravy made from their braising liquid (page 420), along with Minted Peas (page 68) and Mashed Potatoes (page 80) or swede (rutabaga).

Serves: 6
Prep time: 40 minutes, plus 90 minutes soaking
Cook time: 50 minutes
{ 🔪 } { ✎ }

- caul fat
- 500 g / 1 lb 2 oz pig's or lamb's liver
- 500 g / 1 lb 2 oz boneless, skinless belly pork
- 200 g / 7 oz smoked streaky (lean) bacon
- 1 pig's or 2 lambs' hearts
- 100 g / 3½ oz (¾ cup plus 2 teaspoons) oatmeal or breadcrumbs
- 6 sage leaves, chopped
- ½ teaspoon dried or fresh thyme leaves
- ¼ teaspoon ground mace
- ¼ teaspoon ground allspice
- ¼ teaspoon ground black pepper
- 1 teaspoon sea salt
- about 1.5 litres / 50 fl oz (6¼ cups) beef stock
- salt

- To serve:
- Minted Peas (page 68)
- Mashed Potatoes (page 80)

* Put the caul fat into a bowl, cover with salted water and leave to soak as directed on page 155.
* Preheat the oven to 160°C / 325°F / Gas Mark 3.
* Cut the meat and offal and process them together on the coarse plate of a mincer (grinder) positioned over a large bowl. Add the remaining ingredients to the bowl, except the caul fat and stock, and mix together. Shape the mixture into 100 g / 3½ oz portions. You should have about 12.
* Lay the soaked caul fat out on a clean work counter and cut into 12 equal squares. Spoon the meatball mixture onto the caul fat squares and wrap the fat around each mixture. Arrange in a medium roasting pan, with the ends of the caul fat wrapped underneath each faggot. Pour over enough beef stock to come halfway up the faggots and bake in the oven for 50 minutes. Drain the stock, setting some aside for gravy, and skimming away the fat. Serve with Minted Peas and Mashed Potatoes.

UNITED KINGDOM
*

BEEF WELLINGTON

Embraced widely as a British dish, the Wellington is almost certainly a close adaptation of the French *fillet du boeuf en croute*. The 'Wellington' name itself has dubious origins as well, stemming not from the famous eponymous Duke, but from American cookbooks of the early twentieth century. The recipe was first published in British cookbooks of the 1970s, and in the last several decades many myths have spawned seeking to tie the dish to the military commander. However dubious those stories are, or how 'British' this dish is, they make it no less enjoyable – the lavish centrepiece of any occasion.

An impressive party dish and a feat for the aspiring home cook, a Beef Wellington consists of a piece of fillet (tenderloin) wrapped in pâté or mushroom duxelles and baked in an immaculate pastry crust. It is served in thick slices, with the centre still a warm pink. Tradition dictates it should be served alongside a Madeira sauce made with beef stock, however a horseradish sauce – as suggested by English food writer Caroline Conran – makes just as much sense.

Serves: 6 generously
Prep time: 1 hour, plus 1¼ hours resting
Cook time: 1 hour 40 minutes
{⌀}

- 1 quantity Rough Puff Pastry (page 247), made with 400 g/14 oz (3⅓ cups) strong white flour
- 1 onion, chopped
- 300 g/11 oz chestnut (cremini) mushrooms
- 1 handful flat-leaf parsley leaves
- 60 g/2¼ oz (½ stick) butter
- 100 ml/3½ fl oz (⅓ cup plus 1 tablespoon) red wine
- 2 tablespoons beef dripping or lard
- 1.5 kg/3¼ lb piece beef fillet (tenderloin), centre-cut
- plain (all-purpose) flour, for dusting
- several slices Parma ham or prosciutto (optional)
- 75–100 g/2½–3½ oz chicken liver pâté (optional)
- 1 egg beaten with ½ teaspoon salt, for egg wash
- salt and pepper

- For the pancakes (optional):
- 150 g/5 oz (1¼ cups) plain (all-purpose) flour
- 1 egg
- 300 ml/10 fl oz (1¼ cups) full-fat (whole) milk
- 1 teaspoon rapeseed (canola) oil per pancake

* Line a large baking sheet with baking (parchment) paper and set aside. Make the pastry following the recipe on page 247 and leave to rest for 30 minutes before using.
* For the pancakes (if using), sift the flour into a large bowl, add the egg and milk and whisk together to form a completely smooth batter.
* Heat a large frying pan or skillet over a medium-high heat, add the oil, enough to just coat the pan, pouring away any excess, then add a ladleful of the batter. Turn or angle the pan to let the batter coat the bottom of the pan completely and cook for 2 minutes, or until the bottom is golden brown. Turn over and cook the other side for another 2 minutes. Transfer to a plate and repeat with the remaining batter. You should have enough to make 3–4 pancakes. They don't need to be kept warm.
* For the Wellington's duxelles filling, put the onion, mushrooms and parsley leaves into a food processor and blend coarsely. Melt the butter in a large frying pan or skillet over a medium heat, add the onion mixture and fry, seasoning well with salt and pepper, for 20 minutes, or until quite dry. Add the wine, increase the heat and cook for 15 minutes, or until the pan is dry. Transfer to a medium bowl and leave to cool.
* Wipe the pan clean, put over a high heat and render the dripping. Add the beef fillet (tenderloin) to the pan and cook for 30 seconds on each side, or until browned all over. Transfer to a plate and leave to cool.
* Roll out the pastry on a lightly floured work counter into a rectangle large enough to roll the beef up, about 7–8 cm/2¾–3¼ inches longer than the beef, and wide enough to wrap with about 2 cm/¾ inch of overlap. This exact measure will vary from cut to cut. Remember, the beef will shrink a little when cooked.
* If using the pancakes or thin slices of Parma ham or prosciutto, line the pastry with them. Spread over the pâté (if using) followed by the mushroom mixture. Remember, only the mushroom mixture is essential, so if you are not feeling particularly extravagant, feel free to leave out the other additions.
* Put the beef on top and roll it up in the pastry, cutting off any excess. Bind the seam with some egg wash, then turn it over so the seam is on the bottom and the ends are tucked underneath the Wellington. Seal with egg wash and cut off any excess pastry.
* Put onto the prepared baking sheet and brush all over with egg wash. Cover with clingfilm (plastic wrap) and put into the fridge for 45 minutes to firm up.
* Preheat the oven to 200°C/400°F/Gas Mark 6.
* Remove the Wellington from the fridge and score a pattern on the top, if desired. Bake in the oven for 50 minutes until golden brown, then leave to rest for 20 minutes before slicing.
* **Notes:** You can make a smaller Wellington using a third of the ingredients, and cooking for about 30 minutes.

ENGLAND
*

FORCEMEAT BALLS
OLD ENGLISH 'MEATBALLS'

Forcemeats are traditional English mixtures of meat or fish that are used as stuffing or cooked as small meatballs to be served alongside meat or in stews or savoury pies. The notion of 'forcing' stretches back to medieval times and the earliest English cookbooks but has actually survived to become the foundation of what we know today as stuffing. Forcemeat, however, is an even broader concept than today's stuffing, as evidenced by a full page of suggestions made by English cookery writer Nell Heaton in her 1947 work *The Complete Cook*. Heaton suggests making forcemeat using a base of anything from breadcrumbs and potatoes to minced (ground) beef and minced mushrooms. She offers nearly two dozen recommendations for flavourings. As such, the recipe below should be used primarily as a starting point and an inspiration for your own experimentation.

Serves: 6
Prep time: 15 minutes
Cook time: 10 minutes
{♨}{⌀}{✕}

- 125 g/4¼ oz streaky (lean) bacon, smoked or unsmoked
- 250 g/9 oz (5 cups) fresh breadcrumbs
- 90 g/3¼ oz beef suet, shredded
- 1 tablespoon chopped flat-leaf parsley
- 1 teaspoon chopped thyme or winter savory
- grated zest of ½ lemon
- 1 egg
- lard for frying (optional)
- 1 poultry, rabbit or hare liver (optional)

* Finely chop the bacon in a food processor or using a sharp knife, then put it into a large bowl and add the breadcrumbs, suet, herbs and grated lemon zest and gently mix together. Beat the egg in a small bowl, then add it to the mixture and combine thoroughly.
* Roll the mixture into 30–40 g/1–1½ oz balls using a dessertspoon for consistency. The forcemeat balls can then be fried in a little lard in a large frying pan or skillet for 5 minutes, or until golden brown, and used as required.
* Notes: If serving the balls with poultry, rabbit or hare, you can mash the liver of the animal with a fork and gently mix it in with the beaten egg.

WALES / ENGLAND
*
HASLET

This traditional country meatloaf is made from minced (ground) pork and offal and baked in a wrapping of caul fat. It should be served in slices with sharp mustard, Piccalilli (page 446) or chutney, and a mustardy Watercress Salad (page 62). Haslet slices also make great light lunches or they can be fried as a breakfast sausage or served in a sandwich.

Makes: 1 loaf
Prep time: 20 minutes
Cook time: 1 hour
{ ᴗ• }

- 150 g/5 oz (3 cups) fresh breadcrumbs
- about 75 ml/2½ fl oz (⅓ cup) full-fat (whole) milk
- 500 g/1 lb 2 oz (2¼ cups) minced (ground) pork
- 250 g/9 oz pig's liver, minced (ground) or chopped (optional)
- 250 g/9 oz unsmoked streaky (lean) bacon, minced (ground) or chopped
- 1 onion, very finely chopped
- ½ teaspoon ground mace
- ½ teaspoon ground nutmeg
- ½ teaspoon dried sage
- salt and pepper

- To serve:
- crusty bread
- English mustard
- pickle

* Preheat the oven to 180°C/350°F/Gas Mark 4. Line a 900 g/2 lb loaf pan with baking (parchment) paper.
* Put the breadcrumbs into a large bowl, pour in the milk and leave to soak for 10 minutes, then drain the excess liquid.

* Put the soaked breadcrumbs into a large bowl with the remaining ingredients and mix together. Season with salt and pepper. Pack the mixture into the prepared loaf pan and level the top with the flat side of a knife or spatula.
* Bake in the oven for 1 hour, or until the meatloaf is hot to touch and well-browned on top. If using a meat thermometer, the temperature should read 72°C/162°F. Eat immediately or leave to cool and serve later.

ENGLAND
*
BEEF OLIVES

An 'olive' – in this sense at least – is a British culinary term for a thin roll of meat, wrapped around a filling of stuffing or even sausage meat and cooked in gravy. It is a dish that stretches back to at least the 1600s (The Compleat Cook, 1658), if not even further, to medieval times as The Oxford Companion to Food suggests.
Traditionally made with any cut of red meat, today beef olives are the most common by far, and make a wonderfully comforting, warming winter meal. They should be served with their own gravy, steamed vegetables and creamy Mashed Potatoes (page 80).

Serves: 4
Prep time: 30 minutes
Cook time: 1 hour 10 minutes
{ ᴗ• }

- 6 large thin slices beef rump (round)
- 6 tablespoons fresh breadcrumbs
- 50 g/2 oz (¼ cup) shredded beef suet
- 2 anchovy fillets, chopped
- 1 onion, chopped
- grated zest of 1 lemon
- 1 tablespoon chopped flat-leaf parsley
- ½ teaspoon chopped thyme leaves
- 1 egg
- 30 g/1 oz (2 tablespoons) beef dripping or lard
- 300 ml/10 fl oz (1¼ cups) beef stock
- salt and pepper

- To serve:
- steamed vegetables
- Mashed Potatoes (page 80)

* Preheat the oven to 180°C/350°F/Gas Mark 4.
* Use a steak tenderizer or a rolling pin to flatten the slices of beef and make them as thin as possible.
* Put the remaining ingredients, except the fat and stock, into a large bowl and mix together to make a stuffing. Season with salt and pepper and divide the mixture equally into 6 portions. Spoon the stuffing into the centre of the beef slices, roll each slice up lengthways and secure with a cocktail stick or toothpick or small skewer.
* Heat the fat in a large frying pan or skillet over a medium-high heat, add the beef olives and fry for 2 minutes on each side, or enough for each side to colour. Arrange in a large baking dish and pour over the stock. Bake in the oven for 1 hour, or until tender. Serve with steamed vegetables and Mashed Potatoes.

UNITED KINGDOM
*

RISSOLES OF BEEF

Rissoles are a delicious reprisal of left-over roast beef: finely chopped or minced (ground), then fried. Serve with any left-over gravy and Champ (page 81) made from cold roast or boiled potatoes.

Makes: 12
Prep time: 15 minutes
Cook time: 10 minutes

{♨}{✗}

- 500 g/1 lb 2 oz left-over roast beef
- 250 g/9 oz (5 cups) fresh breadcrumbs
- 1 teaspoon chopped thyme
- 1 tablespoon finely chopped flat-leaf parsley
- grated zest of ½ lemon
- 1 egg, beaten with 1 tablespoon water or milk
- 30 g/1 oz (2 tablespoons) beef dripping
- left-over beef gravy, reheated, to serve

* Finely chop or mince (grind) the left-over beef and put it into a large bowl. Add the remaining ingredients, except the dripping, and combine thoroughly with your hands or using a wooden spoon. Divide the mixture into 12 equal patties, flattening them until they are about 1 cm/½ inch thick.
* Heat the dripping in a large heavy frying pan or skillet over a medium heat until melted, then add the patties, in batches if necessary, and fry for 4 minutes on each side until cooked through and golden. Serve with the hot beef gravy.

UNITED KINGDOM
*

ROAST FORERIB OF BEEF

A bone-in forerib of beef makes for a superlative roast. When selecting a piece of meat for roasting, always go bigger than you would intend: you will get more flavour and the meat will shrink a little while cooking anyway. Plus, few things are better than a lunch of cold roast beef sandwiches. When it comes to serving a roast, it's hard to improve on the classic accompaniments: a bowl of buttered cabbage or greens, crisped and fluffy Roast Potatoes (page 86), Yorkshire Puddings (page 282) warm from the oven, and a great jug (pitcher) of beef Gravy (page 420). There are times for going off-script, but this shouldn't be one of them. Don't forget a jar of English mustard or a small pot of creamy Horseradish Sauce (page 415) – this is their moment to shine.

Serves: 10
Prep time: 10 minutes, plus 30 minutes resting
Cook time: about 1½ hours

{♨}

- 1 forerib of beef on the bone with plenty of fat covering it, at least 3 ribs in size, about 3–3.5 kg/ 6 lb 10 oz–7 lb 11 oz
- 1–2 tablespoons rapeseed (canola) oil
- salt and pepper

- To serve:
- Yorkshire Puddings (page 282)
- Roast Potatoes (page 86)
- buttered cabbage
- Gravy (page 420)

* Preheat the oven to 240°C/475°F/Gas Mark 9, or as high as it will go.
* Weigh the meat and calculate the roasting time, allowing 25 minutes per 1 kg/2¼ lb for rare, 35 minutes for medium and 45 minutes per 1 kg/2¼ lb for well-done.
* Put the meat onto a trivet or clean wire rack set on top of a large roasting pan. Rub the fatty side of the meat with a little oil and season well with salt and pepper. Roast for 20 minutes, fatty-side facing up, then reduce the oven temperature to 180°C/350°F/Gas Mark 4 to cook for the remainder of its roasting time. Leave to rest for at least 30 minutes before carving. Use the dripping fat and roasting pan to make Yorkshire Puddings as it rests. Serve with Roast Potatoes, buttered cabbage and Gravy.

ENGLAND
*

BOILED BEEF
WITH
CARROTS AND SUET DUMPLINGS

Don't let anyone deign this dish as beneath them: it is simple, yes, but the marriage of flavours is both classic and incredibly warming. The slow-cooked beef is simmered (not boiled) in a meat-rich stew and later crowned with bronzed Suet Dumplings (page 244). Ladle the meat, vegetables and dumplings into shallow bowls and break apart the flaky dumplings so that they can soak up all that delicious gravy.

Serves: 6
Prep time: 30 minutes
Cook time: 3 hours

{♨}{🍲}

- 500 g/1 lb 2 oz rolled beef brisket or salted beef brisket
- 30 g/1 oz (2 tablespoons) beef dripping
- 6 carrots, peeled
- 2 stalks celery, sliced
- 1 onion, sliced
- 2 bay leaves
- 6 sprigs thyme, tied with kitchen string
- 150 ml/5 fl oz (⅔ cup) stout or red wine or beef stock
- 450 ml/15 fl oz (1⅓ cups plus 2 tablespoons) beef stock
- 1 quantity Suet Dumplings flecked with grated horseradish (page 244)
- salt and pepper

* Preheat the oven to 150°C/300°F/Gas Mark 2.
* Season the beef. Heat the dripping in a casserole dish or Dutch oven over a high heat, add the beef and cook for 6–7 minutes until browned all over. Remove the beef and set aside on a plate, then add the vegetables to the dish and cook for 5 minutes, or until browned. Add the beef back to the pan together with the bay leaves and thyme. Pour in the wine or stout (if using) and stock, then bring to a simmer, cover with a lid and cook in the oven for 2 hours.
* Meanwhile, prepare the dumplings following the recipe on page 244 and rolling into 6 balls.
* After 2 hours, increase the oven temperature to 200°C/400°F/Gas Mark 6. Remove the beef from the oven, add the dumplings, put the lid back on and return the pot to the oven. Cook for 20 minutes, then uncover and cook for another 10 minutes, or until pale golden brown.

ENGLAND: SUSSEX

*

SUSSEX STEWED STEAK

This is a very simple wholesome recipe that involves little preparation, only time. The result is a tender, juicy steak bathed in a rich gravy and ready to be served with Mashed Potatoes (page 80).

Serves: 6
Prep time: 15 minutes
Cook time: 3 hours
{♨}

- 1 onion, sliced
- 2 tablespoons plain (all-purpose) flour
- 1.2–1.5 kg/2½–3¼ lb stewing or braising steak in one piece, such as braising (chuck) steak
- 150 ml/5 fl oz (⅔ cup) port or stout, or a mixture
- 2 tablespoons Mushroom Ketchup (page 426) or Worcestershire sauce
- salt and pepper
- Mashed Potatoes (page 80), to serve

* Preheat the oven to 140°C/275°F/Gas Mark 1.
* Put the onion slices in a layer across the bottom of a casserole dish or Dutch oven.
* Put the flour into a large bowl, then add the steak and toss until coated. Put the steak onto the onion, then pour over the alcohol and ketchup and season well with salt and pepper.
* Cover tightly with a lid, using aluminium foil to make it extra secure, and stew in the oven for 3 hours, or until the steak is tender. Serve with Mashed Potatoes.

UNITED KINGDOM

*

SIRLOIN STEAKS
WITH
PEPPERCORN SAUCE

Hereford and Aberdeen Angus are just two of the many British breeds of cattle that are not only famous for the quality of their meat, but have international steakhouse chains named in their honour. Traditionally, British beef steaks were grilled (broiled) or pan-seared and basted, as they cooked, in dripping. Well-cooked quality meat shouldn't need any sauce, but for those who are insistent on it, a creamy Peppercorn Sauce (page 418) is most common.

Serves: 2
Prep time: 10 minutes, plus up to 2 hours resting
Cook time: 15–20 minutes
{♨}

- 2 sirloin steaks, about 250 g/9 oz each
- 1 tablespoon beef dripping
- 15 g/½ oz (1 tablespoon) butter
- 1 sprig rosemary or thyme or 1 tablespoon chopped flat-leaf parsley (optional)
- sea salt and pepper

- To serve:
- 1 quantity Peppercorn Sauce (page 418), warmed
- Roast Potatoes (page 86)
- boiled asparagus

* Pat the steaks dry with paper towels and season with sea salt. Leave to rest at room temperature for at least 30 minutes and up to 2 hours before cooking.
* Heat the dripping in a large frying pan or skillet over a high heat. Once it has fully rendered, reduce the heat to medium-high and add the butter and herbs, if using.
* Sprinkle a little pepper over each steak, then add a steak to the pan. Use a pair of kitchen tongs to set the steak on its edge to render the fat, then cook for 3–4 minutes on each side, allowing more time for thicker steaks. A meat thermometer inserted into the thickest part of the steak should read at least 52°C/126°F, and closer to 57°C/135°F (for medium rare), or 63°C/145°F (for medium). While the steak is cooking, remember to baste it regularly with the liquid fat, tilting the pan slightly so that the liquid pools at one end, then spooning it over the meat. Once the steak is cooked, remove from the pan and leave to rest for at least 5–10 minutes. It will keep cooking when taken off the heat. Repeat with the remaining steak.
* Serve with the warmed Peppercorn Sauce, Roast Potatoes, and boiled asparagus.

UNITED KINGDOM
*

ROAST SIRLOIN OF BEEF

Sirloin (top round) makes for another classic roasting piece of beef; serve as for the Roast Forerib of Beef (page 180).

Serves: generous 6, plus left-overs
Prep time: 10 minutes, plus 20 minutes resting
Cook time: 1 hour 25 minutes
{⌀}

- 1 x 2-kg/4½-lb piece boned, rolled sirloin (top round)
- ½ tablespoon beef dripping or lard
- salt and pepper

* Preheat the oven to 240°C/475°F/Gas Mark 9, or as high as it will go.
* Calculate the roasting time, allowing 25 minutes per 1 kg/2¼ lb for rare, 30 minutes per 1 kg/2¼ lb for medium and 35 minutes per 1 kg/2¼ lb for (just) well-done.
* Season the beef all over with salt and pepper. Heat the fat in a large roasting pan on the stove over a medium-high heat, then add the beef and cook for 5 minutes, or until browned all over. Transfer to the oven for 20 minutes, then reduce the oven temperature to 180°C/350°F/Gas Mark 4, for the remainder of its roasting time. Leave the beef to rest for at least 20 minutes before carving.

UNITED KINGDOM
*

BEEF POT-ROAST

To be served with ample English mustard and horseradish cream. Buttered cabbage and potatoes also make for excellent accompaniments. If you cannot find silverside of brisket, look for topside (top round) or even short ribs.

Serves: 6
Prep time: 20 minutes
Cook time: 2¼–3¼ hours
{⌀}{⌀}

- 1 x 1-kg/2¼-lb piece silverside or brisket
- 30 g/1 oz (2 tablespoons) beef dripping or butter
- 1 onion, sliced
- 2 cloves garlic, sliced
- 6 carrots, halved
- bouquet garni of 2 bay leaves, 1 sprig rosemary and 3 sprigs thyme all tied together with kitchen string
- 250 ml/8 fl oz (1 cup) red wine or beer
- 500 ml/17 fl oz (2 cups plus 1 tablespoon) beef stock
- salt and pepper

- To serve:
- English mustard
- horseradish cream

* Preheat the oven to 160°C/325°F/Gas Mark 3.
* Season the meat all over with salt and pepper. Heat the dripping or butter in a large casserole dish or Dutch oven over a medium-high heat, add the meat and cook for

5 minutes, or until browned all over. Remove from the pan and set aside.
* Reduce the heat to medium, add the onion and garlic to the pan and fry for 12–15 minutes until golden brown. Add a little more fat if the pan has dried out. Return the beef to the pan, then tuck in the carrots and bouquet garni and pour in the wine or beer and stock. Cook in the oven for 2 hours for silverside and 3 hours for brisket, or until tender. Serve with English mustard and horseradish cream.

UNITED KINGDOM
*

CORNED BEEF HASH

The term hash comes from the French *hacher* ('to chop') and is broadly used to describe small slices or chunks of meat that are stewed or fried with vegetables and, nowadays, potatoes. Many old British recipe books feature substantive chapters on a multitude of different hashes to be made from left-over meat, but today the only well-known hash is one made from corned beef. The corned beef hash became popular in the 1900s and retained its popularity due to wartime rationing, when canned corned beef was more accessible than fresh meat. Today, diners might prefer making theirs with less-processed salt beef. Serve as breakfast or lunch with fried eggs and the condiment of your choosing.

Serves: 6
Prep time: 30 minutes
Cook time: 3½ hours
{⌀}{⌀}

- 500 g/1 lb 2 oz salt beef, diced or cut into chunks
- 500 g/1 lb 2 oz potatoes, skin on
- 80 g/3 oz lard or butter, plus 60 g/2¼ oz lard or 2 tablespoons rapeseed (canola) oil
- 2 yellow onions, chopped
- 2–3 tablespoons chopped flat-leaf parsley
- 6 eggs
- salt and pepper

* Poach the salt beef following the final step of the recipe on page 184, then chop into medium pieces, about 2 cm/¾ inch.
* Cook the potatoes in a large saucepan of water for 15 minutes, or until tender. Drain, leave to cool, then cut into dice.
* Melt the 80 g/3 oz lard or butter in a large frying pan or skillet over a medium heat, add the onions and fry for 12 minutes, or until golden. Add the beef, potatoes and parsley and gently mix together. Increase the heat to medium-high, press down and cook for 3–4 minutes, until golden brown, then turn over and cook the other side in the same way. The mixture will break up when turned, but that's fine. Season with salt and pepper and transfer to a warmed bowl.
* When ready to eat, heat the 60 g/2¼ oz lard or 2 tablespoons oil in a large frying pan or skillet over a high heat, add the eggs and fry for 2 minutes, or until all the whites have turned opaque and are cooked through. Serve the hash with the fried eggs on top.

Roast sirloin of beef

SCOTLAND

*

MINCE
AND
TATTIES

Mince and tatties is a traditional Scottish dish, one of those deceptively simple ones where, as you eat, you think to yourself, 'How can this be so good?' The key is well-browned fatty beef mince (ground beef) and onions. They are cooked in a little oatmeal, then simmered in a rich beef stock and dark beer until the mixture is thick. A friend once asked me for a recipe recommendation – something 'dark and ambrosial', he said. This is just what he was after. The sort of recipe that makes you pine for cold, dreary days, just as an excuse to make this. Serve over creamy Mashed Potatoes (page 80).

Serves: 2
Prep time: 10 minutes
Cook time: 1 hour
{🔥} {◦•}

- 1 tablespoon rapeseed (canola) oil or beef dripping
- 1 large white onion, finely diced
- 1 small carrot, finely diced
- ½ small neep/swede (rutabaga), peeled and finely diced
- 350 g/12 oz (1½ cups) good-quality steak mince (ground steak), about 15% fat
- good pinch of finely chopped thyme leaves
- 15 g/½ oz (1 tablespoon) fine oatmeal
- 1 teaspoon ground white pepper
- 260 ml/8¾ fl oz (1 cup plus 2 teaspoons) Porter
- strong beef stock made from shin (shank) bones, reduced to 570 ml/19 fl oz (2¼ cups plus 1 teaspoon)
- 1 bay leaf
- 1 teaspoon Bovril
- dash of Mushroom Ketchup (shop-bought or homemade, page 426)
- dash of Worcestershire sauce (optional)
- 350 g/12 oz floury (baking) potatoes, such as Maris Piper or Yukon Gold, peeled and cut into large chunks
- 30 g/1 oz (2 tablespoons) butter
- salt

* Heat the oil or dripping in a large frying pan or skillet over a medium heat, add the onion, carrot, swede (rutabaga) and a good pinch of salt and sauté for 4–5 minutes until beginning to soften. Increase the heat slightly and add the mince (ground steak) and cook for 10 minutes, or until very well-browned, breaking up the meat with a wooden spoon as you go. Add the thyme, oatmeal and white pepper and stir in well, then cook for 5 minutes. Pour in the Porter and stir over the heat, scraping up all the bits stuck on the bottom of the pan, then add the stock, bay leaf, Bovril, Mushroom Ketchup and Worcestershire sauce, if using. Reduce the heat and simmer for 40 minutes, until the sauce has thickened and taken on a deeper colour. Check and adjust the seasoning, if necessary.
* Meanwhile, bring a large saucepan of well-salted water to the boil. Carefully add the potatoes and boil for 15–20 minutes until tender and a fork pierces easily through them. Drain, return to the pan and leave to steam-dry.
* Add the butter to the potatoes, then mash together. Check the seasoning and add salt and more butter to taste as desired. Serve the mince and tatties inelegantly.

ENGLAND: LONDON

*

SALT BEEF

British salt-brined beef is often associated with London's large Ashkenazi Jewish population. Jewish (and Irish) immigrants salted beef first out of necessity, but the tradition carried on as taste for the preparation grew. It is commonly served in thick cuts or deli-style slices.

When making salt beef, it is absolutely imperative that you use a curing salt, otherwise your beef will end up a very unappetizing grey colour. Serve boiled salt beef with carrots and Suet Dumplings (page 244), or slice into thick chunks and pile onto a bagel with English mustard and pickled cucumbers. Eat warm.

Makes: enough cure for 2–3 kg/
4½ lb–6 lb 10 oz beef brisket
Prep time: 10 minutes, plus 1 week curing
Cook time: 3–3½ hours
{◦•}

- 450 g/1 lb (1¾ cups plus 2 tablespoons) sea salt
- 50 g/2 oz (¼ cup) curing salts
- 400 g/14 oz (2 cups) soft brown sugar
- 1 teaspoon juniper berries, crushed
- 1 teaspoon black peppercorns, crushed
- 3 bay leaves
- 1 large sprig rosemary or thyme
- 1 x 2–3 kg/4½–6 lb 10 oz piece beef brisket

- To serve:
- root vegetables of choice
- Suet Dumplings (page 244)

* Put 3 litres/101 fl oz (12 cups) water, the salts and sugar into a stockpot and heat over a medium heat, stirring until the salt and sugar have dissolved. Add the remaining ingredients, except the brisket, and slowly bring to the boil. Reduce the heat and simmer for 10 minutes, then remove from the heat and leave to cool. Once cooled, strain into a large bowl.
* Put the brisket into a large saucepan or container and cover with the curing liquid. Cover with a lid and leave to cure in the fridge for at least a week, turning it regularly.
* After a week, strain, discard the curing liquid and cover the beef with fresh water. Bring to the boil, then reduce the heat and simmer for 2½–3 hours, depending on the weight of the meat, until tender. Drain and leave the beef to rest on a chopping (cutting) board before slicing and serving with root vegetables, Suet Dumplings or in slices in a sandwich.

Mince and tatties

UNITED KINGDOM
*

ALOO GOSHT
MEAT AND POTATO CURRY

A Punjabi staple curry – hearty and simple, this is still made by many Pakistani Punjabi families who migrated to Britain. Most Pakistanis would make this with mutton on the bone, but you can also use beef or lamb.

Serves: 4–6
Prep time: 12 minutes
Cook time: 50–60 minutes, plus 10 minutes resting
{🐂}{🌶}

- 1 teaspoon coriander seeds
- 50 ml/1¾ fl oz (3½ tablespoons) vegetable oil, plus 3–4 tablespoons extra
- 1 large red onion, finely chopped
- 1 cm/½ inch piece of fresh root ginger, peeled and grated
- 2 garlic cloves, very finely chopped
- 1 kg/2¼ lb stewing beef, or mutton on the bone, cut into 5–6 cm/2–2½ inch chunks
- 1–2 teaspoons salt
- ½ teaspoon ground turmeric
- 1 teaspoon plain paprika (not smoked)
- 1 teaspoon chilli powder
- 2 tomatoes, finely chopped
- 500 g/1 lb 2 oz floury (baking) potatoes, such as Maris Piper or Yukon Gold, peeled and quartered
- plain basmati rice or Naan Bread (page 275), to serve

- To garnish:
- 1 teaspoon garam masala
- 2 tablespoons chopped coriander (cilantro) leaves
- 2 fresh green chillies, finely chopped

* Put the coriander seeds into a frying pan or skillet over a medium heat and dry-roast, stirring constantly, for 30 seconds, or until they start to smell fragrant. Transfer to a spice grinder or pestle and mortar and grind to a powder.
* Heat the 50 ml/1¾ fl oz (3½ tablespoons) oil in a large saucepan with a lid over a medium heat, add the onion, ginger and garlic and cook for 7–8 minutes until the onions are light brown. Add the mutton pieces, salt, turmeric, paprika and chilli powder, then add 150 ml/5 fl oz (⅔ cup) water and reduce the heat to medium-low. Cover the pan with the lid and cook for 15–20 minutes until the mutton is tender and the curry is reddish brown, checking the water has not dried up. If it does, add about 20 ml/¾ fl oz (4 teaspoons) water to ensure that the mutton is just covered.
* Increase the heat to medium-high, add the remaining 3–4 tablespoons vegetable oil, tomatoes and reserved ground coriander. Stir-fry to allow the oil in the pan to cook the tomatoes and create a thick red sauce with oil separating and rising to the surface of the curry.
* Add the potatoes and 200–300 ml/7–10 fl oz (¾ cup plus 1 tablespoon–1¼ cups) water, depending on how watery you prefer the curry (traditionally it is quite watery), then reduce the heat to medium-low and cook for 10–15 minutes until the potatoes are tender. The curry should be red with oil rising to the surface but watery. If this has not happened yet, keep the saucepan over a very low heat for another 5–10 minutes, but make sure not to overcook the potatoes.

* Turn off the heat, cover with the lid and let the curry rest in its own heat for about 10 minutes before serving. When ready to serve, transfer to a serving dish and garnish with garam masala, chopped coriander (cilantro) and chopped green chillies. This is best served with plain basmati rice or Naan Bread.

NORTHERN IRELAND / ENGLAND
*

SPICED BEEF

Spiced beef is a riff on the traditional salt beef cure. It is usually served at Christmas time – especially in Ireland – where it either deputizes for or is served alongside a glazed Christmas ham. As with Salt Beef (page 184), some form of curing salt is essential to the meat maintaining its colour when cooked.

Serves: about 6
Prep time: 30 minutes, plus 1 week curing
Cook time: 3½ hours
{🐂}{🌶}

- 2 tablespoons black peppercorns
- 2 tablespoons allspice berries
- 2 tablespoons juniper berries
- 90 g/3¼ oz (½ cup) soft dark brown sugar
- 120 g/4 oz (½ cup) sea salt
- 50 g/2 oz (¼ cup) curing salts
- 1 x 1.5–2-kg/3¼–4½-lb piece rolled brisket
- beef stock (optional)
- plain (all-purpose) flour (optional)

* Put the spices into a pestle and mortar, spice grinder or coffee grinder and coarsely grind, then transfer to a medium bowl. Add the sugar, sea salt and curing salts and mix together. Put the beef into a tub or container and sprinkle with the curing mixture, making sure the meat is well covered. Pay attention to the sides where it is rolled – poke some mixture into those ends. Cover with a lid and leave to chill in the fridge, turning and coating every day for 1 week.
* After 1 week, preheat the oven to 140°C/275°F/Gas Mark 1. Rinse the beef under cold running water, then put it into a tight-fitting casserole dish or Dutch oven and pour in enough water to reach halfway up the sides of the beef. Cover with a lid and cook for 3½ hours.
* The beef can be eaten at this point, with the cooking liquor heated with some beef stock and thickened with plain (all-purpose) flour as a sauce. If using for cold cuts, wrap in baking (parchment) paper and chill in the fridge overnight.

SCOTLAND

SQUARE SAUSAGE
LORNE SAUSAGE/SASSERMAET

This well-spiced beef sausage is formed in a square loaf pan and fits very neatly sandwiched between bread made in the same mould, which made it a very handy packed lunch for industrial workers. The dish is especially popular in Glasgow, where it's also known by the name 'Lorne sausage'. To serve, fry and eat with breakfast, or on a buttered roll. In the words of Glasgow-born comedian Billy Connolly, 'above all, at least once in your life, have a roll and square sliced sausage and cup of tea'.
Notes: Sassermaet is a Shetland sausage very similar to Lorne sausage, although historically it was a salted beef mince (ground beef) made from Shetland kye (a native breed of cattle).

Serves: 8
Prep time: 30 minutes, plus 8–12 hours chilling
Cook time: 16–20 minutes
{🧂}{🍖}{🍳}

- ½ teaspoon ground allspice
- ½ teaspoon ground black pepper
- ½ teaspoon ground white pepper
- ¼ teaspoon ground cloves
- ¼ teaspoon grated nutmeg
- ½ teaspoon ground cinnamon
- 2 teaspoons salt
- 1.5 kg/3¼ lb (6⅔ cups) minced (ground) beef
- beef dripping or lard, for frying

* Line a 900 g/2 lb loaf pan with baking (parchment) paper or clingfilm (plastic wrap).
* Put the spices and salt into a small bowl and mix well. Put the minced (ground) beef into a large bowl, tip in the spice mixture and combine well. Pack the mixture tightly into the prepared loaf pan, then cover with clingfilm (plastic wrap) and leave to chill in the fridge overnight.
* The next day, remove from the loaf pan and cut into 1.5 cm/⅝ inch thick slices. Heat a little beef dripping in a large frying pan over a medium heat, add the slices and fry, turning occasionally, for 8–10 minutes until nicely browned on both sides. You may need to do this in batches.

NORTHERN IRELAND

NORTHERN IRISH VEGETABLE ROLL

This fatty beef sausage is traditionally made with leeks and spring onions (scallions). Unique to Northern Ireland, it is typically sliced into circles and served as part of an Ulster Fry (page 26).

Serves: 6
Prep time: 10 minutes, plus 3–12 hours chilling
Cook time: 10 minutes
{🍖}{🍳}

- 500 g/1 lb 2 oz (2¼ cups) beef mince (ground beef)
- 125 g/4¼ oz (2½ cups) fresh breadcrumbs
- 1 teaspoon salt
- ½ teaspoon ground black pepper
- ½ teaspoon mixed spice
- 3 spring onions (scallions) or 1 shallot, finely chopped
- 100 g/3½ oz cooked or left-over cooked vegetables, such as leeks, carrot, parsnip, swede (rutabaga), finely chopped (optional)
- 1 egg, beaten
- lard, beef dripping or sunflower oil, for frying

* Line a 900 g/2 lb loaf pan with clingfilm (plastic wrap) or baking (parchment) paper.
* Put all the ingredients, except the fat, into a large bowl and mix together well, using enough water, 1 tablespoon at a time, to make a cohesive sausage meat that is sticky but still firm. Pack well into the prepared loaf pan, cover with clingfilm and chill in the fridge for 3 hours, or preferably overnight, until set.
* When ready to cook the roll, remove it from the pan and cut it into 1 cm/½ inch thick slices. Heat 1 teaspoon of fat in a large frying pan or skillet over a medium heat, add the slices and fry on both sides, turning occasionally, for 8 minutes, or until cooked through. You may need to do this in batches.

SCOTLAND
*

POTTED HOUGH

In Scotland, a tough or typically undesirable cut of meat, like beef shin (shank), called 'hough', would be boiled for hours, and the slow-cooked shredded meat set in its own jelly, to later be served with buttered Oatcakes (page 260). A common variation of this recipe was potted heid, made with the meat from a sheep's head, after making Powsowdie (page 53).

The recipe below is a family one from Scottish chef Pamela Brunton, whose great-grandmother Margaret Fraser lived with her as a teen, and always kept a jar of this potted hough in the fridge. If you don't have a big enough pan to accommodate a whole beef shin, then use 450 g/ 1 lb beef shin pieces and 900 g/2 lb beef shin bone or veal knuckle pieces. You will also need proper stock, otherwise you will need to add some gelatine so the meat can set in its jelly.

Serves: 6–8
Prep time: 30 minutes, plus 1 hour resting
and 8–12 hours cooling
Cook time: 6 hours

{♠}{✦}

- 1 whole Highland beef shin (shank) on the bone,
about 1.3 kg/2 lb 13 oz
- beef, pork or chicken stock to cover the bone
- ½ teaspoon allspice berries
- ½ teaspoon black peppercorns
- 1 blade mace
- 1 bay leaf
- fine sea salt and pepper

- To serve:
- pickled items, such as onions and mustard seeds
- fresh chives, chive flowers, chervil or parsley
- thick-cut toast

* Preheat the oven to 200°C/400°F/Gas Mark 6.
* Season the shin (shank) lightly with fine salt, then put the meat onto a large baking sheet and roast in the oven for 10–20 minutes until deep brown all over. Make sure to turn the meat frequently. (If you are using the alternative – meat plus bones – then roast the bones in the oven and brown the pieces of seasoned shin in ½ tablespoon oil in a hot pan for 4–5 minutes.)
* Put the roasted meat and bones (if using) into a large stockpot and add the beef stock, topping up (topping off) with water, if necessary, to cover the bone and meat. Bring almost to the boil, skimming off any scum and excess fat that floats to the top with a slotted spoon. Reduce the heat to the gentlest shimmering simmer, add the spices and cover the surface of the liquid with a circle of baking (parchment) paper, with a little hole cut in the centre for the steam to escape.
* Simmer very gently for 4–5 hours for a whole shin on the bone or 3 hours for pieces of shin. When the meat is tender and beginning to fall off the bone, remove from the heat and leave to rest in the liquor for an hour or so.
* Transfer the meat to a tray or plate. Strain the liquor through a sieve lined with muslin (cheesecloth) into a bowl or container and leave to cool in the fridge until

any remaining fat rises to the surface and solidifies.
* Scrape the fat off the now-jellied liquor with a spoon. Return the braising liquor to a clean saucepan and cook over a medium heat for 10–12 minutes, until it has reduced by about half and is very flavourful. The potted hough is served cold, so it must be especially well-flavoured when warm.
* Meanwhile, shred the beef shin meat with your fingers into thin fibres. It should be easily soft enough. Season with fine salt and pepper and pack into moulds, either 1 large container, such as a casserole dish, or small ramekins. When the cooking liquor is reduced and flavourful, pour it over the shredded meat in its container and cover with clingfilm (plastic wrap). Chill in the fridge overnight, or until the jelly is set.
* Serve with pickled items, such as onions and mustard seeds; chives or chive flowers, chervil or parsley. Use thick toast, which must be hot, so the jelly melts and turns the bread into a delicious beefy dumpling in your very hands.

UNITED KINGDOM
*

BRAISED OXTAILS

Oxtails should be slow cooked until the meat falls off the bone. Traditionally, once braised, the oxtail would be allowed to cool overnight – the flavours will have time to saturate and deepen – and then skimmed of its top layer of fat before reheating.

Serves: 6
Prep time: 40 minutes
Cook time: 3–3½ hours

{✦}

- 4 tablespoons plain (all-purpose) flour
- 3 oxtails, trimmed of fat and cut into thick pieces
- 60 g/2¼ oz (4 tablespoons) beef dripping or lard
- ½ teaspoon smoked paprika or chilli (red pepper) flakes
- 2 carrots, chopped
- 2 onions, chopped
- 4 stalks celery, chopped
- 4 cloves garlic, lightly crushed
- bouquet garni of flat-leaf parsley stalks, 4 sprigs thyme,
2 sprigs rosemary, 4 bay leaves tied together
with kitchen string
- 1 x 750 ml/25 fl oz bottle red wine
- 400 g/14 oz can chopped plum tomatoes
- 750 ml/25 fl oz (3 cups) beef stock
- 2 tablespoons tomato purée (paste)
- 3 tablespoons chopped flat-leaf parsley leaves
- salt and pepper

- To serve:
- Mashed Potatoes (page 80)
- English mustard

* Preheat the oven to 140°C/275°F/Gas Mark 1.
* Spread the flour out on a large plate and season with 1 teaspoon each of salt and pepper. Dust the oxtail pieces in the seasoned flour before shaking off any excess.
* Melt the fat in a heavy frying pan or skillet over a medium-high heat, add the oxtail pieces and fry for 5

minutes, or until browned on all sides. Cook them slowly, and in batches if necessary. Once all the oxtail pieces are browned, transfer them to a casserole dish or Dutch oven.

* Add the paprika or chilli (red pepper) flakes, vegetables and garlic to the frying pan or skillet, then season with salt and pepper and brown them in the fat over a medium heat for 10–15 minutes. Transfer to the casserole dish or Dutch oven with the bouquet garni.

* Pour a little of the red wine into the frying pan or skillet and stir over the heat, scraping up all the crispy bits stuck on the bottom of the pan, then pour into the dish with the rest of the bottle, the plum tomatoes, beef stock and tomato purée (paste). Bring to a simmer over a low heat, then cover with a lid and braise in the oven for 2½–3 hours until the meat is tender and coming away from the bone. Remove the meat from the dish and keep warm.

* Strain the liquor into a fresh saucepan, pushing the juice out of the vegetables with a spoon and cook over a medium heat for 10–12 minutes until reduced by a third. Taste and season, then add the oxtail to the pan and heat through for 5 minutes. Sprinkle with the parsley and serve with Mashed Potatoes and sharp English mustard.

UNITED KINGDOM
*

PICKLED
AND
POACHED OX TONGUE

Ox tongue is a rich and fatty cut of beef, which was commonly pickled and preserved through winter. To serve, poach, slice thinly and serve with Damson Sauce (page 416) or Rhubarb/Damson Ketchup (page 426).

Serves: 6–8
Prep time: 15 minutes, plus 1 week curing
Cook time: 3 hours
{🦴}{🔪}{🍶}

- 1 ox tongue
- 1 onion, quartered
- 1 teaspoon black peppercorns
- 3 bay leaves
- 3 sprigs thyme
- 3 sprigs flat-leaf parsley

- For the brine:
- 500 g/1 lb 2 oz (2 cups) salt
- 500 g/1 lb 2 oz (2½ cups) dark brown sugar
- 1 teaspoon pink curing salt
- 12 juniper berries, crushed
- 12 allspice berries, crushed
- 1 teaspoon black peppercorns, crushed
- 2 bay leaves
- 6 sprigs thyme

- To serve:
- Boiled New Potatoes (page 84)
- Damson Sauce (page 416) or Rhubarb/Damson Ketchup (page 426)

* For the brine, put all the ingredients into a stockpot. Pour in 2.5 litres/85 fl oz (10 cups) water and heat over

a high heat, stirring to dissolve the salt and sugar, then reduce the heat and simmer for 15 minutes. Leave to cool, then strain into a large bowl. Add the tongue to the bowl, then put an upturned bowl over the top to keep it submerged. Leave to pickle in the fridge for 1 week.

* After 1 week, remove the tongue, rinse off the cure, and put it into a large saucepan. Cover with water and add the onion, peppercorns and herbs. Bring slowly to a bare simmer over a low heat and cook for 3 hours, skimming away any scum that rises to the top with a slotted spoon. Test if the tongue is cooked through by inserting a skewer; it should be tender enough to easily pierce.

* Remove the tongue from the pan and leave to cool slightly. Peel away the skin, cut off any gristle and neaten the tongue up at the root end. Slice thinly and serve with Boiled New Potatoes and Damson Sauce or Ketchup spooned over the slices of tongue.

UNITED KINGDOM
*

ROAST BONE MARROW ON TOAST

Hot bone marrow on toast was a popular Victorian savoury – a course that, like today's cheese course, was intended to clear the palate, and often followed sweet puddings. The bones were often cooked by steaming, although British-Italian chef Charles Francatelli parboiled his. Once cooked, the marrow was scooped out, seasoned with salt, lemon juice and flat-leaf parsley, then served on hot toast. Today, bone marrow on toast has enjoyed a great resurgence in popularity as the signature dish of iconic London restaurant St. JOHN, where the bones are roasted whole and served alongside slices of toast, a fresh parsley salad and plenty of good salt.

Serves: 4–8
Prep time: 20 minutes
Cook time: 12–15 minutes
{🦴}{🔪}{🍶}{🥄}

- 4 pieces centre-cut marrow bones, 8–10 cm/3¼–4 inches in length, split lengthways (ask your butcher to do this)

- To serve:
- Watercress Salad with Capers (page 62)
- 1 handful flat-leaf parsley, chopped
- Mustard Dressing (page 427), optional
- slices thick brown or sourdough bread, toasted

* Preheat the oven to 180°C/350°F/Gas Mark 4. Line a baking sheet with baking (parchment) paper.

* Arrange the marrow bones on the prepared baking sheet, flat-side up, and roast in the oven for 12–15 minutes until the marrow begins to melt slightly. Remove and leave to cool slightly.

* Meanwhile, prepare the Watercress Salad following the recipe on page 62 and add the parsley. Drizzle over the Mustard Dressing (if using), then serve the salad with the slices of toast and half a bone each. Spoon out the marrow onto the toast and top with some of the salad.

UNITED KINGDOM
*
CALF'S LIVER
AND
BACON

An iconic combination that is thankfully still served at greasy spoon cafés up and down the country. Use a fatty bacon so that, once fried, its rendered fat can be used to cook the liver. Serve them both together in an Onion Gravy (page 420), alongside Mashed Potatoes (page 80) or Chips (page 84) with green peas.

Serves: 4
Prep time: 20 minutes, plus 2–8 hours soaking
Cook time: 30 minutes
{ꞏ•}

- 4 slices rose calf's liver, 1 cm / ½ inch thick,
outer membrane removed
- full-fat (whole) milk
- 1 quantity Onion Gravy (page 420)
- 3 tablespoons plain (all-purpose) flour
- 40 g / 1½ oz (2 tablespoons plus 2 teaspoons) lard, plus
extra if needed
- 4 rashers (slices) smoked streaky (lean) bacon
- salt and pepper

- To serve:
- Mashed Potatoes (page 80) or Chips (page 84)
- freshly cooked peas

* Put the liver into a large bowl, add enough milk to cover, then cover with clingfilm (plastic wrap) and leave to soak in the fridge for a minimum of 2 hours or overnight.
* The next day, make the Onion Gravy following the recipe on page 420 and keep warm.
* Drain the liver and pat dry with paper towels. Spread the flour out on a plate and season with ¾ teaspoon each of salt and pepper. Toss the liver in the seasoned flour, shaking off any excess, and set aside.
* Melt the lard in a large frying pan or skillet over a medium-high heat, add the bacon and fry for several minutes until crisped. Remove and keep warm. Add the liver to the pan. If the pan has dried out, add a little more lard, but if there's bacon fat left in the pan there's no need. Increase the heat to high and flash-fry the liver for 2 minutes on each side. Add the Onion Gravy to the pan with the liver, along with the bacon, and heat through for 3–4 minutes. Serve with Mashed Potatoes or Chips and peas.

ENGLAND: LANCASHIRE
*
TRIPE
AND
ONIONS

Once beloved across the Midlands and north of England, tripe could be found at most traditional markets, where entire stalls were dedicated to its sale. More than that, Lizzie Boyd, the editor of *British Cookery* (1976) suggests that 'tripe parlours' were also the logical precursors to today's chip shops. Here is an adapted take on the classic British preparation, to be served with creamy Mashed Potatoes (page 80).

Serves: 4
Prep time: 45 minutes
Cook time: 3½ hours
{ꞏ•}

- 800 g / 1¾ lb honeycomb tripe
- 1 onion, peeled and studded with a few cloves
- 3 bay leaves
- 1 bunch flat-leaf parsley stalks

- For the onions and sauce:
- 1 tablespoon rapeseed (canola) oil
- 500 g / 1 lb 2 oz onions, sliced
- 100 g / 3½ oz (7 tablespoons) unsalted butter
- 50 g / 2 oz (6 tablespoons) plain (all-purpose) flour
- 500 ml / 17 fl oz (2 cups plus 1 tablespoon) full-fat (whole) milk
- malt vinegar, for sprinkling
- 2 tablespoons chopped flat-leaf parsley
- coarse sea salt and white pepper
- Mashed Potatoes (page 80) or bread and butter, to serve

* Put the tripe into a large saucepan, cover with cold water and add a handful of coarse salt. Bring to the boil, then drain out the water. Cover again with more cold water and bring to the boil once more. Repeat, then after the third time, fill the pan with water, add the tripe, the onion studded with cloves, the bay leaves and parsley stalks and cook over a medium heat for 3 hours, or until a knife can go through the tripe without resistance. Strain and leave to cool.
* Meanwhile, heat the oil in a clean large saucepan over a medium heat. Add the sliced onions and cook for 10–12 minutes until soft and golden. As the onions cook, cut the tripe into small pieces.
* Melt the butter in another saucepan over a medium-low heat for 2 minutes, or until foaming. Stir in the flour and cook for 2 minutes, stirring frequently to prevent lumps and without colouring. Slowly whisk in the milk, making sure it is fully combined before you add more, then simmer for 20 minutes, stirring frequently until thickened. Add the sliced onions and tripe and cook for another 20 minutes. Sprinkle with a dash of vinegar, some white pepper and chopped parsley, and serve immediately with Mashed Potatoes or bread and butter.
* Notes: You can also add ½ teaspoon chopped fresh thyme leaves, then bake this mixture under a Shortcrust Pastry (page 247) lid in an oven preheated to 220°C / 425°F / Gas Mark 7 for 25 minutes, then reduce the oven temperature to 180°C / 350°F / Gas Mark 4 and bake for another 20 minutes until golden brown.

Calf's liver and bacon

SCOTLAND
*

HAGGIS
WITH
NEEPS AND TATTIES

The haggis is a tremendous savoury pudding, and by reputation Scotland's foremost culinary export. The squeamish may recoil at its composition: sheep's offal – typically liver, heart and lungs – oatmeal, suet and spices. Traditionally, the mixture is stuffed into the sheep's stomach bag and boiled for hours. The result is rightly considered, as Scottish national poet Robert Burns deftly put it, the 'great chieftain o' the puddin' race'.

Once common to all of Britain, the haggis became a distinctly Scottish speciality in the eighteenth century. Every year on 25th January, Burns Suppers are held across Scotland, where haggis is traditionally served beside mashed neeps and tatties. A Whisky Cream Sauce (page 418) is often poured over the top, but this tradition is more recent.

Serves: at least 6 with lots for left-overs
Prep time: 2 hours
Cook time: 4½ hours
{♨}{🔪}{🍴}

- 1 sheep's stomach bag (optional)
- 1 sheep's pluck (heart, liver, lungs)
- 300 g/11 oz (2½ cups) fine or medium oatmeal
- 200 g/7 oz (1 cup plus 1 tablespoon) beef suet, shredded
- 3 onions, finely chopped
- 1 tablespoon salt
- 2 teaspoons coarsely ground pepper
- ½ teaspoon cayenne pepper (optional)
- 1 nutmeg, freshly grated
- 1 litre/34 fl oz (4¼ cups) beef stock

* If using the stomach bag, wash and rinse its inside until well cleaned. Set aside.
* Put the pluck into a large saucepan, cover with cold water and simmer over a low heat for 90 minutes. Meanwhile, toast the oats in a large, dry frying pan or skillet, stirring constantly, for 5 minutes, or until golden brown.
* Remove the lights (the lungs) from the pluck, trim away the gristle and either finely chop or mince (grind) the heart, liver and lungs into a large bowl. Add the suet, onions, salt and spices and stir in the stock. If using the stomach, fill it with the mixture and sew up the hole with a needle and thread. Alternatively, fill 1–2 pudding basins (ovenproof bowls) with the mixture, cover with baking (parchment) paper and aluminium foil and secure with kitchen string.
* If using the stomach, boil in a large saucepan of water, or if using pudding basins, steam for 3 hours. Keep checking the stomach and burst any air bubbles, making sure that the pan/steamer doesn't boil dry. Remove the haggis and leave to cool for 30 minutes.

- For the neeps and tatties:

Serves: 4
Prep time: 20 minutes
Cook time: 1¼ hours
{🍴}

- 1 x 500-g/1-lb 2-oz Haggis or 1 x 500-g/1-lb 2-oz Veggie Haggis (page 77)
- 750 g/1 lb 10 oz neeps/swede (rutabaga), peeled and cut into large chunks
- 750 g/1 lb 10 oz potatoes, such as Maris Piper, peeled and cut into large chunks
- 150 g/5 oz (1¼ sticks) butter
- salt and pepper
- 1 quantity Whisky Cream Sauce (page 418) or Gravy (page 420), to serve

* Fill a large saucepan with water and, when simmering, add the Haggis. Simmer gently over a medium-low heat for 1 hour. Halfway through the cooking time, put the swede (rutabaga) into another large saucepan and the potatoes into another, then cover both with water and simmer them for 25 minutes, or until they are very tender. Drain well, then return them to their respective pans and mash using a masher or hand-held blender. Beat half the butter into each using a wooden spoon and season with salt and pepper.
* Cut open the haggis and place a neat spoonful on each plate followed by the same of mashed potatoes and mashed swede (rutabaga). Serve with Whisky Sauce or Gravy in a jug (pitcher) or sauce boat.

WALES
*

ROAST RACK OF LAMB
WITH
LAVER SAUCE

Saltmarsh lamb and laver sauce is a classic Welsh combination. The lambs graze along Welsh coasts, eating everything from samphire and purslane to seaweed. The laver sauce accentuates those flavours in the meat.

Serves: 6
Prep time: 5 minutes
Cook time: 50–60 minutes
{♨}{🔪}{🍴}

- 2 racks of lamb of similar size (if you ask your butcher in advance they will be able to split a best end of neck to make 2 matching pieces)
- 300 ml/10 fl oz (1¼ cups) laver
- grated zest and juice of 1 orange
- squeeze of lemon juice or dash of vinegar
- salt and pepper

* Preheat the oven to 220°C/425°F/Gas Mark 7.
* Season the lamb, then put the racks into a large roasting pan leaning up against the other, the ribs crossing, like an old-fashioned tent. Cover the bones with aluminium foil to prevent them burning and roast for 45 minutes for rare, to 55 minutes for medium. Set aside to rest while you make the laver sauce.
* Heat the laver in a medium saucepan with the orange zest and juice over a medium heat for 5 minutes, or until hot. Add a squeeze of lemon or vinegar. Season with salt and pepper and pour in any juices from the roasting pan and stir in until combined. Serve with the lamb.

Haggis with neeps and tatties

UNITED KINGDOM
*

BOILED LEG OF LAMB
WITH
OYSTER STUFFING

In Victorian times, legs of lamb or mutton were often cooked at a low boil or simmer until the meat was soft and tender, then sliced and served with a white caper or white onion sauce. If the leg is tunnel-boned beforehand, then the cavity will be ideal for stuffing. This recipe pays homage to a surprisingly excellent marriage of flavours – lamb and oyster – but most any herby stuffing or forcemeat will work as well. Serve with Minted Peas (page 68) and boiled, buttered new potatoes, as well as the sauce of your choosing.
Notes: In her classic work, *English Food* (1974), Jane Grigson suggests that the flavour of the lamb leg will improve if you let it cool overnight in its own cooking liquid – a worthwhile trick if you have the time to spare.

Serves: 6
Prep time: 30 minutes
Cook time: 1½ hours
{ ᴗ }

- 1 quantity Oyster Stuffing (page 243)
- 1 leg of lamb, about 2.5 kg/5½ lb, tunnel boned (ask the butcher to do this for you)
- 2 carrots, sliced
- 2 onions, sliced
- 2 stalks celery, sliced
- 4 bay leaves
- 500 ml/17 fl oz (2 cups plus 1 tablespoon) lamb or beef stock
- 100 ml/3½ fl oz (⅓ cup plus 1 tablespoon) white wine
- 30 g/1 oz (2 tablespoons) butter
- 30 g/1 oz (3¾ tablespoons) plain (all-purpose) flour
- salt and pepper
- 1 quantity White Onion Sauce (page 418) or White Caper Sauce (page 422), to serve (optional)

* Make the Oyster Stuffing following the recipe on page 243 and set aside.
* Preheat the oven to 180°C/350°F/Gas Mark 4.
* Stuff the leg cavity with the stuffing, then fold the end of the leg over, securing with a metal skewer. Put the vegetables and bay leaves into the bottom of a large roasting pan. Sit the leg on top, season with salt and pepper, then pour the stock and wine into the pan. Cover well with aluminium foil and cook in the oven for 16 minutes per 500 g/1 lb 2 oz, until the meat is soft and pulling apart. Remove the leg from the oven, uncover, take it out of the pan and leave it to rest on a chopping (cutting) board for 20–30 minutes.
* Meanwhile, strain the stock into a jug (pitcher). Melt the butter in a medium saucepan over a medium heat, stir in the flour and cook, stirring constantly, for 3–4 minutes until pale golden brown. Slowly whisk in the strained stock, making sure it is fully combined before you add more. Simmer for 10 minutes, then check the seasoning. Pass through a sieve into a sauce boat or jug and serve with the lamb and the White Onion Sauce or White Caper Sauce, if desired.

UNITED KINGDOM
*

LAMB SCRUMPETS

To make these scrumpets, wonderfully tender strips of lamb are breaded and then fried until golden brown and crispy. Serve with a fruity ketchup – like Rhubarb (page 426).

Serves: 2–4
Prep time: 6 hours, plus 4 hours chilling
Cook time: 2½ hours
{ ᴗ }

- 1 x 300–400-g/11–14-oz piece lamb breast, bones removed
- vegetable oil, for rubbing and deep-frying
- 3 cloves garlic, crushed
- 2 sprigs rosemary
- 2 sprigs thyme
- 60 g/2¼ oz (½ cup) plain (all-purpose) flour
- 2 eggs, beaten
- 70 g/2½ oz (1½ cups minus 1 teaspoon) fresh breadcrumbs
- salt and pepper

- To serve:
- aioli and a lemon wedge
- Rhubarb Ketchup (page 426)

* Preheat the oven to 160°C/325°F/Gas Mark 3.
* Rub the lamb breast with oil and season with salt and pepper, then put it into a roasting pan with the garlic, rosemary and thyme and a splash of water. Cover with aluminium foil and roast for 2 hours, or until tender.
* Remove the lamb from the oven and transfer to the fridge for at least 4 hours. When it is cooled and set, cut the lamb into strips. Heat enough vegetable oil for deep-frying, about halfway up a deep, heavy saucepan, until it reaches 180°C/350°F on a thermometer.
* Put the flour into a shallow dish, then put the eggs into another and the breadcrumbs into a third dish. Toss the breast strips first into the flour, then dip them into the eggs and then into the breadcrumbs until completely coated. Carefully lower the strips, a few at a time, into the hot oil and deep-fry for 3–5 minutes, until golden brown. Remove with a slotted spoon and leave to drain on paper towels. Season well and serve with a pot of aioli, a lemon wedge or alongside some Rhubarb Ketchup.

UNITED KINGDOM
*

ROAST SADDLE OF LAMB

A lamb's saddle is a very large cut of meat composed of both sides of the loin and makes for a sumptuous feast. If boned and rolled, you may want to fill the middle with the stuffing of your choice.
Lamb is traditionally served with its own gravy and a bright Mint Sauce (page 414), especially in warmer months, although a Redcurrant Jelly (page 434) is also common in winter. Great bowls of Boiled New Potatoes (page 84) and creamed or buttered greens are handsome accompaniments.

Serves: 12
Prep time: 5 minutes
Cook time: according to weight, plus 20 minutes resting

{☙}

- 1 saddle of lamb, boned and dressed (ask the butcher to do this for you)
- salt and pepper

- To serve:
- Mint Sauce (page 414) or Redcurrant Jelly (page 434)
- Gravy (page 420)

* Preheat the oven to 240°C/475°F/Gas Mark 9 or as high as it will go.
* Weigh the meat and calculate the roasting time, allowing 30 minutes per 1 kg/2¼ lb plus 20 minutes for medium. For well-done, allow 35 minutes per 1 kg/2¼ lb plus 20 minutes. Season the lamb all over with salt and pepper, then put it onto a trivet or clean wire rack set on top of a large roasting pan. Roast in the oven for 20 minutes, then reduce the oven temperature to 180°C/350°F/Gas Mark 4 for the remainder of its roasting time. Leave to rest for at least 20 minutes before removing the string and carving. Serve with your sauce of choice and Gravy.

WALES
*

ROAST LEG OF LAMB
WITH
GINGER, HONEY, CIDER AND ROSEMARY
COES OEN RHOST GYDA SINSIR, MÊL, SEIDR A RHOSMARI

This recipe was a popular Sunday lunch in Wales. Smothered in sweet spices and herbs, the lamb's fragrance and flavour would last long in the memory.

Serves: 4–6
Prep time: 30 minutes
Cook time: about 45 minutes

{☙}

- 1 small leg of lamb, about 1.3 kg/2 lb 13 oz
- 2.5 cm/1 inch piece fresh root ginger, peeled and cut into slivers
- 25 g/1 oz (2 tablespoons) butter, plus extra 1 tablespoon, softened
- 2 tablespoons honey
- 1 tablespoon chopped rosemary
- 100 ml/3½ fl oz (⅓ cup plus 1 tablespoon) cider
- 1 tablespoon plain (all-purpose) flour

* Preheat the oven to 200°C/400°F/Gas Mark 6.
* Using a sharp knife, make small cuts in the leg of lamb and insert the ginger. Melt the 25 g/1 oz (2 tablespoons) butter in a small saucepan over a medium-low heat for 2 minutes, then add the honey and rosemary and mix together. Spread the mixture over the lamb.
* Put the lamb into a large roasting pan, pour in the cider

and cover loosely with aluminium foil. Roast, allowing 15–20 minutes per 450 g/1 lb. When half-cooked, uncover and continue roasting, basting frequently with juices from the roasting pan.
* Remove the lamb from the oven, lift out of the pan and keep warm, covered loosely with aluminium foil. Put the softened butter and flour into a small bowl and, using your fingertips, mix together. Pour the juices into a heatproof bowl and stir, removing the excess fat. Set aside.
* Put the roasting pan on the stove over a medium heat, pour in a little cider and stir to scrape up all the crispy bits stuck on the bottom. Bring to the boil, then pour in the non-fatty juices and thicken to preference with a little of the kneaded butter. Serve with the lamb.

UNITED KINGDOM
*

SLOW-ROASTED LAMB SHOULDER

Cooked low and slow, this recipe yields a shoulder that is wonderfully tender and giving. Serve with Roast or Mashed Potatoes (pages 86 or 80), Mint Sauce (page 414) or Rowan Jelly (page 434).

Serves: 6
Prep time: 15 minutes
Cook time: 5¾ hours

{☙}

- 2 onions, sliced
- 2 sprigs rosemary
- 2.5–3 kg/5½ lb–6 lb 10 oz shoulder of lamb
- 4 cloves garlic, very thinly sliced
- 6 anchovies, halved
- 100 ml/3½ fl oz (⅓ cup plus 1 tablespoon) red wine
- 250 ml/8 fl oz (1 cup) beef stock
- 30 g/1 oz (2 tablespoons) butter
- 30 g/1 oz (3¾ tablespoons) plain (all-purpose) flour
- salt and pepper
-
- To serve:
- Roast or Mashed Potatoes (pages 86 or 80)
- Mint Sauce (page 414) or Rowan Jelly (page 434)

* Preheat the oven to 160°C/325°F/Gas Mark 3.
* Arrange the onions in a layer on the bottom of a roasting pan, then sit the rosemary on top. Put the meat on top, then, using a sharp pointed knife, make incisions all over. Push the garlic and anchovies into the incisions. Pour the wine and stock around the meat and season the skin well with salt and pepper. Cover tightly with aluminium foil and roast in the oven for 5½ hours, or until tender.
* Remove the meat from the oven and put it onto a chopping (cutting) board to rest. Meanwhile, strain the juices through a sieve into a jug and skim away the fat with a spoon.
* Melt the butter in a medium saucepan over a medium-low heat, then stir in the flour and cook for 5 minutes, stirring constantly until the roux turns deep golden brown. Slowly whisk in the strained juices, a third at a time, making sure there are no lumps. If unsure, sieve again into a jug or sauce boat. Serve with the meat, Roast or Mashed Potatoes and Mint Sauce or Rowan Jelly.

UNITED KINGDOM
*

BARNSLEY CHOPS
WITH
ROSEMARY AND GARLIC

The Barnsley chop is a hefty cut of lamb: a two-sided lamb chop, cut across the loin (or saddle). They are prepared and served in much the same way as lamb chops – and simply take a couple more minutes to cook on each side. Serve with Minted Peas (page 68), Redcurrant Jelly (page 434) and Mashed Potatoes (page 80).

Serves: 2
Prep time: 30 minutes, plus 1 hour marinating
Cook time: 15 minutes
{🖐}{🌶}

- 2 Barnsley chops, about 300 g / 11 oz each or
4 lamb chops, about 150 g / 5 oz each
- 1 tablespoon olive oil
- salt and pepper

- For the rosemary and garlic marinade (optional):
- 1 clove garlic, very finely chopped
- 3 sprigs rosemary, leaves picked and very finely chopped
- 2 teaspoons freshly ground salt
- 1 teaspoon freshly ground black pepper
- 2–3 tablespoons olive oil

- To serve:
- Mashed Potatoes (page 80)
- Minted Peas (page 68)
- Redcurrant Jelly (store-bought or homemade. page 434)
- Gravy (page 420)

* If using the marinade, put the garlic, rosemary, salt, pepper and olive oil into a small bowl and stir well to ensure the mixture is evenly mixed. Pat both chops dry with paper towels, then put them into a large, shallow dish and spread the rosemary and garlic mixture over both sides of each chop. Cover with clingfilm (plastic wrap) and leave to marinate in the fridge for at least 1 hour.
* Leave the Barnsley chops to come to room temperature for at least 30 minutes before cooking. Pat them dry with paper towels and season to taste with salt and pepper.
* Heat a large heavy frying pan or skillet over a medium-high heat and add the oil. When hot, add the chops and cook them on one side for 5–6 minutes, depending on thickness, until browned, then, using kitchen tongs, turn the chops upright and crisp the fat on the base of the pan. The rendered fat should be more than enough for cooking the other sides but add another 1 tablespoon of oil if the pan is still dry. Turn onto the opposite side and cook for another 5–6 minutes. Insert a meat thermometer into the centre of the chops: it should read at least 62°C / 144°F. Once cooked, leave to rest for a few minutes before serving with Mashed Potatoes, Minted Peas, Redcurrant Jelly and Gravy.
* Notes: For smaller lamb chops, cook in the same manner but for just a couple of minutes less on both sides.

UNITED KINGDOM
*

LAMB VINDALOO

Outside of India, vindaloo has come to mean one of the hottest curries one can eat. In India, however, a vindaloo is a regional curry from the coastal state of Goa, which was for many years a stronghold of the Portuguese. Many Goan recipes have a strong Portuguese influence – such as the vinegar in the recipe below – and the curry itself is not measured on a scale of heat. Rather, as many historians will say, it was a sauce made with *vino* (wine, which was later replaced with vinegar) and *alho* (garlic), loosely combining to its name, vindaloo.
Goa is famous for its hot and spicy dishes, which help to make you sweat – and by extension, cool you down.
In Britain, the spiciness and heat has been amped up over the years, with many recipes or restaurants opting for heat over flavour.

Serves: 4
Prep time: 15 minutes, plus 20 minutes soaking
Cook time: 1 hour 10 minutes
{🖐}{🍖}{🌶}

- 10 dried red Kashmiri chillies (or 6–7 for a milder curry), broken in half and seeds shaken out
- 8 cloves garlic, chopped
- 2.5 cm / 1 inch piece fresh root ginger, skin scraped and chopped
- 4 tablespoons malt vinegar
- 3 cloves
- 2 teaspoons cumin seeds
- 1 small cinnamon stick
- ½ teaspoon ground black pepper
- 2 onions, sliced
- 2 tablespoons vegetable oil
- 600 g / 1 lb 5 oz boneless, trimmed lamb shoulder, cubed
- salt

* Put the chillies, garlic and ginger into a small bowl, add the vinegar and ½ teaspoon of salt and leave to soak for 20 minutes.
* Heat a large frying pan or skillet over a high heat, add the cloves, cumin seeds, cinnamon and pepper and dry-toast for 40 seconds until just smoking, then add these to the soaking chillies. Add the onions and the chilli mixture to a blender and whizz to a purée, adding a little water to help turn the blades. This is the vindaloo masala.
* Heat the oil in a large, heavy saucepan over a high heat, add the lamb and fry for 3–4 minutes to seal but not brown the meat, then tip in the vindaloo masala. Stir to blend and coat the lamb. Rinse out the blender with a little water and add this to the pan. Bring to the boil, then reduce the heat to medium, cover with a lid and cook for 1 hour, or until the lamb is tender. Serve.

Barnsley chops with rosemary and garlic

UNITED KINGDOM
*

NIHARI

Nihari is a defining dish of Pakistani cuisine and has evolved according to local flavour preferences. In Karachi, in the south of Pakistan, for instance, it is made fairly hot and even more spicy. When eating Nihari, the stew juices are usually mopped up with Naan (page 275), kulcha (leavened bread found in Lahore and Amritsar) or Roti (page 263). It is always topped with individual garnishes that enliven the flavour, including ginger, garam masala, lemon, caramelized onions, coriander (cilantro) and/or mint.
This recipe has also found its way into Britain and is often enjoyed in British Pakistani restaurants and homes. British Pakistanis have adapted this recipe by using lamb shanks or even chicken instead of the traditional mutton. Poppy seeds are often left out as well.

Serves: 4–6
Prep time: 15 minutes
Cook time: 3¼ hours
{✌}

- 4 tablespoons vegetable oil
- 2 tablespoons ghee
- 2.5 cm/1 inch piece fresh root ginger,
  peeled and finely grated
- ½ tablespoon very finely chopped garlic
- 3 large lamb shanks
- 1 teaspoon cayenne pepper or 1½ tablespoons Kashmiri
  red chilli powder
- 2 teaspoons salt, or to taste
- 1 tablespoon plain (all-purpose) flour, sifted
- 1 tablespoon wholemeal (whole wheat) flour, sifted
  (I prefer atta flour, which is used to make chappatis)
- Naan Bread (page 275), to serve

- For the spice blend:
- 1 tablespoon fennel seeds
- 1 cinnamon stick
- 2 black cardamom pods
- 10 green cardamom pods
- 2 star anise
- 1½ tablespoons coriander seeds
- 1 tablespoon cumin seeds
- 2 blades mace
- ½ teaspoon grated nutmeg
- 2 tablespoons white poppy seeds
- 15 cloves
- ¾ tablespoon black peppercorns
  or 2–3 pippali long peppers

- For the condiments:
- 150 g/5 oz (5 cups) chopped coriander (cilantro) leaves
- 5 cm/2 inch piece fresh root ginger, peeled and very
  thinly sliced into matchsticks
- 2 green bird's eye chillies or another thin chilli, finely
  chopped
- 175 g/6 oz (2 cups) crispy fried onions
- 4 lemons, cut into wedges

* Put all the spice blend ingredients into a spice or coffee grinder and grind together. Set aside.

* Heat the oil and ghee in a large saucepan over a medium heat, add the ginger and garlic and fry for 3–4 minutes until the raw smell leaves the pan. Add the lamb and fry for 5 minutes, or until the meat is sealed all over. Add the cayenne pepper, salt and the spice blend, except for 1 tablespoon, and fry until the spice blend is fragrant. If it sticks to the pan, add a splash of water as you go.
* Pour in about 2–2.5 litres/68–85 fl oz (8½–10 cups) water until the meat is submerged, then reduce the heat to medium-low, cover with a lid and cook for about 1 hour. Keep checking to see that the meat is simmering but not boiling.
* After about 1 hour, remove about 250 ml/8 fl oz (1 cup) of the liquid from the meat and pour into a small heatproof bowl, then stir in the flours until combined. Pour it back into the main pan and stir in evenly. Add another 250 ml/8 fl oz (1 cup) water, cover again, then reduce the heat to very low and cook gently for 2 hours, or until the meat falls off the bones.
* Serve hot topped with coriander (cilantro), ginger, bird's eye chillies, fried onions, lemons and the reserved spice blend. Eat with Naan Bread.

WALES / ENGLAND
*

KIDNEYS ROASTED IN THEIR OWN FAT

Ask your butcher to help you in sourcing lambs' kidneys still enclosed in a layer of suet. When trimmed slightly and then roasted simply, the meat comes out pink and juicy and can be sliced and served with good bread and English mustard or Brown Sauce (page 426).

Serves: 6
Prep time: 20 minutes
Cook time: 30 minutes
{🔪}{✌}

- 6 lambs' kidneys still surrounded in their fat
- salt and pepper
- caul fat (optional)

- To serve:
- good-quality bread
- English mustard or Brown Sauce (page 426)

* Preheat the oven to 220°C/425°F/Gas Mark 7.
* Remove any blood vessels from the kidneys. If any of the kidneys are without fat, trim some of the fat from the fattier parts to cover. Season with salt and pepper.
* If a lot of trimming has occurred, it may be a good idea to wrap the kidneys in caul fat. Put the kidneys onto a trivet in a large roasting pan and roast for 30 minutes. Leave to rest for 10 minutes before serving with bread, English mustard or Brown Sauce.

SCOTLAND
*

STUFFED LAMBS' HEARTS

Hearts were a common feature on Scottish dinner tables well into the 1940s and 50s: the celebrated Glasgow-born author and artist Alasdair Gray proclaimed them to be among his favourite foods growing up. The hearts would be stuffed to retain moisture then slow-roasted for a few hours in the oven. Serve hot with Gravy (page 420) and Boiled New Potatoes (page 84) or Mashed Potatoes (page 80).

Serves: 6
Prep time: 30 minutes, plus 8–12 hours soaking
Cook time: 2½–3½ hours
{⚫}

- 6 lambs' hearts
- full-fat (whole) milk
- 1 quantity stuffing or forcemeat of your choice, such as Sage and Onion (page 243) or Skirlie (page 243)
- 12 rashers (slices) smoked streaky (lean) bacon, halved
- about 500 ml/17 fl oz (2 cups plus 1 tablespoon) beef stock and 250 ml/8 fl oz (1 cup) red wine (or just use beef stock)
- 30 g/1 oz (2 tablespoons) butter
- 30 g/1 oz (3¾ tablespoons) plain (all-purpose) flour
- 2 tablespoons redcurrant jelly
- salt and pepper
- Boiled New Potatoes (page 84) or Mashed Potatoes (page 80), to serve

* Put the hearts into a large bowl, cover with milk, then cover with clingfilm (plastic wrap) and leave to soak in the fridge overnight.
* The next day, drain the hearts and set aside. Make the stuffing or forcemeat of your choice following the recipes on pages 242 or 243. Set aside.
* Preheat the oven to 150°C/300°F/Gas Mark 2.
* Using sharp scissors, cut away the sinewy parts inside the top of the hearts. Stuff each heart with the stuffing or forcemeat of your choice, then criss-cross the top of each heart with the bacon halves. Skewer or tie the bacon in place with kitchen string and arrange the hearts in a deep baking dish or roasting pan.
* Pour in the stock and wine (if using). It needs to come about two-thirds up the sides of the hearts. Cover with aluminium foil or a lid and bake in the oven for 2–3 hours until firm. A meat skewer should be able to easily pass through the thickest part. When cooked, remove the hearts from the dish or pan and keep them warm, covered with foil. Set the cooking liquor aside.
* Melt the butter in a medium saucepan over a medium-low heat, then stir in the flour and cook for 5 minutes, stirring constantly until the roux turns a deep golden brown. Slowly whisk in the reserved cooking liquor, a little at a time, making sure there are no lumps. Cook, uncovered, for 20 minutes, before stirring in the redcurrant jelly. Once melted, taste and adjust the seasoning with salt and pepper.
* When ready to serve, remove the string or skewers from the hearts, strain the gravy into a sauceboat or jug (pitcher) and serve with Boiled New Potatoes or Mashed Potatoes.

UNITED KINGDOM
*

SWEETBREADS
WITH
CAPER BUTTER SAUCE

These sweetbreads are fried and lightly crisped in a butter sauce but remain soft and creamy on the inside. Serve with green peas or broad (fava) beans.

Serves: 6
Prep time: 45 minutes, plus 8–12 hours soaking
Cook time: 30 minutes
{⚫}

- 400 g/14 oz lambs' or calves' sweetbreads
- enough full-fat (whole) milk to cover
- 4 tablespoons plain (all-purpose) flour
- pinch of cayenne pepper (optional)
- 2 tablespoons clarified butter
- 1 teaspoon olive oil
- 2 tablespoons small capers
- juice of 1 lemon or 2 tablespoons white wine vinegar
- 100 g/3½ oz (7 tablespoons) very cold unsalted butter, diced
- 1 tablespoon finely chopped flat-leaf parsley
- salt and pepper
- freshly cooked green peas or broad (fava) beans, to serve

* Put the sweetbreads into a large bowl, cover with milk, then cover with clingfilm (plastic wrap) and leave to soak in the fridge overnight.
* The next day, have a large bowl of cold water ready. Fill a large saucepan with water, then add the salt, about 1 teaspoon per 500 ml/17 fl oz (2 cups plus 1 tablespoon) water, and stir to dissolve the salt. Add the sweetbreads and bring to the boil. As soon as the water boils, remove the sweetbreads and put into the bowl of cold water to cool quickly. Remove and pat them dry with paper towels, then remove any sinews.
* If using calves' sweetbreads, cut into thirds or quarters, depending upon the size; lambs' can remain whole. Spread the flour out on a large plate and season with 1 teaspoon each of salt and pepper. Sprinkle over a little cayenne pepper (if using), then toss the sweetbreads evenly in the seasoned flour until coated all over.
* Melt the clarified butter in a large frying pan over a high heat, add the sweetbreads and fry for 4 minutes, turning them over to ensure they crisp evenly but remain soft in the centre. Remove them using a slotted spoon and drain on paper towels.
* As the sweetbreads rest, make the sauce. Put the olive oil into the emptied cooking pan. Add the capers and crush them with the back of a wooden spoon. Add the lemon juice or vinegar and cook over a medium heat for 5 minutes, or until almost dry. Remove from the heat and beat in the butter, dice by dice, using a small whisk until it is very smooth and homogenous – a little less thick than double (heavy) cream. Taste and adjust the seasoning with salt and pepper before adding the parsley. Serve the sweetbreads with the sauce ladled over the top and with freshly cooked green peas or broad (fava) beans.

UNITED KINGDOM
*

DEVILLED KIDNEYS

This breakfast dish of thick-cut spicy kidneys was immensely popular throughout the nineteenth and early twentieth centuries and has enjoyed a resurgence in recent years. The term 'devilled' simply refers to the mixture of spices, cayenne and mustard used to flavour this dish and many others of the same period. Serve devilled kidneys with its pan sauces on thick slices of buttered toast – sourdough ideally – waiting a moment or two before serving to allow the juices to seep into the bread.

Serves: 4
Prep time: 10 minutes, plus 8–12 hours soaking
Cook time: 10 minutes
{🍴}

- 8 lambs' kidneys
- full-fat (whole) milk
- 4 tablespoons Worcestershire sauce
- 4 tablespoons English mustard
- 2 tablespoons cider vinegar
- dash of Tabasco sauce or shake of cayenne pepper
- 60 g/ 2¼ oz (½ stick) butter, plus extra for buttering
- 75 ml/ 2½ fl oz (⅓ cup) double (heavy) cream
- 4 slices bread, cut into 2 triangles each
- 2 tablespoons finely chopped flat-leaf parsley
- pepper

* Put the kidneys into a large bowl, add milk to cover, then cover with clingfilm (plastic wrap) and leave to soak in the fridge overnight.
* The next day, drain the kidneys, then cut them in half and discard any tough outer membrane still intact. Snip out their white cores using sharp scissors. Set the kidneys aside.
* For the sauce, put the Worcestershire sauce, mustard and vinegar into a small bowl and whisk together, adding plenty of pepper and a dash of Tabasco or cayenne. Set aside.
* Heat the butter in a large frying pan or skillet over a high heat for 2 minutes, or until foaming. When it stops foaming, add the kidneys and fry for 2 minutes without disturbing them. Turn them over and cook for another minute, then pour over the sauce. Fry for another 1 minute before mixing in the cream. Cook for 2 minutes, or until the sauce reduces and thickens, making sure the kidneys are well-coated.
* Toast and butter the bread. Spoon 2 kidney halves and a little sauce onto each piece, sprinkle with the chopped parsley and serve.

UNITED KINGDOM
*

CURRIED GOAT

During the mid 1800s, following the abolition of slavery in the Caribbean, the colonies still under British rule sought a new workforce to provide labour on plantations. With the liberation of the enslaved population, the UK government summoned those from the British Raj and Colonial India to work as indentured workers. Their influence redefined the culture of Trinidad, Guyana and parts of Jamaica, St Lucia and Grenada to name a few, directly impacting the cuisine. Curry was introduced as a spice during this time and came to incorporate goat as a substitute for the unavailability of lamb. Curried goat has continued to become a representative of British Caribbean food culture.
This recipe is from Keshia Sakarah, a London-based chef who runs the Brixton eatery Caribé.

Serves: 4–5
Prep time: 20 minutes
Cook time: 2–2½ hours
{🔥}{🍖}{🍴}{🍲}

- 1 kg/ 2¼ lb goat meat, shoulder or leg, or a mixture of both, bone in
- juice of ½ lemon
- 2 tablespoons vegetable oil
- 2 tablespoons curry powder of your choice
- 2 teaspoons ground cumin
- 1 teaspoon ground coriander
- 50 g/ 2 oz (¼ cup) creamed coconut
- 4 cloves garlic, crushed
- 3 thyme sprigs
- 3 bay leaves
- 1 small brown onion, finely chopped
- ½ fresh scotch bonnet chilli (about 10 g/ ¼ oz)
- 2 teaspoons salt
- 2 tablespoons granulated sugar

* Put the goat meat into a large bowl with the lemon juice, then cover with water and set aside. It can stay in the lemon water while you are preparing the rest of the curry.
* Heat the oil in a large, deep casserole dish or Dutch oven over a medium heat, add the curry powder and ground cumin and coriander and cook for 1 minute.
* Measure out 1 litre/ 34 fl oz (4¼ cups) water. Add 100 ml/ 3½ fl oz (⅓ cup plus 1 tablespoon) to the spice mixture and stir to form a paste. Add the remaining water to the pan together with the coconut, garlic, thyme, bay leaves, onion and chilli. You can add a little more chilli if you like more heat. Add the salt and sugar and stir until the coconut has dissolved.
* Strain the goat meat from the lemon water, then add to the pan. Top up (top off) with a little extra water if needed to ensure the goat is covered and bring to the boil. Reduce the heat and simmer for 1½–2 hours until cooked through.

Devilled kidneys

HOT PIES, HOT!
GOOD GEESE AND PIGLETS,
COME AND DINE!
COME AND DINE!

A STREET CRY FROM MEDIEVAL LONDON

One of Britain's proudest culinary traditions is a deceptively simple concept: pastry (pie dough) enveloping a savoury filling. It is an institution of British food culture, and an aspect of our culinary inheritance that's never waned from popularity, remaining a firm favourite over the centuries, from the medieval cookshop and banquet table to the high-street baker, the pie and mash shop and the trendy gastropub.

What does this chapter encompass? Everything from suet crust steak pies to huge pork pies made from hand-raised hot water pastry and some 'honorary' inclusions such as steamed savoury puddings (a cousin to the pie) and the likes of shepherd's pie (a figurative technicality).

It is frankly incredible how many variations we can conceive based on such a straightforward concept of filled pastry. There is the matter of the pastry itself. The choice of filling. The question of temperature. Should it be taken to go? Shared with friends? Served with mash and gravy? Chips (fries) and buttered greens? Eaten from a brown paper bag? Boundlessness might not be the first quality you have in mind when picturing the pie, but surely it is the most appropriate.

It's for this reason that there is a pie and pastry chapter in The British Cookbook, and that these recipes – which would otherwise fit neatly into the chapters of their respective fillings – are all grouped together instead. They are more than the sum of their parts (or in this case, their fillings). They speak to a sort of moment and evoke a nostalgia we can all relate to: the grab-and-go sausage roll, slices of cold pork pie and a pint at lunch, or a heaping of piping hot steak pie on a cold winter's night.

This is inherently a complementary chapter, as it relates to and references nearly every other savoury chapter in this book, and is strengthened by them in the process. Yes, knowing how to make a huge pie from scratch is quite a feat, but it is equally satisfying to riff on a classic, in order to turn last night's left-overs into tonight's quality supper.

Traditionally, seasonality and resource-fulness were key. Fillings might have been made from pigs slaughtered in November, with their lard used for a rich flaky pastry crust. That same could be true of a beef or steak pie with suet crust. While we have recently opted for more familiar, healthier substitutions in the fats we use, it's important to stay connected to the idea that pie-making was once done with great prudence. The main idea I want to impart with this chapter is that these recipes can (and should) act as the starting point for your own innovation. Yes, it's possible to give a lift to the old favourites depending on what's in season or available to you. You will get no extra points for just playing by the rules.

Having said that, there's equally no shame to simply playing the classics. A cottage pie does not need glamming up; a sausage roll or macaroni pie don't require additions. Any way you slice it, it's something good. So read on, dig into the history of Britain's favourites and let inspiration (or indulgence) take you.

SAVOURY PIES AND PASTIES

ENGLAND: LANCASHIRE

*

LANCASHIRE BUTTER PIE

This savoury pie is a speciality across Lancashire, where it's still a common feature at local market stalls. The filling is nearly as straightforward as it sounds: a simple mixture of buttery lightly fried onions and softened diced potato. Serve with Pickled Red Cabbage (page 444), or, for a less traditional approach, a good Rhubarb Ketchup (page 426) or Brown Sauce (page 426).

Serves: 6
Prep time: 50 minutes, plus 40 minutes resting and chilling
Cook time: 1 hour
{ ♨ }

- 1 quantity Shortcrust Pastry (page 247)
- 1 kg/ 2¼ lb potatoes, such as Maris Piper, peeled and cut into chunks, about 4 cm/ 1½ inches thick
- 100 g/ 3½ oz (7 tablespoons) butter, plus extra for greasing
- 3 onions, sliced
- plain (all-purpose) flour, for dusting
- 1 egg, beaten with 1 tablespoon water or milk, for egg wash
- salt and pepper
- Pickled Red Cabbage (page 444) or Rhubarb Ketchup (page 426) or Brown Sauce (page 426), to serve

* Make the pastry following the recipe on page 247 and leave to rest for 20 minutes before using.
* Bring a large saucepan of lightly salted water to the boil. Carefully add the potatoes and cook for 10 minutes until just soft, then drain and set aside to cool.
* Melt the butter in a large frying pan or skillet over a medium heat, add the onions and cook for 10–12 minutes until golden and soft. Remove from the heat and set aside.
* Grease a 1.5 litre/ 50 fl oz pie dish.
* Cut off one-third of the pastry and set it aside, then roll out the remaining two-thirds on a lightly floured counter and use it to line the prepared pie dish. Fill the pie with the onions, then the potatoes and season well with salt and pepper.
* Roll out the remaining pastry to make a lid, then carefully lay it over the dish and seal with egg wash. Use a sharp knife to cut a steam hole in the centre and brush the top with more egg wash. Leave the pie to firm up in the fridge for 20 minutes.
* Meanwhile, preheat the oven to 220°C/ 425°F/ Gas Mark 7. Put a large baking sheet onto the centre shelf to heat up.
* Take the pie out of the fridge, put it onto the hot baking sheet and bake for 20 minutes. Reduce the oven temperature to 180°C/ 350°F/ Gas Mark 4 and cook for another 20 minutes until golden. Leave to cool slightly before eating warm with Pickled Red Cabbage or Rhubarb Ketchup or Brown Sauce.

ENGLAND: LANCASHIRE

*

CHEESE AND ONION PIE

Similar to the Lancashire Butter Pie (see left), this is also a speciality of Lancashire and makes for an indulgent afternoon lunch. Offset the rich filling and buttery crust by pairing with some Pickled Red Cabbage (page 444) or Pickled Beetroot (page 442) and a small salad of leafy greens.

Serves: 6
Prep time: 50 minutes, plus 40 minutes resting and chilling
Cook time: 1 hour
{ ♨ } { ♨ }

- 70 g/ 2½ oz (⅔ stick) butter
- 1 quantity Shortcrust Pastry (page 247)
- 100 g/ 3½ oz Mashed Potatoes (page 80)
- 3 onions, sliced
- plain (all-purpose) flour, for dusting
- 2 eggs, beaten
- 2 teaspoons English mustard
- 100 ml/ 3½ fl oz (⅓ cup plus 1 tablespoon) full-fat (whole) milk
- 75 ml/ 2½ fl oz (⅓ cup) double (heavy) cream
- pinch of ground nutmeg
- 400 g/ 14 oz Cheddar cheese (or Lancashire cheese), grated
- 1 egg, beaten with 1 tablespoon water or milk, for egg wash
- salt and pepper

* Grease a 1.5 litre/ 50 fl oz pie dish with 10 g/ ¼ oz (2 teaspoons) of the butter and set aside.
* Make the pastry following the recipe on page 247 and leave to rest for 20 minutes before using. Make the Mashed Potatoes following the recipe on page 80 and set aside.
* Melt the remaining 60 g/ 2¼ oz (½ stick) of butter in a large frying pan or skillet over a medium heat, add the onions and cook for 10–15 minutes until golden.
* Meanwhile, cut off one-third of the pastry and set it aside, then roll out the remaining two-thirds on a lightly floured work counter and use it to line the prepared pie dish.
* Put the cooked onions into a large bowl with the Mashed Potatoes and mix together. Put the eggs, mustard, milk, cream and nutmeg into another bowl and mix together, then combine both mixtures, along with the cheese, and stir through well. Season with salt and pepper, then pour the filling into the lined pie dish.
* Roll out the remaining pastry to make a lid, then lay it over the dish and seal with egg wash. Use a sharp knife to cut a steam hole in the centre and brush the top with more egg wash. Leave the pie to firm up in the fridge for 20 minutes.
* Preheat the oven to 200°C/ 400°F/ Gas Mark 6.
* Take the pie out of the fridge and cook in the oven for 40 minutes, or until lightly golden brown. Leave to cool slightly, then serve.

SCOTLAND

*

MACARONI PIE

Macaroni has a surprisingly long history in Britain and appears – with cheese – in records dating back as far as *The Forme of Cury* (1390), a cookbook produced during the reign of English monarch Richard II.

This macaroni pie has a much shorter pedigree and hails instead from the bakeries of Scotland, where it is made with a thin hot water pastry crust. The pie can be eaten hot or cold, typically on its own, but sometimes, in the very early hours of morning, on a buttered Breakfast Roll (page 276).

Serves: 6
Prep time: 30 minutes, plus 50 minutes resting and chilling
Cook time: 50 minutes
{👤} {🌱}

- ½ quantity Hot Water Pastry (page 246)
- 125 g/4¼ oz (1¼ cups) macaroni
- 300 ml/10 fl oz (1¼ cups) full-fat (whole) milk, or half single (light) cream and half milk
- 60 g/2¼ oz (½ stick) butter
- 60 g/2¼ oz (½ cup) plain (all-purpose) flour, plus extra for dusting
- 200 g/7 oz Cheddar cheese, grated
- salt and pepper

* Make the pastry following the recipe on page 246 and leave to rest for 10 minutes before using.
* Bring a large saucepan of salted water to the boil. Add the macaroni and cook according to the packet instructions. Drain and set aside.
* Heat the milk and cream (if using) in a large saucepan over a medium heat for 3–4 minutes, or until hot. Remove from the heat and set aside.
* Melt the butter in another large saucepan over a medium heat, stir in the flour and cook for 2–3 minutes. Slowly add the hot milk, whisking constantly. Remove from the heat and add three-quarters of the cheese. Season with salt and pepper, stir in the macaroni and leave to cool.
* Roll out the pastry on a floured work counter and use to line 6 x 140 x 60 mm/5½–2½ inch pie or chef's rings, using a rolling pin to trim away excess. Chill in the fridge for 20 minutes, then fill with the macaroni mixture and sprinkle with the remaining grated cheese. Put into the fridge to firm up for 20 minutes.
* Preheat the oven to 220°C/425°F/Gas Mark 7.
* Bake the pies in the oven for 25 minutes, then reduce the oven temperature to 180°C/350°F/Gas Mark 4 and bake for another 15 minutes, or until the pastry is golden brown. Serve.

ENGLAND: DEVON

*

HOMITY PIE

An open top cheese and vegetable pie popular in West Country England, the homity pie is said to have originated as a recipe of the Women's Land Army – a women's civilian organization that operated during World Wars I and II as a means of boosting agricultural production. Today it is made in a manner much more decadent – with the addition of double (heavy) cream and a lot more cheese.

Serves: 6
Prep time: 30 minutes, plus 40 minutes resting and chilling
Cook time: 1 hour 10 minutes
{👤} {🌱}

- 1 quantity Shortcrust Pastry (page 247)
- 750 g/1 lb 10 oz floury (baking) potatoes, peeled and cut into chunks, about 2.5 cm/1 inch thick
- 60 g/2¼ oz (½ stick) butter
- 1 onion, sliced
- 1 tablespoon chopped flat-leaf parsley
- 300 ml/10 fl oz (1¼ cups) double (heavy) cream
- 200 g/7 oz Cheddar cheese, grated
- ¼ fresh nutmeg, grated
- plain (all-purpose) flour, for dusting
- salt and pepper

* Make the pastry following the recipe on page 247 and leave to rest for 20 minutes before using.
* Boil the potatoes in a large saucepan of salted water for 20 minutes, or until they are tender. Drain well and leave to cool in a large bowl.
* Melt the butter in a large frying pan or skillet over a medium heat, add the onions and fry for 10–12 minutes until they are golden. Transfer the onions to the bowl with the drained potatoes, then break down the potatoes into a very loose mash using a fork or potato masher. Stir in the parsley, cream, cheese, nutmeg and salt and pepper and mix well.
* Roll out the pastry on a lightly floured work counter and use it to line a deep-sided pie dish, about 1.2–1.5 litre/40–50 fl oz capacity. Trim the edges and put the dish into the fridge to firm up for 20 minutes.
* Meanwhile, preheat the oven to 220°C/425°F/Gas Mark 7. Put a baking sheet onto the centre shelf of the oven to heat up.
* Fill the pie dish with the potato filling and slide onto the hot baking sheet. Bake in the oven for 25 minutes, then reduce the oven temperature to 180°C/350°F/Gas Mark 4 and bake for another 15 minutes until golden brown. Leave to cool slightly, then serve.

ENGLAND: CORNWALL

*

STARGAZEY PIE

This Cornish pie earns it name from the pilchards (large Cornish sardines) that gaze skywards from its crimped pastry crust. The Cornish pilchard industry was once a vital lifeline for the local economy. In the eighteenth and nineteenth centuries, thousands of tonnes of pilchards were caught annually and exported for trade.

This pie is still widely made in the small Cornish fishing port of Mousehole, where locals celebrate Tom Bawcock, a mythical fisherman who risked his life to bring a haul of pilchards into port amidst a raging storm. Every year on 23rd December, locals gather at The Ship Inn for Tom Bawcock's Eve, where stargazey pie is made, and afterwards a lantern procession winds through the streets.

The pie itself is rather simple but rustic, with a herby filling of fish, bacon, potato and hard-boiled eggs. Serve warm and with plenty of good Cornish ale.

Serves: 6
Prep time: 40 minutes, plus 1 hour resting and chilling
Cook time: 75 minutes

{•‍•}

- 2 x quantity Shortcrust Pastry (page 247)
- plain (all-purpose) flour, for dusting
- 12 sardines or pilchards or 6 small herrings, boned but leave their heads on (ask the fishmonger to do this for you), plus an extra 6 sardine or pilchard fillets or about 350 g/ 12 oz haddock fillets, cut into bite-sized pieces
- 2 eggs
- 100 g/ 3½ oz (2 cups) fresh breadcrumbs
- 80 g/ 3 oz (¾ stick) butter, melted
- 1 onion, chopped
- 120 g/ 4 oz (⅔ cup) smoked bacon, chopped
- ½ teaspoon chopped thyme or lemon thyme leaves
- 1 tablespoon chopped flat-leaf parsley
- grated zest of 1 lemon
- 2 potatoes, cut into 1 cm/ ½ inch dice
- 50 ml/ 1¾ fl oz (3½ tablespoons) cider
- 50 ml/ 1¾ fl oz (3½ tablespoons) double (heavy) cream
- 1 egg, beaten with 1 tablespoon of water or milk, for egg wash
- 100 ml/ 3½ fl oz (⅓ cup plus 1 tablespoon) fish stock
- salt and pepper

* Make the pastry following the recipe on page 247 and leave to rest for 20 minutes before using.
* Roll out half the pastry on a lightly floured work counter and use it to line a 20 cm/ 8 inch pie dish. Set aside
* Lightly salt the whole fish and set aside.
* Bring a small saucepan of water to the boil, carefully lower the eggs into the water and boil for 10 minutes, or until hard-boiled. Drain and peel off the shells, then cut the eggs into dice. Set aside.
* Put the breadcrumbs, butter, onion, bacon, herbs and grated lemon zest into a large bowl and use a wooden spoon to mix together. Season with salt and pepper. Stuff each fish with a little of the filling (there should still be plenty leftover for filling the pie) and arrange the fish radially from the centre of the bottom, with their heads reaching the pie edge.
* Mix the diced eggs in with the potatoes, pilchard or sardine pieces, cider, cream and remaining filling and spread it across the bottom of the pie.
* Roll out the remaining pastry to a circumference larger

than the dish and carefully lay the pastry over the top. Gently pull back the edges around each fish so that the crust 'ripples' around the pilchards. Crimp and seal with egg wash. Use a sharp knife to cut a steam hole in the centre and brush with more egg wash. Put the pie into the fridge to firm up for 20 minutes.
* Meanwhile, preheat the oven to 200°C/400°F/Gas Mark 6 and put a large baking sheet onto the centre shelf to heat up.
* Put the pie onto the hot baking sheet and bake in the oven for 20 minutes. Reduce the oven temperature to 160°C/325°F/Gas Mark 3 and bake for another 45 minutes.
* Meanwhile, heat the stock in a medium saucepan over a medium heat for 3–4 minutes, or until hot. Remove the pie from the oven and pour the hot stock into the pie through the steam hole. Leave to soak into the filling for 20 minutes before serving.

WALES

*

WELSH COCKLE PIE

Cockle gathering was once a common sight along the beaches of South Wales, where women would wade out into the water with donkeys or mules and wicker baskets to sift cockles from the sand. Now a much more industrialized process takes place, but cockles are still beloved, and a demonstrably Welsh ingredient. They can be served in a multitude of ways: plainly with malt vinegar, cooked in a soft scramble with eggs, or even in a creamy pie – as below. Serve in shallow bowls.

Serves: 6
Prep time: 40 minutes, plus 20 minutes resting
Cook time: 40 minutes

{•‍•}

- 1 quantity Shortcrust Pastry (page 247)
- plain (all-purpose) flour, for dusting
- 1 tablespoon chopped chives
- 2 tablespoons spring onions (scallions), chopped
- 1 litre/ 34 fl oz (4¼ cups) cooked cockles
- 200 g/ 7 oz smoked streaky (lean) bacon, chopped
- 1 egg, beaten with 1 tablespoon water or milk, for egg wash
- 250 ml/ 8 fl oz (1 cup) cockle liquor or fish or chicken stock
- salt and pepper

* Make the pastry following the recipe on page 247 and leave to rest for 20 minutes before using.
* Preheat the oven to 220°C/425°F/Gas Mark 7. Put a baking sheet onto the centre shelf of the oven to heat up.
* Cut off about four-fifths of the pastry, then roll it out on a lightly floured work counter and use it to line a deep pie dish, about 1.5–1.75 litre/ 50–60 fl oz capacity.
* Put the chopped chives and spring onions (scallions) into a small bowl and mix together.
* Layer the ingredients into the pie. First, arrange a layer of cockles in the bottom, then add a layer of the spring onion and chive mixture and then a layer of the bacon. Repeat the layers, seasoning with salt and pepper as you go.
* Roll out the remaining pastry to make a lid and lay it over the dish. Use a sharp knife to cut a few steam holes in the top, then gently press down around the edges and

seal with egg wash. Alternatively, some prefer to make a lattice pattern to top their pie – the choice is yours. Brush the pastry with more egg wash, then pour the stock through the steam holes and carefully put onto the hot baking sheet. Bake in the oven for 20 minutes. Reduce the oven temperature to 180°C/350°F/Gas Mark 4 and bake for another 20 minutes until golden brown. Leave to cool slightly, and serve.

UNITED KINGDOM
*

FISH PIE

This creamy pie is a riff on meat and potato pub classics such as the Cottage or Shepherd's Pie (page 232). The fish pie's filling, however, is less precise and can be made from almost any mix of fish – and shellfish – in a cream sauce.

Serves: 6
Prep time: 50 minutes
Cook time: 1 hour
{ᴖ}

- ½ quantity Mashed Potatoes (page 80)
- 100 g/3½ oz (7 tablespoons) butter
- 400 ml/14 fl oz (1⅔ cups) full-fat (whole) milk
- ½ onion, coarsely sliced
- 1 bay leaf
- pinch of ground nutmeg
- 2 cloves
- 300 g/11 oz cod fillets
- 200 g smoked haddock or other smoked fish fillets
- 1 leek, sliced
- 1 tablespoon chopped tarragon
- 1 tablespoon chopped flat-leaf parsley
- 40 g/1½ oz (⅓ cup) plain (all-purpose) flour
- 75 ml/2½ fl oz (⅓ cup) double (heavy) cream
- 12 king prawns (jumbo shrimp) or 6 scallops, halved crosswise
- salt and pepper

* Preheat the oven to 160°C/325°F/Gas Mark 3.
* Make the Mashed Potatoes following the recipe on page 80 and set aside. Melt 40 g/1½ oz (3 tablespoons) of the butter in a small saucepan over a medium-low heat, then remove from the heat and set aside.
* Bring the milk to simmering point in a large saucepan, add the onion, bay leaf, nutmeg and cloves and simmer for 10 minutes. Cut the fish into bite-sized pieces and add to the milk, then bring back to a simmer and cook for 8 minutes, or until the fish is cooked through and the flesh is opaque. Use a slotted spoon to transfer the cooked fish to a bowl, then strain the liquid into a jug (pitcher) and set aside.
* Melt the remaining 60 g/2¼ oz (½ stick) of the butter in the saucepan over a medium heat, add the leek and herbs and cook for 4–5 minutes, or until soft. Stir in the flour and cook for 2 minutes before whisking in the reserved milk, a little at a time, making sure the sauce is smooth before each addition. Remove the pan from the heat, add the fish and gently fold in, then stir in the cream. Season with salt and pepper and stir in the prawns (shrimp) or scallops. Transfer the mixture to a large pie dish, about 1.75–2 litre/60–68 fl oz capacity, and spoon over the

Mashed Potatoes. Brush the top with the reserved melted butter and bake in the oven for 30 minutes, or until golden. Leave to cool slightly, and serve.

UNITED KINGDOM
*

MUSHROOM PIE

In autumn, swap the shop-bought mushrooms for a mix of foraged or locally sourced wild ones – left whole or cut in half, depending on their size.

Serves: 4
Prep time: 1 hour, plus 50 minutes resting and chilling
Cook time: 1 hour
{ᴖ}

- ½ quantity Rough Puff Pastry (page 247)
- 60 g/2¼ oz (½ stick) butter
- 1 onion, sliced
- 2 cloves garlic, sliced
- ½ teaspoon thyme leaves
- 500 g/1 lb 2 oz chestnut (cremini) or button mushrooms, halved
- 200 g/7 oz (¾ cup plus 1 tablespoon) cream cheese
- 100 ml/3½ fl oz (⅓ cup plus 1 tablespoon) full-fat (whole) milk
- dash of Worcestershire sauce
- 1 tablespoon chopped flat-leaf parsley
- plain (all-purpose) flour, for dusting
- 1 egg, beaten with 1 tablespoon water or milk, for egg wash
- salt and pepper

* Make the pastry following the recipe on page 247 and leave to rest for 30 minutes before using.
* Melt the butter in a large saucepan over a medium heat, add the onion, garlic and thyme and fry for 8–10 minutes until soft. Add the mushrooms, season with salt and pepper and cook for another 6–7 minutes until the mushrooms have released their juices and the pan has dried out. Add the cheese and milk and stir through, then reduce the heat and simmer for 5 minutes, or until the mixture has thickened. Add the Worcestershire sauce and more salt and pepper. Stir in the parsley, then remove from the heat and leave to cool.
* Spoon the mushroom mixture into a large pie dish, about 1–1.5 litre/34–50 fl oz capacity. Roll out the pastry on a lightly floured work counter to make a lid, then carefully lay the pastry over the dish and seal with egg wash. Use a sharp knife to make a steam hole in the top and brush with more egg wash. Let the pie firm up in the fridge for 20 minutes.
* Meanwhile, preheat the oven to 220°C/425°F/Gas Mark 7.
* Bake the pie in the oven for 20 minutes, then reduce the oven temperature to 180°C/350°F/Gas Mark 4 and bake for another 25 minutes, or until the pastry is golden brown and the mixture is bubbling through the steam hole. Serve.

UNITED KINGDOM
*

CHICKEN, LEEK
AND
TARRAGON PIE

A comforting chicken and leek pie with a rough puff pastry lid. The tarragon pairs well with the chicken and gives this rich and creamy filling an extra lift.

Serves: 6
Prep time: 1 hour, plus 1 hour 20 minutes resting and chilling
Cook time: 2 hours
{ₒ•}

- 1 quantity Rough Puff Pastry (page 247)
- 1 medium whole chicken
- 600 ml/ 20 fl oz (2½ cups) chicken stock
- 600 ml/ 20 fl oz (2½ cups) full-fat (whole) milk
- 2 bay leaves
- 1 sprig thyme
- 60 g/ 2¼ oz (½ stick) butter
- 100 g/ 3½ oz (½ cup) dry-cured bacon, chopped
- 2 leeks, sliced
- 3 tablespoons chopped tarragon
- 60 g/ 2¼ oz (½ cup) plain (all-purpose) flour, plus extra for dusting
- 125 ml/ 4¼ fl oz (½ cup) double (heavy) cream
- 1 egg, beaten with 1 tablespoon water or milk, for egg wash
- salt and pepper
- Mashed Potatoes (page 80) and greens, to serve

* Make the pastry following the recipe on page 247 and leave to rest for 30 minutes before using.
* Put the chicken, stock and milk into a large saucepan with salt, pepper, the bay leaves and thyme. Cover with a lid and poach over a low heat for 45 minutes, or until the chicken is cooked and the juices run clear when pierced with a skewer. Remove the chicken and strain the cooking liquor into a jug (pitcher). Set both aside.
* Melt the butter in another saucepan, add the bacon and fry over a medium heat for 5–6 minutes until browned. Add the leeks and tarragon and cook for 12–15 minutes until soft. Stir in the flour, then add the reserved cooking liquor a little at a time, whisking constantly. When it has all been added, simmer for 15 minutes, stirring occasionally.
* Meanwhile, strip the meat from the chicken and cut into even bite-sized pieces, before stirring through the sauce with the cream. Taste and adjust the seasoning, then leave to cool completely.
* Preheat the oven to 220°C/ 425°F/ Gas Mark 7.
* Put the pie filling into a large pie dish, about 2 litre/ 68 fl oz capacity. Roll out the puff pastry on a floured work counter to slightly larger than your dish, then lay it over the top of the dish and brush egg wash around the sides to seal it onto the pie dish. Trim the edges and crimp with a fork. Use a knife to cut a steam hole in the centre and brush with more egg wash. Bake in the oven for 25 minutes. Reduce the oven temperature to 180°C/ 350°F/ Gas Mark 4 and cook for another 20 minutes, or until golden brown and piping hot. Serve with Mashed Potatoes and greens.

UNITED KINGDOM
*

CHICKEN
AND
HAM (OR MUSHROOM) PIE

Another riff on the creamy chicken pie, make yours with diced or shredded ham – or mushrooms. In any case, you'll have sensed a theme: that the exact ingredients of these warming pies can be tailored to personal (or seasonal) taste.

Serves: 6
Prep time: 1 hour, plus 1 hour 20 minutes resting and chilling
Cook time: 1 hour 55 minutes
{ₒ•}

- 1 quantity Rough Puff Pastry (page 247)
- 1 medium whole chicken
- 600 ml/ 20 fl oz (2½ cups) chicken stock
- 600 ml/ 20 fl oz (2½ cups) full-fat (whole) milk
- 2 bay leaves
- 1 sprig thyme
- 60 g/ 2¼ oz (½ stick) butter
- 250 g/ 9 oz cooked ham, diced or 250 g/ 9 oz Portobello mushrooms, quartered
- 2 onions, chopped
- 60 g/ 2¼ oz (½ cup) plain (all-purpose) flour, plus extra for dusting
- 125 ml/ 4¼ fl oz (½ cup) double (heavy) cream
- 2 tablespoons chopped flat-leaf parsley
- 1 egg, beaten with 1 tablespoon water or milk, for egg wash
- salt and pepper

* Make the pastry following the recipe on page 247 and leave to rest for 30 minutes before using.
* Put the chicken, stock and milk into a large saucepan with salt, pepper, the bay leaves and thyme. Cover with a lid and poach over a low heat for 45 minutes, or until the chicken is cooked and the juices run clear when pierced with a skewer. Remove the chicken and strain the cooking liquor into a jug (pitcher). Set both aside.
* Melt the butter in another saucepan over a medium heat, add the diced ham or mushrooms and fry for 5 minutes, or until golden. Add the onions and fry for another 5–6 minutes until soft and golden. Stir in the flour and cook for 5 minutes, or until the roux is pale golden brown. Add the reserved cooking liquor a little at a time, whisking constantly. When it has all been added, simmer for 15 minutes, stirring occasionally.
* Meanwhile, strip the meat from the chicken and cut it into large dice. Mix into the sauce with the cream and parsley, and taste and adjust the seasoning. Remove from the heat and leave to to cool completely.
* Preheat the oven to 220°C/ 425°F/ Gas Mark 7.
* Put the pie filling into a large pie dish, about 2 litre/ 68 fl oz capacity. Roll out the puff pastry on a floured work counter to slightly larger than your dish, then lay it over the top of the dish and secure around the lip of the dish with the egg wash. Trim the edges and crimp with a fork. Use a knife to cut a steam hole in the centre and brush the top of the pie with more egg wash. Bake in the oven for 25 minutes, then reduce the oven temperature to 180°C/ 350°F/ Gas Mark 6 and bake for another 20 minutes, or until golden brown and piping hot. Serve.

Chicken, leek and tarragon pie

UNITED KINGDOM

*

STEAK
AND
ALE PIE

Filled with tender steak slow cooked in a rich ale gravy, and capped with a lid of flaky suet pastry crust, this steak pie is essentially a variation on the famous Victorian steak and kidney pudding. As time and tastes have changed, it has gone on to outshine the classic recipe. Serve with Mashed Potatoes (page 80) or Chips (page 84), more beef gravy, roasted vegetables and cold pints of British ale.

Serves: 4–6
Prep time: 1 hour, plus 1 hour 10 minutes chilling
Cook time: 3½–4½ hours
{•°}

- 1 x 5–7.5 cm/2–3 inch beef shin (shank) bone (full of marrow)
- 4 tablespoons beef dripping
- 1 kg/2¼ lb beef shin (shank), cut into 3–4 cm/ 1¼–1½ inch cubes
- 1 litre/34 fl oz (4¼ cups) good British ale
- 3 banana shallots, halved lengthways
- 6 whole cloves garlic, peeled
- 1 handful rosemary and thyme leaves
- 1 bay leaf
- 2 tablespoons Worcestershire sauce
- 1 quantity Suet Pastry (page 246)
- plain (all-purpose) flour, for dusting and thickening
- butter, for thickening
- 1 egg, beaten with 1 tablespoon of water or milk, for egg wash
- salt and pepper

- To serve:
- Mashed Potatoes (page 80) or Chips (page 84)
- Gravy (page 420)
- roasted vegetables

* Preheat the oven to 220°C/425°F/Gas Mark 7.
* Put the bone marrow onto a baking sheet and roast in the oven for 20 minutes. Remove from the oven and leave to cool (you can set aside and keep the rendered fat for another day). Reduce the oven temperature to 130°C/250°F/Gas Mark ½.
* Heat a large frying pan or skillet over a medium heat and add 1 tablespoon of the dripping. Season the beef well with salt, then, working in 3 batches, add to the pan and fry for 3–4 minutes. Add a glug of the ale each time you remove the beef and stir over the heat, scraping up all the crispy bits that are stuck to the bottom of the pan, then pour the ale into a jug (pitcher) and wipe the pan with paper towels. Set the seared beef and ale aside.
* Wipe the pan clean again, add the remaining dripping and heat over a low heat. Season the shallots, then put into the pan, cut-side down, with the whole garlic cloves and fry for 10 minutes, or until caramelized. Meanwhile, finely chop enough rosemary and thyme leaves to give you 2–3 tablespoons and set aside.
* When the shallots and garlic are caramelized, add the beef back to the pan with the remaining ale, bay leaf, chopped herbs, Worcestershire sauce and a couple of grinds of

pepper. Bring to a simmer, then transfer to a suitably sized casserole dish or Dutch oven. Make sure the mix is almost fully submerged (like a crocodile in a swamp), cover with baking (parchment) paper and a lid or aluminium foil, then put onto the centre shelf of the oven and cook for 2–3 hours until tender and giving when a skewer is inserted into the thickest piece of beef (if it's still a bit tough, be brave and put it back in, checking every 30 minutes or so).
* Meanwhile, make the pastry following the recipe on page 246. Divide the dough in half, roll into 2 balls (for a top and bottom), wrap in clingfilm (plastic wrap) and leave to chill in the fridge for 20 minutes.
* Roll out one of the chilled pastry balls on a lightly floured work counter until it is 3 mm/⅛ inch thick, making sure it is 3 cm/1¼ inches wider all round than your chosen pie dish. Put it in between 2 pieces of clingfilm and set aside. This is for the top. For the bottom, roll out the second ball of pastry as thinly as possible and cut it 4 cm/1½ inches wider than the dish. Put it in between 2 pieces of clingfilm (plastic wrap) and set aside.
* When the beef is ready, remove from the oven and strain the cooking liquid into a small saucepan (make sure to weigh the volume of the liquid). Cook the liquid over a medium heat for a few minutes until it is reduced to a strong concentration of flavour. Season with salt, if necessary. When happy, weigh again, then thicken the liquid with the addition of 20 g/¾ oz (4 teaspoons) each of butter and flour per 300 ml/10 fl oz (1¼ cups) liquid. When thickened, add the beef and shallots to the liquid, mix well and leave to cool completely.
* Once the filling has cooled, line your chosen pie dish with the bottom pastry piece, then add the filling, nestle the roasted marrow bone into the middle of the mix in an upright position and brush egg wash around the sides of the pastry. Cut a small cross in the very middle of the top pastry sheet (big enough to allow the bone to come through the lid) and use the top piece of pastry to cover the top of the pie. Crimp the sides of the pastry onto the dish lip and put into the fridge for 30 minutes to firm up.
* Using a serrated knife, trim the excess pastry away from the pie dish, crimp again and brush with more egg wash, then chill for another 20 minutes. At this stage, your pie is ready to be baked. This can be prepared well in advance.
* Preheat the oven to 200°C/400°F/Gas Mark 6.
* Brush the pastry with more egg wash and bake the pie in the top of the oven for 40–60 minutes until the pastry is golden and the filling is piping hot when tested with a skewer. Serve with Mashed Potatoes or Chips, Gravy and roasted vegetables.

Steak and ale pie

UNITED KINGDOM
*

STEAK, KIDNEY
AND
OYSTER PIE

A somewhat surprising but altogether delightful combination, oysters have graced British steak pies for at least two hundred years. They notably appear as a suggested addition in Eliza Acton's 1845 recipe for 'beef-steak pie' found in *Modern Cookery for Private Families*. Eat with the potatoes of your choosing, buttered greens, more gravy, and a nice cold pint.

Serves: 6–8
Prep time: 1 hour, plus 1 hour 20 minutes resting and chilling
Cook time: 2½ hours
{⋅•⋅}

- 1 quantity Rough Puff Pastry (page 247)
- 150 g/5 oz (1¼ sticks) butter
- 2 large onions, chopped
- about 4 tablespoons plain (all-purpose) flour
- 2 kg/4½ lb casserole beef, diced
- 1 kg/2¼ lb ox kidney, sliced or chopped
- 600 ml/20 fl oz (2½ cups) red wine or stout
- 600 ml/20 fl oz (2½ cups) beef stock or water
- bouquet garni of a few sprigs rosemary and thyme, flat-leaf parsley stalks and 2 bay leaves tied together with kitchen string
- 500 g/1 lb 2 oz mushrooms, sliced
- 1 tablespoon vegetable oil
- 12 oysters, shucked (page 124), liquor reserved
- 2 tablespoons chopped flat-leaf parsley
- plain (all-purpose) flour, for dusting
- 1 egg, beaten with 1 tablespoon of water or milk, for egg wash
- salt and pepper

- To serve:
- potatoes of choice
- buttered greens
- Gravy (page 420)

* Make the pastry following the recipe on page 247 and leave to rest for 30 minutes before using.
* Preheat the oven to 150°C/300°F/Gas Mark 2.
* Melt two-thirds of the butter in a large casserole dish or Dutch oven over a medium heat, add the onions and fry for 7–8 minutes. Remove with a slotted spoon and set aside in a large bowl.
* Spread the flour out on a large plate and season with 1 teaspoon each of salt and pepper. Dust the beef and kidneys in the flour, then add to the dish and cook over a medium-high heat for 6–7 minutes until browned all over. Remove with a slotted spoon and add them to the bowl with the onions. Pour the wine into the casserole dish or Dutch oven and stir over the heat, scraping up all the crispy bits that are stuck to the bottom of the pan. Add the stock or water and the bouquet garni, then slowly bring to a simmer over a medium heat.
* Meanwhile, put the mushrooms into a large frying pan or skillet and fry in the oil over a high heat for 5 minutes, or until well browned. Add the remaining butter and mix

the mushrooms through with the onions, beef and kidneys. Carefully spoon the mixture into the casserole dish or Dutch oven and bake in the oven for 90–120 minutes until the beef is tender.
* When the beef is tender, add the oysters, reserved liquor and parsley and leave to cool completely.
* Increase the oven temperature to 220°C/425°F/Gas Mark 7.
* Remove the bouquet garni and pour the cooled filling into a 3 litre/100 fl oz pie dish.
* Roll out the pastry on a lightly floured work counter to make a lid, then carefully lay the pastry over the top and brush egg wash around the sides to seal it onto the pie dish. Use a sharp knife to cut a steam hole in the centre and brush with more egg wash. Bake in the oven for 25 minutes, or until the pastry is risen and golden. Reduce the oven temperature to 180°C/350°F/Gas Mark 4 and bake for another 35 minutes, or until the centre is piping hot. Serve with potatoes of choice, buttered greens and Gravy.

ENGLAND: DEVON
*

DEVONSHIRE SQUAB PIE

This pie, traditional to Devon and the southwest of England, was originally made with squab (month-old pigeons) but in the course of the eighteenth century its filling changed altogether: out went the squab, and in came a mixture of mutton and apples. Modern bakers might make a further alteration – swapping out mutton for the milder flavours of lamb.

Serves: 6
Prep time: 40 minutes, plus 50 minutes resting and chilling
Cook time: 1½ hours
{⋅•⋅}

- 1 quantity Shortcrust Pastry (page 247) or Beef Dripping Crust (page 246)
- 30 g/1 oz (2 tablespoons) lard or dripping
- 500 g/1 lb 2 oz lamb or mutton, finely diced
- 1 onion, sliced
- 1 teaspoon chopped rosemary
- 200 ml/7 fl oz (¾ cup plus 1 tablespoon) beef or lamb stock
- 1 large Bramley (cooking) apple, peeled, cored and sliced
- 2 teaspoons caster (superfine) sugar
- ½ nutmeg
- plain (all-purpose) flour, for dusting
- 1 egg, beaten with 1 tablespoon water or milk, for egg wash
- salt and pepper

* Make the pastry following the recipe on page 246 or 247 and leave to rest for 20 minutes (shortcrust) and 30 minutes (beef dripping crust) before using.
* Heat the fat in a large frying pan or skillet over a medium heat, add the diced lamb and cook for 5 minutes, or until browned all over. Add the onion and rosemary and season well with salt and pepper. Cook for 10–15 minutes until the onion is well coloured and soft. Remove from the heat and leave to cool.
* Tip the cooled lamb mixture into a deep pie dish, about 2 litre/68 fl oz capacity, then pour in the stock. Put the

apple slices and sugar into a small bowl and mix together, then arrange on top of the lamb. Grate the nutmeg over the top of the apples.

* Roll out the pastry on a lightly floured work counter to make a lid, then carefully lay the pastry over the dish and seal with egg wash. Use a sharp knife to cut a steam hole in the centre and brush the top with more egg wash. Let the pie firm up in the fridge for 20 minutes.
* Meanwhile, preheat the oven to 220°C/425°F/Gas Mark 6.
* Bake the pie in the oven for 20 minutes, then reduce the oven temperature to 160°C/325°F/Gas Mark 3 and cook for another 50–55 minutes until golden brown and bubbling. Leave to cool slightly, then serve.

SCOTLAND
*

SCOTCH PIE

These small, hand-held pies are made using a thin crust of hot water pastry and usually have a filling of well-spiced mutton, lamb or beef – with mutton being the most traditional, but the least common these days. They are often served at bakeries, takeaway restaurants or sports stadiums across Scotland.

Eat warm or cold, on its own, or topped with baked beans and Mashed Potatoes (page 80).

Serves: 6
Prep time: 40 minutes, plus 30 minutes resting and chilling
Cook time: 1½ hours
{•••}

- 1 quantity Hot Water Pastry (page 246)
- plain (all-purpose) flour, for dusting
- 1 kg/2¼ lb (8⅓ cups) minced (ground) lamb, mutton or beef
- ¼ teaspoon ground nutmeg
- ¼ teaspoon ground mace
- 200 ml/7 fl oz (¾ cup plus 1 tablespoon) beef or lamb stock
- 1 egg, beaten with 1 tablespoon water, for egg wash
- salt

- To serve (optional):
- Mashed Potatoes (page 80)
- baked beans

* Make the pastry following the recipe on page 246 and leave to rest for 10 minutes before using.
* Roll out two-thirds of the pastry on a lightly floured work counter and use it to line 6 x 140 x 60 mm/5½–2½ inch pie or chef's rings.
* Put the minced (ground) meat into a large bowl, add the spices and ½ teaspoon of salt and, using your hands or a wooden spoon, mix the spices and salt through the meat. Spoon the mixture into the pie rings and pour over the stock.
* Roll out the remaining pastry and cut out 6 circles to the size of the rings, then put them on top of the pies and secure with egg wash. Use a sharp knife to cut a steam hole in the centre of the lids and brush with egg wash. Put the pies into the fridge to firm up for 20 minutes.
* Meanwhile, preheat the oven to 200°C/400°F/Gas Mark 6 and put a baking sheet onto the centre shelf to heat up.
* Carefully put the pies onto the hot baking sheet and bake in the oven for 30 minutes. Reduce the oven temperature to 180°C/350°F/Gas Mark 4 and bake for 1 hour. Serve with Mashed Potatoes and baked beans, if desired

---

WALES
*

WELSH KATT PIE

The Katt Pie was once a popular feature of the Templeton Fair in Pembrokeshire, Wales, where it was baked annually for over 200 years. According to the Welsh food writer Bobby Freeman, the name 'Katt' comes from a London pie shop – owned by Christopher Cat – that was famous for its sweet mutton pies.

At the time of its creation, many sweet pies were still made with minced (ground) meat, so the inclusion of mutton wouldn't have thrown its customers off. The Katt Pie is still made today in Pembrokeshire households, but typically with minced (ground) lamb instead of mutton. Serve hot.

Serves: 6
Prep time: 50 minutes, plus 40 minutes resting and chilling
Cook time: 1 hour
{•••}

- 1 (generous) quantity Shortcrust Pastry (page 247)
- plain (all-purpose) flour, for dusting
- 400 g/14 oz (1¾ cups) minced (ground) lamb
- 100 g/3½ oz beef or lamb suet
- 200 g/7 oz (¾ cup plus 1 tablespoon) currants
- 40 g/1½ oz (¼ cup) candied orange peel (optional)
- 60 g/2¼ oz (⅓ cup) soft brown sugar
- ½ teaspoon thyme leaves
- ¼ teaspoon ground nutmeg
- 1 egg, beaten with 1 tablespoon of water or milk, for egg wash

* Make the pastry following the recipe on page 247 and leave to rest for 20 minutes before using.
* Roll out half the pastry on a floured work counter and use to line a pie plate, 24–26 cm/9½–10½ inches wide.
* Put all the remaining ingredients, except the egg wash, in a large bowl and mix thoroughly to combine. Spoon the mixture into the pastry-lined plate.
* Roll out the remaining pastry to the circumference of the pie plate and carefully lay the pastry over the pie plate. Trim off the excess pastry, then gently press down around the edges and seal with egg wash. Use a sharp knife to make a steam hole in the top and brush with more egg wash. Let the pie firm up in the fridge for 20 minutes.
* Meanwhile, preheat the oven to 200°C/400°F/Gas Mark 6.
* Bake the pie in the oven for 20 minutes, then reduce the oven temperature to 180°C/350°F/Gas Mark 4 and bake for another 40 minutes. Serve hot.

UNITED KINGDOM
*

GAME PIE

A rich game pie is ideally made using the left-overs from a roast but will work just as well with uncooked oven-ready birds. The following recipe is versatile and intended for adaptation – swap in seasonal produce or any game meat and its stock, and leave the overall measurements unchanged. Serve this pie warm with plenty of Mashed Potatoes (page 80) and Gravy (page 420).

Serves: 6
Prep time: 1 hour, plus 40 minutes resting and chilling
Cook time: 50 minutes
{ᵔ}

- 2 x quantity Shortcrust Pastry (page 247)
- 3–4 oven-ready game birds (1 pheasant and 2 pigeons weighing 1.5–2 kg/3¼–4½ lb in total),
or about 1 kg/2¼ lb meat from precooked/roasted birds along with their bones and carcass
- bouquet garni of 2 sprigs thyme, flat-leaf parsley stalks, 2 pieces pared orange zest, 2 bay leaves tied together with kitchen string
- 30 g/1 oz (2 tablespoons) lard
- 100 g/3½ oz smoked streaky bacon rashers (slices), chopped
- 1 onion, chopped
- 2 carrots, diced
- 2 stalks celery, diced
- 1½ teaspoons salt
- ½ teaspoon black pepper
- 50 g/2 oz (½ cup minus 2 teaspoons) plain (all-purpose) flour
- 100 ml/3½ fl oz (⅓ cup plus 1 tablespoon) port
- 2 teaspoons chopped flat-leaf parsley
- plain (all-purpose) flour, for dusting
- 1 egg, beaten with 1 tablespoon water or milk, for egg wash

- To serve:
- Mashed Potatoes (page 80)
- Gravy (page 420)

* Make the pastry following the recipe on page 247 and leave to rest for 20 minutes before using.
* Split the birds down the back and through the breast to make 2 approximate halves. Pack them into a large stockpot with the bouquet garni and cover with about 750 ml/25 fl oz (3 cups) water. Simmer over a medium-low heat for 45 minutes, or until tender, then strain, keeping the liquor. Put the carcasses onto a chopping (cutting) board and pick or cut the meat off the bones, setting the meat aside in a large bowl.
* Heat the lard in a saucepan over a medium heat, add the bacon and fry for 8 minutes, then remove and set aside. Add the onion to the pan and cook for another 12–15 minutes until golden brown. Add the vegetables, season with ½ teaspoon of the salt and the pepper, then cover with a lid and cook gently for 10 minutes, or until soft.
* Sift the flour into the pan and stir in, then stir in the port and then some of the reserved cooking liquor, stirring to make a rather thick sauce. Stir in the cooked meat and parsley and season with the remaining salt.
* Roll out two-thirds of the pastry on a lightly floured work

counter and use it to line a pie dish, 1.5 litre/50 fl oz capacity, then pour in the filling. Roll out the remaining pastry to make a lid, then carefully lay it over the dish and seal with egg wash. Use a sharp knife to cut a steam hole in the centre and brush the top with more egg wash. Let the pie firm up in the fridge for 20 minutes.
* Meanwhile, preheat the oven to 220°C/425°F/Gas Mark 7.
* Bake the pie in the oven for 20 minutes, then reduce the oven temperature to 180°C/350°F/Gas Mark 4 and bake for another 30 minutes until golden brown. Serve with Mashed Potatoes and Gravy.

ENGLAND: SHROPSHIRE AND CHESHIRE

FIDGET PIE

This rustic Shropshire pie is made with a layered filling of diced bacon or gammon (ham), potatoes and apples. These days, some modern bakers forgo the top layer of shortcrust for a piping of creamy mustard mash.

Serves: 4
Prep time: 30 minutes, plus 40 minutes resting and chilling
Cook time: 1 hour
{ᵔ}

- 1 quantity Shortcrust Pastry (page 247)
- 500 g/1 lb 2 oz potatoes, peeled and sliced
- 400 g/14 oz (2¼ cups) gammon (ham), diced
- 2 onions, sliced
- 2 Bramley (cooking) apples, peeled, cored and sliced
- 1 tablespoon soft brown sugar
- 250 ml/8 fl oz (1 cup) homemade chicken or pork stock or shop-bought stock and 3 gelatine leaves soaked in cold water (optional)
- plain (all-purpose) flour, for dusting
- 1 egg, beaten with 1 tablespoon water or milk, for egg wash
- salt and pepper

* Make the pastry following the recipe on page 247 and leave to rest for 20 minutes before using.
* Arrange alternate layers of the potatoes, diced gammon (ham), onions and apples in a large pie dish, about 2 litre/68 fl oz capacity, until they are all used up. Season between the layers with the sugar, salt and pepper. Pour in the stock. If you're not using homemade stock, you may want to add some gelatine to the shop-bought variety. Do so by heating a little stock in a saucepan until hot, squeezing out the excess cold water from the soaked gelatine leaves and adding them to the hot stock, stirring until they are fully dissolved. Top up (top off) with more water until you have 250 ml/8 fl oz (1 cup) of the now-gelatinous stock.
* Roll out the pastry on a lightly floured work counter to make a lid, then lay the pastry over the dish and seal with egg wash. Use a sharp knife to cut a steam hole in the centre and brush the top with more egg wash. Let the pie firm up in the fridge for 20 minutes.
* Meanwhile, preheat the oven to 220°C/425°F/Gas Mark 7.
* Bake the pie in the oven for 20 minutes, then reduce the oven temperature to 180°C/350°F/Gas Mark 4 and bake for another 40 minutes. Serve.

UNITED KINGDOM
*

PIGEON PIE

This traditional pigeon pie is made with a layer of suet pastry, which, once cooked, is pushed into the filling and topped with another layer of puff pastry. The first layer of pastry is meant to act like suet dumplings, absorbing the juices from the rich stock, and taking the place of mashed or boiled potatoes – as in a stew.

Notes: Those with means often included a layer of chopped beef or steak at the bottom of pigeon pies – whether or not it had a dumpling crust.

Serves: 6
Prep time: 2½ hours, plus 1 hour 20 minutes chilling
Cook time: 2½ hours
{↝•}

- ½ quantity Suet Pastry (page 246)
- ½ quantity Rough Puff Pastry (page 247)
- 40 g/1½ oz (3 tablespoons) butter or lard
- 6 oven-ready pigeons
- 200 g/7 oz button mushrooms
- 150 g/5 oz smoked streaky (lean) bacon, diced
- 1 onion, diced
- 2 stalks celery, diced
- 30 g/1 oz (3¾ tablespoons) plain (all-purpose) flour
- 500 ml/17 fl oz (2 cups plus 1 tablespoon) beef or game stock
- 100 ml/3½ fl oz (⅓ cup plus 1 tablespoon) port
- 12 allspice berries
- 12 juniper berries
- bouquet garni of 2 bay leaves, 3 sprigs thyme and 2 sprigs rosemary tied together with kitchen string
- plain (all-purpose) flour, for dusting
- 1 egg, beaten with 1 tablespoon of water or milk, for egg wash
- salt and pepper

* Make the Suet Pastry following the recipe on page 246 and leave to chill for 20 minutes before using.
* Make the Rough Puff Pastry following the recipe on page 247 and leave to rest for 30 minutes before using.
* Melt the butter or lard in a large saucepan over a medium heat, add the pigeons and cook for 10 minutes, or until browned all over. Remove the birds using a slotted spoon and set aside.
* Add the mushrooms to the pan, increase the heat to medium-high and fry for 5 minutes, or until browned. Remove using a slotted spoon and set aside. Add the bacon to the pan and fry over a medium-high heat for 10–12 minutes until crispy. Add the onion and celery, reduce the heat to medium and fry for 8 minutes, or until soft. Add the flour and stir thoroughly. Beat in the stock using a wooden spoon, then beat in the port until the sauce is smooth. Put the pigeons, mushrooms and herbs into the pan. Crush the berries, then tie them in a little muslin (cheesecloth) bag and add them to the pan with the bouquet garni. Season well, cover with a lid and simmer gently over a medium heat for 1 hour, or until the pigeons are tender.
* Remove the pigeons and leave to cool. When cool, cut the breasts from the carcass with a short sharp knife, then remove the thigh meat and smaller parts with your hands. Chop the meat into neat pieces. Remove and discard the bouquet garni and spice bag from the pan, then add the

pigeon meat and stir through. Pour the mixture into a large pie dish, about 1.5–1.75 litre/50–60 fl oz capacity.
* Preheat the oven to 180°C/350°F/Gas Mark 4.
* Roll out the Suet Pastry and carefully lay the pastry over the dish. Bake in the oven for 20–25 minutes until the suet layer has risen and cooked through. Remove the pie from the oven, break up the suet crust and, using a fork, push it into the filling. Increase the oven temperature to 220°C/425°F/Gas Mark 7.
* Roll out the Rough Puff Pastry on a lightly floured work counter to make a lid, then carefully lay the pastry over the top and seal with egg wash. Use a sharp knife to make a steam hole in the top and brush with more egg wash. Bake the pie again for 25 minutes, or until the pastry has risen and is crisp. Reduce the oven temperature to 180°C/350°F/Gas Mark 4 and bake for another 10–15 minutes until bubbling hot. Serve.

ENGLAND
*

BACON
AND
EGG PIE

This quiche-like pie is simple enough to make in the morning, and perfect for a savoury breakfast. Serve in generous slices alongside a dollop of Brown Sauce (page 426) or Rhubarb Ketchup (page 426).

Serves: 4–6
Prep time: 25 minutes, plus 20 minutes resting
Cook time: 40 minutes
{↝•}

- 2 x quantity Shortcrust Pastry (page 247)
- plain (all-purpose) flour, for dusting
- 4 eggs
- 300 ml/10 fl oz (1¼ cups) double (heavy) cream
- 200 g/7 oz dry-cured smoked streaky (lean) bacon, chopped
- 1 egg, beaten with 1 tablespoon water or milk, for egg wash
- salt and pepper
- Brown Sauce (page 426) or Damson Ketchup (page 426), to serve

* Make the pastry following the recipe on page 247 and leave to rest for 20 minutes before using.
* Preheat the oven to 220°C/425°F/Gas Mark 7. Put a baking sheet onto the centre shelf to heat up.
* Roll out two-thirds of the pastry on a lightly floured work counter and use it to line a shallow 20 cm/8 inch pie dish or tart pan. Put the eggs and cream into a medium bowl and whisk together, then season with a little salt and pepper. Arrange the bacon on the bottom of the pastry in the dish, then pour over the egg mixture.
* Roll out the remaining pastry to make a lid, then carefully lay it over the dish and seal with egg wash. Use a sharp knife to cut a steam hole in the centre and brush the top with more egg wash. Carefully put the dish onto the hot baking sheet and bake in the oven for 20 minutes. Reduce the oven temperature to 180°C/350°F/Gas Mark 4 and bake for another 20 minutes. Serve warm with Brown Sauce or Rhubarb Ketchup.

SCOTLAND: FIFE
*

RABBIT
AND
BACON PIE

This rich rabbit and bacon pie is based on a traditional Kingdom of Fife pie, often cited in historic Scottish cookbooks, but which otherwise seems lost to time. The recipe was adapted by Fife-based chef James Ferguson, proprietor of the Kinneuchar Inn, who has garnered a reputation for his own pies.

Serves: 4
Prep time: 2 hours, plus 3¼ hours resting and chilling
Cook time: 3–3½ hours
{•'}

- For the pastry:
- 500 g/ 1 lb 2 oz (4 cups plus 4 teaspoons) strong bread flour
- 100 g/ 3½ oz (¾ cup plus 2 teaspoons) wholemeal (whole wheat) spelt flour, plus extra for dusting
- 1 teaspoon fine sea salt
- 60 g/ 2¼ oz (4 tablespoons) lard
- 350 g/ 12 oz (3 sticks) cold unsalted butter, diced into 1 cm/ ½ inch cubes
- 150 ml/ 5 fl oz (⅔ cup) full-fat (whole) milk
- 1 tablespoon white wine vinegar
- 1 egg, beaten with 1 tablespoon water or milk, for egg wash
- 1 egg and a splash of milk, beaten, to glaze

- For the filling:
- 2 eggs
- 1 tablespoon lard
- 1 wild rabbit, cut into pieces (ask your butcher)
- 400 g/ 14 oz smoked streaky (lean) bacon, cut into 1 cm/ ½ inch chunks
- 8 round shallots, peeled
- 5 cloves garlic, peeled
- 2 fresh bay leaves
- 50 g/ 2 oz (1⅔ cups) sage, leaves picked and chopped
- 500 ml/ 17 fl oz (2 cups plus 1 tablespoon) dry cider
- 500 ml/ 17 fl oz (2 cups plus 1 tablespoon) chicken stock
- 100 g/ 3½ oz (7 tablespoons) butter
- 100 g/ 3½ oz (¾ cup plus 2 teaspoons) plain (all-purpose) flour
- 2 teaspoons Dijon mustard
- salt and pepper

- For the forcemeat balls:
- rabbit's liver, heart, kidneys, finely chopped
- 150 g/ 5 oz (⅔ cup) smoked streaky (lean) bacon, minced (ground)
- 100 g/ 3½ oz (2 cups) fresh white breadcrumbs
- 1 egg, beaten
- 1 teaspoon ground white pepper
- few gratings of nutmeg
- 1 tablespoon medium-dry sherry

- To serve:
- buttered kale

* To make the pastry, put the flours and salt into a large bowl, add the lard and rub it in with your fingertips until

fully incorporated. Add the butter to the flour mix and lightly coat all the cubes (do not work the butter into the flour). Make a well in the centre and stir in the milk, 150 ml/ 5 fl oz (⅔ cup) chilled water and the vinegar. You should now have a lumpy pastry. Cover with clingfilm (plastic wrap) and leave to rest at room temperature for 45 minutes. Once rested, roll out on a floured work counter to a rectangle 1.5 cm/⅝ inch thick. Fold into thirds, turn 90 degrees and roll to 1.5 cm/⅝ inch thick again. Wrap in clingfilm and leave to chill in the fridge for 30 minutes. Repeat this process 3 times.

* For the filling, bring a small saucepan of water to the boil, carefully add the eggs and boil for 7 minutes, or until soft-boiled. Drain, peel off the shells and set aside.

* Heat the lard in a large frying pan or skillet over a medium heat. Season the rabbit, then add to the pan and fry for 5–7 minutes, or until browned all over. Transfer to an ovenproof casserole dish or Dutch oven deep and wide enough to accommodate all the ingredients.

* Add the bacon to the frying pan or skillet and fry over a medium heat for 8 minutes, or until browned. Add the shallots and garlic and cook for 5 minutes, or until soft but not coloured. Add the bay and sage, then put into the pan with the rabbit.

* Preheat the oven to 170°C/ 325°F/ Gas Mark 3.

* Put the casserole dish or Dutch oven onto the stove over a medium heat and bring everything to a nice sizzle, then immediately add the cider. Cook for several minutes, until the cider is reduced by half, then add enough stock to just cover, being careful to not flood (think paddling pool not swimming pool!). Cover the dish with a lid and cook in the oven for 2 hours, or until the rabbit comes easily off the bone.

* Strain everything through a fine-mesh sieve into a large heatproof bowl and set the cooking liquor aside. Put the shallots and bacon into another heatproof bowl. Remove all the rabbit meat from the bones and combine with the shallot and bacon mix.

* Melt the butter in a large saucepan over a medium-low heat. Add the flour and cook, stirring constantly, for 3–4 minutes, or until it smells biscuity. Pour in the reserved cooking liquid and simmer over a low-medium heat for 10 minutes, or until the sauce thickens to a consistency that coats the back of a spoon. Add the mustard and adjust the seasoning if necessary. Combine with the rabbit and leave to cool completely.

* For the forcemeat balls, put all the ingredients into a large metal bowl and mix together until combined. Add salt cautiously as the bacon packs a punch. Roll the mixture into 30 g/ 1 oz balls and set aside.

* To assemble the pie, roll out two-thirds of the pastry on a lightly floured work counter until it is 3 mm/ ⅛ inch thick, then use to line a 28 cm/ 11 inch pie dish, allowing some overhang. Add the rabbit filling, then nestle in the forcemeat balls and boiled eggs, keeping the eggs whole. Roll out the remaining pastry and carefully lay the pastry over the dish. Gently press down around the edges and seal with the egg wash. Let the pie firm up in the fridge for 1 hour.

* Preheat the oven to 200°C/ 400°F/ Gas Mark 6. Put a large baking sheet onto the centre shelf to heat up.

* Trim off the excess pastry from around the edge of the pie, brush the pie with the glaze, then cut a small steam hole in the centre. Put the pie onto the hot baking sheet and bake in the oven for 20 minutes. Reduce the oven temperature to 180°C/ 350°F/ Gas Mark 4 and bake for another 30 minutes, or until golden and bubbling. Serve with buttered kale.

Rabbit and bacon pie

ENGLAND
*

ROOK PIE

This English country pie was traditionally made with rooks – a cousin to the crow – and invariably included chopped vegetables and hard-boiled eggs, or diced beef – as in traditional pigeon pies. Today, pigeon breasts will work just as well. Serve warm with Mashed Potatoes (page 80) and buttered greens.

Serves: 6
Prep time: 30 minutes, plus 40–50 minutes resting and chilling
Cook time: 1 hour 40 minutes
{✿}

- ½ quantity Rough Puff Pastry (page 247) or Shortcrust Pastry (page 247)
- 60 g/2¼ oz (½ stick) butter
- 200 g/7 oz (¾ cup plus 2 tablespoons) diced beef
- 1 onion, thinly sliced
- 1 carrot, sliced
- 2 stalks celery, sliced
- 1 small bunch thyme, leaves picked
- 60 ml/2 fl oz (¼ cup) red wine
- 150 ml/5 fl oz (⅔ cup) beef stock
- 6 pigeon breasts, cut into large chunks
- plain (all-purpose) flour, for dusting
- 1 egg, beaten with 1 tablespoon of water or milk, for egg wash
- salt and pepper

- To serve:
- Mashed Potatoes (page 80)
- buttered greens

* Make the pastry following the recipe on page 247 and leave to rest for 20–30 minutes, depending on which pastry you are using.
* Melt half the butter in a large sauté pan over a medium-high heat, add the beef and fry for 7–8 minutes until browned all over. Add the vegetables and thyme and cook for 5–7 minutes, until the onions have softened. Add the wine and stock, season with a little salt and pepper, then cover with a lid and braise for 1 hour.
* Meanwhile, heat the remaining butter in a large frying pan or skillet over a medium heat, add the pigeon breasts and fry for 3–4 minutes, or until browned all over. Add the pigeon to the simmering beef and vegetables and cook for another 30 minutes. Remove the pan from the heat and leave to cool completely. Spoon the cooled filling into a pie dish.
* Roll out the pastry on a lightly floured work counter to a circumference larger than the dish and carefully lay the pastry over the top, making sure there is some overhang. Brush egg wash around the sides to seal it onto the pie dish. Use a sharp knife to cut a few steam holes in the top and brush with more egg wash. Put into the fridge to firm up for 20 minutes.
* Meanwhile, preheat the oven to 220°C/425°F/Gas Mark 7.
* Bake the pie for 25 minutes, or until the pastry has risen and is crisp. Reduce the oven temperature to 180°C/350°F/Gas Mark 4 and bake for another 25 minutes, or until bubbling hot. Leave to cool slightly before serving warm with Mashed Potatoes and buttered greens.

UNITED KINGDOM
*

SAUSAGE ROLLS

A simple but much beloved British treat, the filling of a humble sausage roll practically invites experimentation using different flavours and spices. The stalls of almost any British market are testament to just how many successful combinations can been made. Serve this flaky treat warm or cold, with English mustard.

Serves: 4
Prep time: 30 minutes, plus 1 hour resting and chilling
Cook time: 25 minutes
{✿}

- 1 quantity Rough Puff Pastry (page 247)
- plain (all-purpose) flour, for dusting
- 400 g/14 oz sausage meat
- 1 egg, beaten with 1 tablespoon of water or milk, for egg wash
- English mustard, to serve

* Make the pastry following the recipe on page 247 and leave to rest for 30 minutes before using.
* Divide the pastry into 4 equal portions and roll out on a lightly floured work counter into long, even rectangles. Divide the sausage meat mixture into 4 equal portions and roll out on the work counter into sausages at least 4 cm/1½ inches thick, and as long as the pastry strips. Put a sausage down the centre of one of the pieces, neaten the edges, then fold the pastry over the top. Moisten with egg wash, crimping the edges with a fork to seal. Alternatively, put the sausage 2–3 mm/¹⁄₁₆–⅛ inch from the edge of one side, fold the pastry over the top and similarly crimp and seal with the egg wash. Repeat with the other 3 sausages and pastry strips. Put the sausage rolls into the fridge to firm up for 30 minutes.
* Preheat the oven to 220°C/425°F/Gas Mark 7. Line a large baking sheet with baking (parchment) paper.
* Remove the rolls from the fridge and trim the edges if necessary. You can also halve them at this point if desired. Arrange the sausage rolls on the prepared baking sheet and brush with egg wash. Bake for 25 minutes, or until golden brown and the sausage is at least 74°C/165°F when a temperature probe is inserted. Leave to cool slightly, then eat warm, or chill and eat cold with sharp English mustard.

UNITED KINGDOM
*

BLACK PUDDING SAUSAGE ROLLS

A riff on the beloved favourite, and every bit as good.

Makes: 7–8
Prep time: 25–30 minutes,
plus 1½ hours resting and chilling
Cook time: 40 minutes
{ᵔᵕ}

- 1 quantity Rough Puff Pastry (page 247)
- 1 tablespoon vegetable oil
- 200 g/7 oz white onion, diced
- 4 g/1 teaspoon thyme, plus optional extra 4 g/
1 teaspoon leaves to garnish
- 4 g/1 teaspoon chopped rosemary leaves
- 300 ml/10 fl oz (1¼ cups) apple cider
- 300 g/11 oz black pudding (blood sausage)
- 600 g/1 lb 5 oz pork sausage meat
- 300 g/11 oz (1⅓ cups) minced (ground) pork shoulder
- 20 g/¾ oz (4 teaspoons) wholegrain mustard
- 20 g/¾ oz (4 teaspoons) Dijon mustard
- plain (all-purpose) flour, for dusting
- 2 egg yolks beaten with 2 tablespoons water,
for egg wash
- salt and pepper

- To serve:
- English mustard
- pickles

* Make the pastry following the recipe on page 247 and
leave to rest for 30 minutes before using.
* Heat the oil in a large saucepan over a medium heat, add
the onion, thyme and rosemary and cook gently for 5
minutes. Add the cider and cook for 10 minutes, or until
it is reduced and the pan is dry. Transfer to a bowl, cover
with clingfilm (plastic wrap) and chill in the fridge.
* Cut the black pudding (blood sausage) into dice about
5 mm/¼ inch, then put into a large bowl with the
cooled onion, the sausage meat, minced (ground) pork
and mustards. Season with a little salt and pepper and
mix together. Divide the mixture into 200 g/7 oz balls,
then form into 7–8 sausages. Transfer to a baking sheet to
firm up in the fridge while you roll out the pastry.
* Preheat the oven to 200°C/400°F/Gas Mark 6. Line a
large baking sheet with baking (parchment) paper.
* Roll out the pastry on a lightly floured work counter and
cut into squares large enough to wrap the sausage (as if
in a blanket). Remove the sausages from the fridge and
place each one down the middle of one square, or about
2 mm/¹⁄₁₆ inch from the edge of one side. If the sausage
is placed down the middle of the square, then fold up
both sides and seal with egg wash at the top. If placed
at the side, fold over the far end of the pastry, crimp
the edge with a fork, and seal. Either way make sure
the edges have been pressed together with a fork, before
brushing the top with egg wash and sprinkling with
thyme leaves (if using) and salt to garnish.
* Arrange the sausage rolls on the lined baking sheet and
bake in the oven for 20–25 minutes. Eat warm or cool
with English mustard and pickles.

ENGLAND: LEICESTERSHIRE
*

PORK PIE

The iconic British pork pie is made with a thick hand-raised
hot water pastry crust, and a filling of diced uncured pork.
Leicestershire's connection to hand-raised pork pies (Melton
Mowbray especially) dates back to the eighteenth century at
least, although the first mention of Melton Mowbray pork
pies wasn't for another hundred years. Over time, they have
become the gold standard of traditional pork pies. Resist the
temptation to serve these warm – the filling needs time to
cool and set.

Makes: 6
Prep time: 50 minutes, plus 1 hour resting and chilling
Cook time: 2½ hours
{ᵔᵕ}

- 1 quantity Hot Water Pastry (page 246)
- 1 kg/2¼ lb lean pork (uncured), diced
- 250 g/9 oz unsmoked streaky (lean) bacon, finely
chopped (or another 250 g/9 oz diced lean pork)
- 1 teaspoon mixed spice
- 2 teaspoons anchovy essence
- 1 teaspoon each salt and pepper
- 3 tablespoons brandy or water
- plain (all-purpose) flour, for dusting
- 1 egg, beaten, for egg wash
- 4 leaves gelatine
- 300 ml/10 fl oz (1¼ cups) chicken or pork stock

- To serve:
- English mustard
- fruity chutney
- pickles or Piccalilli (page 446)

* Make the pastry following the recipe on page 246 and
leave to rest for 10 minutes before using.
* Put the pork, bacon, spice, anchovy essence, salt, pepper
and brandy into a large bowl and, using your hands, mix
together until everything is evenly mixed through.
* Roll out two-thirds of the pastry on a lightly floured
work counter and use it to line a 15–18 cm/6–7 inch
cake pan. Fill with the pork mixture, packing it down.
* Roll out the remaining pastry to make a lid, then lay it
over the pan and seal with egg wash. Use a sharp knife
to make a steam hole in the top and brush with more egg
wash. Let the pie firm up in the fridge for 20 minutes.
* Preheat the oven to 200°C/400°F/Gas Mark 6.
* Bake the pie in the oven for 20 minutes, then reduce the
oven temperature to 160°C/325°F/Gas Mark 3 and bake
for another 2 hours. Leave to cool for 30 minutes before
removing it from its pan.
* Soak the gelatine leaves in water for 5–10 minutes until
soft. Heat the stock in a saucepan over a medium heat for
5 minutes, or until hot. Squeeze out any excess water from
the gelatine, then add to the hot stock and stir through
until fully dissolved. Pour the stock into the pie through the
steam hole and leave to cool in the fridge before serving with
English mustard, chutney, pickles or Piccalilli (page 446).

ENGLAND
*
ASCOT PIE

A rectangular, jelly-set pork pie, baked with a hot water pastry crust. It is typically served in square slices with English mustard. You can turn an Ascot pie into a gala pie by slicing off the ends of 4–5 hard-boiled eggs, laying the eggs end to end down the centre of the pork filling and covering with the rest of the meat filling.

Serves: 6
Prep time: 40 minutes, plus 1 hour resting and chilling
Cook time: 2½ hours
{ᴗ•}

- 1 quantity Hot Water Pastry (page 246)
- plain (all-purpose) flour, for dusting
- 1 kg/2¼ lb diced pork or 500 g/1 lb 2 oz diced pork and 500 g/1 lb 2 oz diced veal
- 250 g/9 oz (1½ cups minus 4 teaspoons) dry-cured bacon, chopped
- 2 teaspoons salt
- 1 egg beaten with 1 tablespoon water or milk, for egg wash
- 2 leaves gelatine
- about 250 ml/8 fl oz (1 cup) pork stock
- pepper
- English mustard, to serve

* Make the pastry following the recipe on page 246 and leave to rest for 10 minutes before using.
* Roll out the pastry on a lightly floured work counter, then cut off two-thirds of the pastry and use to line a 900 g/2 lb loaf pan.
* Put the pork, bacon, salt and a little pepper into a large bowl and mix well until combined, then fill the pastry-lined pan with the meat mixture.
* Roll out the remaining pastry to use as a lid, then carefully lay the pastry over the pan and seal with egg wash. Use a sharp knife to make 2 steam holes in the centre and brush the top with more egg wash. Put the pie into the the fridge for 20 minutes to firm up.
* Meanwhile, preheat the oven to 200°C/400°F/Gas Mark 6.
* Put the loaf pan onto a large baking sheet and bake in the oven for 30 minutes. Reduce the oven temperature to 160°C/325°F/Gas Mark 3 and bake for another 90 minutes. Leave the pie to cool for 30 minutes before removing from the pan.
* Meanwhile, soak the gelatine leaves in a bowl of water for 5–10 minutes until soft. Heat the stock in a medium saucepan over a medium heat for 5 minutes, or until hot. Squeeze out any excess water from the gelatine, then add it to the hot stock and stir until fully dissolved. Pour the stock into the pie through the steam holes and leave to cool in the fridge before serving with English mustard.

UNITED KINGDOM
*
HUNTSMAN PIE

This riff on a traditional pork pie is made with layers of diced pork and chicken breast, and topped off with a sage and onion stuffing. Popular at pie stands in local markets up and down the country, the huntsman pie should be served cold with English mustard, chutney or Piccalilli (page 446).

Serves: 6
Prep time: 25 minutes, plus 1 hour resting and chilling
Cook time: 2 hours
{ᴗ•}

- ½ quantity Hot Water Pastry (page 246)
- 1 quantity Sage and Onion Stuffing (page 243)
- 30 g/1 oz (2 tablespoons) butter
- 1 onion, sliced
- 1 teaspoon chopped sage leaves
- 250 g/9 oz pork sausage meat
- plain (all-purpose) flour, for dusting
- 500 g/1 lb 2 oz (2¼ cups) diced pork shoulder
- 125 g/4¼ oz (¾ cup) unsmoked bacon, chopped
- 1 skinless, boneless chicken breast, diced
- 2 leaves gelatine
- 200 ml/7 fl oz (¾ cup plus 1 tablespoon) hot chicken stock
- salt and pepper

* Make the pastry following the recipe on page 246 and leave to rest for 10 minutes before using.
* Make the stuffing following the recipe on page 243 and set aside.
* Melt the butter in a large saucepan over a medium heat, add the onion and sage and fry for 5 minutes, or until soft. Transfer to a large bowl and leave to cool, then mix with the sausage meat.
* Roll out the pastry on a lightly floured work counter and use it to line a 15 cm/6 inch cake pan.
* Mix the pork and bacon together in a large bowl and season well with salt and pepper. Pack into the cake pan, then arrange the chicken in a layer on top. Press the sausage meat into a circle and lay it on top of the chicken, tucking it inside the edges. Using your finger, make a steam hole in the centre. Mould the stuffing into a circle large enough to sit on top of the sausage meat, then put it on top, making sure it goes to the very edge, meeting the pastry all the way around. Make a large steam hole in the centre. Let the pie firm up in the fridge for 20 minutes.
* Meanwhile, preheat the oven to 200°C/400°F/Gas Mark 6.
* Bake the pie for 20 minutes, then reduce the oven temperature to 160°C/325°F/Gas Mark 3 and cook for another 90 minutes. Remove from the oven and leave to cool for 30 minutes before removing from its pan.
* Meanwhile, soak the gelatine leaves in a bowl of water for 5–10 minutes until soft. Heat the stock in a saucepan over a medium heat for 5 minutes, or until hot. Squeeze out any excess water from the gelatine, then add it to the hot stock and stir until fully dissolved. Pour the stock into the steam hole. If it has sealed itself, make a hole at the edge of the stuffing and sausage meat and pour in the stock. Leave to cool in the fridge before serving.

PORK
AND
APPLE PIE

This twist on a traditional pork pie is topped with diced apples, the tips of which turn a distinctively dark brown as they cook.

Serves: 6
Prep time: 50 minutes, plus 40 minutes resting and chilling
Cook time: 50 minutes
{•*}

- 2 x quantity Shortcrust Pastry (page 247)
- 90 g/3¼ oz (6 tablespoons) butter
- 500 g/1 lb 2 oz (2¼ cups) diced pork
- 100 g/3½ oz smoked bacon, chopped
- pinch of ground nutmeg
- 100 ml/3½ fl oz (⅓ cup plus 1 tablespoon) cider
- plain (all-purpose) flour, for dusting
- 2 dessert apples, peeled, quartered and diced
- 60 g/2¼ oz (⅓ cup) light brown sugar
- salt and pepper

* Make the pastry following the recipe on page 247 and leave to rest for 20 minutes before using.
* Melt the butter in a large saucepan over a medium-high heat, add the pork and bacon and fry until browned all over. Season well with salt and pepper and the nutmeg, then spoon over the cider. Remove from the heat and leave to cool.
* Divide the pastry into 6 balls and roll each one out on a lightly floured work counter into a circle large enough to fit 6 x 12 cm/4½ inch pie dishes. Fill the lined dishes with the cooled pork mixture.
* Put the apples and sugar into a medium bowl and mix together, then arrange on top of the pies. Let the pies firm up in the fridge for 20 minutes.
* Meanwhile, preheat the oven to 220°C/425°F/Gas Mark 7. Put a large baking sheet onto the centre shelf to heat up.
* Put the pies onto the hot baking sheet and bake in the oven for 20 minutes. Reduce the oven temperature to 180°C/350°F/Gas Mark 4 and bake for another 20 minutes.

PATTIES

Patties in the Caribbean come in all forms, shapes and sizes. Most commonly known here by the British Caribbean community are the half-moon shaped, super buttery and flaky kind, deep filled with everything from ackee and saltfish to callaloo. Originally, these are said to have been brought to the islands by the British, where they were called Cornish Pasties (page 224) – a name by which they are still known in St Lucia. Over time they have developed to incorporate curry powder or turmeric, which gives them their distinctively bright yellow colour.

Serves: 6
Prep time: 15 minutes, plus 4½–5½ hours chilling
Cook time: 1 hour
{•*}

- For the pastry:
- 320 g/11¼ oz (2⅔ cups) plain (all-purpose) flour, plus extra for dusting
- 1½ teaspoons curry powder or ground turmeric or an even mix of both
- 1 teaspoon salt
- 140 g/5 oz (1¼ sticks) butter, divided into 20 g/¾ oz (4 teaspoons), softened, and 120 g/4 oz (1 stick)

- For the filling:
- 600 g/1 lb 5 oz skinless, boneless chicken, thighs or breast, finely chopped
- juice of ½ lemon
- 15 g/½ oz (1 tablespoon) curry powder
- 7.5 g/¼ oz (1½ teaspoons) ground cumin
- 1 tablespoon green seasoning
- 2 garlic cloves, crushed
- ½ scotch bonnet chilli, finely chopped
- 1 spring onion (scallion), finely chopped
- 15 ml/½ fl oz (1 tablespoon) vegetable oil
- salt and pepper

* First, make the pastry. Put the flour, spices and salt into a large bowl and mix together. Add the 20g/¾ oz (4 teaspoons) butter and rub it in until it is absorbed into small grains in the flour. While mixing, gradually add 160 ml/5¼ fl oz (⅔ cup) water to form a smooth dough. Leave to chill in the fridge for 30 minutes.
* Roll the dough out on a floured work counter until it is about 1.5 cm/⅝ inch thick. Spread the remaining butter into the centre of the dough and fold in all 4 corners of the dough like an envelope. Ensure it is sealed so the butter does not seep out of the dough, then roll the pastry out lightly lengthways, folding the dough into three. Wrap in clingfilm (plastic wrap) and chill in the fridge for 1 hour. Repeat this process 3–4 times as this creates the layers of the pastry, then the pastry is done.
* For the filling, wash the chicken with the lemon juice and some water, then discard the water.
* Put the chicken into a large bowl with the remaining ingredients, except the oil, then season to taste with salt and pepper. Cover the bowl with clingfilm (plastic wrap) and leave to marinate in the fridge for about 30 minutes.
* When the chicken is ready to be cooked, heat the oil in a large saucepan over a medium-high heat, add the chicken and the marinade and cook for 4–5 minutes, or until is browned all over. Add 100 ml/3½ fl oz (⅓ cup plus 1 tablespoon) water, cover with a lid and cook for another 20 minutes, or until the chicken is cooked through. Using a slotted spoon, remove the chicken from the sauce and leave it to cool.
* To assemble, preheat the oven to 160°C/325°F/Gas Mark 3. Line a large baking sheet with baking (parchment) paper. Roll out the pastry on a work counter until it is 1 cm/½ inch thick and cut out circles using a 15 cm/6 inch pastry cutter. Put a small amount of the chicken, breaking it up if necessary, into the centre of each pastry circle, then fold the pastry over and seal all around the edges with water. Arrange the patties on the prepared baking sheet and bake in the oven for 25–30 minutes until golden brown.

ENGLAND: CORNWALL

*

CORNISH PASTY

The Cornish pasty has its roots in the nineteenth century as a portable meal for workers, and was a favourite among miners especially. In a short period of time, the pasty became so ingrained in Cornish baking that an often repeated joke claims that the Devil never travelled into Cornwall 'for fear of the Cornish woman's habit of putting anything and everything into a pasty'.

To this day, this half-moon pastry is filled with any number of savoury (and sometimes sweet) fillings – both traditional and modern – but there is also a commonly accepted classic recipe. It calls for chopped (not minced/ground) beef, as well as potato, swede (rutabaga), onions and plenty of freshly ground black pepper. As the beef cooks, the steam and juices from it cook and commingle with the vegetables and give great depth to its flavour.

Makes: 4 large or 6 smaller pasties
Prep time: 50 minutes, plus 40 minutes resting and chilling
Cook time: 50 minutes
{ ✎ }

- 2 x quantity Shortcrust Pastry (page 247)
- 200 g/7 oz white onion, diced
- 200 g/7 oz swede (rutabaga), peeled and diced
- 300 g/11 oz potatoes, such as Maris Piper, peeled and diced
- ¼ teaspoon chopped thyme (optional)
- 300 g/11 oz raw fatty steak, chopped into small chunks, traditionally any braising (chuck) steak will do, but if you prefer you may try sirloin instead
- plain (all-purpose) flour, for dusting
- 4–6 tablespoons beef stock or water
- 1 egg, beaten with 1 tablespoon water or milk, for egg wash
- salt and pepper

* Line a large baking sheet with baking (parchment) paper.
* Make the pastry following the recipe on page 247 and leave to rest for 20 minutes before using.
* Put all the vegetables and thyme (if using) into a large bowl. Season very well with salt and pepper and mix with your hands. Add the meat, season again and mix it in well.
* Divide the pastry into 4 equal portions. Form into balls and roll each one out on a lightly floured work counter into circles the size of small dinner plates (about 18 cm/7 inches). Divide the filling between the 4 circles, spooning each portion onto one half of the circle, up to about 5 mm/¼ inch from its edge. Sprinkle 1 tablespoon of the beef stock or water into each, then fold over the empty half of each pastry circle to form a crescent or half-moon shape and seal with egg wash. Using a fork, crimp the edges down all along the seal, then brush egg wash all over. Use a sharp knife to cut a steam hole in the top, then repeat with each pasty. Put the pasties onto the prepared baking sheet and leave to chill and firm up in the fridge for 20 minutes.
* Preheat the oven to 200°C/400°F/Gas Mark 6.
* Put the baking sheet into the oven and bake for 30 minutes. Reduce the oven temperature to 180°C/350°F/ Gas Mark 4 and bake for another 20 minutes. Check that the pasties are ready by inserting a skewer or the tip of a sharp knife into the potatoes and if they are tender, they are done. Leave to cool slightly before eating warm.

ENGLAND: BEDFORDSHIRE

*

BEDFORDSHIRE CLANGER

This hefty log-like suet pastry has two separate fillings: savoury at one end, sweet at the other. Originally a complete lunch for farm workers in East England, it is still made by local Bedfordshire bakery Gunn's, who sell their clangers with a range of different sweet and savoury fillings – feel free to experiment with your own!

Serves: 4
Prep time: 1 hour, plus 20 minutes chilling
Cook time: 40 minutes
{ ✎ } { 🏛 }

- 2 x quantity Suet Pastry (page 246)
- plain (all-purpose) flour, for dusting
- ½ quantity Apple Pie filling (page 384), or any other fruit pie filling, cold
- ½ quantity Cornish Pasty filling (see left), or any other savoury pie filling, cold
- 1 egg, beaten with 1 tablespoon water or milk, for egg wash

* Make the pastry following the recipe on page 246 and leave to chill in the fridge for 20 minutes. Make the Apple Pie filling and the Cornish Pasty filling and make sure they are cold before using.
* Preheat the oven to 200°C/400°F/Gas Mark 6. Line 2 large baking sheets with baking (parchment) paper.
* Divide the pastry into 4 equal portions and roll out on a work counter into long rectangles, trimming the edges to even out the sides. Set the trimmings aside.
* Start filling the pastry. Turn one of the pastry strips so that the long end is closest to you, then put a few spoonfuls of the apple mixture down the middle of one half of the pastry, about 1 cm/½ inch from the edge closest to you. Use a little of the trimmings to make a dividing 'wall' of pastry, then spoon the savoury filling onto the other half. You want to keep the fillings fairly close to you, so you can easily fold the pastry over. Fold the pastry over and seal with the egg wash. Use a sharp knife to cut some steam holes in the top and repeat with the other pieces of dough. If desired, you can put the fillings down the middle, then fold up from both sides and seal with the egg wash.
* Put the clangers on the prepared baking sheets and bake in the oven for 20 minutes. Reduce the oven temperature to 160°C/325°F/Gas Mark 3 and bake for another 20 minutes. Serve warm.

Cornish pasty

SCOTLAND: ANGUS
*

FORFAR BRIDIES

Bridies are meaty half-moon-shaped pastries that originated in bakeries across central Scotland at the end of the nineteenth century. At that time, meat was only served on special occasions, and the bridie was mainly a weekend treat. To this day they are still a popular Saturday lunch for Forfar locals. Once cooked, leave to cool slightly before eating warm.

Makes: 6
Prep time: 50 minutes, plus 40 minutes resting and chilling
Cook time: 50 minutes
{ᵔ•ᵔ}

- 2 x quantity Shortcrust Pastry (page 247)
- 500 g/ 1 lb 2 oz (2¼ cups) minced (ground) or finely chopped beef
- 90 g/ 3¼ oz beef suet
- 1 onion, very finely chopped
- plain (all-purpose) flour, for dusting
- 4 tablespoons beef stock or water
- 1 egg, beaten with 1 tablespoon water or milk, for egg wash
- salt and pepper

* Make the pastry following the recipe on page 247 and leave to rest for 20 minutes before using. Line a large baking sheet with baking (parchment) paper.
* Put the beef, suet and onion into a large bowl and mix together. Season very well with salt and pepper. Divide the pastry into 6 equal pieces on a lightly floured work counter, then shape into balls and roll each one out into circles about the size of a small dinner plate (about 18 cm/ 7 inches).
* Spoon the filling onto one half of each of the 6 pastry discs, putting it up to 5 mm/ ¼ inch from the edge, and no further than halfway across. Sprinkle with a little beef stock or water. Fold the other half of the pastry over to make a horseshoe, crescent or half-moon shape and seal with the egg wash. Crimp the edges down all along the seal, then brush egg wash all over. Use a sharp knife to cut a steam hole and repeat with each pastry disc. Put the pastries onto the prepared baking sheet and put into the fridge to firm up for 20 minutes.
* Meanwhile, preheat the oven to 200°C/ 400°F/ Gas Mark 6.
* Put the baking sheet into the oven and bake for 30 minutes, then reduce the oven temperature to 180°C/ 350°F/ Gas Mark 4 and bake for another 20 minutes. Check that the bridies are ready by inserting a skewer or the tip of a sharp knife into the centre, and if they are tender, they are done. Leave to cool a little before eating warm.

UNITED KINGDOM
*

CHEESE
AND
ONION PASTY

A popular variation on the traditional Cornish pasty, which can be made with any mature-flavoured melting cheese.

Serves: 4
Prep time: 50 minutes, plus 40 minutes resting and chilling
Cook time: 50 minutes
{ᵔ•ᵔ}

- 30 g/ 1 oz (2 tablespoons) butter (optional)
- ½ quantity Cheese and Onion Pie filling (page 206), made with mature Cheddar cheese or a cheese of your choice
- 2 x quantity Shortcrust Pastry (page 247)
- plain (all-purpose) flour, for dusting
- 4 tablespoons beef stock or water
- 1 egg, beaten with 1 tablespoon water or milk, for egg wash
- salt and pepper

* Line a large baking sheet with baking (parchment) paper.
* Make the Cheese and Onion Pie filling following the recipe on page 206.
* Make the pastry following the recipe on page 247 and leave to rest for 20 minutes before using.
* Divide the pastry into 4 equal portions on a lightly floured work counter, then shape into balls and roll each one out into circles about the size of a small dinner plate (about 18 cm/ 7 inches).
* Spoon the filling onto one half of each of the 4 pastry discs, putting it up to 5 mm/ ¼ inch from the edge, and no further than halfway across. Sprinkle with a little beef stock or water. Fold the other half of the pastry over to make a half-moon shape and seal with the egg wash. Crimp the edges down all along the seal, then brush egg wash all over. Use a sharp knife to cut a steam hole and repeat with each pastry disc. Put the pastries onto the prepared baking sheet and put into the fridge to firm up for 20 minutes.
* Preheat the oven to 200°C/ 400°F/ Gas Mark 4.
* Put the baking sheet into the oven and bake for 30 minutes, then reduce the oven temperature to 180°C/ 350°F/ Gas Mark 4 and bake for another 20 minutes. Leave to cool slightly before eating warm.

Forfar bridies

WALES / ENGLAND: LANCASHIRE
*

LANCASHIRE HOTPOT

This is a rich, layered lamb or mutton stew crowned with thinly sliced and bronzed potatoes. The term hotpot has, over time, gone on to refer more generally to any meat stew with a top layer of potatoes – but this is the classic version.

Serves: 4
Prep time: 20 minutes
Cook time: 2–2½ hours
{•⁕}

- 50 g/2 oz (3½ tablespoons) butter
- 4 lambs' kidneys, about 250 g/9 oz in total
- plain (all-purpose) flour, for dredging
- 2 tablespoons rapeseed (canola) oil
- 12 lamb (or mutton) cutlets, long bones removed, or one scrag end of neck, cut into large pieces (about 900 g/2 lb)
- 2 onions, thinly sliced
- 750 g/1 lb 10 oz potatoes, peeled and thinly sliced
- 400 ml/14 fl oz (1⅔ cups) beef stock or water
- Worcestershire sauce or Yorkshire relish, to taste (optional), plus extra to serve
- Pickled Red Cabbage (page 444), to serve

* Preheat the oven to 160°C/325°F/Gas Mark 3.
* Melt the butter in a small saucepan over a medium-low heat, then remove from the heat and set aside.
* Remove any membrane from the kidneys, then cut in half and remove the white core using a pair of sharp scissors. Chop the kidneys into small pieces and set aside.
* Spread the flour out on a large plate. Heat the oil in a deep casserole dish over a medium-high heat. Toss the cutlets in the flour, shake off any excess and add to the pot. Cook for 2–3 minutes each side, until well-browned.
* Reduce the heat and arrange alternating layers of onions, lamb, kidney and potatoes, seasoning frequently.
* Pour in stock or water to come about four-fifths of the way up the pot, add Worcestershire sauce to taste (if using), then finish with a layer of potatoes. Brush with the melted butter and cook in the oven for 2–2½ hours until the meat is tender. If the potatoes begin to brown too much, cover with a lid or aluminium foil. Serve with Pickled Red Cabbage and Worcestershire sauce or relish.

ENGLAND: EAST SUSSEX AND SUSSEX
*

CHIDDINGLY BEEF HOTPOT

This beef hotpot is from the southeast of England, where it was allegedly created by Edward Shoosmith in 1917. Chiddingly is characterized by layers of olives, an unusual addition, that is left out altogether in some later recipes.

Serves: 4
Prep time: 20 minutes
Cook time: 2½ hours
{⌨}{�️}{•⁕}{⏲}

- 500 g/1 lb 2 oz diced stewing/braising beef
- 100 g/3½ oz (¾ cup plus 2 teaspoons) green olives, stoned (pitted) and chopped
- 2 onions, thinly sliced
- 2 stalks celery, thinly sliced
- pinches of ground cloves
- pinches of ground allspice
- 2 tablespoons wine or cider vinegar
- 500 g/1 lb 2 oz potatoes, peeled and thinly sliced
- about 400 ml/14 fl oz (1⅔ cups) beef stock
- salt and pepper

* Preheat the oven to 160°C/325°F/Gas Mark 3.
* Arrange a layer of the beef in a large casserole dish or Dutch oven, then add a layer of olives, onions and celery. Repeat each layer, seasoning as you go, with salt and pepper and small pinches of ground cloves and allspice. There should be 3–4 layers of each ingredient.
* Sprinkle the vinegar over the top and cover the top with a neat layer of potatoes. Pour in the stock, cover, and cook in the oven for 2 hours, or until the beef is tender.
* Uncover, then increase the oven temperature to 200°C/400°F/Gas Mark 6 and cook for another 30 minutes, or until the potatoes are golden brown. Serve.

ENGLAND: CUMBRIA
*

CUMBRIAN TATTIE POT

Also known as a Westmorland tattie pot, this is a riff on the traditional hotpot, often using beef instead of lamb, but distinguished by its inclusion of black pudding (blood sausage). This dish is especially good for those dark nights when the rain shuts you indoors and the warming depth of the usual hotpot isn't enough.

Serves: 4
Prep time: 20 minutes
Cook time: 3½ hrs
{⏸}{•⁕}{⏲}

- 500 g/1 lb 2 oz beef shin (shank) or an equal weight of diced lamb/mutton shoulder
- 2 small black puddings (blood sausages)
- 2 onions, sliced
- 1 tablespoon pearl barley
- 450 ml/15 fl oz (1⅔ cups plus 2 tablespoons) beef or lamb stock
- 1 tablespoon Worcestershire sauce (optional, mixed into the stock)
- 750 g/1 lb 10 oz potatoes, such as Maris Piper
- salt and pepper

* Preheat the oven to 160°C/325°F/Gas Mark 3.
* Cut the beef shin (shank) and black pudding (blood sausage) into large pieces and put them into a casserole dish or Dutch oven with the onions and barley. Season well with salt and pepper, then pour over the stock.
* Cut the potatoes into thin slices, leaving the skin on if preferred, and arrange on top of the beef.
* Cover with a lid or with aluminium foil and cook in the oven for 3 hours. Uncover, increase the oven temperature to 200°C/400°F/Gas Mark 6 and cook for another 30 minutes, or until the potatoes turn golden brown. Serve.

Lancashire hotpot

ENGLAND: LINCOLNSHIRE AND NORFOLK
*

PIG'S FRY CASSEROLE

Pig's fry is a mix of offal including the liver and heart, and often the lights (lungs), kidney sweetbreads and even some fat. They are all dredged in flour, fried and baked in a casserole dish or Dutch oven underneath a layer of potatoes. This dish was once also common to Norfolk, where it was served with Norfolk Dumplings (page 244) instead of potatoes – which would work just as well.

Serves: 6
Prep time: 20 minutes
Cook time: 1 hour 25 minutes
{•} {🍲}

- 750 g/1 lb 10 oz floury (baking) potatoes, such as Maris Piper or Yukon Gold
- 2 tablespoons plain (all-purpose) flour
- 1 kg/2¼ lb pig's fry (a typically varying assortment of pig's offal)
- 60 g/2¼ oz (½ stick) butter or lard
- 1 onion, sliced
- 1 carrot, diced
- 1 celery, diced
- 2 teaspoons dried sage
- 750 ml/25 fl oz (3 cups) chicken stock
- salt and pepper

* Preheat the oven to 180°C/350°F/Gas Mark 4.
* Peel the potatoes and cut into 5 mm/¼ inch thick slices. Spread the flour out on a large plate and season with ½ teaspoon each of salt and pepper, then toss the pieces of meat in the seasoned flour.
* Melt the fat in an ovenproof casserole dish or Dutch oven over a medium-high heat, add the meat and fry for 10–12 minutes until browned. Remove with a slotted spoon and set aside.
* Add the vegetables and sage to the pan and fry over a medium heat for 10 minutes, or until the onions have softened. Put the browned meat back into the pan, season with salt and lots of pepper, then pour in the stock and arrange the potatoes on top. Cover with a lid and bake in the oven for 45–60 minutes until the meat and potatoes are very tender. If desired, uncover for the final 15–20 minutes of the cooking time to brown the potatoes, but be careful the dish doesn't dry up or burn at the edges. Serve.

UNITED KINGDOM
*

SAUSAGE
AND
BACON CASSEROLE

This warming casserole could easily adapt to include a variety of different beans, peas or lentils.

Serves: 6
Prep time: 30 minutes
Cook time: 1 hour 10 minutes
{❄} {🥄} {•}

- 20 g/¾ oz (4 teaspoons) lard
- 12 traditional English sausages (i.e. Cumberland, page 164)
- 120 g/4 oz smoked streaky (lean) bacon, diced
- 2 onions, sliced
- 2 cloves garlic, chopped
- 2 carrots, diced
- 2 stalks celery, diced
- 2 bay leaves
- 1 tablespoon tomato purée (paste)
- 500 ml/17 fl oz (2 cups plus 1 tablespoon) chicken stock
- 300 ml/10 fl oz (1¼ cups) cider
- 1 teaspoon chopped sage leaves
- 2 tablespoons flat-leaf parsley, chopped
- 60 g/2¼ oz (⅓ cup) soft brown sugar
- 1 tablespoon cider vinegar
- salt and pepper

* Preheat the oven to 160°C/325°F/Gas Mark 3.
* Melt the lard in a large ovenproof saucepan over a high heat, add the sausages and fry for 4 minutes, or until browned all over. (They don't need to be fully cooked at this stage.) Using tongs, remove the sausages from the pan and set aside.
* Add the bacon to the pan and fry for 5 minutes, or until it starts to go crispy. Add the onions, garlic, carrot, celery and bay leaves and stir through so that the mixture is evenly dispersed. Season with salt and pepper and fry for 10–15 minutes until the onion has picked up a little colour. Add the tomato purée (paste) and cook for 1–2 minutes until it turns a few shades darker. Pour in the stock and cider, then add the sage, parsley, sugar and vinegar. Stir and add the sausages. Bake in the oven for 45 minutes. If you don't have an ovenproof pan, then transfer to a casserole dish or Dutch oven before baking in the oven.

WALES
*

LEEK
AND
STILTON TART
TARTEN GENNIN A CHAWS STILTON

Cookery writer Theodora Fitzgibbon suggests that tarts like this one first came to Wales as an adaptation of the French *flan de poireau*. The leek, of course, has been a staple of the Welsh kitchen since time immemorial, so it's easy to understand its seamless adoption.
This recipe swaps out the French flan's Gruyère or Comté for a stronger English or even Welsh cheese – Stilton, Cheddar or Caerphilly, depending on your preference. Serve warm with a leafy green salad.

Serves: 6
Prep time: 40 minutes, plus 40 minutes resting and chilling
Cook time: 1 hour–1 hour 20 minutes
{ 🌶 }{ 🥓 }

- 1 quantity Shortcrust Pastry (page 247)
- plain (all-purpose) flour, for dusting
- 60 g/2¼ oz (½ stick) butter
- 2 leeks, thinly sliced
- ½ teaspoon thyme leaves
- 1 tablespoon flat-leaf parsley, chopped
- 180 g/6 oz Stilton, Cheddar or Caerphilly cheese, grated or crumbled
- 4 eggs
- 150 ml/5 fl oz (⅔ cup) full-fat (whole) milk
- 150 ml/5 fl oz (⅔ cup) double (heavy) cream
- salt and pepper
- leafy green salad, to serve

* Make the pastry following the recipe on page 247 and leave to rest for 20 minutes before using.
* Preheat the oven to 200°C/400°F/Gas Mark 6.
* Roll out the pastry on a lightly floured work counter and use it to line a 23 cm/9 inch tart pan. Trim the edges to neaten it before putting the pan into the fridge to firm up for 20 minutes.
* Crumple a large square of baking (parchment) paper (larger than the tart), fold it out and lay it in the tart pan so that the sides overhang. Fill the paper with ceramic baking beans or pie weights and bake in the oven for 25 minutes, or until the edges are golden brown. Remove the baking beans and paper and return to the oven for 7–8 minutes to cook the base. Remove from the oven and set aside, then reduce the oven temperature to 180°C/350°F/Gas Mark 4.
* Melt the butter in a large frying pan or skillet over a medium heat, add the leeks and herbs and cook for 12–15 minutes, or until the leeks are softened. Season with salt and pepper. Spoon the leeks over the pastry and sprinkle with the cheese. Add the eggs, milk and cream to a medium bowl and whisk together. Season with pepper and a little more salt, then pour into the tart pan. Bake in the oven for 30–40 minutes until the eggs are just set. Leave to cool slightly, and serve with a leafy green salad.

WALES
*

PASTAI PERSLI

This recipe for 'parsley pie' comes from the Gower, in South Wales, and is an adaptation of a French quiche Lorraine – with the inclusion of its eponymous ingredient, and the exclusion of cheese.

Serves: 6
Prep time: 40 minutes, plus 40 minutes resting and chilling
Cook time: 1¼ hours
{ 🥓 }

- 1 quantity Shortcrust Pastry (page 247)
- plain (all-purpose) flour, for dusting
- 20 g/¾ oz (4 teaspoons) butter
- 125 g/4¼ oz bacon or ham, diced
- 6 eggs
- 200 ml/7 fl oz (¾ cup plus 1 tablespoon) single (light) cream
- 2 tablespoons chopped flat-leaf parsley
- salt and pepper

* Make the pastry following the recipe on page 247 and leave to rest for 20 minutes before using.
* Preheat the oven to 200°C/400°F/Gas Mark 6.
* Roll out the pastry on a lightly floured work counter and use it to line a 23 cm/9 inch tart pan. Trim the edges to neaten it before putting the pan into the fridge to firm up for 20 minutes.
* Crumple a large square of baking (parchment) paper (larger than the tart), fold it out and lay it in the tart pan so that the sides overhang. Fill the paper with a kitchen weight, such as ceramic baking beans or pie weights and bake in the oven for 25 minutes, or until the edges are golden brown. Remove the baking beans and paper and return to the oven for 7–8 minutes to cook the base. Remove from the oven and set aside, then reduce the oven temperature to 160°C/325°F/Gas Mark 3.
* Melt the butter in a large frying pan or skillet over a medium-high heat, add the bacon or ham and fry for 10 minutes, or until crisp. Spread the bacon or ham over the bottom of the pastry case (shell). Put the eggs and cream into a large bowl and whisk to combine, then stir in the parsley and a little seasoning. Pour the mixture into the pastry case and bake in the oven for 30 minutes, or until set but still a little wobbly. Leave to cool slightly, and serve.

UNITED KINGDOM
*
COTTAGE PIE

This pub classic has its likely origins in the late eighteenth century, when similar meat and potato pies became popular throughout Britain. Originally made from left-over roast beef, today it is more common to use fresh mince (ground beef), which is then cooked down with diced vegetables in a rich gravy. The filling is then topped with buttery mashed potatoes and sometimes an extra gilding of grated cheese.

Serves: 6
Prep time: 30 minutes
Cook time: 1½ hours
{🏛}{🌶}

- 30 g/1 oz (2 tablespoons) lard or beef dripping
- 600 g/1 lb 5 oz (5 cups) minced (ground) beef
- 1–2 tablespoons rapeseed (canola) oil (optional)
- 1 onion, chopped
- 1 stalk celery, chopped
- 1 carrot, diced
- 1 bay leaf
- ½ teaspoon dried thyme
- 1 tablespoon tomato purée (paste)
- 400 ml/14 fl oz (1⅔ cups) beef stock
- 100 ml/3½ fl oz (generous ⅓ cup) red wine or beef stock
- 450 g/1 lb potatoes, peeled and cut into chunks
- 1 tablespoon cornflour (cornstarch)
- 30 g/1 oz Parmesan or other hard cheese, grated (optional)
- salt and pepper

- To serve:
- Worcestershire sauce
- condiment of your choice, such as Tomato Ketchup (page 425) or Brown Sauce (page 426)

* Heat the fat in a deep frying pan or skillet over a medium-high heat, add the minced (ground) beef and fry, stirring constantly, for 8–10 minutes until browned all over. Using a slotted spoon, transfer the meat to a large bowl and set aside. Tip away any fat, leaving about 2 tablespoons in the pan. If the pan has dried out, add up to 2 tablespoons of rapeseed (canola) oil.
* Add the vegetables and herbs to the pan, then reduce the heat to medium and fry for 10–15 minutes until soft and browned. Add the tomato purée (paste) and fry for another 2 minutes, before spooning the meat back into the pan and pouring over the stock and wine (if using). Bring to a simmer over a medium heat, cover with a lid and cook for at least 30 minutes, or until tender.
* Meanwhile, cook the potatoes in a saucepan of boiling water for 15 minutes, or until tender, then drain and mash. Set aside.
* Preheat the oven to 200°C/400°F/Gas Mark 6.
* Put the cornflour (cornstarch) into a small bowl and whisk in a little water to a paste consistency, then tip into the meat mixture to thicken the gravy. Simmer, uncovered, for another 5–10 minutes until the sauce forms a thick, rich gravy. Season with salt and pepper, then pour into a baking dish and spoon or pipe over the potatoes. Sprinkle with grated cheese, if desired, and bake in the oven for 30 minutes, or until golden brown. Serve with Worcestershire sauce and your condiment of choice.

UNITED KINGDOM
*
SHEPHERD'S PIE

A good shepherd's pie is made in much the same manner as a cottage pie (see left), but using lamb instead of beef mince (ground beef). Food writers such as Alan Davidson have speculated that this version of the classic meat and potato pie originated in northern England and Scotland, where mutton and lamb were more prevalent in local diets.

Serves: 4
Prep time: 10 minutes
Cook time: 1 hour 50 minutes
{🌶}

- 50 ml/1¾ fl oz (3½ tablespoons) vegetable oil
- 1 large onion, finely chopped
- 500 g/1 lb 2 oz (4 cups) lamb mince (ground lamb)
- 1 tablespoon plain (all-purpose) flour
- 2 bay leaves
- 2 sprigs thyme
- 450 ml/15 fl oz (1⅔ cups plus 2 tablespoons) lamb stock
- 100 g/3½ oz (⅔ cup) tomato purée (paste)
- 2 teaspoons Worcestershire sauce
- 700 g/1 lb 8½ oz potatoes, peeled and cut into chunks
- 55 ml/1¾ fl oz (3½ tablespoons) milk
- 85 g/3 oz (¾ stick) butter
- 1 egg yolk
- salt and pepper

- To serve:
- Worcestershire sauce
- condiment of your choice, such as Tomato Ketchup (page 425) or Brown Sauce (page 426)

* Heat half the oil in a large saucepan over a medium heat, add the onion and cook for 5 minutes.
* Meanwhile, heat the remaining oil in a large frying pan over a medium-high heat, add the meat and fry, stirring constantly, for 8–10 minutes until browned all over, breaking up any lumps with the back of the spoon.
* Sift the flour into the onions (this helps to thicken the juices) and make sure they are evenly coated in it, then add the bay leaves and thyme and stir through. Set aside about 60 ml/2 fl oz (¼ cup) of the stock, then pour the rest into the pan and add the tomato purée (paste), Worcestershire sauce and the cooked meat.
* Pour the reserved stock into the empty meat pan and stir over the heat, scraping up all the crusty and browned bits stuck on the bottom of the pan. Pour this into the saucepan and bring the mixture to the boil, adding a pinch of salt and pepper. Reduce the heat and simmer for about 45 minutes, stirring frequently.
* Meanwhile, preheat the oven to 180°C/350°F/Gas Mark 4.
* Fill a large saucepan two-thirds full with water, add a pinch of salt, then bring to the boil. Add the potatoes and boil for 15–20 minutes until tender. Drain, then return the potatoes to the pan and add the milk, butter and egg yolk and mash until smooth. Season with salt and pepper.
* Spoon the meat into a baking dish and spread the mash on top, then drag a fork through to mark it. Bake for 45 minutes, or until the top is golden brown. Serve with Worcestershire sauce and your condiment of choice.

Shepherd's pie

UNITED KINGDOM
*

STEAK
AND
KIDNEY STEAMED PUDDING

This sumptuous pudding dates back to the nineteenth century (and its roots much further), but luckily it has aged marvellously. Tender beef and diced kidney cooked down in a rich gravy, the juices of which soak into its soft suet pastry shell. While the filling mixture is the same for pie and pudding versions of this recipe, the eating is different: the steamed suet pastry picks up a softer, almost bready texture which makes it perfect for mopping up gravy.

Serves: 4
Prep time: 30 minutes, plus 20 minutes chilling
Cook time: 6½ hours
{ల•}

- For the suet pastry:
- 125 g/4¼ oz suet, shredded
- 250 g/9 oz (2 cups) self-raising flour
- butter, for greasing
- plain (all-purpose) flour, for dusting
- salt

- For the filling:
- 100 g/3½ oz (¾ cup plus 2 teaspoons) plain (all-purpose) flour
- 50 g/2 oz (3½ tablespoons) mustard powder
- 1 tablespoon vegetable oil (optional)
- 700 g/1 lb 8½ oz beef, such as shin (shank), oxtail, cheek
- 1 ox kidney, diced (ask your butcher for the suet to still be attached), or about 500 g/1 lb 2 oz mushrooms, quartered
- 200 g/7 oz onions, diced
- 2 bay leaves
- few sprigs thyme
- 2 tablespoons Worcestershire sauce
- 1 litre/34 fl oz (4¼ cups) beef or chicken stock or water or beer
- salt and pepper
- potatoes, buttered greens and Gravy (page 420), to serve

* For the pastry, put the suet, flour and a pinch of salt into a large bowl and pour in enough cold water to make a smooth, firm dough. Chill in the fridge for 20 minutes.
* Grease a 1.7 litre/3 pint pudding basin (ovenproof bowl) with butter and leave to chill in the fridge.
* When ready, cut one-quarter off the dough for the lid and set aside, then roll out the remaining pastry on a well floured work counter and use to line the prepared pudding basin, then chill in the fridge. Roll out the lid to slightly larger than the basin and refrigerate.
* For the filling, if you have fresh suet, render some for frying the meat by melting it slowly over a low heat. Otherwise, heat the oil in the pan.
* Spread the flour out on a large plate and season with the mustard powder, salt and pepper. Roll the pieces of beef in the seasoned flour, then add to the pan and fry for 5–10 minutes, until browned all over Remove and set aside, then repeat with the kidneys. Add the onions to the pan and cook for 5 minutes, or until soft, then add

the beef, kidneys, bay leaves, thyme, Worcestershire sauce and stock. Bring to the boil, then reduce the heat and simmer for 3 hours. Remove from the heat and leave to cool completely.
* Fill the lined basin with the filling, then carefully put the lid on top, wetting it slightly round the edge to secure, and wrap in aluminium foil. Put it into a large saucepan and pour in hot water until it is halfway up the sides of the bowl. Bring to the boil, then reduce the heat to a simmer. Cover with a lid, making sure the water doesn't go below the halfway mark, and steam for 3 hours. Serve with potatoes, buttered greens and Gravy.

ENGLAND: NORFOLK
*

NORFOLK PLOUGH PUDDING

This savoury steamed pudding was traditionally made in East Anglia on Plough Monday, the first Monday after Epiphany (6th January), when Christmas festivities ended and the new farming calendar began.

Serves: 6
Prep time: 35 minutes, plus 20 minutes chilling
Cook time: 3½ hours
{ల•}

- 1 quantity Suet Pastry (page 246)
- 400 g/14 oz sausage meat
- 100 g/3½ oz (½ cup) streaky (lean) bacon, diced
- 1 teaspoon chopped sage leaves
- 60 ml/2 fl oz (¼ cup) pork or vegetable stock
- butter, for greasing
- self-raising flour, for dusting
- potatoes, buttered greens and Gravy (page 420), to serve

* Make the pastry following the recipe on page 246 and leave to chill in the fridge for 20 minutes.
* Put the meats, sage and stock into a large bowl and stir through very well until combined. Set aside.
* Grease a 900 ml/30 fl oz pudding basin (ovenproof bowl) with butter. Roll out three-quarters of the pastry on a lightly floured work counter into a circle that will fit the basin. Fold it into quarters, pick it up and put the corner into the centre of the bottom of the basin and unfold the pastry, making sure there are no air bubbles (carefully pop them with a sharp knife). Spoon the filling into the lined basin. Roll out the remaining pastry to make the lid, then lay it over the bowl and seal with a little water. Use a knife to cut a steam hole in the centre.
* Cover the top with a double layer of pleated baking (parchment) paper and aluminium foil and secure it with kitchen string. Steam in a steamer for 3½ hours, topping up with boiling water, if necessary.
* If you don't have a steamer, put an upturned saucer in the bottom of a large saucepan, put the basin on top (make sure it doesn't touch the bottom of the pan) and fill halfway with water. Bring to the boil, then reduce the heat to a simmer. Cover with a lid, making sure the water doesn't go below the halfway mark, and steam for 3½ hours. Turn out and serve with potatoes of choice, buttered cabbage and Gravy.

Steak and kidney steamed pudding

ENGLAND: KENT
*

KENTISH CHICKEN PUDDING

Kentish chicken puddings were originally made with boiling fowls: older, tougher chickens whose meat was reserved for long-simmering stews and pie fillings. Since the 1950s, younger chickens have been used.

Serves: 4
Prep time: 1 hour, plus 20 minutes chilling
Cook time: 4 hours 20 minutes
{ᴥ}

- 1 quantity Suet Pastry (page 247)
- 90 g/3¼ oz (6 tablespoons) butter, plus extra for greasing
- 120 g/4 oz (⅔ cup) smoked bacon, chopped
- 90 g/3¼ oz (¾ cup) plain (all-purpose) flour, plus extra for dusting
- 600 g/1 lb 5 oz boneless chunks of chicken, preferably thighs
- 1 onion, chopped
- 200 g/7 oz mushrooms, sliced
- 400 ml/14 fl oz (1⅔ cups) chicken stock
- 1 tablespoon chopped flat-leaf parsley
- salt and pepper

* Make the pastry following the recipe on page 247 and leave to chill in the fridge for 20 minutes before using.
* Melt 60 g/2¼ oz (½ stick) of the butter in a large saucepan over a medium-high heat, add the bacon and fry for 5 minutes, or until golden. Remove with a slotted spoon and set aside in a heatproof bowl.
* Spread a little flour on a plate, then dust the chicken pieces in the flour and season with salt and pepper. Reduce the heat under the pan to medium, add the chicken and sauté for 8–10 minutes until golden brown.
* Remove the chicken pieces using a slotted spoon and set aside with the bacon. Add the onion to the pan and fry for 10 minutes, or until softened. Add the mushrooms and cook for another 8–10 minutes, adding an extra 30 g/1 oz (2 tablespoons) of butter, if needed.
* Remove the onion and mushrooms using a slotted spoon and set aside with the chicken. Add the flour to the pan and stir and mix with the fat, cooking for 1 minute before adding the stock, a little at a time, as you whisk it into the roux mixture. When all the stock has been added, simmer for 10 minutes. Taste and adjust the seasoning, if necessary, then mix into the chicken and bacon with the parsley. Leave to cool.
* Grease a 1 litre/24 fl oz pudding basin (ovenproof bowl) with butter. Roll out three-quarters of the pastry on a floured work counter into a circle that will fit the basin. Fold it into quarters (this makes it easier to move), pick it up and put the corner into the centre of the bottom of the basin and unfold the pastry, making sure there are no air bubbles – if there are, carefully pop them with a knife.
* Spoon the cold chicken mixture into the lined basin. Roll out the remaining pastry so it is slightly larger than the basin, brush the edges with water and lay the pastry over the bowl. Gently press all around the edge, then trim off any excess pastry and cut a steam hole in the centre.
* Cover with a double pleated layer of baking (parchment) paper and aluminium foil and secure with kitchen string.
* Steam in a steamer for 3½ hours, topping up (topping off) with boiling water, if necessary. If you don't have a steamer, then put an upturned saucer in the bottom of a large saucepan, put the basin on top (it's important the basin doesn't touch the bottom of the pan) and carefully fill halfway with water. Bring to the boil, then reduce the heat to a simmer. Cover with a lid, making sure the water doesn't go below the halfway mark, and steam for 3½ hours.

ENGLAND
*

TOAD IN THE HOLE

Fried sausages baked in a fluffy, crispy Yorkshire pudding, this much beloved English classic has been around since the 1700s when batter puddings first became popular. A favourite anytime meal for all ages. Serve with Onion Gravy (page 420), steamed vegetables and Mashed Potatoes (page 80).

Serves: 6
Prep time: 20 minutes
Cook time: 1 hour
{ᴥ}

- 1 quantity Yorkshire Pudding batter (page 282)
- 2–3 tablespoons lard, dripping or sunflower oil
- 12 thin or 6 thick Cumberland or Lincolnshire sausages (page 164)
- ¼ teaspoon chopped thyme leaves (optional)

- To serve:
- Mashed Potatoes (page 80)
- Onion Gravy (page 420)

* Make the Yorkshire Pudding batter following the recipe on page 282.
* Preheat the oven to 220°C/425°F/Gas Mark 7.
* Put enough fat into a large roasting pan so that the entire bottom is quite liberally covered with it, then put it into the oven for at least 10 minutes, or until it is very hot.
* Meanwhile, heat a little more fat in a large frying pan or skillet over a medium heat, add the sausages and fry for 5–6 minutes until browned. They don't need to be cooked through at this stage. Remove and set aside. If using the thyme leaves, whisk them through the batter.
* Remove the roasting pan from the oven, arrange the sausages in the hot fat and pour the batter around them. Carefully put the roasting pan into the oven as quickly as possible and cook for 20 minutes, or until crisp and well-risen. Reduce the oven temperature to 180°C/350°F/Gas Mark 4 and cook for another 30 minutes. Don't open the oven door midway through cooking, as the Yorkshire pudding will deflate. Serve with Mashed Potatoes and Onion Gravy.

Toad in the hole

IT WAS A DINNER NESSET LOVED.
FIRST CAME NORFOLK DUMPLINGS,
LIGHT AS PUFF-BALLS, MADE WITH REAL BREWER'S YEAST,
FLOATING IN RICH BROWN HARE GRAVY.

MATHENA BLOMEFIELD,
THE BULLEYMUNG PIT: THE STORY OF A NORFOLK FARMER'S CHILD, 1946

The recipes found in this small but highly important chapter are the workhorses of British baking, and the unsung heroes of the best stews and roasts.

Great British baking needs a foundation, and pastry (pie dough) provides that at every occasion: a flaky suet crust for steak pie, hot water pastry for a good hand-raised Melton Mowbray pork pie, rough puff for Eccles cakes, fat and sticky, a buttery shortcrust for all sorts of sweet and savoury, and so on. It can be worrying how much pastry to make for a given recipe, but here's the trick: always over-estimate. One of the fun things about British baking is that it accounts for this sort of overspill with plenty of recipes for small jam tarts, cheese straws, and so on. And, of course, pastry can be frozen

as well – defrosted and whipped into something spontaneous when the feeling takes you a month later. Dumplings may not, on the face of it, seem particularly British in today's world, but the word does in fact originate in seventeenth-century England, with the recipes coming from Norfolk. There, dumplings were traditionally made with the excess from the weekly bread dough, and would be quite simple in flavour. A richer variety could be made with suet, and these are perhaps the most popular sort today as they are a little more indulgent, and can be easily adapted to incorporate herbs, cheese and plenty of other flavourings.

Stuffings originate as another left-over from the bread-baking process – this time from the excess dried bread, which would be ground into

breadcrumbs and served as the base of the recipe. Stuffings come to us from the forcemeats of old: these meat mixtures vary considerably but are typically much meatier than your average stuffing.

There is something so satisfying, cyclical (and relevant) about utilizing excess, and the clever use of left-overs, and something so indicative of British cooking, which seems to be that central notion of making the absolute most of everything you have.

So, dog-ear or bookmark this chapter. It's one you will keep coming back to.

STUFFING, DUMPLINGS, PORRIDGE AND PASTRY

UNITED KINGDOM
*

APRICOT STUFFING

A classic accompaniment to Christmas turkeys and roasts of all kinds, this recipe makes enough for one chicken or a stuffed shoulder of lamb. Double the recipe for a turkey.

Makes: enough for 1 chicken or a stuffed lamb shoulder
Prep time: 15 minutes
Cook time: 12–17 minutes
{🐛}

- 60 g/2¼ oz (4 tablespoons) butter
- 1 onion, chopped
- 1 teaspoon chopped thyme leaves
- 30 g/1 oz (¼ cup) roasted hazelnuts or almonds, chopped (optional)
- 100 g/3½ oz (scant ½ cup) dried apricots, chopped
- 200 g/7 oz (4 cups) fresh breadcrumbs
- 1 tablespoon chopped flat-leaf parsley leaves
- 6 sage leaves, chopped
- grated zest of 1 lemon
- 1 egg, beaten
- salt and pepper

* Melt the butter in a medium saucepan over a medium-low heat, add the onion and thyme leaves and fry for 10–15 minutes until the onion is soft and golden.
* Meanwhile, put the nuts (if using), the apricots, breadcrumbs, parsley, sage and lemon zest into a large bowl and mix together until combined. Season with salt and pepper.
* Add the onion and any buttery juices, then add the egg and lightly mix together with clean hands. Use to stuff your chosen meat, or cook on its own in a baking dish in an oven preheated to 190°C/375°F/Gas Mark 5 for 25–30 minutes.

UNITED KINGDOM
*

CHESTNUT STUFFING

A traditional stuffing for roast birds, chestnut stuffing has been made in England since the 1840s when Eliza Acton included it in her book *Modern Cookery for Private Families*. When making this recipe for turkey, double the ingredients.

Makes: enough for 1 chicken or a stuffed lamb shoulder
Prep time: 15 minutes
Cook time: 12–17 minutes
{🐛}

- 50 g/2 oz (3½ tablespoons) butter
- 1 onion, chopped
- 1 clove garlic, finely chopped
- 200 g/7 oz (1½ cups) cooked and peeled chestnuts, chopped
- 90 g/3¼ oz (4½ cups) fresh breadcrumbs
- 1 tablespoon chopped flat-leaf parsley
- 1 egg, beaten
- salt and pepper

* Melt the butter in a medium saucepan over a medium-low heat, add the onion and garlic and fry for 10–15 minutes until soft and golden.
* Meanwhile, put the chestnuts, breadcrumbs and parsley into a large bowl and mix together. Season with salt and pepper. Add the onion, garlic and any buttery juices from the pan, then add the egg and lightly mix together with clean hands. Use to stuff your chosen meat, or cook on its own in a baking dish in an oven preheated to 190°C/375°F/Gas Mark 5 for 25–30 minutes.

UNITED KINGDOM
*

HERB STUFFING

This stuffing is a perfect go-to recipe for Sunday roast chicken, but would work just as well in a lamb shoulder. The herbs used in this recipe are meant as a guide, so change it up based on your preferences.

Makes: enough for 1 chicken or a stuffed lamb shoulder
Prep time: 15 minutes
Cook time: 25 minutes

- 50 g/2 oz (3½ tablespoons) butter
- 90 g/3¼ oz smoked bacon, chopped (optional)
- 1 onion, chopped
- ½ teaspoon chopped thyme or lemon thyme leaves
- ½ teaspoon finely chopped rosemary or winter savory leaves
- 60 g/2¼ oz (½ cup) hazelnuts, chopped (optional)
- 90 g/3¼ oz (1¾ cups) fresh breadcrumbs
- 1 tablespoon chopped flat-leaf parsley
- 1 teaspoon finely chopped chervil or chives
- 1 egg, beaten
- salt and pepper

* Melt the butter in a medium saucepan over a medium-high heat, add the bacon and fry for 10–12 minutes until it begins to crisp. Add the onion, thyme and rosemary or savory leaves, then reduce the heat to medium and fry for 8–10 minutes until the onion is soft and golden.
* Meanwhile, put the hazelnuts (if using), the breadcrumbs and the remaining herbs into a large bowl and mix together until combined. Season with salt and pepper.
* Add the onion and bacon along with any juices from the pan, then add the egg and lightly mix together with clean hands. Use to stuff a chicken or cook on its own in a baking dish in an oven preheated to 190°C/375°F/Gas Mark 5 for 25–30 minutes..

UNITED KINGDOM

*

SAGE
AND
ONION STUFFING

A classic all-purpose stuffing used for roast birds and red or white meat. Double the ingredients for a turkey.

Serves: 6
Prep time: 15 minutes
Cook time: 10–12 minutes
{☷}{⌁}{✗}

- 60 g/2¼ oz (4 tablespoons) butter
- 1 onion, chopped
- 8 large sage leaves, chopped
- 90 g/3¼ oz (1¾ cups) fresh breadcrumbs
- 1 tablespoon chopped flat-leaf parsley
- 1 egg, beaten
- salt and pepper

* Melt the butter in a large frying pan or skillet over a medium-low heat, add the onion and sage and fry for 8–10 minutes until golden.
* Meanwhile, put the breadcrumbs and parsley into a large bowl and mix until combined. Season with salt and pepper. Add the onion and any buttery juices from the pan, then add the egg and lightly mix with clean hands.
* Use to stuff roast turkey or chicken or cook on its own in a baking dish in an oven preheated to 190°C/375°F/ Gas Mark 5 for 25–30 minutes.

UNITED KINGDOM

*

OYSTER STUFFING

The notion of a stuffing made from fresh oysters may seem a bit excessive these days, but native oysters were once plentiful (and cheap) enough to eat with abandon. In the late eighteenth century, in oyster bars and taverns across the UK, that was certainly the custom. This stuffing was traditionally used for a boiled leg of mutton or lamb but would work just as well with a lamb shoulder.

Serves: 6
Prep time: 15 minutes
{⚓}{⌁}{✗}

- 12 oysters
- ½ teaspoon thyme leaves
- 60 g/2¼ oz (⅓ cup) smoked ham or bacon, chopped
- 150 g/5 oz (3 cups) fresh breadcrumbs
- 1 tablespoon chopped flat-leaf parsley
- pinch each of ground nutmeg, mace and cayenne pepper
- 1 egg, beaten

* Shuck the oysters following the instructions on page 124 and drain, reserving their liquor in a bowl. Coarsely chop the oysters and put into a large bowl with the remaining ingredients, except the egg, then lightly stir together until combined. Using a wooden spoon, lightly fold in the egg to make a crumbly but moist mixture. If the stuffing is a little too dry, add 1 tablespoon of the reserved oyster liquor. Use the stuffing for mutton or lamb leg.
* **Notes:** You can reserve the remaining oyster liquor for Oyster Sauce (page 422).

SCOTLAND

*

SKIRLIE

A traditional Scottish serving of oatmeal and onions fried in fat (traditionally suet), skirlie is often likened to a skinless mealy pudding (page 177). The name comes from the Scots word, 'skirl', which means to emit a shriek – an allusion to the sounds emitted by the mixture as it fries. Serve as a stuffing, a side dish for roast birds, such as chicken, or on its own to combat the sort of Scots malaise that descends with the first of the November storms.
This recipe comes from Scottish chef Pamela Brunton.

Serves: 4 as a side
Prep time: 10 minutes
Cook time: 15–25 minutes
{♨}{⚓}{⌁}{🍲}

- 125 g/4½ oz (1 cup) pinhead oatmeal
- 50 g/2 oz chicken fat (from the top of a stock or the pan of a roasted bird), butter or suet
- 1 brown onion, finely diced
- 125 ml/4¼ fl oz (½ cup) hot chicken broth or water (optional)
- salt and pepper

* Preheat the oven to 180°C/350°F/Gas Mark 4.
* Spread the oatmeal out on a baking sheet and toast in the oven for 10 minutes, keeping an eye on it to prevent it burning.
* Meanwhile, melt the fat in a medium saucepan over a low heat, add the onion and ½ teaspoon salt and cook for 10 minutes, or until the onion is translucent and warmly golden. Add the toasted oatmeal and stir until it absorbs the fat. At this point you can legitimately stop, season and eat; this is how many ate their skirlie in the past.
* However, for those who prefer the chew of hydrated oat over a more sandy texture, now is the time to add the hot chicken stock or water. This will make the oatmeal clump immediately into a sticky mass. Reduce the heat to very low and cook, stirring frequently, for 5–10 minutes, or as long as it takes for the oats to absorb the stock, for the starch to cook fully and the oats to dry somewhat, separating again into an open, crumbly pudding. Season enthusiastically with pepper and add a little more salt if needed. It should be slightly spicy.

ENGLAND: NORFOLK

NORFOLK DUMPLINGS
NORFOLK 'SWIMMERS'

Norfolk has a long and proud attachment to bread dumplings, traditionally made for serving with stews. In fact, the word 'dumpling' originated in the local Norfolk dialect in the 1600s as a word to describe these large doughballs, which were typically left-over from weekly bread-baking. The term 'swimmers' is a reference to how they float on the surface of the stew – a necessary feature of any good dumpling.

Serves: 4–6
Prep time: 20 minutes, plus 30–45 minutes rising
Cook time: 15–20 minutes
{ ☙ }

- 225 g/8 oz (1¾ cups plus 1 tablespoon) plain (all-purpose) flour
- 1 tsp salt
- 1 x 7-g/¼-oz sachet instant dried yeast
- 100–125 ml/3½–4¼ fl oz (⅓ cup plus 1 tablespoon– ½ cup) warm milk or water
- 1 litre/34 fl oz (4¼ cups) beef stock or water

* Sift all the dry ingredients together into a large bowl, then gradually mix in three-quarters of the warm milk or water and mix to form a stiff dough. Add the rest of the milk if it's too dry. Knead the dough for several minutes, until firm, then cover the bowl with a clean, damp dish towel and leave to rise for at least 30–45 minutes until it has doubled in size.
* Divide the risen dough into 4 equal portions, then shape each portion into a ball.
* Bring the beef stock or water to the boil in a large saucepan. Carefully lower the dumplings into the pan, cover with a lid and cook for 15–20 minutes (depending on how large the dumplings are). As the name 'swimmers' suggest, they will swim on the surface of the pan.
* When the dumplings are cooked, using a slotted spoon, remove them from the pan and leave to cool for a moment before serving, sliced into wedges, alongside a stew, casserole or a joint of beef.

UNITED KINGDOM

SUET DUMPLINGS

Suet dumplings, bronzed in the top of a stew pot, are one of the great pleasures of traditional English cooking. Flecked with parsley or filled with a bite of horseradish, they are typically served with stews and casseroles – or indeed any sort of boiled beef. Soaked in rich meaty juices, these stodgy morsels provide a level of comfort and indulgence no loaf of bread can afford.

In her book *English Recipes*, Shelia Hutchins also describes a tantalizing account of large suet dumplings, sliced and set in the dripping pan under a beef roast, where they would lightly fry until brown, and be served together with the meat.

Serves: 4–6
Prep time: 10 minutes
Cook time: 25–30 minutes
{ ☙ }

- 100 g/3½ oz (¾ cup plus 2 teaspoons) self-raising flour, plus extra for dusting
- 50 g/2 oz beef suet
- pinch of salt
- pinch of pepper
- 1 tablespoon finely chopped flat-leaf parsley (optional)
- ½ teaspoon finely chopped thyme leaves (optional)
- ½ teaspoon creamed horseradish (optional)
- piece of bone marrow (optional)

* Put the flour and suet together in a large bowl, add salt and pepper and, if using, the herbs. Mix until combined. Slowly add about 75 ml/2½ fl oz (⅓ cup) water, using a butter knife to mix it in until it forms a single ball of dough. It should be as soft as possible, but not so wet that it cannot be worked with floured hands.
* Dust your hands lightly with flour, then divide the dough into 4 large or 6 small portions and roll into dumplings, then use as desired. Preheat the oven to 200°C/400°F/ Gas Mark 6 and cook in a casserole or stew for 25–30 minutes with the lid on. If you like them browned, then remove the lid for at least the last 10 minutes.
* **Notes:** For horseradish or bone marrow dumplings, make a hole in the dumplings and place ½ teaspoon of creamed horseradish or a piece of bone marrow inside, then seal it in the centre of the dumplings and cook as desired.

SCOTLAND / WALES

OATMEAL DUMPLINGS
TROLLIES

Oatmeal dumplings were once common to Scotland and Wales, where oats grew in abundance. In Scotland they were typically savoury and cooked in stews – sometimes in the shape of a rooster (called 'Fitless Cock'). In Wales so-called 'trollies' were typically made the size of a golf ball, with currants and spices, and boiled in either stock or fresh water. Trollies could be served with the stew or in place of pudding, split and spread with butter while steaming hot.

Serves: 4
Prep time: 15 minutes
Cook time: 30–40 minutes
{ ☗ } { ☙ }

- 200 g/7 oz (1⅔ cups) oatmeal
- 50 g/2 oz (½ cup minus 2 teaspoons) plain (all-purpose) flour
- 70 g/2¾ oz (½ cup minus 1 tablespoon) shredded beef suet
- 1 white onion, finely chopped
- 1 egg, beaten

* Put all the ingredients, except the egg, into a large bowl and mix together until combined. Form a well in the centre, then add the egg and mix with the dry ingredients to form a fairly stiff dough. Add a little milk or water if the dough is too dry to hold together. Using wet hands,

divide the mixture into 16 portions and shape into balls.

* Poach the balls in a soup, stew or casserole, or bring a large saucepan of lightly salted water to a gentle simmer and poach them for 30–40 minutes.
* Notes: To make these sweet, swap the chopped onion for 80 g/ 3 oz (⅓ cup) currants and a pinch of ground nutmeg and serve with a small piece of butter and a drizzle of golden syrup.

UNITED KINGDOM
*

OAT PORRIDGE

Oat porridge (oatmeal) was originally quite a simple affair: oats, water and a little salt. In fact, until the proliferation of cheap sugar, syrups and jam, Scots rarely ate sweet porridge. Moreover, when porridge was served with milk or cream, it was usually served in a separate bowl, so as to keep them warm and cool respectively. When making porridge, a wooden implement called a spurtle would be used to gently ensure that clumps of oats did not form – you can use the back end of a wooden spoon if you like. Serve with honey and jam, or toppings of your choice.

Serves: 1
Prep time: 5 minutes
Cook time: 10–20 minutes
{👅}{🍃}{🐄}{🍴}{🔪}{𝕏}

- 360 ml/ 12 fl oz (1½ cups) full-fat (whole) milk, water or a mixture of the two
- 120 g/ 4 oz (1¼ cups) porridge (steel-cut) oats
- pinch of salt

- To serve (optional):
- sugar
- honey
- jam
- butter
- golden syrup
- a little extra milk or cream

* Heat the milk/ water in a medium saucepan over a medium heat. Gradually add the oats to the liquid, mixing well with a wooden spoon to prevent lumps forming. Bring to a simmer, add a small pinch of salt, then reduce the heat to low. Cook for 8 minutes, or until your desired thickness is achieved. Spoon into bowls, add the sweetener of your choice and cool the edges with a little extra milk, if desired.
* Notes: This recipe is based on a 1:3 ratio and will make a rather liquidy porridge, but if you desire something thicker, either cook the mixture for longer, or change the ratio of oats to liquid to 1:2. Additionally, you can soak the oats overnight, which will speed up the cooking time.

SCOTLAND / WALES
*

SOWANS
SUCENS

Sowans is a fermented oat dish traditional to Scotland and Wales. A dish borne out of poverty, it was traditionally made from the husks of oats, which, even after milling, had some starch and possibly even a little meal left on them. After being soaked with water or buttermilk for a few days, the mixture was strained off and left to sit for a further day or two. Of what remained, the starchy liquid was the sowans, and would be boiled down with water before eating like a sort of oat jelly or thick yogurt with whatever you would flavour porridge (oatmeal) with.
This traditional recipe has been modernized by Glasgow-based Scottish chef Craig Grozier, utilizing rolled oats and oat bran instead of oat husks.

Prep time: 1–2 weeks
{👅}{🍃}{🐄}{🍴}{🔪}

- 200 g/ 7 oz oat bran
- 100 g/ 3½ oz rolled oats
- 22 g/ 1 oz Maldon sea salt
- 45 g/ 1½ oz whey (page 34)

* Add the bran and oats to a sterilized 2 litre/ 68 fl oz Kilner (canning) jar (page 464). In a large pot, whisk 1.2 litres/ 40 fl oz distilled water at 37°C/ 99°F with the salt and whey. Pour this over the bran and oats and ensure they are both fully submerged in the brine.
* Seal the jar and leave in a warm place for 1–2 weeks. The amount of time depends on climate, ambient heat of the room, etc. If it's warm, 7 days should be good; if it's cold, it may take up to 2 weeks.
* At the end of this period it should have picked up a lactic smell, like an oaty yogurt. (If there's a different, odd smell that doesn't feel right, you've gone wrong somewhere and need to start again.)
* Pass the mixture through a muslin- (cheesecloth-) lined sieve, squeezing out and collecting all the liquid in a bowl. Pour the liquid into a clean Kilner jar and leave to settle for a couple of days. The liquid will split. A starchy white substance will settle on the bottom (the sowans) and a yellow liquid on the top (the swats).
* Pour off most of the swats and reserve it. It has probiotic properties and tastes akin to kefir. Store the starch (sowans) in the fridge with a layer of swats on top.

For the sowans:

- 25 g/ 1 oz sowans
- golden syrup, honey or jam, to serve

* Whisk 250 ml/ 8 fl oz water and the sowans together in a small saucepan.
* Bring to the boil over a low-medium heat, stirring often, and simmer for 5–10 minutes, or until it thickens to a thick, cream-like consistency – when lifting a wooden spoon through the mixture, the run-off from the spoon should form a tail. Add a spoonful of golden syrup, honey or jam to the sowans to flavour it.
* Notes: Add more or less sowans, depending on how thick you like it.

WALES
*

FLUMMERY

Flummery, or llymru as the Welsh first called it, was a traditional Celtic dish. Fine oatmeal was steeped in water or buttermilk for several hours, then the liquid strained off and boiled until it turned into a brown blancmange. This recipe was adapted into 'twentieth-century' flummery by Welsh cookery writer Gilli Davies.

Serves: 4
Prep time: 15 minutes, plus 8–12 hours soaking
{🌶}{🔪}{🍴}

- 100 g/3½ oz (¾ cup plus 4 teaspoons) medium oatmeal
- 2 tablespoons heather honey
- 1 tablespoon fresh lemon juice
- 225 g/8 oz seasonal fresh fruit
- 150 ml/5 fl oz (⅔ cup) double (heavy) cream

* Put the oatmeal into a medium bowl, cover with cold water and leave to soak overnight.
* The next day, strain off any excess water and stir in the honey, lemon juice and fresh fruit. Put the cream into another bowl and softly whip with electric beaters, then fold gently into the oatmeal mixture. Serve the flummery at breakfast or as a pudding. It makes a delicious, healthy, filling snack.

UNITED KINGDOM
*

BEEF DRIPPING CRUST

A flavourful savoury pastry made from beef dripping. Use this pastry for savoury pies and pastries.

Makes: about 500 g/1 lb 2 oz dough
Prep time: 10 minutes, plus 30 minutes chilling
{🔪}{🍴}{🔪}

- 200 g/7 oz beef dripping, chilled
- 400 g/14 oz (3⅓ cups) plain (all-purpose) flour, sifted
- ½ teaspoon salt

* Remove the dripping from the fridge and grate on the coarser side of a box grater into a cold bowl (ensuring it is cold will help give the dough a flaky texture).
* Put the flour and salt into a large bowl, add the grated dripping and mix together until combined, then gradually add 100 ml/3½ fl oz (⅓ cup plus 1 tablespoon) cold water until the dough binds together.
* Knead very briefly into a ball, cover in clingfilm (plastic wrap) and chill in the fridge for at least 30 minutes before using.

UNITED KINGDOM
*

HOT WATER PASTRY

Hot water pastry is ideal for hand-raised pies and works equally well in everything from a large Pork Pie (page 221) or as the thin pastry shell of a small Scotch Pie (page 215).

Makes: about 800 g/1¾ lb dough
Prep time: 10 minutes, plus 10 minutes resting
Cook time: 2 minutes
{🔪}{🔪}{🍴}{⏲}

- 175 g/6 oz (1 cup) lard
- ½ teaspoon salt
- 250 g/9 oz (2 cups) plain (all-purpose) flour, sifted, plus extra for dusting
- 250 g/9 oz (2 cups) strong white flour, sifted

* Pour 175 ml/6 fl oz (¾ cup) hot water into a small saucepan, add the lard and gently warm over a low heat for a couple of minutes until the lard has melted. Add the salt and stir to dissolve.
* Meanwhile, put both flours into a large bowl and mix well using a wooden spoon. While stirring, gradually add the water and melted lard to form a dough. Alternatively, use a stand mixer fitted with a paddle attachment to make the dough.
* Put the dough onto a lightly floured work counter and knead well for 30 seconds, or until the dough is smooth, then cover in clingfilm (plastic wrap) and leave to rest at room temperature for 10 minutes (otherwise the dough will be too elastic).
* Use the dough immediately. If necessary, divide it into 2 pieces, then cover one while shaping the other.

UNITED KINGDOM
*

SUET PASTRY

This rich, flaky pastry can be used in many savoury British pies or puddings – and a handful of sweet ones too. It is the go-to pastry for classics ranging from Steak and Kidney Steamed Pudding (page 234) to Jam Roly Poly (page 354).

Makes: about 400 g/14 oz
Prep time: 10 minutes, plus 20 minutes chilling
{🔪}{🔪}{🍴}

- 200 g/7 oz (1⅔ cups) self-raising flour, sifted, plus extra for dusting
- pinch of salt
- 100 g/3½ oz beef suet, shredded

* Put the flour, salt and suet into a bowl and mix together. Slowly add about 150 ml/5 fl oz (⅔ cup) water and mix using a knife until the dough comes together into a ball.
* Turn the dough out onto a lightly floured work counter and knead briefly, until it is soft but not sticky to the touch. Cover with clingfilm (plastic wrap) and leave to chill in the fridge for 20 minutes. Once the dough has chilled, use as required.

UNITED KINGDOM

ROUGH PUFF PASTRY

This flaky pastry is less labour intensive than a proper puff pastry. In British baking, it is used for certain sweet and savoury puddings, and even some small cakes such as the Eccles Cake (page 298).

Makes: about 1 kg/ 2¼ lb
Prep time: 30 minutes, plus 1 hour 20 minutes chilling
{👤}{🍴}

- 500 g/ 1 lb 2 oz (4 cups plus 4 teaspoons) strong white flour, sifted, plus extra for dusting
- ½ teaspoon salt
- 375 g/ 13 oz (3½ sticks) very cold, unsalted butter, diced
- 30 ml/ 1 fl oz (2 tablespoons) lemon juice

* Put the flour, salt and butter into a large bowl and mix together by squashing the pieces of butter between your thumb and forefinger, without rubbing them in or breaking them up. Add the lemon juice and 220 ml/ 7¼ fl oz (¾ cup plus 2 tablespoons) very cold water, then mix until the dough is just incorporated. Avoid overworking the dough.
* Roll the dough into a ball, cover with clingfilm (plastic wrap) and leave to chill in the fridge for 20 minutes.
* Roll the rested dough out on a lightly floured work counter into a rectangle about 30 x 20 cm/ 12 x 8 inches. Fold the dough into thirds – fold the top third down to the centre and the bottom third up to the centre and over the top third – then turn it 90 degrees clockwise and roll out it out again to roughly the same size. Repeat the process, then fold the dough into 3 again. Wrap in clingfilm (plastic wrap) and leave to chill in the fridge for 30 minutes.
* Once rested, repeat the rolling and folding another 2 times. The pastry is now ready. Cover in clingfilm and rest for another 30 minutes before using. The dough will keep in the fridge for up to 3 days and up to 1 month in the freezer.

UNITED KINGDOM

SHORTCRUST PASTRY

Shortcrust, a rich pastry made with butter (or a combination of butter and lard), is the go-to pastry crust for many of Britain's sweet and savoury pies – along with some biscuits, cakes and traybakes.

Makes: about 450 g/ 1 lb
Prep time: 10 minutes, plus 20 minutes resting
{🍴}

- 250 g/ 9 oz (2 cups) plain (all-purpose) flour, sifted
- pinch of salt
- 125 g/ 4½ oz (9 tablespoons) cold butter, diced (or 60 g/ 2¼ oz butter and 60 g/ 2¼ oz lard)
- 1 egg, at room temperature

* Put the flour and salt into a large bowl and mix together. Add the fats and rub them in with your fingertips until the mixture resembles breadcrumbs. (If using a stand mixer fitted with a paddle attachment, do this on the slowest speed.) Make a well in the centre, add the egg and 60 ml/ 2 fl oz (¼ cup) water, then mix in, drawing in the flour to form a dough.
* Gradually, bring the dough together with your hands and knead briefly, just 2–3 times until smooth. Avoid overworking the dough. Cover with clingfilm (plastic wrap) and leave to rest in the fridge for 20 minutes. The dough will keep in the fridge for up to 3 days, and up to 1 month in the freezer.
* **Variation:** For a sweet shortcrust, which makes about 500 g/ 1 lb 2 oz, follow the same method as above, using 250 g/ 9 oz (2 cups) plain (all-purpose) flour, sifted, pinch of salt, 100 g/ 3½ oz (7 tablespoons) cold butter, diced, and 2 eggs, at room temperature.

UNITED KINGDOM

SWEET SHORTCRUST PASTRY

Use this sweetened shortcrust pastry for all pies and tarts that are not overly sweet already.

Makes: enough for 1 double-crusted 20 cm/ 8 inch pie or 2 x base-lined 20 cm/ 8 inch tarts
Prep time: 30 minutes, plus 1 hour chilling
{👤}{🍴}

- 340 g/ 12 oz (2¾ cups plus 2 teaspoons) stoneground, high-extraction, unbleached flour
- 140 g/ 5 oz (1 cup plus 4 teaspoons) stoneground wholemeal (whole wheat) flour (or an additional 140 g/ 5 oz unbleached flour)
- 110 g/ 3¾ oz (½ cup) caster (superfine) sugar
- ½ teaspoon sea salt flakes
- 280 g/ 10 oz (2½ sticks) unsalted butter, cold, diced
- 2 egg yolks
- 100 ml/ 3½ fl oz (⅓ cup plus 1 tablespoon) double (heavy) cream

* Put the flours, sugar and sea salt into a large bowl or a stand mixer fitted with a paddle attachment. Add the diced butter and, if making by hand, begin to rub it in with your fingertips until the mixture resembles coarse breadcrumbs with some pea-sized butter pieces remaining. If using the stand mixer, mix on low-medium speed until the mixture resembles this texture.
* Mix the egg yolks and cream together in another bowl, then gradually add this to the flour and butter mixture. If using your hands, bring the mixture together in the bowl. If using the mixer, continue to mix gently until a dough just begins to form. The mixture will look crumbly at first but it will quickly come together so don't overhandle it or mix it too fast.
* Once the dough comes together, divide it into 2 equal portions, flatten each into a circle and wrap in clingfilm (plastic wrap). Chill in the fridge for at least 1 hour before using. Store in the fridge for up to 2 days or freeze for up to 1 month.

...AND NEW-BAKED SCONES AND PANCAKES
STRAUCHT FRAE THE GIRDLE.
AND THE SCONES AND ROWTH O HIGH-TEA
CAKES THAT GARS YOUR TEETH WATTER...

DUNCAN GLEN, FROM UPLAND MAN, 1997

This chapter is a celebration of a shared baking tradition across much of northern Britain: the iron griddle. Here, for the average folk, these breads predate the oven-baked variety. And there is something truly joyous about these small cakes and breads, eaten still warm from the griddle and dusted with sugar, or spread with butter and broken into soup.

In Britain, the griddle is known by many names, but has for centuries been a fixture of kitchens. In Scotland and northern England, this cooking device was traditionally known as a girdle, in Ireland a baking iron, and in Wales it was dubbed a bakestone or 'planc'.

Originally these devices were made from stone (sandstone or slate) and heated by the fire, but by the eighteenth and nineteenth centuries they were mostly cast iron, meaning they could be sat directly above the flames. The Scottish and English variants of this iron plate have metal hoop arms and a ring over the top from which they could be suspended over a fire. The Welsh bakestone has a handle cut into the design for hanging over the fire.

In Scotland, the griddle was the go-to device for cooking what were broadly known as 'cakes' or bannocks, which invariably simply referred to the round shape and size of the bake rather than its composition. These cakes were typically made from barley, and until the advent of bicarbonate of soda (baking soda), more closely resembled a modern flatbread. They would also dry out quite quickly, so needed to be eaten while warm and fresh. In parts of northern England, the griddle might be used for making a Norse-influenced bake called riddlebread or havercake. This was a thin, elongated oatcake that could be dried, and stored away, to be eaten like crackers.

As Britain's obsession with home-baking kicked off in the nineteenth century, the griddle came to be used more for sweet cakes than for savoury. We can easily picture the greased flat top of a griddle cooking Scotch pancakes (or drop scones), girdle scones, pikelets, Welsh cakes and singin' hinnies, each served with a choice of butter and golden syrup, honey or jam.

There are still regions such as Shetland, where traditional griddle breads, like the flour or barley bannock, or even oatcakes, are still cooked in circles on a griddle, but this is a device now almost exclusively used in home kitchens – as even the busiest Welsh bakeries will prefer the much wider flat top of a contemporary metal plancha.

When cooking with a griddle, be sure to give it plenty of time to heat up (about 10–15 minutes) and make sure to prepare the surface appropriately: either greased (as in pancakes or pikelets) or floured (as in oatcakes or breads).

GRIDDLE CAKES

AND

BREADS

ENGLAND
*

ENGLISH CRUMPETS

A toasted crumpet, spread with good butter and jam, is nothing to be scoffed at. I would go so far as to say that when paired with a great big mug of something hot and soothing, it makes an ideal start to the day.

The earliest recipe for crumpets comes from Elizabeth Raffald in her 1769 book *The Experienced English Housekeeper*, but similar sorts of griddle breads exist in recipe books as far back as the fourteenth century and seem to be common to ancient Celtic cultures. The crumpet is still closely related to a handful of griddle breads and cakes, not least of which is the near-identical Pikelet (see right).

Crumpets should be light and airy, with a distinctive many-holed top, and a nice open texture that produces, in the wise words of Dorothy Hartley, 'a suitable concavity for the butter'. What's the right amount of butter to use then? Well, Hartley imparts wisdom straight from the legendary chef Alexis Soyer when she says a small piece, roughly 15 g/ ½ oz (1 tablespoon).

Makes: 12
Prep time: 10 minutes, plus 1 hour rising
Cook time: 45 minutes
{👤}{📍}

- 160 ml/5½ fl oz (⅔ cup plus 2 teaspoons) full-fat (whole) milk
- 250 g/9 oz (2 cups) plain (all-purpose) flour
- 1 teaspoon caster (superfine) sugar
- 8 g/¼ oz (2½ teaspoons) instant dried yeast
- ½ teaspoon salt
- ½ teaspoon bicarbonate of soda (baking soda)
- vegetable oil or lard, for greasing

- To serve:
- butter
- jam or honey

* Heat the milk gently in a medium saucepan over a low heat for 3–5 minutes until lukewarm, then remove from the heat and set aside. Heat 160 ml/5½ fl oz (⅔ cup plus 2 teaspoons) water in the same way until lukewarm.
* Put all the dry ingredients into a large bowl, make a well in the centre, then gradually beat in the warmed milk. When smooth, beat in the warmed water. Cover with a clean, damp dish towel and leave to rise for about 1 hour in a warm place, until the mixture has expanded and bubbles have formed on the surface.
* Preheat a griddle, frying pan or skillet over a medium-low heat. Oil the griddle or pan as well as 4 crumpet rings. Put the rings carefully onto the hot surface, then ladle the batter into each ring, filling enough for it to come just over halfway up the ring. Cook for 8–9 minutes until bubbles form and the batter starts to firm up. Remove the rings, turn the crumpets over and cook the other side for 3–4 minutes. They will be lighter in colour and a little less cooked on the second side, but this is totally normal. Remove from the pan and repeat with the remaining batter.
* Leave the crumpets to cool before serving warm with butter and jam or honey.

WALES / ENGLAND: MIDLANDS
*

PIKELETS
GIRDLE CAKES

Pikelets are made from a batter quite similar to that used for the Crumpet (see left), but cooked without the use of metal rings. The result is a thinner, equally bubbly griddle cake, which can be enjoyed in much the same way: eaten warm with butter, jam and a mug of tea.

Despite their similarities in shape, texture and taste, pikelets and crumpets may actually have different origins. While crumpets once varied in flour and size (ranging as large as a dinner plate), pikelets have always enjoyed their present shape. Many in Wales, including food writer Bobby Freeman, have suggested that the name pikelet is an English corruption of the Welsh *bara pyglyd*, or *bara picklet*, and that their popularity in the Midlands comes as the result of close cross-border exchange.

Makes: about 18
Prep time: 10 minutes
Cook time: 10 minutes
{📍}{🍴}

- 440 g/15½ oz (3⅔ cups) plain (all-purpose) flour, sifted
- 1 teaspoon salt
- 5 g/⅛ oz (2 teaspoons) baking powder
- 15 g/½ oz (1 tablespoon) caster (superfine) sugar
- 1 egg
- 125 ml/4¼ fl oz (½ cup) full-fat (whole) milk
- lard, animal fat or oil, for frying
- marmalade or jam, to serve

* Preheat a girdle or heavy frying pan or skillet over a medium heat.
* Put all the dry ingredients, except the sugar, into a large bowl and mix thoroughly. Separate the egg yolk from the white into 2 bowls and beat each one separately. Put the milk and 125 ml/4¼ fl oz (½ cup) water into a jug, then beat in the egg yolk. Pour the egg yolk mixture into the dry ingredients and mix thoroughly using a whisk, making a batter-like texture.
* Meanwhile, add the sugar to the egg white and, using either electric beaters or a stand mixer fitted with a whisk attachment, whisk until soft peaks form. Using a spoon, fold the egg whites into the pikelet mixture (make sure that the whites are fully incorporated but not overmixed).
* Rub the girdle with a piece of lard, animal fat or oil, removing any excess with paper towel. Using a small ladle, carefully spoon the mixture onto the girdle (you may need to do this in batches) and cook for 1–2 minutes on each side until coloured on both sides. Remove and repeat until the batter is used up. Eat hot straight from the girdle with a generous amount of marmalade or jam.

English crumpets

SCOTLAND

*

SCOTTISH CRUMPETS

The Scottish crumpet is like its English cousin, writ large and baked without rings: one side is bubbly and airy, the other smooth and a deep amber brown. Scottish crumpets are to be served warm, spread with butter and jam or golden syrup and eaten rolled up.

Makes: 12
Prep time: 5 minutes
Cook time: 50 minutes
{🍴}{🥄}

- 45 g/1½ oz (3 tablespoons) unsalted butter
- 375 g/13 oz (3 cups plus 1 tablespoon) plain (all-purpose) flour
- 8 g/¼ oz (2 teaspoons) baking powder
- 4 g/⅛ oz (1 teaspoon) fine salt
- 45 g/1½ oz (¼ cup) caster (superfine) sugar
- 2 eggs
- 400 ml/14 fl oz (1⅔ cups) full-fat (whole) milk
- butter or vegetable oil, for frying

- To serve:
- butter
- jam, honey or golden syrup

* Preheat a large, heavy frying pan or skillet over a medium-high heat. Preheat the oven to 80°C/176°F/lowest Gas Mark (optional).
* Meanwhile, melt the butter in a small saucepan over a medium-low heat. Remove from the heat and set aside.
* Sift the flour, baking powder, salt and sugar into a medium bowl.
* Beat the eggs and milk together in another medium bowl until smooth, then stir in the melted butter.
* Using a whisk, slowly incorporate the egg mixture into the dry ingredients, making sure that no lumps form (beating vigorously only if necessary, but avoid overworking the batter). Continue to gradually add the remaining egg mixture until a smooth texture is achieved (similar to that of thick double (heavy) cream), scraping the bottom of the bowl to ensure the batter is thoroughly mixed.
* Reduce the heat under the frying pan or skillet to medium, rub the butter or oil around the frying pan or skillet (repeating the process in between crumpets), then spoon a 115 ml/4 fl oz ladleful of the mixture into the centre of the pan, creating a thin crumpet about 10 cm/4 inches in diameter. Cook each crumpet for 2–3 minutes until bubbles start to form and the batter begins to dry out. The crumpet should brown on the base but still be tacky. Flip over and cook for another minute until pale golden on top with small bubbles showing. Serve immediately or keep the crumpets in the preheated oven until they are all cooked.
* Serve with butter, or jam, honey or golden syrup.

SCOTLAND / WALES / ENGLAND

*

SCOTCH PANCAKES
DROP SCONES/CREMPOG/FFROES

Scotch pancakes are in many ways a smaller version of the light and fluffy American-style pancakes, to which they are undoubtedly related. They are made from a thick batter of eggs, milk and flour, which is then spooned out and dropped (hence the name) onto a hot, greased girdle. The pancakes are cooked for a few minutes on one side until bubbles form and the bottom is a golden brown. They are then flipped and cooked until the other side reaches the same colour.

Makes: about 15
Prep time: 10 minutes
Cook time: 30 minutes
{🍴}{🥄}

- vegetable oil or butter, for greasing
- 20 g/¾ oz (4 teaspoons) butter, plus extra to serve
- 280 g/10 oz (2⅓ cups) self-raising flour
- 100 g/3½ oz (½ cup) caster (superfine) sugar
- pinch of salt
- 2 eggs, beaten
- 260 ml/9 fl oz (1 cup plus 2 teaspoons) full-fat (whole) milk
- butter, honey or jam, to serve

* Preheat a girdle, heavy frying pan or skillet over a low heat and grease liberally. Preheat the oven to 80°C/176°F/lowest Gas Mark.
* Melt the butter in a small saucepan over a low heat. Remove from the heat and set aside.
* Sift the flour, sugar and salt together into a large bowl. Separately combine the beaten eggs and milk in a jug (pitcher), before adding the melted butter. Make a well in the centre of the dry mix, then add the wet ingredients, stirring inwards from the edges to incorporate the ingredients into a smooth batter.
* Test a pancake in the heated girdle by adding a tablespoon of the batter to the pan and cooking for 2–3 minutes, or until bubbles appear on the surface. Flip over to cook the other side for 2–3 minutes. You are looking for an even brown top and a good rise when flipped. Too runny and the batter will spread and not rise; too thick and it will be very heavy. If the top browns unevenly, add more melted butter. If the top does not brown at all, increase the heat on the stove. Put the drop scone on an ovenproof plate and keep warm in the oven. Repeat until you have used up all of the batter. Serve warm with butter and honey or jam.

Scottish crumpets

BLAANDA BREAD

A bannock-style griddle bread from Shetland, the blaanda would have been made using equal parts of beremeal (a variety of barley) and Shetland black oats. The word 'blaanda' likely comes from Norn, the extinct Scandinavian language spoken on Scotland's northern islands until the mid-nineteenth century.

Serves: 6–8
Prep time: 10 minutes
Cook time: 20 minutes
{●} {◞•}

- 150 g/5 oz (1¼ cups) fine oatmeal
- 150 g/5 oz (1¼ cups) barley flour (ideally beremeal), plus extra for dusting
- 1 teaspoon bicarbonate of soda (baking soda)
- 60 g/2¼ oz (½ stick) salted butter
- up to 150 ml/5 fl oz (⅔ cup) full-fat (whole) milk

* Preheat a bakestone or griddle over a medium-low heat.
* Sift the oatmeal, flour and bicarbonate of soda (baking soda) into a bowl, add the butter and rub it in with your fingertips until it resembles breadcrumbs. Add as much of the milk as needed, starting with about half and then adding a little at a time, mixing to form a stiff dough.
* Form the dough into a ball about 1 cm/½ inch thick, and press out into a circle large enough to fit on the bakestone or griddle. Lightly dust the griddle with flour, then put the dough onto it and cook for 10 minutes on one side. Flip it over and cook for another 10 minutes. You may need to reduce the heat if the bread is taking on too much colour.

SODA BREAD
NORTHERN IRISH SODA FARLS

In Northern Ireland, white soda bread is not baked as a loaf in the oven, but rather as a flat circle on a griddle. As each loaf cooks, it is cut into four equal parts, or farls. Serve with butter and jam, or as part of an Ulster Fry (page 26).

Serves: 4
Prep time: 10 minutes
Cook time: 20 minutes
{●} {◞•}

- 300 g/11 oz (2½ cups) plain (all-purpose) flour, plus extra for dusting
- 1 teaspoon baking powder
- ½ teaspoon salt
- 260 ml/8¾ fl oz (1 cup plus 2 teaspoons) buttermilk

* Preheat a heavy pan or flat griddle over a medium heat, making sure to not grease the pan.
* Put the flour, baking powder and salt into a large bowl and mix together until combined. Make a well in the centre and pour in the buttermilk. Stir quickly using a wooden spoon, then tip onto a floured work counter and shape into a circle. Press flat until it is 1.5 cm/⅝ inch thick, then cut into quarters. Cook in the hot pan or griddle for 10 minutes, then flip over and cook for another 10 minutes until golden brown on both sides.

GIRDLE SCONES
SODA SCONES

Girdle-baked scones predate the oven-baked variety, and while the two use the same dough, the difference in cooking method lends a noticeably different bake. When prepared for the girdle, the scones are shaped into smaller, thinner farls (wedges) and pick up a golden crust and a soft steamy inside. They should be served while still warm.

Serves: 6
Prep time: 15 minutes
Cook time: 30 minutes
{◞•} {✕}

- 450 g/1 lb (3¾ cups) plain (all-purpose) flour, plus extra for dusting
- 1 teaspoon salt
- 2 teaspoons baking powder
- 100 g/3½ oz (7 tablespoons) unsalted butter
- 100 g/3½ oz (½ cup) caster (superfine) sugar
- 100 g/3½ oz (⅔ cup) sultanas (golden raisins) or raisins (optional)
- 300 ml/10 fl oz (1¼ cups) buttermilk or full-fat (whole) milk
- butter, lard or oil, for frying

- To serve:
- butter, jam and Clotted Cream (page 34, optional)

* Preheat a girdle or heavy frying pan or skillet over a medium heat.
* Sift the flour, salt and baking powder together into a large bowl, add the butter and rub it in with your fingertips until it resembles breadcrumbs. Add the sugar and sultanas (golden raisins) or raisins (if using) and mix well. Make a well in the centre of the mixture and gradually mix in the buttermilk using a rubber spatula until the dough starts to come together.
* Turn the scone dough out onto a lightly floured work counter and divide into 3 equal pieces. Gently knead each portion until the dough starts to become smooth, without overworking it. Using a floured rolling pin, evenly roll out each piece into a circle about 2.5 cm/1 inch thick, then, using a sharp knife, cut each circle into quarters.
* Using a paper towel, evenly apply your preferred fat to the girdle, then put the scones onto the girdle and cook for 5 minutes on one side (you may need to do this in batches). Flip over and repeat on the other side, ensuring a uniform golden brown colour and that the scone sounds hollow when tapped. Remove from the pan and leave the scones to cool slightly before serving.
* Slice the warm scones in half and serve with butter, and/or a generous amount of your favourite jam and an optional spoonful of Clotted Cream.

Soda bread

SCOTLAND: SHETLAND

*

BARLEY BANNOCKS
BEREMEAL BANNOCKS

In Scotland, the term 'bannock' refers to a flat round bread baked on a griddle. Traditionally the most common type were barley bannocks, which were unleavened flatbreads. According to Scottish food writer Catherine Brown, they were baked very thin and then rolled up with butter and eaten while hot.

Today, barley bannocks are typically made with a 50/50 ratio of barley and wheat, buttermilk and a leavening agent. Soft and light, modern barley bannocks are not dissimilar in shape and texture to a Soda Farl or Girdle Scone (page 256), although they have a deeper, almost malty flavour. Leave them to cool just slightly in a clean dish towel before slicing and spreading with butter.

In Orkney and Shetland, beremeal bannocks are still made from an ancient heritage cultivar of barley, called bere, which has even greater depth of flavour. An old water-powered mill called Barony Mill is the main local producer and exporter of beremeal.

Makes: 12
Prep time: 25 minutes
Cook time: 30 minutes
{◉}{✷}

- 200 g/7 oz (1⅔ cups) beremeal or barley flour
- 100 g/3½ oz (¾ cup plus 2 teaspoons) plain (all-purpose) flour, plus extra for dusting
- large pinch of salt
- 2 teaspoons bicarbonate of soda (baking soda)
- 1 level teaspoon cream of tartar
- 25 g/1 oz (2 tablespoons) butter
- 300 ml/10 fl oz (1¼ cups) buttermilk
- butter, cold meat (salt beef, lamb), cheese or soup, to serve

* Sift all the dried ingredients into a large bowl, add the butter and rub it in with your fingertips until it resembles breadcrumbs. Add the buttermilk and mix to form a soft dough using your hands.
* Divide the dough into 3 equal portions. Pat each into a circle and put onto a lightly floured work counter. Flatten each one slightly to about 1 cm/½ inch thick, then divide into quarters.
* Heat a griddle or large flat pan over a medium heat, add the bannocks and cook for about 5 minutes on each side. Remove and leave to cool, covered, by a dish towel.
* Bannocks freeze well and are particularly good served slightly warm. Serve with butter, cold meat, cheese, or a bowl of wholesome soup.

SCOTLAND: SHETLAND

*

FLOUR BANNOCKS
AND
SAAFT TAMMIES

In the early twentieth century, wheat became much more affordable and accessible on Shetland and began to replace beremeal as the key ingredient in the islands' distinctive bannocks. Flour bannocks are softer, along the lines of a Soda Farl or Girdle Scone (page 256) and can be served in much the same way. A popular adage says, 'You can get more butter into a cool bannock than a hot one.'

Saaft tammies are a local speciality made from the same dough as flour bannocks that has been sweetened and flecked with dried fruit. The thin bannocks are then fried in oil and spread with golden syrup before serving. An act of pure indulgence.

Makes: 12
Prep time: 25 minutes
Cook time: 30 minutes
{◉}{✷}

- 330 g/11¾ oz (2¾ cups) white self-raising flour
- 40 g/1½ oz (3 tablespoons) butter, softened
- 3 teaspoons baking powder
- 1 egg
- 250 ml/8 fl oz (1 cup) full-fat (whole) milk
- salt

* Preheat a griddle over a medium heat.
* Meanwhile, put the flour into a large bowl, add the butter and rub it in with your fingertips until it resembles breadcrumbs. Add a good pinch of salt and then the baking powder and stir well. Make a well in the centre and add the egg and a small amount of the milk and knife it through. Add enough of the milk to make the dough soft but not sticky.
* Divide the dough into 3 equal portions. Handling each portion lightly, pat each into a circle, then divide into quarters. The griddle should be medium-hot. Cook each bannock for 5 minutes on one side, then turn over and cook the edges for a few moments until golden brown and cooked through, before removing from the pan and leaving to cool in a folded dish towel.
* **Notes:** For saaft tammies, add 15 g/½ oz (1 tablespoon) caster (superfine) sugar and 50 g/2 oz (⅓ cup) raisins or currants, then shallow-fry them in 1 cm/½ inch hot vegetable oil. Serve the saaft taamies warm, spread with a little golden syrup.

Barley bannocks

NORTHEAST OF SCOTLAND

*

SAUTY BANNOCKS

Fastern's Even was once a beloved Scottish festival celebrated on Shrove Tuesday in the northeast of the country, especially in Aberdeenshire. Schoolchildren were given a holiday for what they excitedly called Bannocks and Brose Day. Accounts from the 1850s state that families gathered together and bannocks (griddle cakes) of all sorts were made with great merriment well into the evening.

These oatmeal griddle cakes were one such bannock and are made with a thick batter of dropping consistency. The 'sauty' aspect of the bannock refers either to the addition of salt or the magic 'soot' thrown into them. They should be cooked on both sides and kept warm before serving with butter, jam or honey – like Scotch Pancakes (page 254).

Serves: 4
Prep time: 10 minutes, plus 8–12 hours resting
Cook time: 30 minutes
{👻}{✴}

- 280 ml/9½ fl oz (1 cup plus 2 tablespoons) full-fat (whole) milk
- 175 g/6 oz (1½ cups) fine oatmeal
- ½ teaspoon bicarbonate of soda (baking soda)
- ½ teaspoon salt
- 1 tablespoon golden syrup
- 1 egg, beaten
- vegetable oil, for frying

- To serve:
- butter
- jam or honey

* Heat the milk gently in a medium saucepan over a low heat for 3–5 minutes until lukewarm. Remove from the heat and set aside.
* Put the dry ingredients into a large bowl and mix together, then make a well in the centre. Whisk the milk and golden syrup together, then add to the centre of the well and beat using a wooden spoon to form a smooth batter. Cover with clingfilm (plastic wrap) and leave to rest in the fridge overnight.
* The next day, preheat the oven to 80°C/176°F/lowest Gas Mark and preheat a griddle or frying pan or skillet over a medium heat for several minutes to warm up.
* Beat the egg into the batter.
* Lightly oil the griddle, then spoon the mixture out into small pancakes, about 10 cm/4 inches, and cook for 2 minutes, or until the underside is golden brown. Flip over and cook for another minute or so. Put the cooked pancakes onto an ovenproof plate and keep warm in the oven. Repeat until all the mixture is used up. Serve with butter, jam or honey.

SCOTLAND / WALES / ENGLAND

*

OATCAKES
BARA CEIRCH

Until the late nineteenth and early twentieth century, in many areas of the United Kingdom, oatcakes were more common than wheaten bread. Oatcakes could be made from a simple paste of ground oats, water and sometimes a little bacon fat or butter. Scottish travellers and soldiers alike carried a bag of oats to make these thin cakes when they were on the road.

Traditionally, oatcakes were cooked until their edges began to curl upwards, then toasted and dried out in front of a fire. The latter can be done by continuing to cook them on a much lower setting for another few minutes. In Scotland and Wales especially, oatcakes were eaten almost daily, and with most meals. Now they are most frequently served at the end of a long dinner, after or alongside sweet puddings, with good cheese and thick fruit pastes or a spiced chutney.

Makes: 12 oatcakes or farls
Prep time: 15 minutes, plus 10–15 minutes chilling
Cook time: 30 minutes
{🥣}{✴}

- 100 g/3½ oz (1 cup) pinhead oats
- 40 g/1½ oz (scant ½ cup) porridge (steel-cut) oats
- 180 g/6 oz (1½ cups) fine Scottish oatmeal
- 4 g/⅛ oz (scant 1 teaspoon) fine salt
- 20 g/¾ oz (1 tablespoon plus 2 teaspoons) soft light brown sugar
- 85 g/3 oz (6 tablespoons) fat, such as lard or beef dripping or goose/duck fat
- cheese, jams or pickles, to serve

* Preheat the oven to 170°C/325°C/Gas Mark 3.
* Spread the pinhead and porridge (steel-cut) oats out on a baking sheet and toast in the oven for 8–10 minutes until lightly golden.
* Put the oats, oatmeal, salt and sugar into a bowl and mix together. Add your chosen fat and rub it in with your fingertips until it resembles breadcrumbs. Using a rubber spatula, stir in 70 ml/2¼ fl oz (¼ cup plus 2 teaspoons) boiling water and mix thoroughly. The mixture should be sticky but not dry. Add a little more water if necessary.
* Put the mixture between 2 sheets of baking (parchment) paper about 20 x 30 cm/8 x 12 inches and roll out until it is 5 mm/¼ inch thick. Alternatively, divide the mixture into 2 equal portions, put each between 2 sheets of baking paper and spread into 2 discs, about 20 cm/8 inches in diameter. Chill in the freezer for 10–15 minutes.
* Line a baking sheet with baking paper. Take the oatcake mixture out of the freezer, then remove the paper it's wrapped in from both sides before it starts to defrost. Using a 6 cm/2½ inch ring cutter, cut out the oatcakes, putting them on the prepared baking sheet evenly spaced apart. Alternatively, remove and unwrap the 2 x 20 cm/8 inch discs, put them onto the prepared baking sheet and score each into 6 wedges evenly using a sharp knife.
* Bake in the centre of the oven for 15–20 minutes until golden brown, turning the baking sheet halfway through.
* Remove from the oven and leave to cool completely. For the wedges, cut through the scored oatcakes, then leave them to cool. Serve with cheese and any jams or pickles.

WALES / ENGLAND: MIDLANDS AND DERBYSHIRE
*

STAFFORDSHIRE OATCAKES
DERBYSHIRE OATCAKES

Large pancakes made from a batter of fine oatmeal and flour and baked on a griddle-top surface or in a frying pan or skillet. The result is a soft pancake with a bubbly surface and enjoyably sour oaty taste. In Staffordshire, these are often served for breakfast, topped or filled with any number of breakfast staples like bacon, sausage, eggs and cheese. These oatcakes are also traditional to Derbyshire (although made at a much smaller size). In Anglesey, a similar oatmeal pancake (*bara bwff*) was also made for Shrove Tuesday.

Makes: 12
Prep time: 15 minutes, plus 30–45 minutes standing
Cook time: 30 minutes
{ᴥ•}

- 400 ml / 14 fl oz (1⅔ cups) full-fat (whole) milk
- 15 g / ½ oz (1 tablespoon) fresh yeast or 3 g / ⅛ oz (1 teaspoon) instant dried yeast
- 25 g / 1 oz (2 tablespoons) caster (superfine) sugar
- 265 g / 9¼ oz (2¼ cups) fine oatmeal
- 185 g / 6½ oz (1½ cups) strong wholemeal (whole wheat) flour, sifted
- 10 g / ¼ oz (2 teaspoons) salt
- lard, dripping or butter, for frying

- To serve
- butter and jam, marmalade, or savoury ingredients such as cheese, tomato, bacon, egg and mushrooms

* Gently warm 475 ml / 16 fl oz (2 cups) water and the milk in a medium saucepan over a low heat until it reaches 32–35°C / 90–95°F on a thermometer. If it exceeds this temperature, leave to cool before using.
* Put the yeast into a medium bowl, then pour over the warmed milk and water mixture and stir until the yeast has dissolved. Add 5 g / ¼ oz (1 teaspoon) of the sugar and mix until completely dissolved. Cover and leave in a warm place for 10–15 minutes to activate the yeast. The mixture will foam and bubbles will start to form.
* Meanwhile, put the oatmeal, flour, the remaining sugar and the salt into a large bowl and mix together. Add the activated yeast mixture, then, using a rubber spatula, mix into the batter until fully incorporated. Cover with clingfilm (plastic wrap) and leave to stand for 20–30 minutes until small bubbles start to appear on top.
* Preheat a 25 cm / 10 inch heavy nonstick frying pan or skillet over a medium-high heat. Line a large baking sheet with baking (parchment) paper.
* Rub a little of your chosen fat around the pan, add a ladleful of the batter into the centre of the pan (avoid tapping or mixing the batter), then quickly rotate the pan to cover the bottom and fry, keeping the heat at a constant medium temperature, for 1–2 minutes on each side until golden brown. Once cooked, remove the oatcake with a spatula and put onto the lined baking sheet. Cover with a dish towel and repeat with the remaining batter, rubbing the pan with your chosen fat each time. Keep warm and serve with your chosen accompaniments.

ENGLAND: YORKSHIRE AND LANCASHIRE
*

YORKSHIRE OATCAKES
HAVERBREAD/HAVERCAKE/CLAPBREAD

Two types of oatcake are traditional to Yorkshire: a batter oatcake (not unlike the Staffordshire variety, see left), and one made from a dough, which could be dried and kept indefinitely. Both bear a strong resemblance to old Nordic breads, and unsurprisingly so. The root word 'haver' is essentially the same as modern forms of the Swedish, Danish and Norwegian word for 'oat' – '*havre*'.

In *Traditional Foods of Britain*, Yorkshire-born food writer Laura Mason describes the elaborate preparation process: the batter underwent a lacto-fermentation akin to sourdough bread before it was thinned on a special chequered wooden board and finally slid – or later, flung – onto a hot griddle surface to create a long oval shape. The oatcakes were cooked on one side, leaving their tops nice and soft. This soft side was spread with butter, and sometimes additional sweet or savoury toppings. The batter version of the Yorkshire oatcake could also be dried, which gave it a long shelf-life. These dried oatcakes were served alongside stews, a pairing which became known as 'stew and hard'.

Makes: 2 large oatcakes
Prep time: 15 minutes
Cook time: 30 minutes
{�}{ᴥ•}

- 175 g / 6 oz (1½ cups) fine oatmeal, plus extra for dusting
- 60 g / 2¼ oz (½ cup) plain (all-purpose) flour, sifted
- ¼ teaspoon salt
- ¼ teaspoon bicarbonate of soda (baking soda)
- 30 g / 1 oz (2 tablespoons) butter, at room temperature

* Preheat a griddle, large frying pan or skillet over a medium heat and preheat the oven to 180°C / 350°F / Gas Mark 4.
* Put all the dry ingredients into a medium bowl, make a well in the centre and add the butter and 150 ml / 5 fl oz (⅔ cup) boiling water. Using a wooden spoon, mix to form a firm dough, then leave to cool for 5 minutes.
* Tip the dough onto a work counter lightly dusted with oatmeal and knead until smooth, adding a little water if needed. Divide the dough into 2 even-sized balls, then roll out the balls to circles about 3–4 mm / ⅛–¼ inch thick.
* Dust the griddle with oatmeal, reduce the heat to low and cook the oatcakes for 10–12 minutes until the edges begin to curl. Flip over and cook the other side for 2–4 minutes. Transfer the oatcakes to a nonstick baking sheet and cook in the oven for 10 minutes, or until cooked and slightly dried.
* **Notes:** This recipe is for a rather thick haverbread, but there were also thinner ones around, and, according to food historian Peter Brears, there is a yeasted variety in West Yorkshire.

SCOTLAND: ORKNEY /
ENGLAND: NORTHUMBERLAND

*

SINGIN' HINNIES
FATTY CUTTIES

These griddle cakes are made with an enriched dough of butter and lard, which 'sings' as it hits the hot griddle. Popular in Northumberland, they bear an uncanny resemblance to Welsh Cakes (see right), although some hinnies are thick enough to slice in half and serve with butter and jam – a very good prospect indeed. Similar griddle cakes were also traditionally made in northern Scotland, on the Orkney Islands, where they were called 'fatty cutties'.

Makes: 12
Prep time: 15 minutes
Cook time: 15 minutes
{♥}

- 500 g/1 lb 2 oz (4 cups plus 2 teaspoons) self-raising flour, sifted, plus extra for dusting
- ½ teaspoon salt
- ¼ teaspoon bicarbonate of soda (baking soda)
- ½ teaspoon cream of tartar
- 125 g/4¼ oz (9 tablespoons) cold butter, diced
- 125 g/4¼ oz (9 tablespoons) cold lard, diced
- 180 g/6 oz (¾ cup plus 1 teaspoon) currants
- 90 ml/3¼ cups (6 tablespoons) milk
- lard, for frying

- To serve:
- butter
- jam

* Put the flour into a large bowl with the salt, bicarbonate of soda (baking soda) and cream of tartar and mix briefly with a whisk. Add the butter and lard and rub them in with your fingertips until the mixture resembles breadcrumbs, then add the currants. Add the milk and mix to form a soft but not sticky dough that is still firm enough to roll (similar to the dough for scones). You may need an extra tablespoon of milk, but if unsure, go for a slightly wetter mixture.
* Divide the dough into 12 even pieces and roll each one out on a lightly floured work counter into 5 mm/ ¼ inch discs.
* Heat a nonstick frying pan or skillet over a medium-low heat and grease with a little lard. Working in batches, add the singin' hinnies and fry for 5–7 minutes, turning once or twice until golden brown. Serve with butter and jam.

WALES
*

WELSH LIGHT CAKES
LEICECS

Leicecs are a lighter, sweeter version of the traditional Welsh *crempog* or pancake (page 254) made using soured cream and/or buttermilk. They are baked in small cakes, 7.5– 10 cm/3–4 inches wide (the size of a Scotch Pancake) and eaten warm with butter. Traditionally, they were served in Welsh farmhouses as a teatime snack for visitors to enjoy with their cup of tea.

Makes: 10–12
Prep time: 10 minutes, plus resting time
Cook time: 15 minutes
{♥}

- 150 g/5 oz (1¼ cups) plain (all-purpose) flour
- 85 g/3 oz (½ cup minus 1 tablespoon) caster (superfine) sugar
- pinch of salt
- ½ teaspoon bicarbonate of soda (baking soda)
- 20–80 ml/¾–3 fl oz (4 teaspoons–⅓ cup) buttermilk
- 2 tablespoons soured cream
- 2 eggs, beaten
- butter, oil or lard, for greasing
- butter, to serve

* Preheat a griddle, large frying pan or skillet over a medium heat.
* Put the flour, sugar and salt into a large bowl and make a well in the centre.
* Put the bicarbonate of soda (baking soda) into a small bowl, add a splash – about 20 ml/¾ fl oz (1½ tablespoons) – of buttermilk and mix together until combined and the bicarbonate of soda has dissolved. Add the soured cream and mix together, then whisk in the eggs. Gradually whisk the egg and buttermilk mixture into the well in the centre of the dry ingredients until it forms a smooth, light batter. Add more buttermilk, if necessary.
* Grease the griddle, frying pan or skillet with your chosen fat and spoon out tablespoons of the batter. They should form cakes about 7.5–10 cm/3–4 inches wide. Cook for 2 minutes, or until bubbles begin to appear on the surface and the bottom has turned an even golden brown. Flip over and cook for another 2 minutes, or until golden brown.
* Serve hot, well-buttered, individually or in stacks. In the old days, light cakes were also made much larger, buttered, stacked and quartered.

WALES
*

WELSH CAKES
PICE AR Y MAEN

Welsh cakes are named after the griddle upon which they
are baked – which is why their name (in Welsh) varies so
much throughout the country. Regional variations for these
cakes abound, but typically they are made with a dough
enriched with butter and lard and flecked with currants.
The dough is rolled out to a thickness of 6–7 mm/¼ inch,
and sliced into circles, about 7–8 cm/2¾–3¼ inches wide.
Cooked on both sides, the top and bottom should be firm,
and the centre soft and a little crumbly.

Makes: 24
Prep time: 15 minutes
Cook time: 45 minutes
{ᴖ•}

- 500 g/1 lb 2 oz (4 cups plus 2 teaspoons) self-raising
flour, sifted, plus extra for dusting
- pinch of salt
- pinch of ground mace
- 250 g/9 oz (2¼ sticks) cold butter, diced or 125 g/4¼ oz
(9 tablespoons) butter and 125 g/4¼ oz (9 tablespoons)
lard, plus extra for frying
- 100 g/3½ oz (½ cup minus 1 tablespoon) currants
- 125 g/4¼ oz (½ cup plus 2 tablespoons) caster
(superfine) sugar, plus extra for dusting
- 2 eggs
- 75 ml/2½ fl oz (⅓ cup) full-fat (whole) milk

* Put the flour, salt and mace into a large bowl and mix
briefly using a whisk. Add the fat(s) and rub in with
your fingertips until the mixture resembles breadcrumbs.
Stir in the currants and sugar. Put the eggs into a medium
bowl and beat, then add three-quarters of the milk and
mix together. Pour the wet mixture into the flour and
mix using a wooden spoon to form a light, soft dough.
If it seems crumbly at all, add the remaining milk.
* Roll the dough out on a lightly floured work counter
until it is 5 mm/¼ inch thick, then cut it into 24 x
7 cm/2¾ inch circles using a ring cutter (use a minimal
amount of flour).
* Heat a large nonstick frying pan or skillet over a medium-
low heat. Lightly grease the pan with butter or lard and,
working in batches, cook the cakes for 3–4 minutes on
each side until golden brown. Dust or coat with sugar
while hot and serve while warm.

UNITED KINGDOM
*

ROTI

Roti is a staple bread that's eaten throughout Asia and takes
on many forms. Since the early 1800s, when indentured
workers from India migrated to the Caribbean, roti, along
with many of their other food traditions, incorporated itself
into the local diet and became a beautiful representation of
the Afro-Indian subculture. During the Windrush era (page
16), many of the earliest settlers who travelled to the UK were
from Trinidad and formed a strong community in London.

Makes: 4
Prep time: 10 minutes, plus 60–90 minutes resting
Cook time: 5 minutes
{ᴖ} {ᴖ•}

- 340 g/12 oz (2¾ cups plus 2 teaspoons) plain
(all-purpose) flour, plus extra for dusting
- 1 teaspoon baking powder
- 1 teaspoon caster (superfine) sugar
- 2 teaspoons salt
- 4 tablespoons butter or vegetable fat
- 2 tablespoons vegetable oil

* Sift the flour, baking powder, sugar and salt into a large bowl
and mix together to combine. Add the oil, then gradually
add 175 ml/6 fl oz (¾ cup) water, kneading to form a soft
dough. Divide the dough into 4 'loyas' or balls and leave to
rest for 30–60 minutes, covered with a dish towel.
* Roll out each ball of dough on a lightly floured work
counter, then spread 1 tablespoon of butter over each one.
Make a cut from the centre out to the edge and roll into
a cone. Press the peak and flatten the centre of the cone.
Leave to rest for another 15–30 minutes. Once the dough
has rested, roll out on a floured work counter.
* Preheat a *tawa* (a flat metal griddle), frying pan or skillet
over a medium-high heat. Once hot, brush with oil,
then, cooking one roti at a time, put one onto the *tawa*
and leave for 30 seconds, or until bubbles start to form.
Brush the roti with oil and turn over to cook the other
side in the same way.
* When the roti is cooked on both sides, use a *dabla*
(wooden spatula) to break up the roti to give the ripped
up, flaky appearance. Alternatively, wrap the roti in a
clean cloth and beat with your hands or using a *bailna*
(wooden rolling pin).
* Put the finished roti into a dish towel. Repeat with the
remaining roti, then serve.

WALES
*

BAKESTONE BREAD
BARA PLANC

Before it was common for Welsh homes to have their own oven ranges, bread would be baked once a week in a local bakery oven. Typically, one small loaf's worth of dough was left behind to be baked at home, where it would be cooked flat on the griddle. This sort of dough was typically a plain white bread dough (still a luxury in its own right) but could be enriched or flecked with currants for a special occasion.

Serves: 4
Prep time: 30 minutes
Cook time: 40 minutes
{●}{✹}

- 120 ml/4 fl oz (½ cup) full-fat (whole) milk
- 400 g/14 oz (3⅓ cups) plain (all-purpose) flour
- ½ teaspoon salt
- ½ teaspoon caster (superfine) sugar
- 1 teaspoon instant dried yeast
- 15 g/½ oz (1 tablespoon) butter, softened

* Heat the milk gently in a medium saucepan over a low heat for 3–5 minutes until lukewarm, then remove from the heat and set aside.
* Sift the flour, salt and sugar into a large bowl and stir in the yeast. Make a well in the centre and add the milk and butter. Mix with your hands until combined. Alternatively, use a stand mixer fitted with a dough hook attachment.
* When combined, knead the dough until smooth and springy. This will take 6 minutes in a mixer and about 12 minutes if kneading by hand. Using your hands, form into a tight ball and press down flat with your fingers.
* Leave the dough to rest as you let a bakestone, skillet or griddle warm up over a medium-low heat for 5 minutes. Put the dough onto the flat cooking surface and cook for 20 minutes. Turn over and cook for another 20 minutes. Remove and leave to cool on a wire rack.

SCOTLAND
*

SOUR SKONS

To make sour skons, oatmeal is steeped in buttermilk or whey for a number of days before being worked into a dough with flour and caraway seeds. Cook on a griddle before splitting and serving as for Soda Farls (page 256).

Makes: 8
Prep time: 15 minutes, plus 3 days soaking
Cook time: 20 minutes
{●}{✹}

- 90 g/3¼ oz (¾ cup) medium oatmeal
- 120 ml/4 fl oz (½ cup) buttermilk or whey
- 120 g/4 oz (1 cup) plain (all-purpose) flour
- 1 teaspoon bicarbonate of soda (baking soda)
- 1 teaspoon caster (superfine) sugar
- 1 teaspoon caraway seeds (optional)

* Put the oatmeal and buttermilk into a large bowl and mix together, then cover with clingfilm (plastic wrap) and leave to soak in the fridge for 3 days.
* When ready to make the skons, preheat a dry heavy frying pan, skillet or griddle over a medium heat.
* Mix the remaining ingredients into the oatmeal and buttermilk, then form the mixture into a circle and flatten or roll it out until it is 1 cm/½ inch thick. Mark out 8 wedges, by just scoring it with the tip of a sharp knife but not cutting it, then cook in the pan for 8 minutes, or until slightly risen and golden brown. Flip over and cook the other side for another 8 minutes until well risen and golden brown. Serve.

WALES
*

BAKESTONE TURNOVER
TEISEN AR Y MAEN/TARTEN PLANC

Turnovers were a popular feature of Welsh farmhouse baking; made from a butter and lard pastry, they were filled with fresh seasonal fruit – apples, blackberries, gooseberries and so forth – then baked until golden and eaten warm.

Makes: 1 very large turnover or 2 medium
Prep time: 25 minutes
Cook time: 30 minutes
{✹}

- 250 g/9 oz (2 cups) self-raising flour, plus extra for dusting
- pinch of salt
- 60 g/2¼ oz butter, diced
- 60 g/2¼ oz lard, diced
- 120 g/4 oz (½ cup plus 4 teaspoons) caster (superfine) sugar, plus an extra 4 tablespoons
- 1 egg, beaten
- 2 tablespoons full-fat (whole) milk
- 100 g/3½ oz fruit, such as peeled and thinly sliced apple, blackberries, gooseberries, etc.

* Sift the flour and salt into a bowl, add the butter and lard and rub in with your fingertips until the mixture resembles breadcrumbs. Stir in the 120 g/4 oz sugar, then fork in the egg and add the milk. Mix well to form a dough, then roll it out on a floured work counter to a 25–28 cm/10–11 inch circle.
* Put the fruit and remaining sugar into another bowl and mix together. Sprinkle the fruit mixture over the half of the dough closest to you, then fold the half further away from you over the top of the fruit to make a half-moon shape. Seal the edges with a little water and crimp using a fork.
* Heat a bakestone or griddle over a medium heat. Put the bread onto the hot pan and cook for 10–15 minutes until golden brown, then flip it over and cook for another 10–15 minutes until the bottom half is golden. Serve warm.
* If desired, you can also bake the turnover in the oven. Preheat the oven to 180°C/350°F/Gas Mark 4 and line a baking sheet with baking (parchment) paper. Put the turnover onto the baking sheet and bake for 15 minutes. Flip it over and bake for another 10–15 minutes until golden brown on both sides.

Bakestone turnover

…MY BREAD IS SWEET AND NOURISHING,
MADE FROM MY OWN WHEAT,
GROUND IN MY OWN MILL,
AND BAKED IN MY OWN OVEN.

TOBIAS SMOLLETT,
THE EXPEDITION OF HUMPHRY CLINKER, 1771

For much of British history, bread-baking could not be done from home. Most home kitchens either lacked a proper oven, or at least one capable of reaching the required temperatures. Thus, it became a routine (often weekly) activity with its own rituals. Dough would be prepared from home kitchens and then brought to the town's local baker to fire in their oven. (With the exception of some home kitchens in Cornwall and parts of Wales, where large pots might be inverted and turned into a proto-oven, or bread might be steamed within a jar.) In whatever manner the bread dough was prepared, the excess might be mixed with a little dried fruit and cooked as a thin cake on a bakestone or griddle, or shaped into dumplings for a stew.

There is an old Roman saying, loosely translating to 'know the colour of one's bread'; this adage was equally apt in medieval and early modern times. The whiter your flour, the more elevated your status. White wheat flour was aspirational, and largely out of reach for the average Briton until as late as the middle of the nineteenth century. From medieval times, the finest loaf of bread was known as manchet and was made from well-bolted (sieved) flour. For more common folk, bread was often what we would consider 'wholemeal' (whole wheat) or 'brown bread', and sometimes made from a mix of grain ('maslin'), like barley, rye or oats – or even peasemeal.

In the nineteenth century, the changing shape of the home kitchen, with its brand-new oven range, enabled a great revolution in bread-baking. Many British loaves originated during these times, like the crispy-crusted Coburg, the double-tiered cottage loaf, and even the small bridge rolls for light bites and teatime sandwiches. Of course, there was also the hefty baker's loaf style of bread known as 'plain loaf' or 'batch bread'. These tall loaves are square or rectangular, baked four or nine to a pan, and make for excellent toast.

The new English concept of the 'sandwich', invented in the eighteenth century, was already familiar to many by this point, but really exploded over the rest of the nineteenth century. While Britons are enthusiastic about their sandwiches, this book does not explore the art of sandwich-making itself, and most references to classic sandwiches – like ham and mustard, cheese and pickle, egg mayonnaise – are listed in their respective chapters.

Finally, one of the greatest and most territorial aspects of British bread-baking tradition is that of the morning roll, a light bread roll, which is typically filled with fried breakfast meats like bacon or sausage. Across the UK, this simple roll changes shape – in width, height, texture and crust. It can be known by more than a dozen names as well, such as bap, barm, batch, scuffler, teacake, stottie, oggie, and so on. The names vary by region, often without clear geographic distinctions, but despite that, the appreciation for this mainstay grab-and-go breakfast is deeply felt.

OVEN-BAKED BREADS

BREADS

AND

SAVOURY

BAKES

UNITED KINGDOM
*

BASIC BREAD DOUGH
(WHITE OR WHOLEMEAL)

This basic bread dough has been popular in Britain for several generations. It will produce a soft white interior and can be baked in loaf pans or in more elaborate freestanding shapes such as the Cob (see right) or Cottage Loaf (see right) and Bridge Rolls (page 278).

Makes: 2 loaves or 12 rolls
Prep time: 30 minutes, plus 2¾–3 hours rising and proving
Cook time: 20–50 minutes

{✿}{♠}{⚬}{🔔}

- 1 kg/ 2¼ lb (8⅓ cups) strong white bread flour,
  plus extra for dusting
- 14 g/ ½ oz (4 teaspoons) instant dried yeast
- 20 g/ ¾ oz (4 teaspoons) fine sea salt
- vegetable oil, for oiling

* Pour 700 ml/ 23½ fl oz (2¾ cups plus 2 teaspoons) water into a large saucepan and heat over a medium heat until it reaches 24°C/75°F on a thermometer.
* Put the flour, yeast and salt into a large bowl and mix together. Make a well in the centre and gently pour in the warm water and mix to a soft dough. Alternatively, use a stand mixer fitted with a dough hook attachment and mix on medium speed for 5 minutes, or until the dough is smooth and elastic. If mixing by hand, turn the dough out onto a lightly floured work counter and knead for 10 minutes, or until the dough is smooth and elastic.
* Put the dough into an oiled bowl, cover with oiled clingfilm (plastic wrap) or clean, damp dish towel and leave in a warm place to rise for 1 hour, or until doubled in size.
* Gently turn the risen dough out onto a lightly floured work counter and knead gently to knock the dough back to remove any air bubbles. Return to the bowl, cover again and leave to prove in a warm place for 1 hour, or until it has doubled in size.
* Meanwhile, lightly oil 2 x 900 g/ 2 lb loaf pans and line with baking (parchment) paper. If making rolls, line 2 baking sheets with baking paper.
* Once the dough has proved, turn it out onto a lightly floured work counter and divide it either in half for loaves or into 12 equal portions for rolls. Shape and put into the pans or onto the baking sheets. Cover and leave to prove for 45–60 minutes in a warm place until the dough fills the pans or doubles in size. At this stage, you can put the bread into the fridge to chill overnight and bake fresh the next morning, removing it from the fridge for 1 hour to prove before baking.
* Meanwhile, preheat the oven to 200°C/ 400°F/ Gas Mark 6.
* Bake the rolls for 15–20 minutes or the loaves for 40 minutes. If baking loaves, remove them from the pans after 40 minutes and bake for another 5–10 minutes. The loaf/ rolls should be golden brown and sound hollow when tapped on the bottom. Leave to cool before slicing.
* **Variations:** This is a versatile recipe and it provides a good template from which to experiment and play. For a bread with a softer crumb, try adding 20 g/ ¾ oz (4 teaspoons) fat, such as oil, melted butter or lard. You can also experiment with replacing some of the water content with milk, beer or fruit juice. The flour can

also happily be swapped about – add in a percentage of spelt, wholemeal (whole wheat), rye or granary. Using more wholemeal flour will make the dough drier, so compensate for this by adding more water to your dough, and add it gradually until you have a smooth dough. For a loaf that's half wholemeal and half white flour, try adding an extra 100 ml/ 3½ fl oz (⅓ cup plus 1 tablespoon) water. Add toasted seeds, flakes, grains, dried fruit, nuts, herbs, and if the addition might absorb moisture from the dough, either soak the seeds, nuts, etc. before adding them or increase the water content of the dough.
* If you are short of time or like a soft crust, this loaf can also be baked from a cold oven. In this case don't preheat the oven, just put the bread or rolls into a cold oven and switch it on to 200°C/ 400°F/ Gas Mark 6 and proceed as above.

ENGLAND
*

COTTAGE LOAF

The cottage loaf is baked as two circles of Basic Bread Dough (see left) – one on top of the other. The circles converge as they bake, forming the loaf's distinctive shape.

Makes: 1 loaf
Prep time: 30 minutes, plus 2 hours rising and proving
Cook time: 30–35 minutes

{✿}{♠}{⚬}{🔔}

- 850 g/ 1 lb 14 oz Basic Bread Dough (see left)
- extra strong white bread flour, for dusting

* Follow the directions for making the Basic Bread Dough (see left). Once the dough has risen for the first time, gently turn the risen dough out onto a lightly floured work counter and knead gently to knock the dough back to remove any air bubbles, then cut off a third of the dough. Make the cob shape by forming a ball with the dough and tucking your hands under it, tightening the surface of the dough and turning it slightly as you go. Repeat with the other piece of dough.
* Dust a large baking sheet with flour and set aside. Put the small loaf directly on top of the large one, flour the first 3 fingers of one hand and plunge them down through the dough to the work counter, then repeat one more time. Your 2 pieces should be well-fused together. Put the bread onto the prepared baking sheet, cover with a large plastic bag or large bowl and leave in a warm place to prove for 1 hour, or until it has doubled in size and feels springy to the touch.
* To achieve a really good crust, preheat the oven to 220°C/ 425°F/ Gas Mark 7 and put a roasting pan on the bottom of the oven.
* When the loaf is ready, boil the kettle and put the loaf onto the middle shelf of the oven, then carefully pour the boiling water into the roasting pan and quickly shut the door. Bake for 30–35 minutes until brown, crusty and the bottom sounds hollow when tapped with your finger. Leave to cool on a wire rack.

ENGLAND
*

COB
COBURG LOAF

This crusty loaf of bread is characterized by patterns scored into its top: frequently a criss-cross pattern, or slashes that form a crown of sorts when baked. Despite the linguistic similarities, the word cob is actually derived from the Old English word 'copp', which means 'top' or 'head'. The loaf picked up the Coburg name in the nineteenth century, after the marriage between the British Royal Family and the German dynasty of Saxe-Coburg-Gotha.

Makes: 1 loaf
Prep time: 30 minutes,
plus 1 hour 20 minutes rising and proving
Cook time: 35 minutes
{�}{♠}{↩}{🏔}

- 650 g/1 lb 7 oz Basic Bread Dough (see left)
- extra strong white bread flour, for dusting

* Follow the directions for making the Basic Bread Dough (see left). Once the dough has risen for the first time, gently turn the risen dough out onto a lightly floured work counter and knead gently to knock the dough back to remove any air bubbles. Make the cob shape by forming a ball with the dough and tucking your hands under it, tightening the surface of the dough and turning it slightly as you go.
* Dust a large baking sheet with flour, then put the dough onto it, cover with a large plastic bag or large bowl and leave to prove in a warm place for 20 minutes, or until doubled in size.
* To achieve a really good crust, preheat the oven to 220°C/425°F/Gas Mark 7 and put a roasting pan on the bottom of the oven.
* When the loaf is ready, slash the top with a sharp serrated knife to make a cross shape. Boil the kettle or a pan of water and put the loaf onto the middle shelf of the oven, then carefully pour the boiling water into the roasting pan and quickly shut the door.
* Bake for 15 minutes, then reduce the oven temperature to 200°C/400°F/Gas Mark 6 and bake for another 15–20 minutes until brown, crusty and the bottom sounds hollow when tapped with your finger. Leave to cool on a wire rack.

UNITED KINGDOM
*

BLOOMER BREAD

Bloomer bread is a thick and crusty loaf made from Basic Bread Dough (see left), and marked by four or five evenly spaced slashes across its top. While the edges are crusty, the interior is nice and soft: slice and use as sandwich bread or serve with any good soup or stew.

Makes: 1 loaf
Prep time: 30 minutes,
plus 1 hour 20 minutes rising and proving
Cook time: 30 minutes
{☰}{♠}{↩}{🏔}

- 500 g/1 lb 2 oz (4 cups plus 2 teaspoons) strong white bread flour, plus extra for dusting
- 10 g/¼ oz (2 teaspoons) salt
- 1 teaspoon instant dried yeast
- vegetable oil, for oiling

* Pour 350 ml/12 fl oz (1½ cups) water into a medium saucepan and heat gently over a low heat until warm. Remove from the heat and set aside.
* Sift the flour into a large bowl and add the salt and yeast. Make a well in the centre and pour in the warm water. Mix well to form a soft dough. Alternatively, use a stand mixer fitted with a dough hook attachment and mix on medium speed for 5 minutes, or until the dough is smooth and elastic. If mixing by hand, turn the dough out onto a lightly floured work counter and knead for 10 minutes, or until the dough is smooth and elastic. Shape into a tight ball and put into an oiled bowl. Cover with a clean, damp dish towel and leave to rise in a warm place for 1 hour, or until doubled in size.
* Dust a large baking sheet with flour and set aside. Gently turn the risen dough out onto a lightly floured work counter and knead gently to knock the dough back to remove any air bubbles. Press the dough out into a rectangle, about 30 x 25 cm/12 x 10 inches, and roll the dough up from one of the long edges. Taper the ends to create a rounded shape. Put the dough onto the prepared baking sheet, cover again and leave to prove for 20 minutes, or until it has doubled in size.
* Preheat the oven to 220°C/425°F/Gas Mark 7.
* When the dough is ready, lightly flour it, then, using a sharp knife, make 3–4 diagonal slashes down its length. Slide the baking sheet into the oven and bake for 30 minutes until brown, crusty and the bottom sounds hollow when tapped with your finger. Remove from the oven and leave to cool on a wire rack.

NORTHERN IRELAND / SCOTLAND
*

PLAIN LOAF
BATCH BREAD/SQUARE LOAF

These soft floury loaves are traditionally baked in large batches, which are later pulled or sliced apart. As a result, most loaves stay soft and crustless on their sides. Batch bread can be replicated at home and without a commercial oven by creating four mini loaves in a small pan. They are best eaten on the day they are baked or used as toast on the days afterwards. Deliciously moreish, they make the perfect chip butty or fried egg and Square Sausage sandwich (page 187).

Makes: 4 mini batch loaves or 1 large loaf
Prep time: 30 minutes, plus 2–4 hours rising and proving
Cook time: 35–45 minutes
{ö} {•}

- 200 ml / 7 fl oz (¾ cup plus 1 tablespoon) full-fat (whole) milk
- 40 g / 1½ oz (3 tablespoons) butter, plus extra melted butter for greasing and brushing
- 500 g / 1 lb 2 oz (4 cups plus 2 teaspoons) strong white bread flour, plus extra for dusting
- 10 g / ¼ oz (2 teaspoons) fine table salt
- 5 g / ⅛ oz (1 teaspoon) caster (superfine) sugar
- 6 g / ⅛ oz (1 teaspoon) instant dried yeast
- 50 g / 2 oz sourdough starter (optional), page 275
- vegetable oil, for oiling
- butter and jam, to serve

* Pour the milk into a large saucepan and heat over a low heat until it reaches 24°C / 75°F on a thermometer. Remove from the heat and set aside. Pour 100 ml / 3½ fl oz (⅓ cup plus 1 tablespoon) water into a medium saucepan and heat over a medium heat until it reaches 24°C / 75°F on a thermometer. Remove from the heat and set aside.
* Melt the butter in a small saucepan over a low heat for 2 minutes, then remove from the heat and set aside.
* Put the flour, salt, sugar and yeast into a large bowl or stand mixer fitted with a dough hook attachment and whisk lightly to combine.
* Put the milk, melted butter, sourdough starter (if using) and the warm water into another large bowl and stir to combine.
* Add the wet mix to the dry ingredients and mix to form a soft dough. If using a stand mixer, mix on slow speed to combine for a few minutes, then increase the speed to medium and mix until the dough is uniform and cleaning the sides of the bowl. If working by hand, bring the ingredients together in the bowl, then as soon as you have a dough, turn it out onto a lightly floured work counter and knead for 10 minutes, or until the dough is smooth and elastic. Put the dough into an oiled bowl, cover with clingfilm (plastic wrap) or a clean, damp dish towel and leave to rise at room temperature for 1–2 hours until doubled in size.
* Meanwhile, line a 900 g / 2 lb loaf pan with baking (parchment) paper and lightly grease with melted butter. Once the dough is risen, turn it out onto a lightly floured work counter. If you are making a single large loaf, shape the dough and carefully put it into the prepared pan. If you are making batch loaves, divide the dough into 4 equal pieces, then gently shape each piece into a small loaf shape and brush each one all over with melted butter before putting them side by side in the prepared pan. Cover the pan. At this point you can put the pan into the fridge and leave overnight to bake fresh the next morning.

* If baking immediately, or when removing from the fridge the next day, leave the bread to prove in a warm place for 1–2 hours until it has doubled in size and risen almost to the top of the pan.
* Preheat the oven to 230°C / 450°F / Gas Mark 8.
* Once the dough is ready, brush the tops of the loaves with some melted butter and carefully put a small baking sheet or roasting pan on top of the bread to create a lid. Bake for 15 minutes, then remove the baking sheet or roasting pan lid and bake for another 15 minutes, or until the top is a dark brown and the internal temperature is 92°C / 198°F or above. If you want a really Glasgow-style dark top, increase the oven temperature to its highest setting for the last 5 minutes.
* Remove the bread from the oven and leave to cool for 5 minutes, then turn it out of the pan and carefully separate the individual loaves if you have batch baked. Leave to cool completely or tear apart and slather with jam and butter.

UNITED KINGDOM
*

FARMHOUSE LOAF

This is a rustic-style farmhouse loaf, made using a 50/50 mix of white and wholemeal (whole wheat) flour. It's a bread suited to almost every occasion.

Makes: 1 large loaf
Prep time: 30 minutes, plus 2 hours rising and proving
Cook time: 30 minutes
{ö} {♠} {•} {▲}

- 250 g / 9 oz (2 cups) strong white bread flour, plus extra for dusting
- 250 g / 9 oz (2 cups) strong wholemeal (whole wheat) flour
- 10 g / ¼ oz (2 teaspoons) salt
- 1 teaspoon instant dried yeast
- vegetable oil, for oiling

* Pour 375 ml / 13 fl oz (1½ cups) water into a medium saucepan and heat over a medium heat until warm. Remove from the heat and set aside.
* Sift the flours into a large bowl, then add the salt and yeast. Make a well in the centre and pour in the warm water. Mix to form a soft dough. Alternatively, use a stand mixer fitted with a dough hook attachment and mix on medium speed for 6 minutes, or until the dough is smooth and elastic. If mixing by hand, turn the dough out onto a lightly floured work counter and knead for 12 minutes, or until the dough is smooth and elastic.
* Shape the dough into a tight ball, then put it into an oiled bowl. Cover with a clean, damp dish towel and leave to rise in a warm place for 1½ hours, or until doubled in size.
* Dust a large baking sheet with flour. Gently turn the risen dough out onto a lightly floured work counter and knead gently to knock the dough back to remove any air bubbles. Shape into a tight ball and put it onto the

prepared baking sheet, cover again and leave to prove in a warm place for 30 minutes, or until doubled in size.

* Meanwhile, preheat the oven to 220°C/425°F/Gas Mark 7.
* When the dough is ready, dust the top with flour, then, using a sharp knife, cut 3–4 diagonal slashes across the top. Slide the baking sheet into the oven and bake for 30 minutes until brown, crusty and the bottom sounds hollow when tapped with your finger. Remove from the oven and leave to cool on a wire rack.

UNITED KINGDOM
*

GRANARY BREAD

Granary flour is a sort of brown wholemeal (whole wheat) flour to which malted wheat has been added. This brown loaf, mixed through with chopped nuts, should be used for sandwiches that call for a more robust bread.

Makes: 1 large loaf
Prep time: 30 minutes, plus 2 hours rising and proving
Cook time: 35 minutes
{👤}{◆}{🔪}

- 500 g/1 lb 2 oz (4 cups plus 2 teaspoons) granary flour, plus extra for dusting
- 10 g/¼ oz (2 teaspoons) salt
- 1 teaspoon instant dried yeast
- 60 ml/2¼ fl oz (¼ cup) walnut oil
- vegetable oil, for oiling
- 50 g/2 oz (½ cup minus 2 teaspoons) chopped walnuts

* Pour 320 ml/11 fl oz (1¼ cups plus 4 teaspoons) water into a medium saucepan and heat over a medium heat until warm. Remove from the heat and set aside.
* Sift the flour into a large bowl and add the salt and yeast. Make a well in the centre and pour in the warm water and the oil. Mix to form a soft dough. Alternatively, use a stand mixer fitted with a dough hook attachment and mix on medium speed for 5 minutes, or until the dough is smooth and elastic. If mixing by hand, turn the dough out onto a lightly floured work counter and knead for 10 minutes, or until the dough is smooth and elastic.
* Shape the dough into a tight ball, put it into an oiled bowl, cover with clingfilm (plastic wrap) or a clean, damp dish towel and leave to rise in a warm place for 1½ hours, or until doubled in size.
* Lightly dust a large baking sheet with flour. Gently turn the risen dough out onto a lightly floured work counter and knead gently to knock the dough back to remove any air bubbles. Knead in the nuts and form into a tight ball. Put the dough onto the prepared baking sheet, cover again and leave to prove in a warm place for 30 minutes, or until it has doubled in size.
* Meanwhile preheat the oven to 220°C/425°F/Gas Mark 7.
* When the dough is ready, dust the top with flour, then, using a sharp knife, cut 3–4 diagonal slashes across the top. Slide the baking sheet into the oven and bake for 30 minutes until brown, crusty and the bottom sounds hollow when tapped with your finger. Remove from the oven and leave to cool on a wire rack.

NORTHERN IRELAND
*

STOUT BREAD

This Irish seeded loaf is flavoured with stout beer, a little dark treacle (blackstrap molasses) and a small handful of oats. The result is a dark loaf that's easy to bake at home and a good friend to soups and stews of all manner. Serve as for Wheaten Bread (page 276).

Makes: 1 loaf
Prep time: 15 minutes
Cook time: 1 hour
{👤}{🌱}

- vegetable oil or butter, for greasing
- 450 g/1 lb (3¾ cups) wholemeal (whole wheat) flour
- 75 g/2¾ oz (½ cup plus 1 tablespoon) plain (all-purpose) flour
- 10 g/¼ oz (2 teaspoons) salt
- 10 g/¼ oz (2 teaspoons) bicarbonate of soda (baking soda)
- 60 g/2¼ oz (½ cup) mixed seeds
- 20 g/¾ oz (¼ cup minus 2 teaspoons) porridge oats
- 1 egg
- 15 ml/½ fl oz (1 tablespoon) neutral oil
- 10 g/¼ oz (2 teaspoons) treacle (blackstrap molasses)
- 230 ml/7¾ fl oz (1 cup minus 4 teaspoons) buttermilk
- 320 ml/11 fl oz (1¼ cups plus 4 teaspoons) stout
- butter, to serve

- To glaze:
- 40 g/1½ oz (2 tablespoons) treacle (blackstrap molasses)
- 20 ml/¾ fl oz (4 teaspoons) stout
- seeds of choice

* Preheat the oven to 200°C/400°F/Gas Mark 6. Grease a 900 g/2 lb loaf pan generously.
* Put all the dry ingredients into a large bowl and mix together. Put all the wet ingredients into another bowl and mix together. Make a well in the centre of the dry ingredients and slowly stir the wet into the dry until incorporated. Don't be alarmed – the mix should be rather wet. Pour the batter into the prepared loaf pan (it should come two-thirds of the way up the sides) and bake for 1 hour, or until a small knife inserted into the loaf comes out clean and the loaf sounds hollow when tapped on the bottom.
* Remove the bread from the oven and make the glaze. Put the treacle (blackstrap molasses) and stout into a small bowl and stir until combined, then brush it over the top. Sprinkle with seeds before the bread cools. Serve with butter.

NORTHERN IRELAND
*

TREACLE BREAD

This is a rather rustic and dark loaf, made with wholemeal (whole wheat) flour and occasionally a small amount of fine oatmeal (or oat flour).

Makes: 1 loaf
Prep time: 20 minutes
Cook time: 30–40 minutes
{👤}{🔥}

- 250 g/9 oz (2 cups) wholemeal (whole wheat) flour, plus extra for dusting
- 200 g/7 oz (1⅔ cups) plain (all-purpose) flour
- 50 g/2 oz (½ cup minus 2 teaspoons) fine oatmeal
- 1 teaspoon salt
- 1 teaspoon bicarbonate of soda (baking soda)
- 250 ml/8 fl oz (1 cup) buttermilk
- 2 tablespoons treacle (blackstrap molasses)
- butter, to serve

* Preheat the oven to 200°C/400°F/Gas Mark 6. Dust a large baking sheet with flour.
* Sift the dry ingredients into a large bowl and mix well. Make a well in the centre. Pour the buttermilk into a jug (pitcher) and add the treacle (blackstrap molasses). Whisk to combine, then tip into the well and use your hands to mix thoroughly. Shape the mixture into a circle and put onto the prepared baking sheet.
* Using a sharp knife, cut a cross into the surface of the loaf and bake for 30–40 minutes until golden brown. Leave to cool on a wire rack before cutting into slices and serving with butter.

UNITED KINGDOM
*

SOURDOUGH BREAD

Sourdough bread, made from a lacto-fermented starter, has a poorly documented history here in Britain. While today it is one of the country's most sought-after styles of bread, there's little evidence to suggest a tradition that stretches back any further than the last couple of decades.
Before baker's yeast was mass-produced, loaves of bread were 'naturally' leavened – this much we know. And it is quite possible that the English ate wholemeal (whole wheat) sourdough bread: Elizabeth David suggests that at least the Cornish did, when they used the left-over leaven in something they called 'kettle bread', which was made in a covered pot over a peat hearth. But this was a barley bread, and it is important to remember how rare wheat bread was until the nineteenth century.
Regardless of its long tradition, a country loaf made from British heritage wheat can hold its own against anything from Europe. This recipe comes from talented bakers Sam and Anna Luntley, two of Britain's finest.

Makes: 2 small country-style loaves
Prep time: 1 hour, plus 11–15 hours resting and chilling
Cook time: 45 minutes
{👤}{♦}{🍴}{🔥}

- 610 g/1 lb 5 oz (5 cups) strong white bread flour, plus extra for dusting
- 150 g/5 oz (1¼ cups) wholemeal (whole wheat) bread flour
- 115 g/4 oz sourdough leaven (see right)
- 15 g/½ oz (1 tablespoon) salt

* Pour 560 ml/19 fl oz (2¼ cups) water into a medium saucepan and heat over a medium heat until it reaches 24°C/75°F on a thermometer. Remove from the heat and set aside.
* Put the flours, sourdough leaven and warm water into a large bowl and mix to form a smooth, loose dough. Cover with clingfilm (plastic wrap) or a clean, damp dish towel and leave to rest at room temperature for 30 minutes.
* Add the salt and another 50 ml/1¾ fl oz (3½ tablespoons) water to the dough and, using your hands, mix well. The dough will initially seem to break apart, but keep moving and working it until it comes back to a smooth dough. Cover again and leave to rest at room temperature for 40 minutes.
* After 40 minutes, it is time to do the first fold of the dough. Keeping the dough in the bowl, use wet hands to pick up one edge of the dough, stretch it upwards and fold it over the rest of the dough, then turn the bowl 45 degrees and repeat the process, stretching and folding the dough over itself – you are developing the strength of the dough as well as beginning to work some air in. Repeat this process 3–4 times with a 40-minute rest between each fold until the dough feels light, airy and active.
* When the dough feels ready, turn it out onto a lightly floured work counter and divide it into 2 equal pieces, then shape each into tight circles. Leave the dough to rest on the work counter for 20 minutes. Do a final shape of the dough, then put them into 2 proving baskets and leave to chill in the fridge overnight.
* The next day, preheat the oven to 230°C/450°F/Gas Mark 8. Put a lidded cast-iron pot into the oven to heat up. When the oven is at the correct temperature and the pot is hot, remove the bread from the fridge. Take the pot out of the oven and gently and carefully turn the bread out into the pot. Using a sharp knife, cut an even score across the top of the bread, then quickly put the lid on and bake for 20 minutes.
* After 20 minutes, uncover and bake for another 20 minutes. Towards the end of baking, keep an eye on the bread and reduce the oven temperature slightly if it is browning too fast. Remove the bread from the pot and return to the oven for another 5 minutes. To test if your bread is fully baked, it should sound hollow when tapped on the bottom and a temperature probe should read 92°C/198°F or over in the centre of the loaf. Leave to cool before slicing.

UNITED KINGDOM
*

OAT PORRIDGE SOURDOUGH

In this riff on a basic sourdough recipe, cooled or left-over porridge (oatmeal) is worked into the dough, creating a loaf that's surprisingly light and moist, with an almost custardy texture.

Makes: 2 small country-style loaves
Prep time: 1 hours, plus 11–15 hours resting and chilling
Cook time: 1 hour
{ӥ} {♠} {♣} {◦•}

- 200 g / 7 oz (2 cups) porridge (steel-cut) oats, rye flakes, spelt flakes, barley flakes or a mixture, plus extra for rolling
- 760 g / 1 lb 10 oz brown bread flour, plus extra for dusting
- 115 g / 4 oz sourdough leaven (see below)
- salt

* Begin by making the porridge (oatmeal). Preheat the oven to 180°C / 350°F / Gas Mark 4.
* Spread the oats out onto a large baking sheet and bake in the oven for 10 minutes, or until lightly toasted. Remove from the oven and tip into a medium saucepan. Pour in 400 ml / 14 fl oz (1⅔ cups) water and cook over a medium heat for 8–10 minutes, until the oats are soft and form a thick porridge. Season to taste with salt and leave to cool completely to room temperature. (This can be done a day in advance and stored at room temperature.)
* Follow the directions for the Sourdough Bread (see left), adding the porridge mix, 15 g / ½ oz (1 tablespoon) salt and another 50 ml / 1¾ fl oz (3½ tablespoons) water after the dough has been left to rest for the first 30 minutes.
* Once the dough has had its final shape, gently wet the top with a little water and roll in some extra oats before you put it into the proving basket and leave to chill in the fridge overnight.
* The next morning, follow the directions for baking on page 274.

For the sourdough leaven / starter:

* Many books have been written on the subject of sourdough bread and creating a sourdough leaven, and it's impossible to do it justice here, so you may want to do some wider reading on this. As a general rule, combine equal parts flour and tepid water in a plastic container or Kilner (canning jar) and leave for 3 days at room temperature. After 3 days, discard around 75 per cent of the leaven before adding equal parts flour and water again. Repeat this discarding and feeding daily until your leaven is bubbling and active. You can check if it is ready to use by doing a float test: drop 1 teaspoon of the leaven into a bowl of room temperature water and if it floats it is ready to go.

UNITED KINGDOM
*

NAAN BREAD

In India, naans are cooked in a tandoor oven made of clay and fuelled by coal. Tandoors are extremely heavy and bulky, and take a long time to get to temperature, so they are impractical for Indian home kitchens. Ovens are similarly uncommon – as no part of the cuisine requires one – which makes the naan, as a home-baked bread, much more of a reality in Britain than abroad.

Makes: 12
Prep time: 20 minutes,
plus 1 hour 40 minutes standing and rising
Cook time: 15 minutes
{ӥ} {◦•}

- 1½ teaspoons instant dried yeast
- 1 teaspoon caster (superfine) sugar
- 380 g / 13½ oz (3 cups plus 4 teaspoons) self-raising flour, plus extra for dusting
- 1 tablespoon full-fat (whole) plain yogurt
- 2 tablespoons vegetable oil, plus extra for oiling
- salt

* Pour 100 ml / 3½ fl oz (⅓ cup plus 1 tablespoon) water into a medium saucepan and heat over a medium heat until warm. Remove from the heat and pour into a large bowl. Add the yeast and sugar and whisk until the yeast has dissolved. Leave to stand for 10 minutes.
* Sift the flour and 1 teaspoon of salt into another large bowl, then add the yeast mixture, yogurt and 1 tablespoon of the oil and mix well, adding more warm water if necessary, to form a soft, springy but not sticky dough. Tip the dough out onto a lightly floured work counter and knead for 5 minutes, or until the dough is smooth. Put the dough into an oiled bowl, cover with clingfilm (plastic wrap) or a clean, damp dish towel and leave to rise in a warm place for 1½ hours until doubled in size.
* Preheat the oven to 220°C / 425°F / Gas Mark 7.
* Gently turn the risen dough out onto a lightly floured work counter and knead gently to knock the dough back to remove any air bubbles. Divide into 12 balls and roll into 12 round or oblong mini naans. Put half of the naans onto a large baking sheet and bake in the centre of the oven for 3–4 minutes until cooked through. Remove from the oven and repeat with the remaining naans.

SOFT BAPS

MORNING ROLLS/BREAKFAST ROLLS

Bread rolls vary across the United Kingdom, ranging in size and texture, and they might have soft, crispy, or even 'well-fired' tops. But surely the greatest differences are in the regional names used to describe such a roll. Whether you call yours a morning roll, cob, bun, bap, barm, stotty, oggie or even teacake – and these are just a few – breakfast rolls are glorious when buttered and consumed with your filling of choice. On most mornings a simple bacon roll is more than fine, but Square Sausage (page 187), Potato Scone (page 90) and a fried egg or hash brown has retrieved me from many a sorry state.

To avoid this entry becoming a book of its own, a 'standard' recipe is given here, but it should be said, or even encouraged, that you should try some different rolls. Make it an excuse to travel and support greasy spoon caffs nationwide.

Makes: 8
Prep time: 30 minutes, plus 10–15 hours rising, chilling and proving
Cook time: 12–15 minutes

{👤}{🍴}

- 35 g/1¼ oz (2 tablespoons plus 1 teaspoon) unsalted butter
- 500 g/1 lb 2 oz (4 cups plus 2 teaspoons) strong white bread flour, plus extra for dusting
- 10 g/¼ oz (2 teaspoons) fine sea salt
- 5 g/⅛ oz (1 teaspoon) instant dried yeast
- 175 ml/6 fl oz (¾ cup) full-fat (whole) milk at room temperature
- vegetable oil, for oiling
- 30 g/1 oz (¼ cup) rice flour or semolina (optional), for dusting

* Melt the butter in a small saucepan over a low heat for 2 minutes, then remove from the heat and set aside.
* Pour 175 ml/6 fl oz (¾ cup) water into a large saucepan and heat over a medium heat until it reaches 24°C/75°F on a thermometer.
* Put the flour, salt, yeast, milk, melted butter and warm water into a stand mixer fitted with a dough hook attachment and mix on medium speed for 5–10 minutes until the dough is smooth and elastic. Alternatively, put all the ingredients into a large bowl and mix with your hands to form a soft dough, then turn the dough out onto a lightly floured work counter and knead until you achieve the same smooth dough.
* Put the dough into a lightly oiled bowl, cover with clingfilm (plastic wrap) and leave to rise in a warm place for 1–2 hours until doubled in size.
* Once the dough has risen, tip it out onto a lightly floured work counter and knead lightly for 1–2 minutes, then return to the bowl, cover again and leave in the fridge overnight.
* The next day, line 2 large baking sheets with baking (parchment) paper and put some white bread flour or rice flour into a large bowl. The flour will keep the baps super soft as they bake and the rice flour or semolina will give them a crisper dried crust typical of a Glasgow morning roll.

* Remove the dough from the fridge and put it onto a lightly floured work counter. Divide it into 8 equal pieces, about 100 g/3½ oz each, then shape each piece into a tight ball. Gently toss each dough ball in either the bread flour or rice flour to lightly cover.
* Put 4 dough balls on each prepared baking sheet, spaced about 8 cm/3¼ inches apart, then loosely cover them with clingfilm (plastic wrap) and leave to rise in a warm place for 1 hour, or until doubled in size and beginning to touch each other.
* Preheat the oven to 200°C/400°F/Gas Mark 6. Meanwhile, boil the kettle or a pan of water. Once the oven reaches the correct temperature, carefully pour the boiling water into a large roasting pan and put it into the bottom of the oven. This will create a moist environment for the baps to bake in.
* Bake the baps for 12–15 minutes. As soon as you remove them from the oven, cover with a clean dish towel to capture their steam and maintain a soft crust. If you want to achieve the darker top of the Glasgow morning roll, preheat the grill (broiler) to high and finish the baps under the grill (broiler) for that distinctive charred top.
* It is almost essential that these are eaten the day they are baked but they can also be frozen on the day of baking and refreshed in an oven preheated to 200°C/400°F/Gas Mark 6 once defrosted

---

WHEATEN BREAD

Wheaten bread is the term used in Northern Ireland to describe what we would typically call brown soda bread. Confusingly, in Northern Ireland, Soda Bread (page 256) connotes a soda farl baked in a griddle in a manner similar to a Scottish Girdle Scone (page 256).

As with all soda breads, this is a quick fix. There's no rising, which means this is a simple recipe to whip up in a pinch. Serve buttered for lunch or tea.

Makes: 1 large loaf
Prep time: 20 minutes
Cook time: 40 minutes

{👤}{🍴}

- 500 g/1 lb 2 oz (4 cups plus 2 teaspoons) wholemeal (whole wheat) flour, plus extra for dusting
- 1 teaspoon salt
- 1 teaspoon bicarbonate of soda (baking soda)
- 400 ml/14 fl oz (1⅔ cups) buttermilk
- 1 tablespoon honey or golden syrup
- butter, to serve

* Preheat the oven to 200°C/400°F/Gas Mark 6. Dust a large baking sheet with flour and line with baking (parchment) paper.
* Sift all the dry ingredients into a large bowl and mix together. Make a well in the centre and add the buttermilk and honey or syrup. Combine well, then shape into a large circle and put onto the prepared baking sheet. Using a sharp knife, cut a cross on the top and bake for 40 minutes, or until golden brown. Leave to cool on a wire rack before serving with butter.

Wheaten bread

BRIDGE ROLLS
FINGER ROLLS

These are small, soft bread rolls made in the same way as the Basic Bread Dough (page 270). Once the rolls are baked and cooled, slice and fill with Egg Mayonnaise (page 32), Coronation Chicken (page 134) or any good sandwich filling.

Makes: 12
Prep time: 30 minutes,
plus 1 hour 20 minutes rising and proving
Cook time: 20 minutes
{🌱}{ ✎}

- 175 ml/6 fl oz (¾ cup) full-fat (whole) milk, plus extra for brushing
- 500 g/1 lb 2 oz (4 cups plus 2 teaspoons) strong white bread flour, plus extra for dusting
- 10 g/¼ oz (2 teaspoons) salt
- 1 teaspoon instant dried yeast
- vegetable oil, for oiling

* Pour the milk into a saucepan and heat over a low heat until warm. Pour 175 ml/6 fl oz (¾ cup) water into a separate saucepan and heat over a low heat until warm.
* Sift the dry ingredients into a large bowl and mix together. Make a well in the centre and pour in the warmed water and milk and mix to form a dough. Alternatively, use a stand mixer fitted with a dough hook attachment and mix on medium speed for 5 minutes, or until the dough is smooth and elastic. If mixing by hand, turn the dough out onto a lightly floured work counter and knead for 10 minutes, or until the dough is smooth and elastic. Shape the dough into a tight ball, put into an oiled bowl, cover with oiled clingfilm (plastic wrap) or a clean, damp dish towel and leave to rise in a warm place for 1 hour, or until it has doubled in size.
* Lightly dust 2 large baking sheets with flour and set aside. Gently turn the risen dough out onto a lightly floured work counter and knead gently to knock the dough back to remove any air bubbles, then divide the dough into 12 equal pieces. Roll each piece out into a tight ball, then use the palm of your hand to roll out into fingers, about 12 cm/4½ inches long. Arrange on the floured baking sheets, leaving 4 cm/1½ inch gaps between each one. Cover with a clean damp dish towel and leave to prove in a warm place for 20 minutes, or until they have doubled in size.
* Preheat the oven to 200°C/400°F/Gas Mark 6.
* When the rolls have proved, slide the baking sheets into the oven and bake for 20 minutes, or until pale golden brown. As soon as they come out of the oven, brush the tops with milk and leave to cool on wire racks.

KENTISH HUFFKINS

A large and fairly flat bread roll, the Kentish huffkin is indented with a thumbprint before baking. Serve with breakfast or lunch.

Makes: 12
Prep time: 30 minutes,
plus 1 hour 20 minutes rising and proving
Cook time: 20 minutes
{ ✎}

- 50 g/2 oz (3½ tablespoons) lard
- 500 g/1 lb 2 oz (4 cups plus 2 teaspoons) strong white bread flour, plus extra for dusting
- 10 g/¼ oz (2 teaspoons) salt
- 1 teaspoon instant dried yeast
- vegetable oil, for oiling

* Melt the lard in a small saucepan over a medium heat, then remove from the heat and leave to cool slightly.
* Pour 330 ml/11 fl oz (1⅓ cups) water into a large saucepan and heat over a medium heat until warm. Remove from the heat and set aside.
* Put all the dry ingredients into a large bowl and mix together. Make a well in the centre and pour in the warm water and lard. Mix well to form a soft dough. Alternatively, use a stand mixer fitted with a dough hook attachment and mix on medium speed for 5 minutes, or until the dough is smooth and elastic. If mixing by hand, turn the dough out onto a lightly floured work counter and knead for 10 minutes, or until the dough is smooth and elastic. Shape into a tight ball, put into an oiled bowl, cover with oiled clingfilm (plastic wrap) and leave to rise in a warm place for 1 hour, or until doubled in size.
* Once the dough has risen, dust 1–2 baking sheets with flour. Tip the dough out onto a lightly floured work counter and knead lightly for 1–2 minutes, then divide into 12 equal pieces. Roll each piece into a tight ball, press down to flatten slightly, then press your thumb down 2.5 cm/1 inch into the centre of each one. Arrange on the baking sheets, leaving a 4 cm/1½ inch gap around each one. Cover with a large plastic bag or large bowl and leave to prove in a warm place for 20 minutes, or until doubled in size.
* Preheat the oven to 200°C/400°F/Gas Mark 6.
* When the rolls are ready, slide the baking sheets into the oven and bake for 20 minutes, or until pale golden brown. As soon as they come out of the oven, cover with clean dish towels, which will give them a soft texture.

SPRING ONION ROLLS
GIBBONS

'Gibbons' is a south Wales term for spring onions (scallions). The recipe for these savoury rolls comes from Welsh baker Lynda Kettle and can be adapted into larger loaves or even shaped into rolled savoury buns, in the manner of a Chelsea Bun (page 290).

Makes: 12
Prep time: 30 minutes, plus 30 minutes rising
Cook time: 15 minutes
{🌶}{🌱}

- 25 g / 1 oz (2 tablespoons) butter, plus extra for greasing
- 1 kg / 2¼ lb (8⅓ cups) wholemeal (whole wheat) flour, plus extra for dusting
- 1 teaspoon salt
- 50 g / 2 oz (5½ tablespoons) instant dried yeast
- ½ teaspoon soft brown sugar
- 100 g / 3½ oz gibbons or spring onions (scallions), green and white parts chopped
- 1 tablespoon chopped flat-leaf parsley
- 2–3 tablespoons full-fat (whole) milk

* Grease a large baking sheet with butter.
* Pour 900 ml / 30 fl oz (3¾ cups) water into a medium saucepan and heat over a medium heat until warm. Remove from the heat and set aside.
* Put the flour and salt into a large bowl and mix together, then leave in a warm place for about 10 minutes. Sprinkle in the yeast and sugar and stir well.
* Pour in the warm water and mix to a firm dough. Alternatively, use a stand mixer fitted with a dough hook attachment and mix on medium speed for 5 minutes, or until the dough is smooth and elastic. If mixing by hand, turn the dough out onto a lightly floured work counter and knead for 10 minutes, or until the dough is smooth and elastic.
* Roll or pull the dough into a large rectangular shape, about 60 cm / 24 inches long and 30 cm / 12 inches wide. Sprinkle over the gibbons and parsley, then roll up from a long side like a Swiss (jelly) roll. Using a sharp knife, cut the dough into sections or buns and stand them up on their ends on the prepared baking sheet.
* Put the buns fairly close together, so that they will touch when risen. Cover and leave to rise in a warm place for 30 minutes.
* Preheat the oven to 220°C / 425°F / Gas Mark 7.
* When the rolls have risen, brush the tops with the milk and bake for about 15 minutes, or until golden.

TEACAKES
MORNING BREAD ROLLS

In most of the UK, teacakes are light, sweet rolls with dried fruit or candied peel. In parts of Yorkshire, Lancashire and Cumbria, however, 'teacake' is local parlance for a simple round bread roll, made in the manner below.

Makes: 8
Prep time: 30 minutes, plus 2 hours rising and proving
Cook time: 25–30 minutes
{🌱}

- 250 ml / 8 fl oz (1 cup) full-fat (whole) milk
- 500 g / 1 lb 2 oz (4 cups plus 2 teaspoons) strong bread flour, plus extra for dusting
- 5 g / ⅛ oz (1 teaspoon) instant dried yeast
- 10 g / ¼ oz (2 teaspoons) salt
- 1 tablespoon caster (superfine) sugar
- 60 g / 2¼ oz (½ stick) butter or lard, softened
- 1 teaspoon rapeseed (canola) oil, for oiling
- 100 g / 3½ oz dried fruit (optional)

* Pour the milk into a saucepan and heat gently over a low heat until warm. Remove from the heat and set aside.
* Sift the flour into a stand mixer fitted with a dough hook attachment and add the yeast, salt and sugar. Make a well in the centre and pour in the warmed milk together with the butter or lard, then slowly mix for 6 minutes, or until the dough is smooth and elastic. Shape the dough into a ball, put into an oiled bowl, cover with clingfilm (plastic wrap) or a clean, damp dish towel and leave to rise in a warm place for 1½ hours, or until doubled in size.
* Once the dough has risen, knead gently to knock the dough back to remove any air bubbles, then knead in the dried fruit (if using). Divide the dough into 8 equal pieces and roll them up into very tight balls on a lightly floured board. Roll out a little and flatten them slightly to make rounded loaf shapes.
* Line a large baking sheet with baking (parchment) paper and arrange the buns on it, leaving a 2 cm / ¾ inch gap between each one. Cover again and leave to prove for 30 minutes, or until they have doubled in size.
* Once the buns are ready, put them into a cold oven and heat the oven to 200°C / 400°F / Gas Mark 6. Bake for 25–30 minutes until golden brown. As soon as they come out of the oven, cover with a clean, damp dish towel to keep them soft.

ENGLAND
*

ENGLISH MUFFINS

We are all familiar with today's shop-bought 'English muffins', but muffins were traditionally home-baked and sold by muffin men on city streets well into the 1900s. A photo of a muffin man – muffin tray neatly balanced on his head and a clanging bell in hand – will make you nostalgic for a life you never lived.

English muffins are traditionally cooked on a griddle until browned on top and bottom, and then toasted. The proper procedure for serving a toasted muffin is not to slice it in half with a knife, but rather to pull it apart from top and bottom so that it splits at the soft middle. Slide slices of butter into the middle of the muffin, close and allow the butter to warm before serving.

Makes: 16
Prep time: 30 minutes, plus 1½ hours rising and proving
Cook time: 1 hour 10 minutes
{❂} {☞}

- 360 ml/12 fl oz (1½ cups plus 2 teaspoons) full-fat (whole) milk
- 16 g/½ oz (1 tablespoon) fresh yeast or 8 g/¼ oz (½ tablespoon) instant dried yeast
- 30 g/1 oz (2½ tablespoons) caster (superfine) sugar
- 2 eggs
- 40 g/1½ oz (3 tablespoons) butter
- 640 g/1 lb 6 oz (5 ⅓ cups) strong white bread flour, plus extra for dusting
- 6 g/⅛ oz (1 teaspoon) salt
- 6 g/⅛ oz (1 teaspoon) baking powder
- vegetable oil, for oiling
- semolina, for sprinkling and rolling
- preserves or honey, to serve

* Pour the milk and 50 ml/1¾ fl oz (3½ tablespoons) water into a small saucepan and heat gently over a low heat until it reaches 25–35°C/77–95°F on a thermometer.
* Pour the warmed milk and water into a stand mixer, add the yeast and a sprinkle of sugar and whisk briefly to dissolve. Leave the mixture in a warm place for 10 minutes to activate the yeast.
* Once the yeast mixture has started to foam, add the eggs, butter, flour, salt, remaining sugar and the baking powder. Using the dough hook attachment, mix on low speed for 5 minutes to combine all the ingredients, scraping the bowl occasionally, then mix on medium speed for another 10 minutes, or until the dough is smooth and elastic. The dough should come away easily from the sides of the bowl.
* Put the dough into a lightly oiled medium bowl, cover with clingfilm (plastic wrap) or a dish towel and leave to rise in a warm place for 1 hour, or until it is almost doubled in size.
* Spread some of the semolina out on a large plate. Line a large baking sheet with baking (parchment) paper and sprinkle with a generous amount of semolina.
* Tip the risen dough onto a lightly floured work counter, then weigh the mixture and divide into 16 equal pieces. Using the palm of your hand, roll each piece of dough in a circular motion on the work surface, applying a little pressure to form a tight ball, then roll each ball in semolina to coat, before arranging them on the prepared baking sheet. Gently cover the baking sheet with clingfilm

(plastic wrap), making sure it isn't too tight. Leave the muffins to prove for 20–30 minutes until doubled in size.
* Meanwhile, preheat a large heavy frying pan or skillet over a medium heat and preheat the oven to 170°C/325°F/ Gas Mark 3.
* Sprinkle an even layer of semolina in the frying pan or skillet, then gently transfer 4 muffins into the pan, making sure there is enough space for them to expand and cook evenly. Cook for 5–7 minutes on each side until golden brown, before transferring them to a baking sheet and baking in the oven for 10–12 minutes to ensure the muffins are completely cooked. Repeat the process with the remaining muffins.
* To serve, carefully tear the muffins in half, then lightly toast each half and enjoy with your favourite preserve, honey or savoury preference. Ideal for breakfast, they can also be frozen once baked.

NORTHEAST OF ENGLAND
*

STOTTIE ROLLS

These large, chewy rolls are popular in the northeast of England where they are commonly eaten with butter and jam or ham and Pease Pudding (page 76).

Makes: about 5
Prep time: 20 minutes, plus at least 1 hour rising
Cook time: 20 minutes
{❂} {☞}

- 170 ml/6 fl oz (¾ cup) full-fat (whole) milk
- 650 g/1 lb 7 oz (5½ cups minus 2 teaspoons) strong white bread flour, plus extra for dusting
- 7 g/¼ oz sachet instant dried yeast
- ½ teaspoon ground white pepper
- ½ teaspoon granulated sugar
- 1 tsp salt
- vegetable oil, for oiling
- butter and jam, to serve

* Pour 260 ml/9 fl oz (1 cup plus 2 teaspoons) water and the milk into a medium saucepan and heat over a low heat until just warm. Remove from the heat and set aside.
* Sift all the dry ingredients into a stand mixer fitted with a dough hook attachment and mix together. Make a well in the centre and add the liquid, then, using the dough hook attachment, slowly knead for 5 minutes until glossy and elastic. You could also make the dough by hand. Cover the dough with oiled clingfilm (plastic wrap) and leave to rise in a warm place for at least 1 hour, or until it has doubled in size.
* Preheat the oven to 180°C/350°F/Gas Mark 4. Line a large baking sheet with baking (parchment) paper.
* Once the dough is ready, tip it out onto a lightly floured work counter. Divide it into 5 equal pieces and roll it out into circles about 2–3 cm/¾ –1¼ inches thick. Make a small indentation in the top of each circle using your finger, and transfer to the lined baking sheet. Bake in the oven for 20 minutes. Leave to cool slightly before eating with butter and jam.

English muffins

ENGLAND: YORKSHIRE
*

YORKSHIRE PUDDINGS

These simple batter puddings are made in an exacting manner by their legion of fanatics. Ideally cooked in hot beef dripping, a flavourful Yorkshire pudding, with its soft melting inside and crispy exterior, is a requisite accompaniment to any good roast. Traditionally, Yorkshire puddings were eaten with gravy before the beef, as a sort of proto-appetizer. They could also be saved for afters, and topped with a drizzling of golden syrup or whisked butter and sugar. Today, they are most typically served on a big plate, commingling with the meat and vegetables, and with a rich gravy poured over the top.

When cooking them, the main things to keep in mind are the flavour and the heat of your fat, and the fact that if you open the oven door before they are properly baked they will deflate.

This recipe comes from Yorkshire-born chef James Ferguson, whose grandmother Beatrice cooked Yorkshire puddings following this recipe for the Sunday lunch, as well as for dessert (with sugar and butter whisked together).

Makes: about 24 small or about 6 large puddings
Prep time: 15 minutes, plus 4 hours resting time
Cook time: 18–20 minutes
{•'}

- 4 eggs
- 350 ml/12 fl oz (1½ cups) full-fat (whole) milk, plus a little extra (optional)
- 225 g/8 oz (1¾ cups plus 1 tablespoon) plain (all-purpose) flour
- 10–15 g/¼–½ oz (2–3 teaspoons) beef dripping (per pudding), or, if you must, vegetable oil
- salt and pepper

* Put the eggs and milk into a jug (pitcher) and mix together. Put the flour into a large bowl and slowly and gently whisk in the milk and egg mixture. Don't overwhisk – lumps are fine. Don't season the mixture yet. Leave the batter to rest at room temperature for at least 4 hours, covered with clingfilm (plastic wrap).
* When ready to cook, preheat the oven to 200°C/400°F/Gas Mark 6.
* Put 2 x 12 hole muffin trays or a 6 hole muffin tray into the oven to heat up for 10 minutes, then add a good piece of beef dripping (no one wants a Yorkshire cooked in vegetable oil but it will work) to each hole.
* Season the batter with a good pinch of salt and a few twists of black pepper, then loosen the consistency of the batter with a little milk, if necessary – it should be like single (light) cream. Pour the batter into the muffin holes until they are half full and bake in the oven for 20 minutes (do not open the oven door!), or until the bottom is soft and the sides are crunchy. Serve immediately.

UNITED KINGDOM
*

CHEESE STRAWS

These thin and flaky cheese pastries make for excellent snacking and are a favourite of parties and large gatherings. The straws are made from a simple pastry, with the cheese, spice and other flavourings worked straight into the dough. That makes it easy to swap in different cheeses or additional flavourings such as Marmite. Even as far back as May Byron's *Pot-Luck* (1914), there was variation, and Byron notes no fewer than six different versions.

Makes: 24
Prep time: 25 minutes, plus 30–45 minutes chilling
Cook time: 8–10 minutes
{●} {•'}

- 100 g/3½ oz (¾ cup plus 2 teaspoons) plain (all-purpose) flour, plus extra for dusting
- 2 g/½ teaspoon salt
- 2 g/½ teaspoon paprika, plus extra for seasoning
- 50 g/2 oz (3½ tablespoons) unsalted butter, cut into pieces
- 50 g/2 oz good-quality Cheddar cheese, finely grated
- 1 egg yolk, beaten
- 25 ml/1 fl oz (2 tablespoons) full-fat (whole) milk
- 1 egg
- 50 g/2 oz good-quality Parmesan cheese, finely grated
- Maldon sea salt, crushed

* Preheat the oven to 180°C/350°F/Gas Mark 4. Line 2 large baking sheets with baking (parchment) paper.
* Put the flour, salt and paprika into a large bowl and mix together. Add the butter and rub in with your fingertips until the mixture has a breadcrumb-like texture. Add the Cheddar, followed by the beaten egg yolk and milk, and incorporate slowly but thoroughly, without overworking, until a dough forms. Wrap the dough in clingfilm (plastic wrap) and leave to rest in the fridge for 30–45 minutes.
* Once the dough is chilled, put the whole egg into a small bowl, add 1 tablespoon water or milk and beat to combine. Set aside. Roll the dough out on a lightly floured work counter into a 25 x 15 cm/10 x 6 inch rectangle about 5 mm/¼ inch thick. Using a ruler and a sharp knife, cut the dough into 24 strips, about 15 cm/6 inches long and 1 cm/½ inch wide, and arrange them on the prepared baking sheets. Brush with the beaten egg mixture, then sprinkle with the Parmesan and a little extra paprika and crushed sea salt.
* Bake in the oven for 8–10 minutes until pale golden brown. Leave to cool before serving or enjoy warm straight out of the oven.

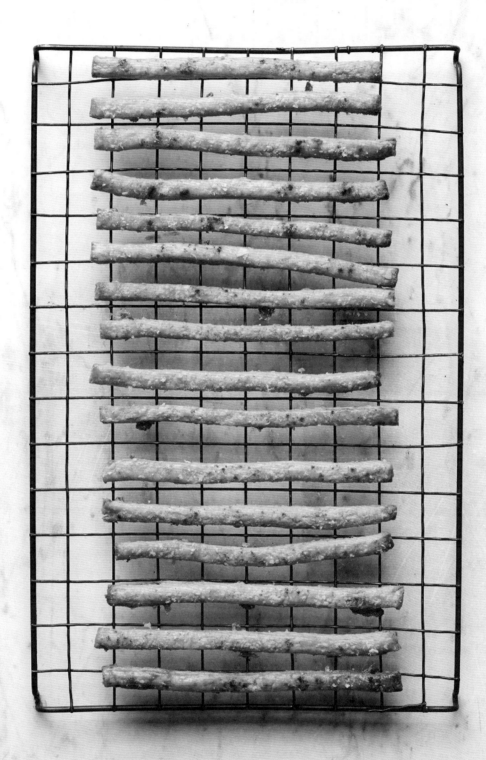

Cheese straws

THERE'S A CHARM IN THE SOUND,
WHICH NOBODY SHUNS,
OF SMOKING HOT, PIPING HOT,
CHELSEA BUNS

AN EIGHTEENTH-CENTURY RHYME,
VIA ELIZABETH DAVID'S *ENGLISH BREAD AND YEAST COOKERY*, C. 1977

This chapter begins our exploration of the sweeter side of British baking, diving deep into all manner of cakes and buns: from buttery sponge cakes and spiced buns to fruity tea loaves and sticky gingerbreads.

Britain's traditional bakes are rooted in centuries of evolving taste, ingredients and technique. Gingerbread is a great example of this: originating nearly a millennium ago as a well-spiced medieval sweet more in line with the size and thickness of today's biscuits (cookies), it evolved into a deeply flavoured cake, to be wrapped in baking (parchment) paper and left to mature.

Today's gingerbread is invariably a moister loaf-style of cake, yet you can still find dozens of regional gingerbreads and ginger cakes across Britain that work as a sort of snapshot of this very gradual progression: biscuit-like gingerbread bars, oaty Yorkshire parkin and Orkney broonie, and the deep, dark square ginger biscuits known fondly as parlies.

Buttery sponge cakes have a distinctively British feel to them as well and were traditionally baked for occasions big and small: everything from harvest celebrations to mid-afternoon moments, to be enjoyed with a glass of Madeira. Popular flavourings could be caraway seeds, candied mixed peel or cinnamon and honey – perhaps not all at once. These cakes weren't meant to be great expressions of a baker's innovative mind; they were simple pleasures, to be eaten as they were, or, as most things, spread with a little extra butter. Still to this day, dolled-up multi-tiered cakes, sandwiched with fillings or spread with rich layers of buttercream, have never really found their own voice in Britain – although the Victoria sponge sandwich is one very happy exception to that rule.

Then there are fruitcakes and fruity tea loaves. In a sense, two sides of the same (often-maligned) coin. A grossly simplified distinction might be that the former are baked with a lot of butter, and the latter without – they are merely spread with it before serving. These well-spiced and fruited bakes have an abundance of regional variations that run the length and breadth of the British Isles, rivalling the great gingerbread for variety in all its shapes and sizes.

The bun is another surprisingly ancient British treat, having been baked since at least the late medieval period, with dedicated bun houses operating in London not long after. The many great British buns have also varied considerably over time. The Bath bun, for instance, is a bake of considerable richness, more akin to a brioche than what is commonly found today. A little subtlety of flavour goes a long way, and many British buns, like the hot cross bun, are quite subtle in their flavour, but they're not meant to be eaten plainly: they should, as you may by now have guessed, be sliced, toasted and spread with butter (and marmalade). Again, the very sweet, very sticky Chelsea bun is a notable exception to this.

Finally, we arrive at the biscuit, and perhaps this is more forewarning than anything: while there are few things more British than a cupboard well-stocked with biscuits, they do largely exist outside of the home baking tradition, with many varieties having been invented by commercial bakeries. This chapter makes a few exceptions to this understanding, and celebrates some old favourites along the way. After all, it's hard to turn down something enveloped in chocolate.

CAKES, BUNS AND BISCUITS

ENGLAND: LONDON
*

HOT CROSS BUNS

These iconic spiced buns are traditionally baked for Good Friday, and have been ever since the late sixteenth century, when Elizabethan law first decreed that they could only be made around certain holidays. *The Oxford Companion to Food* suggests that marking the buns with a cross is an Anglo-Saxon tradition that dates back to pagan times when buns were marked with a cross for Ēostre, a goddess of light and the namesake of Easter in the UK.
Today's hot cross buns are made with plenty of candied peel and dried fruit, and they should be toasted and buttered. Any left-over buns can, once slightly stale, be made into a superlative Bread and Butter Pudding (page 360).

Makes: 12
Prep time: 45 minutes, plus 2–3 hours rising and proving
Cook time: 15–20 minutes
{👁}{🍃}

- 150 g/5 oz (1 cup) sultanas (golden raisins)
- 75 g/2¾ oz (½ cup) raisins
- 75 g/2¾ oz (⅓ cup) dried apricots, chopped
- 75 g/2¾ oz (⅔ cup) dried cranberries
- 75 g/2¾ oz (½ cup minus 2 teaspoons) dried figs, chopped
- grated zest of 1 orange
- 1 tablespoon mixed spice
- 350 g/12 oz (3 cups minus 2 teaspoons) plain (all-purpose) flour, plus extra for dusting
- 230 g/8 oz (2 cups minus 2 teaspoons) strong brown bread flour
- 40 g/1½ oz cold unsalted butter, diced
- 50 g/2 oz (¼ cup) caster (superfine) sugar
- 10 g/¼ oz (2 teaspoons) fine sea salt
- 8 g/¼ oz (about 2¼ teaspoons) instant dried yeast
- 2 eggs
- 160 ml/5¼ fl oz (⅔ cup) full-fat (whole) milk, at room temperature, about 24°C/75°F
- 50 g/2 oz sourdough starter (optional)
- sunflower oil, for oiling
- butter, to serve (optional)

- For the cross paste and glaze:
- 5 g/⅛ oz (1 teaspoon) unsalted butter
- 100 g/3½ oz (¾ cup plus 4 teaspoons) plain (all-purpose) flour
- pinch of salt
- pinch of caster (superfine) sugar
- 100 g/3½ oz (⅓ cup plus 1 tablespoon) honey

* Put all the dried fruits, orange zest and mixed spice into a large bowl, mix to combine and set aside. Put the flours into a stand mixer fitted with a dough hook attachment. Add the butter and rub it in with your fingertips until it resembles fine breadcrumbs. Add the sugar, salt, yeast, eggs, milk and sourdough starter (if using), together with 160 ml/5¼ fl oz (⅔ cup) water at room temperature, about 24°C/75°F. Mix on slow speed at first until combined, then increase the speed to medium and mix for 10 minutes to form a smooth and elastic dough that comes away from the sides of the bowl as it mixes. Add the spiced fruit mixture and mix on slow speed for another 2–3 minutes until the fruit is evenly dispersed throughout the dough.

* Put the dough into a lightly oiled bowl, cover with clingfilm (plastic wrap) or a damp dish towel and leave to rise at room temperature for 1–2 hours until almost doubled in size. Once the dough is risen, you can either chill it overnight to bake the next morning, or shape to bake the same day.
* Line 2 large baking sheets with baking (parchment) paper and set aside.
* To shape the dough, turn it out onto a lightly floured work counter and divide it into 12 equal pieces, about 140 g/5 oz each. Gently shape the pieces into balls by cupping your hand over the dough and rolling in a circular motion on the work surface. If it is sticky, use flour on your hands and the surface.
* Put 6 buns evenly spaced onto each prepared baking sheet. Cover loosely with clingfilm and leave to rise in a warm place for 1 hour, or until almost doubled in size.
* Meanwhile, prepare the cross paste. Melt the butter in a small saucepan over a low heat or microwave in a bowl on high for 30–45 seconds. Sift the flour, salt and sugar into a small bowl and slowly whisk in 100 ml/3½ fl oz (⅓ cup plus 1 tablespoon) cold water, followed by the melted butter to make a smooth paste. The paste should be a good consistency to pipe so add a little more flour or water as required. Put the paste into a piping (pastry) bag and set aside.
* Preheat the oven to 180°C/350°F/Gas Mark 4.
* When the buns are ready to bake, pipe on the crosses or whatever design you might choose, then bake in the oven for 15–20 minutes until golden brown, turning the baking sheets around during baking as required to get an even colouring.
* Meanwhile, prepare the glaze. Gently heat the honey and 200 ml/7 fl oz (¾ cup plus 1 tablespoon) water in a small saucepan over a low heat for 2 minutes until dissolved. Bring to a simmer and cook for another 2 minutes until it has reduced slightly.
* Remove the cooked buns from the oven and put the baking sheets onto wire racks to cool. Leave to set for 5 minutes, then brush the buns liberally with the honey glaze. Devour immediately or leave to cool and then enjoy toasted with lashings of butter over the next few days.

Hot cross buns

ENGLAND: LONDON

*

CHELSEA BUNS

These sticky sweet buns are made from a yeasted dough that's rolled thin and spread with a buttery currant filling. Once rolled up they are baked in neat squares, then brushed (or doused, if desired) in a syrupy glaze, which makes uncoiling them an enjoyably messy experience. As the name suggests, Chelsea buns hail from west London, where they were a speciality of the Chelsea Bun House. The Bun House, which was a regular haunt of the reigning British monarchs, was unfortunately demolished in 1839. However, other such institutions have gone on to take their place. The most famous now is perhaps Fitzbillies, which was opened in Cambridge in 1922.

There are no particular serving suggestions for Chelsea buns besides to enjoy them. However, I did once see a bun served still soft and warm from the oven, with a great dollop of Clotted Cream (page 34) beside it. It is a pairing that makes my heart race for a number of reasons. You can begin making the buns the day before you would like to eat them and leave the dough to prove in the fridge overnight, then bake in the morning – a fresh bun makes a delightful breakfast.

Makes: 12

Prep time: 30 minutes, plus 1¾–3 hours rising and proving

Cook time: 15–20 minutes

{●}{♥}

- For the dough:
- 100 g / 3½ oz (7 tablespoons) unsalted butter
- 250 g / 9 oz (2 cups) plain (all-purpose) flour
- 250 g / 9 oz (2 cups) strong white bread flour,
  plus extra for dusting
- 50 g / 2 oz (¼ cup minus 1 teaspoon)
  soft light brown sugar
- 7 g / ¼ oz (2¼ teaspoons) instant dried yeast
- 1 teaspoon fine sea salt
- grated zest of 1 lemon
- 300 ml / 10 fl oz (1¼ cups) full-fat (whole) milk,
  at room temperature
- 1 egg
- sunflower oil for oiling

- For the filling:
- 50 g / 2 oz (3½ tablespoons) unsalted butter
- 50 g / 2 oz (¼ cup minus 1 teaspoon)
  soft light brown sugar
- 150 g / 5 oz (⅔ cup) currants

- For the glaze:
- 60 ml / 2 fl oz (¼ cup) full-fat (whole) milk
- 60 g / 2¼ oz (¼ cup plus 1 teaspoon)
  soft light brown sugar

* For the dough, melt the butter in a small saucepan over a medium-low heat, then remove from the heat and leave to cool slightly. Put the flours, sugar, yeast, salt and lemon zest into a stand mixer fitted with a dough hook attachment and set aside. Pour the melted butter into a large bowl and add the milk and egg. Lightly whisk together until combined, then add to the dry ingredients. Mix on slow speed to incorporate all the ingredients, then increase the speed to medium and mix for 5–10

minutes to form a smooth and elastic dough that comes away from the sides of the bowl as it mixes. Alternatively, mix all the ingredients together in a bowl using electric beaters until incorporated, then turn out onto a lightly floured work counter and knead to a smooth and elastic dough. Put the dough into a lightly oiled bowl, cover with clingfilm (plastic wrap) and leave to rise for 1–2 hours until doubled in size.

* Meanwhile, line the bottom and sides of a deep baking sheet, about 25 x 35 cm / 10 x 14 inches, with baking (parchment) paper. A good tip is to cut the large rectangle of paper, then scrunch it up into a ball, unscrunch it and gently press it into the baking sheet, so no grease is required.

* For the filling, melt the butter in a small saucepan over a medium-low heat, then pour into a large bowl, add the sugar and currants and mix together. Set aside.

* Gently roll out the risen dough on a lightly floured work counter to create a rectangle, about 40 x 25 cm / 16 x 10 inches, ending up with the longest side facing you horizontally. Gently spread the surface of the dough all over with the filling.

* Starting at the long edge closest to you, roll the dough up like a Swiss (jelly) roll, keeping it as neat and tightly rolled as possible. Using a serrated knife, cut the dough into 12 even pieces. Neatly put the 12 pieces into the prepared baking sheet, swirl-side up, in a 3 x 4 formation. Evenly space the buns leaving a little gap between each one so that there is room for them to prove and fill the space. Cover the tray and leave the buns to prove for 45–60 minutes until doubled in size and soft like marshmallows.

* Preheat the oven to 180°C / 350°F / Gas Mark 4.

* Once the buns have proved, bake in the oven for 15–20 minutes until light golden brown all over. A temperature probe inserted into one of the middle buns should read at least 92°C / 198°F when they are done.

* While the buns are baking, make the glaze. Put the milk and sugar into a small saucepan and heat over a low heat until the sugar has completely dissolved. When the buns are ready, remove them from the oven and immediately brush with the glaze, giving the buns a generous soaking. Leave to cool slightly before separating and eating while still slightly warm. These buns are best eaten on the day they are baked but will still be delicious for 2–3 days afterwards if kept in an airtight container.

Chelsea buns

UNITED KINGDOM
*
BELGIAN BUNS

These sweet buns are a cousin to the Chelsea Bun (page 290) and can be made using the same yeasted dough. The main difference is in the filling and topping: Belgian buns are spread with a filling of lemon curd and sultanas (golden raisins), and topped with icing (frosting) and half a glacé (candied) cherry.

Some good advice for the indecisive bakers out there: the creators of this recipe, Sam and Anna Luntley, recommend making a half measure of both the Belgian bun and Chelsea bun fillings and doing a 50/50 bake – six buns of each.

Makes: 12
Prep time: 30 minutes, plus 1¾–3 hours rising and proving
Cook time: 15–20 minutes
{👤}{🌶}

- For the dough:
- 100 g/ 3½ oz (7 tablespoons) unsalted butter
- 250 g/ 9 oz (2 cups) plain (all-purpose) flour
- 250 g/ 9 oz (2 cups) strong white bread flour, plus extra for dusting
- 50 g/ 2 oz (¼ cup minus 1 teaspoon) soft light brown sugar
- 7 g/ ¼ oz (2¼ teaspoons) instant dried yeast
- 1 teaspoon fine sea salt
- grated zest of 1 lemon
- 300 ml/ 10 fl oz (1¼ cups) full-fat (whole) milk, at room temperature
- 1 egg
- sunflower oil, for oiling

- For the filling:
- 100 g/ 3½ oz (⅓ cup) lemon curd
- 150 g/ 5 oz (1 cup) sultanas (golden raisins)

- For the icing (frosting) and to decorate:
- 400 g/ 14 oz (3⅓ cups) icing (confectioners') sugar
- 12 glacé (candied) cherries

* For the dough, melt the butter in a small saucepan over a medium-low heat, then remove from the heat and set aside. Put the flours, soft light brown sugar, yeast, salt and lemon zest into a stand mixer fitted with a dough hook attachment and set aside. Pour the melted butter into a large bowl and add the milk and egg. Lightly whisk together until combined, then add to the dry ingredients.
* Mix on slow speed to incorporate all the ingredients, then increase the speed to medium and mix for 5–10 minutes to form a smooth and elastic dough that comes away from the sides of the bowl as it mixes. Alternatively, mix all the ingredients together in a bowl using electric beaters until incorporated, then turn out onto a lightly floured work counter and knead to a smooth and elastic dough. Put the dough into a lightly oiled bowl, cover with clingfilm (plastic wrap) and leave to rise for 1–2 hours until doubled in size.
* Meanwhile, line the bottom and sides of a deep baking sheet, about 25 x 35 cm/ 10 x 14 inches, with baking (parchment) paper. A good tip is to cut the large rectangle of paper, then scrunch it up into a ball, unscrunch it and gently press it into the baking sheet.
* Roll out the risen dough on a lightly floured work counter to create a rectangle, about 40 x 25 cm/ 16 x 10 inches,

ending up with the longest side facing you horizontally. Gently spread the surface of the dough all over with the lemon curd and sprinkle over the sultanas (golden raisins).

* Starting at the long edge closest to you, roll the dough up like a Swiss (jelly) roll, keeping it as neat and tightly rolled as possible. Using a serrated knife, cut the dough into 12 even pieces. Neatly put the 12 pieces into the prepared baking sheet, swirl-side up, in a 3 x 4 formation. Evenly space the buns, leaving room for them to prove and fill the space. Cover the tray and leave the buns to prove for 45–60 minutes until doubled in size and soft like marshmallows.
* Preheat the oven to 180°C/ 350°F/ Gas Mark 4.
* Once the buns are ready, bake in the oven for 15–20 minutes until light golden brown all over. A temperature probe inserted into one of the middle buns should read at least 92°C/ 198°F when they are done.
* While the buns are baking, make the icing (frosting). Put the icing (confectioners') sugar and 4 tablespoons boiling water into a medium bowl and whisk together to combine into a moderately thick water icing. It should be a spoonable consistency, so add more water if required.
* When the buns are ready, remove them from the oven and dollop a generous spoonful of icing on top of each bun, using the back of the spoon to spread the icing evenly. Top each with a glacé (candied) cherry and leave to cool slightly before separating and eating while still slightly warm. These buns are best eaten on the day they are baked but will still be delicious for 2–3 days afterwards if kept in an airtight container.

ENGLAND: BATH
*
BATH BUNS

Today's Bath buns are small and lightly sweet buns topped with pearl sugar – you can find them at a few of the best-known bakeries and cafés in Bath. The Bath buns of the late eighteenth century are rather more interesting. A venerable group of cookery writers, including Margaret Dods (Christian Isobel Johnstone), Elizabeth David and Jane Grigson, all liken these earlier recipes as closer to a brioche: a taste they prefer to the modern version. The below is an adaptation of one of these older recipes.

Makes: 12
Prep time: 30 minutes, plus 3–5 hours rising and proving
Cook time: 15–20 minutes
{👤}{🌶}

- For the dough:
- 100 g/ 3½ oz (¾ cup plus 2 teaspoons) plain (all-purpose) flour
- 400 g/ 14 oz (3⅓ cups) strong white bread flour, plus extra for dusting
- 250 g/ 9 oz (2¼ sticks) cold unsalted butter, diced
- 100 g/ 3½ oz (½ cup) caster (superfine) sugar
- 7 g/ ¼ oz (2¼ teaspoons) instant dried yeast
- 1 teaspoon fine sea salt
- 2 teaspoons caraway seeds
- 4 eggs, beaten
- 60 ml/ 2 fl oz (¼ cup) full-fat (whole) milk, at room temperature
- vegetable oil, for oiling

- For the glaze and decoration:
- 50 ml/1¾ fl oz (3½ tablespoons) full-fat (whole) milk
- 100 g/3½ oz (½ cup) caster (superfine) sugar
- pearled sugar

- To serve (optional):
- butter, blueberry jam or strong cheese

* For the dough, put the flours into a stand mixer fitted with a dough hook attachment. Add the diced butter and gently rub it in with your fingertips until the mixture resembles fine breadcrumbs. Add the remaining dough ingredients and mix on slow speed until all the ingredients are incorporated. Increase the speed to medium and mix for 5–10 minutes to form a smooth and elastic dough that comes away from the sides of the bowl as it mixes. Form the dough into a ball, then put it into a lightly oiled bowl, cover with clingfilm (plastic wrap), and leave to rise in a warm place for 1 hour.
* Knead the risen dough gently to remove any air bubbles, then fold the dough over onto itself in the bowl. Cover again and leave to prove in a warm place for 1 hour.
* Meanwhile, line 2 large baking sheets with baking (parchment) paper.
* Put the dough onto a lightly floured work counter and divide it into 12 equal pieces, about 80–90 g/3–3¼ oz each. Roll each piece of dough into a neat ball in the palms of your hands – in an action almost like you might use to lather a bar of soap – if the dough is sticky, make sure your hands are well floured. Arrange the dough balls evenly on the prepared baking sheets and loosely cover with clingfilm. Leave the buns to prove for 1–2 hours in a warm place until doubled in size and soft like marshmallows. These buns take slightly longer to prove than other types of bun because their high fat content weighs the dough down.
* Preheat the oven to 180°C/350°F/Gas Mark 4.
* Once the buns are ready, bake in the oven for 15–20 minutes until light golden brown all over. A temperature probe inserted into one of the middle buns should read 92°C/198°F plus when they are done.
* Meanwhile, for the glaze, put the milk and caster (superfine) sugar into a small saucepan and stir over a low heat for 2–3 minutes until the sugar has dissolved.
* When the buns are ready, remove them from the oven and transfer to a wire rack to cool. While they are still hot, brush liberally with the glaze and sprinkle with the pearled sugar. Devour immediately while still warm, or they are delicious for a few days later either reheated in the oven or split and grilled (broiled) with butter, blueberry jam or even a good strong cheese.

ENGLAND: BATH

SALLY LUNN BUNS

The Sally Lunn bun is an enriched English bun closely related to French brioche. Today's version, found almost exclusively at Sally Lunn's tearoom in Bath, is more accurately an overly large soft and slightly sweet bread roll. Such is the roll's size that it's either offered as a whole or half and could comfortably be its own dinner plate. The recipe below is from the historian and baker Justin Cherry. Justin's Sally Lunn is closer to early eighteenth century recipes: buttery and egg-rich, the outside layer of the bun protecting the soft and lush interior.

Makes: 6–12
Prep time: 50 minutes, plus 2 hours rising and chilling
Cook time: 20 minutes
{ ☞ }

- 115 g/4 oz (1 stick) unsalted butter
- 250 ml/8 fl oz (1 cup) double (heavy) cream
- 2 tablespoons demerara (turbinado) sugar
- 400 g/14 oz (3 ⅓ cups) plain (all-purpose) flour
- 1 teaspoon salt
- 3 eggs, plus 1 egg yolk
- 1 tablespoon instant dried yeast
- vegetable oil, for oiling
- butter or lard, for brushing

* Melt the butter, cream and sugar together in a heatproof bowl set over a medium saucepan of gently simmering water, making sure the bottom of the bowl doesn't touch the water. Once combined, remove from the heat and leave to cool to below 43°C/109°F.
* Pour the butter mixture into a stand mixer fitted with a dough hook attachment, then sift in the flour. Add the salt, eggs, egg yolk and yeast and mix on medium speed for 5 minutes. Increase the speed to high and mix for another 2 minutes. Alternatively, put all the ingredients into a bowl and mix by hand for 10–12 minutes. It will be a wet dough. Transfer the dough to an oiled bowl and leave to rise, covered with clingfilm (plastic wrap), in a warm place for 45 minutes, or until doubled in size, then chill in the fridge for 1 hour.
* Lightly oil a large baking sheet and set aside. Now that the dough is easier to work with, divide it into 12 even pieces and, using your hands, roll into small balls. Arrange the dough balls, equally spaced, on the baking sheet, cover with clingfilm, and leave to prove for 15 minutes.
* Meanwhile, preheat the oven to 200°C/400°F/Gas Mark 6.
* When the buns are ready, bake in the oven for 17 minutes, or until golden brown on top. Remove from the oven and transfer to a wire rack. Brush with a little butter or lard.
* Note: Add 4–5 minutes to the bake time if you would like to bake as 6 buns instead of 12.

ENGLAND: CORNWALL
*

CORNISH SAFFRON BUNS

Saffron was produced in the UK into the nineteenth century, but some legends suggest that Cornwall's connection with saffron dates as far back as two millennia, when it was traded with Phoenician merchants from the Middle East. The small amount of saffron imparts both a golden-yellow hue and a faint but slightly astringent flavour to these lightly sweet, spiced treats. A true Cornish classic – split or slice, butter well and enjoy.

Makes: about 20
Prep time: 1 hour, plus 7½ –15½ hours soaking, standing, rising and proving
Cook time: 15 minutes
{❂} {⌁}

- 200 g/ 7 oz (¾ cup plus 1 tablespoon) currants
- 10–15 strands (as much as you dare) good-quality saffron
- 20 g/¾ oz (2 tablespoons) instant dried yeast
- 60 g/ 2¼ oz (½ cup) plain (all-purpose) flour
- 1 kg/ 2¼ lb (8 ⅓ cups) strong white bread flour
- 100 g/ 3½ oz (⅓ cup plus 1 tablespoon) soft dark brown sugar
- 22 g/¾ oz (4 teaspoons) salt
- 450 ml/ 15 fl oz (1⅔ cups plus 2 tablespoons) full-fat (whole) milk
- 4 eggs, beaten
- 80 g/ 3 oz (⅓ cup plus 1 teaspoon) good-quality honey
- rapeseed (canola) oil, for oiling
- 200 ml/ 7 fl oz (¾ cup plus 1 tablespoon) olive oil

- For the glaze:
- 50 g/ 2 oz (¼ cup) golden caster (superfine) sugar
- 50 g/ 2 oz (¼ cup plus 1 teaspoon) honey

* Put the currants into a large heatproof bowl, add 100 ml/ 3½ fl oz (⅓ cup plus 1 tablespoon) boiling water and leave to soak for at least 2 hours, preferably overnight, until the dried fruit puckers and most of the liquid has been absorbed.
* Put the saffron into a small heatproof bowl, add 2 tablespoons just-boiled water and leave to soak until the water is a deep amber colour.
* Put the yeast, 100 ml/ 3½ fl oz (⅓ cup plus 1 tablespoon) warm water and the plain (all-purpose) flour into a large bowl and mix together to a thick, sticky paste. Leave to stand at room temperature for 1 hour, or until active.
* Put the strong white bread flour, the dark brown sugar and salt into another large bowl and set aside.
* Warm the milk in a large saucepan over a low heat until it is hand temperature or about 30°C/ 86°F, then remove from the heat and mix the now-active yeast mixture through the milk. Once it is all well incorporated, add the beaten egg, honey and the saffron and its soaking liquid to the pan and combine well.
* Tip the milk mixture into the centre of the dry ingredients and begin mixing by hand, starting from the centre of the bowl and working outwards until you have a sticky but well-formed mass. Leave to rest for 30 minutes, after which time the flour should be well hydrated and the shaggy mass should be easier to work.
* Tip the currants and any liquid onto the dough and knead in the bowl until extensible. If the dough feels tight and tears on kneading, add a little more milk. Transfer to an oiled bowl, cover with a damp dish towel and leave to rise in a warm place for 1 hour.
* Stretch and fold then rest the dough for another hour, then stretch and fold for a final time, but this time incorporating the olive oil. This may require some work in the bowl. Leave to rest for another hour. After 3 hours the dough should feel billowy and active.
* Line a large baking sheet with baking (parchment) paper. Turn the dough out onto an oiled work counter and divide it into 100 g/ 3½ oz pieces. Shape each piece by rocking the dough in the palm of your hand and using your thumb and little finger (pinky) to tuck the corners of the dough underneath itself until you have a uniform, rounded piece. Tuck any loose currants back under the dough. Put onto the prepared baking tray. Lightly oil the top of your pieces, then lay a sheet of clingfilm (plastic wrap) over the top to prevent them drying out. Leave to prove for 1–2 hours until tripled in size.
* Preheat the oven to 180°C/ 350°F/ Gas Mark 4, and bake the buns in the oven for 10–14 minutes until coloured.
* Meanwhile, for the glaze, put all the ingredients into a saucepan, add 50 ml/ 1¾ fl oz (3½ tablespoons) water and stir over a low heat for 2–3 minutes until the sugar dissolves. Brush the buns with the glaze while still warm.

WALES: CARMARTHENSHIRE
*

LLANDDAROG FAIR CAKES
TEISENNAU FFAIR LLANDDAROG

These rich little cakes were originally made for the Llandarog Fair in Carmarthenshire, where they were especially beloved at the turn of the twentieth century. Traditionally they were baked in an old-fashioned Dutch oven – a covered tray that would sit on the hearth beside the glowing embers, baking the cakes through indirect heat.

Makes: 6
Prep time: 20 minutes
Cook time: 15 minutes
{❂} {⌁}

- 350 g/ 12 oz (3 cups minus 2 teaspoons) self-raising flour, plus extra for dusting
- 225 g/ 8 oz (2 sticks) unsalted butter
- 175 g/ 6 oz (¾ cup plus 1 tablespoon) caster (superfine) sugar, plus extra for dusting
- 100 g/ 3½ oz (⅓ cup plus 1 tablespoon) currants
- 3 tablespoons beer

* Preheat the oven to 190°C/ 375°F/ Gas Mark 5.
* Put the flour into a bowl, add the butter and rub it in with your fingertips until the mixture resembles breadcrumbs. Add the sugar and currants, then add the beer and mix to form a soft dough.
* Roll out the dough on a floured chopping (cutting) board to about 1 cm/ ½ inch thick, then, using a 5 cm/ 2 inch round pastry cutter, cut out 6 circles.
* Arrange the circles on a large nonstick baking sheet and bake in the oven for 15 minutes. Remove from the oven and dust with sugar.

Cornish saffron buns

ENGLAND: LANCASHIRE
*

CHORLEY CAKES

In Lancashire, there are only 20 miles between the towns of Chorley and Eccles, but there's considerably less distance between their two eponymous 'cakes'. Besides a difference in pastry (Eccles Cakes, page 298, call for rough puff), and a simpler, lighter filling, they are almost one and the same. Some bakers will encourage you to butter your Chorley cakes, and, as strange as that sounds, it couldn't hurt to try.

Makes: 6
Prep time: 20 minutes, plus 35 minutes resting and chilling
Cook time: 20 minutes
{⟋}

- ½ quantity Sweet Shortcrust Pastry made with white flour (page 247)
- plain (all-purpose) flour, for dusting
- 150 g/5 oz (⅔ cup) currants
- 6 teaspoons caster (superfine) sugar, plus extra for sprinkling
- full-fat (whole) milk, for brushing

* Make the pastry following the recipe on page 247 and leave to rest for 20 minutes before using.
* Line 1–2 large baking sheets with baking (parchment) paper.
* Divide the dough into 6 equal-sized balls and roll out on a lightly floured work counter into circles about 5 mm/¼ inch thick.
* Sprinkle the currants evenly between the circles and sprinkle a teaspoon of sugar over each one. Bring the outer edges of each dough circle up and over the filling, brushing the edges with milk to seal them together. Turn them over and, using a rolling pin, roll out the circles flat until the currants are almost poking through the dough. Using a sharp knife, make 2 small slashes in the top of each, brush the top with more milk and sprinkle with more sugar. Transfer the cakes to the baking sheets and leave to chill in the fridge for 15 minutes to firm up.
* Preheat the oven to 180°C/350°F/Gas Mark 4. Bake the cakes in the oven for 20 minutes, or until golden brown.

ENGLAND: OXFORDSHIRE
*

BANBURY CAKES

These thin puff-pastry cakes resemble an elongated Eccles Cake (page 298), although there's plenty of evidence to show that the Banbury cake is in fact older, stretching back as far as medieval fairs. Its filling is made of a sweetened mix of dried fruit (currants especially) and spices and can be adapted to taste.

Makes: 12
Prep time: 50 minutes, plus 50 minutes resting and chilling
Cook time: 25 minutes
{◉}{⟋}

- 1 quantity Rough Puff Pastry (page 247)
- plain (all-purpose) flour, for dusting
- 60 g/2¼ oz (½ stick) unsalted butter
- 300 g/11 oz (1¾ cups) mixed dried fruit, such as currants, raisins and sultanas (golden raisins)
- 60 g/2¼ oz (⅓ cup) candied mixed peel
- ½ teaspoon ground nutmeg
- 90 g/3¼ oz (½ cup minus 4 teaspoons) soft dark brown sugar
- 2 tablespoons rum
- ½ teaspoon rose water
- 1 egg, beaten with 1 tablespoon water or milk and a pinch of salt, for egg wash
- demerara (turbinado) or granulated sugar, for sprinkling

* Make the pastry following the recipe on page 247 and leave to rest for 30 minutes before using.
* Line a large baking sheet with baking (parchment) paper.
* Roll out the pastry on a lightly floured work counter into a large oblong shape, leaving it still quite thick. Leave to rest for a few minutes.
* Meanwhile, for the filling, melt the butter in a small saucepan over a low-medium heat for 2 minutes, or until warm, then remove from the heat and set aside. Put the dried fruit, candied mixed peel, nutmeg, dark brown sugar, the melted butter, rum and rose water into a large bowl and mix together.
* Cut the pastry oblong into 12 squares (they don't have to be precise) and divide the filling evenly between each one, spooning it in a line down the centre of each square. Roll the filling up like a sausage roll, using egg wash to seal each one, then seal the ends by pressing together and tucking underneath. Roll out gently to form lozenge shapes. Using a sharp knife, make 2 diagonal slashes on the top of each, then brush with egg wash and sprinkle with demerara (turbinado) or granulated sugar. Transfer the cakes to the prepared baking sheet and leave to chill in the fridge for 20 minutes to firm up.
* Preheat the oven to 220°C/425°F/Gas Mark 7.
* Bake in the oven for 20–25 minutes until puffed up and golden brown, reducing the oven temperature to 180°C/350°F/Gas Mark 4 if they begin to look too dark in colour. Remove from the oven and leave to cool on a wire rack. Eat warm.

Chorley cakes

ENGLAND: LANCASHIRE
*

ECCLES CAKES

An Eccles cake is a flaky butter pastry filled with a sweetly spiced currant mixture, easily recognizable by the three narrow steam holes through which its caramelized filling invariably seeps. The crispy caramelized edges that form are something you should welcome if not seek out especially. In her 1978 classic, *British Cooking*, English food writer Caroline Conran notes that the original eighteenth century recipes called for fresh blackcurrant and mint leaves, showing a clear parallel to Yorkshire's Mint Pasty (page 380). In the last few decades, legendary London restaurant St. JOHN has created a craze over the Eccles cake, which they bake in-house and serve with a wedge of soft, crumbly Lancashire cheese. This particular recipe comes from Andrew Lowkes, of Landrace Bakery in Bath, who makes some of the best Eccles cakes in Britain.

Makes: about 8
Prep time: 1 hour, plus 7–8 hours soaking, chilling and resting
Cook time: 20 minutes
{ }{ }

- For the filling:
- 400 g/14 oz (1¾ cups) currants
- 30 ml/1 fl oz (2 tablespoons) spiced liquor
- 80 g/3 oz (¾ stick) unsalted butter
- 140 g/5 oz (⅔ cup minus 2 teaspoons) soft dark brown sugar
- ½ teaspoon ground mace
- ½ teaspoon ground cinnamon
- ½ teaspoon ground nutmeg

- For the puff pastry:
- 485 g/17 oz (4 cups) strong white bread flour
- 75 g/2¾ oz (¾ stick) unsalted butter, melted
- 12 g/¼ oz (2 teaspoons) salt
- 12 g/¼ oz (2½ teaspoons) caster (superfine) sugar
- 250 g/9 oz (2¼ sticks) salted butter block, beaten into a square, about 5 mm/¼ inch thick
- 1 egg, beaten with 1 tablespoon water or milk, for egg wash
- demerara (turbinado) sugar, for sprinkling

* For the filling, put the currants and liquor into a medium bowl and leave to soak for 1 hour. Melt the butter in a small saucepan over a low-medium heat for 2 minutes, or until melted, then remove from the heat and set aside. Once the currants begin to pucker, put into a large bowl with all the other filling ingredients and mix until combined. Cover with clingfilm (plastic wrap) and leave to chill in the fridge for at least 3 hours, or until well chilled. This mix will improve with age and can be stored refrigerated for up to 3 months, but can be used immediately once cold. Shape into about 8 x 65 g/ 2¼ oz discs and store in the fridge.
* For the puff pastry, put all the ingredients, except the block of butter, into a large bowl, add 240 ml/8 fl oz (1 cup minus 2 teaspoons) cold water and mix together into a dough. Don't worry about kneading. Your pastry will get a sufficient workout in the lamination. Chill in the fridge for 1–2 hours until firm.

* Form the chilled dough into a rectangle that is double the size of the butter square you have bashed into shape. Put the butter square into the centre of the dough rectangle and fold the dough's sides over the top of the butter to enclose it. You should have a square parcel with a butter centre. You want to begin laminating right at the point that the dough and butter are of a similar texture (forget their temperature). If either is too soft/hard, then refrigerate separately or leave out at room temperature until you have a happy equilibrium.
* Working evenly and methodically, use a rolling pin to bash out the butter-dough package into a long strip, keeping the corners at 90 degrees. Fold one end into the middle of the strip and do the same with the other end. This is a book fold. Turn the folded block 90 degrees and repeat. Wrap the dough in clingfilm (plastic wrap) and leave to rest in a cool place (not the fridge) for at least 30 minutes.
* After 30 minutes you should be able to lengthen the block one more time into that same long, rectangular strip, but this time, fold the dough over itself into thirds. This is a single fold.
* Preheat the oven to 220°C/425°F/Gas Mark 7. Line a large baking sheet with baking (parchment) paper and set aside. Roll the well-rested dough to the thickness of 6 mm/¼ inch, then leave to rest on a chilled chopping (cutting) board for at least 15 minutes.
* Using a 10 cm/4 inch cookie cutter, cut about 8 circles out of the rested dough, then put the chilled discs of filling into the centre of the circles. Wrap the pastry over the sides and into the middle of each disc of filling. Arrange the Eccles cakes, seam-side down, on the prepared baking sheet, then brush with egg wash and sprinkle with sugar.
* Using a sharp knife, score the tops 3 times. Bake in the oven for 15 minutes, or until the pastry has puffed up. Reduce the oven temperature to 200°C/400°F/Gas Mark 6 and bake for another 5 minutes, or until coloured to a deep, golden brown and a molten Eccles-rum-spiced caramel is bubbling from the slashes and spilling over. If the sugar on the top starts to caramelize, reduce the oven temperature by 20 degrees. Remove from the oven.

Eccles cakes

WALES / SCOTLAND
*

BARA BRITH
KERRIE LOAF

This is the ubiquitous Welsh fruit loaf made with tea-steeped fruit that 'speckles' the loaf. (The Welsh translation is literally 'speckled bread'.) Earlier recipes use yeast as the raising agent but self-raising flour has become commonplace in almost all modern recipes.

Delightfully easy in its preparation, the bara brith is a moist and spongy loaf that's lightly spiced and coloured by the black tea. There's no butter used in a bara brith, so you will want to apply that slice-by-slice once it's baked. A slice of bara brith, however excellent, is immeasurably lifted by good salted butter. Quite similar to Yorkshire Brack (page 302), and Irish Barmbrack (see right), Welsh food writer Bobby Freeman also relates bara brith to the Scottish 'kerrie loaf'.

Serves: 8
Prep time: 20 minutes, plus 8–12 hours soaking
Cook time: 1½ hours
{♥} {♠} {♣}

- 450 g / 1 lb (3 cups) dried fruit, such as currants, raisins, sultanas (golden raisins)
- 200 ml / 7 fl oz (¾ cup plus 1 tablespoon) strong black tea, hot
- 450 g / 1 lb (3¾ cups) self-raising flour
- 150 g / 5 oz (¾ cup) caster (superfine) sugar
- pinch of salt
- 2 tablespoons marmalade
- 2 eggs, beaten
- 1 teaspoon mixed spice
- 1 teaspoon bicarbonate of soda (baking soda)
- 1 tablespoon honey

* Put the dried fruit into a large bowl, pour in the tea and leave to soak overnight.
* The next day, preheat the oven to 160°C / 325°F / Gas Mark 3. Line the sides and bottom of a 900 g / 2 lb loaf pan with baking (parchment) paper.
* Sift the flour into a large bowl and add all the remaining ingredients, except the honey. Stir well, then add the steeped fruit and tea and mix well using a wooden spoon to disperse the dried fruit evenly throughout the mixture. Pour the batter into the prepared loaf pan and bake in the oven for 1½ hours, although check after 1 hour. To test if it is ready, insert a skewer into the centre of the cake and if it comes out clean it is done.
* Heat the honey and ½ tablespoon water together in a small saucepan over a low heat for 2 minutes, or until warm. When it's done, turn the loaf out of the pan and leave to cool on a wire rack. While it is still warm, brush the top with the warmed honey.

NORTHERN IRELAND
*

BARMBRACK

An Irish fruit bread made with tea-steeped fruit, the barmbrack is nearly identical to Bara Brith (see left). Barmbrack even has the same meaning – 'speckled bread'. The brack, however, often has a few additional ingredients, such as glacé (candied) cherries, a handful of almonds or even a little whiskey. The brack is made in a cake pan, and often made around Halloween time – when a ring would be baked into the bread, giving luck to its finder.

While it's typically baked as a circle, brack is still served in slices (not wedges) with a generous slathering of salted butter.

Serves: 8
Prep time: 20 minutes, plus 8–12 hours soaking
Cook time: 1½ hours
{♥}

- 450 g / 1 lb (3 cups) dried fruit, such as currants, raisins, sultanas (golden raisins)
- 300 ml / 10 fl oz (1¼ cups) strong tea, hot
- 225 g / 8 oz (2 cups minus 1 tablespoon) self-raising flour
- 150 g / 5 oz (⅔ cup) soft light brown sugar
- ½ teaspoon salt
- 1 teaspoon mixed spice
- 2 eggs, beaten
- 60 ml / 2 fl oz (¼ cup) whiskey (optional)
- 30 g / 1 oz (¼ cup minus 1 tablespoon) mixed candied peel
- 30 g / 1 oz (¼ cup minus 2 tablespoons) glacé (candied) cherries, chopped
- 30 g / 1 oz (¼ cup) blanched almonds, chopped (optional)
- 1 tablespoon golden syrup (optional)
- salted butter, to serve

* Put the dried fruit into a large bowl, pour in the tea and leave to soak overnight.
* The next day, preheat the oven to 160°C / 325°F / Gas Mark 3. Line the sides and bottom of a 20 cm / 8 inch round cake pan with baking (parchment) paper.
* Sift the flour into a large bowl, add the sugar, salt, spice, eggs, and whiskey (if using) and mix well. Add the steeped dried fruit together with most of the tea, the candied peel, cherries and almonds (if using), and mix to form a smooth batter. Pour the batter into the prepared cake pan and bake in the oven for 1½ hours, although check after 1 hour. To test if it is ready, insert a skewer into the centre of the cake and if it comes out clean it is done.
* Heat the golden syrup and ½ tablespoon water (if using) together in a small saucepan over a low heat for 2 minutes, or until warm. When it's done, remove the cake from the pan and leave to cool on a wire rack. While it is still warm, brush the top with the warmed syrup, then leave to cool before slicing and serving with salted butter.

Bara brith

ENGLAND

*

TEACAKES
(SWEET ROLLS FOR TOASTING)

These are large flat and lightly sweet yeasted rolls, speckled with dried fruit and glossed with a milk and sugar glaze. They should be sliced, toasted and buttered – to be served with a mug of tea, of course. This recipe comes from Oxford-based baker Kate Hamblin, a teacake aficionado. Like the Hot Cross Bun (page 288), teacakes make for an exquisite Bread and Butter Pudding (page 360).

Makes: 12
Prep time: 45 minutes, plus 11¼–15¼ hours soaking, resting, chilling and proving
Cook time: 12 minutes
{👅}{🌶}

- 80 g/3 oz (⅓ cup) currants
- 80 g/3 oz (½ cup) raisins
- hot, strong English breakfast tea
- ½ cinnamon stick
- ½ nutmeg
- 640 g/1 lb 7 oz strong white bread flour, plus extra for dusting
- 12 g/¼ oz (about 2 teaspoons) salt
- 65 g/2⅓ oz (⅓ cup) caster (superfine) sugar
- 60 g/2¼ oz (½ stick) unsalted butter
- 320 ml/11 fl oz (1¼ cups plus 4 teaspoons) full-fat (whole) milk
- 7 g/¼ oz (2¼ teaspoons) instant dried yeast
- 50 g/2 oz (¼ cup) candied mixed peel
- 3 tablespoons caster (superfine) sugar or honey, for the syrup
- butter, to serve

* Put the dried fruit into a large bowl, pour in enough tea to cover. Cover with clingfilm (plastic wrap) and leave to soak overnight.
* The next day, put the spices into a spice grinder or pestle and mortar and grind finely, then put them into the bowl of a stand mixer fitted with a dough hook attachment. Add the flour, salt and the 65 g/2⅓ oz (⅓ cup) sugar and mix together until combined. Set aside.
* Melt the butter in a small saucepan over a medium-low heat, then remove from the heat and leave to cool. Pour the milk into another small saucepan and heat over a medium heat for 2 minutes, or until lukewarm. Pour the milk into a medium bowl, add the yeast and leave for 10 minutes.
* Pour the milk mixture over the dry ingredients and mix them through on low speed. Add the cooled, melted butter and continue to mix until a dough forms. Leave to rest, covered with clingfilm (plastic wrap) for 15 minutes.
* Strain the fruit, then knead it into the dough together with the candied mixed peel. Mix for another minute until smooth, then cover and leave to rest at room temperature for 1 hour. Chill the dough in the fridge for 2 hours.
* Line a large baking sheet with baking (parchment) paper. Turn the dough out onto a work counter, lightly flour it, then divide it into 12 balls, about 105–110 g/3½–3¾ oz each. Put the balls onto the prepared baking sheet, cover with a dish towel and leave to prove in a warm place for 1 hour, or until puffy and doubled in size.
* Preheat the oven to 220°C/425°F/Gas Mark 7.

* Bake the teacakes on a rack high in the oven for 12 minutes until golden brown.
* Meanwhile, make a simple syrup by putting the 3 tablespoons sugar or honey into a small saucepan, adding 3 tablespoons water and heating over a low heat for 2–3 minutes, stirring until it is thoroughly mixed.
* Once the teacakes are done, brush them with the syrup, then eat while still warm, split and buttered.

ENGLAND: YORKSHIRE

*

YORKSHIRE TEA LOAF
YORKSHIRE BRACK

While Yorkshire brack is made with dried fruit steeped in tea, the 'tea loaf' designation comes from what you serve it with, rather than what's in it! Brack is baked in a circle and is very nearly identical to Bara Brith and Barmbrack (page 300). It should be served in hefty thick slices and spread with salted butter and a few slices of Wensleydale cheese.

Serves: 8
Prep time: 20 minutes, plus 8–12 hours soaking
Cook time: 1½ hours
{👅}{🍴}{🌶}

- 400 g/14 oz (2⅔ cups) mixed dried fruit, such as currants, raisins, sultanas (golden raisins)
- 250 ml/8 fl oz (1 cup) strong tea, hot
- 125 g/4¼ oz (½ cup) soft dark brown sugar
- 275 g/9¾ oz (2¼ cups plus 1 teaspoon) self-raising flour
- 2 eggs, beaten
- salted butter and Wensleydale cheese, to serve

* Put the dried fruit into a large bowl and pour in the hot tea. Cover with clingfilm (plastic wrap) and leave to soak in the fridge overnight.
* The next day, preheat the oven to 160°C/325°F/Gas Mark 3. Line the sides and bottom of a 20 cm/8 inch round cake pan with baking (parchment) paper.
* Put the remaining ingredients into a large bowl and mix well using a wooden spoon until smooth. Add the dried fruit along with the tea it has steeped in and mix well to disperse the fruit.
* Pour the batter into the prepared cake pan and bake in the oven for 1½ hours until golden brown, checking on it after 1 hour. To test if the cake is ready, insert a skewer into the centre and if it comes out clean it is cooked. Leave to cool in the pan for 10 minutes before turning out onto a wire rack to cool completely.

Teacakes

SOUTH OF ENGLAND
*

LARDY CAKE

Lardy cake is a speciality of several southern English counties. It's an indulgent pastry made from bread dough that's enriched with lard, sugar and dried fruit. As it bakes, the outside of the lardy cake starts to crisp and caramelize, but the middle stays gooey, buttery and sweet.

Serves: 6–8
Prep time: 30 minutes, plus 2 hours rising and proving
Cook time: 50–60 minutes
{ᴗ}

- For the dough:
- 300 g/11 oz (2½ cups) strong white bread flour, plus extra for dusting
- 50 g/2 oz (3½ tablespoons) salted butter or lard at room temperature, diced
- 30 g/1 oz (2½ tablespoons) caster (superfine) sugar
- pinch of salt
- 14 g/½ oz (1 tablespoon) fresh yeast or 7 g/¼ oz (2¼ teaspoons) instant dried yeast
- 180 ml/6 fl oz (¾ cup) fat-free milk at room temperature or a little warmer, about 24°C/75°F
- vegetable oil, for oiling
- butter or jam of choice, to serve (optional)

- For the filling:
- 150 g/5 oz (1¼ sticks) salted butter or lard at room temperature, diced, plus extra for greasing
- 75 g/2¾ oz (⅓ cup) demerara (turbinado) sugar, plus extra for lining the pan
- 75 g/2¾ oz (⅓ cup plus 2 teaspoons) caster (superfine) sugar
- 210 g/7 oz (1⅓ cups plus 2 teaspoons) sultanas (golden raisins) or mixed dried fruits of your choice, such as currants and raisins

* For the dough, sift the flour into a large bowl, add the butter or lard and rub it in well with your fingertips until it disappears. Mix in the sugar, salt and yeast, then add the milk and work into a soft dough. Alternatively, use a stand mixer fitted with a dough hook attachment and mix on medium speed for 5 minutes, or until the dough is smooth and elastic. If mixing by hand, turn the dough out onto a lightly floured work counter and knead for 10 minutes, or until the dough is smooth and elastic. Put the dough into an oiled bowl, cover with clingfilm (plastic wrap) and leave in a warm place to rise for 1 hour, or until doubled in size.
* Meanwhile, prepare the filling and pan for laminating and baking. Divide the butter or lard between 3 small bowls, 50 g/2 oz (3½ tablespoons) in each, then add a third of the sugars, 50 g/2 oz (4 tablespoons), and a third of the dried fruits, 70 g/2½ oz (½ cup minus 1 teaspoon), and gently mix to combine.
* Line a 20 cm/8 inch round loose-bottom or springform cake pan with baking (parchment) paper, then grease the paper with butter or lard and dust the inside with a generous sprinkle of demerara (turbinado) sugar. This will create a beautifully caramelized crust. It is also a good idea to wrap the outside bottom of the pan with aluminium foil in case any caramel escapes.

* Roll out the risen dough on a lightly floured work counter into a rectangle about 1 cm/½ inch thick and sprinkle one of the prepared bowls of fat, sugar and fruit mix across the surface of the dough. Fold the dough into thirds by bringing the short edge of the rectangle up and over to cover a third of the dough, then take the other end and fold it up to cover that. The dough block should now be one-third the size you rolled it out to. Turn the dough by a quarter and roll out again to the same size.
* Repeat the process with the second bowl of filling, then do so a third time with the final bowl of filling. Once you have folded up the dough for the final time, roughly shape the block to fit into the prepared cake pan and gently put inside the pan. Cover and leave to prove in a warm place for 1 hour.
* Preheat the oven to 180°C/350°F/Gas Mark 4.
* Bake the cake in the oven for 50–60 minutes until a deep golden brown. Leave to cool in the pan until it is cool enough to handle to stop the outside going soggy and to keep that crisp crust, then remove from the pan and cool on a wire rack. Enjoy slightly warm, with extra butter or jam if you are feeling decadent. This makes a great afternoon treat or a good British breakfast alternative to a croissant. Best eaten the day it is baked but good gently reheated for a few days after.
* **Variations:** For extra flavour, add mixed spices or grated orange or lemon zest or even candied mixed peel to the fruit mix.

ENGLAND: LINCOLNSHIRE
*

LINCOLNSHIRE PLUM BREAD

The main difference between a Lincolnshire plum bread and other 'speckled' fruit loafs is its inclusion of lard in the batter, making it far richer and heavier than its peers. Plum bread is best served with salted butter and slices of Lincolnshire Poacher cheese.

Serves: 8
Prep time: 20 minutes
Cook time: 40 minutes
{ᴗ}

- 250 g/9 oz (2 cups) self-raising flour
- 90 g/3¼ oz (½ cup) lard or half unsalted butter/half lard
- 100 g/3½ oz (½ cup) caster (superfine) sugar
- 100 g/3½ oz (½ cup) mixed dried fruit, such as sultanas (golden raisins), raisins and currants
- 30 g/1 oz (¼ cup minus 2 teaspoons) mixed candied peel
- 1 tablespoon golden syrup
- 60 ml/2 fl oz (¼ cup) full-fat (whole) milk
- 1 egg, beaten
- salted butter and Lincolnshire Poacher cheese, to serve

* Preheat the oven to 150°C/300°F/Gas Mark 2. Line a 500 g/1 lb 2 oz loaf pan with baking (parchment) paper.
* Sift the flour into a large bowl, add the fat and rub it in with your fingertips until it resembles breadcrumbs. Stir in the sugar, dried fruit and mixed candied peel. Put the golden syrup and milk into a small saucepan and stir together over a medium heat for 2 minutes, or until well combined.

* Make a well in the centre of the flour mixture, then add the egg, followed by the milk and syrup mixture and mix into a smooth batter using a wooden spoon. Spoon the batter into the prepared loaf pan and bake in the oven for 30–40 minutes until golden brown. Leave to cool slightly on a wire rack, then turn out and serve in slices with butter and cheese.

SCOTLAND
*

MALT LOAF

Moist and sticky, with a distinctive soft chew, these dark malt loaves pair well with salted butter for an excellent teatime treat. If you have the time, wrap them well in baking (parchment) paper and store in a cool, dark place for a few days before serving.

Makes: 2 loaves
Prep time: 15 minutes
Cook time: 1–1½ hours
{ë}{⌀}

- 225 g/8 oz (⅔ cup) malt extract
- 100 g/3½ oz (¼ cup) black treacle (blackstrap molasses)
- 125 ml/4¼ fl oz (½ cup) black tea, hot
- 300 g/11 oz (2½ cups) wholemeal (whole wheat) flour
- 2 teaspoons baking powder
- ¼ teaspoon mixed spice
- 125 g/4¼ oz (¾ cup plus 2 teaspoons) raisins
- 125 g/4¼ oz (¾ cup plus 2 teaspoons) sultanas (golden raisins)
- 2 eggs, beaten
- butter, to serve

* Preheat the oven to 130°C/250°F/Gas Mark ½. Line 2 x 900 g/2 lb loaf pans with baking (parchment) paper.
* Put the malt extract, treacle (blackstrap molasses) and tea into a large bowl, mix together and leave to cool.
* Sift the flour into another large bowl and add the remaining dry ingredients. Stir through, then add the eggs. Once the eggs have been incorporated, tip in the syrupy tea mixture and mix until well combined.
* Pour the batter into the prepared loaf pans and bake for 1–1½ hours until a skewer inserted into the centre comes out clean. Leave to cool in the pans, then wrap in baking (parchment) paper and store in an airtight tin for 4 days before slicing and eating with butter. The loaves will keep for 2–3 weeks.

ISLE OF MAN
*

MANX BONNAG

The Manx word 'bonnag' is linguistically related to the Scottish 'Bannock' (page 248). Both Celtic-rooted words refer very generally to breads, typically those made on a griddle. The earliest Manx bonnags were very likely made with oats or barley, but modern-day loaves are made almost exclusively with white flour. The bonnag slices and toasts like a rustic bread loaf and should be served well-buttered.

Serves: at least 6
Prep time: 15 minutes
Cook time: 45–55 minutes
{ë}{⌀}

- 300 g/11 oz (2½ cups) plain (all-purpose) flour, plus extra for dusting
- 1 teaspoon bicarbonate of soda (baking soda)
- 80 g/3 oz (¾ stick) unsalted butter, diced
- 80 g/3 oz (½ cup minus 4 teaspoons) caster (superfine) sugar
- 160 g/5¾ oz (1 cup plus 2 teaspoons) raisins or sultanas (golden raisins), optional
- 2 eggs
- 180 ml/6 fl oz (¾ cup) buttermilk

* Preheat the oven to 180°C/350°F/Gas Mark 4. Flour a large baking sheet and set aside.
* Put the flour and bicarbonate of soda (baking soda) into a large bowl, add the butter and rub it in with your fingertips. Mix in the sugar and dried fruit (if using).
* Whisk the eggs and buttermilk together in another bowl, then tip them into the flour mixture, stirring well to incorporate and form a dough.
* Tip the dough onto a lightly floured work counter and knead it briefly before forming into a circle. Cut a cross on the top of the circle and put it onto the prepared baking sheet. Bake in the oven for 45–55 minutes until golden brown.

ENGLAND: YORKSHIRE
*

ROCK CAKES

Rock cakes are named for their crispy, craggy appearance and are an easy teatime bake. Eat while still warm, or if cool, dunk into tea.

Makes: 20–24
Prep time: 20–30 minutes, plus 10–20 minutes chilling
Cook time: 20 minutes
{ë}

- 150 g/5 oz (1¼ cups) self-raising flour
- 150 g/5 oz (1¼ cups) plain flour
- 1 teaspoon baking powder
- ¼ teaspoon fine sea salt
- 125 g/4¼ oz (9 tablespoons) cold unsalted butter, cubed
- 120 g/4 oz (½ cup) currants or mixed dried fruit
- 1 egg, lightly beaten
- 4–5 tablespoons full-fat (whole) milk
- 100 ml/3½ fl oz (⅓ cup plus 1 tablespoon) sour cream

* Preheat the oven to 180°C/350°F/Gas Mark 4. Line a large baking sheet with baking (parchment) paper.
* Put the flours, baking powder and salt into a bowl and mix together. Add the butter and rub it in with your fingertips until the mixture resembles breadcrumbs. Add the currants and toss through the mixture to coat. Make a well in the centre, add the egg, milk and sour cream and use a fork to bring the mixture together to form a dough.
* Scoop 20–24 golf-ball-sized mounds onto the prepared baking sheet and bake for 15 minutes, rotating the baking sheet halfway through.

SCOTLAND / ENGLAND: CORNWALL AND DEVON
*

DEVONSHIRE SPLITS
CORNISH SPLITS/
CHUDLEIGH BUNS/COOKIES

These sweet and lightly enriched bread rolls are a fixture of afternoon cream tea in Cornwall and Devon, where they are often served in place of scones. Splits are served once they have cooled from the oven, split in half (as the name suggests) and spread with a generous amount of Clotted Cream (page 34) and good jam. Occasionally the clotted cream is topped with a drizzle of honey, golden syrup, or black treacle (blackstrap molasses), a traditional combination called 'thunder and lightning'.

Cornish splits and Devonshire chudleighs are almost identical, although the latter tend to be smaller. The main difference is that the Cornish apply their jam before the clotted cream, and Devonians the opposite. Scottish food writer Catherine Brown also notes that a similar treat is traditional to Scotland, where it is known as a 'cookie'.

Makes: 8
Prep time: 1 hour, plus 10–14 hours rising and proving
Cook time: 15–20 minutes
{👤}{🌱}

- For the buns:
- 90 ml/3¼ fl oz (6 tablespoons) full-fat (whole) milk
- 7 g/¼ oz (2¼ teaspoons) instant dried yeast
- 3 large eggs
- 185 g/6 oz (1½ cups) soft wheat flour or plain
  (all-purpose) flour (low-protein flour)
- 185 g/6 oz (1½ cups) strong white bread flour
  (high-protein flour)
- 15 g/½ oz (1 tablespoon) caster (superfine) sugar
- 5 g/⅛ oz (1 teaspoon) fine sea salt
- 150 g/5 oz (1¼ sticks) unsalted butter,
  cool and pliable, cut into thin slices
- vegetable oil, for oiling

- For the filling:
- 600 ml/20 fl oz (2½ cups) double (heavy) cream to whip
  or Clotted Cream (page 34)
- 1 x 370 g/13 oz jar jam of your choice
- icing (confectioners') sugar, for dusting

For the thunder and lightning variation:
- 200–300 ml/7–11 fl oz (¾ cup plus 1 tablespoon–
  1¼ cups) Clotted Cream (page 34)
black treacle (blackstrap molasses), as much as you fancy

* For the buns, bring the milk in a small saucepan just to the boil, then remove from the heat and leave to cool to room temperature. There should be at least 75 ml/ 2½ fl oz (⅓ cup) milk left, allowing for any evaporation, so make any shortfall up with water.
* Once the milk is at a cool room temperature or lukewarm to the touch, pour it into a stand mixer fitted with a dough hook attachment. Add the yeast and stir to encourage the yeast to dissolve. Add the eggs.
* Put the flours, caster (superfine) sugar and salt into a separate bowl and briefly mix together just to evenly distribute the ingredients. Add to the bowl with the milk and egg mixture and mix on low speed for 10 minutes, until the dough comes away from the sides.

* Once the dough is coming away from the sides of the bowl, begin to add the slices of butter, 2 pieces at a time while mixing on slow speed. Mix to incorporate almost completely before adding more butter, scraping down the sides of the bowl with a spatula during the process.
* Once the butter is incorporated, increase the speed to medium-high and mix for 4 minutes, or until all the ingredients are well incorporated. The dough should be soft, smoother in appearance and with no visible streaks of butter.
* Put the dough into a large lightly oiled container with a lid or use a bowl and cover with clingfilm (plastic wrap), then leave to rise in the fridge overnight.
* The next day, line a large baking sheet with baking (parchment) paper. Divide the risen dough into 8 equal portions, each weighing about 85 g/3 oz. Flatten each portion, then gather the edges of the dough, pinching them back into the centre. Flip the dough over and, using the palm of your hand, cup the dough and rotate in a small circular motion, applying pressure to make a neat ball.
* Arrange the balls on the prepared baking sheet, setting them about 2–3 cm/¾–1¼ inches apart, then cover with clingfilm (plastic wrap) or a clean dish towel and leave to prove in a warm place for 2 hours, or until doubled in size. They should look puffed and fluffy and when very gently pressed it should leave an indentation that does not spring back.
* About 20 minutes before the buns have finished proving, preheat the oven to 180°C/350°F/Gas Mark 4.
* Bake the buns for 15–20 minutes until they are lightly golden in colour. Remove from the oven and leave the buns to cool.
* Meanwhile, for the filling, put the double (heavy) cream (if using) into a large bowl and, using electric beaters, whip just to form soft peaks. Stop whipping just before you think it is ready, as it will continue to thicken as you spoon it onto the buns. Alternatively, whip the cream in a stand mixer fitted with a whisk attachment.
* Slice the buns in half, fill with the whipped cream or clotted cream, then add the jam – or treacle (blackstrap molasses) for the thunder and lightning variation. Dust the top of the buns with a little icing (confectioners') sugar before serving.

Devonshire splits

SCOTLAND / ENGLAND: CORNWALL AND DEVON
*

SCONES

In Scotland, the word 'scone' has long been used to refer to flat cakes baked on a hot girdle. In some rural or remote areas, you can still find bakeries and supermarkets selling Girdle Scones (page 256), which, with their distinctive soft browned tops, resemble the Irish Soda farl.

The modern oven-baked scone, crumbly and lightly sweet, originated in Scotland in the nineteenth century and spread far and wide with the advent of the tearoom. Scones are now synonymous with teatime and home baking in all parts of the United Kingdom, and there are many popular sweet and savoury variations. Common additions include cheese, golden syrup, or Clotted Cream (page 34).

Scones are best when served warm, spread with jam and butter or jam and more clotted cream. Such is the intense regionalism over scones, that teasing debates often surface over what spreads to use and in what order.

Makes: 12
Prep time: 20 minutes
Cook time: 15 minutes
{🌀}{🍴}

- 430 g/ 15 oz (3½ cups plus 2 teaspoons) self-raising flour, plus extra for dusting
- pinch of salt
- 70 g/ 2½ oz (⅓ cup plus 1 teaspoon) caster (superfine) sugar
- 1 teaspoon bicarbonate of soda (baking soda)
- 85 g/ 3 oz (¾ stick) very cold unsalted butter, grated
- small handful of sultanas (golden raisins)
- 175 ml/ 6 fl oz (¾ cup) buttermilk, or full-fat (whole) milk soured with a little vinegar or lemon juice
- 1 egg, beaten with a little milk to slacken, for egg wash

* Preheat the oven to 200°C/400°F/Gas Mark 6.
* Sift the flour, salt, sugar and bicarbonate of soda (baking soda) into a large bowl. Add the butter and rub it in with your fingertips until the mixture resembles breadcrumbs. Add the sultanas (golden raisins) at this stage for fruit scones or leave out if you prefer plain ones. Add 150 ml/5 fl oz (⅔ cup) of the buttermilk and mix to form a coarse shaggy dough, adding a little more buttermilk if necessary. Take care not to overwork the dough, but shape it into a circle which sits about 5 cm/2 inches tall on a lightly floured work counter.
* Using a well-floured 6 cm /2.5 inch cutter (which must be as tall if not taller than the circle), cut out 12 individual round scones, taking care not to twist the cutter or pull down the edges, as this will inhibit the rise. If you do not have a cutter, cut triangular scones using a slicing motion with a very sharp knife. Do not apply too much downward pressure or use a sawing motion.
* Brush the top of the scones with the egg wash, but take care not to get any on the sides, as this can inhibit the rise. Transfer to a nonstick baking sheet and bake in the oven for 15 minutes, or until risen and cooked through. Do not open the oven door for at least 10 minutes during baking.

SCOTLAND: THE BORDERS
*

SELKIRK BANNOCKS

This rich yeasted fruit loaf was created by Scottish baker Robbie Douglas in the mid-1800s. The bannocks are made using an enriched bread dough, which is mixed through with sultanas (golden raisins) or raisins. Traditionally they underwent a slow overnight fermentation that helped to further develop the flavour, but most home recipes skip this step.

The Selkirk bannock remains popular to this day, especially along the Scottish Borders, where it is found in most bakeries and supermarkets. When serving, the bannock should be sliced and spread with butter. Left-over bannock will continue to toast well for days to come, and like many fruit loaves and buns, slightly-stale slices of Selkirk bannock make an excellent Bread and Butter Pudding (page 360).

Notes: The 'bannock' in this case refers simply to the round shape of the bread.

Serves: 8
Prep time: 30 minutes, plus 2 hours rising and proving
Cook time: 30–40 minutes
{🌀}{🍴}

- 100 g/ 3½ oz (7 tablespoons) unsalted butter
- 250 ml/ 8 fl oz (1 cup) full-fat (whole) milk or half milk, half water, plus extra milk for brushing
- 500 g/ 1 lb 2 oz (4 cups plus 4 teaspoons) plain (all-purpose) flour, plus extra for dusting
- 1 teaspoon salt
- 1 teaspoon instant dried yeast
- 60 g/ 2¼ oz (¼ cup) soft brown sugar
- vegetable oil, for oiling
- 350 g/ 12 oz (2⅓ cups) sultanas (golden raisins)

* Melt the butter in a small saucepan over a medium-low heat, then remove from the heat and leave to cool slightly. Heat the milk in a medium saucepan over a low heat for 2–3 minutes until warm. Remove from the heat and set aside.
* Sift the flour into a stand mixer fitted with a dough hook attachment and add the salt, yeast and sugar. Make a well in the centre, then add the melted, cooled butter and warm milk. Mix on medium speed for 5 minutes to form a smooth dough. Alternatively, put the ingredients into a large bowl, then mix into a dough and knead for 10 minutes, or until smooth. Shape the dough into a ball and put it into an oiled bowl. Cover with clingfilm (plastic wrap) and leave to rise in a warm place for 1½ hours, or until doubled in size.
* Flour a large baking sheet. Knead the risen dough gently to remove any air bubbles, then knead in the sultanas (golden raisins). Shape into a ball, flatten slightly and put it onto the prepared baking sheet. Cover with a plastic bag, a damp cloth or an inverted bowl and leave to prove for 30 minutes, or until doubled in size.
* Meanwhile, preheat the oven to 200°C/400°F/Gas Mark 6.
* Brush the bannock with extra milk and bake in the oven for 30–40 minutes until a deep golden brown. Reduce the oven temperature to 180°C/350°F/Gas Mark 4 if the top is browning too much. Remove from the oven and leave to cool on a wire rack before serving. This can be eaten warm or cold, and is great toasted.

Scones

ENGLAND: NORTH YORKSHIRE
*

WHITBY LEMON BUNS

A speciality of the North Yorkshire seaside town, Whitby buns are sweet and enriched, sometimes flecked with dried fruit, but always topped with a lemon icing (frosting). They have been baked since 1865 by Elizabeth Botham and Sons, a Whitby-based baker, and one of the very few to regularly produce them.

Makes: 12
Prep time: 30 minutes, plus 2 hours rising and proving
Cook time: 30 minutes
{☻}{✍}

- 250 ml/8 fl oz (1 cup) full-fat (whole) milk
- 500 g/1 lb 2 oz (4 cups plus 4 teaspoons) strong white bread flour, plus extra for dusting
- 5 g/2 teaspoons instant dried yeast
- 10 g/¼ oz (2 teaspoons) salt
- 60 g/2¼ oz (⅓ cup minus 1 teaspoon) caster (superfine) sugar
- 1 egg
- 50 g/2 oz (3½ tablespoons) unsalted butter, softened
- vegetable oil, for oiling
- 125 g/4¼ oz (½ cup) lemon curd

- For the icing (frosting):
- 100 g/3½ oz (¾ cup plus 2 teaspoons) icing (confectioners') sugar
- 2 tablespoons lemon juice

* Heat the milk in a medium saucepan over a low heat for 2–3 minutes, or until warm. Remove from the heat and set aside. Sift the flour into a large bowl and add the yeast, salt and caster (superfine) sugar. Mix together, then make a well in the centre. Beat the egg into the warmed milk, then pour it into the well and add the butter. If you have a stand mixer, use the dough hook attachment to knead for about 6 minutes, or until the dough is tacky, glossy, smooth and stretchy. Alternatively, mix together with your hands in the bowl, then knead by hand on a lightly floured work counter for 10 minutes.
* Form the dough into a ball, then put it into a large oiled bowl and cover with clingfilm (plastic wrap) or a damp dish towel. Leave to rise in a warm place for 1½ hours, or until doubled in size.
* Gently turn the risen dough out onto a lightly floured work counter and knead gently to knock the dough back to remove any air bubbles. Divide the dough into 12 equal pieces and roll out on a lightly floured chopping (cutting) board. Put a spoonful of lemon curd into the centre, then fold over the sides of the dough and shape into tight balls.
* Line a large baking sheet with baking (parchment) paper and arrange the buns on it, leaving about 2 cm/¾ inch space between each one. Cover with a large plastic bag or a tea towel and leave to prove in a warm place for 30 minutes, or until they have doubled in size.
* Remove the cover and put the buns into a cold oven. Heat the oven to 200°C/400°F/Gas Mark 6 and bake for 20–25 minutes until golden brown. Leave to cool on a wire rack.
* When nearly cool, put the icing (confectioners') sugar and lemon juice into a bowl and mix until combined. Once the buns are cool, dip each one into the icing (frosting) and smooth over the bun using a palette knife.

ENGLAND: BRISTOL
*

MOTHERING BUNS

These lightly sweet buns are iced (frosted) and then dipped one at a time into hundreds and thousands (small sprinkles), giving them their cheery coating. Traditional to Bristol, they have been baked for years as a special treat for Mothering Sunday (Mother's Day).

Makes: 12
Prep time: 30 minutes, plus 2 hours rising and proving
Cook time: 20–25 minutes
{☻}{✍}

- 250 ml/8 fl oz (1 cup) full-fat (whole) milk
- 500 g/1 lb 2 oz (4 cups plus 2 teaspoons) strong white bread flour, plus extra for dusting
- 5 g/2 teaspoons instant dried yeast
- 10 g/¼ oz (2 teaspoons) salt
- 60 g/2¼ oz (⅓ cup minus 1 teaspoon) caster (superfine) sugar
- 1 egg
- 50 g/2 oz (3½ tablespoons) unsalted butter, softened
- vegetable oil, for oiling

- To decorate:
- 100 g/3½ oz (¾ cup plus 2 teaspoons) icing (confectioners') sugar
- about 3 tablespoons hundreds and thousands (sprinkles)

* Heat the milk in a medium saucepan over a low heat for 2–3 minutes, or until warm. Remove from the heat and set aside. Sift the flour into a large bowl and add the yeast, salt and caster (superfine) sugar. Mix together, then make a well in the centre. Beat the egg into the warmed milk, then pour it into the well with the butter. If you have a stand mixer, use the dough hook attachment to knead for about 6 minutes, or until the dough is tacky, glossy, smooth and stretchy. Alternatively, mix together with your hands in the bowl, then knead by hand on a lightly floured work counter for 10 minutes.
* Form the dough into a ball, then put it into a large oiled bowl and cover with clingfilm (plastic wrap) or a damp dish towel. Leave to rise in a warm place for 1½ hours, or until doubled in size.
* Gently turn the risen dough out onto a lightly floured work counter and knead gently to knock the dough back to remove any air bubbles. Divide into 12 equal pieces and roll into tight balls on a floured chopping (cutting) board.
* Line a large baking sheet with baking (parchment) paper and arrange the buns on it, leaving about 2 cm/¾ inch space between each one. Cover with a large plastic bag or a dish towel and leave to prove for 30 minutes, or until they have doubled in size.
* Preheat the oven to 200°C/400°F/Gas Mark 6.
* Remove the cover and bake in the oven for 20–25 minutes until golden brown. Leave to cool on a wire rack.
* Put the icing (confectioners') sugar and 2 tablespoons water into a bowl and mix until combined. Put the hundreds and thousands (sprinkles) into another bowl. Once the buns are fully cooled, dip each one into the icing (frosting) and smooth it over the bun using a small palette knife. Dip each bun, icing-side down, into the hundreds and thousands (sprinkles) until coated.

WALES
*

WELSH OVERNIGHT CAKE
TEISEN DROS NOS

The batter for this light Welsh fruitcake needs overnight resting – and makes a convenient excuse for an early morning bake. Some Welsh families also used this cake base for their Simnel Cake (page 318) and, made with less milk, as a dough for spiced Welsh Cakes (page 263).

Serves: 8
Prep time: 15 minutes, plus 8–12 hours resting
Cook time: 1 hour
{👤} {🌶}

- 125 g/4¼ oz (9 tablespoons) unsalted butter, at room temperature, diced, plus extra for greasing
- 250 g/9 oz (2 cups) plain (all-purpose) flour
- 65 g/2¼ oz (⅓ cup) caster (superfine) sugar
- 60 g/2¼ oz (¼ cup plus 2 teaspoons) demerara (turbinado) sugar
- 125 g/4¼ oz (¾ cup plus 2 teaspoons) sultanas (golden raisins)
- 50 g/2 oz (¼ cup plus 1 teaspoon) candied mixed peel (optional)
- ½ teaspoon grated nutmeg
- ½ teaspoon ground ginger
- ½ teaspoon ground cinnamon
- 150 ml/5 fl oz (⅔ cup) full-fat (whole) milk
- ½ teaspoon bicarbonate of soda (baking soda)
- 1 tablespoon cider vinegar

* Line the base and sides of a 20 cm/8 inch round cake pan with baking (parchment) paper and grease with butter.
* Sift the flour into a large bowl. Add the butter and rub it in with your fingertips until the mixture resembles fine breadcrumbs. Mix in the sugars, sultanas (golden raisins), candied mixed peel (if using) and spices. Add the milk and mix to a soft batter.
* Put the bicarbonate of soda (baking soda) and vinegar into a glass bowl and mix together. Add this to the batter and mix well until it is incorporated. Spoon the batter into the prepared pan and smooth over the top using a palette knife. Cover the pan with a clean dish towel and leave to rest in a cool place overnight.
* The next day, preheat the oven to 150°C/300°F/Gas Mark 2. Bake the cake for 1 hour, or until it is golden brown and a skewer inserted into the centre of the cake comes out clean. Leave to cool completely in the pan. This is delicious the day it is baked, but also keeps well for up to 2 weeks wrapped in baking paper in an airtight container.
* **Variations:** This is an easy cake to vary by changing the kinds of dried fruits and spices used. You could also add grated orange or lemon zest, candied mixed peel and vanilla extract. The overnight method used here is a traditional one, which suited baking the cake in the residual heat of the farm's bread oven early in the morning. For a more modern approach without the need to rest the cake batter overnight, replace the plain (all-purpose) flour with self-raising flour, omit the vinegar and bicarbonate of soda (baking soda) entirely and add 1 beaten egg along with the milk. Follow the baking directions as in the main recipe.

WALES
*

MOIST CAKE
TEISEN LAP

Teisen lap is a light fruitcake, which in the late nineteenth century became a favourite of lunchboxes on account of its excellent keeping qualities. According to the Welsh food writer Bobby Freeman, this cake was especially popular with the miners and tin workers of the South Wales Valleys.

Serves: 6
Prep time: 15 minutes
Cook time: 50–55 minutes
{👤} {🌶}

- butter or lard, for greasing
- 220 g/7¾ oz (1¾ cups plus 2 teaspoons) self-raising flour, plus extra for dusting
- ½ teaspoon salt
- ½ teaspoon ground nutmeg
- 100 g/3½ oz (7 tablespoons) unsalted butter, diced
- 40 g/1½ oz (¼ cup) lard, diced
- 100 g/3½ oz (½ cup) caster (superfine) sugar
- 100 g/3½ oz (½ cup plus 2 teaspoons) mixed dried fruit, such as currants, raisins and sultanas (golden raisins)
- 2 eggs
- 140 ml/4¾ fl oz (½ cup minus 2 teaspoons) full-fat (whole) milk or buttermilk

* Preheat the oven to 180°C/350°F/Gas Mark 4. Grease a 20–25 cm/8–10 inch pie plate well with lard or butter.
* Sift the flour into a large bowl, add the salt and ground nutmeg and mix together. Add the fats and rub them in with your fingertips until the mixture resembles breadcrumbs. Mix in the sugar and mixed dried fruit and make a well in the centre.
* Put the eggs and milk or buttermilk into another bowl and beat together until combined. Pour the mixture into the well and combine the wet and dry ingredients thoroughly using a wooden spoon. Tip the mixture onto a lightly floured work counter and knead briefly, then roll or press out until it is about 2.5 cm/1 inch thick. Alternatively, roll or press out to the width of the pie plate.
* Bake in the oven for 15 minutes, then reduce the oven temperature to 140°C/275°F/Gas Mark 1 and bake for another 35–40 minutes until golden brown. Remove from the oven, turn out of the plate and leave to cool on a wire rack. Store covered in an airtight container for about a week.

SCOTLAND: DUNDEE
*

DUNDEE CAKE

A rich and buttery fruitcake topped with distinctive concentric rings of whole blanched almonds. There are no spices used in a Dundee cake. Beyond the sultanas (golden raisins) the main flavouring comes from orange zest and peel – the original recipe is said to originate with the Dundee's famous Seville marmalade industry.

Serves: 8–10
Prep time: 20 minutes
Cook time: 1½ hours
{ॐ}

- 200 g/7 oz (1¾ sticks) salted butter, at room temperature, plus extra, melted, for greasing
- 220 g/7¾ oz (1¾ cups plus 2 teaspoons) plain (all-purpose) flour
- 200 g/7 oz (¾ cup plus 2 tablespoons) soft light brown sugar
- grated zest of 1 orange
- 4 eggs
- 100 g/3½ oz (1 cup) ground almonds
- 50 g/2 oz (¼ cup minus 4 teaspoons) orange marmalade
- 40 g/1½ oz (¼ cup) candied mixed peel
- 400 g/14 oz (2⅔ cups) sultanas (golden raisins)
- 60 ml/2 fl oz (¼ cup) sherry
- 80 g/3 oz (⅔ cup) whole blanched almonds
- 20 g/¾ oz (1 tablespoon plus 2 teaspoons) caster (superfine) sugar
- 60 ml/2 fl oz (¼ cup) full-fat (whole) milk

* Preheat the oven to 150°C/300°F/Gas Mark 2. Using a little melted butter, grease and line the bottom and sides of a 20 cm/8 inch round loose-bottom or springform cake pan with baking (parchment) paper and set aside.
* Sift the flour into a large bowl and set aside. Put the butter, soft light brown sugar and orange zest into a stand mixer fitted with a paddle attachment (or mix by hand) and cream together, starting on slow speed to incorporate and gradually increasing the speed until the mix is light and fluffy, scraping down the sides of the bowl with a spatula as required.
* Once the butter and sugar are pale and airy, slowly add the eggs, one at a time. With each egg, also add 1 tablespoon of flour and mix on medium speed until the egg is well incorporated, scraping down the sides of the bowl. Add the second egg and another 1 tablespoon of flour and mix to incorporate. Repeat this process until you have incorporated all the eggs. Use a spatula to gently fold in the remaining flour, followed by the ground almonds, marmalade, candied mixed peel, sultanas (golden raisins) and sherry.
* Spoon the batter into the prepared pan. Smooth the top with a spatula and arrange the blanched almonds carefully in concentric circles.
* Bake in the oven for 90 minutes, checking after 70 minutes. The cake should be golden in colour, be gently risen, equal in texture all over and a skewer should come out clean from the centre.
* Just before the cake is ready, put the caster (superfine) sugar and milk into a small saucepan and warm over a low heat for 2–3 minutes, stirring until the sugar has dissolved. As soon as the cake is removed from the oven,

brush the glaze over the top, then return it to the oven for 2–3 minutes for the glaze to set.
* Remove the cake from the oven and leave to cool in its tin on a wire rack.
* The cake is delicious the day it is baked, even while still slightly warm, but as with all good fruitcakes, this cake improves with age and will keep for up to a few months if well wrapped in baking (parchment) paper in an airtight container.

WALES: ANGLESEY
*

ANGLESEY CAKE
CACEN SIR FÔN

In the eighteenth century, across Wales – and the island of Anglesey in particular – black treacle (blackstrap molasses) was added to cakes to give them an appearance of richness. Anglesey cakes, darkened with black treacle, were often served at weddings by families too poor to afford wedding cakes. Today, the Anglesey cake survives as a moist, dark brown delicacy with the recipe, sometimes known as 'granny's recipe', being handed down from generation to generation.

Serves: 8
Prep time: 30 minutes
Cook time: 50–60 minutes
{ॐ} {⸱}

- 100 g/3½ oz (7 tablespoons) unsalted butter, softened, plus extra for greasing
- 75 g/2¾ oz (⅓ cup) soft brown sugar
- 1 egg, beaten
- 1 tablespoon black treacle (blackstrap molasses)
- 275 g/9¾ oz (2¼ cups) self-raising flour
- ½ teaspoon salt
- 1 teaspoon ground ginger
- 1 teaspoon mixed spice
- 200 ml/7 fl oz (¾ cup plus 1 tablespoon) full-fat (whole) milk
- ½ teaspoon bicarbonate of soda (baking soda)
- 175 g/6 oz (1 cup) mixed dried fruit

* Preheat the oven to 170°C/325°F/Gas Mark 3. Grease a 20 cm/8 inch round cake pan with butter and line the sides and bottom with baking (parchment) paper.
* Put the butter and sugar into a large bowl and, using a wooden spoon, mix together until pale and fluffy. Beat in the egg, then stir in the treacle (blackstrap molasses).
* Sift the flour, salt, ginger and mixed spice together into another bowl, then stir it into the creamed mixture.
* Put the milk into a medium bowl, add the bicarbonate of soda (baking soda) and mix together until the bicarbonate of soda has dissolved. Gradually add this to the creamed mixture, then stir thoroughly. Add the dried fruit and stir through.
* Spoon the batter into the prepared cake pan and bake in the oven for 50–60 minutes until a skewer inserted into the centre of the cake comes out clean. Leave to cool in the tin for 5 minutes, then transfer to a wire rack to cool. The cake is best kept for 24 hours before cutting and keeps well in an airtight tin.

Dundee cake

SCOTLAND

BLACK BUN
SCOTCH BUN

Originally a spiced bun made with bread dough, as the name suggests, over time the Scottish black bun has evolved into a dark and richly spiced fruitcake wrapped in shortcrust pastry (basic pie dough).

The black bun is traditionally served at Hogmanay (Scottish New Year's Eve) and has also been one of several traditional gifts given by 'first-footers', the first entrants to a home on New Year's Day. If carefully wrapped and stored somewhere dark and dry, it will keep well for weeks.

Serves: 8–10
Prep time: 1 hour, plus 30 minutes chilling
Cook time: 2 hours
{❅}

- For the pastry (pie dough):
- 100 g/3½ oz (¾ cup plus 2 teaspoons) plain (all-purpose) flour, plus extra for dusting
- 100 g/3½ oz (¾ cup plus 2 teaspoons) wholemeal (whole wheat) flour
- ½ teaspoon baking powder
- 2 pinches fine sea salt
- 2 pinches caster (superfine) sugar
- 100 g/3½ oz (7 tablespoons) unsalted cold butter, diced, plus a little extra melted butter for greasing
- 1 egg, beaten with 1 tablespoon water or milk and a pinch of salt, for egg wash
- granulated sugar for dusting

- For the filling:
- 150 g/5 oz (1¼ cups) plain (all-purpose) flour
- 50 g/2 oz (½ cup) ground almonds
- 700 g/1 lb 8½ oz (4 cups) mixed dried fruit, such as the traditional currants and sultanas (golden raisins); you can also include raisins, figs, prunes, dates, candied mixed peel
- 1 teaspoon mixed spice
- ½ teaspoon ground black pepper
- 10 g/¼ oz piece fresh root ginger, peeled and finely grated
- 100 g/3½ oz (½ cup minus 2 teaspoons) dark soft brown sugar
- ½ teaspoon bicarbonate of soda (baking soda)
- grated zest of 1 orange
- grated zest of ½ lemon
- 1 egg
- 50 ml/1¾ fl oz (3½ tablespoons) full-fat (whole) milk
- 20 g/¾ oz (4 teaspoons) marmalade
- 20 g/¾ oz (4 teaspoons) black treacle (blackstrap molasses)
- 30 ml/1 fl oz (2 tablespoons) brandy or whisky

* For the pastry (pie dough), sift the flours, baking powder, salt and caster (superfine) sugar into a bowl. Add the butter and rub in with your fingertips until it resembles coarse breadcrumbs. While mixing, slowly add 75 ml/ 2½ fl oz (⅓ cup) ice-cold water until a dough forms. Be careful not to overwork it. Wrap in clingfilm (plastic wrap) and leave in the fridge for at least 30 minutes.
* Meanwhile, brush a 900 g/2 lb loaf pan with the melted butter to completely coat the bottom and sides. Set aside.
* For the filling, put all the dry ingredients into a large bowl. Put the egg, milk, marmalade and treacle (blackstrap

molasses) into a small bowl or jug and lightly beat until combined. Add this milky mixture to the dry ingredients and mix to combine, adding the brandy or whisky as you do. Set aside.
* Preheat the oven to 160°C/325°F/Gas Mark 3.
* Put the chilled dough onto a lightly floured work counter and cut off a quarter and set aside. Roll the remaining dough out to a large enough rectangle to line the bottom and sides of the loaf pan and about 2 mm thick. Gently press the dough into the loaf pan, leaving an excess of about 1 cm/½ inch, trimming off any excess as necessary and set aside.
* Carefully spoon the fruitcake mixture into the pastry case (shell). Roll out the remaining dough to about 2 mm thick and cut out a rectangle to fit the top of the pan. Lightly brush the dough edge with the egg wash and put the rolled-out dough on top, pinching the edges to seal as you go, creating a crust or edge to the top. Brush egg wash all over the top. If you have any excess pastry scraps, roll these out, cut out leaves, petals or any additional decoration you desire and arrange on top. Brush egg wash all over to finish and sprinkle with granulated sugar.
* Bake in the oven for 2 hours, rotating the bun 180° after 1 hour, until it is golden brown. Remove from the oven and leave to cool completely in the pan. It will keep well for many weeks wrapped in baking (parchment) paper in an airtight container.

UNITED KINGDOM

SEED CAKE

Caraway seeds are very traditional to British baking; recipes for seed cakes both rich and plain are found in English cookbooks dating back as far as the early seventeenth century. Today's variety is essentially a soft and buttery sponge flavoured with the caraway seeds. It should be served warm and alongside a cup of tea.

Serves: 8
Prep time: 20 minutes
Cook time: 45 minutes
{❅}

- 170 g/6 oz (1½ sticks) unsalted butter, softened, or 85 g/3 oz (¾ stick) softened butter and 85 g/ 3 oz (½ cup) dripping, plus extra for greasing
- 170 g/6 oz (¾ cup plus 4 teaspoons) caster (superfine) sugar
- 3 eggs
- 1 tablespoon full-fat (whole) milk
- 170 g/6 oz (1⅓ cups plus 2 teaspoons) self-raising flour
- 60 g/2¼ oz (⅔ cup) ground almonds
- ½ teaspoon baking powder
- ½ teaspoon salt
- 1 tablespoon caraway seeds

* Preheat the oven to 160°C/325°F/Gas Mark 3. Grease a 450 g/1 lb loaf pan with butter and line with baking (parchment) paper.
* Put the butter and sugar into a stand mixer fitted with a paddle attachment and beat together until light and fluffy (or mix by hand). Meanwhile, put the eggs and milk into a small bowl and beat together using a fork.

Sift the flour into a medium bowl, add the ground almonds, baking powder, salt and caraway seeds and mix briefly using a whisk to distribute the ingredients evenly.

* Once the butter and sugar are aerated, add a third of the egg mixture, followed by a third of the dry ingredients to the mixer, mixing thoroughly in between. Alternate between the wet and dry ingredients, scraping down the bowl frequently until everything has been incorporated.
* Pour the cake batter into the loaf pan and bake in the oven for 45 minutes, or until golden brown and a skewer inserted into the centre of the cake comes out clean. If it doesn't come out clean, return it to the oven for another 10 minutes. Remove from the oven and serve warm.

WALES
*

SHEARING CAKE
THRESHING CAKE/CACEN GNEIFIO

Each spring this cake was baked across Wales to coincide with and celebrate the sheep-shearing season. The cake's batter was originally made with bacon fat or bacon dripping instead of butter, distinguishing it from the buttery rich Seed Cake (see left).

Serves: 8
Prep time: 20 minutes
Cook time: 1 hour
{🌙}{🌶}

- 225 g/8 oz (2 sticks) unsalted butter, softened and diced, plus extra for greasing
- 150 g/5 oz (⅔ cup) soft brown sugar
- 2 eggs, well beaten
- 75 ml/2½ fl oz (⅓ cup) full-fat (whole) milk
- 225 g/8 oz (2 cups minus 1 tablespoon) plain (all-purpose) flour, sifted
- ½ teaspoon baking powder
- 2 teaspoons caraway seeds
- pinch of salt
- 1 whole nutmeg, grated, to taste
- 100 g/3½ oz (½ cup plus 2 teaspoons) candied mixed peel (optional)
- grated zest and juice of 1 lemon

* Preheat the oven to 180°C/350°F/Gas Mark 4. Grease a 20 cm/8 inch cake pan with butter and line with baking (parchment) paper.
* Put the butter and sugar into a stand mixer fitted with a paddle attachment and beat until light and fluffy.
* Meanwhile, put the eggs and milk into a small bowl and beat together using a fork.
* Sift the flour into a medium bowl, add the baking powder and caraway seeds and mix together. Add a third of the egg mixture, followed by a third of the flour mix and beat for 2 minutes, scraping down the bowl in between. Repeat the process until all the egg mix and flour mix is used up. Beat for another 2 minutes to ensure the mix is smooth and incorporated. Add the salt, nutmeg, candied mixed peel (if using), grated lemon zest and juice, then fold in using a wooden spoon until fully distributed. The cake batter should be quite loose; if necessary, add a little more milk to adjust the consistency.

* Pour the cake batter into the cake pan and bake in the oven for 20 minutes, then reduce the oven temperature to 150°C/300°F/Gas Mark 2 and bake for another 40 minutes, or until a skewer inserted into the centre of the cake comes out clean. Remove from the oven, leave to cool in the pan for 10 minutes before turning out and leaving to cool on a wire rack.

UNITED KINGDOM
*

ARCTIC ROLL

This riff on the Swiss Roll Cake (page 319) – which features a jam and ice cream filling – first cropped up in frozen food aisles in the late 1950s. The Arctic Roll was wildly popular in the 1980s, but over the last decade has enjoyed a nostalgia-induced revival. You might not be able to replicate the store original at home, but perhaps you can do one better.

Serves: 6
Prep time: 1 hour, plus 3–4 hours freezing
Cook time: 15 minutes
{🌙}{🌶}

- 1 litre/34 fl oz (4¼ cups) vanilla ice cream
- 3 large eggs
- 100 g/3½ oz (½ cup) caster (superfine) sugar
- 75 g/2¾ oz (½ cup plus 1 tablespoon) plain (all-purpose) flour
- butter, for greasing
- 300 g/11 oz (1 cup) raspberry jam

* Preheat the oven to 180°C/350°F/Gas Mark 4. Transfer the ice cream from the freezer to the fridge to soften.
* Crack the eggs into a large bowl, add the sugar and whisk using electric beaters until pale and fluffy. Sift in the flour and stir until fully combined.
* Grease a rimmed baking sheet, about 25–35 cm/10–14 inches, all over with some of the butter, line with baking (parchment) paper, then grease the paper as well. Pour in the sponge batter and bake in the oven for 10–15 minutes until cooked through and a toothpick comes out clean.
* Put a piece of baking paper a little wider than the sponge onto a work counter, then flip the sponge out of the baking sheet onto the paper, discarding the paper that was in the baking sheet and which is now on top of the sponge. Carefully roll the sponge, bottom sheet of paper and all, into a cylinder and leave to cool for 20 minutes.
* When the sponge is still very slightly warm, carefully unroll it and spread the jam all over. Spread the softened ice cream over the jam in dollops, leaving just 5 cm/2 inches free at one end to form the seal when rolled. Use only as much ice cream as you need – don't overfill it.
* Begin rolling the sponge back up using the baking paper to help you lift the sponge up over itself. Roll it just tightly enough that the last 5 cm/2 inches of uncovered sponge connects with the outside of the roll from the end you are rolling from. Some ice cream and jam may start to spill out of the side, but don't worry. Use the baking paper to keep the roll together, then twist and push the excess paper into each end of the roll to help keep the contents in. Lay the roll in a large dish with the connecting ends of sponge facing down and leave in the freezer for 3–4 hours before serving in slices.

ENGLAND
*

BATTENBERG CAKE
'CHAPEL WINDOWS' CAKE

A Battenberg cake seems a rather involved and elaborate task – an alternating pink and yellow sponge, neatly layered with jam and then carefully wrapped in marzipan. But broken down there's a lot less to fear, provided you take your time. Perhaps home bakers of the late nineteenth century had a bit more patience, as this cake was quite popular in Victorian baking books, where it often ran under a more telling name – 'Chapel Windows'. Unfortunately, despite plenty of speculation – including a Victorian wedding – there's no accepted story behind the famous Battenberg name.

Serves: 8
Prep time: 45 minutes, plus 1 hour chilling
Cook time: 25 minutes
{👤}

- 175 g/6 oz (1½ sticks) unsalted butter, softened, plus extra for greasing
- 3 eggs
- 175 g/6 oz (¾ cup plus 2 tablespoons) caster (superfine) sugar
- 175 g/6 oz (1½ cups) self-raising flour, sifted
- 3–4 drops red or pink food colouring
- 200 g/7 oz (¾ cup) apricot jam
- 400 g/14 oz marzipan
- icing (confectioners') sugar, for rolling

* Preheat the oven to 180°C/350°F/Gas Mark 4. Lightly grease a 26 x 16.5 cm/10 x 6½ inch cake pan with butter and line the bottom and sides with baking (parchment) paper. Using a piece of aluminium foil, create a divider in the centre of the pan by folding the aluminium foil over itself several times, ensuring it divides the pan widthwise in a straight line.
* Put a medium saucepan of water over a medium heat. Put the eggs and 25 g/¾ oz (2 tablespoons) of the sugar into a metal bowl and set the bowl over the pan of water, making sure the bottom of the bowl doesn't touch the water. Whisk the eggs and sugar together for 5–7 minutes until pale and smooth. Meanwhile, put the butter and the remaining sugar into a stand mixer fitted with a paddle attachment and beat until pale and aerated.
* Once both mixtures are pale and aerated, slowly add the egg to the butter mix, then gently fold in the sifted flour until the batter is completely smooth. Divide the batter into 2 equal quantities, adding 3–4 drops of food colouring to one part. Mix thoroughly, then spoon both mixes into opposite sides of the prepared pan. Bake in the centre of the oven for 25 minutes, turning halfway through. Remove from the oven and leave to cool in the pan for 5–10 minutes before turning out and leaving to cool completely on a wire rack.
* To assemble the cake, cut the sponge in half and, separating the different colours, trim the sides and top of each, creating 2 even rectangular strips of sponge, then slice in half lengthwise. Form 4 individual bands of sponge, 2 of each colour, about 13 cm/5 inches long, 3 cm/1¼ inches high and 4 cm/1½ inches wide. The bands must be even in proportion.
* Heat the apricot jam in a small saucepan over a low heat for a few minutes until warm, then brush it over 2 sides

of each piece and sandwich them together, creating a chequered pattern. Once they are firmly stuck together, knead and roll out the marzipan into a rectangle, 30 x 16 cm/12 x 6¼ inches with a little icing (confectioners') sugar to about 2 mm thick. Brush the marzipan with apricot jam, then put the sponge at one end, applying a little pressure, and gently roll the sponge, ensuring the marzipan doesn't tear. Press the edges so that it seals, then carefully trim the excess marzipan where the seam overlaps. Gently smooth the marzipan using the palm of your hand to remove any air pockets and leave to chill in the fridge for 1 hour before serving.

ENGLAND: CUMBRIA
*

WESTMORLAND PEPPER CAKE

A little pepper goes a long way in this spiced fruitcake, once popular in the historic county of Westmorland (now a part of Cumbria). Similar to the Cumberland Rum Nicky (page 396), the ingredients in this cake underscore the strong link between Cumbrian ports such as Whitehaven, and the spice trades in the West Indies.

Serves: 8
Prep time: 20 minutes
Cook time: 1 hour
{👤}{🌶}

- 120 g/4 oz (⅔ cup minus 2 teaspoons) caster (superfine) sugar
- 120 g/4 oz (⅓ cup) black treacle (blackstrap molasses)
- 60 g/2¼ oz (½ stick) unsalted butter
- 120 g/4 oz (⅔ cup) mixed dried fruit, such as currants, raisins and sultanas (golden raisins)
- 30 g/1 oz (¼ cup minus 1 tablespoon) candied mixed peel
- 240 g/8½ oz (2 cups) plain (all-purpose) flour
- pinch of salt
- ¼ teaspoon freshly ground black pepper
- ¼ teaspoon ground ginger
- ¼ teaspoon ground cloves
- 2 eggs, beaten

* Preheat the oven to 160°C/325°F/Gas Mark 3. Line the sides and bottom of a 20 cm/8 inch round cake pan with baking (parchment) paper.
* Put the sugar, treacle (blackstrap molasses), butter, mixed dried fruit and candied mixed peel into a medium saucepan over a medium heat and stir for 2–3 minutes until the butter has melted and the sugar dissolved.
* Meanwhile, sift the flour, salt and spices into a large bowl and make a well in the centre. Pour in the treacle mixture and stir through. Add the eggs and mix thoroughly until combined.
* Pour the batter into the prepared cake pan and bake in the oven for 1 hour, or until a skewer inserted into the centre of the cake comes out clean. Leave to cool for 5 minutes in the tin, then turn out onto a wire rack.

Battenberg cake

UNITED KINGDOM
*

CHRISTMAS CAKE

A British Christmas cake follows in much the same vein as a Christmas Pudding (page 350) – they are both heavily spiced, densely packed with dried fruit and similarly fed the same 'diet' of rum or brandy in the weeks before they are served. The main differences are the fat used – butter in the cake and traditionally suet in the pudding – and the layer of apricot jam and marzipan or royal icing, which are invariably used to coat the cake.

Serves: 8
Prep time: 50 minutes,
plus 3–4 weeks maturing and firming up
Cook time: 2¾–3 hours
{ 🌣 }

- 900 g/2 lb (5 cups plus 2 tablespoons) mixed dried fruit, such as currants, raisins and sultanas (golden raisins)
- 125 g/4¼ oz (1 cup minus 1 teaspoon) whole roasted almonds
- 125 g/4¼ oz (¾ cup) chopped candied mixed peel
- 125 g/4¼ oz (½ cup) glacé (candied) cherries, rinsed
- 300 g/11 oz (2½ cups) self-raising flour
- 1½ teaspoons mixed spice
- grated zest of 1 lemon
- 250 g/9 oz (2¼ sticks) salted butter, softened
- 250 g/9 oz (1 cup plus 2 tablespoons) soft dark brown sugar
- 1 teaspoon vanilla extract
- 1 tablespoon black treacle (blackstrap molasses)
- 6 eggs
- 120 ml/4 fl oz (½ cup) brandy, plus extra for feeding
- 1 quantity Royal Icing (page 429)

* Preheat the oven to 140°C/275°F/Gas Mark 1. Line a 20 cm/8 inch round cake pan with baking (parchment) paper.
* Put the dried fruit, almonds, candied mixed peel and cherries into a large bowl and mix together. Sift in the flour, add the mixed spice and lemon zest and stir through until everything is coated in the flour.
* Put the butter and dark brown sugar into another large bowl and, using a wooden spoon, beat them together until they are pale and fluffy. Stir in the vanilla extract and treacle (blackstrap molasses). Beat the eggs into the butter and sugar mixture, one at a time, then mix through well and add the fruit and flour together with enough brandy to slacken the mixture to a dropping consistency. Pour the batter into the prepared cake pan, shaping a small indent in the centre so that when it bakes, it rises with a reasonably flat top.
* Bake in the oven for 2¾–3 hours, but check it after 2½ hours. To test if the cake is cooked, insert a skewer into the middle and if it comes out clean it's done. Leave to cool in the pan.
* Keep the cake in an airtight container to mature for 3–4 weeks, 'feeding' it every week with 2–3 tablespoons brandy evenly distributed across the cake.
* When ready to ice (frost) the cake, make the Royal Icing following the recipe on page 429. Cover the cake with the Royal Icing using a palette knife dipped in hot water. Smooth and neaten the sides and top and decorate. Leave for at least 3 days so that the Royal Icing can firm up. Serve in slices.

* VARIATION: If desired, a classic combination is to layer jam and marzipan underneath the icing (frosting). Heat 2 tablespoons apricot jam and 1 tablespoon water in a small saucepan over a medium heat, and, when boiling, strain it through a sieve into a small heatproof bowl, then brush it over the top and sides of the cake. Using at least 500 g/1 lb 2 oz ready-to-roll marzipan, roll out a third into a circle, about 3–4 mm/⅛–⅙ inch thick. Use the cake's pan as a guide for the size of the marzipan circle. Put the disc onto the top of the cake. Measure the height of the cake and roll out the remaining marzipan, cutting into rectangles of the appropriate width for the sides. Adhere the marzipan to the side of the cake, then leave to dry for 2 days before icing (frosting) the cake.

UNITED KINGDOM
*

SIMNEL CAKE

This is a light fruitcake that's often baked around Easter. It boasts a layer of marzipan across the middle of the cake, and a further, more elaborate layer on top including 11 marzipan balls which are apparently made to represent Jesus's disciples.

Serves: 8
Prep time: 20 minutes, plus 1 hour resting
Cook time: 2–2½ hours
{ 🌣 }

- For the marzipan:
- 60 g/2¼ oz (⅓ cup minus 1 teaspoon) caster (superfine) sugar
- 170 g/6 oz (1½ cups minus 2 teaspoons) icing (confectioners') sugar
- 220 g/7¾ oz (2¼ cups) ground almonds
- 1 egg, beaten

- For the cake:
- 225 g/8 oz (2 sticks) unsalted butter, softened
- 225 g/8 oz (1 cup plus 2 tablespoons) caster (superfine) sugar
- 4 eggs
- 225 g/8 oz (1¾ cups plus 1 tablespoon) self-raising flour
- 2 teaspoons mixed spice
- grated zest of 1 orange
- grated zest of 1 lemon
- 350 g/12 oz (2 cups) mixed dried fruit, such as currants, raisins and sultanas (golden raisins)
- 100 g/3½ oz (⅓ cup plus 1 tablespoon) whole glacé (candied) cherries
- 2 tablespoons apricot jam
- 1 egg, beaten, for egg wash

* For the marzipan, put the sugars and ground almonds into a large bowl and mix together. Add the egg and mix it thoroughly into the sugars and almond. Tip the mixture onto a work counter and knead for 2–3 minutes until it is completely smooth. Wrap in clingfilm (plastic wrap) and leave to rest in the fridge for at least 1 hour.
* Preheat the oven to 140°C/275°F/Gas Mark 1. Line the bottom and sides of a 20 cm/8 inch round cake pan with baking (parchment) paper.
* For the cake, put the butter and sugar into a large bowl and, using a wooden spoon, beat together until pale and

fluffy. Add the eggs one at a time, then fold in the flour, spice and citrus zests. Mix through well, then fold in the fruit. Pour half of the batter into the prepared cake pan.
* Roll out half the marzipan on a work counter and cut it into a 20 cm/8 inch diameter circle (it should fit neatly over the cake). Put this on top of the cake batter in the pan before covering with the remaining batter. Set the marzipan trimmings aside as they will be used later to form decorations for the top of the cake.
* Bake in the oven for 2–2½ hours, then remove from the oven and leave to cool in the pan.
* Heat the apricot jam in a small saucepan over a low heat for 2–3 minutes until warm, then strain through a sieve into a heatproof bowl. Roll out the remaining marzipan on a work counter and cut out a 20 cm/8 inch circle. Brush the top of the cake with the apricot jam, then lay the marzipan on top and crimp the edges with a fork. Brush the marzipan with the beaten egg, then roll 11 equal-sized balls from the marzipan trimmings and arrange around the edge. Brush the balls with more egg wash and brown using a chef's torch or put under a hot grill (broiler).

UNITED KINGDOM
*

SWISS ROLL

A Swiss (jelly) roll is a light sponge cake spread with jam or icing (frosting), which is then rolled up and set into a log shape. It closely resembles a Jam Roly Poly (page 354), but the latter is made using a flaky suet pastry.

Serves: 6
Prep time: 20 minutes
Cook time: 20 minutes
{●} {◡•}

- 4 eggs
- 110 g/3¾ oz (½ cup plus 2 teaspoons) caster (superfine) sugar, plus extra for dusting
- 80 g/3 oz (⅔ cup) self-raising flour
- icing (confectioners') sugar, for dusting

- For the jam:
- 200 g/7 oz (1⅔ cups) fresh or frozen raspberries
- 120 g/4 oz (⅔ cup) caster (superfine) sugar
- 20 ml/¾ fl oz (4 teaspoons) lemon juice

- For the filling:
- 200 ml/7 fl oz (¾ cup plus 1 tablespoon) double (heavy) cream
- 50 g/2 oz icing (confectioners') sugar
- 350 g/12 oz (1¼ cups) Lemon Curd (shop-bought or homemade, page 432) (optional)

* Preheat the oven to 170°C/325°F/Gas Mark 3. Line a 23 x 33 cm/9 x 13 inch Swiss (jelly) roll pan with baking (parchment) paper.
* For the jam, heat the raspberries and sugar in a small saucepan over a medium-high heat for 5 minutes until it's almost the correct jam-like texture. Add the lemon juice, mix and set aside.
* For the sponge, put the eggs and caster (superfine) sugar into a stand mixer fitted with a whisk attachment and whisk on medium speed until light, fluffy and pale. Sift

the flour into a large bowl, then gently start folding the flour into the mixture using a hand whisk and finish using a spatula to scrape the bottom of the bowl, mixing to form a sponge batter. Pour the batter into the prepared pan and bake in the oven for 10–12 minutes until a skewer inserted into the cake comes out clean.
* Meanwhile, lay a piece of baking paper slightly bigger than the pan flat on the work counter and dust evenly with caster sugar.
* Remove the sponge from the oven and flip directly onto the sugar-dusted paper and leave to cool, without removing any of the paper.
* Meanwhile, for the filling, put the cream and icing (confectioners') sugar into the cleaned bowl of a stand mixer fitted with a whisk attachment and whip on low speed to soft peaks. Alternatively, whip the cream in a large bowl with electric beaters.
* With the cooled sponge lengthwise, remove the top layer of paper and start to spread the jam or curd all over the sponge, leaving a 2 cm/¾ inch gap on the longest side furthest away from you. Repeat with the whipped cream, spreading it about 5 mm/¼ inch thick, then start to gently but firmly roll the sponge away from you, ensuring the filling stays inside, into a log shape. Put it on a serving plate seam-side down, dust lightly with icing sugar and trim the edges.

UNITED KINGDOM
*

MADEIRA CAKE

This buttery cake is similar to a Victoria sponge (page 320) but made using a higher proportion of flour. The result is a denser close-textured sponge frequently served with a cup of tea or a glass of Madeira – the fortified Portuguese wine from which its name originates.

Serves: 8
Prep time: 20 minutes
Cook time: 50–60 minutes
{●} {◡•}

- 150 g/5 oz (1¼ sticks) unsalted butter, softened
- 150 g/5 oz (¾ cup) caster (superfine) sugar
- grated zest of 1 lemon
- 4 eggs, beaten
- 225 g/8 oz (1¾ cups plus 1 tablespoon) self-raising flour
- sherry or Madeira, to serve

* Preheat the oven to 180°C/350°F/Gas Mark 4. Line a 900 g/2 lb loaf pan with baking (parchment) paper.
* Put the butter, sugar and grated lemon zest into a large bowl and, using a wooden spoon, mix them together until they are pale and fluffy. Gradually beat in the eggs, adding a little extra flour if the mixture begins to split. Once the eggs have been incorporated, sift in the flour and mix carefully to a smooth consistency. Pour the batter into the prepared pan and bake in the oven for 50–60 minutes until a skewer inserted into the centre of the cake comes out clean. Remove from the oven, turn out from the pan and leave to cool on a wire rack. Serve mid-afternoon alongside a glass of sherry, Madeira or the like.

UNITED KINGDOM
*

VICTORIA SPONGE CAKE

The classic British sponge is a light and fluffy cake made with equal parts of butter, sugar and flour, beaten together with eggs. A popular way to serve sponge cake is to sandwich it with jam and sweetened whipped cream – this is the method you will find in the recipe below. The combination is said to originate with Queen Victoria, who enjoyed her cakes split and spread with a layer of jam. The Victoria sandwich has since become a staple of tearooms, bakeries and cafés, and an iconic cake for all occasions.

Serves: 6–8
Prep time: 30 minutes
Cook time: 1 hour 20 minutes
{ 🌡 } { ✿ }

- unsalted butter, at room temperature (amount depending on weight of eggs), plus extra, melted, for greasing
- 4 eggs
- caster (superfine) sugar (amount depending on weight of eggs)
- self-raising flour (amount depending on weight of eggs)
- 250 ml/8 fl oz (1 cup) double (heavy) cream
- 4 tablespoons strawberry jam
- 1 handful ripe strawberries, sliced or quartered
- icing (confectioners') sugar, for dusting

* Preheat the oven to 150°C/300°F/Gas Mark 2. Using a little melted butter, grease a 20 cm/8 inch loose-bottom or springform cake pan and line the bottom and sides with baking (parchment) paper.
* Weigh the eggs in their shells to determine the weight of the other cake ingredients,. For example, if the eggs weigh 240 g/8½ oz in total, then you will need 240 g/8½ oz of butter, sugar and flour.
* Sift the flour into a large bowl and set aside.
* Put the butter and sugar into a stand mixer fitted with a paddle attachment and beat on slow speed to incorporate, then gradually increase the speed and beat until the mix is light and fluffy, scraping down the sides with a spatula.
* Once the butter and sugar are pale and airy, add the eggs, one at a time. With each egg also add 1 tablespoon of flour and mix on medium speed until the egg is well incorporated, scraping down the sides of the bowl. Repeat this process until you have incorporated all the eggs.
* Remove the bowl from the mixer and, using a spatula, gently fold in the remaining flour. Spoon the cake batter into the prepared pan and bake in the oven for 1 hour 20 minutes, checking after 1 hour. The cake should be golden in colour, gently risen, equal in texture all over and a skewer insterted into the centre of the cake should come out clean. Remove from the oven and leave to cool still in the pan on a wire rack.
* Meanwhile, put the cream into a large bowl and whisk to soft peaks. Once the cake is cold, turn it out of the pan and carefully slice it horizontally into 3 equal parts. Put the bottom third onto a serving plate and spread with half the jam, followed by half the cream and half the strawberry pieces dotted across the cream. Gently put the middle cake slice onto the top and repeat the process with the remaining jam, cream and strawberries. Top with the final cake slice and dust liberally with icing (confectioners') sugar to finish.

UNITED KINGDOM
*

LEMON DRIZZLE CAKE

A fixture of British teatime, this cake is said to have been introduced to the UK in the pages of the London-based *Jewish Chronicle* by Manchester-born cookery writer Evelyn Rose in the late 1960s. This recipe has been adapted slightly by the Glasgow-based baker Anna Luntley. It features oat flour, which gives the cake a soft, moist crumb.

Makes: 1 large loaf
Preparation: 20 minutes
Cooking time: 1 hour
{ 🌡 } { ✿ }

- 270 g/9½ oz (2½ sticks) unsalted butter at room temperature, plus a little melted butter for greasing
- 200 g/7 oz (1⅔ cups) plain (all-purpose) flour
- 70 g/2¾ oz (½ cup plus 2 teaspoons) oat flour
- 2¾ teaspoons baking powder
- 270 g/9½ oz (1⅓ cups) caster (superfine) sugar, plus extra for sprinkling
- 1 teaspoon vanilla extract (optional)
- pinch of salt
- 4 eggs
- grated zest and juice of 4 lemons
- splash of milk
- about 200 g/7 oz (¾ cup plus 2 tablespoons) demerara (turbinado) sugar

* Preheat the oven to 140°C/275°F/Gas Mark 1. Grease a 900 g/2 lb loaf pan with the melted butter and line with baking (parchment) paper.
* Weigh the flours and baking powder into a bowl.
* Put the butter, caster (superfine) sugar, vanilla extract (if using) and salt together in a stand mixer fitted with a paddle attachment and starting slowly, beat together, gradually increasing the speed and scraping down the sides of the bowl as needed, until the mixture is light and fluffy, 3–4 minutes.
* Add the eggs, one at a time, together with 1 tablespoon of the dry ingredients at each addition. Beat gently until the egg and flours are well combined before scraping down the sides of the bowl and adding the next egg.
* Once all the eggs are incorporated, gently fold in the remaining dry ingredients, together with the lemon zest and milk to create a smooth, light batter. You can mix by hand with a spatula or on the slowest mixer speed.
* Spoon the cake batter into the prepared loaf pan and bake in the middle of the oven for 1 hour, or until the cake is well risen, deep golden and a skewer or toothpick inserted into the centre of the cake comes out clean.
* Meanwhile, for the lemon syrup, put the lemon juice into a small saucepan and add an equal weight of demerara (turbinado) sugar. Heat over a low heat, stirring to dissolve the sugar. Once the sugar has completely dissolved, increase the heat and bring to the boil, then reduce the heat and simmer for 5 minutes.
* Once the cake is baked, leave to cool in the pan for 5 minutes to give the crumb a chance to set. Brush the top with the lemon sugar syrup (it's fine if the impatient baker resorts to pouring the syrup over the cake). Leave to cool in the pan for another 20 minutes, before turning out onto a wire rack. Sprinkle with caster sugar, coating the top and sides, and leave to cool completely.

Victoria sponge cake

ENGLAND: HEREFORDSHIRE AND OXFORDSHIRE

*

OLD ENGLISH CIDER CAKE

Despite its billing as an 'Old English' cake, this recipe must date back no further than the 1850s, when we first start to see cider used in English cookbooks. Often attributed to a cider-producing region like Herefordshire, we can't be as precise about the origin of this particular recipe.

Moist, and with flavourful notes from the cider and nutmeg, it makes the perfect addition to (or total replacement of) afternoon tea.

Serves: 8
Prep time: 50 minutes
Cook time: 40–45 minutes
{ } { }

- 110 g/3¾ oz (1 stick) unsalted butter, diced, at room temperature, plus extra butter, melted, for greasing
- 110 g/3¾ oz (½ cup minus 2½ teaspoons) soft light brown sugar
- 110 g/3¾ oz (1 cup minus 2 teaspoons) plain (all-purpose) flour
- 110 g/3¾ oz (1 cup minus 2 teaspoons) wholemeal (whole wheat) flour
- 1 teaspoon bicarbonate of soda (baking soda)
- ½ teaspoon grated nutmeg
- 2 eggs
- 330 ml/11 fl oz (1⅓ cups) local cider
- 85 g/3 oz (⅓ cup plus 2 teaspoons) demerara (turbinado) sugar, plus extra for sprinkling (optional)
- pouring cream, to serve (optional)

- For the honey cream cheese icing (frosting) (optional):
- 100 g/3½ oz (7 tablespoons) unsalted butter, at room temperature
- 50 g/2 oz (¼ cup minus 2 teaspoons) set honey
- 100 g/3½ oz (¾ cup plus 2 teaspoons) icing (confectioners') sugar
- 200 g/7 oz (¾ cup plus 1 tablespoon) full-fat (whole) cream cheese, any liquid drained off

* Preheat the oven to 150°C/300°F/Gas Mark 2. Line the bottom and sides of a 20 cm/8 inch round cake pan or 900 g/2 lb loaf pan with baking (parchment) paper and grease with melted butter.
* Put the butter and soft light brown sugar into a stand mixer fitted with a paddle attachment and beat until light and fluffy (or mix by hand). Sift the flours and bicarbonate of soda (baking soda) into another bowl and stir in the nutmeg.
* Once the butter and sugar are creamed, add the eggs, one at a time along with a spoonful of the flour mixture. Scrape down the bowl after each addition and make sure the egg is well-incorporated before adding the next one. Once all the eggs have been added, remove the bowl from the mixer and, using a plastic spatula, fold in half of the remaining flour mix. Fold in 160 ml/5¼ fl oz (⅔ cup plus 2 teaspoons) of the cider, followed by the remaining flour mix and stir until the batter is smooth. Pour into the prepared cake pan and bake in the oven for 40–45 minutes until risen and golden brown.

* Meanwhile, pour the remaining cider and the demerara (turbinado) sugar into a small saucepan and stir over a low heat for 2–3 minutes until the sugar has dissolved, then simmer for 10–15 minutes until the liquid is reduced by about half.
* When the cake is ready, remove from the oven, turn out of the pan and leave to cool on a wire rack. Brush the cake liberally with the cider sugar syrup and sprinkle with a little extra demerara (turbinado) sugar, if desired. This cake is delicious served still warm with cold pouring cream, or you can leave to cool completely and keep for up to 5 days in an airtight container.
* This cake would have traditionally been eaten plain but it can be made that little bit more special if iced (frosted) with the honey cream cheese frosting. Put the butter and honey into a large bowl and, using a handheld electric whisk, beat until light and fluffy. Add the icing (confectioners') sugar and beat until very pale and fluffy. Gradually add the cream cheese, a third at a time, beating well after each addition until well incorporated and the texture is thick and creamy. Spoon onto the top of the cooled cake and spread evenly using a palette knife.

ENGLAND: LONDON

*

TOTTENHAM CAKE
HACKNEY CAKE

This traybake cake, with its bright pink icing (frosting), evokes memories of British school dinners (lunches) for many. The cake originates in nineteenth-century North London, where its distinctive icing was allegedly made by locally sourced mulberries. True or not, there's nothing so fruity (or nutritious) about today's version: a simple, gleeful, sugary school dessert.

Serves: 8
Prep time: 30 minutes
Cook time: 25–30 minutes
{ } { }

- For the cake:
- 200 g/7 oz (1¾ sticks) butter, softened, plus extra for greasing
- 180 g/6 oz (1 cup minus 4 teaspoons) caster (superfine) sugar
- 3 large eggs
- 180 g/6 oz (1½ cups) self-raising flour, sifted
- 20 g/¾ oz cornflour (cornstarch)
- ½ teaspoon baking powder
- 3–4 tablespoons milk
- Custard (page 33), to serve

- For the icing (frosting):
- 250 g/9 oz icing (confectioners') sugar
- red food colouring
- sprinkles of your choice

* Preheat the oven to 170°C/325°F/Gas mark 3. Grease a 15 x 20 cm (6 x 8 inch) baking pan with butter, and line the base and sides with baking (parchment) paper.
* In the bowl of a stand mixer fitted with a paddle attachment, beat together the butter and sugar for several minutes until pale and fluffy (or mix by hand).

* Add the eggs, one at a time, mixing each time until well incorporated, then fold in the flour and baking powder using a spatula. Finally, fold in the milk until the mix falls off the spatula in soft, pillowy dollops.
* Spoon into the prepared tin and bake for 25–30 minutes until golden brown, or until a skewer or toothpick inserted into the centre comes out clean. Remove from the oven and allow to cool.
* While the cake cools, make the icing (frosting). Sift the icing (confectioners') sugar into a bowl, make a well in the middle and gradually add 2–3 tablespoons of hot water, mixing until you have a smooth, thick icing. Stir in a few drops of food colouring, to reach your desired colour, then spread over the cooled cake, adding sprinkles before leaving the icing to set.
* Cut into squares and serve in a pool of warm Custard.

UNITED KINGDOM
*
STICKY GINGER CAKE

This richly spiced cake is studded with stem (preserved) ginger. Both moist and spongy, this is more along the lines of a ginger loaf than a traditional British gingerbread.

Serves: 6
Prep time: 20 minutes, plus 3–4 days resting
Cook time: 35–40 minutes
{☉}{☂}

- 180 g/6 oz (¾ cup plus 2 teaspoons) soft brown sugar
- 80 g/3 oz (¾ stick) unsalted butter
- 100 g/3½ oz (¼ cup plus 2 tablespoons) golden syrup
- 2 tablespoons black treacle (blackstrap molasses)
- 150 g/5 oz (1¼ cups) self-raising flour
- 1 teaspoon mixed spice
- 1 teaspoon nutmeg
- 1 teaspoon ground ginger
- grated zest of ½ lemon (optional)
- pinch of salt
- 60 g/2¼ oz stem (preserved) ginger,
finely chopped or grated
- 2 tablespoons ginger syrup from the stem ginger jar
- 200 ml/7 fl oz (¾ cup plus 1 tablespoon) full-fat
(whole) milk
- 1 egg

* Preheat the oven to 150°C/300°F/Gas Mark 2. Line a 450 g/1 lb loaf pan with baking (parchment) paper.
* Put the sugar, butter, golden syrup and treacle (blackstrap molasses) into a large saucepan and heat gently over a low heat for 5 minutes until the sugar has dissolved and the butter melted. Stir well. Make sure it does not boil.
* Meanwhile, sift the flour into a large bowl and add the spices, lemon zest and salt. Pour in the hot syrups, add the stem (preserved) ginger and ginger syrup and mix thoroughly using a wooden spoon or balloon whisk. Beat in the milk, followed by the egg.
* Pour the cake batter into the prepared loaf pan and bake in the oven for 35–40 minutes until a skewer or toothpick inserted into the centre of the cake comes out clean. Remove from the oven and leave to cool in the pan. Once cool, cover and leave in a cool, dark place for 3–4 days before eating.

ENGLAND: CUMBRIA
*
CUMBRIAN GINGERBREAD

This traditional gingerbread is like a spicy-sweet and crumbly shortbread biscuit (cookie) – a far cry from the moist, spongy varieties so popular today. One of the best-known gingerbread bars hails from a tiny Cumbrian village, Grasmere, where in 1855 it was created by Victorian cook and baker Sarah Nelson. A local shop still bakes the gingerbread, but the exact recipe remains a secret. Once baked, slice into bars and serve warm. It should keep for at least a week.

Makes: 12
Prep time: 15 minutes
Cook time: 20–25 minutes
{☉}{☂}

- 150 g/5 oz (1¼ cups) wholemeal (whole wheat) flour
- 150 g/5 oz (1¼ cups) fine oatmeal
- 1½ teaspoons ground ginger
- ¼ teaspoon ground black pepper
- ¼ teaspoon ground cloves
- ½ teaspoon baking powder
- pinch of fine sea salt
- 150 g/5 oz (⅔ cup) soft light brown sugar
- 150 g/5 oz (1¼ sticks) unsalted butter, chilled and cubed

* Preheat the oven to 180°C/350°F/Gas Mark 4. Line a 23 x 33 cm/9 x 13 inch Swiss (jelly) roll pan with baking (parchment) paper.
* Put the flour, oatmeal, spices, baking powder and salt into a food processor and pulse briefly to combine. Add the sugar and pulse again to mix. Add the diced butter and pulse until the mixture resembles coarse breadcrumbs.
* Press two-thirds of the mixture into the prepared pan, making sure it is well compacted and evenly spread. Sprinkle the remaining mixture over the top like a loose crumble. Bake in the oven for 20–25 minutes until an even golden brown all over.
* Remove from the oven and, using a wet butter knife, portion the gingerbread into 12 bars while still hot in its pan. Leave in the pan to cool completely before gently removing. It is delicious eaten on the day of baking, but keeps well in an airtight container for up to 5 days.

NORTH OF ENGLAND: YORKSHIRE
*

YORKSHIRE PARKIN

Parkin is a form of oatmeal gingerbread common to Yorkshire and other parts of England where oats were grown in abundance. Dark and treacly, parkin makes the perfect accompaniment to mid-autumn holidays like Bonfire Night – an occasion for which it is often made. Once baked, cover well and allow to mature and soften up for a few days before serving.

Serves: 12
Prep time: 20 minutes
Cook time: 45 minutes
{🌢} {🥄}

- 400 g/14 oz (3½ sticks) unsalted butter
- 200 g/7 oz (¾ cup plus 1 tablespoon)
soft dark brown sugar
- 100 g/3½ oz (¼ cup plus 2 tablespoons) black treacle
(blackstrap molasses)
- 350 g/12 oz (1 cup) golden syrup
- 350 g/12 oz (3 cups minus 2 teaspoons) self-raising flour
- 2 teaspoons baking powder
- 2 tablespoons (12 g/¼ oz) ground ginger
- 4 teaspoons ground nutmeg
- 2 teaspoons mixed spice
- 250 g/9 oz (2 cups) medium oatmeal
- 4 eggs, beaten
- 120 ml/4 fl oz (½ cup) full-fat (whole) milk

* Preheat the oven to 140°C/275°F/Gas Mark 1. Line a 30 x 20 cm/12 x 8 inch cake pan with baking (parchment) paper.
* Put the butter, sugar, treacle (blackstrap molasses) and golden syrup into a saucepan and slowly stir over a low heat for 2–3 minutes until the sugar has dissolved and the butter melted.
* Sift the flour, baking powder and spices into a large bowl. Add the oatmeal and mix together. Beat the sweet liquid mixture from the saucepan into the bowl using a wooden spoon, then gradually incorporate the beaten eggs and milk, alternating between splashes of the 2, and stirring constantly.
* Tip the cake batter into the prepared cake pan and bake in the oven on the central rack for 45 minutes, or until deep brown and a skewer inserted into the centre of the cake comes out clean. Remove from the oven and leave to cool in its pan. Take it out of the pan and, if you can, cover with baking paper and keep it in a cool, dark place for at least 3 days before slicing and eating.

SCOTLAND: ORKNEY / ENGLAND: YORKSHIRE
*

ORKNEY BROONIE

While the name suggests that this gingerbread hails from the Orkney Islands in northern Scotland, most recipes for Orkney Broonie are near-identical to Yorkshire Parkin (see left). The only difference seems to be that some versions of Orkney Broonie are baked as a plainer amber-hued loaf cake.

Serves: 8
Prep time: 15 minutes
Cook time: 30–60 minutes
{🌢} {🥄}

- 70 g/2½ oz (⅔ stick) unsalted butter,
plus extra for greasing
- 100 g/3½ oz (¾ cup plus 2 teaspoons) plain
(all-purpose) flour
- 100 g/3½ oz (¾ cup plus 2 teaspoons) medium oatmeal
- ½ teaspoon bicarbonate of soda (baking soda)
- pinch of salt
- 2 teaspoons ground ginger
- 100 ml/3½ fl oz (⅓ cup plus 1 tablespoon) buttermilk
or 50 g/2 oz (¼ cup) plain yogurt
- 50 ml/1¾ fl oz (3½ tablespoons) full-fat (whole) milk
- 1 egg
- 70 g/2½ oz (⅓ cup) soft light brown sugar
- 50 g/2 oz (¼ cup minus 3 tablespoons) black treacle
(blackstrap molasses)
- butter, to serve

* Preheat the oven to 150°C/300°F/Gas Mark 2. Line a 450 g/1 lb loaf pan or 20 x 20 cm/8 x 8 cm traybake pan with baking (parchment) paper and grease with butter.
* Put the flour, oatmeal, bicarbonate of soda (baking soda), salt and ginger into a large bowl and mix together until combined. Put the buttermilk or yogurt, milk and egg into another bowl and lightly whisk together until combined.
* Put the butter, sugar and treacle (blackstrap molasses) into a medium saucepan and gently stir over a low heat for 2–3 minutes until the sugar has dissolved, the butter has melted and it just starts to bubble. Whisking constantly, pour the warm butter and sugar mixture into the milk and egg mix and whisk to incorporate. Next, pour this mixture into the dry mix, again whisking to combine thoroughly and ensure there are no lumps.
* Pour the batter into the prepared pan and bake in the oven for 30–40 minutes for a shallow traybake or 45–60 minutes for a loaf cake, until it is a deep brown colour. Remove from the oven and leave to cool completely, then wrap tightly in clingfilm (plastic wrap) and aluminium foil. This is best baked ahead and eaten after 3 days or left for up to a week as the cake will become moister, firmer and increasingly delicious. Devour with extra butter and a cup of tea.

Yorkshire parkin

WALES
*

BARA SINSIR
OLD WELSH GINGERBREAD

This traditional Welsh gingerbread is distinctive for the lack of its principal ingredient, ginger. In this case, the black treacle (blackstrap molasses) and candied mixed peel does most of the legwork in terms of spicing and colouring the cake.

Serves: 6
Prep time: 15 minutes
Cook time: 45–60 minutes
{♥}{✧}

- 120 g/4 oz (8 tablespoons) unsalted butter
- 500 g/1 lb 2 oz (4 cups plus 2 teaspoons) self-raising flour
- 150 g/5 oz (⅔ cup) light brown sugar
- pinch of salt
- 140 g/5 oz (1 cup) raisins
- 60 g/2¼ oz (⅓ cup) candied mixed peel
- 3 tablespoons black treacle (blackstrap molasses)
- 2 eggs, beaten
- 90 ml/3¼ fl oz (6 tablespoons) full-fat (whole) milk

* Preheat the oven to 160°C/325°F/Gas Mark 3. Line a 900 g/ 2 lb loaf pan with baking (parchment) paper.
* Melt the butter in a medium saucepan over a low-medium heat for 2 minutes, or until melted, then remove from the heat and set aside.
* Put the flour, sugar and salt into a large bowl and mix together. Add the raisins and candied mixed peel, then beat in the melted butter, treacle (blackstrap molasses) and eggs and, when smooth, mix in the milk. Pour the batter into the prepared loaf pan and bake in the oven for 45–60 minutes until risen and golden brown. Remove from the oven and leave to cool in the pan.

ENGLAND: DEVON
*

DEVONSHIRE HONEY CAKE

The National Trust serves a version of this moist honey cake at many of the stately homes and estates they manage in the southwest of England. Its taste will vary slightly depending on the honey – the flowers the bees pollinate will affect the taste of the honey and by extension the cake. If you have the option, go for something local and flavourful. Serve warm with a cup of tea.

Serves: 8
Prep time: 15 minutes
Cook time: 45–55 minutes
{♥}{✧}

- 230 g/8 oz (2 sticks plus 1 teaspoon) unsalted butter
- 255 g/9 oz (1 cup plus 2 tablespoons) honey
- 115 g/4 oz (½ cup) soft dark brown sugar
- 3 eggs
- 300 g/11 oz (2½ cups) self-raising flour

* Preheat the oven to 140°C/275°F/Gas Mark 1. Line the bottom and sides of a 20 cm/8 inch round cake pan with baking (parchment) paper.
* Put the butter, honey and sugar into a medium saucepan and stir over a low heat for 2–3 minutes, or until melted. Pour into a large bowl and leave to cool slightly. Beat in the eggs one at a time, then sift and gradually stir in the flour. Mix thoroughly, then pour the batter into the prepared cake pan. Bake in the oven for 45–55 minutes until a skewer inserted into the centre of the cake comes out clean. Remove from the oven and leave to cool still in the pan on a wire rack.

WALES
*

WELSH CINNAMON CAKE

This lightly spiced cake is spread with a layer of jam and baked with a thin topping of soft meringue.
The Welsh cookery writer Bobby Freeman suggests that the meringue indicates it was served especially for guests and special occasions.

Serves: 6–8
Prep time: 30 minutes
Cook time: 30 minutes
{♥}{✧}

- 120 g/4 oz (8 tablespoons) unsalted butter, softened
- 120 g/4 oz (⅔ cup minus 2 teaspoons) caster (superfine) sugar, plus 45 g/1½ oz (¼ cup minus 1 teaspoon) extra
- 3 eggs, separated
- 240 g/8½ oz (2 cups) self-raising flour
- 1 teaspoon ground cinnamon
- 2 tablespoons full-fat (whole) milk
- 2 teaspoons jam of your choice

* Preheat the oven to 200°C/400°F/Gas Mark 6. Line the bottom and sides of a 20 cm/8 inch loose-bottomed cake pan with baking (parchment) paper.
* Put the butter and the 120 g/4 oz (⅔ cup minus 2 teaspoons) sugar into a large bowl and, using a hand-held electric whisk, beat until pale and fluffy. Beat in the 3 egg yolks. Add the flour and cinnamon and mix in, then beat in the milk. Pour the batter into the prepared pan and bake in the oven for 20 minutes until a skewer or toothpick inserted into the centre of the cake comes out clean. Remove from the oven, turn out of the pan and leave to cool on a wire rack.
* Melt the jam in a small saucepan over a low heat for 2–3 minutes. Alternatively, melt in a microwave for 20 seconds, then brush all over the cooled cake.
* Put the egg whites and a third of the remaining 45 g/1½ oz (¼ cup minus 1 teaspoon) sugar into a large, clean bowl and, using electric beaters, whisk on high speed until incorporated, then add the remaining sugar, a little at a time, until it is thick and glossy. Spread the meringue over the cake using a palette knife, then put the cake back into the oven for 10 minutes, or until the meringue is golden brown. Remove from the oven and leave to cool.

ENGLAND: DORSET AND DEVON

*

DORSET APPLE CAKE

The west country of England, Dorset and Devon especially, are known for their apples. Recipes like this one, a buttery sponge with slices of apple and a crispy top, have been a household favourite for several generations. Slices of apple cake make excellent eating all day long – some might even suggest a slice as a sweet nibble for breakfast.

Serves: 8
Prep time: 20 minutes
Cook time: 1 hour 15 minutes
{◉} {☀}

- 150 g/5 oz (1¼ sticks) unsalted butter,
plus extra for greasing
- 2 eggs
- 150 g/5 oz (⅔ cup) soft light brown sugar
- 250 g/9 oz (2 cups) wholemeal (whole wheat)
self-raising flour
- 250 g9 oz windfall apples or eating apples of your choice,
cored and cut into 1–2 cm/½–¾ inch dice
- 30 ml/1 fl oz (2 tablespoons) full-fat (whole) milk
- demerara (turbinado) sugar, for sprinkling
- Clotted Cream (page 34), to serve

- For additional flavourings (optional):
- 2 teaspoons ground spice, such as cinnamon or nutmeg
- 100 g/3½ oz (½ cup plus 1 tablespoon) dried fruits,
such as raisins or sultanas (golden raisins)
- 1 teaspoon grated lemon zest
- 1 teaspoon vanilla extract
- extra apple pieces, for topping
- honey, for drizzling

* Preheat the oven to 150°C/300°F/Gas Mark 2. Grease a round 20 cm/8 inch cake pan with butter and line the bottom and sides with baking (parchment) paper.
* Melt the butter in a medium saucepan over a low-medium heat for 2 minutes, or until melted, then remove from the heat and set aside. Put the eggs and light brown sugar into a large bowl and whisk using a balloon whisk until well combined and lightly frothy. Fold in the flour until it is all incorporated. The mixture will seem fairly stiff and dry at this stage. Fold in the melted butter, then fold in the chopped apples and milk, plus any of the additional ingredients you desire. Spoon the batter into the prepared cake pan and smooth the top using the back of the spoon. Top with the extra apple pieces (if using) and sprinkle liberally with demerara (turbinado) sugar and bake in the oven for 1¼ hours, checking every 5 minutes after the first hour, until the cake is risen and deep golden brown. Remove from the oven and leave to cool slightly. If you prefer a softer top, cover the cake with a clean dish towel as it cools or liberally drizzle the cake with honey.
* This cake is delicious eaten while still slightly warm on the day it is baked with a hefty dollop of Clotted Cream or similar, but it also keeps well for a few days in an airtight container or well wrapped in baking paper, either eaten at room temperature or reheated. If desired, ice (frost) this cake with a honey cream cheese frosting (page 322).
* **Variations:** This is a versatile cake to play with. Use pears instead of the apple and add a few tablespoons of chai latte powder to the mix. You can also replace the

wholemeal (whole wheat) flour with plain self-raising flour for a less earthsome-tasting cake. Cherries or other fresh berries would also work well in the summer.

ENGLAND: CORNWALL

*

CORNISH HEAVY CAKE
HEVVA CAKE

A rich and crumbly flat cake traditionally baked by the wives of Cornish fishermen. The name 'hevva' apparently comes from the cry 'hes va', which was used by clifftop scouts to alert fishermen to shoals of pilchards, 'hes', in this case, being the Cornish word for a shoal of fish. Before putting the cake into the oven, score a criss-cross pattern two-thirds of the way through the cake. The pattern is said to represent a fisherman's net – which is a cute touch – but has the added advantage of making the hevva easier to break apart. Serve warm with a mug of tea, and if desired, a little more butter or Cornish clotted cream.

Serves: 6
Prep time: 20 minutes
Cook time: 40–45 minutes
{☀}

- 500 g/1 lb 2 oz (4 cups plus 2 teaspoons) self-raising
flour, plus extra for dusting
- 250 g/9 oz (1⅓ cups plus 2 teaspoons) lard, diced,
or half lard and half butter
- 125 g/4 ¼ oz (½ cup plus 1 tablespoon) granulated sugar
- 250 g/9 oz (1⅓ cups plus 2 teaspoons) dried fruit, such
as currants, sultanas (golden raisins) or raisins, or a mix
- 30 g/1 oz (¼ cup minus 2 teaspoons)
candied mixed peel (optional)
- 100 ml/3½ fl oz (⅓ cup plus 1 tablespoon)
full-fat (whole) milk
- butter or Clotted Cream (page 34), to serve

- For the gloss:
- 2 tablespoons full-fat (whole) milk
- large pinch of granulated sugar

* Preheat the oven to 180°C/350°F/Gas Mark 4. Grease a 20 x 20 cm/8 x 8 inch baking pan with butter.
* Put the flour into a large bowl, add the fat and rub it in until it resembles breadcrumbs. Stir in the sugar, dried fruit and candied mixed peel (if using), then add the milk and mix to form a dough. Knead the dough on a floured work counter only once to bring the mixture together, then press into the prepared pan and, using a sharp knife, make cuts in a criss-cross fashion across the top.
* Bake in the oven for 40–45 minutes until a skewer inserted into the centre of the cake comes out clean. Remove from the oven.
* For the gloss, put the milk and granulated sugar into a small bowl and mix together, then brush it over the top of the cake. Leave the cake to cool for 30 minutes before removing it from the pan and cooling on a wire rack. Serve with butter or Clotted Cream.

UNITED KINGDOM
*

BLACK CAKE

Although similar to fruitcake, black cake has an identity all its own, embodying the extremities of labour and luxury. Black cake is a descendent of British plum (Christmas) pudding mostly found in parts of the former and current British West Indies, such as Barbados, Montserrat and Guyana since the eighteenth century. People from these communities now living in the UK have continued this tradition. Aside from dried fruit, the heavy presence of rum, sugar and molasses are reminiscent of a time when the economic priority of sugar cane production, powered by the ills of servitude, anchored British interest in the Caribbean. Black cake is most commonly eaten during Christmas time and its ritualistic process can start as early as the Christmas prior. Dried fruits are ground into a fine paste, then soaked in rum indefinitely. This process of grinding makes the cake extra moist while maintaining its richness and density.

Serves: 10–12
Prep time: 30 minutes
Cook time: 1¾ hours
{ }

- For the fruit mix:
- 500 g/ 1 lb 2 oz (3⅓ cups) raisins
- 250 g/ 9 oz (1⅔ cups) sultanas (golden raisins)
- 125 g/ 4¼ oz (¾ cup) candied mixed peel
- 125 g/ 4¼ oz (½ cup) dried glacé (candied) cherries
- 250 ml/ 8 fl oz (1 cup) dark rum or sherry

- For the cake batter:
- 450 g/ 1 lb (4 sticks) unsalted butter, softened
- 450 g/ 1 lb (2 cups) dark brown muscovado sugar
- 9 eggs
- grated zest of 1 lemon
- grated zest of 1 orange
- 1 teaspoon vanilla extract
- 1 teaspoon almond extract
- 300 g/ 11 oz (2½ cups) plain (all-purpose) flour
- 2 teaspoons baking powder

- For the browning:
- 4 tablespoons molasses or black treacle (blackstrap molasses)
- 4 tablespoons dark rum or sherry

* Preheat the oven to 160°C/ 325°F/ Gas Mark 3. Line the bottom and sides of a 23 cm/ 9 inch round cake pan with baking (parchment) paper.
* For the fruit mix, put all the dried fruits into a food processor and blend. As they start to break down, gradually add the rum or sherry to the food processor. The fruit will form a paste. At this point you can decide how smooth you would like the fruitcake to be. Set the paste aside.
* For the cake batter, put the butter and sugar into a large bowl and, using a wooden spoon, mix together until pale and fluffy. Crack the eggs into another bowl and gradually whisk into the cake batter along with the lemon and orange zest, vanilla and almond extract. The batter may curdle at this stage but don't worry.
* Sift the flour and baking powder into another bowl, then fold into the cake batter using a large spoon or spatula. Do this gradually to ensure the batter does not become lumpy. Once the flour is evenly combined into the batter, set aside while you prepare the browning.
* Heat the molasses or treacle (blackstrap molasses) and rum or sherry in a medium saucepan over a low heat for 2–3 minutes until the liquids have incorporated evenly, then remove from the heat and leave to cool.
* Fold 1 kg/ 2¼ lb of the reserved fruit paste into the cake batter until it is evenly mixed in. The remaining fruit paste can be left to mature in an airtight container in the fridge until you bake another black cake. Finally, fold the browning into the mix.
* Spoon the cake batter into the prepared cake pan and bake on the centre shelf of the oven for 1¾ hours. Don't open the oven for the first hour of baking otherwise the centre of the cake can sink. To check if the cake is cooked, insert a skewer into the centre of the cake and if it comes out clean, it is done. Remove the cake from the oven and leave to cool, then serve.

ENGLAND: KENT
*

KENTISH COBNUT CAKES

The Kentish cobnut is a type of hazelnut famous to the Kent region since the seventeenth century. Eaten both fresh and lightly roasted, they also make a great addition to lightly spiced autumnal cakes like the one below.

Serves at least 8
Prep time: 20 minutes
Cook time: 30–40 minutes
{ }

- 180 g/ 6 oz (1½ sticks) unsalted butter, diced
- 120 g/ 4 oz (⅓ cup) golden syrup
- 80 g/ 3 oz (⅓ cup plus 1 teaspoon) demerara (turbinado) sugar
- 150 ml/ 5 fl oz (⅔ cup) double (heavy) cream
- 3 pieces stem (preserved) ginger, finely chopped
- 2 eggs, beaten
- 260 g/ 9 oz (2 cups plus 4 teaspoons) self-raising flour
- 1 tablespoon ground ginger
- 120 g/ 4 oz (1 cup) cobnuts or hazelnuts, coarsely chopped

* Preheat the oven to 180°C/ 350°F/ Gas Mark 4. Line the bottom and sides of a 20 cm/ 8 inch round cake pan with baking (parchment) paper.
* Put the butter, syrup and sugar into a small saucepan and heat over a low heat for 2–3 minutes, stirring until the sugar has dissolved and the butter has melted. Remove from the heat and pour into a large bowl. Stir in the cream, stem (preserved) ginger and the eggs. Sift in the flour and ginger before adding the nuts and mixing until the batter is smooth.
* Pour the batter into the prepared pan and bake in the oven for 30–40 minutes until a skewer inserted into the centre of the cake comes out clean. Leave to cool in the pan for 5 minutes, then transfer to a wire rack.

SCOTLAND
*

TIFFIN

This Scottish 'fridge cake' is made from a base of crushed biscuits (cookies), unsweetened cocoa powder and dried fruits, which is then draped in a thick layer of chocolate. Tiffin is highly adaptable and can be made or topped with different types of chocolate or sweets (candies). Slice into squares or bars.

Serves: about 12
Prep time: 10 minutes
Cook time: 20 minutes, plus 3½ hours setting
{👁}{⌁}

- 18 digestive biscuits
(shop-bought or homemade, page 340)
- 120 g/4 oz (1 stick) unsalted butter
- 60 g/2¼ oz (½ cup) unsweetened cocoa powder
- 120 g/4 oz (⅓ cup plus 2 teaspoons) golden syrup
- 200 g/7 oz (1⅓ cups) sultanas (golden raisins)
- 200 g/7 oz milk chocolate, broken into small pieces

* Line a 20 x 20 cm/8 x 8 inch baking pan with baking (parchment) paper.
* Carefully crush the biscuits (cookies) using a rolling pin. You don't want fine crumbs, so there's no need to be overzealous! Set the crumbs aside.
* Put the butter, cocoa and golden syrup into a small saucepan and heat over a low heat, stirring occasionally, for 3–4 minutes until melted. Remove from the heat and tip into a large bowl. Add the sultanas (golden raisins) and crushed biscuits and, using a wooden spoon, mix together, making sure they are thoroughly combined. Spoon the mixture into the prepared pan, press down firmly and smooth out with a spoon or palette knife. Leave to chill in the fridge for 2 hours to firm up.
* Put the chocolate into a heatproof bowl and set over a saucepan of gently simmering water, making sure the bottom of the bowl doesn't touch the water and melt the chocolate slowly. Keep an eye on the chocolate to ensure it doesn't burn.
* When fully melted, pour it over the tiffin base, spreading it evenly over the top using a palette knife. Put the pan back into the fridge to cool for at least 1½ hours, or until set. You can leave it overnight, if desired. Remove the tiffin from the pan and cut into squares.

SCOTLAND: ABERDEEN
*

ABERDEEN CRULLAS

These plaited (braided) pastries are very much like the Dutch/Dutch-American cruller – hence the similar linguistic root. The earliest existing recipe for Aberdeen crullas dates back to 1829, in Mrs Dalgairns's *The Practice of Cookery*. The pastry was likely brought to Scotland's east coast by Americans, if not from the Dutch directly, as Dutch traders and fishermen settled along Scotland's east coast starting from the 1600s.

Serves: 8
Prep time: 40 minutes
Cook time: 20 minutes
{⌁}

- lard or sunflower oil, for deep-frying
- 100 g/3½ oz (7 tablespoons) unsalted butter, softened
- 100 g/3½ oz (½ cup) caster (superfine) sugar, plus extra for dusting
- 2 eggs
- 200 g/7 oz (1⅔ cups) plain (all-purpose) flour, plus extra for dusting

* Heat enough lard or oil for deep-frying in a large, deep saucepan or deep fryer until it reaches 190°C/375°F on a thermometer.
* Meanwhile, put the butter and sugar into a large bowl and, using a wooden spoon, mix them together until they are pale and fluffy. Beat in the eggs, then sift in the flour and mix to a dough.
* Tip the dough out onto a lightly floured work counter and roll into an oblong shape. Cut into 8 even, short strips. Separate the strips on the work counter, so there is enough space to prepare each one. Make 3 evenly spaced cuts into each pastry strip, running four-fifths of the way up, then plait (braid) each strip of pastry. Deep-fry in batches for 3–4 minutes until golden brown, flipping them after a minute or two to ensure they are evenly cooked. Remove using a slotted spoon and leave to drain on paper towels. Dust the tops of each crulla with sugar and leave to cool a little before eating.

SCOTLAND: ABERDEEN

*

BUTTERIES
ROWIES

In typical deprecating Scottish humour, these pastries have the unglamorous epithet of 'roadkill croissants' – and yes, Scots are less particular about laminated layers, but these pastries are not to be missed. Made with very generous amounts of butter and lard, and just slightly savoury, butteries should be eaten fresh, or toasted and spread – again – with butter and jam or honey.

Makes: 16
Prep time: 30 minutes, plus 1 hour rising and proving
Cook time: 15–20 minutes
{ᵕᵕ}

- For the dough:
- 1 tablespoon caster (superfine) sugar
- 20 g/¾ oz (4 teaspoons) fresh yeast or 5 g/
2 teaspoons instant dried yeast
- 390 ml/13½ fl oz (1⅔ cups minus 2 teaspoons)
water (37°C/98.6°F)
- 500 g/1 lb 2 oz (4 cups minus 4 teaspoons) strong white
bread flour, plus extra for dusting

- For the fat:
- 140 g/5 oz (1¼ sticks) unsalted butter, softened,
plus extra for greasing and to serve
- 115 g/4 oz (⅔ cup) lard, softened
- 30 g/1 oz (2 tablespoons) salt
- 1 tablespoon caster (superfine) sugar
- 150 g/5 oz (1¼ cups) strong white bread flour

* For the dough, put all the ingredients into a large bowl, add 390 ml/13 fl oz (1⅔ cups minus 2 teaspoons) blood temperature (37°C/98.6°F) water and mix together. Do not overwork the dough and just mix it enough to combine all the ingredients. It should be loose and a little sticky. Cover the dough with clingfilm (plastic wrap) or a dish towel and leave to rise at room temperature for 30 minutes.
* Meanwhile, for the fat, put all the ingredients into a stand mixer fitted with a paddle attachment and beat until it is all combined and the mixture is a creamy consistency. Set aside.
* Grease a large baking sheet with butter. Tip the risen dough out onto a heavily dusted work counter and roll it to a rectangle about 5 mm/¼ inch thick. Spread a third of the fat mixture evenly over the top, then fold the dough over in thirds, then roll this out gently again to 5 mm/¼ inch. Repeat this process until all the fat mixture is used up.
* Divide the dough into 16 even pieces and very carefully roll each one into a loose ball, then transfer to the prepared baking sheet. Cover again and leave to prove in a warm place for 30 minutes, or until they have doubled in size.
* Meanwhile, preheat the oven to 200°C/400°F/Gas Mark 6.
* When the butteries have doubled in size, bake in the oven for 15–20 minutes until lightly coloured on top. Remove from the oven and leave to cool. Served them toasted with more butter.

SCOTLAND / ENGLAND

*

FUDGE DOUGHNUTS

Custard-filled fudge doughnuts are a special favourite in bakeries across Britain: from the high-street bakery chains to traditional family-run operations like the excellent fifth-generation Fisher & Donaldson based in Fife and Dundee. In England, these doughnuts are also invariably known as toffee or caramel custard doughnuts, but this version is a modern take on the classic by Glasgow-based baker Anna Luntley. Enjoy with a cup of tea and a bit of sun.

Makes: 12
Prep time: 30 minutes, plus 2–4 hours rising and proving
Cook time: 15–20 minutes
{ᵕ} {ᵕᵕ}

- For the dough:
- 250 g/9 oz (2 cups) strong white bread flour,
plus extra for dusting
- 250 g/9 oz (2 cups) strong brown bread flour
- 60 g/2¼ oz (¼ cup) soft light brown sugar
- 1½ teaspoons fine sea salt
- 17 g/¾ oz (4 teaspoons) fresh yeast or 5 g/
2 teaspoons instant dried yeast
- 330 ml/11 fl oz (1⅓ cups) full-fat (whole) milk,
at room temperature
- 130 g/4½ oz (9 tablespoons) unsalted butter,
at room temperature, diced
- 2 eggs, beaten
- sunflower oil, for oiling and deep-frying

- For the custard cream:
- 500 ml/17 fl oz (2 cups plus 1 tablespoon)
full-fat (whole) milk
- 1 vanilla pod (bean), split lengthwise in half
and seeds scraped out
- 6 egg yolks
- 120 g/4 oz (⅔ cup) caster (superfine) sugar
- 40 g/1½ oz (⅓ cup) cornflour (cornstarch)
- 50 g/2 oz (3½ tablespoons) unsalted butter,
diced and chilled
- 400 ml/14 fl oz (1⅔ cups) double (heavy) cream

- For the fudge glaze:
- 300 g/11 oz (2¾ sticks) unsalted butter
- 300 g/11 oz (1⅓ cups) soft light brown sugar
- 150 ml/5 fl oz (⅔ cup) double (heavy) cream
- 1 teaspoon vanilla extract
- pinch of fine sea salt
- 100 g/3½ oz good-quality white chocolate,
finely chopped

* For the dough, put the flours, sugar, salt and yeast into a large bowl and set aside. Put the milk, butter and eggs into a stand mixer fitted with a dough hook attachment and mix on slow speed until they are combined. Add the dry ingredients to the bowl and mix on slow speed until combined, then increase the speed to medium and mix for 5–10 minutes to form a smooth dough that comes away from the sides of the bowl as it mixes.
* Transfer the dough to a lightly oiled bowl, cover with clingfilm (plastic wrap) or a damp dish towel and leave to rise in a warm place for 1–2 hours until doubled in size.

* Knead the risen dough gently to remove any air bubbles then fold the dough over onto itself in the bowl. Cover again and leave to prove in a warm place for 1–2 hours until doubled in size.

* Meanwhile, prepare the custard cream. Pour the milk and vanilla seeds into a medium saucepan. Put all the other ingredients into separate bowls (the yolks should be in the largest bowl, which eventually all the other ingredients will fit into).

* Gently warm the milk over a medium heat for 2–3 minutes until it begins to steam, stirring gently to disperse the vanilla seeds. Once the milk begins to steam, combine the egg yolks and caster (superfine) sugar and whisk by hand to incorporate. Add the cornflour (cornstarch) to this mixture and whisk to incorporate.

* Carefully remove the milk from the heat and gradually add half the hot milk to the egg yolk mixture, a little at a time, and whisking in well with each addition to prevent the eggs scrambling. Once half of the hot milk is incorporated, pour it all back into the pan with the remaining milk and return to a medium heat. Whisk well to incorporate, then continue whisking to prevent the custard from sticking to the bottom of the pan. Keep the pan on the heat until the mixture comes to the boil. Once the custard starts to boil, whisk energetically for another 2 minutes. Keep the custard moving constantly to prevent sticking, burning or lumps, then remove from the heat and immediately whisk in the butter, whisking for another 2 minutes until the butter is incorporated and gently starts to cool the custard. Transfer the custard from the hot pan to a plastic bowl, cover the surface with clingfilm (plastic wrap) and leave to cool completely. Once cool, chill in the fridge until needed. It can be made up to 2 days ahead.

* Once the dough has proved, line 2 large baking sheets with baking (parchment) paper. Put the dough onto a lightly floured work counter and divide it into 12 equal pieces, about 90–100 g/ 3¼–3½ oz each. Roll each piece of dough into a neat ball in the palm of your hand in an action almost like you might use to lather a bar of soap. If the dough is sticky make sure your hands are well floured. Arrange the 12 dough balls evenly across the prepared baking sheets and loosely cover with clingfilm (plastic wrap). Leave to prove for 1–2 hours in a warm place until doubled in size and soft like marshmallow.

* Meanwhile, make the fudge glaze. Melt the butter in a medium saucepan over a low heat for 2–3 minutes. Add the light brown sugar and gently stir until the sugar has completely dissolved. Increase the heat and simmer until it comes to a rolling bubble. Remove the pan from the heat and carefully pour in the cream – the mixture should bubble and splutter a little. Stir in the cream until it is fully incorporated, then add the vanilla extract, salt and chocolate and stir until melted. Leave to cool to room temperature.

* Once the doughnuts are fully proved – they should feel soft and pillowy – heat enough oil for deep-frying to 180°C/350°F on a thermometer. It is best to use a deep fryer, but a large saucepan with about 7.5 cm/3 inches of oil and a digital thermometer will work. Working in batches of 3, carefully lower the doughnuts into the hot oil and deep-fry for 3 minutes. Using a slotted metal spoon, gently flip the doughnuts over and deep-fry for another 3 minutes. Remove with a slotted spoon and leave to drain and cool on paper towels.

* While the doughnuts are cooling, whip the cream for the custard filling in a stand mixer fitted with a whisk attachment to soft peaks. Alternatively, whip the cream in a large bowl with electric beaters. Add the chilled vanilla custard and whip again until it is incorporated and thick. Be careful not to whip it too far as it can begin to deflate – you want to stop whipping just as the custard cream is holding itself in thick pillows. Gently spoon the cream into a piping (pastry) bag ready to fill the doughnuts.

* The doughnuts should be filled when they are completely cool, otherwise the cream will melt and make a soggy doughnut. For peace of mind, the doughnuts can be chilled for a short while before filling.

* To fill the doughnuts, use the point of a small sharp knife to make an incision into the centre of the doughnut, then wiggle the knife around to open up a cavity inside the bun. You can also use your fingers at this point to make sure that there is plenty of room for the filling. Insert the nozzle of the piping bag into the doughnut and squeeze until fully laden with cream, about 80–100 g/ 3–3½ oz is a good amount to aim to get inside each doughnut.

* Once filled, remove any excess cream from the outside of the doughnut and ice (frost) each with a generous spoonful of the fudge glaze, spreading a little as needed using a palette knife.

* If not serving immediately, chill the doughnuts until later, but they are best enjoyed at room temperature on the day they are made.

* **Notes:** It is always a good idea to deep-fry one doughnut first and test your times and temperature as doughs can vary slightly. Fry one first using the guidelines above, then remove from the pan and drain on paper towel. Once cool enough to touch, tear it in half to check that the doughnut is cooked through. You may want to alter the frying times accordingly.

UNITED KINGDOM
*
YUM YUMS

A flaky plaited (braided) pastry that is deep-fried and glazed with icing (frosting), the yum yum is neither croissant nor doughnut but has nevertheless become a beloved staple of high-street bakeries.

Makes: 12–15
Prep time: 1 hour,
plus 1 hour 20 minutes resting and proving
Cook time: 20 minutes
{👤}{ - • }

- 220 ml/7½ fl oz (¾ cup plus 3 tablespoons) full-fat (whole) milk or water
- 500 g/1 lb 2 oz (4 cups plus 2 teaspoons) strong white bread flour, plus extra for dusting
- 1 teaspoon salt
- 1 teaspoon instant dried yeast
- 40 g/1½ oz (¼ cup minus 2 teaspoons) caster (superfine) sugar
- 80 g/3 oz (¾ stick) unsalted butter, diced
- 2 eggs, beaten
- vegetable oil, for oiling and deep-frying
- 200 g/7 oz (1⅔ cups) icing (confectioners') sugar

* Heat the milk or water in a medium saucepn over a low heat for 3–4 minutes, or until warm. Remove from the heat and set aside. Sift the flour into a large bowl and add the salt, yeast, caster (superfine) sugar and butter. Make a well in the centre and add the warm milk and eggs. Mix to form a dough. Don't rub in the butter – it needs to be in chunks. Alternatively, mix in a stand mixer fitted with a dough hook atachment. Put the dough into an oiled bowl, cover with clingfilm (plastic wrap) and leave to rest for 20 minutes.
* Roll out the dough on a lightly floured work counter to make a rectangle, then fold the rectangle into thirds, turn and roll again. (Turn it onto itself twice.) Repeat this process 3 times, then put the folded dough into a rectangular oiled container, cover with clingfilm and leave to rest in the fridge for 30 minutes.
* Roll out the rested dough into a wide, thin rectangle, about 25 x 15 cm/10 x 6 inches, then cut the rectangle into 12–15 equal-sized strips depending on exactly how wide the pastry is. Cut each strip down its centre, leaving it attached at both ends, then twist the pastry once (the top half turning one direction, and the bottom the opposite) and set back down. Put the yum yums onto a lightly oiled baking sheet, cover again and leave to prove in a warm place for 30 minutes, or until doubled in size.
* Heat enough oil for deep-frying in a large, deep saucepan or deep fryer until it reaches 170°C/344°F on a thermometer.
* Meanwhile, for the icing (frosting), put the icing (confectioners') sugar and 3 tablespoons water into a large bowl and mix together. The icing should be runny enough to brush. Set aside.
* Working in batches of 3–4, carefully lower the yum yums into the hot oil and deep-fry, turning occasionally, for 5 minutes, or until crispy and golden brown. Remove the yum yums with a slotted spoon and drain on paper towels. When somewhat cool, transfer to a wire rack and brush each one lightly with the icing.

SCOTLAND
*
SNOWBALLS

In Scotland, two famous sweets bear the name 'snowball'. This one is a cakey biscuit (cookie), sandwiched with jam and covered in desiccated (unsweetened shredded) coconut. The other is a chocolate and coconut-covered marshmallow – but there's room for both in our lives.

Serves: 4
Prep time: 30 minutes, plus 1–2 hours setting
Cook time: 20 minutes
{👤}

- 160 g/5¾ oz (1⅓ cups) self-raising flour
- 80 g/3 oz (¾ stick) unsalted butter, diced
- 80 g/3 oz (½ cup minus 4 teaspoons) caster (superfine) sugar
- 1 egg, beaten
- 100 g/3½ oz (¾ cup minus 2 teaspoons) icing (confectioners') sugar
- about 3 tablespoons desiccated (unsweetened shredded) coconut
- 4 tablespoons raspberry jam

* Preheat the oven to 180°C/350°F/Gas Mark 4.
* Sift the flour into a large bowl, add the butter and rub it in with your fingertips until the mixture resembles breadcrumbs, then stir in the caster (superfine) sugar and the egg to make a dough.
* Divide the dough into 8 equal pieces and use your hands to roll them into very smooth, evenly round balls. You will want them to bake very uniformly. Arrange on a large baking sheet and bake in the oven for 20 minutes, or until pale golden brown. Remove from the oven and leave to cool on a wire rack.
* Put the icing (confectioners') sugar into a large bowl, add about 2 tablespoons water and beat together with a wooden spoon to make a fairly runny icing. Keeping them on the rack, pour the icing (frosting) over the cakes, using a knife to spread it. Leave for 5 minutes so the excess icing can drip away, then sprinkle well with the desiccated (unsweetened shredded) coconut. Alternatively, put the desiccated coconut into a medium bowl and dip each cake into the coconut to coat. Leave to set for 1–2 hours before slicing them in half and sandwiching together again with the jam.

WALES: ANGLESEY
*

ABERFFRAW CAKES
ANGLESEY SHORTBREAD

These shortbread biscuits (cookies) are baked in a scallop-shell mould (or large cockle shells), and are unique to the Isle of Anglesey in northwest Wales.

Makes: 6
Prep time: 15 minutes
Cook time: 20 minutes
{👤}{🔪}{🥛}

- 80 g/3 oz (¾ stick) unsalted butter, plus extra for greasing
- 120 g/4 oz (1 cup) plain (all-purpose) flour, plus extra for dusting
- 40 g/1½ oz (¼ cup minus 2 teaspoons) caster (superfine) sugar, plus extra for sprinkling

* Preheat the oven to 180°C/350°F/Gas Mark 4.
* Melt the butter in a small saucepan over a medium-low heat, then remove from the heat and set aside.
* Sift the flour into a large bowl and stir in the melted butter. Add the sugar and mix to form a firm cake batter, then divide into 6 equal pieces on a lightly floured work counter.
* Grease and then flour a scallop-shaped mould and press the mixture into the mould. Repeat with the other pieces, then arrange on a large baking sheet and bake in the oven for 20 minutes, or until pale golden brown.
* Turn the cakes out of the moulds and onto a wire rack, sprinkle with extra sugar and leave to cool.

UNITED KINGDOM
*

ABERNETHY BISCUITS

These light and flaky caraway biscuits (cookies) surprisingly bear no relation to the Scottish town. Instead, they are named for the English surgeon, John Abernethy (1764–1831). According to *The Oxford Companion to Food*, the biscuits were created after Abernethy suggested that a local baker add sugar and caraway seeds to the plain biscuits they sold.

Makes: 12
Prep time: 20 minutes
Cook time: 20 minutes
{👤}{🔪}

- 230 g/8 oz (2 cups minus 2 teaspoons) plain (all-purpose) flour, plus extra for dusting
- 90 g/3¼ oz (6 tablespoons) unsalted butter
- 90 g/3¼ oz (½ cup minus 2 teaspoons) caster (superfine) sugar
- ½ teaspoon baking powder
- ½ teaspoon caraway seeds (optional)
- 1 tablespoon full-fat (whole) milk
- 1 egg, beaten

* Preheat the oven to 160°C/325°F/Gas Mark 3. Line a large baking sheet with baking (parchment) paper.

* Sift the flour into a large bowl, add the butter and rub it in with your fingertips until the mixture resembles breadcrumbs. Add the sugar, baking powder and caraway seeds (if using) and mix together. Make a well in the centre of the mixture and slowly pour in the milk, followed by the beaten egg and mix together.
* Tip the mixture onto a lightly floured work counter and knead briefly to bring the dough together. Roll the dough out to a thickness of 3–4 mm/⅛–⅙ inch thick and cut into 12 circles about 5–6 cm/2–2½ inches wide. Arrange them on the prepared baking sheet and bake in the oven for 20 minutes, or until all sides of the biscuits have turned a pale golden. Remove from the oven and cool on a wire rack.

SCOTLAND: EDINBURGH
*

PARLIAMENT CAKES
PARLIES

These ginger shortbread biscuits (cookies) were created in the nineteenth century by one Mrs Flockhart, also known as 'Lucky Fykie', the owner and proprietor of a hotel-cum-grocery store in Edinburgh's Waverley neighbourhood. The parlies, which are traditionally cut into squares, became highly popular with Lucky's clientele, which included many lawyers, bankers and even members of parliament.

Makes: 24
Prep time: 10 minutes, plus 10–15 minutes chilling
Cook time: 15–20 minutes
{👤}{🔪}

- 120 g/4 oz (½ cup) muscovado sugar
- 50 g/2 oz (¼ cup minus 3 tablespoons) black treacle (blackstrap molasses)
- 120 g/4 oz (1 stick) unsalted butter
- 1 egg
- 230 g/8 oz (2 cups minus 2 teaspoons) self-raising flour, sifted
- 10 g/¼ oz (2 teaspoons) ground ginger

* Preheat the oven to 170°C/325°F/Gas mark 3. Line 2–3 large baking sheets with baking (parchment) paper.
* Put the muscovado sugar, treacle (blackstrap molasses) and butter into a medium saucepan and stir over a low heat for 2–3 minutes, or until the sugar has completely dissolved. Add the egg and whisk briefly to emulsify the mixture. Add the flour and ginger, then begin to incorporate the mix with a spatula until the ingredients come together to form a dough.
* Roll the dough out between 2 sheets of baking paper to about 4 mm/⅙ inch thick, then chill in the fridge for 10–15 minutes.
* Remove the dough from the fridge and peel back the paper from both sides. Using a knife, cut the dough into 24 x 5 cm/2 inch squares, then arrange onto the prepared baking sheets, leaving space between each one. Use a fork to prick each biscuit (cookie) several times, then bake in the oven for 15–20 minutes until they are a rich dark brown. Remove from the oven and leave to cool completely on a wire rack before serving.

SCOTLAND / NORTHERN IRELAND
*

EMPIRE BISCUITS

Shortbread biscuits (cookies) spread with icing (frosting) and sandwiched with a layer of jam, Empire biscuits are said to be a heftier version of the elegant Austrian *Linzerkekse*. Originally known by the name German biscuits, they were redubbed during the course of World War I.

Makes: 12
Prep time: 30 minutes
Cook time: 10 minutes
{ⵣ} {⚫}

- 225 g/8 oz (2 sticks) unsalted butter, softened
- 100 g/3½ oz (½ cup) caster (superfine) sugar
- 250 g/9 oz (2 cups) plain (all-purpose) flour, plus extra for dusting
- about 150 g/5 oz (½ cup) raspberry jam
- 200 g/7 oz (1⅔ cups) icing (confectioners') sugar
- 12 glacé (candied) cherries, halved, to decorate

* Preheat the oven to 180°C/350°F/Gas Mark 4. Line 2–3 large baking sheets with baking (parchment) paper.
* Put the butter and caster (superfine) sugar into a large bowl and, using a wooden spoon, beat them until pale and fluffy. Add the flour and mix to form a dough. Tip the dough out onto a lightly floured work counter and roll it out to a rectangle about 3–4 mm/⅛–⅙ inch thick. Cut into 24 circles about 6 cm/2½ inches wide. Arrange on the prepared baking sheets, spaced slightly apart, and bake in the oven for 10 minutes, or until pale golden brown. Remove from the oven and leave to cool on a wire rack. When cool, sandwich together 2 biscuits (cookies) with a layer of raspberry jam.
* Put the icing (confectioners') sugar into a large bowl, add 2 tablespoons water and beat together using a wooden spoon to make an icing (frosting). Using a spoon, spread the biscuits with the icing. Decorate with a halved glacé (candied) cherry, the flat half facing downwards.

SCOTLAND / NORTH OF ENGLAND
*

PERKINS BISCUITS

Perkins are oatmeal and ginger biscuits (cookies) that are closely related to the Yorkshire Parkin (page 324). Oddly enough, these biscuits are most often found in regions where parkin is not.

Makes: 12
Prep time: 15 minutes, plus 30 minutes chilling
Cook time: 15 minutes
{ⵣ}

- 100 g/3½ oz (¾ cup plus 2 teaspoons) medium oatmeal, plus 2 handfuls for rolling
- 100 g/3½ oz (¾ cup plus 2 teaspoons) plain (all-purpose) flour
- ¾ teaspoon bicarbonate of soda (baking soda)
- 1 teaspoon ground ginger
- 1 teaspoon ground cinnamon
- pinch of fine sea salt
- 50 g/2 oz (3½ tablespoons) cold unsalted butter, diced
- 60 g/2¼ oz (¼ cup plus 2 teaspoons) soft light brown sugar
- 30 g/1 oz (1½ tablespoons) golden syrup
- 30 g/1 oz (1½ tablespoons) black treacle (blackstrap molasses)
- 1 egg, lightly beaten
- strong cheese, to serve (optional)

* Preheat the oven to 180°C/350·F/Gas Mark 4.
* Put the oatmeal, flour, bicarbonate of soda (baking soda), spices and salt into a large bowl. Add the butter and rub it in until it resembles fine breadcrumbs. Mix in the sugar.
* Put the golden syrup and treacle (blackstrap molasses) into a small saucepan and gently melt over a low heat for 3–4 minutes until liquid. Pour the warm syrups into the dry mix and gently mix in together with the beaten egg to form a soft dough.
* Cover the bowl with clingfilm (plastic wrap) and leave to chill in the fridge for at least 30 minutes, or until firm enough to handle.
* Meanwhile, line 2 large baking sheets with baking (parchment) paper and pour 2 handfuls of oatmeal into a small bowl. When the dough is firm, remove it from the fridge and divide it into 12 golf-ball-sized pieces. Shape these into balls, then roll each ball in the oatmeal to coat.
* Evenly space out 6 balls on each prepared baking sheet, about 7 cm/2¾ inches apart, as they will spread during baking, and bake in the oven for 15 minutes, turning the baking sheets halfway through to ensure the biscuits are evenly baked. Remove from the oven and leave to cool on the baking sheets. These biscuits are delicious freshly baked but even better after a day in an airtight container. They will keep well for up to a week and are perfect served with a cup of tea, or even with a strong slice of cheese and a light beer.
* **Variations:** To make these biscuits even more true to their Scottish origins, replace the plain (all-purpose) flour with 50 g/2 oz (½ cup minus 2 teaspoons) oat flour and 50 g/ 2 oz (½ cup minus 2 teaspoons) barley flour, instead of rolling in oatmeal to finish. They were also sometimes just topped with a blanched almond half before baking.

Empire biscuits

SOUTHWEST OF ENGLAND: CORNWALL
*

CORNISH FAIRINGS

These spicy ginger biscuits (cookies) have a distinctive cracked surface. They are traditional to parts of the southwest of England – Cornwall especially – where for hundreds of years they were given as gifts and bought at country fairs.

Makes: 12
Prep time: 15 minutes
Cook time: 10–15 minutes
{ }

- 220 g/7¾ oz (1¾ cups plus 2 teaspoons) plain (all-purpose) flour, plus extra for dusting
- 1½ teaspoons bicarbonate of soda (baking soda)
- 1½ teaspoons baking powder
- 2 teaspoons ground ginger
- 1 teaspoon ground cinnamon
- ¼ teaspoon ground coriander
- ¼ teaspoon ground nutmeg
- ¼ teaspoon fine sea salt
- 100 g/3½ oz (7 tablespoons) cold unsalted butter, diced
- 50 g/2 oz (¼ cup) caster (superfine) sugar
- 50 g/2 oz (¼ cup minus 2 teaspoons) demerara (turbinado) sugar
- 100 g/3½ oz (¼ cup plus 2 teaspoons) golden syrup
- Clotted Cream (page 34) or strawberry ice cream, to serve (optional)

* Preheat the oven to 160°C/325°F/Gas Mark 3. Line 2 large baking sheets with baking (parchment) paper.
* Sift the flour, bicarbonate of soda (baking soda), baking powder, spices and salt into a large bowl. Add the butter and rub it in with your fingertips until it resembles fine breadcrumbs. Mix in the sugars.
* Put the golden syrup into a small saucepan and gently melt over a low heat for 3–4 minutes until liquid. Pour the warm syrup into the dry mix and gently mix together to form a soft dough, turning out onto a lightly floured work counter to knead lightly if required.
* Divide the dough into 12 pieces, about 35 g/1¼ oz each, then roll into 12 balls. Evenly space out 6 balls on each prepared baking sheet and bake in the oven for 15 minutes, turning the baking sheets halfway through to ensure the biscuits (cookies) are evenly baked. Remove from the oven and leave to cool on the baking sheets. These are delicious eaten fresh and keep well in an airtight container for up to 5 days. They are also great sandwiched together with Clotted Cream or strawberry ice cream as a Cornish summer dessert, or to use in a cheesecake base.
* **Variations:** Some recipes make an addition of candied mixed peel, or these can be finished with a water icing (frosting) to be given as a gift – traditionally a gift given from a man to his sweetheart along with sweet almonds, macaroons and candied angelica.

UNITED KINGDOM
*

GARIBALDI BISCUITS

These popular biscuits (cookies) derive their name from the nineteenth-century Italian general and patriot, Giuseppe Garibaldi, who played a major role in the unification of the modern Italian state. The biscuits bear no relation to anything Italian, however. They are made by sandwiching two thin layers of buttery biscuit dough with a sweetened currant middle. In this way, they are much like a biscuit-bar take on the much thicker Fruit Slice (page 390). Both biscuit and slice are often known by similar morbid monikers like Fly Cemetery and Fly Pie (page 390) – a reference to the currant filling.

Makes: 24
Prep time: 30 minutes,
plus 1¾–2¾ hours soaking and chilling
Cook time: 20–25 minutes
{ } { }

- 110 g/3¾ oz (½ cup minus 2½ teaspoons) dried currants
- 50 ml/1¾ fl oz (3½ tablespoons) brandy
- 230 g/8 oz (2 cups minus 2 teaspoons) plain (all-purpose) flour, sifted, plus extra for dusting
- 110 g/3¾ oz (½ cup plus 2 teaspoons) caster (superfine) sugar
- 80 g/3 oz (¾ stick) unsalted butter, diced and chilled
- 80 ml/2¾ fl oz (⅓ cup) full-fat (whole) milk, chilled
- 1 egg, lightly beaten
- 1 teaspoon ground cinnamon

* Put the currants and brandy into a small bowl, mix together, then leave to soak for 1–2 hours. Drain the excess brandy after soaking and set aside.
* Meanwhile, put the flour and 60 g/2¼ oz (⅓ cup minus 1 teaspoon) of the sugar into a medium bowl and mix together. Add the cold, diced butter and rub it in with your fingertips until the mixture resembles breadcrumbs. Add the cold milk and gently mix until the dough is combined. Cover with clingfilm (plastic wrap) and leave to chill in the fridge for 45 minutes.
* Meanwhile, preheat the oven to 180°C/350°F/Gas Mark 4. Line a large baking sheet with baking (parchment) paper.
* Divide the dough in half, then roll out both pieces on a lightly floured work counter into 2 rectangles, about 20 x 30 cm/8 x 12 inches each. Lightly brush 1 of the rectangles with some of the beaten egg, then sprinkle evenly with half the remaining sugar and half the cinnamon. Sprinkle all the currants over the dough. Put the second rectangle directly on top of the first, then, using a rolling pin, gently roll over the doughs, applying even pressure to stick them together. Brush the top with the remaining beaten egg, then sprinkle with the remaining sugar and cinnamon.
* Using a sharp knife, cut the biscuits (cookies) into 4 x 7 cm/1½ x 2¾ inch rectangles and arrange on the prepared baking sheet. You should have 24 in total. Bake in the oven for 20–25 minutes until lightly golden. Remove from the oven, leave to cool a little on the baking sheet, then transfer to a wire rack to cool completely.

ENGLAND: LANCASHIRE
*

GOOSNARGH CAKES

Hailing from a small Lancashire village, these are round shortbread-style biscuits (cookies) flavoured with caraway seeds and dusted with sugar.

Makes: 12
Prep time: 20 minutes
Cook time: 18–20 minutes
{👅}{💀}

- 120 g/4 oz (1 stick) unsalted butter, softened
- 60 g/2¼ oz (⅓ cup minus 1 teaspoon) caster (superfine) sugar
- 180 g/6 oz (1½ cups) plain (all-purpose) flour, plus extra for dusting
- 1 teaspoon caraway seeds (optional)
- granulated sugar, for sprinkling

* Preheat the oven to 180°C/350°F/Gas Mark 4. Line a large baking sheet with baking (parchment) paper.
* Put the butter and caster (superfine) sugar into a large bowl and, using a wooden spoon, mix them together until they are pale and fluffy. Sift in the flour and caraway seeds (if using) and mix well to form a dough.
* Tip the dough out onto a lightly floured work counter and use a 6 cm / ½ inch cutter to create 12 x 5 mm/¼ inch thick circles. Arrange the circles on the prepared baking sheet, sprinkle with the granulated sugar and bake in the oven for 18–20 minutes until golden brown. Remove from the oven and leave to cool on a wire rack.

NORTHERN IRELAND
*

FLAKEMEAL BISCUITS

Don't despair if you draw a blank searching supermarket aisles for 'flakemeal' – it's an Irish term for porridge (rolled) oats and these are simple but tasty oatmeal and coconut biscuits (cookies).

Makes: about 20
Prep time: 10 minutes, plus 10 minutes chilling
Cook time: 30 minutes
{👅}

- 85 g/3 oz (¾ cup) plain (all-purpose) flour, plus extra for dusting
- 200 g/7 oz (2 cups) flakemeal or porridge (rolled) oats
- 200 g/7 oz (1¾ sticks) unsalted butter, diced
- 80 g/3 oz (½ cup minus 4 teaspoons) caster (superfine) sugar, plus extra for dusting
- 50 g/2 oz (½ cup plus 1 tablespoon) desiccated (unsweetened shredded) coconut

* Preheat the oven to 180°C/350°F/Gas Mark 4. Line 2 large baking sheets with baking (parchment) paper.
* Sift the flour into a large bowl and add the porridge (rolled) oats. Add the butter and rub it in with your

fingertips until the mixture resembles breadcrumbs, then add the sugar and coconut and combine well into a dough. Cover with clingfilm (plastic wrap) and leave to chill in the fridge for 10 minutes.
* Roll the dough out on a lightly floured work counter to about 5 mm–1 cm/¼–½ inch thick. Cut into 20 circles using a 6 cm/2½ inch cookie cutter or a knife, re-rolling and re-cutting the trimmings, then arrange on the prepared baking sheets, spaced slightly apart, and bake in the oven for 30 minutes. Transfer to a wire rack and dust with sugar while still warm.

UNITED KINGDOM
*

FLAPJACKS

A chewy biscuit- (cookie-) like traybake, flapjacks are made from a simple, almost sinful mixture of porridge (steel-cut) oats, brown sugar, butter and a little golden syrup. Brits have been using the word 'flapjack' as far back as the seventeenth century, when it originally referred to pancakes or thin tarts. In America, flapjacks are still synonymous with the breakfast staple, but here in Britain it has referred to this oaty treat since the 1930s.
Flapjacks are easily adaptable. Common additions include both chocolate and raisins, but they take well to nuts and other dried fruits and sweets (candies).

Makes: 12
Prep time: 15 minutes
Cook time: 25–30 minutes
{👅}{🍴}{🥄}{💀}

- 250 g/9 oz (2¼ sticks) unsalted butter
- 2 tablespoons golden syrup
- 200 g/7 oz (¾ cup plus 2 tablespoons) demerara (turbinado) or soft light brown sugar
- 350 g/12 oz (3½ cups) porridge (steel-cut) oats
- 80 g/3 oz dried fruit (optional)

* Preheat the oven to 180°C/350°F/Gas Mark 4. Line the bottom and sides of a square 20 cm/8 inch cake pan with baking (parchment) paper.
* Put the butter, syrup and sugar into a large saucepan and melt slowly over a medium heat for 2–3 minutes, combining the mixture as it heats. Once fully combined, tip the mixture into a large bowl and stir in the oats and fruit (if using). Mix to a thick paste, then spoon into the prepared pan, pressing down hard with the back of a wooden spoon or a palette knife to make sure the mixture is levelled out and tightly pressed into the pan. Bake in the oven for 25–30 minutes until golden brown. Remove from the oven and cut into 12 squares or bars before leaving to cool in the tin. They will keep well for at least a week when stored in an airtight container.

SCOTLAND
*

SHORTBREAD
AND
PETTICOAT TAILS

Shortbread biscuits (cookies) follow a basic rule of one part sugar to two parts butter and three parts flour. While they are commonly associated with Scotland, there are actually numerous shortbread-style biscuits in England, such as Shrewsbury biscuits, or Goosnargh Cakes (page 337), which also contain caraway seeds. More recently, they have become the base layer of popular fridge bakes such as Millionaire's Shortbread (see right), which is topped with layers of caramel and chocolate.

In her classic work, *Food in England* (1954), Dorothy Hartley states that shortbread biscuits had been baked for centuries by the time petticoat tails were created in the seventeenth century. Baked in a scored circle with the centre cut out, the blunted ends of each crumbly 'tail' held together better than points – and apparently resembled popular Elizabethan petticoats.

Makes: 30 shortbread fingers or 12 petticoat tails
Prep time: 20 minutes
Cook time: 25 minutes
{☻}{↵}

- vegetable oil, for oiling
- 200 g/7 oz (1⅔ cups) plain (all-purpose) flour
- 100 g/3½ oz (¾ cup plus 2 teaspoons) cornflour (cornstarch)
- 100 g/3½ oz (¾ cup plus 2 teaspoons) icing (confectioners') sugar
- 200 g/7 oz (1¾ sticks) unsalted butter, very soft at room temperature
- granulated sugar, for sprinkling

* For shortbread fingers, preheat the oven to 160°C/325°F/ Gas Mark 3. Lightly oil a 23 x 33 cm/9 x 13 inch Swiss (jelly) roll pan.
* Sift the flours and icing (confectioners') sugar into a large bowl. Add the butter and rub it in with your fingertips until it starts to come together as a dough. Tip the dough into the prepared pan, pressing the mix together and evenly distributing and flattening the dough around the pan. Once the dough is even and flat, use a sharp knife to make incisions about halfway through the dough, creating 3 bands lengthways and then scoring each band into 10 fingers without cutting through to the pan underneath. Using a fork, pierce each finger 3 times through the surface of the dough.
* Bake in the oven for 20–25 minutes until very pale golden brown. Remove from the oven, score the shortbread again, if necessary, and leave to cool for 5–10 minutes before sprinkling with granulated sugar. Remove from the pan and leave to cool completely on a wire rack.
* To adapt as petticoat tails, lightly oil a 25 cm/10 inch loose-bottomed tart pan. Flatten the dough into the pan evenly, then use a sharp knife to make 6 incisions about halfway through the dough, creating 12 even segments. Using a small 4 cm/1½ inch ring cutter, cut a circle from the centre, then pierce each segment with a fork 3 times through the surface of the dough. Follow the baking directions above.

SCOTLAND
*

MILLIONAIRE'S SHORTBREAD

These biscuits (cookies) have picked up the moniker 'millionaire's shortbread' in Scotland, where they were known for being a popular and indulgent treat.

Makes: 24
Prep time: 1 hour, plus 3 hours setting
Cook time: 40 minutes
{☻}{↵}

- vegetable oil, for oiling
- 1 quantity Shortbread dough (see left)
- 150 g/5 oz (1¼ sticks) unsalted butter
- 150 g/5 oz (⅔ cup) soft brown sugar
- 1 x 397 g/14 oz can condensed milk
- 250 g/9 oz dark (semisweet) chocolate, 55–70% cocoa solids, chopped into small pieces
- 100 g/3½ oz milk chocolate, 40% cocoa solids, chopped into small pieces

* Preheat the oven to 160°C/325°F/Gas Mark 3. Lightly oil a 23 x 33 cm/9 x 13 inch Swiss (jelly) roll pan and set aside.
* Make the Shortbread dough following the recipe on the left. Evenly flatten the dough into the pan, then use a sharp knife to divide the dough into 24 squares, 5.5 x 5.5 cm/ 2.1 x 2.1 inches. Bake in the oven for 20–25 minutes until very pale golden brown. Leave to cool in the pan.
* Melt the butter and soft brown sugar in a heavy saucepan (making sure it is big enough that the ingredients do not exceed a third of the pan), over a low heat for 5 minutes. Add the condensed milk and bring to the boil. (Be extremely careful while making the caramel, especially when stirring.) Reduce the heat and simmer for 5 minutes, or until the caramel changes slightly to a dark golden brown colour and has a soft fudge texture.
* Carefully pour the caramel over the cooled shortbread, then quickly and evenly spread using a palette knife into each corner. Leave to cool and set at room temperature for 1 hour.
* Melt the chocolate in a heatproof bowl set over a saucepan of gently simmering water, making sure the bottom of the bowl doesn't touch the water. Ideally, the chocolate temperature should not exceed 32°C/90°F. A higher temperature will cause the fats in the chocolate to separate from the solids. Using a palette knife, spread the melted chocolate evenly over the cooled and set caramel and leave to set for at least a couple of hours until firm.
* To serve, heat a large knife with boiling water, dry it with a dish towel and cut through the biscuits in one swift movement. Continue the process for every slice, wiping the knife clean in between cuts.

Millionaire's shortbread

UNITED KINGDOM
*

DIGESTIVE BISCUITS

These British biscuits (cookies) were invented by Scottish doctors in the middle of the nineteenth century and had the stated purpose of aiding digestion. Today's digestive biscuits have nothing medicinal about them – they are typically coated in chocolate and sometimes caramel, or made with a buttery crumbly oat mixture. The only thing that's surprising about them is that they are rarely baked at home. They make a delectable – and very dunkable – companion to a cup of tea.

Makes: 18–20
Prep time: 50 minutes, plus 30 minutes chilling
Cook time: 12 minutes
{♨}{☕}

- 65 g/2¼ oz (⅓ cup) caster (superfine) sugar
- 1 teaspoon baking powder
- 1 teaspoon flaky sea salt
- 165 g/5¾ oz (1⅓ cups plus 1 teaspoon) wholemeal (whole wheat) flour, plus extra for dusting
- 35 g/1¼ oz (⅓ cup) wheatgerm or bran or if these are unavailable use an additional 35 g/1¼ oz (4 tablespoons) wholemeal flour
- 115 g/4 oz (1 stick) cold unsalted butter, diced into cubes, about 1 x 1 cm/½ x ½ inch
- about 50–60 ml/1¾–2 fl oz (3½–4 tablespoons) full-fat (whole) milk

* Put the sugar, baking powder, salt, flour and wheatgerm or bran into a food processor and process to evenly mix the dry ingredients together. Add the butter cubes and pulse briefly to coat the butter with the dry ingredients, then process until the butter is evenly dispersed throughout. Add enough whole milk to just bind the mixture together to form a dough. Depending upon the type of flour and wheatgerm or bran you use, you may find you don't need all the milk. It is important not to add more than needed to bring the dough together or it will become very sticky and difficult to roll and cut out.
* When the dough has come together, tip it out of the bowl and dust it lightly with a little extra flour so it is easy to handle. Put it between 2 sheets of baking (parchment) paper and roll it out as evenly as possible until it is 5 mm/¼ inch thick, then leave to chill in the fridge for 30 minutes to firm up. This will make it easier to cut.
* Once the dough has chilled, line 2–3 large baking sheets with baking paper. Use a 6 cm/2½ inch round cutter to cut the biscuits and arrange on the prepared baking sheets, well spaced out. Continue to cut out as many biscuits as you can, rerolling all the trimmings until all the dough is used up. Using a fork or skewer, prick holes in the top of the biscuits.
* Chilling the biscuits at this stage will help give nicely defined edges but it is up to you, and they can be baked immediately, if desired. They can also be stored in the freezer for up to 1 month to be baked whenever the urge strikes. To bake, preheat the oven to 160°C/325°F/Gas Mark 3 and bake for 6 minutes, then rotate and bake for another 6 minutes, or until the edges are beginning to take on a little colour and crisp up. Remove from the oven and leave to cool on a wire rack.

* **Variations:** To make these into chocolate digestives, simply melt about 80 g/3 oz of your choice of milk or dark (semisweet) chocolate and coat one side of the biscuits. If you have the time and inclination to temper the chocolate then go for it, but if you want a quick and easy cheat, then work quickly once the biscuits come out of the oven, turn them over as soon as you can without burning yourself and cover the underside of each with a sprinkling of chopped chocolate. It will begin to melt and you can use a palette knife to smooth the melted chocolate to the edges.

UNITED KINGDOM
*

BRANDY SNAPS

Crisp and rather lacy wafers, brandy snaps are baked flat and rolled while they are still warm and pliable. Despite their name, the brandy in both the biscuit (cookie) and the cream filling are optional – many recipes leave both out completely.

Makes: about 24
Prep time: 20 minutes
Cook time: 30–40 minutes
{♨}{☕}

- 75 g/2¾ oz (¾ stick) unsalted butter
- 75 g/2¾ oz (¼ cup) golden syrup
- 75 g/2¾ oz (⅓ cup) demerara (turbinado) sugar
- 75 g/2¾ oz (½ cup plus 1 tablespoon) plain (all-purpose) flour
- pinch of salt
- 1 teaspoon ground ginger
- 1 teaspoon lemon juice
- 1 teaspoon brandy (optional)

- For the piping cream (optional):
- 150 ml/5 fl oz (⅔ cup) whipping cream
- 1 tablespoon icing (confectioners') sugar
- ½ teaspoon brandy (optional)

* Preheat the oven to 200°C/400°F/Gas Mark 6. Line 2 large baking sheets with baking (parchment) paper.
* Put the butter, syrup and demerara (turbinado) sugar into a large saucepan and stir over a medium heat for 3–4 minutes until melted. Make sure it doesn't boil. Remove the pan from the heat, then sift in the flour and add the salt, ginger, lemon juice and brandy (if using). Mix well.
* Put 6 teaspoons of the mixture onto each prepared baking sheet, making sure they are well spaced out as they spread considerably during baking. Bake in the oven for 8–10 minutes until a rich brown, then remove from the oven and, while still warm, shape each snap around the handle of a wooden spoon, forming a tube that can later be filled. Use a palette knife to help if necessary, then leave to cool completely. If the snaps cool too quickly before shaping them, return them to the oven to warm up.
* If desired, whip the cream, icing (confectioners') sugar and brandy (if using) in a large bowl using electric beaters until floppy. Alternatively, use a stand mixer fitted with a whisk attachment. Transfer to a piping (pastry) bag with a star-shaped nozzle and pipe into the tubes.

Brandy snaps

WHEN GOOD KING ARTHUR RULED THE LAND,
HE WAS A GOODLY KING:
HE STOLE THREE PECKS OF BARLEY MEAL,
TO MAKE A BAG-PUDDING.

A BAG-PUDDING THE KING DID MAKE,
AND STUFFED IT WELL WITH PLUMS;
AND IN IT PUT GREAT LUMPS OF FAT,
AS BIG AS MY TWO THUMBS.

THE KING AND QUEEN DID EAT THEREOF,
AND NOBLEMEN BESIDE;
AND WHAT THEY COULD NOT EAT THAT NIGHT,
THE QUEEN NEXT MORNING FRIED

A NINETEENTH-CENTURY NURSERY RHYME

Pudding. A rather nebulous word with enough meanings as to somehow be both less and more descriptive than the general term 'desserts'. When British people say pudding, they mean many things at once: there are savoury puddings and there are sweet puddings, there are hot puddings and cold puddings, bread puddings and milk puddings, steamed puddings and sponge puddings – and that's just the start. Somewhat confusingly, you would also find a pie, trifle or even ice cream on a restaurant's pudding menu, but none of these are puddings in its narrower sense. So, what is going on here, and can anyone possibly explain what a pudding is?

WHAT IS A PUDDING?

The English word 'pudding' comes to us from the Latin *botellus*, or sausage, and so shares its etymological root with the French black pudding (blood sausage), *boudin noir*. Indeed, the earliest puddings, in the original meaning, were humble sausages filled with a mixture of blood, suet and cereal (groats), and boiled in the intestines (small) or stomach lining (much larger) of an animal like a pig or sheep.

The contents of a traditional pudding could be sweet as well as savoury, and this was especially true by the seventeeth century, and even more so by the eighteenth and nineteenth centuries. These sweet puddings incorporated spices, dried fruit and sugar in addition to the traditional mixture of animal fat (suet) and a fine meal made from barley, oats or wheat. The pudding as an idea was then already quite versatile,

and could be made in most home kitchens, as the only device it required was a pot for boiling. The animal guts also gradually fell out of favour as a cooking utensil. British food historian Constance Anne Wilson cites a 1617 recipe for a sweet college pudding as the earliest mention of a pudding cloth – a reusable muslin- (cheesecloth-) like alternative to intestines. That is not to say that all traditional sweet puddings lost that innate connection with the animal itself – the Scottish fruit pudding, or Shetland's sweet puddeens, are still traditionally cooked using intestines and stomach linings from a sheep (respectively).

While some traditional puddings – like the Scottish puddeens or clootie dumpling – are still boiled, most are now steamed, typically in a large pot with a special pudding basin (ovenproof bowl). The mixture has evolved to mirror a sponge batter: favouring butter over suet, and almost always wheat flour over the more traditional barleymeal. Christmas pudding is one notable exception, and is still commonly made with suet. Once cooked, however, they are eaten the same way: turned out, sliced and served with a generous helping of custard, pouring cream – or in the case of Christmas pudding, brandy butter. And as the old adage suggests, left-over steamed puddings are fantastic when fried up for breakfast the following morning.

PUDDING, PIE AND AFTERS

Eventually, pudding's place as an after-dinner serving became ubiquitous,

giving rise to the word's catch-all connotation of any such sweet dish. There were plenty of other types of puddings as well. Along with the traditional boiled and steamed puddings, there were milk puddings such as rice pudding, posset and burnt cream, and bread puddings made from sweet mixtures of dried bread or breadcrumbs and a spiced custard mixture, like old-fashioned English bread pudding, bread and butter pudding and cabinet pudding.

As we broaden our understanding of what a pudding is, and can be, we arrive at our broadest understanding of the word: a sweet dish following a savoury meal. It is due to this use of the word that we would see a pie or tart on a pudding menu. Both of these sweet bakes involve pastry (pie dough) encasing a sweet filling, although tarts lack a pastry lid – this is a basic but important distinction. Like puddings, pies are served with custard, cream or ice cream. Tarts, on the other hand, lean more towards cream or even crème fraîche.

Despite all this seriousness, classification and dichotomy, it's important to not lose sight of the fact that puddings are joyous, often celebratory occasions. Nothing can quite cap an excellent meal – or save a poor one – in the same way. And such is my own great love for good pudding, that I swapped sweet for savoury, and began writing this book backwards, starting with this chapter.

PUDDINGS

AND

PIES

UNITED KINGDOM

APPLE CHARLOTTE

Apple Charlotte belongs to the noble family of bread puddings, and this one is a particular delight – the outside crisp and buttery, the centre soft with caramelized apples. It would be rude not to serve this autumnal treat with great jugs (pitchers) of Toffee Sauce (page 358) or Custard (page 33), or both, ideally.

Serves: 6
Prep time: 30 minutes
Cook time: 1 hour
{ॏ} {⋅•}

- 500 g/1 lb 2 oz Bramley (cooking) apples, peeled, cored and sliced
- 500 g/1 lb 2 oz dessert apples, such as Russet or Cox's Pippin, peeled, cored and sliced
- 110 g/3¾ oz (½ cup plus 2 teaspoons) caster (superfine) sugar
- 2 egg yolks
- 210 g/7 oz (1¾ sticks plus 2 teaspoons) unsalted butter
- 1 x 800g/1 lb 12oz loaf bread, cut into slices 5 mm/¼ inch thick, crusts removed
- Toffee Sauce (page 358) or Custard (page 33), to serve

* Preheat the oven to 180°C/350°F/Gas Mark 4.
* Put the apples, 60 g/2¼ oz (⅓ cup) of the sugar and 60 g/2¼ oz (½ stick) of the butter into a large saucepan and cook over a medium heat for 15 minutes, or until the apples have softened and cooked down a little. Keep an eye on the pan and stir occasionally to keep the apples from sticking or burning. Remove the pan from the heat, add the egg yolks and stir them through. Leave to cool for 1 minute.
* Heat the remaining 150 g/5 oz (1¼ sticks) butter in a medium saucepan over a low-medium heat for 2 minutes, or until melted. Brush the bread slices with the melted butter and arrange two-thirds of it inside a large soufflé dish, overlapping the slices and pressing down firmly. Add the apples as a layer, then cover the apples with the remaining bread. Sit an ovenproof plate on top of the pudding and set a 1 kg/2¼ lb baking weight on top of it – you want to apply pressure to the pudding as it bakes.
* Bake in the oven for 30 minutes, then reduce the oven temperature to 160°C/325°F/Gas Mark 3 and bake for another 30 minutes until golden brown. Remove from the oven and leave to stand for 20 minutes before turning out onto a plate and serving with Toffee Sauce or Custard.

UNITED KINGDOM

BAKED APPLE DUMPLINGS

Enveloped in a layer of Sweet Shortcrust Pastry (page 247), these little packages have a buttery sweet apple filling. Serve with plenty of Custard (page 33) or ice cream.

Serves: 4
Prep time: 50 minutes, plus 20 minutes resting
Cook time: 35–40 minutes
{ॏ} {⋅•}

- ½ quantity Sweet Shortcrust Pastry (page 247) made with plain (all-purpose) flour, plus extra for dusting
- 4 medium eating apples, such as Cox's Pippin or Russet, peeled and cored
- juice of ½ lemon
- 4 tablespoons light brown sugar
- ½ teaspoon ground cinnamon
- ¼ teaspoon ground cloves
- 4 small pieces butter, 60 g/2¼ oz (½ stick) in total
- 1 egg, beaten with 1 tablespoon milk or water, for egg wash
- Custard (page 33) or ice cream, to serve

* Make the pastry following the recipe on page 247 and leave to rest for 20 minutes before using.
* Preheat the oven to 190°C/375°F/Gas Mark 5.
* Divide the dough into 4 equal portions on a lightly floured work counter, then roll them out into equal circles of about 3–4 mm/⅛–⅙ inch thick and large enough to enclose the apples.
* Brush the apples with a little of the lemon juice to prevent discolouration. Put the brown sugar and spices into a small bowl and mix together until combined.
* Put an apple into the centre of a dough circle and fill its core with 1 tablespoon of the spice and sugar mixture. Press in a small piece of butter. Using a sharp knife, make 4 evenly spaced cuts in the dough, starting 5 mm/¼ inch from the base of the apple. Fold the dough upwards over the apple, cut away any excess and use the egg wash to seal the strips together at the sides, as well as on top. At this stage you can also roll up the trimmings and make leaves to decorate the dumpling. Make sure to seal these onto the pastry and brush with egg wash as well. Brush with more egg wash and place the apple on a large baking sheet. Repeat with the remaining apples.
* Bake in the oven for 35–40 minutes until a rich, deep golden brown. Remove from the oven and leave to cool for 2 minutes before serving with Custard or ice cream.

ENGLAND: DEVON

DEVONSHIRE IN-AND-OUT PUDDING
EXMOOR IN-AND-OUT PUDDING

The name of this Devonshire recipe is a reference to the ease with which it is put together: the apples are dusted or tossed in sugar and spices, then covered with a butter or suet sponge batter – similar in essence to an Eve's Pudding (see right). Serve while still warm with a good thick cream.

Serves: 6
Prep time: 30 minutes
Cook time: 45 minutes
{ॏ}

- 600 g/ 1 lb 5 oz Bramley (cooking) apples,
peeled, cored and diced
- 180 g/ 6 oz (¾ cup plus 1 teaspoon) soft light brown sugar
- ½ teaspoon mixed spice
- 120 g/ 4 oz (1 stick) unsalted butter, softened
or 120 g/ 4 oz (⅔ cup) beef suet, shredded
- 120 g/ 4 oz (1 cup) self-raising flour
- 2 eggs
- 60 g/ 2¼ oz (⅔ cup) ground almonds
- ¼ teaspoon almond extract

* Preheat the oven to 180°C/350°F/Gas Mark 4.
* Put the apples into a deep pie dish, about 1.2–1.5 litre/
40–50 fl oz capacity, and sprinkle with 60 g/ 2¼ oz
(¼ cup plus 1 teaspoon) of the sugar, the mixed spice
and a splash of water.
* Put the butter and remaining sugar into a large bowl and,
using a wooden spoon, beat until pale and fluffy. Sift in
the flour, then add the eggs, ground almonds and almond
extract and mix well to make a smooth batter. Spoon the
batter evenly over the apples, then bake in the oven for
45 minutes, or until risen and golden brown.

UNITED KINGDOM
*

BAKED ALMOND PUDDING

When baked, the top of this pudding crisps while the centre
remains cake-like – much like an Eve's Pudding (see right)
but without the apples. Plums would also make a nice
addition to this pudding – cut 6–7 into large chunks, toss
with a pinch of ground cinnamon and pack into the casserole
dish or Dutch oven before spooning the batter over the top.

Serves: 4–6
Prep time: 10 minutes
Cook time: 30–40 minutes
{❂} {⌣•}

- 120 g/ 4 oz (1 stick) unsalted butter, softened
- 120 g/ 4 oz (1¼ cups) ground almonds
- ¼ teaspoon almond extract
- 4 eggs
- 30–60 ml/ 1–2 fl oz (2–4 tablespoons) sweet sherry
- grated zest and juice of ½ lemon
- 120 g/ 4 oz (⅔ cup) caster (superfine) sugar
- 600 ml/ 20 fl oz (2½ cups) double (heavy) cream
- 1 heaped tablespoon fresh breadcrumbs

* Preheat the oven to 180°C/350°F/Gas Mark 4. Grease a
shallow 20 cm/ 8 inch baking dish with a small piece of
the butter.
* Put the remaining butter, ground almonds and almond
extract into a large bowl and mix together using a wooden
spoon until combined.
* Add the eggs, one at a time, and beat until each one is
incorporated. Add the sherry and lemon zest and juice and
mix into the mixture, then add the sugar and cream and
mix in. Finally, add the fresh breadcrumbs, stir through,
ensuring the batter is smooth and well mixed, then pour
into the prepared baking dish. Bake in the oven for 30–40
minutes until set. Serve.

UNITED KINGDOM
*

EVE'S PUDDING
MOTHER EVE'S PUDDING

Traditionally a steamed sponge with chopped apples, the
modern Eve's Pudding, or Mother Eve's Pudding, is a lovely
autumnal pudding consisting of a sweet apple mixture baked
with a buttery sponge cake on top. Once baked, leave to cool
slightly before spooning the pudding into shallow bowls and
pouring over Custard (page 33).
This pudding adapts quite easily to fit virtually any fruit
that's in season, although soft fruits such as raspberries or
blackberries won't need the same softening as apples.

Serves: 6
Prep time: 30 minutes
Cook time: 45–60 minutes
{❂} {⌣•}

- 1 large Bramley (cooking) apple, about 250 g/
9 oz, peeled, cored and chopped
- 210 g/ 7¼ oz (1 cup plus 2 teaspoons)
caster (superfine) sugar
- 120 g/ 4 oz (1 stick) very soft butter,
plus extra for greasing
- 2 eggs
- 120 g/ 4 oz (1 cup) self-raising flour, sifted
- ½ teaspoon mixed spice (optional)
- 1–2 tablespoons full-fat (whole) milk
- Custard (page 33), to serve

* Put the chopped apples into a large saucepan with 90 g/
3¼ oz (½ cup minus 2 teaspoons) of the sugar and a dash
of water and stew over a medium heat for 15–20 minutes
until soft. Remove from the heat while it still has some
texture and leave to cool.
* Meanwhile, preheat the oven to 180°C/350°F/Gas Mark 4.
Grease a 1.5 litre/ 50 fl oz soufflé dish with butter.
* Put the butter and remaining 120 g/ 4 oz (⅔ cup) sugar
into a large bowl and, using a wooden spoon, mix them
together until they are pale and fluffy. Slowly beat in the
eggs, then fold in the flour and mixed spice (if using) and
mix thoroughly, slackening with 1–2 tablespoons milk,
if necessary.
* Spoon the apple mixture into the bottom of the prepared
dish and spread the cake batter over the top. Bake in
the oven for 45–60 minutes until the sponge topping is
a deep golden brown. Serve with Custard.

ENGLAND: MIDLANDS
*
BAKEWELL PUDDING

The Bakewell pudding was popularized long before its now-famous variation, the Bakewell Tart (page 378), came into being in the early twentieth century. The pudding consists of a puff pastry base spread with a layer of raspberry or strawberry jam and a rich egg custard, flavoured with almond that's set on top. Popular legend suggests that Bakewell pudding was created by mistake in the Derbyshire town of Bakewell, but multiple published recipes predate this myth. Incidentally, *The Oxford Companion to Food* suggests the pudding's origin stretches back even further into the fifteenth century, in the form of a medieval pastry tart called the 'flathon': one popular flathon was filled with a rich egg custard set over candied fruit, and another used a paste of almonds and sugar. Our modern variation may be a convergence of the two.

Serves: a generous 6
Prep time: 50 minutes,
plus 1 hour 20 minutes resting and chilling
Cook time: 1¼ hours
{👤}

- ½ quantity Rough Puff Pastry (page 247)
- plain (all-purpose) flour, for dusting
- 180 g/6 oz (1½ sticks) unsalted butter
- 2 eggs
- 8 egg yolks
- 175 g/6 oz (¾ cup plus 2 tablespoons) caster (superfine) sugar
- 75 g/2¾ oz (¾ cup) ground almonds
- ¼ teaspoon almond extract
- grated zest of 1 lemon
- ½ teaspoon mixed spice
- 5 tablespoons raspberry jam

* Make the pastry following the recipe on page 247 and leave to rest for 30 minutes before using.
* Roll out the pastry on a lightly floured work counter until it is 3 mm/⅛ inch thick and use it to line a 20 cm/8 inch tart case (shell). Prick the pastry all over with a fork and leave to chill in the fridge for 30 minutes.
* Meanwhile, preheat the oven to 170°C/325°F/Gas Mark 3.
* Line the tart case with baking (parchment) paper and fill with baking beans or pie weights. Blind bake in the oven for 25–30 minutes until the sides are golden brown. Remove from the oven, take out the beans or weights and paper and bake the case again for 7 minutes, or until the bottom has dried out. Remove from the oven and increase the temperature to 180°C/350°F/Gas Mark 4.
* Leave the tart case to cool while you make the filling mixture. Heat the butter in a medium saucepan over a low-medium heat for 2 minutes, or until melted. Remove from the heat and leave to cool.
* Put the eggs, egg yolks and sugar into a bowl and, using a balloon whisk, whisk until very thick. Fold in the cooled, melted butter, ground almonds, almond extract, lemon zest and mixed spice until combined. Spread the jam over the bottom of the tart case and pour the custardy filling over the top. Bake in the oven for 40 minutes, or until the filling is set, reducing the oven temperature to 160°C/325°F/Gas Mark 3 if the pastry is beginning to brown too much. Allow to cool a little before serving.

SCOTLAND
*
CLOOTIE DUMPLING

This is a delightful Scottish spiced pudding, often made for Christmas or Hogmanay (Scottish New Year's Eve), and still in the traditional manner – by boiling in a pudding cloth or 'cloot'. The pudding cloth is dusted in flour first, which helps to form the distinctive skin of the pudding, something you would miss if you steamed the mixture.

Serves: a generous 4 with left-overs
Prep time: 20 minutes
Cook time: 2¼ hours,
{🥄}

- plain (all-purpose) flour, for dusting
- caster (superfine) sugar, for dusting
- Custard (page 33), ice cream, lightly sweetened whipped cream, or butter, to serve

- For the dry mix:
- 175 g/6 oz (3½ cups) fresh breadcrumbs
- 175 g/6 oz (1½ cups) self-raising flour
- 1 teaspoon bicarbonate of soda (baking soda)
- 175 g/6 oz (1 cup) suet granules (or vegetarian 'suet')
- 100 g/3½ oz (⅓ cup plus 1 tablespoon) soft brown or muscovado sugar
- ½ teaspoon salt
- 275 g/9¾ oz (1½ cups) mixed dried fruit, such as raisins, sultanas (golden raisins) and currants, or dried peel
- 1 teaspoon each ground ginger and cinnamon
- ¼ teaspoon ground cloves
- 2 teaspoons mixed spice

- For the wet mix:
- 1 egg
- 2 tablespoons black treacle (blackstrap molasses)
- 150 ml/5 fl oz (⅔ cup) full-fat (whole) milk

* Put a dinner plate into the bottom of a large saucepan to prevent contact with direct heat, then fill with water and heat until it is simmering. Wet a cloth – ideally one with dimples or ridges – and wring out any excess moisture.
* Put all the ingredients for the dry mix into a large bowl and mix together, then put all the ingredients for the wet mix into another bowl and mix together. Combine both mixes and bring together to make a ball of dough. The wet mix combines better if you slightly heat the milk to melt the treacle (blackstrap molasses).
* Lay the damp cloth flat on a work counter and dust with plain (all-purpose) flour and sugar.
* Form the dough into a ball and dust all over with flour. Leave to stand for a few minutes, then put onto the cloth. Fold the sides of the cloth up and tie together above the dumpling. Leave some room for expansion. Put the dumpling into the pan of simmering water, then cover with a lid and simmer for 2 hours. Towards the end of this time, preheat the oven to 180°C/350°F/Gas Mark 4.
* Remove the cooked dumpling from the pan, leave to cool for 10–15 minutes, then unwrap it and put it onto a baking sheet. Bake for 15 minutes, or until a good skin forms. Remove from the oven and leave to cool thoroughly before slicing. It can be reheated or toasted and is best served with Custard, ice cream or lightly sweetened whipped cream, or fried with butter.

Bakewell pudding

UNITED KINGDOM
*

CHRISTMAS PUDDING

A richly spiced and densely fruited suet pudding, the
Christmas pudding is steamed slowly for hours, then left to
slowly mature in a cool, dark space for several months. There
the pudding is fed 1–2 tablespoons of alcohol each week,
before being re-steamed on Christmas Day. It is a process
that has changed little in the last 200 years.

According to *The Oxford Companion to Food*, today's Christmas
puddings are rooted in the medieval 'plum pottage', a savoury
spiced porridge-like dish made with dried fruit. Over time,
'plum' has become synonymous with dried fruit, and the
term 'plum puddings' confusingly attributed to both the
recognizable Christmas pudding and a variation that is
noticeably more subdued.

Today's Christmas pudding dates back to the nineteenth
century, when it became the culmination of a centuries-
long obsession with spiced and fruited cakes and puddings,
and the idea that 'more is more'. Although too spiced and
boozy for some, a thick slice of warm Christmas pudding
with brandy butter or brandy cream is nothing to scoff at.

Serves: 10
Prep time: 1 hour, plus 8–12 hours marinating
Cook time: 5 hours, plus 1–2 hours additional steaming
{ᵔ}

- 140 g/5 oz (¾ cup plus 2 teaspoons) shredded beef suet
- 120 g/4 oz (¾ cup) sultanas
  (golden raisins)
- 120 g/4 oz (¾ cup) raisins
- 250 g/9 oz (1 cup plus 2 tablespoons) currants
- 250 g/9 oz (1 cup plus 2 tablespoons) dark brown sugar
- 1 teaspoon mixed spice
- 1 teaspoon grated nutmeg
- ½ teaspoon ground cinnamon
- 130 g/4½ oz (2⅔ cups) fresh breadcrumbs
- 400 g/14 oz Bramley (cooking) apples, peeled and grated
- grated zest of 1 lemon
- grated zest and juice of 1 orange
- 2 eggs
- 75 ml/2½ fl oz (⅓ cup) sweet sherry
- 100 ml/3½ fl oz (⅓ cup plus 1 tablespoon) dark rum
- 75 g/2¾ oz (½ cup plus 1 tablespoon)
  self-raising flour, sifted
- unsalted butter, for greasing
- Brandy Sauce (page 427), to serve

* Put the suet, dried fruits, sugar, spices and breadcrumbs
  into a large bowl and mix thoroughly, making sure that
  everything is evenly distributed. Add the grated apple,
  lemon zest and orange zest and juice and mix again. Put
  the eggs, sherry and rum into a small bowl and beat
  together, then pour into the pudding mix.
* Using a spatula, mix all the ingredients together thoroughly,
  making sure that everything is coated with moisture.
  Cover the bowl with clingfilm (plastic wrap) and leave
  the mixture in the fridge to marinate overnight.
* The next day, mix the pudding mixture again thoroughly,
  then gradually add the flour. Grease two 570 ml/20 fl oz
  pudding basins (ovenproof bowls) with butter and
  divide the mixture equally between the prepared bowls.
  Cover each one with a lid, or make them from a large
  pleated square made from a double layer of baking

(parchment) paper and aluminium foil, and secure them
around the top of the pudding basins with kitchen string.
* Put the bowls into a steamer and cook for 5 hours.
  Alternatively, put a pudding basin on an inverted saucer
  in a large saucepan. Cover the saucer with a small square
  of muslin (cheesecloth) and set the bowl on top, then
  fill the saucepan a third of the way full with water.
  Bring to the boil, then reduce the heat and simmer for 5
  hours, making sure to top up (top off) the water level as
  necessary halfway through cooking. You may have to cook
  the puddings separately.
* Remove the puddings from the steamer and set aside in a
  cool, dark place until needed. Reheat the puddings in the
  steamer for 1–2 hours, before serving with Brandy Sauce.

SCOTLAND: SHETLAND
*

PUDDEEN

The puddeen is a Shetland cousin to the Clootie Dumpling
(page 348) and cooked in the manner of Haggis (page 192)
– in the sheep's stomach bag. After simmering for several
hours, the pudding would be dried off, sliced and served
for breakfast or afternoon tea. It can be eaten either on its
own or fried with a little bacon. This recipe is made in a
pudding cloth or muslin (cheesecloth) bag – more like a
Clootie Dumpling – as stomach bags are tough to come by.

Serves: a generous 6
Prep time: 30 minutes
Cook time: 4½ hours
{ᵔ}

- 1 kg/2¼ lb (8⅓ cups) plain (all-purpose) flour
- 600 g/1 lb 5 oz shredded sheep's suet
- 700 g/1 lb 8½ oz (4 cups) mixed dried fruit
- 15 g/½ oz (2½ tablespoons) mixed spice
- 400 g/14 oz (1¼ cups minus 2 teaspoons) golden syrup
- 2 onions, finely chopped
- 1 litre/34 fl oz (4¼ cups) full-fat (whole) milk
- salt

* Put all the ingredients, except the salt, into a large bowl
  and mix together with a wooden spoon and then a clean
  hand. When thoroughly combined, the mixture should be
  moderately sticky. Transfer to a large muslin (cheesecloth)
  bag and push well into the corners. Sew or tie shut with
  strong kitchen string.
* Bring a large saucepan of lightly salted water to the boil,
  then very carefully lower the puddeen into the pan.
  Reduce the heat to a simmer and cook gently for 4½
  hours, or until it darkens. Remove from the pan, carefully
  uncover and serve while hot.

Christmas pudding

ENGLAND
*

CASTLE PUDDINGS

Castle puddings are simple sponge puddings baked in small dariole moulds. They make convenient individual puddings and were popular with children in the early/mid-1900s.

Serves: 6
Prep time: 20 minutes
Cook time: 20–25 minutes
{⟨ðŸ‘⟩}{⟨⟩}

- 120 g/4 oz (1 stick) unsalted butter,
plus extra for greasing
- 2 eggs
- 120 g/4 oz (⅔ cup) caster (superfine) sugar
- 120 g/4 oz (1 cup) self-raising flour
- grated zest of ½ lemon or ½ teaspoon vanilla extract
- 1 tablespoon full-fat (whole) milk (optional)
- Custard (page 33) or jam of choice, to serve

* Preheat the oven to 180°C/350°F/Gas Mark 4. Grease 6 dariole moulds with butter.
* Put the eggs into a large bowl and whisk using electric beaters until thick and frothy. Add the sugar in a steady stream, whisking constantly. Sift in the flour, then fold it in using a wooden spoon. Add the grated lemon zest or vanilla and stir it through. If the mixture gets too tough, add 1 tablespoon milk.
* Divide the batter among the prepared moulds, pouring it two-thirds of the way up the moulds. Arrange the moulds on a large baking sheet, evenly spaced out, and bake in the oven for 20–25 minutes until well-risen and golden brown. Remove from the oven and leave to cool slightly before turning out and serving with Custard or jam.

UNITED KINGDOM
*

BASIC STEAMED SPONGE

To my mind, there are few better ways to end a meal than with a steamed sponge: soft with a slight wobble, capped with jam or syrup and drizzled (or doused) with a rich pouring custard. Armed with only a spoon, I will always make short work of one – leaving nothing behind.
This is a basic recipe for a steamed sponge pudding that is both excellent and versatile. Try testing out a few of the variations below, or experiment with other flavour combinations and toppings.

Serves: 6
Prep time: 20 minutes
Cook time: 1½–2 hours
{⟨ðŸ‘⟩}{⟨⟩}

- 175 g/6 oz (1½ sticks) unsalted butter, at room temperature, plus extra for greasing
- 3 tablespoons jam or Lemon Curd (page 432) or golden syrup or dried fruit or stewed apple or apricots (variations below)

- 125 g/4¼ oz caster (superfine) sugar or soft brown sugar
- 3 eggs
- 175 g/6 oz (1½ cups) self-raising flour, sifted
- pinch of salt
- 30 ml/1 fl oz (2 tablespoons) full-fat (whole) milk
- Custard (page 33) or chocolate sauce, to serve

* Heavily grease a 1.2 litre/40 fl oz pudding basin (ovenproof bowl) with butter and put your desired filling in the bottom.
* Put the butter and sugar into a stand mixer fitted with a paddle attachment and mix together on medium speed until pale. Reduce the speed to low and beat in the eggs, one at a time, adding a third of the flour with each egg to prevent curdling. Add the salt and increase the speed to medium and beat for 2–3 minutes until smooth, scraping the bowl down occasionally. Fold in the milk to loosen the mixture slightly.
* Spoon the batter into the prepared basin, cover with a lid, or make one from a large pleated square made from a double layer of baking (parchment) paper and aluminium foil, and secure it around the top of the pudding basin with kitchen string. Put the bowl into a steamer and cook for 1½–2 hours until a skewer inserted into the sponge comes out clean. Alternatively, put the basin on an inverted saucer inside a large saucepan. Cover the saucer with a small square of muslin (cheesecloth) and set the basin on top. Fill the saucepan a third full with water, bring to the boil, then reduce the heat and simmer, making sure to top up (top off) the water halfway through steaming.
* To serve, gently loosen the sponge from the sides of the bowl using a knife, then turn out onto a warmed plate and serve with Custard, chocolate sauce or equivalent.
* **Variations:** For the jam sponge, fresh fruit (optional) can be folded through the mixture, before adding the jam to the base of the basin and then pouring over the pudding mixture. Warm an extra 3 tablespoons of jam to serve over the sponge after cooking (optional).
* For a treacle sponge, use soft brown sugar and add 3 tablespoons golden syrup to the mixture at the same time as the sugar. Pour 3 tablespoons of warmed golden syrup into the base of the basin before adding the pudding mixture. Warm an extra 3 tablespoons of syrup to serve over the sponge after cooking (optional).
* For a chocolate sponge, replace 20 g/¾ oz (2⅓ tablespoons) of the flour with unsweetened cocoa powder, and chocolate sauce can be poured into the basin prior to the sponge batter, if desired.
* For a lemon sponge, add the grated zest of 2 lemons and 40 ml/1½ fl oz (2 tablespoons plus 2 teaspoons) of lemon juice to the sponge batter, then put lemon curd into the basin prior to the sponge batter.
* For a stewed apple or apricot sponge, make a compote by heating 150–200 g/5–7 oz fruit, 50 ml/1¾ fl oz (3½ tablespoons) water, 40 g/1½ oz (¼ cup plus 2 teaspoons) caster (superfine) sugar and 20 ml/¾ fl oz (4 teaspoons) lemon juice over a low heat for 15 minutes. Chill and put into the basin prior to the sponge batter.
* For a dried fruit sponge, soak 100 g/3½ oz (½ cup plus 2 teaspoons) mixed dried fruit, such as sultanas (golden raisins), raisins and currants in orange juice, tea or brandy, overnight, then drain and fold through the sponge batter. Use a little of the liquid to slacken the batter instead of the milk.

Basic steamed sponge

ENGLAND: OXFORD AND CAMBRIDGE
*

COLLEGE PUDDING

There are nearly 70 colleges at the universities of Oxford and Cambridge, and the majority of them have their own pudding, a tradition that is said to date back to the early seventeenth century. Plenty of Oxbridge colleges still serve these puddings as part of their traditional three-course formal-hall dinners.

While there are differences between each pudding, the majority are fairly simple and made from a combination of suet, breadcrumbs and dried fruit. The recipe below is for a richer variation, and includes an egg, brandy and a little spice. After cooking, leave to cool slightly before slicing into wedges and serving with jugs (pitchers) of good Custard (page 33).

Serves: 6
Prep time: 15 minutes
Cook time: 2 hours
{ᵒ•ᵒ}

- unsalted butter, for greasing
- 220 g/ 7¾ oz (4½ cups minus 1 teaspoon) fresh white breadcrumbs
- 60 g/ 2¼ oz (¼ cup) soft brown sugar
- ½ teaspoon ground nutmeg
- good pinch of salt
- 100 g/ 3½ oz (½ cup plus 2 teaspoons) shredded beef suet or 150 g/ 5 oz (1¼ sticks) unsalted butter
- 1 egg, beaten
- 90 ml/ 3 fl oz (6 tablespoons) brandy or milk, or a mixture
- 80 g/ 3 oz (½ cup) mixed dried fruit
- grated zest of 1 lemon
- Custard (page 33), to serve

* Grease a 900 ml/ 30 fl oz pudding basin (ovenproof bowl) with butter.
* Put the breadcrumbs, sugar, nutmeg and salt into a large bowl and mix together, then add the suet or butter and mix again. Beat in the egg, followed by the brandy or milk, and, finally, add the dried fruit and grated zest.
* Spoon the batter into the prepared basin, cover with a lid, or make one from a large pleated square made from a double layer of baking (parchment) paper and aluminium foil, and secure it around the top of the pudding basin with kitchen string.
* Transfer to a steamer and steam for 2 hours. Alternatively, put the basin on an inverted saucer within a large saucepan. Cover the saucer with a small square of muslin (cheesecloth) and set the basin on top. Fill the saucepan a third full with water, bring to the boil, then reduce the heat and simmer for 2 hours, making sure to top up (top off) the water halfway through steaming. Turn out and serve with Custard.

UNITED KINGDOM
*

JAM ROLY POLY

A flaky suet sponge rolled up with a layer of jam, this is a classic nursery pudding that's stayed a favourite over the last 200 years. A slightly sinful combination of sweet and stodge, made all the more delicious with lashings of Custard (page 33).

Serves: 6
Prep time: 30 minutes, plus 20 minutes chilling
Cook time: 40–60 minutes
{ᵒ•ᵒ}

- 1½ x quantity Suet Pastry (page 246)
- plain (all-purpose) flour, for dusting
- 225–250 g/ 8–9 oz jam of choice
- 3–4 tablespoons fresh breadcrumbs (optional)
- butter, for greasing
- full-fat (whole) milk, for sealing
- 1 egg, beaten, for glazing
- caster (superfine) sugar, for dusting
- Custard (page 33), to serve

* Make the pastry following the recipe on page 246 and leave to chill for 20 minutes before using.
* Preheat the oven to 180°C/ 350°F/ Gas Mark 4, ensuring there are 2 shelves inside it.
* Roll out the dough on a lightly floured work counter into a rectangle about 30 x 20 cm/ 12 x 8 inches (the longer side being a little shorter than the roasting pan). Using a palette knife, spread the jam evenly over the dough, leaving a 2 cm/ ¾ inch gap around a longer edge and 2 shorter edges. If the jam is runny, sprinkle with the breadcrumbs. Lightly brush the 3 edges with the milk, then, starting with the longer edge that's covered in jam nearest to you, firmly roll up the dough away from you like a Swiss (jelly) roll. Apply pressure on the seal and the ends of the dough so that the jam stays inside.
* Put a piece of aluminium foil about 40 cm/ 16 inches long onto the work counter, then heavily grease a piece of baking (parchment) paper with butter and put it on top of the foil. Transfer the roll onto the paper. Brush the dough with the egg, generously sprinkle with the sugar and wrap gently in the paper, making a pleat along the top, then secure with the foil firmly at the ends.
* Bring 1 litre/ 34 fl oz (4¼ cups) water to the boil and reduce the oven temperature to 160°C/ 325°F/ Gas Mark 3. Put a 23 x 33 cm/ 9 x 13 inch roasting pan onto the lower shelf of the oven and the roly poly on the top shelf. Quickly and carefully pour the boiling water into the roasting pan and bake for 40–60 minutes. Remove the roly poly from the oven and leave to cool for 10 minutes before unwrapping.
* Remove the roly poly from the foil and paper, divide it into even portions and serve with hot Custard.

Jam roly poly

WALES
*

SNOWDON PUDDING
PWDIN ERYRI

This steamed suet pudding was devised in 1887 by Alice Corbett at the Victoria Hotel, situated at the foot of Mount Snowdon. The pudding, cutely presented with a summit of raisins, became popular as a rib-sticking treat for hikers after a long day up Wales' tallest mountain.

Traditionally, this pudding was served with a sweet and syrupy red wine sauce, or 'saws gwin'. You can make your own saws gwin using a couple of glasses of wine, a little lemon peel, a piece of butter and 1 tablespoon of sugar – cook the mixture slowly for about 10 minutes until it thickens, then serve with the pudding and Custard (page 33).

Serves: 4–6
Prep time: 10 minutes
Cook time: 1½ hours
{🌶}{🍷}

- unsalted butter, for greasing
- 120 g/4 oz (2½ cups) fresh white breadcrumbs
- 120 g/4 oz (⅔ cup) shredded beef suet
- 20 g/¾ oz (¼ cup minus 2 teaspoons) cornflour (cornstarch)
- 90 g/3¼ oz (½ cup minus 4 teaspoons) soft light brown sugar
- grated zest of 1 lemon
- 90 g/3¼ oz (⅓ cup) lemon marmalade
- 3 eggs, beaten
- 60 g/2¼ oz (½ cup minus 1 tablespoon) raisins, with a small handful set aside
- Custard (page 33), to serve

* Grease a 500 ml/17 fl oz pudding basin (ovenproof bowl) with plenty of butter.
* Put the breadcrumbs, suet, cornflour (cornstarch), sugar and grated lemon zest into a large bowl and mix together. Mix in the marmalade and eggs, then fold in most of the raisins. Put the remaining raisins into the bottom of the prepared basin, then pour in the pudding batter. Cover with a lid, or make one from a large pleated square made from a double layer of baking (parchment) paper and aluminium foil, and secure it around the top of the pudding basin with kitchen string.
* Put the basin into a steamer and steam for 1½ hours. Alternatively, put an inverted saucer into a large saucepan. Cover the saucer with a small square of muslin (cheesecloth) and set the basin on top, then fill the saucepan a third full with water. Bring to the boil, then reduce the heat and simmer for 1½ hours. Make sure that you check and top up (top off) the water level as necessary halfway through cooking.
* Remove the pudding from the steamer and leave to stand for 15–20 minutes before turning out onto a plate. Serve with Custard.

ENGLAND
*

SPOTTED DICK
SPOTTED DOG

A steamed sponge pudding that's speckled with currants and lightly spiced with cinnamon, the spotted dick has been made in much the same way since it first appeared in Alexis Soyer's *A Shilling Cookery for The People* in 1845. Its enduring appeal is easy to understand: served warm and with plenty of Custard (page 33), it is simple and soothing.

Serves: 6
Prep time: 15 minutes
Cook time: 1½–2 hours
{🍷}

- unsalted butter, for greasing
- 80 g/3 oz (½ cup minus 4 teaspoons) caster (superfine) sugar, plus extra for sprinkling
- 300 g/11 oz (2½ cups) self-raising flour, sifted
- 1 teaspoon baking powder
- 150 g/5 oz (1 cup minus 2 tablespoons) shredded beef suet
- 120 g/4 oz (½ cup) currants
- grated zest of 2 lemons
- 200–250 ml/7–8 fl oz (¾ cup–1 cup) full-fat (whole) milk
- Custard (page 33), to serve

* Generously grease a 1 litre/34 fl oz pudding basin (ovenproof bowl) with butter, then sprinkle the bowl with the extra sugar and coat it by rotating the bowl and covering the butter completely.
* Put the flour, baking powder, suet, currants, the 80 g/3 oz sugar and the grated lemon zest into a large bowl and mix thoroughly until combined. Gradually stir in 200 ml/7 fl oz of the milk until it is the consistency of a thick cake batter, adding extra milk if needed. Spoon the batter into the prepared basin. Cover with a lid, or make one from a large pleated square made from a double layer of baking (parchment) paper and aluminium foil, and secure it around the top of the pudding basin with kitchen string.
* Put the basin into a steamer and steam for 1½–2 hours. Alternatively, put an inverted saucer into a large saucepan. Cover the saucer with a small square of muslin (cheesecloth) and set the basin on top, then fill the saucepan a third full with water. Bring to the boil, then reduce the heat and simmer for 1½–2 hours. Make sure that you check and top up (top off) the water level as necessary halfway through cooking. The pudding is ready when a skewer or toothpick inserted into the sponge comes out clean.
* Remove the pudding from the steamer and leave to stand for 5–10 minutes, then turn out onto a large plate and serve with Custard.

Spotted dick

ENGLAND: OXFORDSHIRE
*
HOLLYGOG PUDDING

This farmhouse pudding is from the village of Kiddington, on the outskirts of the Cotswolds in south-central England. It is a brilliant self-saucing golden syrup roly-poly, the top of which caramelizes as it bakes. Once baked, slice and serve with more golden syrup and Custard (page 33) or cream.

Serves: 6
Prep time: 30 minutes
Cook time: 30–45 minutes
{👤}{🌱}

- 150 g/5 oz (1¼ sticks) unsalted butter, at room temperature, diced, plus extra for greasing
- 4 tablespoons golden syrup, plus an extra 4 tablespoons to serve (optional)
- 280 g/10 oz (2⅓ cups) plain (all-purpose) flour, plus extra for dusting
- pinch of salt
- 2 tablespoons caster (superfine) sugar
- 5–6 tablespoons full-fat (whole) milk, plus extra for sealing
- Custard (page 33), to serve

- To finish:
- about 250 ml/8 fl oz (1 cup) full-fat (whole) milk
- 40 g/1½ oz (3 tablespoons) unsalted butter, cut into slivers
- 2 tablespoons caster (superfine) sugar, for dusting (optional)

* Preheat the oven to 200°C/400°F/Gas Mark 6. Grease a deep ovenproof dish with a lip of at least 2.5 cm/1 inch with butter.
* Heat the golden syrup in a small saucepan over a low heat for a few minutes until warm, then set aside.
* Sift the flour, salt and the 2 tablespoons sugar together into a bowl, then stir to combine. Add the 150 g/5 oz (1¼ sticks) butter and rub in with your fingertips until the mixture resembles fine breadcrumbs. Add the milk, a little at a time, until a stiff dough is formed. Turn the dough out onto a lightly floured work counter and roll out into a rectangle about 5 mm/¼ inch thick.
* Using a palette knife, spread the warmed golden syrup evenly over the dough, leaving a 2 cm/¾ inch gap around a longer edge and 2 shorter edges. Lightly brush the 3 edges with the tablespoon of milk, then, starting with the longer edge that's covered in syrup nearest to you, firmly roll the dough up away from you. Apply pressure on the seal and the ends of the pastry so that the syrup stays inside.
* Put the pudding into the prepared dish, then pour in enough of the milk for the sauce so that it comes about halfway up the sides of the dish. Lay the slivers of butter evenly on top of the pudding, then dust with the caster (superfine) sugar, if desired.
* Bake in the oven for 30–45 minutes until the top is golden brown and caramelized. Remove and leave to cool until warm before slicing and serving with Custard and a little more warmed golden syrup.

ENGLAND
*
STICKY TOFFEE PUDDING

A moist cake saturated in a rich toffee sauce, the sticky toffee pudding was only popularized in the 1970s, but has since leapt onto the pages of every self-respecting British pub menu and home cookbook.
In 2008, chef and food writer Simon Hopkinson traced the lineage of the STP back to a Lancashire woman named Patricia Martin, who apparently received the recipe from Canadian Air Force officers who stayed at her hotel during World War II. This story seems likely, Hopkinson notes, because the batter of STP is actually more in line with an American muffin – soft and springy – than a traditional British sponge.

Serves: 6
Prep time: 20 minutes, plus 10 minutes standing
Cook time: 25–35 minutes
{👤}{🌱}

- 90 g/3¼ oz (6 tablespoons) soft unsalted butter, at room temperature, plus extra for greasing
- 180 g/6 oz (1¼ cups) dates, preferably Medjool, stoned (pitted) and chopped
- 3 g/½ teaspoon bicarbonate of soda (baking soda)
- 180 g/6 oz (¾ cup plus 1 teaspoon) soft light brown sugar
- 2 eggs
- 180 g/6 oz (1½ cups) self-raising flour, sifted
- Clotted Cream (page 34) or ice cream, to serve

- For the sauce:
- 200 g/7 oz (¾ cup plus 2 tablespoons) soft dark brown sugar
- 75 ml/2½ fl oz (⅓ cup) double (heavy) cream
- 120 g/4 oz (1 stick) unsalted butter

* Preheat the oven to 160°C/325°F/Gas Mark 3. Grease an 18 cm/7 inch square baking pan or tray with butter and line with baking (parchment) paper.
* Put the dates and bicarbonate of soda (baking soda) into a medium heatproof bowl, pour over 300 ml/10 fl oz (1¼ cups) boiling water, cover with clingfilm (plastic wrap) and leave to stand for 10 minutes.
* Put the butter and soft light brown sugar into a stand mixer fitted with a paddle attachment and mix on medium speed, scraping down the bowl a couple of times during mixing, until it is pale and fluffy. Alternatively, use a large bowl and electric beaters. Slowly incorporate the eggs, one at a time, then fold in the sifted flour and combine thoroughly.
* Using a hand-held blender, blend the date mixture until smooth, then fold this through the pudding batter.
* Pour the pudding batter into the prepared pan or tray and bake in the oven for 25–35 minutes until a knife or skewer inserted into the centre comes out clean. It will also start to crack when it's almost cooked.
* Meanwhile, for the sauce, put all the ingredients into a medium saucepan over a medium heat, stirring occasionally, for 5minutes, or until the sugar has dissolved. About 5 minutes before removing the cooked pudding from the oven, pour a third of the sauce over the top, if desired. Serve with Clotted Cream or ice cream on the side and smother with the remaining sauce.

Sticky toffee pudding

UNITED KINGDOM
*

BREAD
AND
BUTTER PUDDING

There are two fairly different ways of making bread and butter pudding: one in which the bread is layered at an angle across the dish, with the tops protruding slightly above the custard – producing crispy ends and a very custardy base – and a second in which the bread is layered flat, so that the custard soaks evenly into it. This recipe belongs to the second school of thought. While this recipe calls for white bread, you can use virtually any bread or even yeasted buns. In my opinion, a bread and butter pudding made with Hot Cross Buns (page 288) is one of the finest English puddings to look forward to every April.

Serves: 4
Prep time: 15 minutes, plus 30 minutes standing
Cook time: 30–40 minutes
{👥}{🍴}

- 50 g/2 oz (3½ tablespoons) unsalted butter, softened, plus extra for greasing
- 8–10 slices stale bread
- 3 eggs
- 50 g/2 oz (¼ cup) caster (superfine) sugar
- 400 ml/14 fl oz (1⅔ cups) double (heavy) cream
- 1 tablespoon ground cinnamon
- 1 teaspoon mixed spice
- 50 g/2 oz (⅓ cup) sultanas (golden raisins)
- splash of rum or brandy (optional)
- Custard (page 33), Toffee Sauce (page 358) or Butterscotch Sauce (page 428), to serve

* Preheat the oven to 180°C/350°F/Gas Mark 4. Grease a 25 x 20 cm/10 x 8 inch cake pan with butter.
* Butter the bread on both sides and lay in the pan.
* Put the eggs, sugar and cream into a large bowl and whisk until combined. Add the spices, sultanas (golden raisins) and rum (if using) and pour over the bread. Leave to stand for at least 30 minutes.
* Bake in the oven for 30–40 minutes until golden brown. Serve with Custard, Toffee Sauce or Butterscotch Sauce.

ENGLAND
*

OLD-FASHIONED
ENGLISH BREAD PUDDING

This dessert comes as a surprise to those expecting its custardy cousin. Made with loosely the same ingredients, the layers of a bread pudding coalesce into something cake-like, with a texture that's both dense and spongy.

Serves: 4
Prep time: 15 minutes, plus 30 minutes soaking
Cook time: 1 hour
{🍴}

- butter, for greasing
- 350 g/12 oz stale white bread, crusts removed and cut into chunks
- 120 g/4 oz (½ cup) dark brown sugar
- 50 g/2 oz apple, peeled, cored and diced
- 65 g/2¼ oz (⅓ cup plus 1 teaspoon) shredded suet
- 50 g/2 oz (⅓ cup) raisins
- 30 g/1 oz (¼ cup) sultanas (golden raisins)
- 20 g/¾ oz (¼ cup minus 2 tablespoons) candied mixed peel
- 1 egg
- 2 tablespoons dark rum
- ½ teaspoon each ground allspice and cinnamon
- demerara (turbinado) sugar, for sprinkling
- Custard (page 33) or ice cream, to serve

* Preheat the oven to 180°C/350°F/Gas Mark 4. Grease a 25 x 20 cm/10 x 8 inch cake pan with butter.
* Put the bread into a large bowl, pour in enough water to cover and leave to soak for 30 minutes.
* Put all the remaining ingredients, except the demerara (turbinado) sugar into another bowl and mix together until combined. Squeeze out as much water as possible from the bread and add to the bowl, then mix well.
* Pour the mixture into the cake pan and sprinkle with the demerara sugar. Bake in the oven for 1 hour, then serve with Custard or ice cream.

ENGLAND: KENT
*

CHERRY BATTER PUDDING

Batter puddings have been made in England for centuries. This variation is substantially closer to the French clafoutis, but made using the superlative Kentish cherries, which are in season for 6–7 weeks from the end of June.

Serves: 4
Prep time: 15 minutes
Cook time: 30 minutes
{👥}{🍴}

- 30 g/1 oz (2 tablespoons) unsalted butter, plus extra for greasing
- 300 g/11 oz fresh sweet cherries, stoned (pitted)
- 90 g/3¼ oz (¾ cup) plain (all-purpose) flour
- 90 g/3¼ oz (½ cup minus 2 teaspoons) caster (superfine) sugar
- 3 eggs, beaten
- 400 ml/14 fl oz (1⅔ cups) full-fat (whole) milk
- icing (confectioners') sugar, for dusting
- extra-thick cream, to serve

* Preheat the oven to 180°C/350°F/Gas Mark 4.
* Grease a large shallow baking dish with butter and sprinkle over the cherries.
* Heat the butter in a saucepan for 2 minutes until melted. Put the flour and sugar into a large bowl and mix together. Beat in the eggs, then beat in the milk and melted butter to make a smooth batter.
* Pour the batter into the prepared dish and bake in the oven for 30 minutes, or until well risen and golden brown on top. Remove from the oven and dust with a little icing (confectioners') sugar and serve with cream.

Bread and butter pudding

ENGLAND: DEVON
*

DEVONSHIRE APPLE DRUGGET

The most curious thing about this dessert is its name – a drugget being a sort of soft carpet. Perhaps it's a reference to the top of the pudding: a soft layer of breadcrumbs.

Serves: 6
Prep time: 20 minutes
Cook time: 40–55 minutes
{🌢}{✢}

- 90 g/3¼ oz (6 tablespoons) unsalted butter, diced, plus extra for greasing
- 1 kg/2¼ lb Bramley (cooking) apples, peeled, cored and chopped into chunks
- 120 g/4 oz (2½ cups) fresh breadcrumbs
- 90 g/3½ oz (½ cup minus 2 teaspoons) caster (superfine) sugar, plus extra for sprinkling
- 2 eggs, beaten
- grated zest of 1 lemon
- 2 tablespoons marmalade
- ¼ teaspoon mixed spice

* Preheat the oven to 180°C/350°F/Gas Mark 4. Grease a square baking dish with butter.
* Put the apples into a large saucepan with 4 tablespoons water and cook over a medium heat for 10–15 minutes until the apples have broken down to a pulp.
* Transfer the apples to a bowl, add two-thirds of the breadcrumbs, two-thirds of the butter, all the sugar, eggs, lemon zest, marmalade and mixed spice and mix together.
* Pour into the prepared baking dish, then sprinkle over the remaining breadcrumbs, dot with the remaining butter and sprinkle over a little more sugar. Bake for 30–40 minutes until golden and risen.

UNITED KINGDOM
*

RED WINE POACHED PEARS

Poached in a syrupy, spiced red wine, these pears make a handsome winter dessert served upright with a large dollop of cream and a little more of the syrup.

Serves: 4
Prep time: 20 minutes
Cook time: 30 minutes
{🌢}{🔥}{✢}{🍷}

- 4 conference pears
- 500 ml/17 fl oz (2 cups plus 1 tablespoon) red wine
- 90 g/3¼ oz (½ cup minus 2 teaspoons) caster (superfine) sugar, plus extra to taste
- 1 cinnamon stick or star anise
- ¼ teaspoon ground ginger
- whipped cream or ice cream, to serve

* Peel the pears, leaving the stalk intact. Use a melon baller or small paring knife to remove the core from beneath so the pear remains whole. Cut the bottom of each pear so that it can stand upright. Put the pears into a saucepan and pour over the wine. Add the sugar and spices and simmer over a low-medium heat for 15 minutes. Remove the pears using a slotted spoon and keep them warm in a bowl covered with aluminium foil.
* Heat the wine in the pan over a medium-high heat until it is syrupy and coats the back of a spoon, about 15 minutes. Add more sugar if needed, then pour over the pears. Serve with a dollop of cream or scoop of ice cream.

ENGLAND
*

SUMMER PUDDING

A celebration of bright summer fruits, this is a simple English bread pudding that's filled with macerated raspberries and redcurrants. The juicy syrup from the macerated fruit is then brushed or spooned across the surface of the pudding, giving it a distinctive rich deep-red colour. The pudding is set in the fridge, rather than baked.

Serves: a generous 6
Prep time: 10 minutes,
plus up to 24 hours macerating and chilling
Cook time: 20 minutes
{🌢}{✢}

- 200 g/7 oz (1⅔ cups) redcurrants
- 200 g/7 oz (1⅓ cups) blackcurrants
- 175 g/6 oz (1 cup) raspberries
- 100 g/3½ oz (¾ cup) blackberries
- 175 g/6 oz (¾ cup plus 2 tablespoons) caster (superfine) sugar
- 800 g/1 lb 12 oz loaf stale white bread or a large stale Madeira Cake (page 319)
- ice cream, to serve

* Put the fruits and sugar into a large bowl and mix together. Cover with clingfilm (plastic wrap) and leave to macerate in the fridge overnight.
* The next day, transfer the fruit mixture with all its liquid into a large saucepan and simmer over a low heat for 20 minutes, stirring, until the sugar has dissolved. Remove from the heat and set aside.
* Cut the bread or cake into 1 cm/½ inch thick slices, removing the crusts. Cut the slices into thick rectangular strips and use them to line the sides of a 900 ml/30 fl oz pudding basin (ovenproof bowl). Cut a circle from a slice of bread and put it onto the bottom of the basin. Use a little of the fruit juices to seal the edges of the bread.
* Pour in all the fruit and a little more of the juice, setting the remaining juice aside, then cut out a wider circle of bread to use as a lid. Put a small plate onto the top, then put the basin into the fridge and put a weight or heavy can or jar onto the plate to weight it down. Leave to chill in the fridge overnight.
* The next day, use a spatula to free the pudding from the sides of the basin, then carefully turn it out onto a plate. Brush the reserved syrup over the top, making sure the entire pudding is painted a deep red colour. Serve with ice cream.

Summer pudding

ENGLAND
*

CABINET PUDDING
DIPLOMAT'S/CHANCELLOR'S/ NEWCASTLE PUDDING

Cabinet pudding is a moulded bread pudding made with left-over slices of cake (sponge, ideally), dried fruit and a sweet custard that's often spiked with liquor. The pudding is usually steamed in a decorative mould, then served in slices – a remnant of Victorian times and tastes.

Serves: 6
Prep time: 20 minutes, plus 2 hours soaking
Cook time: 1½ hours
{👤}{👃}

- 60 g/2¼ oz (½ stick) unsalted butter, diced, plus extra for greasing
- 40 g/1½ oz (¼ cup) candied mixed peel or stem (preserved) ginger, chopped
- 90 g/3¼ oz (½ cup minus 2 tablespoons) dried or glacé (candied) cherries
- 90 g/3¼ oz (⅔ cup minus 2 teaspoons) sultanas (golden raisins)
- 250 g/9 oz stale sponge cake, cut into 1–1.5 cm/½–5/8 inch wide cubes
- 300 ml/10 fl oz (1¼ cups) full-fat (whole) milk, or 150 ml/5 fl oz (⅔ cup) milk and 150 ml/5 fl oz (⅔ cup) double (heavy) cream
- 60 ml/2 fl oz (¼ cup) brandy or more milk
- 30 g/1 oz (2½ tablespoons) caster (superfine) sugar
- grated zest of 1 lemon
- 3 eggs

* Generously grease a 900 ml/30 fl oz pudding basin (ovenproof bowl) with butter and sprinkle the candied mixed peel or ginger over the bottom of the basin together with a third of the dried fruit. Move the bowl around to distribute the fruit, making sure it goes up the sides of the bowl too.
* Put some of the cubes of cake into the basin in a single layer, then add a layer of dried fruit and dot with pieces of butter. Repeat until the ingredients are used up, finishing with a layer of cake.
* Put the milk or cream/milk mixture, brandy (if using), sugar, lemon zest and eggs into a large bowl and whisk together. Pour this liquid into the basin, cover with clingfilm (plastic wrap) and leave to soak in the fridge for at least 2 hours.
* Remove the pudding basin from the fridge and remove the clingfilm. Make a large pleated square from a double layer of baking (parchment) paper and aluminium foil and secure it around the top of the pudding basin with kitchen string. Put into a steamer and steam for 1½ hours. Alternatively, put an inverted saucer into a large saucepan. Cover the saucer with a small square of muslin (cheesecloth) and set the basin on top, then fill the saucepan a third full with water. Bring to the boil, then reduce the heat and simmer for 1½ hours. Make sure that you check and top up (top off) the water level as necessary halfway through cooking.
* Leave to stand for 15–20 minutes before turning out and serving.

ENGLAND: SUSSEX
*

SUSSEX POND PUDDING

The Sussex pond pudding gets its name from the sweet butter sauce that pools out when it's cut open – rather like today's Fondant (see right) – and dates as far back as the 1670s. The modern version includes a strong lemon component, with many recipes calling for a whole lemon or lemon slices to be set into the pudding before steaming. This recipe, by English pastry chef Richard Phillips, calls for a lemon confit instead. As with any steamed pudding, serve with Custard (page 33).

Serves: 6
Prep time: 1½ hours, plus 30 minutes chilling
Cook time: 4½–5 hours
{👃}

- 1½ x quantity Suet Pastry (page 246)
- 2 lemons
- 120 g/4 oz (1 stick) unsalted butter, cold and diced, plus extra for greasing
- plain (all-purpose) flour, for dusting
- 120 g/4 oz (½ cup) light brown sugar
- 10 slices lemon confit
- salt
- ice cream, Clotted Cream (page 34) or double (heavy) cream, to serve

- For the lemon confit:
- 8 lemons, unwaxed
- 500 g/1 lb 2 oz (2½ cups) caster (superfine) sugar

* For the lemon confit, half-fill a medium saucepan with cold water and put 6 of the lemons into the pan. Bring the water to a simmer over a high heat, then boil the lemons for 2–3 minutes. Remove the lemons from the boiling water and refresh them under cold running water for 5 minutes. Repeat the process another 4 times (5 times in total). This process will remove the bitterness. Cut the lemons into 1 cm/½ inch slices, remove any pips (seeds) and set aside. Juice the remaining 2 lemons and set aside.
* Preheat the oven to 150°C/300°F/Gas Mark 2.
* Pour 500 ml/17 fl oz (2 cups plus 1 tablespoon) water into a saucepan, add the sugar and simmer over a low-medium heat for 5 minutes, stirring, until the sugar has dissolved. Remove from the heat and add the lemon juice.
* Arrange the lemon slices in rows, slightly overlapping, on a large nonstick baking sheet or in a roasting pan. Gently pour the syrup over the lemons, then cover completely with a piece of baking (parchment) paper. Pierce a few holes in the paper with a knife (allowing some of the moisture to escape) and cover with aluminium foil. Put into the oven for 50–60 minutes until the lemon slices are translucent. Remove the foil and paper and cook for another 20–30 minutes until the syrup is reduced and sticky. Remove from the oven and leave to cool or put directly into a sterilized jar (page 464) to use later.
* For the pudding, make the pastry following the recipe on page 246, grating the zest of the 2 lemons and adding it to the dough, then leave to chill for 20 minutes before using. Set the lemons aside.
* Generously grease a 1 litre/34 fl oz pudding basin (ovenproof bowl) with butter.
* Roll the lemon-flavoured dough out on a lightly floured work counter into 2 circles, one about 33 cm/13 inches

in diameter and 1 cm / ½ inch thick, and the other about 15 cm / 6 inches in diameter.

* Lay the larger circle of dough over the prepared basin and gently work and push the dough into the bottom with your fingers, applying pressure so the dough sticks to the sides of the bowl. Leave the basin and the pastry lid to chill in the fridge for 10 minutes.

* Using a knife, cut the two fresh lemons into 5 slices, removing any seeds, and set aside.

* Remove the bowl and dough lid from the fridge and start to build the pudding. Put 2 slices of lemon confit and 2 slices of fresh lemon into the bottom of the basin and sprinkle 20 g / ¾ oz (1 tablespoon plus 2 teaspoons) of the sugar and 20 g / ¾ oz (4 teaspoons) of the butter and a pinch of salt over the top. Repeat the process until you have 5 layers of lemons with sugar and butter packed between them, seasoned with a little salt.

* Moisten the rim of the pastry, then put the smaller circle of pastry over the lemons, applying pressure, and seal both pieces of pastry together by firmly squeezing them. Cover the top with a lid made from a large pleated square made from a double layer of baking (parchment) paper and aluminium foil, and secure it around the top of the pudding basin with kitchen string.

* Put the basin into a steamer and steam for 2½–3 hours. Alternatively, put an inverted saucer into a large saucepan. Cover the saucer with a small square of muslin (cheesecloth) and set the basin on top, then fill the saucepan a third full with water. Bring to the boil, then reduce the heat and simmer for 2½–3 hours. Make sure that you check and top up (top off) the water level as necessary halfway through cooking. The pudding is ready when a skewer or toothpick inserted into the sponge comes out clean.

* Remove the pudding from the steamer and leave to stand for 5–10 minutes, then turn out onto a large plate and serve with ice cream, Clotted Cream or double (heavy) cream.

UNITED KINGDOM
*

CHOCOLATE FONDANTS

Fondants are the typical British term for what can also be described as a 'molten' or 'melt-in-the-middle' pudding – small individual cakes with soft centres and a sweet sauce filling. These chocolate fondants are perhaps the most well known. Serve while still warm with a scoop of ice cream.

Serves: 6
Prep time: 30 minutes, plus 2 hours setting
Cook time: 15 minutes
{👤} {🌶}

- 100 g / 3½ oz dark (semisweet) chocolate
(at least 70% cocoa solids), chopped or use buttons
- 100 g / 3½ oz (7 tablespoons) unsalted butter
- 140 g / 5 oz (¾ cup minus 2 teaspoons)
caster (superfine) sugar
- 3 eggs, plus 1 egg yolk
- 15 g / ½ oz (1¾ tablespoons)
plain (all-purpose) flour, sifted
- ice cream, to serve

For lining the moulds:
- unsalted butter, softened

- 25 g / 1 oz (¼ cup minus 1 teaspoon)
unsweetened cocoa powder
- 25 g / 1 oz (¼ cup minus 2 tablespoons)
caster (superfine) sugar

- For a simple chocolate sauce:
- 180 ml / 6 fl oz (¾ cup) full-fat (whole) milk
- 240 g / 8½ oz dark (semisweet) chocolate
(at least 70% cocoa solids), chopped

* First, prepare the fondant moulds. Using a pastry brush, evenly apply a generous yet thin layer of butter to six 5.5 x 5 cm / 2½ x 2¼ inch rings, brushing from top to bottom in straight lines. Put the cocoa powder and sugar into a small bowl and mix together, then spoon it over the butter, making sure it is completely coated. Leave in the fridge to set for 2 hours.

* For the fondants, put the chocolate and butter into a heat-proof bowl set over a large saucepan of gently simmering water, making sure the bottom of the bowl doesn't touch the water, and heat until the chocolate and butter have melted and combined. Make sure it doesn't exceed 40°C / 104°F, then set aside. Meanwhile, put the sugar, eggs and egg yolk into a stand mixer fitted with a whisk attachment and whisk on medium speed until pale, fluffy, thick and well aerated.

* Using a spatula, begin to gently fold the chocolate mixture into the egg mixture. Before it is completely incorporated, add the flour and fold in until the mixture is smooth, making sure to scrape the bottom of the bowl. Put the batter into a piping (pastry) bag fitted with a plain nozzle, then pipe the batter into the chilled moulds until they are two-thirds full. Leave to chill in the fridge for 2 hours, or until firm. The fondants can be made and kept up to a day in advance.

* Preheat the oven to 180°C / 350°F / Gas Mark 4.

* Put the chilled fondants onto a large baking sheet and cook in the oven for 8 minutes. Turn and cook for another 5 minutes. To test, insert a cocktail stick or toothpick into the centre and if it comes out covered in hot liquid fondant batter and with a cake-like crust, they are done. Remove from the oven and leave to cool for 1–2 minutes, before lifting the fondants onto a serving plate and removing the moulds.

* While the fondants are cooking, make the chocolate sauce. Pour the milk into a medium saucepan and bring to a simmer over a low heat, add the chocolate and whisk until smooth. Remove from the heat and pour into a small jug (pitcher).

* Serve the fondants with a scoop of ice cream and the chocolate sauce on the side.

ENGLAND
*

DEBDEN CHOCOLATE PUDDING

This chocolate pudding uses a fun technique that's become popular in modern British desserts: sponge batter is poured into a baking dish and covered by a sweet layer (of, for instance, dried fruit, spices, sugar or cocoa powder), before being topped with one of water. When baked, a seemingly magical transformation occurs – the top is crisp and cakey chocolate sponge and the bottom is oozing with a thick fudgy sauce. A Debden is surprisingly chocolatey, though, given the small amount included in the recipe.

Just as with a steamed pudding, there's endless room here for tinkering with the flavouring of both the cake and the sauce once you master the method.

Serves: 6
Prep time: 15 minutes
Cook time: 50–60 minutes
{👤}{🔥}

- 30 g/1 oz (2 tablespoons) unsalted butter, plus extra for greasing
- 125 g/4¼ oz (1 cup plus 1 teaspoon) plain (all-purpose) flour
- 2 teaspoons baking powder
- ½ teaspoon fine sea salt
- 175 g/6 oz (¾ cup plus 1 tablespoon) granulated sugar
- 25 g/1 oz dark (semisweet) chocolate, broken into pieces
- 150 ml/5 fl oz (⅔ cup) full-fat (whole) milk
- 50 g/2 oz (¼ cup minus 1 teaspoon) demerara (turbinado) sugar
- 50 g/2 oz (¼ cup) caster (superfine) sugar
- 3 tablespoons unsweetened cocoa powder, sifted
- pouring cream, to serve

* Preheat the oven to 170°C/325°F/Gas Mark 3. Lightly grease a shallow 900 ml/30 fl oz ceramic baking dish with butter.
* Sift the flour and baking powder into a large bowl, then stir in the salt and granulated sugar.
* Put the chocolate and butter into a heatproof bowl set over a large saucepan of gently simmering water, making sure the bottom of the bowl doesn't touch the water, and heat until the chocolate and butter have melted and combined. Remove from the heat and stir in the milk, then add this to the flour mixture and stir well to incorporate into a smooth batter. Pour the batter into the prepared baking dish and smooth out.
* Sprinkle the demerara (turbinado) sugar evenly over the top, then sprinkle with the caster (superfine) sugar, creating another even layer. Sprinkle the cocoa powder in an even layer on top of the sugars. Finally, gently pour 175 ml/6 fl oz (¾ cup) cold water over the top of the pudding, being careful not to disturb the sugar and cocoa layers too much.
* Carefully transfer to the oven and bake for 50–60 minutes until a crisp top has formed and the edges are bubbly with a chocolate fudge sauce. Remove from the oven and leave to cool.
* This is best enjoyed at room temperature with cold pouring cream. It will keep well, covered, in the fridge for a few days, but bring back to room temperature to serve.

SCOTLAND
*

SCOTTISH FRUIT PUDDING

Fruit pudding is made similar to White Pudding (page 177) – with beef suet, oats and spices – to which dried fruit, sugar, and sometimes even black treacle (blackstrap molasses) are added. It is similar in texture to an oaty white pudding but has the sweet spices and dried fruit of a Clootie Dumpling (page 348).

Once the pudding is cooked it is ready to eat, but you could store it in the fridge and use later, or slice and fry it in lard or oil over a medium heat for 2 minutes on each side. Alternatively, fry until lightly crisp and serve it with a Full Breakfast (page 26), or spread it across a thick slice of buttered bread. A warm mug of tea and some chill morning air are two more unbeatable serving suggestions.

Serves: 6
Prep time: 40 minutes, plus 8–12 hours soaking
Cook time: 45 minutes
{🔥}

- natural pig casing
- 240 g/8½ oz (2 cups) medium oatmeal
- 240 g/8½ oz (1⅓ cups) shredded beef suet
- 240 g/8½ oz (2 cups) plain (all-purpose) flour
- ½ teaspoon baking powder
- 1 teaspoon ground cinnamon
- 1 teaspoon finely chopped rosemary
- 1 teaspoon finely chopped sage
- 2 onions, chopped
- 1 tablespoon soft dark brown sugar
- 320 g/11½ oz (1¾ cups plus 1 tablespoon) mixed dried fruit, such as currants, raisins and sultanas (golden raisins)
- 160 g/5¾ oz (¾ cup) glacé (candied) cherries, halved
- grated zest of 2 lemons
- grated zest of 2 oranges
- 2 eggs, beaten
- salt

* Put the pig casing into a large bowl, cover with water and leave to soak overnight.
* The next day, put the oatmeal into a dry frying pan or skillet and toast over a medium-high heat for 5 minutes, or until golden brown. Put into a large bowl with the remaining ingredients, except the eggs, casing and salt, and mix together. When evenly mixed, add the eggs and mix to combine.
* Tie the casing at one end and, using a wide-mouthed funnel, stuff the mixture in to loosely fill the casing, removing as many air bubbles as possible. Tie loosely at the other end.
* Bring a large saucepan of salted water to a simmer over a medium-low heat. Poach the pudding very gently for 45 minutes, pricking the casing with a pin wherever air bubbles appear. Remove with a slotted spoon and leave to drain. Serve.

Debden chocolate pudding

SCOTLAND

*

CRANACHAN

According to the Scottish food writer Catherine Brown, cranachan was originally served family-style in separate bowls all laid out at once: a bowl of toasted oats, one of freshly whipped cream, another of soft seasonal fruits (such as raspberries or blackberries), a jar of good heather honey and a little whisky. Each guest would then take the time to mix and make their own, adding ingredients in the proportions they prefer. Serve yours in this way or follow the restaurant-style preparation below.

While cranachan is typically served for Burns Supper or other Scottish holidays, it makes most sense to serve it throughout summer, when Scottish soft fruits are at their very best.

Serves: 6
Prep time: 5 minutes
Cook time: 15 minutes
{👅}{🍴}{🔪}{✖}

- 60 g/2¼ oz (½ cup) medium oatmeal
- 600 ml/20 fl oz (2½ cups) double (heavy) cream
- 3 tablespoons honey
- 2 tablespoons whisky
- 100 g/3½ oz (½ cup minus 2 teaspoons) raspberries, with an additional 100 g/3½ oz (½ cup minus 2 teaspoons) sieved to create a purée, if desired

* Put the oatmeal into a dry frying pan or skillet and toast over a medium-high heat for 5 minutes, or until golden brown and aromatic. Remove from the heat and leave to cool.
* Meanwhile, put the cream into a stand mixer fitted with a whisk attachment and whip on medium speed until it is just set and a little floppy. Alternatively, whip the cream in a large bowl using electric beaters. Add the honey and whisky and stir through until combined.
* Put alternate layers of the cream, toasted oats, whole raspberries and raspberry purée (if using) into 6 tall sundae glasses, saving some oats and raspberries for the top. Serve.

UNITED KINGDOM

*

PAVLOVA

Named after Anna Pavlova, a famous prima ballerina of the early 1900s, this dessert actually originates in Australia and New Zealand, where Pavlova once toured in 1926.

If the pavlova appears demonstrably British, then perhaps it is because it shares its basic composition – meringue, whipped cream and strawberries – with the Eton Mess (page 370). Importantly, however, the meringue in a pavlova is made with the addition of cornflour (cornstarch) and vinegar, which gives it a crisp shell but a soft, airy inside. Finished with a generous layer of sweetened whipped cream and topped with fresh strawberries (or any good seasonal fruit), it transcends as a hallmark of British summertime.

Serves: 6
Prep time: 20 minutes, plus 1 hour cooling
Cook time: 45–60 minutes
{👅}{🍴}

- 4 egg whites, at room temperature
- 200 g/7 oz (1 cup) caster (superfine) sugar
- 1 teaspoon white vinegar of choice
- 1 teaspoon cornflour (cornstarch)
- 30 g/1 oz (¼ cup) crushed hazelnuts (optional)
- 300 ml/10 fl oz (1¼ cups) double (heavy) cream
- 2 tablespoons icing (confectioners') sugar
- fresh fruit of choice, such as strawberries, cherries, poached rhubarb, passionfruit, etc., to serve

* Preheat the oven to 150°C/300°F/Gas Mark 2.
* Put the egg whites into a stand mixer fitted with a whisk attachment and whisk on medium speed until stiff peaks form. Alternatively, whisk the egg whites in a large bowl with electric beaters. Once it reaches roughly one and a half times its original volume, gradually add the caster (superfine) sugar, one spoonful at a time. When three-quarters of the sugar has been added, mix in the vinegar and cornflour (cornstarch), then whisk in the remaining sugar. Fold in the hazelnuts (if using).
* Line a large, heavy baking sheet with baking (parchment) paper, using a little of the meringue at the corners to hold it in place. Spoon or pipe the meringue into a circle, about 15 cm/6 inches in diameter, making sure the edges are higher, creating a crater in the centre.
* Reduce the oven temperature to 120°C/250°F/Gas Mark ½ and bake the pavlova in the oven for 45–60 minutes until crisp but not browned. Turn the oven off with the door ajar and leave the pavlova in the oven for 1 hour, or until completely cool.
* Put the cream and icing (confectioners') sugar into a large bowl and whip until it forms soft peaks. Spoon the whipped cream over the meringue and decorate with fresh fruit of your choice to serve.

Cranachan

ENGLAND
*

ETON MESS

A traditional English dessert said to have originated at the famous boarding school, Eton College, in the late nineteenth century. It is a perfect dish for warm summertime evenings – a fairly loose mixture of freshly whipped cream, crushed meringue and fresh, ripe strawberries. If you don't have time to make the meringue, then use six shop-bought meringue nests.

Serves: 6
Prep time: 30 minutes
Cook time: 1½–2 hours
{🍴}{🥄}{🌶}

- 700 g/1 lb 8½ oz fresh strawberries
- 30 g/1 oz (2½ tablespoons) caster (superfine) sugar or vanilla sugar
- 600 ml/20 fl oz (2½ cups) double (heavy) cream
- 20 g/¾ oz (¼ cup minus 2 teaspoons) icing (confectioners') sugar, sifted
- 2 tablespoons strawberry jam

- For the meringues:
- 4 egg whites
- pinch of salt
- 280 g/10 oz (1½ cups minus 4 teaspoons) caster (superfine) sugar
- 1 tablespoon white wine vinegar

* Preheat the oven to 150°C/300°F/Gas Mark 2.
* For the meringues, put the egg whites and salt into a stand mixer fitted with a whisk attachment and whisk on medium speed to stiff peaks, then increase the speed to high and gradually add the caster (superfine) sugar, a spoonful at a time. Scrape down the bowl, add the vinegar, then continue to whisk on high speed for 6–8 minutes until the meringue is white and glossy.
* Line 2 large baking sheets with baking (parchment) paper, using a little of the meringue in the corners to hold the paper in place. Spoon the meringue onto the paper to make 6 circular nests.
* Reduce the oven temperature to 120°C/250°F/Gas Mark ½, then bake the meringues for 1½–2 hours until they are completely dry, keeping the door slightly ajar using the handle of a wooden spoon, to allow the moisture to escape. Once dried, leave the meringues to cool completely.
* Meanwhile, cut the strawberries into halves or quarters, depending on their size, then put into a large bowl, add the caster (superfine) or vanilla sugar and mix together. Leave to stand for no longer than 20 minutes while the meringue cools.
* Put the cream and icing (confectioners') sugar into the cleaned bowl of a stand mixer fitted with a whisk attachment and whip on medium speed to soft peaks. Alternatively, whip the cream and icing (confectioners') sugar together in a large bowl using electric beaters.
* Gently fold 500 g/1 lb 2 oz of the strawberries and their juice, the jam and crushed up meringue in separate layers into the cream. Avoid mixing them up too much, so there are prominent layers. Spoon into a 25 cm/10 inch bowl or 6 individual trifle or sundae glasses and decorate with the reserved strawberries and meringue. Serve immediately.

ENGLAND
*

BURNT CREAM

A rich vanilla custard with a layer of caramelized sugar on top, the burnt cream has a long tradition dating back to English cookbooks of the eighteenth century – if not even earlier, as Jane Grigson suggests. Despite its history, the burnt cream has been overshadowed by its French counterpart, the crème brûlée (itself the French for 'burnt cream'). While they look and taste quite the same, cookery writer Simon Hopkinson notes that burnt creams are meant to be a touch less sweet. They are also sometimes flavoured with fruit, a prospect that seems less likely across the Channel. Sometimes burnt creams are also associated with Cambridge University's Trinity College, where they are invariably known as a Trinity (or Cambridge) cream.
Serve as for crème brûlée: on its own, or with a small handful of fresh soft fruit.

Serves: 6
Prep time: 10 minutes
Cook time: 1 hour
{🍴}{🥄}{🌶}

- 1 vanilla pod (bean), split in half lengthways and seeds scraped out
- 600 ml/20 fl oz (2½ cups) double (heavy) cream
- 8 egg yolks
- 110 g/3¾ oz (½ cup plus 2 teaspoons) caster (superfine) sugar
- about 6 teaspoons granulated sugar
- 1 small handful fresh soft fruit, to serve (optional)

* Preheat the oven to 150°C/300°F/Gas Mark 2.
* Put the vanilla seeds and pod (bean) into a large saucepan with the cream and slowly bring to a simmer over a low heat. Cook for 5 minutes, allowing the vanilla to infuse into the cream.
* Meanwhile, put the egg yolks and caster (superfine) sugar into a large bowl and whisk together. While whisking, pour the infused cream through a sieve onto the yolks. When fully incorporated, divide this mixture evenly among 6 ramekins and put them all into a large roasting pan. Carefully pour just-boiled hot water into the pan, enough to reach halfway up the sides of the ramekins, and bake in the oven for 40–50 minutes until the custards are set. Remove from the oven, dry the bottom of the ramekins using a dish towel, then cover and leave to chill in the fridge until cooled.
* When the custards have cooled, remove them from the fridge and sprinkle the granulated sugar over the top of each ramekin. Using a chef's blowtorch, carefully caramelize the tops. Alternatively, preheat the grill (broiler) to medium and put the ramekins under the hot grill for a few minutes. The heat source does make this method inconsistent and prone to burning, so watch them carefully. Serve with fresh soft fruit, if desired.

Eton mess

UNITED KINGDOM
*

RHUBARB PIE

Forced rhubarb has been common in the UK since the late 1870s, when 'forcing sheds' warmed by cheap coal became common in West Yorkshire. Forced rhubarb comes into season in the dead of winter and provides a much-needed burst of vibrance in colour and flavour. In those dark months, a warm slice of rhubarb pie and cool cream can feel like the promise of spring.

Serves: 8
Prep time: 50 minutes,
plus 1 hour resting and chilling
Cook time: 55 minutes
{👤}{🍷}

- 1½ x quantity Shortcrust Pastry (page 247)
- unsalted butter, for greasing
- plain (all-purpose) flour, for dusting
- 1 kg/ 2¼ lb rhubarb, forced if available, trimmed
- 30 g/ 1 oz (¼ cup) cornflour (cornstarch)
- 150 g/ 5 oz (¾ cup) caster (superfine) sugar
- 1 egg, beaten with 1 tablespoon water or milk, for egg wash
- 4 g/ 1 teaspoon salt
- demerara (turbinado) sugar, for sprinkling
- cream or ice cream, to serve (optional)

* Make the pastry following the recipe on page 247 and leave to rest for 20 minutes before using.
* Grease a 23 cm/ 9 inch loose-bottom tart pan with butter. Line a large baking sheet with baking (parchment) paper.
* Roll out the dough on a lightly floured work counter evenly into 2 circles, about 25 cm/ 10 inches in diameter and 3 mm/ ⅛ inch thick.
* Lay one circle of dough over the prepared pan and gently work and push the dough into the edges using your fingers or use a lightly floured piece of dough. Slide it onto the prepared baking sheet, prick the bottom all over with a fork and chill in the fridge for 10 minutes, along with the second circle.
* Meanwhile, chop 800 g/ 1¾ lb of the rhubarb into even 2 cm/ ¾ inch batons, then juice the remaining rhubarb (you should have around 100 ml/ 3½ fl oz / ⅓ cup plus 1 tablespoon). Put the cornflour (cornstarch) into a medium bowl, add the chopped rhubarb and roll it in the cornflour until coated. You may need to do this in batches.
* Put the rhubarb juice and caster (superfine) sugar into a medium saucepan and bring it to the boil over a high heat. Add the coated rhubarb, then reduce the heat to a simmer and cook, stirring constantly, for 5 minutes, or until the mixture thickens but the rhubarb still has a bite. Remove from the heat, leave to cool slightly, then transfer to the fridge to chill for 30 minutes.
* Preheat the oven to 180°C/ 350°F/ Gas Mark 4.
* Remove the pastry case (shell) from the fridge and brush evenly with egg wash, then distribute the chilled rhubarb filling evenly over the bottom. Using a 2 cm/ ¾ inch ring cutter, cut a hole in the centre of the second circle of dough, brush egg wash on one side and place egg-wash side up over the filling, sealing and crimping the dough over the pan. Brush the top of the dough with more egg wash, then sprinkle with demerara (turbinado) sugar.

Bake in the oven for 40 minutes, turning halfway through. Check the pie after 30 minutes. It should be golden brown. If the edges start to colour too much, reduce the oven temperature to 160°C/ 325°F/ Gas Mark 3 and cover with aluminium foil.
* Remove the pie from the oven and leave to cool for 30 minutes. Serve on its own, or with cream or ice cream, if desired.

UNITED KINGDOM
*

FLOATING ISLANDS

This delightful Anglo-French dessert is composed of soft spoonfuls of meringue floating in a thin crème anglaise – or in Britain, custard of the cook's desired thickness. The earliest English versions of this recipe, found in nineteenth-century cookbooks, prepared it with jam as well..

Serves: 6
Prep time: 40 minutes
Cook time: 25 minutes
{👤}{🥄}{🍷}

- 1 quantity Custard (page 33)
- about 750 ml/ 25 fl oz (3 cups) full-fat (whole) milk
- 4 egg whites (use the yolks to make the custard)
- 200 g/ 7 oz (1 cup) caster (superfine) sugar

* Make the Custard following the recipe on page 33 and leave to cool.
* Pour the milk into a large sauté pan and slowly heat over a medium heat to scalding point or 83°C/ 181°F on a thermometer. Don't let it get hot enough to boil.
* Meanwhile, put the egg whites and 2 tablespoons of the sugar into a large bowl and, using electric beaters, whisk until fluffy. Add the remaining sugar, 1 tablespoon at a time, until you have a thick and glossy meringue.
* Using 2 spoons, scoop about a sixth of the meringue and pass the meringue repeatedly between the spoons until the mixture is a smooth oval shape. Carefully scrape the meringue into the milk using the spoon to help, and leave the meringue to poach for 2 minutes. Turn it over using the spoons and poach for another 2 minutes. Remove and leave to drain and cool on a clean dish towel. Clean the spoons of any meringue and repeat with the remaining mixture.
* Divide the Custard between 6 dessert bowls and put a meringue into the centre of each one. Serve.

Floating islands

ENGLAND
*

SHERRY TRIFLE

A delicately assembled, layered dessert featuring sherry-soaked sponge, custard, jam and jelly (flavoured gelatine) and cream, the trifle is the centrepiece of summertime celebrations and Yuletide tables alike. While it's easy for the trifle to look pretty inside a serving bowl, it's important to ensure that each layer maintains its shape, so that you get a little of each in every bite. Such is the depth of admiration for and significance of the trifle that noted food writers Helen Saberi and Alan Davidson co-wrote a small volume called *Trifle*, published in 2001, solely on the topic.

Serves: 6
Prep time: 50 minutes, plus 10–14 hours chilling
Cook time: 20–35 minutes
{♨}

- For the jelly (flavoured gelatine):
- 1½ leaves gelatine
- 250 g/9 oz fresh raspberries
- 50 g/2 oz (¼ cup) caster (superfine) sugar

- To build:
- 16 sponge (lady) fingers
- 100 ml/3½ fl oz (⅓ cup plus 1 tablespoon) dessert wine
- 100 ml/3½ fl oz (⅓ cup plus 1 tablespoon) sherry or Madeira
- 120 g/4 oz (½ cup minus 4 teaspoons) raspberry jam
- 250 g/9 oz fresh raspberries
- 600 ml/20 fl oz (2½ cups) Custard (page 33) made with 1 teaspoon extra cornflour (cornstarch)

- For the syllabub:
- 300 ml/10 fl oz (1¼ cups) double (heavy) cream
- 2 tablespoons icing (confectioners') sugar
- 60 ml/2 fl oz (¼ cup) sweet sherry or Madeira
- juice of ½ lemon

- To decorate:
- 50 g/2 oz (½ cup plus 2 teaspoons) flaked (slivered) almonds, toasted
- cocktail cherries

* For the jelly (flavoured gelatine), put the gelatine leaves into a small bowl, cover with very cold water and leave to soak for 5–10 minutes until completely soft. Usually 1 gelatine leaf can set 250 ml/8 fl oz (1 cup) liquid, so check the packet instructions.
* Meanwhile, put the raspberries, caster (superfine) sugar and 375 ml/13¾ fl oz (1½ cups) water into a heatproof bowl, cover the bowl with clingfilm (plastic wrap) and set over a large saucepan of gently simmering water. Heat for 10–15 minutes to about 50–60°C/122–140°F to avoid stewing the raspberries. Strain the liquid into a heatproof bowl, squeeze the gelatine to remove the excess water, then add the squeezed-out gelatine leaves to the raspberry infusion and stir until the gelatine has dissolved. (If the infusion is cold, warm a quarter of the mixture and gently mix the gelatine into that, then stir the warmed mixture into the remaining raspberry infusion.)
* To build the trifle, cut each of the sponge (lady) fingers into 3 pieces and put into the bottom of a 1 litre/ 34 fl oz glass bowl or 6 individual trifle or sundae dishes.

Pour the wine and sherry over the fingers and leave to soak for 5–10 minutes. Meanwhile, put the jam and a little water to loosen, if necessary, into a small saucepan and heat over a low heat for 5 minutes until warm. Carefully spread the jam over the sponge fingers, then sprinkle with the fresh raspberries. Pour in the cool liquid raspberry jelly, filling to about a third of the glass, then cover and leave to set in the fridge for 1 hour.
* Meanwhile, make the Custard following the recipe on page 33. Once the jelly has set, pour the Custard over the layer of jelly, filling to another third of the glass. Set aside.
* For the syllabub, whip the cream using electric beaters or in a stand mixer fitted with a whisk attachment to almost soft peaks. Put the icing (confectioners') sugar into a medium bowl, add the sherry and lemon juice and stir until the sugar has dissolved. Pour the mixture into the cream and briefly whisk until just combined.
* Spread or pipe the syllabub over the top of the Custard, then chill in the fridge for 1 hour, or ideally overnight.
* Decorate with toasted flaked (slivered) almonds and cocktail cherries and serve.

ENGLAND
*

POOR KNIGHTS
OF WINDSOR

This version of what the French call *pain perdu*, or Americans French toast, has been known to English kitchens since medieval times – but is commonly considered more a pudding than a breakfast dish.

Prep time: 10 minutes
Cook time: 15 minutes
Serves: 4
{♨}{♨}

- 4 slices bread, preferably brioche, with or without crusts
- 8 tablespoons sweet sherry
- 200 g/7 oz (1¾ sticks) unsalted butter
- 4 egg yolks
- 60 g/2¼ oz (⅓ cup plus 1 teaspoon) caster (superfine) sugar
- sweetened whipped cream or jam of choice, to serve

* Preheat the oven to 80°C/176°F/lowest Gas Mark.
* Put the bread onto a large plate and sprinkle over half the sherry. Meanwhile, melt a third of the butter in a frying pan or skillet over a medium heat.
* Put the egg yolks into a large shallow bowl and beat with a fork, then dip the bread slices into the yolks until suitably soaked. Working in batches, carefully put each slice of bread into the frying pan or skillet and fry for 2 minutes on each side until golden. Remove from the pan, put onto a large ovenproof plate and keep warm in the oven while you fry the remaining slices.
* To make the sauce, put the remaining butter into a saucepan and heat for 2 minutes until melted. Add the sugar and heat, stirring, for 2 minutes, until the sugar has dissolved. When bubbling gently, beat in the remaining sherry and remove from the heat. Plate the poor knights, smothered in some of the sauce, with the rest served alongside with whipped cream and jam.

Sherry trifle

WALES / ENGLAND
*

BAKED RICE PUDDING
CLIPPING TIME PUDDING/
PWDIN REIS

Rich and creamy rice puddings have been baked in homes across Britain for a few hundred years. In Wales, they even formed part of a weekly routine and were frequently served as part of a Sunday dinner. These puddings are cooked low and slow, sometimes for 3–4 hours until the skin on top has started to turn a nice golden caramel colour.
British rice pudding is made using a round grain of rice known simply as pudding rice, but if you can't get your hands on some, you can substitute with an Arborio or paella rice. A particularly indulgent version of rice pudding was made in farmhouses across England during sheep-shearing season. Called 'clipping time pudding', it was enriched with roasted bone marrow or suet, dried fruits and spices, and was particularly popular in Cumbria and Kent.

Serves: 4–6
Prep time: 5 minutes
Cook time: 2 hours
{🍴}{•}

- 30 g/ 1 oz (2 tablespoons) unsalted butter, diced,
plus extra for greasing
- 100 g/ 3½ oz (½ cup) pudding rice
- 50 g/ 2 oz (¼ cup) caster (superfine) sugar
- 1 vanilla pod (bean), split in half lengthways
and seeds scraped out
- 1 litre/ 34 fl oz (4¼ cups) full-fat (whole) milk
- stewed fruit or jam of your choice, to serve

- To make into Clipping Time pudding, add:
- 115 g/ 4 oz (⅔ cup) dried fruit, such as raisins,
or a mix of dried fruit
- 30 g/ 1 oz roasted bone marrow
instead of the butter (page 189)
- ½ teaspoon ground cinnamon
- ½ teaspoon ground nutmeg

* Preheat the oven to 140°C/ 275°F/ Gas Mark 1. Grease an ovenproof dish with a capacity of just over 1 litre/ 34 fl oz with butter.
* Sprinkle the pudding rice into the prepared dish, then sprinkle in the sugar and dried fruit (if using). Dot with the butter and/ or marrow (if using) and add the vanilla seeds and pod (bean) and ground spices (if using). Pour in the milk and bake in the oven for 2 hours, or until the skin has become a golden caramel in colour.
* While baking, stir every 30 minutes to prevent the rice forming lumps and clumping together. Remove from the oven and serve with stewed fruit or a couple of spoonfuls of jam.

UNITED KINGDOM
*

KHEER

Kheer is a cardamom-infused rice pudding that is loved by Pakistanis. In Britain some families make it with pudding rice or any short-grain rice, but in Pakistan it is only ever made with basmati.

Serves: 4
Prep time: 10 minutes
Cook time: 50–60 minutes
{🌱}{🍴}

- 100 g/ 3½ oz (½ cup) pudding rice
or any short-grain rice
- 500 ml/ 17 fl oz (2 cups plus 1 tablespoon)
full-fat (whole) milk
- 4–5 cardamom pods, bashed open and seeds crushed
- 100 g/ 3½ oz (⅓ cup) sweetened condensed milk
- 30 g/ 1 oz (2½ tablespoons) caster (superfine) sugar,
or more to taste
- 1 tablespoon finely crushed pistachios, to decorate

* Cook the rice in a medium saucepan of boiling water over a medium heat for 10 minutes, or until overcooked and mushy. Strain the rice into a heatproof bowl and mash with a fork until soft and it resembles porridge (oatmeal). Set aside.
* Pour the full-fat (whole) milk into a large (ideally nonstick) saucepan, add the crushed cardamom seeds, bring to the boil, then reduce the heat to a simmer, stirring to ensure that it doesn't stick and burn on the bottom of the pan. Add the crushed rice, condensed milk and sugar and cook gently for 20–35 minutes until the milk has reduced by half. Taste and adjust the sweetness with more sugar, if desired.
* Kheer will become thick and gloopy once done, so pour it immediately into 4 serving bowls (traditionally unglazed terracotta), decorate with the crushed pistachios and leave to chill in the fridge. Serve once cold.

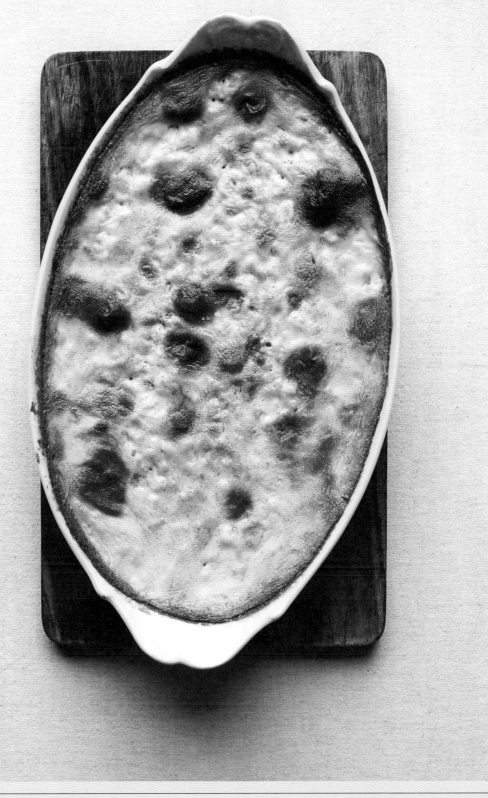

Baked rice pudding

BANOFFEE PIE

I'm always surprised when the British assume this to be an American recipe. In fact, it was invented in the 1970s at a hotel in East Sussex. Perhaps this misnomer came from the fact that supermarkets in the 1980s sold it under the moniker 'American pie'. Either way, the banoffee pie has become a modern British classic. It involves very little cooking, and is more of an assembly job. It just needs time to firm up in the fridge, then it's perfect for serving cold on summer days.

Serves: 6
Prep time: 5 minutes, plus 1½ hours setting
Cook time: 30 minutes
{ } { }

- 210 g/7 oz (1¾ sticks plus 2 teaspoons) unsalted butter
- 12 digestive biscuits (shop-bought or homemade, page 340)
- 80 g/3 oz (⅓ cup plus 1 teaspoon) light brown sugar
- 400 g/14 oz can sweetened condensed milk
- 3 ripe bananas
- 300 ml/10 fl oz (1¼ cups) double (heavy) cream
- 1 tablespoon icing (confectioners') sugar
- 30 g/1 oz milk or dark (bittersweet) chocolate, flaked or shaved

* Cut out a circle of baking (parchment) paper to fit across the bottom of a loose-bottom 20 cm/8 inch tart or cake pan.
* Heat the butter in a medium saucepan over a low-medium heat for 2 minutes, or until melted. Remove from the heat and set aside.
* Crush the biscuits in a food processor, if available (or put the biscuits in a plastic bag and bash to crumbs using a rolling pin). Put the crumbs into a large bowl and stir in half the melted butter to make a paste. Tip the biscuits into the prepared pan and press them down flat. Leave to set in the fridge for 30 minutes.
* Meanwhile, for the caramel, put the remaining melted butter and the light brown sugar into a heavy saucepan and cook over a low heat for 5 minutes, or until the sugar has dissolved. Add the condensed milk and bring the mixture to the boil. Cook for 2 minutes, or until it turns a deep brown colour. Keep stirring constantly so the caramel doesn't stick to the bottom of the pan. Set aside.
* Remove the biscuit-base lined pan from the fridge and spread the bottom with a layer of the caramel, then slice the bananas and arrange in a single layer on top. Whip the cream and icing (confectioners') sugar in a stand mixer fitted with a whisk attachment or in a bowl using electric beaters until floppy, then spread or pipe it into a thick layer over the bananas. Sprinkle the chocolate shavings over the whipped cream and leave to chill in the fridge for at least 1 hour, or until firm. Serve.
* **Notes:** You can swap a 400 g/14 oz can of dulce de leche for the homemade caramel mixture, if desired.

BAKEWELL TART

One of Britain's iconic desserts, the Bakewell tart exploded into popularity in the early twentieth century as a variation of the much older Bakewell Pudding (page 348), swapping out the pudding's puff pastry for shortcrust, and egg custard for a soft but cakey frangipane filling, sometimes topped with slivered almonds or a layer of icing (frosting) and glacé (candied) cherries. It can also be made as a traybake.

Serves: 6
Prep time: 50 minutes,
plus 30 minutes resting and chilling
Cook time: 35–50 minutes
{ }

- 1 quantity Shortcrust Pastry (page 247)
- plain (all-purpose) flour, for dusting
- 1 egg, beaten with 1 tablespoon water, for egg wash

- For the almond cream filling:
- 100 g/3½ oz (7 tablespoons) unsalted butter, softened, plus extra for greasing
- 100 g/3½ oz (½ cup) caster (superfine) sugar
- 2 eggs
- 1 g almond extract (optional)
- 100 g/3½ oz (1 cup) ground almonds
- 30 g/1 oz (3¾ tablespoons) self-raising flour
- 200 g/7 oz (¾ cup) jam of choice, such as cherry, raspberry or apricot
- 30 g/1 oz (⅓ cup) slivered almonds

* Make the pastry following the recipe on page 247 and leave to rest for 20 minutes before using.
* Preheat the oven to 170°C/325°F/Gas Mark 3. Grease a 20 cm/8 inch loose-bottom tart pan or ring with butter. Line a large baking sheet with baking (parchment) paper.
* Roll out the dough until it is 3 mm/⅛ inch thick, then carefully lay the dough over the pan and gently work and push the dough into the corners using your fingers or a lightly floured piece of dough. Slide onto the prepared baking sheet, prick the bottom of the case (shell) all over with a fork, then chill in the fridge for 10 minutes.
* Meanwhile, for the filling, put the butter and sugar into a bowl and, using a wooden spoon, beat together until smooth. Add the eggs, almond extract, ground almonds and flour and beat for another 4–8 minutes, making sure you scrape the bottom of the bowl occasionally to ensure there are no lumps of butter. Set aside.
* Line the rested tart case (shell) with baking paper and fill with baking beans or pie weights. Blind bake for 15–20 minutes until lightly golden in colour. Remove from the oven, inspect for cracks and fill with a little more dough, if necessary. Brush with a little egg wash, then bake again for 5 minutes. Leave to cool.
* Spread the jam evenly over the bottom of the tart case, leaving 1 cm/½ inch around the edges, then spoon or pipe the filling first around the edges, then work your way to the centre. The jam should be completely covered. Level the filling using a spatula, then sprinkle with the slivered almonds. Bake for 15–25 minutes until evenly golden brown. If it starts to get too brown reduce the oven temperature to 160°C/325°F/Gas Mark 3. Leave to cool before serving.

Banoffee pie

WALES / ENGLAND
*

QUEEN OF PUDDINGS
MANCHESTER PUDDING/
MONMOUTH PUDDING

These are three names for the same, or remarkably similar puddings. Each features a soft base like a bread pudding, made from a breadcrumb and custard-like mixture, which is then spread with a thick layer of jam and crowned with soft meringue. Serve while still warm in shallow bowls, either on its own or with Custard (page 33).

Serves: 6
Prep time: 20 minutes,
plus 10–15 minutes standing
Cook time: 55 minutes
{👁}{👄}

- 60 g/ 2¼ oz (½ stick) unsalted butter,
plus extra for greasing
- 3 eggs, separated
- 180 g/ 6 oz (1 cup minus 4 teaspoons)
caster (superfine) sugar
- 500 ml/ 17 fl oz (2 cups plus 1 tablespoon)
full-fat (whole) milk
- grated zest of 1 lemon
- 120 g/ 4 oz (1¾ cups plus 1 teaspoon) breadcrumbs
(day old are better, slightly stale)

- For the jam:
- 200 g/ 7 oz fresh or frozen fruit, such as red fruits,
raspberry, cherry, blackcurrant or gooseberries
- 120 g/ 4 oz (⅔ cup) caster (superfine) sugar
- 20 ml/ ¾ fl oz (4 teaspoons) lemon juice

* Lightly grease an 18 cm/ 7 inch casserole dish or baking dish with butter.
* Put the egg yolks and 60 g/ 2¼ oz (⅓ cup plus 1 teaspoon) of the sugar into a large heatproof bowl and beat together using a wooden spoon until combined.
* Put the milk, butter and grated lemon zest into a large saucepan and heat gently over a low heat until it is simmering and about 85°C/ 185°F on a thermometer. While whisking, gradually pour the milk mixture over the egg yolks until it is all incorporated.
* Sprinkle the breadcrumbs over the bottom of the prepared dish, then pour in the custard mix and leave to stand for 10–15 minutes.
* Preheat the oven to 160°C/ 325°F/ Gas Mark 3.
* Meanwhile, for the jam, heat the fruit and sugar in a small saucepan over a medium-high heat for 15 minutes, or until the mixture reaches your desired texture (it should be almost jam-like). Add the lemon juice, stir until combined, then remove from the heat and set aside.
* After leaving the pudding to stand, bake in the oven for 15 minutes, or until just set. Don't overcook. Remove from the oven and leave to cool for 5–10 minutes. Leave the oven on. Evenly cover the pudding with the jam.
* Reduce the oven temperature to 130°C/ 250°F/ Gas Mark ½.
* Meanwhile, put the egg whites into a stand mixer fitted with a whisk attachment and whisk on medium speed until soft peaks form. While whisking, gradually add the remaining sugar until you have a fluffy and glossy meringue.
* Decorate the pudding by either spreading or piping the meringue over the pudding, then bake for 25–30 minutes until the meringue is a pale golden brown and crisp. Serve.
* **Notes:** If you don't want to make the jam then use 3 tablespoons of jam of your choice.

ENGLAND: YORKSHIRE
*

YORKSHIRE CURRANT
AND
MINT PASTY

These sweet little pasties feature a filling that's not found outside Yorkshire. They are sometimes also baked in flat circles – similar to a large Chorley Cake (page 296).

Serves: 6
Prep time: 30 minutes, plus 20 minutes resting
Cook time: 25 minutes
{👄}

- 1 quantity Shortcrust Pastry (page 247)
made using half butter and half lard
- plain (all-purpose) flour, for dusting
- 300 g/ 11 oz (1⅓ cups) currants
- 90 g/ 3¼ oz (½ cup) candied mixed peel
- 2 tablespoons chopped mint
- 90 g/ 3¼ oz (⅓ cup plus 1 tablespoon)
soft dark brown sugar
- 90 g/ 3¼ oz (6 tablespoons) unsalted butter, softened
- ½ teaspoon ground nutmeg
- 1 egg, beaten with 1 tablespoon water or milk,
for egg wash
- granulated sugar, for sprinkling

* Make the pastry following the recipe on page 247 and leave to rest for 20 minutes before using.
* Preheat the oven to 200°C/ 400°F/ Gas Mark 6.
* Divide the pastry into 6 equal pieces and roll each piece into a circle, about 2–3 mm/ 1/16–⅛ inch thick on a lightly floured work counter.
* Put the currants, peel, mint, brown sugar, butter and nutmeg into a large bowl and mix together, then divide equally between the 6 circles, putting the filling onto one half of each circle. Brush egg wash around one edge and fold the pasties shut, crimping the edges by pressing down with a fork. Brush the top and sides with more egg wash and sprinkle with granulated sugar. Put the pasties onto 1–2 large baking sheets and bake in the oven for 25 minutes, or until golden brown.

Queen of puddings

UNITED KINGDOM
*

CLASSIC APPLE CRUMBLE

Fruit crumble was most likely the creation of wartime rationing in the 1930s and '40s. Marguerite Patten, who herself became famous as a wartime recipe writer, points out that the earliest recipes for apple crumble with oats come from a 1940s Ministry of Food pamphlet. This appears to have been a Scottish edition, which was only later picked up throughout the rest of the nation.

At any rate, fruit crumble is a gloriously simple affair: stewed fruit tossed with sugar, baked with a crumbly topping that crisps and caramelizes as it cooks. The result is sweet, tart, buttery and crunchy; the only thing missing is the creamy richness of a Custard (page 33) or a good-quality ice cream, which should be on hand as you serve the crumble.

Serves: 6
Prep time: 20 minutes
Cook time: 35 minutes
{ }

- 750 g/1 lb 10 oz Bramley (cooking) apples, peeled, cored and diced
- 250 g/9 oz eating apples, such as Granny Smith, Cox's or Braeburn, peeled, cored and diced
- 75 g/2¾ oz (⅓ cup) light brown sugar or caster (superfine) sugar
- lemon juice, to taste
- Custard (page 33), to serve

- For the crumble:
- 200 g/7 oz (1⅔ cups) plain (all-purpose) flour
- 150 g/5 oz (1¼ sticks) salted butter, diced
- 100 g/3½ oz (1 cup) rolled oats
- 175 g/6 oz (¾ cup) demerara (turbinado) or granulated sugar
- 50 g/2 oz (⅓ cup) nuts of choice, chopped (optional)

* Put the apples into a large bowl, toss with the light brown or caster (superfine) sugar, then transfer to a large saucepan, pour in 100 ml/3½ fl oz (⅓ cup plus 1 tablespoon) water and cook over a medium heat for 10–15 minutes until soft. If using soft fruits, omit the water. Add lemon juice to taste, then pour into a 23 cm/9 inch square baking dish and leave to cool completely.
* Preheat the oven to 180°C/350°F/Gas Mark 4.
* For the crumble, put the flour into a large bowl, add the butter and rub it coarsely into the flour with your fingertips. Stir in the oats, demerara (turbinado) or granulated sugar and nuts (if using). Spoon the topping over the fruit, levelling coarsely with a fork. Bake in the oven for 35 minutes, or until golden and bubbling. Serve hot with Custard.
* Variations: Apple and cinnamon: Add 1 teaspoon ground cinnamon, or to taste, to the apples and mix thoroughly prior to cooking.
* Apple and blackberry: Add 150 g/5 oz (1¼ cups) fresh blackberries prior to baking the crumble.
* Quince: Reduce the sweetness accordingly.
* Gooseberry: Increase the sweetness accordingly.

* Apricot and lavender: Use apricot halves and adjust the sweetness accordingly; infuse a lavender sprig into the apricot compote.
* Cherry: Use stoned (pitted) cherries and adjust sweetness accordingly.
* Plum: Use halved plums and adjust sweetness accordingly.
* Rhubarb: Increase the sweetness accordingly.
* Strawberry: Reduce the sweetness accordingly.
* Mixed red fruit: Adjust the sweetness accordingly.

ENGLAND: YORKSHIRE
*

BILBERRY PLATE TART
MUCKY MOUTH TART

Despite the name, this is actually a pie (with a top and bottom layer of shortcrust). These sweet pies, sometimes called 'mucky mouth' pies, earned their name from the bilberry's deep purple stain. Bilberries, whortleberries or blaeberries (Scotland), are a cousin to the American blueberry, and native to northern Europe. By comparison, whinberries are slightly smaller and slightly more tart. Originally baked in rather shallow pie plates, they should be served still warm with ice cream or Clotted Cream (page 34).

Serves: 8
Prep time: 50 minutes, plus 40–50 minutes resting
Cook time: 40 minutes
{ } { }

- 1 quantity Shortcrust Pastry (page 247)
- plain (all-purpose) flour, for dusting
- 400 g/14 oz (3¼ cups) bilberries
- 120 g/4 oz (⅔ cup) caster (superfine) sugar
- 1 tablespoon cornflour (cornstarch)
- 1 egg, beaten with 1 tablespoon water or milk, for egg wash
- granulated or demerara (turbinado) sugar, for sprinkling
- ice cream or Clotted Cream (page 34), to serve

* Make the pastry following the recipe on page 247 and leave to rest for 20 minutes before using.
* Roll out half the dough on a lightly floured work counter and use it to line a 24–26 cm/9½–10½ inch pie plate.
* Put the bilberries, sugar and cornflour (cornstarch) into a large bowl and mix together, then spoon into the pie plate.
* Roll out the remaining pastry to a make lid, then carefully lay it over the pie plate and seal with egg wash. Use a sharp knife to cut a steam hole in the centre and brush the top with more egg wash. Sprinkle with granulated or demerara (turbinado) sugar, then leave to chill in the fridge for 20–30 minutes to firm up.
* Preheat the oven to 220°C/425°F/Gas Mark 7. Put a large baking sheet onto the centre shelf to heat up.
* Carefully put the pie plate onto the hot baking sheet and bake in the oven for 20 minutes. Reduce the oven temperature to 180°C/350°F/Gas Mark 4 and bake for another 20 minutes. Remove from the oven and serve warm with ice cream or Clotted Cream.

Classic apple crumble

UNITED KINGDOM
*
ENGLISH APPLE PIE

English bakers have traditionally made their apple pies with shortcrust pastry instead of puff. This recipe from Leeds-based baker Sarah Lemanski is inspired by a family recipe from Florence White's *Good Things in England*, published in 1932. Lemanski uses a very rich Sweet Shortcrust Pastry (page 247), and an apple stock made from the apple peels and cores.

Serves: 8
Prep time: 1 hour,
plus 1 hour 20 minutes resting and chilling
Cook time: 2 hours
{👁}{🌙}

- 1 quantity Sweet Shortcrust Pastry (page 247)
- 600 g / 1 lb 5 oz Bramley (cooking) apples
- 15 g / ½ oz (1 tablespoon) unsalted butter, plus extra for greasing
- 40 g / 1½ oz (3¼ tablespoons) caster (superfine) sugar
- 40 g / 1½ oz (3¼ tablespoons) soft light brown sugar
- 400 g / 14 oz dessert apples, such as Cox's Orange Pippin, Russet or other flavourful variety
- juice of 1 small lemon
- ½ teaspoon ground cinnamon
- ¼ teaspoon freshly grated nutmeg
- ¼ teaspoon flaky sea salt
- ½ tablespoon plain (all-purpose) flour, plus extra for dusting
- 1 egg, beaten, for egg wash
- demerara (turbinado) sugar, for sprinkling

* Make the pastry following the recipe on page 247 and leave to rest for 20 minutes before using.
* Meanwhile, peel and core the Bramley (cooking) apples, setting the cores and peel aside, then cut the apples into chunks, about 2 x 2 cm / ¾ x ¾ inch.
* Put a frying pan or skillet, large enough to accommodate all the Bramley (cooking) apple chunks, over a low-medium heat and add the butter. Once melted, add the apple chunks and both sugars and cook for 20–30 minutes until the apples have broken down to a fluff-filled purée. The mixture should look dry with no residual water.
* Meanwhile, core the dessert apples. There's no need to peel, but again set the cores aside, and cut into chunks, about 2 x 2 cm / ¾ x ¾ inch. Put into a large bowl with the lemon juice to prevent discolouration.
* Put the apple peel and cores into a separate medium saucepan and add enough cold water to just cover. Bring to the boil, then reduce the heat and simmer for 20 minutes. This will create an apple stock that will be intense in flavour and enriched with pectin, contributing a more pronounced apple flavour and a thickened filling. Remove from the heat and leave to cool completely.
* Once the Bramley (cooking) apples have cooked down, remove the pan from the heat and add the ground cinnamon and nutmeg and leave to cool. When the filling has cooled, stir through the dessert apples, including the lemon juice, sea salt and 50 ml / 1¾ fl oz (3½ tablespoons) apple stock. Taste to check for sweetness and adjust if required by adding a little more sugar. Set the filling aside.
* Lightly grease a 23 cm / 9 inch pie dish with butter. Roll out half the pastry on a lightly floured work counter until

it is 4 mm / ⅙ inch thick and 5 cm / 2 inches wider than the pie dish. Carefully lift the pastry into the dish and press firmly around the bottom and up the sides to ensure good contact between dough and dish. There should be some overhang but not too much, so trim as needed.
* Using a small sieve or tea strainer, sprinkle the ½ tablespoon flour evenly over the pastry base. Add the cooled filling and leave the pie to chill in the fridge.
* Meanwhile, roll out the second circle of pastry on a lightly floured work counter until it is 4 mm / ⅙ inch thick and 2.5–5 cm / 1–2 inches wider than the pie dish. Remove the pie from the fridge and carefully lay the dough over the top. Gently press the pastry to expel any large air bubbles and press around the edges to seal. Use a sharp knife to trim the pastry edges and cut 2 steam holes in the centre. Leave the pie to chill in the fridge for 1 hour.
* Preheat the oven to 180°C / 350°F / Gas Mark 4. Put a large baking sheet or a baking stone into the oven to heat up.
* Remove the pie from the fridge, brush egg wash all over the top and sprinkle with demerara (turbinado) sugar. Immediately put the pie onto the baking sheet or stone and bake for 30 minutes. Rotate and bake for another 30–40 minutes until you can see juices bubbling from the steam holes in the centre. There may also be juice bubbling around the edge which is nothing to worry about. If the pie is getting too dark in colour, cover it with aluminium foil but remove this for at least 10 minutes towards the end of baking to allow any excess steam to escape.
* Remove the pie from the oven and leave to cool before serving. The pie will keep well in the fridge for up to 3 days. It is much easier to cut once completely cold and individual portions can then be reheated to serve as needed.

ENGLAND: YORKSHIRE
*
YORKSHIRE CURD TART

Made with fresh curds and currants, and with plenty of butter and sugar, these tarts are like early predecessors of the modern cheesecake. It's important that you do use curds and not cream cheese or cottage cheese, as it's essential to getting the right texture. This recipe is an adaptation of the classic provided by Jane Grigson in *English Food* (1974).
You can serve these tarts warm, but unsurprisingly (given the cheesecake relation), I prefer them chilled.

Serves: 6
Prep time: 65 minutes, plus 1 hour resting, chilling and draining
Cook time: 50–55 minutes
{👁}{🌙}

- 1 quantity Sweet Shortcrust Pastry (page 247)
- 80 g / 3 oz (¾ stick) unsalted butter, softened, plus extra for greasing
- plain (all-purpose) flour, for dusting
- 225 g / 8 oz (1 cup) shop-bought or homemade Curd Cheese (page 391), made with full-fat (whole) milk
- 1 egg, beaten with 1 tablespoon water or milk for egg wash
- 60 g / 2¼ oz (⅓ cup plus 1 teaspoon) caster (superfine) sugar
- 2 eggs, beaten

- 40 g/1½ oz (⅔ cup) breadcrumbs
(day old are best, slightly stale)
- 125 g/4¼ oz (½ cup) currants
- ¾ teaspoon ground allspice
- salt
- 1 nutmeg, for grating

* Make the pastry following the recipe on page 247 and leave to rest for 20 minutes before using.
* Preheat the oven to 170°C/325°F/Gas Mark 3. Grease a 20 cm/8 inch loose-bottom tart pan with butter. Line a large baking sheet with baking (parchment) paper.
* Roll out the dough on a lightly floured work counter to a circle about 3 mm/⅛ inch thick. Lay the dough over the prepared pan and gently work and push the dough into the corners with your fingers or use a lightly floured piece of dough. Slide it onto the prepared baking sheet, prick the bottom all over with a fork, then chill in the fridge for 10 minutes.
* Put a sieve over a small bowl, gently mix the curd cheese, then pour into the sieve and leave to drain for 30 minutes.
* Meanwhile, once the pastry case (shell) has rested, remove it from the fridge and line with baking paper, then fill with baking beans or pie weights. Blind bake in the oven for 15–20 minutes until lightly golden in colour. Remove from the oven, inspect for cracks (fill with a little more dough if necessary), then brush all over with egg wash. Return to the oven for another 5 minutes, then remove from the oven and leave to cool slightly.
* Increase the oven temperature to 200°C/400°F/Gas Mark 6.
* Meanwhile, put the butter and sugar into a stand mixer fitted with a paddle attachment and beat together on medium speed until pale and fluffy. Alternatively, beat the butter and sugar together in a large bowl using electric beaters. Add the drained curd cheese and incorporate thoroughly, making sure to scrape down the bowl. Gradually fold in the beaten eggs, breadcrumbs and currants using a wooden spoon, then season with allspice and 2 pinches of salt. Spoon the filling into a piping (pastry) bag with nozzle and pipe the mixture into the tart case, flattening slightly with a spatula, if necessary.
* Bake in the oven for 10 minutes, then reduce the oven temperature to 180°C/350°F/Gas Mark 4 and bake for another 20 minutes, or until golden brown with a slight wobble. Check after 10 minutes. Reduce the oven temperature further if the tart begins to get too much colour. Remove from the oven and leave to cool on a wire rack until it reaches room temperature.
* Finely grate a dusting of nutmeg over the tart, then using a large knife, cut through the tart in one swift movement, continuing for every slice and wiping the knife in between.

ENGLAND: YORKSHIRE
*

WILFRA CAKES

Despite the name, these are in essence shortcrust apple pies, baked with a generous helping of crumbly Wensleydale cheese. They were baked each year in the small Yorkshire town of Ripon, marking Wilfra Week – a festival that celebrated the life of St Wilfrid, a seventh-century English saint. The tradition of eating sweet cakes and pies with cheese is well-documented and still popular throughout Yorkshire.

For these pies, you can use either sharp crisp dessert apples or Bramley (cooking) apples. If using Bramley apples, peel and core them, otherwise leave the peel on and just core the dessert apples.

Serves: a generous 6
Prep time: 50 minutes,
plus 1 hour 20 minutes resting and chilling
Cook time: 45–50 minutes
{●} {♥}

- 1 quantity Sweet Shortcrust Pastry (page 247)
- unsalted butter, for greasing
- plain (all-purpose) flour, for dusting
- 50 g/2 oz (1 cup) fresh breadcrumbs
- 550 g/1 lb 4 oz apples,
weight once cut into 2 mm/1/16 inch thick slices
- 70 g/2½ oz (⅓ cup) demerara (turbinado) sugar,
plus a little extra for sprinkling
- 70 g/2½ oz Wensleydale cheese, grated
- 1 egg, lightly beaten, for egg wash
-

* Make the pastry following the recipe on page 247 and leave to rest for 20 minutes before using.
* Lightly grease a 23 cm/9 inch tart pan or pie plate.
* Roll out half the dough on a lightly floured work counter to a circle, about 2–3 mm/1/16–⅛ inch thick. Keep the remaining dough chilled.
* Lay the dough on the bottom of the prepared pan or plate and sprinkle over half the breadcrumbs in an even layer. Arrange the apple slices over the top, leaving a 1.5– 2 cm/⅝–¾ inch border around the edge. Sprinkle with the remaining breadcrumbs, followed by the demerara (turbinado) sugar and then the grated cheese.
* Roll out the other half of the dough on a lightly floured work surface, to a little larger than the circumference of the tart pan, so it can accommodate the height of the filling. Using water and a pastry brush, gently brush the border of the pastry bottom and cover the filling with the dough. Trim off any excess dough and seal well, crimping in a decorative manner of your choosing or use a fork to secure the top and bottom crusts. Leave to chill in the fridge for at least 1 hour, or until firm.
* When ready to bake, preheat the oven to 200°C/400°F/ Gas Mark 6. Put a heavy baking sheet or baking stone into the oven to heat up.
* Remove the pie from the fridge and brush the egg wash over the the top, adding a sprinkle of demerara (turbinado) sugar. Using a sharp knife, make 2–3 slits in the top of the pie to allow steam to escape. Put the pie onto the preheated baking sheet and reduce the oven temperature immediately to 180°C/350°F/Gas Mark 4. Bake for 10 minutes, then reduce the oven temperature to 170°C/325°F/Gas Mark 3 and bake for another 25 minutes. Rotate the pie and bake for another 10–15 minutes until golden brown.

ENGLAND
*

CUSTARD TART

A rich egg custard, baked in a pastry case (shell), has been a part of the British kitchen – for the royals at least – since medieval times. Today, that tart is typically made with Sweet Shortcrust Pastry (page 247) and dusted with a little nutmeg.

Serves: 6
Prep time: 40 minutes,
plus 30 minutes resting and chilling
Cook time: 1½ hours
{☗} {✦}

- ½ quantity Sweet Shortcrust Pastry (page 247), made using unbleached flour rather than wholemeal
- unsalted butter, for greasing
- plain (all-purpose) flour, for dusting
- 1 egg, beaten with 1 tablespoon milk/water, for egg wash

- For the custard mix:
- 200 ml/7 fl oz (¾ cup plus 1 tablespoon) rich, full-fat (whole) milk
- 400 ml/14 fl oz (1⅔ cups) double (heavy) cream
- 3 eggs, plus 1 egg yolk
- 90 g/3¼ oz caster (superfine) sugar
- 1 nutmeg, for grating

* Make the pastry following the recipe on page 247 and leave to rest for 20 minutes before using.
* Preheat the oven to 170°C/325°F/Gas Mark 3, removing all the racks except the bottom one. Grease a 20 cm/ 8 inch loose-bottomed tart pan or ring with butter. Line a large baking sheet with baking (parchment) paper.
* Roll out the dough on a lightly floured work counter until it is about 3 mm/⅛ inch thick. Lay the dough over the prepared pan and gently push it into the corners with your fingers or a floured piece of dough. Slide onto the prepared baking sheet, then prick the bottom all over with a fork and leave to chill in the fridge for 10 minutes.
* Once rested, remove the pastry case (shell) from the fridge and line with baking paper, then fill with baking beans or pie weights. Blind bake in the oven for 20–30 minutes until golden in colour. Remove from the oven, inspect for cracks (fill with a little more dough if necessary), then brush with a little egg wash. Return to the oven for 5 minutes, then leave to cool.
* Reduce the oven temperature to 130°C/250°F/Gas Mark ½.
* For the custard mix, heat the milk and cream in a saucepan over a medium heat until it reaches 83°C/181°F. Put the eggs, egg yolk and sugar into a bowl and whisk until smooth, then gradually pour in the milk and cream, whisking constantly. Sieve the mix into a jug (pitcher).
* Put the tart back into the oven, pull the shelf out slightly and carefully fill the case as full as possible with the custard mix. Grate over the nutmeg. Carefully push the shelf back in, gently close the door and bake for 35–45 minutes until just set – the centre should still wobble and it will continue to cook slightly. Turn the oven off, door ajar, and leave to cool in the oven for 15 minutes.
* To serve, leave the tart to cool completely (not in the fridge), then cut into portions by heating a large knife in boiling water, then drying it on a clean dish towel and cutting through the tart in one swift movement. Repeat for every slice, wiping the knife in between.

ENGLAND: MANCHESTER AND LANCASHIRE
*

MANCHESTER TART

Manchester tarts are a variant of the custard tart that's set in the fridge rather than baked.

Serves: a generous 6
Prep time: 40 minutes,
plus 1 hour 50 minutes resting and chilling
Cook time: 30–40 minutes
{☗} {✦}

- ½ quantity Sweet Shortcrust Pastry (page 247)
- unsalted butter, for greasing
- plain (all-purpose) flour, for dusting
- 6 egg yolks
- 1 teaspoon vanilla extract
- 150 g/5 oz (¾ cup) caster (superfine) sugar
- 90 g/3¼ oz (¾ cup) plain (all-purpose) flour
- 500 ml/17 fl oz (2 cups plus 1 tablespoon) full-fat (whole) milk
- 175 ml/6 fl oz (¾ cup) double (heavy) cream
- 50 g/2 oz (½ cup plus 2 teaspoons) desiccated (dry unsweetened) coconut
- 3 tablespoons raspberry jam
- 2 ripe bananas, sliced (optional)
- 150 ml/5 fl oz (⅔ cup) double (heavy) cream
- 1 tablespoon icing (confectioners') sugar

* Make the pastry following the recipe on page 247 and leave to rest for 20 minutes before using.
* Grease a 20 cm/8 inch loose-bottomed tart pan or ring with butter. Line a large baking sheet with baking (parchment) paper.
* Roll out the dough on a lightly floured work counter until it is 3 mm/⅛ inch thick. Lay the dough over the prepared pan and gently work it into the corners. Slide onto the prepared baking sheet, then prick the bottom all over with a fork and chill in the fridge for 30 minutes.
* Preheat the oven to 170°C/325°F/Gas Mark 3.
* Once rested, remove the pastry case (shell) from the fridge and line with baking paper, then fill with baking beans or pie weights. Blind bake for 25–30 minutes until lightly golden. Remove from the oven, inspect for cracks (fill with a little more dough if necessary), then leave to cool.
* For the crème patissière filling, put the egg yolks, vanilla and 100 g/3½ oz (½ cup) caster (superfine) sugar into a bowl and beat together. Sift in the flour and mix again.
* Heat the milk in a medium saucepan over a medium heat for 3–4 minutes, or until it is about to boil. Add this to the yolk mixture, then pour back into the saucepan and whisk for 5 minutes, or until very thick. Strain the custard through a sieve into a large bowl, then cover with clingfilm (plastic wrap) and leave to cool in the fridge.
* Meanwhile, whip the cream and remaining sugar together in a large bowl using electric beaters. Whisk the cold custard to get it smooth again, then fold in the cream until it is incorporated.
* To finish, spread the jam over the bottom of the tart case (shell) and arrange the banana slices in a layer on top (if using). Spread the custard mixture over the bananas. Whip the cream and icing (confectioners') sugar together in a bowl until it forms soft peaks, and pipe around the edges of the tart. Chill in the fridge for at least 1 hour before serving.

Custard tart

WALES: MONTGOMERYSHIRE (POWYS)
*
GOOSE BLOOD TART

A rather unusual-sounding Christmas pie traditionally made in parts of Montgomeryshire (Powys), Wales. The blood was likely taken from the same geese that would later be roasted for dinner. While a sweet blood tart may sound strange to us now, it bakes and tastes as if it were a rich, almost chocolatey ganache. Although, again, this is probably one for reference.

Serves: 6
Prep time: 50 minutes, plus 20 minutes resting
Cook time: 2½–3½ hours
{⁀}

- fresh blood of 2 geese, less than 24 hours old (ask for a splash of vinegar to be added to prevent it coagulating), then shaken and passed through a fine sieve or muslin (cheesecloth) to remove any clots
- 1 quantity Shortcrust Pastry (page 247)
- 120 g/4 oz (¾ cup plus 1 teaspoon) raisins
- 90 g/3¼ oz (½ cup minus 4 teaspoons) currants
- 90 g/3¼ oz (⅔ cup minus 2 teaspoons) sultanas (golden raisins)
- 300 g/11 oz (1⅓ cups) soft light brown sugar
- 150 g/5 oz (½ cup) shredded beef suet
- 2 teaspoons mixed spice
- 8 twists of black pepper
- 2 teaspoons fine salt
- 2 tablespoons golden syrup, or enough to bind the mixture
- plain (all-purpose) flour, for dusting
- 1 egg, beaten with 1 tablespoon water or milk, for egg wash
- demerara (turbinado) sugar, for sprinkling

* Pour the blood into a heatproof bowl and set over a large saucepan of simmering water. Put 2 pieces of clingfilm (plastic wrap) on top of each other to make a double layer and place directly onto the blood, forcing any air out (to avoid added oxidization), then cover it with a lid and steam over a medium heat for 2–3 hours, topping up (topping off) the water at regular intervals. Once the blood has solidified, remove from the pan and leave to cool completely at room temperature.
* Make the pastry following the recipe on page 247 and leave to rest for 20 minutes before using.
* Preheat the oven to 200°C/400°F/Gas Mark 6.
* Break up 450 g/1 lb of the cooled blood between your fingers into breadcrumb-sized pieces over a large bowl. Add the dried fruit, light brown sugar and suet to the bowl, mixing well between each addition. Sprinkle in the spice and seasonings and mix thoroughly. Finally, add the golden syrup and mix until well combined. It shouldn't be overly loose and should be similar in texture to mincemeat, so add more syrup if necessary.
* Put a ceramic pie bird into the centre of a 25 cm/10 inch dinner plate, then spread the mixture over the plate, leaving a 2 cm/¾ inch gap around the edges, mimicking the shape of a flying saucer.
* Roll out the dough on a lightly floured work counter to a circle, about 30 cm/12 inches in diameter and 5 mm/¼ inch thick, making a slit for the pie bird. Brush the edges of the plate with egg wash, then carefully lay the dough over the blood mixture. Gently press out any excess air, then trim the dough using a knife and crimp the edges with a fork. Brush the pastry evenly with egg wash, sprinkle with demerara (turbinado) sugar and, using a sharp knife, make 2 slits in the dough or roll up 2 rectangular pieces of aluminium foil to create chimneys.
* Bake in the oven for 30 minutes, or until golden brown.
* Note: If you prefer more pastry (pie dough), brush the plate with butter and add an extra layer of dough directly onto the plate before adding the blood mixture, then continue to follow the recipe above.

ENGLAND: KENT
*
GYPSY TART

A favourite of school dinners in Kent, and understandably so, as this tart's mousse-like filling is simple and wickedly sweet, consisting of only dark brown sugar whisked into evaporated milk. Slices of the tart are often served alongside thin slices of a cored green apple.

Serves: 6
Prep time: 40 minutes,
plus 50 minutes resting and chilling
Cook time: 55–60 minutes
{⁀}

- ½ quantity Sweet Shortcrust Pastry (page 247) made with plain (all-purpose) flour, plus extra for dusting
- 410 g/14 oz can evaporated milk
- 250 g/9 oz (1 cup plus 1 tablespoon) soft dark brown sugar
- 6 green Cox apples, cored and sliced, to serve

* Make the pastry following the recipe on page 247 and leave to rest for 20 minutes before using.
* Roll out the dough on a lightly floured work counter and use it to line a 20 cm/8 inch tart pan or ring. Prick the bottom all over with a fork and leave to chill in the fridge for 30 minutes to firm up.
* Meanwhile, preheat the oven to 170°C/325°F/Gas Mark 3.
* Line the tart case (shell) with baking (parchment) paper and fill with baking beans or pie weight, then blind bake in the oven for 25–30 minutes until the edges of the dough are golden. Remove the beans or pie weights and paper and return to the oven for another 10 minutes to cook the bottom. Remove from the oven, inspect for cracks (fill with a little more dough if necessary), then set aside.
* Increase the oven temperature to 180°C/350°F/Gas Mark 4.
* Put the condensed milk and sugar into a large bowl and whisk using electric beaters until light and fluffy, then pour into the case (shell) and bake in the oven for 20 minutes, or until just set. Remove from the oven and serve with sliced apple.

Goose blood tart

SCOTLAND: THE BORDERS

*

PARADISE SLICE
BORDER TART

Made as a traybake in Scotland since the 1980s, the Paradise Slice bears a resemblance to the Bakewell Tart (page 378), but its layer of almond sponge layer is flavoured with coconut and studded with sultanas (golden raisins) and glacé (candied) cherries.

In the Scottish Borders, the same ingredients are baked into a tart case (shell) and dubbed a Border Tart. Alex Dalgetty & Sons – the fifth-generation bakers famous for their Ecclefechan Tart (page 396) and Selkirk Bannocks (page 308) – produce an excellent Border Tart that's prepared in much the same way as the recipe below.

Serves: 8
Prep time: 40 minutes, plus 30 minutes chilling
Cook time: 1¼ hours
{ⅱ}

- 140 g/5 oz (1 cup plus 4 teaspoons) plain (all-purpose) flour, plus extra for dusting
- pinch of salt
- 30 g/1 oz (2½ tablespoons) caster (superfine) sugar, plus extra for sprinkling
- 85 g/3 oz (¾ stick) cold unsalted butter, diced, plus extra, melted, for greasing (optional)
- 1 egg yolk
- 5 tablespoons raspberry jam
- cream or ice cream, to serve (optional)

- For the filling:
- 110 g/3¾ oz (1 stick) unsalted butter, at room temperature
- 160 g/5¾ oz (¾ cup plus 2 teaspoons) caster (superfine) sugar, plus extra for sprinkling
- 2 eggs, plus 1 egg white
- 100 g/3½ oz (1 cup) ground almonds
- 90 g/3¼ oz (1 cup minus 2 teaspoons) desiccated (unsweetened shredded) coconut
- 90 g/3¼ oz (⅔ cup) sultanas (golden raisins)
- 70 g/2½ oz (⅓ cup) glacé (candied) cherries

* Sift the flour, salt and sugar into a large bowl. Add the butter and rub it in with your fingertips until it resembles coarse breadcrumbs. Add the egg yolk, along with 1 tablespoon cold water if necessary, to form a smooth dough. Wrap the dough in clingfilm (plastic wrap) and leave to chill in the fridge for 30 minutes.

* Preheat the oven to 170°C/325°F/Gas Mark 3. Line the bottom and sides of a 20 x 20 cm/8 x 8 inch square brownie pan or a 20 cm/8 inch tart pan with baking (parchment) paper, if required. If you have a nonstick pan, then simply brush with a little melted butter.

* Roll out the chilled dough on a lightly floured work counter, large enough to line the brownie or tart pan, and about 4 mm/⅙ inch thick. Press the dough into the pan, neaten the edges and prick the bottom all over with a fork. Line with baking (parchment) paper and fill with baking beans or pie weights. Blind bake in the oven for 30 minutes, or until pale golden brown.

* Meanwhile, for the filling, put the butter and sugar into a large bowl and, using electric beaters, beat together until well incorporated but not long enough to get too pale or fluffy. You don't want to add too much air. Beat in the eggs and egg white until just incorporated, then, using a spatula, fold in the almonds and coconut, followed by the sultanas (golden raisins) and cherries. Set aside.

* Once the pastry base is baked, remove from the oven and leave to cool slightly before removing the baking beans or pie weights and paper. Spread the raspberry jam liberally over the pastry base, then the pour in the filling mixture and gently smooth over.

* Reduce the oven temperature to 160°C/325°F/Gas Mark 3 and bake the tart for 40–45 minutes until deep golden brown, checking after 20 minutes and turning to ensure even colouring. Remove the tart from the oven and sprinkle with a few pinches of caster (superfine) sugar. Leave to cool in the pan before removing and portioning as desired. This is delicious served warm as a dessert with cream or ice cream or enjoyed at room temperature with an afternoon cup of tea. It will keep well for up to 5 days in an airtight container.

SCOTLAND / NORTH OF ENGLAND

*

FRUIT SLICE
FLY CEMETERY/FLY CAKE

Two layers of thick shortbread pastry sandwich a sweet currant filling in this beloved traybake – often given the rather morose moniker 'fly cemetery' by school kids (and former school kids) on account of the filling. Recipes for similar style traybakes abound, as the format is easily adaptable. The traditional filling is just fruit, butter and sugar, so it takes well to spicing up (literally), or figuratively, with other dried fruit like dates or figs. Fly cakes, popular in northern England, includes a majority of the latter.

Makes: 12
Prep time: 20 minutes, plus 30 minutes chilling
Cook time: 40–50 minutes
{ⅱ} {⌁}

- For the dough:
- 500 g/1 lb 2 oz (4 cups plus 4 teaspoons) plain (all-purpose) flour, plus extra for dusting
- good pinch of fine sea salt
- good pinch of caster (superfine) sugar
- 280 g/10 oz (2½ sticks) cold unsalted butter, diced, plus extra, melted, for greasing
- 1 egg, beaten
- 1 tablespoon caster (superfine) sugar

- For the filling:
- 200 g/7 oz (¾ cup plus 1 tablespoon) currants
- 150 g/5 oz (1 cup) sultanas (golden raisins)
- 150 g/5 oz (¾ cup plus 4 teaspoons) dried figs, chopped or 75 g/2¾ oz (½ cup) extra sultanas (golden raisins) and currants
- 180 g/6 oz (1½ sticks) unsalted butter
- 180 g/6 oz (¾ cup plus 1 tablespoon) soft light brown sugar
- grated zest of 1 orange (optional)
- grated zest of 1 lemon (optional)
- 2 teaspoons mixed spice
- 1 tablespoon whisky (optional)

* For the dough, put the flour, salt and sugar into a large bowl. Add the butter and rub it in with your fingertips. Do this quite sparingly as you want to leave some big pieces of butter, about the size almonds in the flour. Gradually add 250 ml/8 fl oz (1 cup) ice-cold water and bring together to form a dough. Gently roll the dough out on a lightly floured work counter into a rectangle about 30 x 20 cm/12 x 8 inches. Fold the rectangle up like a letter, bringing one of the shorter edges one-third of the way up the length of the dough and lightly pressing down, then bringing the opposite end over to cover that third. Wrap the folded dough in baking (parchment) paper and leave to chill in the fridge for at least 30 minutes.
* Meanwhile, grease a large rimmed baking sheet, about 27 x 20 cm/10¾ x 8 inches, with melted butter. Set aside.
* For the fruit filling, put all the filling ingredients into a medium saucepan and gently warm over a medium heat, stirring to melt the butter and dissolve the sugar. Allow it to start to bubble at the edges, then remove from the heat and set aside.
* Preheat the oven to 180°C/350°F/Gas Mark 4.
* Remove the rested dough from the fridge, unwrap and put it onto a lightly floured work counter. Cut the dough in half and set one half aside. Roll out the remaining half to create the base for the traybake. It should be large enough to fill the bottom of the baking sheet, to come up the sides by 2–3 cm/¾–1¼ inches and leave a 1 cm/½ inch excess. Press the dough into the prepared sheet, then spoon the fruit filling into the tray and spread to cover the pastry base in a smooth, even layer. Roll out the other half of the dough to make a top layer, the same size as the tray. Gently lay the pastry over the fruit filling, pinching the edges with the overlap from the base pastry to seal in the fruit filling. Lightly brush the top with the beaten egg and pierce the dough in several places using a sharp knife to allow steam to escape during baking. Sprinkle with the sugar and bake in the oven for 40–50 minutes until golden brown.
* Carefully remove from the baking sheet as soon as it is cool enough to prevent it sticking, then leave to cool completely before slicing into 12 pieces using a serrated knife. This is delicious on the day it is baked but it is also good for up to a week in an airtight container. A cup of tea is the perfect afternoon companion, as is a slice of mature cheese and a wee tipple after dinner.
* **Variation:** This recipe is an amalgamation of traditional recipes from both England and Scotland where similar Fruit Slice-style bakes have long been favourites in traditional bakeries under different names and slight variations. To make a more traditionally Scottish version of this traybake, replace the rough puff pastry with a Sweet Shortcrust Pastry (page 247) and replace the sultanas (golden raisins) and figs with an additional 300 g/11 oz (1⅓ cups) currants and leave out the citrus zest. To make a more English version you can add diced Bramley (cooking) apples and toasted walnuts into the fruit mix, but just make sure your total weight of dried fruit, apple and nuts comes to 500 g/1 lb 2 oz. This recipe would work well with shop-bought puff or sweet shortcrust pastry.

ENGLAND
*

MAIDS OF HONOUR TARTS

These tartlets are made from rough puff pastry and filled with a sweetened mixture of fresh curds. Some recipes, flecked with currants, resemble Yorkshire Curd Tarts (page 384), while others (such as the recipe below) have a base of lemon curd or jam.

Makes: 12
Prep time: 50 minutes,
plus 1¼ hours chilling, resting and draining
Cook time: 35–45 minutes
{ⱷ}{ᴗ•}

- 1 quantity Rough Puff Pastry (page 247)
- 900 ml/30 fl oz (3¾ cups) full-fat (whole) milk
- 4 teaspoons white wine vinegar
- plain (all-purpose) flour, for dusting
- 125 g/4¼ oz (9 tablespoons) unsalted butter, softened
- 90 g/3¼ oz (½ cup minus 2 teaspoons) caster (superfine) sugar
- grated zest of 1 lemon
- pinch of salt
- 2 eggs
- 12 teaspoons Lemon Curd (shop-bought or homemade, page 432)

* Make the pastry following the recipe on page 247 and leave to chill for 30 minutes before using.
* For the curd cheese, pour the milk into a large saucepan and bring it slowly to a simmer over a low heat. Remove from the heat and stir in the vinegar. Leave to stand for 10 minutes. Line a colander or sieve with a piece of wet muslin cloth (cheesecloth), place it over a bowl and pour the curdled milk into it. Leave to drain for 30 minutes.
* Preheat the oven to 170°C/325°F/Gas Mark 3.
* Roll out the pastry on a lightly floured work counter until it is 2–3 mm/¹⁄₁₆–⅛ inch thick, then, using a 9 cm/3½ inch round cutter, cut out 12 circles. Put the circles into a 12-hole (-cup) muffin tray and prick the bottoms with a fork. Line each hole with a piece of baking (parchment) paper and fill with baking beans or pie weights. Bake the pastry cases (shells) for 20 minutes, or until golden brown. Remove from the oven, take out the beans or weights and paper and return to the oven for another 3–4 minutes. Remove from the oven and set aside.
* Reduce the oven temperature to 160°C/325°F/Gas Mark 3.
* Turn the cheese curd out into a large bowl, add the butter, sugar, grated lemon zest, salt and eggs and mix together until combined. Spoon 1 teaspoon of the curd mixture into the bottom of each tart, then divide the lemon curd evenly between them. Bake in the oven for 12–15 minutes until the filling is set. Remove from the oven and the muffin tray and leave to cool on a wire rack.

ENGLAND
*

LEMON TART

Lemon tarts can be found in English cookbooks dating back as far as Hannah Glasse's *The Art of Cookery, Made Plain and Easy* (1747). Glasse's tarts, however, were made from puff pastry and featured a filling of stewed apples with lemon juice. Today's lemon tarts, by sharp contrast, are a delicious shortcrust tart with sweet lemon curd fillings. Some people prefer their lemon tarts baked in a shallow base, nice and set, but I've always preferred a deeper dish and gentler bake – I like my lemon tarts with custard-like silkiness and a slight wobble.

You can also use this filling, or a shop-bought or homemade Lemon Curd (page 432), to make little lemon tartlets in the same way as the Jam Tarts (see right).

Serves: 6
Prep time: 65 minutes, plus 40 minutes resting, infusing and chilling
Cook time: 1¼ hours
{👅}{🥄}

- ½ quantity Sweet Shortcrust Pastry (page 247)
- unsalted butter, for greasing
- plain (all-purpose) flour, for dusting
- 1 egg, beaten with 1 tablespoon milk or water, for egg wash

- For the filling:
- 200 ml/7 fl oz (¾ cup plus 1 tablespoon) full-fat (whole) milk
- 200 ml/7 fl oz (¾ cup plus 1 tablespoon) double (heavy) cream
- grated zest and juice of 4 lemons
- 6 eggs
- 200 g/7 oz (1 cup) caster (superfine) sugar

* Make the pastry following the recipe on page 247 and leave to rest for 20 minutes before using.
* Preheat the oven to 170°C/325°F/Gas Mark 3. Grease a 20 cm/8 inch tart ring, 4 cm/1½ inches deep with butter.
* Roll out the dough on a very lightly floured work counter to a circle about 3 mm/⅛ inch thick. Lay the dough over the prepared ring and gently work and push it into the corners with your fingers or a lightly floured piece of dough. Slide it onto a large baking sheet, then prick the bottom all over with a fork and leave to chill in the fridge for 10 minutes.
* Once rested, remove the pastry case (shell) from the fridge and line with baking (parchment) paper, then fill with baking beans or pie weights. Blind bake in the oven for 15–20 minutes until lightly golden in colour. Remove from the oven, inspect for cracks (fill with a little more dough if necessary), then brush all over with egg wash. Return to the oven for another 5 minutes, then remove from the oven and leave to cool. Reduce the oven temperature to 130°C/250°F/Gas Mark ½.
* Meanwhile, for the filling, put the milk and cream into a medium saucepan and gently heat over a medium heat for 3–4 minutes until simmering. Add the grated lemon zest and leave to infuse for 5–10 minutes off the heat.
* Put the eggs and sugar into a medium bowl and whisk until pale. Add the lemon juice, then, while whisking, slowly add the hot lemon infusion to the egg mixture

until it is all incorporated. Pour the custard mixture into a medium saucepan and heat over a low heat until it reaches 70°C/158°F on a thermometer. Strain the mixture through a fine-mesh sieve into a large jug (pitcher).
* Put the tart case (shell) into the centre of the oven and carefully pour the warm filling mixture to the brim of the tart case, adding as much as possible. Carefully push the shelf back into the oven and gently close the door. Bake for 30 minutes, or until the filling wobbles in the centre, but does not ripple when you gently tap the ring. Remove from the oven and leave to cool completely at room temperature.

UNITED KINGDOM
*

JAM TARTS

These tartlets are traditionally made with offcuts of shortcrust pastry and must be one of the simplest treats you can whip up at the last minute. Use any good seasonal fruit jam. If you still have pastry (pie dough) left after rolling out the tartlets, use the excess to top the jam fillings with decorative hearts or stars.

Makes: 12
Prep time: 30 minutes, plus 20 minutes resting
Cook time: 20 minutes
{👅}{🥄}

- ½ quantity Sweet Shortcrust Pastry (page 247)
- butter, for greasing
- plain (all-purpose) flour, for dusting
- 12 tablespoons jam of your choice (see recipe) or fruit curd

- For the jam (optional):
- 200 g/7 oz fresh or frozen fruit
- 120 g/4 oz (⅔ cup) caster (superfine) sugar
- 20 ml/¾ fl oz (4 teaspoons) lemon juice

* Make the pastry following the recipe on page 247 and leave to rest for 20 minutes before using.
* Preheat the oven to 170°C/325°F/Gas Mark 3. Grease a 12-hole (-cup) muffin pan with butter, then lightly flour.
* For the jam, if making, heat the fruit and sugar in a small saucepan over a medium-high heat for 20 minutes, or until it's to your desired texture. Add the lemon juice, stir until combined, then remove from the heat and set aside.
* Roll the dough out on a lightly floured work counter to about 5 mm/¼ inch thick. Using an 8 cm/3¼ inch cutter, cut out 12 circles. Put a dough circle into each hole (cup) of the muffin pan, then fill each circle with 1 tablespoon of the jam (if using) or curd. Bake in the oven for 20 minutes, or until golden. Remove from the oven and leave to cool on a wire rack.

Lemon tart

ENGLAND
*

TREACLE TART
(NORFOLK TREACLE TART)

What is now known to Brits as golden syrup was once simply 'light treacle'. The filling of this beloved British tart is made from a can of such syrup, a spoonful of a little dark treacle (blackstrap molasses) and thickened with fresh breadcrumbs. The result is decidedly sweet and just a little gooey; each slice should be served with a dollop of Clotted Cream (page 34).

Most modern recipes for treacle tart tone down its sweetness, and call for both eggs and cream. In doing so, they take inspiration from a traditional variation, the Norfolk treacle tart, which eschews the recipe's breadcrumbs for a similar weight in butter, resulting in a custardy filling.

Serves: 6
Prep time: 50 minutes,
plus 35–40 minutes resting and chilling
Cook time: 1 hour 10 minutes–1 hour 25 minutes
{●}{•}

- 1 quantity Shortcrust Pastry (page 247)
- unsalted butter, for greasing
- plain (all-purpose) flour, for dusting
- 1 egg, beaten with 1 tablespoon water
or milk, for egg wash
- Clotted Cream (page 34), to serve

- For the treacle filling:
- 675 g/1 lb 7 oz (2 cups) golden syrup
- 50 g/2 oz (2½ tablespoons) black treacle
(blackstrap molasses)
- 40 ml/1½ fl oz (2 tablespoons plus 2 teaspoons)
lemon juice
- grated zest of 1 lemon
- 2 eggs, plus 1 egg yolk, lightly beaten
- 75 ml/2½ fl oz (⅓ cup) double (heavy) cream
- 10 g/1¼ oz (2 teaspoons) salt
- 175 g/6 oz (2¾ cups) breadcrumbs
(day old are best, slightly stale)

* Make the pastry following the recipe on page 247 and leave to rest for 20 minutes before using.
* Preheat the oven to 170°C/325°F/Gas Mark 3. Grease a 23 cm/9 inch loose-bottom tart pan with butter. Line a large baking sheet with baking (parchment) paper.
* Roll out the dough on a lightly floured work counter to a circle, about 3 mm/⅛ inch thick. Lay the dough over the pan and gently work and push the dough into the corners with your fingers or use a lightly floured piece of dough. Slide it onto the prepared baking sheet, prick the bottom all over with a fork and leave to chill in the fridge for 10 minutes.
* Once rested, remove the pastry case (shell) from the fridge and line with baking paper, then fill with baking beans or pie weights. Blind bake in the oven for 15–20 minutes until lightly golden in colour. Remove from the oven, inspect for cracks (fill with a little more dough if necessary), then brush all over with egg wash. Return to the oven for another 5 minutes, then remove from the oven and leave to cool slightly. Reduce the oven temperature to 150°C/300°F/Gas Mark 2.

* Meanwhile, for the filling, put the golden syrup, treacle (blackstrap molasses) and lemon juice and zest into a medium saucepan and stir over a medium heat for 3–4 minutes, or until it is all incorporated. Remove the pan from the heat, add the lightly beaten eggs and egg yolk, followed by the cream and mix using a whisk until smooth. Season with the salt. Put the breadcrumbs into a large bowl and pour the mixture over them. Mix briefly, then leave to stand for 5–10 minutes so the breadcrumbs can soak up the moisture.
* Pour the filling into the tart case (shell), spread evenly and bake in the oven for 40–50 minutes until it is slightly golden and almost solid (it will continue to cook slightly). Remove from the oven and leave to cool in the tin on a wire rack until it is at room temperature. Serve with Clotted Cream.

ENGLAND: WEST MIDLANDS
*

OLDBURY TARTS

Oldbury tarts are more accurately small hand-raised gooseberry pies made with a Hot Water Pastry Crust (page 246). They were once an early summer staple of fairs in the West Midlands.

Makes: 6 pies
Prep time: 45 minutes, plus 1 hour 10 minutes resting
Cook time: 25 minutes
{•}

- 1 quantity Hot Water Pastry (page 246)
- plain (all-purpose) flour, for dusting
- 500 g/1 lb 2 oz fresh gooseberries, topped and tailed
- about 200 g/7 oz (¾ cup plus 2 tablespoons)
soft light brown sugar
- 90 g/3¼ oz (6 tablespoons) unsalted butter
- 1 egg, beaten with 1 tablespoon water
or milk, for egg wash

* Make the pastry following the recipe on page 246 and leave to rest for 10 minutes before using.
* Take two-thirds of the dough and divide it into 6 even-sized balls. Roll out each ball on a lightly floured work counter into a circle that's 22 cm/8½ inches in diameter. Set the remaining dough aside.
* Use each of the dough circles to line a chef's ring, measuring 6 x 9 cm/2½ x 3½ inches, so that the dough has neat walls shaped by the ring itself. Put the rings onto a large baking sheet and leave to chill in the fridge for 1 hour.
* Preheat the oven to 220°C/425°F/Gas Mark 7. Line a large baking sheet with baking (parchment) paper.
* Put the rings onto the prepared baking sheet. Divide the gooseberries and sugar evenly between the pies and dot with the butter.
* Roll out 6 lids from the remaining pastry on a lightly floured work counter, then carefully lay the lids over the rings and brush with egg wash over the top to help seal the edges. Brush all over with more egg wash and bake in the oven for 25 minutes, or until golden brown. Remove from the oven and leave to cool for 20 minutes before carefully taking off the rings.

Treacle tart

ECCLEFECHAN TART

A popular tart from a small village in the Scottish Borders, this recipe is now common to the entire Borders region, and along with Border Tart (page 390), made with an almond-coconut sponge, can still be found at many traditional bakeries in the area. One of the best is Alex Dalgetty & Sons, a fifth-generation baker also specializing in Selkirk Bannocks (page 308) and Black Buns (page 314). Ecclefechan tarts are quite sweet and ideally just a little gooey – almost like a fruity pecan pie (without the nuts). They are particularly moreish, and can be served on their own, or with a big dollop of Clotted Cream (page 34).

Serves: 6
Prep time: 50 minutes, plus 30 minutes resting
Cook time: 50–55 minutes
{👤}{🌶}

- 1 quantity Shortcrust Pastry (page 247)
- 110 g/3¾ oz (7¾ tablespoons) unsalted butter, softened, plus extra for greasing
- plain (all-purpose) flour, for dusting
- 1 egg, beaten with 1 tablespoon milk or water, for egg wash

- For the filling:
- 3 eggs
- 90 g/3¼ oz (½ cup minus 2 teaspoons) caster (superfine) sugar
- 90 g/3¼ oz (½ cup minus 4 teaspoons) soft dark brown sugar
- 300 g/11 oz (1¾ cups) mixed dried fruit (equal amounts of raisins, currants and fresh redcurrants if available)
- 1 teaspoon ground cinnamon
- grated zest and juice of 1 lemon

* Make the pastry following the recipe on page 247 and leave to rest for 20 minutes before using.
* Preheat the oven to 170°C/325°F/Gas Mark 3. Grease a 25 cm/10 inch loose-bottom tart pan or ring with butter. Line a large baking sheet with baking (parchment) paper.
* Roll out the dough into a circle 3 mm/⅛ inch thick. Carefully lay the dough over the prepared pan and gently work and push it into the corners with your fingers or a lightly floured piece of dough. Slide onto the prepared baking sheet, then prick the bottom all over with a fork and leave to chill in the fridge for 10 minutes.
* Once rested, remove the pastry case (shell) from the fridge and line with baking paper, then fill with baking beans or pie weights. Blind bake in the oven for 15–20 minutes until lightly golden in colour. Remove from the oven, inspect for cracks (fill with a little more dough if necessary), then brush with a little egg wash. Return to the oven for another 5 minutes, then remove from the oven and leave to cool.
* Meanwhile, for the filling, cream the butter, eggs and sugars in a stand mixer fitted with a paddle attachment and mix together until smooth. Add the dried fruit, cinnamon, lemon zest and juice and mix in by hand using a wooden spoon until thoroughly incorporated. Set aside.
* Increase the oven temperature to 180°C/350°F/Gas Mark 4. Spread the filling over the bottom of the tart and bake for 30 minutes, or until the pastry is golden and a crust has formed on the filling.

CUMBERLAND RUM NICKY

Rural Cumbria, although far from major population centres, was the beneficiary of food ingredients from the ports of Maryport and Whitehaven: sugar, rum, dates, ginger and nutmeg. This pie, or 'plate cake' as it is known in Cumbria, became a teatime treat that could be enjoyed as a change from plain north country fare. This recipe comes from heritage wheat farmer Andrew Whitley, whose former Cumberland bakery once made dozens of such pies a week.

Serves: 8
Prep time: 50 minutes,
plus 3 hours soaking and chilling
Cook time: 30 minutes
{👤}{🌶}

- 200 g/7 oz (1⅔ cups) fine wholemeal (whole wheat) flour or partially sifted, plus extra for dusting
- 100 g/3½ oz (7 tablespoons) slightly salted butter
- 75 g/2¾ oz (⅓ cup plus 2 teaspoons) raw cane sugar
- yogurt, crème fraîche or soured cream, to serve

- For the filling:
- 25 g/1 oz (¼ cup minus 2 teaspoons) sultanas (golden raisins)
- 20 ml/¾ fl oz (4 teaspoons) rum
- 20 g/¾ oz (4 teaspoons) unsalted butter
- 40 g/1½ oz (¼ cup minus 1 tablespoon) raw cane sugar
- pinch each of ground nutmeg and cloves
- 100 g/3½ oz (⅔ cup) dried chopped dates
- 40 g/1½ oz (¼ cup minus 1 tablespoon) chopped crystallized (candied) ginger

* For the filling, put the sultanas (golden raisins) into a small bowl, add the rum and leave to soak for 1 hour.
* Put the butter, sugar and spices into a bowl and mix together. Add the dates, ginger and soaked sultanas and mix until blended. Cover with clingfilm (plastic wrap) and chill in the fridge for 2 hours.
* For the pastry, put the flour into a large bowl, add the butter and rub it in with cold fingertips until the mixture resembles breadcrumbs.
* Put the sugar into a small saucepan, add 2 tablespoons water and stir over a low heat for 2 minutes, or until dissolved. Pour the sugar into the bowl and mix carefully using a fork until it just comes together as a dough.
* Preheat the oven to 180°C/350°F/Gas Mark 4.
* Divide the dough in half. On a lightly floured work surface, roll out one half of the dough to 4 mm thick, to a diameter of 25 cm / 10 in, or that will slightly overhang the edges of the pie plate. Roll the filling into a disc about 5 mm/¼ inch smaller in diameter than the pastry-covered plate and put this disc onto the dough.
* Roll out the remaining pastry on a lightly floured work counter and either cut it using a lattice cutter or make your own strips about 7 mm/¼ inch wide and long enough to stretch over the plate. Moisten the pastry that is visible around the rim with a little water. Arrange the pastry strips in a diamond lattice pattern (7–8 strips per direction should do) and trim the edges neatly.
* Bake in the oven for 30 minutes, or until the pastry is light golden. Serve cold or slightly warm with yogurt, crème fraîche or soured cream.

Cumberland rum nicky

UNITED KINGDOM
*

MINCE PIES

Few things mark the arrival of the festive season and simultaneously bring so much joy as mince pies do. These little pies date back centuries to a time when, yes, the fillings were made with minced (ground) meat. However, in the early nineteenth century it became popular to prepare the mincemeat filling without the meat in advance so that it had time to mature and deepen in flavour. After some time it became even more popular to skip the meat altogether, giving us the 'mincemeat' filling we know today: packed with dried fruit, spices and soft brown sugar – and sometimes with a little brandy.

The fillings for mince pies can, and ideally should, be made in advance and left to mature in sealed and sterilized jars (page 464) for at least 2 weeks. However, they are still good when whipped up last minute. Make them in abundance, as they quickly disappear.

Makes: 12
Prep time: 30 minutes, plus a minimum of 5 hours soaking and cooking the filling and at least 2 weeks maturing
Cook time: 25–30 minutes
{⋅•}

- For the mincemeat:
- 375 g/13¼ oz (2 cups plus 2 tablespoons) mixed dried fruit (125 g/4¼ oz (½ cup) each currants, raisins and sultanas (golden raisins))
- 120 ml/4 fl oz (½ cup) brandy
- 100 g/3½ oz (¾ cup plus 4 teaspoons) minced (ground) beef (optional)
- 200 g/7 oz (1 cup plus 2 tablespoons) shredded beef suet
- 125 g/4¼ oz (½ cup) soft dark brown sugar
- 30 g/1 oz (¼ cup minus 2 teaspoons) mixed candied peel
- ¼ teaspoon ground cinnamon
- ¼ teaspoon grated nutmeg
- 175 g/6 oz Bramley (cooking) apples, peeled, cored and grated
- grated zest and juice of 1 lemon

- To build the pies:
- 1 quantity Shortcrust Pastry (page 247)
- unsalted butter, for greasing
- plain (all-purpose) flour, for dusting
- 1 egg, beaten with 1 tablespoon water or milk, for egg wash
- granulated or demerara (turbinado) sugar, for sprinkling

* For the mincemeat, put the dried fruits into a large bowl, add the brandy and leave to soak for 1 hour, or overnight. Pour out the excess brandy into a small bowl and set aside, then put the soaked fruits into a large heatproof bowl and add all the remaining mincemeat ingredients, except the reserved excess brandy, and mix together. Cover with aluminium foil and leave to marinate for 1 hour.
* Preheat the oven to 110°C/225°F/Gas Mark ¼.
* Put the filling into the oven for 3 hours, then remove from the oven and leave to cool, stirring occasionally to emulsify the fat back into the mixture. Add the reserved excess brandy, mix thoroughly and pack into sterilized jars (page 464), leaving a 1 cm/½ inch headspace. Cover and seal, then leave to mature in a cool, dark place for at least 2 weeks (see introduction).

* When you are ready to make the pies, make the pastry following the recipe on page 247 and leave to rest for 20 minutes before using.
* Preheat the oven to 180°C/350°F/Gas Mark 4. Grease a 12-hole (-cup) mince pie pan or bun tray with butter and lightly flour each hole.
* Roll out the dough on a lightly floured work counter until it is 5 mm/¼ inch thick. Cut out 12 x 8 cm/3¼ inch circles for the bases and 12 x 6 cm/2½ inch circles for the lids, marking a cross in the centre of the lids.
* Line the prepared pan or tray with the bases, then put 2 teaspoons of the mincemeat into each one. Brush with egg wash, then lay the lids on top and press down, applying pressure on the edges. Lightly glaze the mince pies with more egg wash and sprinkle with the granulated or demerara (turbinado) sugar.
* Bake in the oven for 25–30 minutes until golden brown, then remove from the oven and leave to cool on a wire rack.

SCOTLAND: SHETLAND
*

WHIPKULL

This sweetened egg custard should be eaten with the help of Shortbread Biscuits (page 338).

Makes: 2
Prep time: 10 minutes, plus 2–3 hours soaking
Cook time: about 20 minutes
{☻}{⋅•}

- 25 g/1 oz (¼ cup minus 2 teaspoons) raisins
- 4 tablespoons rum
- 3 egg yolks
- 50 g/2 oz (¼ cup) caster (superfine) sugar
- 125 ml/4¼ fl oz (½ cup) whipping cream
- Shortbread Biscuits (page 338), to serve

* Put the raisins into a small bowl and cover with 2 tablespoons of the rum. Leave to soak for 2–3 hours.
* Put a large heatproof bowl over a small saucepan of boiling water over a low heat, making sure the bottom of the bowl doesn't touch the water. The heat should be enough to keep the water at a simmer. Put the egg yolks, sugar and remaining rum into the bowl and keep stirring until very thick, about 20 minutes.
* Remove from the heat and leave to cool, then fold in the whipping cream. Transfer to 2 small ramekins, divide the rum-soaked raisins evenly between the ramekins and serve with Shortbread Biscuits.

Mince pies

ENGLAND
*

GOOSEBERRY FOOL

A summertime dessert made from a sweetened, whipped double (heavy) cream and softened gooseberries. Serve with Shortbread Biscuits (page 338) for dipping or spoon out the fool.

Serves: 6
Prep time: 15 minutes
Cook time: 10–12 minutes
{👁}{🍴}{🌢}{✗}

- 250 g/ 9 oz (2 cups plus 4 teaspoons) gooseberries, topped and tailed
- 150 g/ 5 oz (¾ cup) caster (superfine) sugar
- pared zest of 1 lemon
- dash of Muscat wine (optional)
- 600 ml/ 20 fl oz (2½ cups) double (heavy) cream
- 2 tablespoons icing (confectioners') sugar
- ratafia or Shortbread Biscuits (page 338), to serve

* Put the gooseberries into a large saucepan with the caster (superfine) sugar, lemon zest, Muscat (if using) and a little water and cook over a medium heat for 10–12 minutes until the gooseberries are soft. Taste and add more sugar, if desired. Remove from the heat and leave to cool completely.
* Put the cream and icing (confectioners') sugar into a large bowl and whip until it is a little floppy, then fold in the gooseberries. Divide the mixture between 6 serving glasses and serve with the ratafia or Shortbread Biscuits.

———

ENGLAND
*

LEMON POSSET

Originally a hot drink popular with medieval nobles, posset was once made from sweetened and spiced milk, which was then curdled with wine, ale or lemon juice.
Like the Syllabub (see right), posset has gradually evolved since the seventeenth century from a drink to a creamy set dessert that's often flavoured, as in this case, with citrus. Early trifle recipes also featured a chilled layer of posset.

Serves: 6
Prep time: 15 minutes, plus 2–12 hours chilling
Cook time: 10 minutes
{👁}{🌢}

- 600 ml/ 20 fl oz (2½ cups) double (heavy) cream
- 80 g/ 3 oz (⅓ cup plus 1 tablespoon) caster (superfine) sugar
- grated zest of 2 unwaxed lemons
- 110 ml/ 3¾ fl oz (½ cup minus 1 tablespoon) lemon juice (about 3 lemons)

- To serve:
- fresh raspberries
- raspberry sauce
- Shortbread Biscuits (page 338) or a citrus sorbet or citrus salad with orange/ grapefruit, etc

* Bring the cream, sugar and grated lemon zest to the boil in a large saucepan, stirring to dissolve, then reduce the heat and simmer gently for 5 minutes. Leave to cool completely in the fridge.
* Put the cooled cream into a stand mixer fitted with a whisk attachment, add the lemon juice and start to whip on medium speed, keeping a close eye on the machine. Whip until a semi-firm or a lightly whipped cream texture is achieved, then finish slowly by hand. There is a fine line between not whipping the mixture enough and whipping it too much as the acid thickens the cream noticeably and will eventually also split the mixture.
* Quickly pour or pipe the cream mixture into 6 serving dishes, tap the dishes on a work counter and cover with clingfilm (plastic wrap). Leave to chill in the fridge for 2 hours, or overnight.
* Serve the posset with fresh raspberries, raspberry sauce and shortbread or a citrus sorbet or citrus salad with orange/ grapefruit, etc.

———

ENGLAND
*

SYLLABUB

Much like the Posset (see left), our earliest syllabub recipes date back several hundred years, to a time when it first took the form of a warm and frothy milk drink, curdled with wine, cider or lemon juice. As a drink, the syllabub fell out of popularity in the nineteenth century before enjoying a modest resurgence in modern times as a dessert of sweetened and whipped cream spiked with wine and/ or brandy.

Serves: 6
Prep time: 15 minutes, plus 8–12 hours infusing
{👁}{🌢}

- 100 ml/ 3½ fl oz (⅓ cup plus 1 tablespoon) sweet wine, such as Muscat
- 60 ml/ 2 fl oz (¼ cup) brandy
- finely grated lemon zest and juice of 1 lemon
- 75 g/ 2¾ oz (⅓ cup plus 2 teaspoons) caster (superfine) sugar
- 300 ml/ 10 fl oz (1¼ cups) double (heavy) cream
- ½ nutmeg, for grating or 1 teaspoon ground nutmeg, for sprinkling
- Shortbread Biscuits (page 338), to serve

* Put the wine, brandy, lemon zest and juice and sugar into a large bowl and stir together until combined and the sugar has dissolved. Cover with clingfilm (plastic wrap) and leave to infuse in the fridge overnight.
* The next day, pour in the cream and whisk for several minutes until floppy. Spoon into cups and grate over some fresh nutmeg or sprinkle with the ground nutmeg before serving.

Gooseberry fool

NORTHERN IRELAND
*

FIFTEENS

The rather cutely named Fifteens – there's fifteen of each principal ingredient – is a Northern Irish recipe that comes together like a traybake but requires only a simple assembly job and some chilling in the fridge. Make it a day in advance for children's parties, so it has ample time to set.

Serves: 6
Prep time: 15 minutes, plus 2–12 hours setting

- 15 digestive biscuits
(shop-bought or homemade, page 340), crushed
- 15 marshmallows, quartered
- 15 glacé (candied) cherries, coarsely chopped
- about 175 ml/6 fl oz (¾ cup) condensed milk
- 4 tablespoons desiccated (unsweetened shredded) coconut

* Put the biscuits in a plastic bag and carefully crush using a rolling pin.
* Put the crushed biscuits, marshmallows and cherries into a large bowl and pour in the condensed milk. Stir very well to make a sticky dough.
* Spread the desiccated (unsweetened shredded) coconut quite thickly over a work counter and pour or spoon the mixture over the coconut. Roll the mixture in the coconut, making it into a thick sausage shape. Wrap the mixture tightly in clingfilm (plastic wrap) and leave to set for at least 2 hours and ideally overnight in the fridge.
* Once set, uncover and slice into circles.

UNITED KINGDOM
*

BLANCMANGE

Blancmange is a sweetened milk jelly, often flavoured with almonds, thickened with either gelatine or cornstarch and set in a mould. In modern times the dish has achieved notoriety for its artificial colours, and is a mainstay of children's birthday parties, but blancmange has surprising origins as a slightly sweet dish common to most of medieval Europe. Known then by the same name (itself an Anglicized form of the French blancmanger, or 'white food'), blancmange consisted of shredded chicken, almond milk and rice. This recipe is, thankfully, for the modern variant. It should be served well chilled with some fresh or poached fruit and a little whipped cream.

Serves: 6
Prep time: 15 minutes, plus 4 hours setting
Cook time: 20 minutes
{⚏}{⦁ʼ}

- 600 ml/20 fl oz (2½ cups) full-fat (whole) milk
- 1 teaspoon almond extract
- 200 ml/7 fl oz (¾ cup plus 1 tablespoon)
double (heavy) cream
- 100 g/3½ oz (½ cup) caster (superfine) sugar
- 8 leaves gelatine
- fresh or poached fruit and whipped cream, to serve

* Heat the milk, almond extract and cream in a large saucepan over a medium heat for 5 minutes, or until just starting to bubble. Stir in the sugar and gelatine and heat for another 3–5 minutes, just until the sugar and gelatine have dissolved. Don't let the milk boil. Usually 1 gelatine leaf can set 250 ml/8 fl oz (1 cup) liquid, so check the packet instructions.
* Remove the pan from the heat, leave to cool for a few minutes, then strain the mixture through a sieve to remove any lumps. Pour the mixture into a jelly mould, cover and leave to chill for at least 4 hours to let the blancmange set. If you don't have a jelly mould, use a heatproof dish.
* To remove the blancmange, put the outside of the jelly mould briefly into some warm water to release the blancmange from the sides of the mould. Put a plate over the top of the jelly mould and flip it carefully. The blancmange should release easily. Serve with fresh or poached fruit and whipped cream.

NORTH OF SCOTLAND / WALES
*

BEESTING PUDDING
PWDIN LLAETH BRITH

'Beest' is another name for what we typically call colostrum, the first milk of a mammal – in this case a cow – after it has given birth. This milk is rich in flavour and protein, and when baked it sets like an eggless custard. Beesting is first sweetened or spiced (with cinnamon or nutmeg) and once baked and cooled, it is cut into slices and served with fresh or macerated red fruit. Another one for reference, as you will not find colostrum in the supermarket!

Serves: 6
Prep time: 10 minutes
Cook time: 40 minutes
{⚏}{⧉}{⦁ʼ}{⌂}

- 300 ml/10 fl oz (1¼ cups) full-fat (whole) milk
- 150 g/5 oz (¾ cup) caster (superfine) sugar
- 4 g/1 teaspoon salt
- 600 g/1 lb 5 oz colostrum

* Preheat the oven to 170°C/325°F/Gas Mark 3. Put a large roasting tray onto the lower rack of the oven and carefully pour in enough boiling water until it is almost half full.
* Heat the milk in a medium saucepan over a medium heat for 2–3 minutes until warm, then add the sugar and salt and stir for another 2–3 minutes until they have dissolved. Don't heat the milk excessively. Remove from the heat and leave to cool.
* When the mixture has cooled, add the colostrum and mix together, then pour into a casserole dish. Carefully put the casserole dish into the roasting tray, ensuring the water is the same height as the milk mixture and bake for 40 minutes, checking halfway through cooking. Reduce the cooking time to 30 minutes if the pudding starts to set (it should wobble but not ripple when nudged).
* Leave to cool completely before serving.

Fifteens

UNITED KINGDOM

BUTTERMILK PUDDING

This creamy pudding is similar in texture to a panna cotta, with the added tang of buttermilk. Similar types of puddings have been made in England for centuries, such as the 'tea cream' described by eighteenth-century cook and tavern owner John Farley. To adapt this recipe to Farley's tea cream, swap the buttermilk for the same amount of full-fat (whole) milk and warm to scalding heat before infusing with 60 g/ 2¼ oz (½ cup plus 2 teaspoons) of tea leaves for 30 minutes. Strain and proceed according to the recipe below.
To serve, turn the buttermilk pudding out from its ramekin or mould and spoon fresh fruit or compote over the top. Rhubarb works especially well.

Serves: 6
Prep time: 5 minutes, plus up to 12 hours soaking
and setting
Cook time: 10 minutes
{🝧}{🝨}{🝪}

- 2½ gelatine leaves
- 300 ml/ 10 fl oz (1¼ cups) fresh buttermilk
- 100 g/ 3½ oz (½ cup) caster (superfine) sugar
- 200 ml/ 7 fl oz (¾ cup plus 1 tablespoon)
double (heavy) cream
- fresh fruit or compote, to serve

* Put the gelatine leaves into a small bowl of very cold water, making sure they are submerged, and leave to soak for 5–10 minutes until completely soft. Usually 1 gelatine leaf can set 250 ml/ 8 fl oz (1 cup) liquid, so check the packet instructions.
* Heat 150 ml/ 5 fl oz (⅔ cup) of the buttermilk in a medium saucepan over a low heat to 37°C/ 98.6°F (any hotter and the buttermilk may split). Squeeze the gelatine to remove the excess water, then add the gelatine and sugar to the warmed buttermilk and stir to dissolve. Making sure there are no lumps, stir the remaining buttermilk and the double (heavy) cream into the mixture and pour into 1 large or 6 individual dishes. Cover and leave in the fridge to set, preferably overnight.
* To serve, turn the buttermilk pudding out of the dish or dishes and spoon fresh fruit or compote over the top.

NORTHERN IRELAND / SCOTLAND

CARRAGEEN PUDDING

Carrageen moss is an edible seaweed common to the shores of Ireland and Scotland. It has a natural gelatinous quality when cooked and was traditionally used as a thickener in milk puddings, imparting a subtle but pleasurable saline flavour. Serve just as you would any other milk pudding, with fresh fruit or compote.

Serves: 6
Prep time: 20 minutes, plus up to 12 hours soaking
and setting
Cook time: 30 minutes
{🝧}{🝨}{🝪}

- 30 g/ 1 oz dried carrageen
- 200 ml/ 7 fl oz (¾ cup plus 1 tablespoon)
full-fat (whole) milk
- 30 ml/ 1 fl oz (2 tablespoons) Irish whiskey or brandy
- 100 g/ 3½ oz (½ cup) caster (superfine) sugar
- 200 ml/ 7 fl oz (¾ cup plus 1 tablespoon)
double (heavy) cream

* Put the carrageen into a small bowl, cover with cold water and leave to soak for 20 minutes. Strain and put into a large saucepan with 600 ml/ 20 fl oz (2½ cups) fresh water. Bring to a simmer over a low-medium heat and cook for 20–25 minutes until the mixture has thickened.
* Pour the milk and alcohol into another large saucepan and slowly heat over a medium heat until it reaches scalding point or 83°C/ 181°F on a thermometer. Add the sugar and stir over the heat for 2–3 minutes until the sugar has completely dissolved.
* Squeeze the carrageen gel through muslin (cheesecloth), then remove the milk pan from the heat and whisk the carrageen into the milk until it is well combined.
* Put the cream into a large bowl and lightly whip to just before soft peak stage, then fold into the milk mixture. Pour the mixture into an 850 ml/ 29 fl oz mould. Cover and leave to set in the fridge overnight.
* The next day, carefully submerge the mould around halfway into very hot water. Leave to stand for a few seconds, then turn it out onto a plate and serve.

UNITED KINGDOM

*

TRADITIONAL MILK ICE CREAM

A very smooth, creamy and rich traditional ice cream with no added flavourings. Quality ingredients are absolutely essential. After trying this, you will never go back to vanilla.

Makes: about 600 g/ 1 lb 5 oz
Prep time: 50–60 minutes,
plus 3–3½ hours chilling and freezing
Cook time: 15 minutes
{ǐ}{☖}{☙}

- 350 ml/ 12 fl oz (1½ cups) full-fat (whole) milk, preferably local and good quality
- 150 ml/ 5 fl oz (⅔ cup) double (heavy) cream, preferably local, good quality and high in fat, or Clotted Cream (shop-bought or homemade, page 34)
- 30 ml/ 1 fl oz (2 tablespoons) liquid glucose
- 5 egg yolks
- 120 g/ 4 oz (⅔ cup) caster (superfine) sugar

* Put the milk, cream and glucose into a large saucepan over a medium-high heat and gradually bring to the boil, about 5–10 minutes. Once it is boiling, remove from the heat, cover with a lid and leave to infuse for 5–10 minutes.
* Meanwhile, put a medium metal mixing bowl over a large bowl of ice, ready to cool the custard once it is cooked.
* Put the egg yolks and sugar into another large bowl and whisk using a balloon whisk until pale and frothy. While whisking constantly, slowly pour the cream mixture into the egg yolks until it is all incorporated.
* Rinse and dry the saucepan, add the custard mixture and return to a medium-low heat. Gently heat the custard mixture, scraping the bottom of the saucepan with a spatula constantly until the custard starts to thicken and reaches a temperature of 86°C/ 187°F on a thermometer, or until it coats the back of a spoon. This process shouldn't be rushed as it will split; it should take a generous 5–7 minutes. When it is cooked, strain the custard through a fine-mesh sieve into the metal bowl over the ice bath and leave to cool, stirring occasionally. Once cooled, chill the ice cream mixture thoroughly for at least 2 hours in the fridge.
* Put a freezerproof container or bowl into the freezer prior to churning the ice cream. Pour the chilled custard mixture into an ice-cream machine and churn for 30–45 minutes until it is the desired texture. Transfer the ice cream to the frozen container and freeze for 30–45 minutes before serving.

UNITED KINGDOM

*

STOUT ICE CREAM

The addition of stout (especially a nice, chocolatey variety) makes for a rich and malty ice cream. Serve on its own, topped with a caramel sauce or spooned onto a warm Steamed Ginger Sponge (page 352).

Makes: about 800 g/ 1 lb 12 oz
Prep time: 1 hour 10 minutes,
plus 3¼–4 hours chilling and freezing
Cook time: 15 minutes
{ǐ}{☖}{☙}

- 330 ml/ 11 fl oz (1⅓ cups) strong stout or porter
- 70 g/ 2¾ oz (⅓ cup) dark brown sugar
- 350 ml/ 12 fl oz (1½ cups) double (heavy) cream
- 150 ml/ 5 fl oz (⅔ cup) full-fat (whole) milk
- 40 ml/ 1½ fl oz (2 tablespoons plus 2 teaspoons) liquid glucose
- 6 egg yolks
- 70 g/ 2¾ oz (⅓ cup plus 1 teaspoon) caster (superfine) sugar

* Pour the stout into a medium saucepan, add the dark brown sugar and cook over a medium-high heat for 5–10 minutes, or until reduced by half. Remove from the heat and leave to chill in the fridge.
* Meanwhile, put the cream, milk and glucose into a large saucepan over a medium-high heat and gradually bring to the boil, about 5–10 minutes. Once boiling, remove the pan from the heat, cover with a lid and leave to infuse for 5–10 minutes.
* Put a medium metal mixing bowl over a large bowl of ice, ready to cool the custard once it is cooked.
* Put the egg yolks and sugar into another large bowl and whisk using a balloon whisk until pale and frothy. While whisking constantly, slowly pour the cream mixture into the egg yolks until it is all incorporated.
* Rinse and dry the saucepan, add the custard mix and return to a medium-low heat. Add the stout mixture and gently heat the custard mixture, scraping the bottom of the saucepan with a spatula constantly until the custard starts to thicken and reaches a temperature of 86°C/ 187°F on a thermometer, or until it coats the back of a spoon. This process shouldn't be rushed as it will split; it should take a generous 5–7 minutes. When it is cooked, strain the custard through a fine-mesh sieve into the metal bowl over the ice bath and leave to cool, stirring occasionally. Once cooled, chill the ice cream mixture thoroughly for at least 2 hours in the fridge.
* Put a freezerproof container or bowl into the freezer prior to churning the ice cream. Pour the chilled custard mixture into an ice-cream machine and churn for 40–60 minutes until it is the desired texture. Transfer the ice cream to the frozen container and freeze for 30–45 minutes before serving.

UNITED KINGDOM
*
HONEY PARFAIT

This is delicious topped with walnuts or honeycomb and drizzled with some more honey.

Serves: 6
Prep time: 40 minutes, plus 2 hours freezing
Cook time: 10–15 minutes
{🌙}{🍴}

- 350 ml/12 fl oz (1½ cups) double (heavy) cream
- 150 g/5 oz egg yolks (about 6 or 7)
- 30 g/1 oz (2½ tablespoons) caster (superfine) sugar
- 100 g/3½ oz (7 tablespoons) good-quality local honey, plus extra to decorate
- 20 ml/¾ fl oz (4 teaspoons) lemon juice

- To decorate:
- chopped walnuts or honeycomb

* Line a 450 g/1 lb loaf pan with a double layer of clingfilm (plastic wrap), making sure it overhangs the sides slightly, and put into the freezer.
* Put the cream into a stand mixer fitted with a whisk attachment and whisk on medium speed until lightly whipped. Alternatively, whip the cream in a large bowl using electric beaters. Set aside in the fridge.
* Put the egg yolks, sugar and honey into a medium metal bowl and whisk until smooth and pale. Put the bowl over a large saucepan of boiling water, making sure the bottom of the bowl doesn't touch the water, and reduce the heat to a simmer. Whisk the egg yolk mixture for 8–12 minutes until the texture becomes thick.
* Take the bowl off the heat and whisk slightly, then add the lemon juice. Fold a third of the whipped cream into the honey mixture until it is incorporated, then repeat the process, folding in the remaining cream. Avoid overworking the mixture as you will lose volume. Pour into the prepared loaf pan, cover with clingfilm (plastic wrap) and freeze for 2 hours, or until solid.
* To serve, pull the clingfilm (plastic wrap) from all sides or dip the pan into hot water briefly, put onto a chopping (cutting) board and carefully remove all clingfilm (check thoroughly). Slice evenly into portions and decorate with extra honey, walnuts or honeycomb.

UNITED KINGDOM
*
MARMALADE ICE CREAM

Serve in generous scoops – to be eaten on its own, or perhaps served with a Steamed Chocolate Pudding (page 352).

Makes: about 600 g/1 lb 5 oz
Prep time: 50–60 minutes,
plus 3–3½ hours chilling and freezing
Cook time: 15 minutes
{🌙}{🍴}{🥄}

- 300 ml/10 fl oz (1¼ cups) full-fat (whole) milk
- 200 ml/7 fl oz (¾ cup plus 1 tablespoon) double (heavy) cream
- 30 ml/1 fl oz (2 tablespoons) liquid glucose
- grated zest of 1 orange
- 1 vanilla pod (bean), split in half lengthways and seeds scraped out
- 5 egg yolks
- 120 g/4 oz (⅔ cup) caster (superfine) sugar
- 40 g/1½ oz (¼ cup minus 1 tablespoon) marmalade

* Put the milk, cream and glucose into a large saucepan over a medium-high heat and gradually bring to the boil, about 5–10 minutes. Add the orange zest and vanilla pod (bean) and seeds and whisk the mixture occasionally to stop it from catching on the bottom of the pan. Once it is boiling, remove the pan from the heat, cover with a lid and leave to infuse for 5–10 minutes.
* Meanwhile, put a medium metal mixing bowl over a large bowl of ice, ready to cool the custard once it is cooked.
* While the mixture is infusing, put the egg yolks and sugar into another large bowl and whisk using a balloon whisk until pale and frothy. While whisking constantly, slowly strain the infusion through a fine-mesh sieve into the egg yolks until it is all incorporated. Discard the zest and vanilla pod.
* Rinse and dry the saucepan, add the custard mix and return to a medium-low heat. Gently heat the custard mixture, scraping the bottom of the saucepan with a spatula constantly until the custard starts to thicken and reaches a temperature of 86°C/187°F on a thermometer, or until it coats the back of a spoon. This process shouldn't be rushed as it will split; it should take a generous 5–7 minutes. When it is cooked, strain the custard through a fine-mesh sieve into the metal bowl over the ice bath and leave to cool, stirring occasionally. Once cooled, chill the ice cream mixture thoroughly for at least 2 hours in the fridge.
* Put a freezerproof container or bowl into the freezer prior to churning the ice cream. Pour the chilled custard mixture into an ice-cream machine and churn for 30–45 minutes until it is the desired texture. Transfer the ice cream to the frozen container, fold in the marmalade and freeze for 30–45 minutes before serving.

Honey parfait

BROWN BREAD ICE CREAM

This old-fashioned ice cream is made from crunchy caramelized brown breadcrumbs and was a particular favourite of Queen Victoria, who is said to have preferred hers rippled with honey. This flavour is still hugely popular in Ireland, where you can find it at most traditional ice-cream parlours. Use within a few days of making, as the breadcrumbs will lose their texture and crunch over time.

Serves: 6
Prep time: 10 minutes,
plus 2 hours churning and freezing
Cook time: 25 minutes
{ⓥ}{•ᵛ}

- 300 ml/10 fl oz (1¼ cups) full-fat (whole) milk
- 300 ml/10 fl oz (1¼ cups) double (heavy) cream
- 40 ml/1½ fl oz (2¼ tablespoons) liquid glucose
- 120 g/4 oz egg yolks (6 yolks)
- 100 g/3½ oz (½ cup) caster (superfine) sugar
- 125 g/4¼ oz slices of brown (whole wheat) bread, preferably stale
- 75 g/2¾ oz (⅓ cup) demerara (turbinado) sugar
- 30 g/1 oz (2 tablespoons) unsalted butter

* Put a large freezerproof container into the freezer.
* Bring the milk, cream and liquid glucose to a simmer (85°C/185°F) in a medium saucepan over a medium heat, stirring occasionally to prevent it catching on the bottom of the pan. It will take 5–10 minutes.
* Put the egg yolks and caster (superfine) sugar into a large bowl and whisk until smooth. While whisking, gradually pour in the cream mixture, ensuring that the yolks dissolve into the milk.
* Have a large bowl filled with ice-cold water ready nearby. Pour the mixture back into the pan, then, over a low-medium heat, constantly stir the ice cream with a spatula, gradually heating it to 85°C/185°F. Continue to hold the mixture at this temperature for 1 minute, or until it is thick enough to coat the back of a spoon. Strain into a clean bowl and put it into the ice-cold water until chilled, then set aside in the fridge until needed.
* Meanwhile, put the bread into a food processor and process into crumbs. Add the demerara (turbinado) sugar and mix together. Melt the butter in a frying pan or skillet over a medium heat, then add the breadcrumb mixture and fry for 10 minutes, or until crisp and golden.
* Pour the chilled mixture into an ice-cream machine and churn for 20 minutes, or until it is soft, thick and almost frozen. While still churning, pour in the breadcrumbs and stop when the bread is evenly mixed through. Transfer to a frozen container, cover with a lid and put in the freezer until firm.

KNICKERBOCKER GLORY

An American ice-cream sundae that became popular in the early 1900s, the Knickerbocker Glory has stayed popular in the UK long after it faded into obscurity across the pond.

Serves: 6
Prep time: 30 minutes
Cook time: 5 minutes
{ⓥ}{•ᵛ}

- 250 g/9 oz (1½ cups minus 1 tablespoon) raspberries, setting 1 handful aside
- 3 tablespoons icing (confectioners') sugar
- 150 ml/5 fl oz (⅔ cup) double (heavy) cream
- 30 g/1 oz (⅓ cup plus 1 teaspoon) slivered almonds
- 12 scoops vanilla ice cream or 6 scoops vanilla ice cream and 6 scoops of another flavoured ice cream, such as strawberry
- 150 g/5 oz soft fruit, such as strawberries, quartered, or blueberries
- 6 maraschino cherries, to decorate

* Using a wooden spoon, push the raspberries through a sieve into a large bowl to make a purée. Add 2 tablespoons of the sugar to the raspberry purée and stir through to make a sauce. Set aside.
* Put the remaining sugar and the cream into a large bowl and whip until it is slightly floppy. Set aside.
* Put the almonds into a dry frying pan or skillet and toast over a medium-high heat for 5 minutes, or until just golden. Remove from the heat and set aside.
* Layer the ice creams with the fruit sauce, whipped cream, some of the reserved raspberries and other soft fruit in 6 tall dessert glasses, finishing with a final layer of cream. Sprinkle with the toasted nuts and top each glass with a maraschino cherry and the final few reserved raspberries.

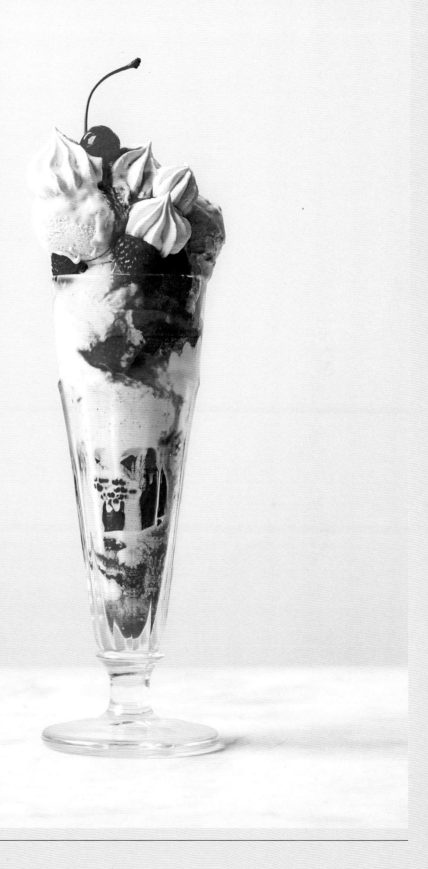

Knickerbocker glory

IT WAS IN VICTORIAN AND EDWARDIAN TIMES
THAT GREAT PRIDE WAS TAKEN
IN HAVING PLENTIFUL STORES OF PRESERVES.
HOUSEWIVES DEPENDED UPON THEIR OWN RESOURCES
AND FILLED CAPACIOUS LARDERS
AND STORE CUPBOARDS WITH
THEIR HOME-MADE HANDIWORK.

MARGUERITE PATTEN,
JAMS, PRESERVES AND CHUTNEYS HANDBOOK, 2001

You might look on this chapter as *The British Cookbook*'s kitchen cupboard, with all the jams, sauces and preserves you will want to take you through the seasons: stocking your own larder with zest, brightness, depth and, of course, sweetness.

There are a couple of different kinds of sauces in this chapter: those you would pour, and those you would use for dipping. While the former should be made fresh each time, the latter can be kept in the fridge and used routinely. Kitchen staples like homemade mayonnaise, brown sauce, English mustard, or the many different types of ketchup, are referenced quite frequently throughout the book and complement a wide range of savoury dishes.

The majority of the pouring sauces are quite simple: many start with a foundation sauce (a sort of bechamel), a gravy or a simple butter sauce. Only the most luxurious sauces will have you embarking on elaborate preparations. Sweet sauces such as butterscotch could be made to pour over your favourite puddings, or set like tablet or fudge to slice up and eat as sweets (candies).

Finally, no British cupboard would be complete without a jar of raspberry jam or a little piccalilli. The preserves in this chapter vary in their usage: lifting everything from cold meat pies to sweet summer puddings. Many of these recipes can and should be adapted to what is in season, so don't take them as being too prescriptive

– they are a starting point to adapt as you like. Homemade preserves may be time-consuming, but the product is always far more enjoyable than the shop-bought counterpart. Homemade candied peel, for instance, is on another level entirely compared to the variety you will get in plastic containers in the shops, and for readers outside of the UK it may be easier to make than find, anyway.

SAUCES, CONFECTIONS AND PRESERVES

UNITED KINGDOM
*

APPLE SAUCE

This is a classic accompaniment to any sort of roast pork. The English food writer Dorothy Hartley recommends making the sauce not on the stove, but in the oven by baking the apples while the pork cooks, then serving the sauce in the dish it was cooked in.

Serves: 4
Prep time: 10 minutes
Cook time: 10–15 minutes
{♨}{♠}{☙}{☕}{✕}

- 500 g/1 lb 2 oz Bramley (cooking) apples, peeled, cored and sliced
- 75 g/2¾ oz (⅓ cup plus 2 teaspoons) caster (superfine) or soft light brown sugar, plus extra to taste
- 30 g/2 oz (2 tablespoons) butter
- salt and pepper

* Put the apples and 2 tablespoons water into a large saucepan and heat over a medium heat for 10–15 minutes until pulpy, but with a little texture. Remember to stir occasionally to prevent the apples catching and burning.
* Stir in the sugar to taste, then add the butter and beat using a wooden spoon. Season with salt and plenty of pepper. Leave to cool before serving.

UNITED KINGDOM
*

MINT SAUCE

This classic British sauce is the undisputed complement to roast lamb, but pairs just as nicely with mutton; the sweet tang of a good mint sauce cuts through the bolder, sometimes gamey flavours found in the meat.

Serves: 6
Prep time: 10 minutes, plus 15 minutes steeping
Cook time: 5 minutes
{♨}{♦}{♠}{♣}{☙}{♟}

- 1 large bunch mint
- 60–90 ml/2–3¼ fl oz (4–6 tablespoons) cider or wine vinegar
- 30 g/1 oz (2½ tablespoons) caster (superfine) sugar

* Separate the mint leaves from the stems. Finely chop the leaves and put them into a heatproof jug (pitcher). Pour 60 ml/2 fl oz (¼ cup) water into a small saucepan and bring to the boil. Once boiling, carefully pour it over the mint leaves, stir through and leave to steep until they are cooled. Add the vinegar and sugar to taste and stir to dissolve the sugar. Taste again, adding more vinegar or sugar if needed, and serve.

ENGLAND
*

CIDER SAUCE

This creamy cider sauce should be served with a pork dish or in lieu of a rich cider gravy.

Serves: 4
Prep time: 5 minutes
Cook time: 10 minutes
{☙}{☕}{✕}

- left-over fat and juices from pan-fried or roasted pork, with the roasting pan set aside as well
- 50 ml/1¾ fl oz (3½ tablespoons) cider vinegar
- 200 ml/7 fl oz (¾ cup plus 1 tablespoon) dry cider
- 1 teaspoon plain (all-purpose) flour
- 20 ml/¾ fl oz double (heavy) cream (optional)
- salt

* Put the roasting pan (the one used to cook the pork) on the stove and heat it over a medium heat. Stir in the left-over roasting juices and melted fat, scraping off any bits of pork still stuck to the pan using a wooden spoon. You can add some of the vinegar to help release any bits of pork as well.
* Increase the heat to high, and, when bubbling, add the cider and vinegar. Cook for 5 minutes, or until reduced by half.
* Whisk in the flour until combined, then cook, stirring frequently, for another 2 minutes, or until the sauce is thickened to your liking. Season, add the cream (if using) and cook for 1 minute until just combined. Serve.

UNITED KINGDOM
*

HORSERADISH SAUCE

A big dollop of creamy horseradish sauce is enough to lift cold slices of roast beef into the realm of fantasy. Serve with good brown bread and smoked salmon for a classic Christmas pairing.

Serves: 6
Prep time: 10 minutes, plus 30 minutes steeping
{♨}{♠}{☙}{♟}

- 4 tablespoons freshly grated horseradish
- 2 tablespoons cider vinegar
- 1 teaspoon caster (superfine) sugar
- 150 ml/5 fl oz (⅔ cup) double (heavy) cream

* Put the grated horseradish into a medium bowl, add the vinegar and leave the horseradish to steep in it for 30 minutes.
* Add the sugar, then stir in the cream and whisk or beat with a spoon until it thickens. Serve immediately.

UNITED KINGDOM
*

CRANBERRY SAUCE

This Christmas staple deserves a place of honour beside the bronzed roast turkey. British cranberry sauce is characterized by the inclusion of a little port. Some modern recipes receive an extra kick from a little chilli and ginger.

Makes: 300 ml/ 10 fl oz (1¼ cups)
Prep time: 5 minutes
Cook time: 15 minutes

{❂}{◆}{♨}{♠}{◞◟}{♨}

- 500 g/ 1 lb 2 oz fresh or frozen cranberries
- juice of 2 oranges and grated zest of 1
- 60 ml/ 2 fl oz (¼ cup) port
- ¼ teaspoon ground ginger
- cinnamon stick
- caster (superfine) sugar, to taste

* Put all the ingredients, except the sugar, into a large saucepan and simmer over a medium-low heat for 10 minutes, or until the cranberries begin to get a bit pulpy. Add sugar to taste, then carefully remove the cinnamon stick and leave to cool. You can either serve the sauce or pour it into a sterilized glass jar (page 464), leaving a 1 cm/½ inch head space, then cover and seal. Store the jar in the fridge for up to 1 month.

WALES
*

LAVER SAUCE

Cooked down with a piece of butter or some juices from the roasting pan, laver can be an excellent serving sauce for lamb or mutton. This sauce is best when served with meat from lamb or sheep that lived along coastal salt marshes, as the laver will intensify its flavour.

Serves: 6
Prep time: 5 minutes
Cook time: 10 minutes

{♨}{◞◟}{♨}{✖}

- 300 ml/ 10 fl oz (1¼ cups) laver
- grated zest and juice of 1 orange
- 30 g/ 1 oz (2 tablespoons) butter (optional)
- 50 ml/ 1¾ fl oz (3½ tablespoons) roasting juices (optional)
- squeeze of lemon juice or dash of apple cider vinegar
- salt and pepper

* Put the laver, orange zest and juices and butter or roasting juices into a large saucepan, mix together, then cook over a medium heat for 10 minutes, or until the laver is heated through. When hot, add a squeeze of lemon or vinegar and mix through. Season with salt and pepper. Keep warm and serve with roast mutton or lamb.

ENGLAND
*

CUMBERLAND SAUCE

A traditional English sauce made from redcurrant jelly and port, Cumberland sauce is a classic accompaniment to pork, lamb, game, such as cold Roast Haunch of Venison (page 154) and gammon (ham). Serve chilled and do not strain out the zest.

Serves: 6
Prep time: 10 minutes
Cook time: 10 minutes

{❂}{◆}{♨}{♠}{◞◟}{♨}{✖}

- 1 orange
- 1 lemon
- 150–250 g/ 5–9 oz redcurrant jelly
(shop-bought or homemade, page 434)
- 150 ml/ 5 fl oz (⅔ cup) port
- 1 tablespoon red wine vinegar
- pinch of ground ginger
- salt and pepper

* Pare the peels from both the orange and lemon and thinly slice them into matchstick slivers. Put the sliced peel into a small saucepan with enough water to generously cover and bring to the boil. Boil for 1–2 minutes before draining out the liquid.
* Return the peel slivers to the saucepan, add the orange and lemon juices, 150 g/ 5 oz of the jelly, the port, vinegar and ginger. Stir through and heat over a low heat for 3–5 minutes. Season, then taste and add more redcurrant jelly, if needed. Leave to cool before serving.

UNITED KINGDOM
*

DAMSON SAUCE

A sweet serving sauce for game or red meat. Use interchangeably with Cumberland Sauce (page 415) – although damson sauce may be served warm.

Serves: 6
Prep time: 5 minutes
Cook time: 30 minutes
{ǔ}{♠}{å}{▮}{⤙}{▤}

- 300 g/11 oz damsons
- 200 ml/7 fl oz (¾ cup plus 1 tablespoon) red wine
- 200 ml/7 fl oz (¾ cup plus 1 tablespoon) port
- 1 star anise or cinnamon stick
- juice of 1 lemon
- juice of 1 orange
- 3 tablespoons redcurrant jelly
(shop-bought or homemade, page 434)
- salt and pepper

* Put the damsons, wine, port and spices into a large saucepan, cover with a lid and bring to the boil. Reduce the heat to medium and simmer for 15 minutes, or until the damsons are very soft and pulpy. Pass the sauce through a sieve into a large bowl, forcing as much pulp as possible with the back of a spoon.
* Clean the pan and pour the damson sauce back into it. Add the lemon and orange juices and jelly and slowly bring to a simmer over a low-medium heat, long enough to allow the jelly to dissolve. Season to taste and add more redcurrant jelly, if desired. Serve.

ENGLAND
*

BREAD SAUCE

This is the last 'descendant' of the many English bread sauces, which were made during medieval times and utilized fresh breadcrumbs primarily as thickener. Today's bread sauce is a creamy and lightly spiced sauce and an essential serving alongside most game birds, such as Roast Pheasant (page 158) or Roast Grouse (page 156).

Serves: 4
Prep time: 15 minutes
Cook time: 30 minutes
{ǔ}{⤙}{▤}

- 1 onion, quartered
- 4 cloves
- 1 bay leaf
- 500 ml/17 fl oz (2 cups plus 1 tablespoon)
full-fat (whole) milk
- 100 g/3½ oz (1½ cups) breadcrumbs from a stale loaf
- pinch of cayenne pepper
- pinch of ground mace
- pinch of ground nutmeg
- 60 g/2¼ oz (½ stick) butter
- 3 tablespoons double (heavy) cream
- salt and white pepper

* Stud the onion with the cloves, then put the onion into a large saucepan, add the bay leaf and milk and heat over a low heat until the milk reaches scalding point or 83°C/ 181°F on a thermometer.
* Simmer very gently for 5–10 minutes, then remove and discard the onion and bay leaf and whisk in the bread-crumbs. Bring to a simmer over a medium-low heat and cook for 15 minutes, or until thick.
* Season well with salt and white pepper, then add the remaining spices. Using a wooden spoon, stir through the butter and cream, then pour into a sauce boat or large bowl and serve.

UNITED KINGDOM
*

WHITE SAUCE
FOUNDATION SAUCE

A British white sauce, sometimes known as 'foundation sauce', is made from a roux of butter and flour, to which milk (and sometimes stock) and spices are added. It is analogous to the French bechamel (and velouté), although its earliest recipes predate the codifying works of French chefs Escoffier and Carême in the nineteenth century.
A legion of sauces can be made using this as a foundation, including Parsley Sauce (page 420), Watercress Sauce (page 424), Onion Sauce (page 418) and Mustard Sauce (page 423). Other common additions to white sauce were capers, dill or chopped fennel.

Makes: 600 ml/20 fl oz (2½ cups)
Prep time: 5 minutes
Cook time: 30 minutes
{ǔ}{⤙}{▤}

- 500 ml/17 fl oz (2 cups plus 1 tablespoon)
full-fat (whole) milk
- 1 small onion, quartered
- 1 bay leaf
- 2 cloves
- ¼ nutmeg or ½ blade mace
- 12 black peppercorns, lightly crushed
- 60 g/2¼ oz (½ stick) butter
- 40 g/1½ oz (⅓ cup) plain (all-purpose) flour
- 100 ml/3½ fl oz (⅓ cup plus 1 tablespoon) single (light)
cream or extra milk
- salt and pepper

* Pour the milk into a large saucepan, add the onion, bay leaf, cloves, nutmeg or mace and peppercorns and bring gently to a simmer over a medium heat. Cover with a lid and simmer for 10 minutes, or until infused. Strain into a jug (pitcher) and set aside.
* Melt the butter in the saucepan over a medium-low heat for 2 minutes, or until foaming. Stir in the flour and cook for 2–3 minutes, stirring frequently to prevent lumps and without colouring. Slowly whisk in the reserved milk, making sure it is fully combined before you add more. Reduce the heat to very low and simmer, stirring frequently, for 15 minutes. Remove from the heat, add the cream or more milk and season to taste with salt and pepper.

Bread sauce

ENGLAND
*

WHITE ONION SAUCE

Onion sauces, both white and brown, have a long tradition in English cooking. A creamy white onion sauce is made using the basic Foundation Sauce (page 416), some double (heavy) cream and a whole onion. It can be served with most boiled meats, though traditionally rabbit, duck, goose and sometimes tripe.

Serves 4
Prep time: 10 minutes
Cook time: 40 minutes
{🍷}{🥄}{🍲}

- 1 large white onion, or equivalent, peeled but left whole
- ½ quantity Melted Butter Sauce (page 420)
or Foundation Sauce (page 416)
- 75 ml/ 2½ fl oz (⅓ cup) double (heavy) cream (optional)
- salt and white pepper

* Put the onion into a small saucepan. Cover with water, bring to a simmer over a low-medium heat and cook for 40 minutes, or until tender.
* Meanwhile, make or heat through the sauce following the recipe on pages 420 or 416.
* Remove the onion from the water and coarsely chop. Once cool enough, blend to a purée in a food processor. Stir into the sauce, then stir in the cream (if using the butter sauce) and season with salt and pepper.

UNITED KINGDOM
*

PEPPERCORN SAUCE

This rich and creamy sauce is an adaptation of the French *sauce au poivre*; the peppercorns are lightly crushed to help release their flavour, but still provide that extra burst of spice. Serve with beef – steak, especially.

Serves: 4
Prep time: 5 minutes
Cook time: 20 minutes
{🍲}{🥄}{🍲}{🍴}

- 1 tablespoon butter
- 2 shallots, finely diced
- 2 teaspoons black peppercorns, lightly crushed
- 30 ml/ 1 fl oz (2 tablespoons) brandy
- 100 ml/ 3½ fl oz (⅓ cup plus 1 tablespoon)
red wine or dry white wine for a lighter sauce
- 200 ml/ 7 fl oz (¾ cup plus 1 tablespoon)
beef or chicken stock
- 75 ml/ 2½ fl oz (⅓ cup) double (heavy) cream
- salt

* Heat the butter in a large saucepan over a medium heat, add the shallots and fry for 8 minutes, or until soft and translucent. Add the crushed peppercorns, then add the brandy and wine and cook for 5 minutes, or until it is reduced by half. Add the stock and cook for another 5 minutes, or until the liquid is reduced by a little more than

half. Add the cream and simmer for 2–3 minutes, or until it has thickened to a good pouring consistency. Season to taste with salt and serve.

UNITED KINGDOM
*

STEAK SAUCE

Traditional British steak sauce is characterized by the use of Mushroom Ketchup (page 426) and sometimes pickled walnut or the liquor from a jar of Pickled Walnuts (page 446). Victorian cookery writer Mrs Beeton was one of the first to put forward such a steak sauce, in her 1861 classic *The Book of Household Management*. It is spicy, tangy and umami.

Serves: 6
Prep time: 10 minutes
Cook time: 25 minutes
{🍲}{🍲}

- 25 g/ 1 oz (2 tablespoons) butter
- 1 onion, finely chopped
- 2 cloves garlic, finely chopped
- 200 g/ 7 oz mushrooms, sliced
- 2 tablespoons Mushroom Ketchup (page 426)
- 2 Pickled Walnuts (page 446), finely diced
- 50–75 ml/ 1¾–2½ fl oz
(¼ cup minus 2 teaspoons–⅓ cup) brandy
- 100 ml/ 3½ fl oz (⅓ cup plus 1 tablespoon) chicken stock
- 250 ml/ 8 fl oz (1 cup) double (heavy) cream
- 2 tablespoons finely chopped flat-leaf parsley
- salt and pepper

* Melt the butter in a large saucepan over a medium heat, add the onion and garlic and fry for 10–15 minutes until they turn golden. Increase the heat to medium-high, add the mushrooms and fry for 6–7 minutes, or until the pan is quite dry. Add the Ketchup and Pickled Walnuts, then add the brandy, stock and cream and cook for another 5 minutes. Remove from the heat, stir through the parsley, season to taste with salt and pepper and serve. This sauce can also be strained, if desired.

SCOTLAND
*

WHISKY CREAM SAUCE

For something so ostensibly Scottish, whisky sauce has a rather thin history. In fact, it seems to be a rather recent invention of Scottish restaurant and hotel kitchens. That shouldn't make it any less enjoyable. Serve with Haggis with Neeps and Tatties (page 192), or try it with steak, in lieu of a peppercorn sauce. Don't waste expensive whisky on this – there's no need to use single malt in this recipe.

Serves: 4
Prep time: 5 minutes
Cook time: 10 minutes
{🍲}{🥄}{🍲}{🍴}

- 1 tablespoon butter
- 1 tablespoon rapeseed (canola) oil
- 2 shallots, finely diced
- 100 ml/3½ fl oz (⅓ cup plus 1 tablespoon) whisky
- 2 teaspoons wholegrain mustard
- 250 ml/8 fl oz (1 cup) double (heavy) cream
- 150 ml/5 fl oz (⅔ cup) beef stock (optional, depending on what meat it will accompany)
- salt and pepper

* Heat the butter and oil in a large saucepan over a medium heat, add the shallots and fry for 10 minutes, or until softened and translucent. Add the whisky and cook for 2 minutes, or until it has evaporated slightly – this may flame up so be careful. Stir in the mustard, then pour in the cream and simmer for 5–10 minutes. Season to taste with salt and pepper. Alternatively, add the mustard and beef stock at the same time and cook for 5–10 minutes, or until reduced by half, then add the cream and continue with the rest of the recipe. Serve.

ENGLAND
*

WOW-WOW SAUCE

This sharp and tangy sauce was originally created by Georgian optician and cook William Kitchiner in the early 1800s. Kitchiner devised this sauce as an ideal pairing for beef, but a thicker condiment version of wow-wow sauce – made more like a tangy English mustard – can be used for meats of all kinds.

Serves: 6
Prep time: 10 minutes
Cook time: 30 minutes

- 500 ml/17 fl oz (2 cups plus 1 tablespoon) beef stock
- 60 g/2¼ oz (½ stick) butter
- 30 g/1 oz (3¾ tablespoons) plain (all-purpose) flour
- 1 tablespoon cider or wine vinegar
- 1 tablespoon Mushroom Ketchup (page 426)
- 1 tablespoon port
- 1 teaspoon English mustard
- 1 teaspoon small capers
- 2 tablespoons finely chopped flat-leaf parsley leaves
- 3 Pickled Walnuts (page 446), cut into very small dice

* Heat the beef stock in a large saucepan over a medium heat for 5 minutes, or until hot. Remove from the heat and set aside.
* Heat the butter in a medium saucepan over a medium-low heat for 2 minutes, or until foaming. Whisk in the flour and cook for 2–3 minutes, then gradually whisk in the hot stock, making sure it is fully combined before you add more. Add the remaining ingredients, except the parsley and walnuts, and simmer for 15 minutes. Remove from the heat, stir through the parsley and walnuts and leave to rest a few seconds to heat through. Serve.

UNITED KINGDOM
*

BRITISH CURRY SAUCE

This Anglicized curry sauce is more the sort you will find in chip shops, rather than Indian restaurants. It will surprise exactly no one, then, that is perhaps better suited to Chips (page 84) drizzled with a little malt vinegar, or thickened and served alongside Battered Fish (page 112).

Serves: 6
Prep time: 10 minutes
Cook time: 35 minutes

{ ✎ } { 🍲 }

- 300 ml/10 fl oz (1¼ cups) chicken or vegetable stock
- 30 g/1 oz (2 tablespoons) butter
- ½ onion, very finely chopped
- 2 cloves
- 30 g/1 oz (3¾ tablespoons) plain (all-purpose) flour
- 1 teaspoon curry powder
- 200 ml/7 fl oz (¾ cup plus 1 tablespoon) full-fat (whole) milk
- 75 ml/2½ fl oz (⅓ cup) double (heavy) cream
- salt

* Heat the stock in a medium saucepan over a medium heat for 5 minutes, or until hot, then remove from the heat and set aside.
* Melt the butter in a large saucepan over a medium heat, add the onion and cloves and fry for 12–15 minutes until the onion is golden. Sift in the flour and curry powder and cook for 2 minutes, before gradually ladling in the hot stock and beating with a whisk as you go to produce a smooth sauce. Reduce the heat to low-medium and simmer for 10 minutes, stirring occasionally. Mix in the milk and simmer for another 5 minutes, before stirring in the cream. Add salt to taste, then strain into a jug (pitcher) and serve.

UNITED KINGDOM

*

GRAVY

I love the ease and versatility of British gravies. Of course, most start the same way: roasting juices and fat, cooked down with stock and often flour; but with the simplest of additions – 1–2 tablespoons of Mint Sauce (page 414) or good Redcurrant Jelly (page 434), a splash of cider or diced onion – they can be tailor-made to pair with the meat in question. Simply put, a jug of good gravy is a roast's best friend.

Serves: 6
Prep time: 5–10 minutes
Cook time: 20–30 minutes
{🥄}{🍴}

- about 300 ml/10 fl oz (1¼ cups) stock of choice
- roasting pan juices (whatever juices are available)
- 30 g/1 oz (3¾ tablespoons) plain (all-purpose) flour, sifted
- 100 ml/3½ fl oz (⅓ cup plus 1 tablespoon) wine, cider or stout

- For onion gravy:
- 60 g/2¼ oz (½ stick) butter
- 2 large white onions, diced
- 1 teaspoon thyme leaves

- For the flavourings (optional):
- 1 tablespoon mustard and cider for pork
- 1 tablespoon Redcurrant Jelly (shop-bought or homemade, page 434) for game
- 1 bunch mint and 1 tablespoon vinegar or 1 tablespoon Mint Sauce (page 414) for lamb
- red wine for beef
- white wine for chicken
- 1 sprig rosemary
- 1 sprig thyme

* Heat the stock in a medium saucepan over a medium heat for 5 minutes, or until hot, then remove from the heat and set aside.
* Pour the juices from the roasting pan into a clear jar or bowl and leave to settle. Skim off as much fat as possible using a slotted spoon, but set aside 1 tablespoon or so in case more liquid is required later.
* If making an onion gravy, heat a large saucepan over a medium heat, add the butter and once it's melted, add the diced onions and thyme and fry for 12–15 minutes until golden brown.
* Add the juices to the pan, then whisk in the flour, adding a little fat from the settled juice, if necessary. Cook for 5 minutes, then add the wine or cider and whisk until smooth.
* Add enough hot stock to the juices to bring to 400 ml/ 14 fl oz (1⅔ cups) in total. Add the hot stock slowly, whisking constantly to keep the sauce smooth. Add the remaining appropriate herbs and flavourings, then simmer for 10 minutes. Taste and adjust the seasoning, remove the herbs and pour into a jug (pitcher). Strain before serving if you prefer a very smooth gravy.

WALES / ENGLAND

*

PARSLEY SAUCE

A classic English parsley sauce is made quite simply by adding chopped parsley and cream to a basic white sauce. In Wales, however, parsley sauce was made by using the starchy water from boiled potatoes, which was thickened with flour and flavoured with just a splash of milk. Parsley sauce can be served with any fish and poured over either gammon (ham) steaks or bacon chops.

Serves: 4
Prep time: 10 minutes
Cook time: 30 minutes
{🥄}{🍴}{🍲}

- 1 quantity Foundation Sauce (page 416) or ½ quantity Foundation Sauce, and ½ quantity fish stock, if serving with fish
- 3 tablespoons finely chopped flat-leaf parsley
- 75 ml/2½ fl oz (⅓ cup) double (heavy) cream
- juice of ½ lemon (optional)
- salt and white pepper

* Make the sauce in a large saucepan following the recipe on page 416. Stir in the parsley and cream. Add the lemon if serving with fish and season with salt and pepper. Serve.

ENGLAND

*

MELTED BUTTER SAUCE

This traditional butter sauce can be poured over cooked meats, or used as the base for more complex sauces.

Serves: 4
Prep time: 5 minutes
Cook time: 20 minutes
{🥄}{🍴}{🍲}{🔪}

- 200 g/7 oz (1¾ sticks) butter, diced and softened
- pinch each of ground pepper and grated nutmeg (optional)
- 20 g/¾ oz (4 teaspoons) plain (all-purpose) flour
- 150 ml/5 fl oz (⅔ cup) water, full-fat (whole) milk or stock (dependent on taste and serving)
- 1 tablespoon lemon juice (optional)
- salt and pepper

* Melt about a third of the butter in a large saucepan over a medium heat. Sprinkle in the spices (if using), then slowly whisk in the flour and cook for another 2–3 minutes, before beating in the liquid until smooth. Once smooth, heat to a bare simmer, then cook for 15 minutes, stirring frequently.
* Reduce the heat to low, add the remaining butter, a few cubes at a time, and whisk until the mixture is smooth again. Add the lemon juice (if using) and salt and pepper to taste. Serve.

UNITED KINGDOM
*

BLACK BUTTER SAUCE

Many old English cookbooks and traditional recipes call for 'black butter sauce', which is really just what the French call *beurre noisette*. Serve over fish with capers or over roast beef.

Serves: 4
Prep time: 5 minutes
Cook time: 10 minutes
{ⓥ}{🌡}{✏}{🍱}{🫙}{✗}

- 250 g/ 9 oz (2¼ sticks) butter, cut into pieces

* Put the butter into a medium saucepan over a low heat and cook, whisking frequently, for 10 minutes, or until the butter solids start to caramelize, turn brown and pick up a nutty aroma. (Watch out, as the butter can go from brown to burned very quickly!)
* Once browned, immediately remove from the heat, strain into a serving jug (pitcher)and set aside to serve.

UNITED KINGDOM
*

SHRIMP SAUCE

A rich sauce based on the luxury fish sauces of Victorian cooking, to be used with any preparation of white or flatfish.

Serves: 4
Prep time: 10 minutes
Cook time: 20 minutes
{✏}

- 300 g/ 11 oz cooked brown shrimps, peeled,
with shells and heads kept on
- 150 g/ 5 oz (1¼ sticks) butter
- 1 tablespoon plain (all-purpose) flour
- pinch of grated mace or nutmeg
- pinch of cayenne pepper
- lemon juice, to taste
- 20 ml/ ¾ fl oz (4 teaspoons)
double (heavy) cream (optional)
- salt

* Put the shrimp shells into a large saucepan, cover with 300 ml/ 10 fl oz (1¼ cups) water and simmer over a low-medium heat for 10 minutes. Strain the shrimp stock into a large container, pressing lightly on the shells as you strain the liquid to extract as much from them as possible. Add as much water as needed to bring the volume back up to 300 ml/ 10 fl oz (1¼ cups). Set aside.
* Melt the butter in another large saucepan over a medium heat, whisk in the flour to make a roux, then cook for 2–3 minutes, stirring frequently to prevent lumps.
* Pour in the shrimp stock a little at a time, stirring constantly to keep the sauce smooth, then cook over a medium heat for 3–5 minutes, or until it starts to thicken. Add the spices, lemon juice to taste and the cream (if using). Cook for another 2–3 minutes, or until slightly thickened to a good pouring consistency. Add the cooked shrimps and check the seasoning. Serve.

UNITED KINGDOM
*

LOBSTER SAUCE

Rich and creamy lobster sauce is traditionally made using the coral (eggs) from lobsters, which, pounded into butter, is then added to a white foundation sauce. Serve with any excellent white fish.

Serves: 4
Preparation time: 10 minutes
Cook time: 20 minutes
{✏}

- meat and coral of 1 cooked lobster
- 175 ml/ 6 fl oz (¾ cup) full-fat (whole) milk
- 175 ml/ 6 fl oz (¾ cup) fish stock
(made using lobster shells, optional)
- ½ onion
- 1 bay leaf
- a few black peppercorns
- 30 g/ 1 oz (2 tablespoons) unsalted butter
- 30 g/ 1 oz (3¾ tablespoons) plain (all-purpose) flour
- pinch cayenne pepper
- lemon juice, to taste
- salt

* Mash and then press the lobster coral through a fine-mesh sieve into a bowl. Chop the meat and set both aside.
* Pour the milk and fish stock into a large saucepan. Add the onion, bay leaf and peppercorns and bring gently to a simmer over a medium-low heat. Simmer for 10 minutes, or until infused, then strain into a jug (pitcher).
* Melt the butter in the pan over a medium-low heat for 2 minutes, or until foaming. Stir in the flour and cook for 2–3 minutes, stirring frequently to prevent lumps. Slowly whisk in the strained milk, a little at a time, making sure it is fully combined before you add more. Repeat until all the milk is used up, then simmer very gently over a low heat, stirring frequently, for 15 minutes, or until it has thickened slightly. Add the mashed coral, chopped meat and cayenne and stir well until completely combined. Season with lemon juice and salt to taste.

UNITED KINGDOM
*

OYSTER SAUCE

This sauce might seem grossly extravagant by today's standards, but in Victorian times oysters were in great abundance. As with other luxury sauces such as Lobster Sauce (page 421), serve with the best quality white fish, such as turbot, brill or the like. Luxury with luxury.

Serves: 6
Prep time: 30 minutes
Cook time: 20 minutes
{⁎}

- 250 ml/8 fl oz (1 cup) full-fat (whole) milk
- 50 g/2 oz (3½ tablespoons) butter
- 50 g/2 oz (6 tablespoons) plain (all-purpose) flour
- 12 oysters, shucked (page 124), liquor reserved and oysters coarsely chopped
- 150 ml/5 fl oz (⅔ cup) double (heavy) cream
- juice of ½ lemon
- pinch of cayenne pepper
- ½ teaspoon anchovy essence (optional)
- salt and pepper

* Pour the milk into a medium saucepan over a medium heat for 3–4 minutes until hot. Remove from the heat and set aside.
* Melt the butter in a large saucepan over a medium heat. Whisk in the flour and cook for 3–4 minutes, stirring constantly, then pour in the hot milk and stir through the chopped oysters. Simmer for 10 minutes, then add the cream, lemon juice, cayenne, and the oyster liquor. If there is not quite enough oyster liquor left, add the anchovy essence. Season to taste with salt and pepper.

UNITED KINGDOM
*

CAPER LEMON BUTTER SAUCE

This spruced-up butter sauce is the ideal pairing for any fish dish, accentuating, but not overpowering the subtle flavours.

Serves: 4
Prep time: 10 minutes
Cook time: 10 minutes
{⁎}{⁎}{⁎}{⁎}{⁎}

- 1 teaspoon rapeseed (canola) oil
- 2 tablespoons small capers
- juice of 1 lemon
- 100 g/3½ oz (7 tablespoons) cold unsalted butter, diced
- 2 teaspoons very finely chopped flat-leaf parsley (optional)
- salt and pepper

* Heat the oil in a small saucepan over a medium heat, add the capers, crushing them with the back of a wooden spoon, then add the lemon juice and bring to the boil over a medium heat for 4–5 minutes until the

liquid has almost evaporated. Remove from the heat and, using a small whisk, beat in the butter, a cube at a time. Season to taste, then add the parsley (if using).
* Pour into a sauce boat and serve.

UNITED KINGDOM
*

ORANGE SAUCE

Sweet and savoury orange sauces appear in English cookbooks as far back as the late seventeenth or early eighteenth century, when they were served with everything from poultry to veal or asparagus. Today, orange sauces are almost exclusively served with duck – a likely inspiration from the French duck à l'orange.

Serves: 6
Prep time: 10 minutes
Cook time: 20 minutes
{⁎}{⁎}

- 30 g/1 oz (2 tablespoons) butter
- 30 g/1 oz (3¾ tablespoons) plain (all-purpose) flour
- 600 ml/20 fl oz (2½ cups) pan juices (if for a roast), topped up (topped off) with beef, game or duck stock
- grated zest and juice of 2 Seville oranges
- 90 ml/3¼ fl oz (6 tablespoons) port
- 30 g/1 oz (2½ tablespoons) caster (superfine) sugar (optional)
- salt and pepper

* Melt the butter in a large saucepan over a medium heat. Whisk in the flour and cook, whisking constantly for 4–5 minutes until it turns a pale golden brown. While whisking, gradually add the pan juices and stock mixture until fully incorporated and the sauce is smooth. Bring to a simmer and cook for 15 minutes, stirring occasionally. Stir in the orange zest and juice, port, salt and pepper. Taste and add sugar, if desired – you may not need it all. Pass through a sieve into a jug (pitcher) and serve.

SCOTLAND
*

EGG SAUCE

This rich egg sauce is of Scottish origin, and traditionally served with white fish. While it is rare if not unknown today, its potential was recognized by the famous French chef Auguste Escoffier, who included a recipe for it in his magnum opus Le Guide Culinaire.

Serves: 4
Prep time: 15 minutes
Cook time: 10 minutes
{⁎}{⁎}{⁎}{⁎}{⁎}

- 4 eggs
- 1 quantity Melted Butter Sauce (page 420) or 300 ml/10 fl oz (1¼ cups) White Sauce (page 416)
- ½ teaspoon English mustard
- salt and pepper

* Bring a medium saucepan of water to the boil, then reduce the heat to low-medium heat and carefully add the eggs using a slotted spoon. Cook for 10 minutes, then drain and cool completely under cold running water. Shell and halve the eggs. Set aside.
* Meanwhile, make the butter sauce in another medium saucepan following the recipe on page 420, then gently heat over a medium-low heat. Scoop out the yolks from the hard-boiled eggs and whisk them into the sauce.
* Finely dice the egg whites and add to a bowl with the mustard. Mix through, then tip them into the sauce. Heat through, season with salt and pepper and serve.

ENGLAND
*

GOOSEBERRY SAUCE

This sauce is typically made to serve alongside mackerel – gooseberries have a natural tartness which helps to cut through oily fish. Grilled (broiled) mackerel with a little gooseberry sauce and a dollop of good English mustard makes for a most excellent al fresco summer lunch.

Serves: 4
Prep time: 5 minutes
Cook time: 10–15 minutes
{♥}{♨}{✋}{♟}{✗}

- 250 g/9 oz gooseberries, topped and tailed
- 60 ml/2 fl oz (¼ cup) white wine
or a dash of cider vinegar
- 60 g/2¼ oz (⅓ cup) caster (superfine) sugar,
or more to taste
- ¼ teaspoon ground ginger
- 30 g/1 oz (2 tablespoons) butter
or 3 tablespoons double (heavy) cream
- salt and pepper

* Heat the gooseberries, 60 ml/2 fl oz (¼ cup) water and the wine or vinegar in a large saucepan over a low-medium heat and cook for several minutes until the gooseberries are very soft. Add the sugar and ginger, then season with salt and pepper. Beat in the butter with a whisk until glossy (if using) or stir in the cream. Add more sugar, if desired and adjust the seasoning, if necessary. Serve.
* Note: If a smooth sauce is required, then after the gooseberries have softened, remove the pan from the heat, pulse the gooseberries with a hand-held blender, then push through a sieve before returning to the heat.

SCOTLAND / ENGLAND
*

MUSTARD SAUCE

In England, fish has been served with a creamy mustard sauce as far back as Thomas Dawson's *The Good Huswifes Jewell* (1596). In Scotland, however, food writer Catherine Brown attributes regional recipes – for fish in mustard sauce – to significant Nordic influence on its western coast. While tradition dictates serving this with fish, it would work just as well with pork or even chicken.

Serves: 4
Prep time: 20 minutes
Cook time: 5 minutes
{♥}{♨}{✗}

- 1 quantity Melted Butter Sauce (page 420) or Foundation
Sauce (page 416)
- 1 teaspoon English mustard
- 2 teaspoons wholegrain mustard
- 75 ml/2 ½ fl oz (⅓ cup) double (heavy) cream (optional)
- granulated sugar (optional)
- salt and pepper

* Make either sauce following the recipe on pages 420 or 416, then heat in a large saucepan over a medium heat for 5 minutes, or until warm. Whisk in the mustards. If you are using a Foundation Sauce as your base, add the cream and stir through. Season to taste with salt and pepper, adding a little sugar or more mustard, if desired. Serve.

UNITED KINGDOM
*

TARTARE SAUCE

Tartare sauce is made from an enticingly simple preparation of mayonnaise, mixed through with chopped herbs, gherkins and capers. Make fresh and serve lightly chilled (if possible) with fish – especially Battered Fish and Chips (page 112).

Makes: 350 ml/12 fl oz
Prep time: 5 minutes
{♥}{♨}{✋}{✗}

- 1 tablespoon finely chopped flat-leaf parsley
- 1 tablespoon finely chopped tarragon
- 2 tablespoons finely chopped gherkins or cornichons
- grated zest of 1 lemon
- 2 tablespoons capers, drained and finely chopped
- 250 g/9 oz (1 cup plus 1 tablespoon)
Mayonnaise (page 427)
- lemon juice, to taste

Put the herbs, gherkins, lemon zest, capers and mayonnaise into a large bowl and stir through well. Taste and add a little lemon juice, if needed. Serve.

ENGLAND
*

WATERCRESS SAUCE

A classic sauce to serve with fish, and a punchier alternative to the more soothing parsley sauce.

Serves: 4
Prep time: 10 minutes
Cook time: 30 minutes
{⌐}{🍲}

- ½ quantity Foundation Sauce (page 416)
- fish stock equal to the amount of Foundation Sauce
- 1 large handful watercress, coarsely chopped
- 75 ml/2½ fl oz (⅓ cup) double (heavy) cream
- juice of ½ lemon
- salt and white pepper

* Make or warm through the Foundation Sauce in a large saucepan following the recipe on page 416, before adding in an equal amount of fish stock. Simmer over a medium heat for 5 minutes, then stir in the watercress and cream and cook for another 2–3 minutes. Stir in the lemon juice, then season with salt and pepper. Serve.

ENGLAND
*

GREEN SAUCE

This is a simple uncooked sauce made from chopped herbs. The name green sauce may conjure up images of Spanish cooking, but, lest we forget, mint sauce is part of the same family – and plenty of these herby sauces date back in English cooking as far as the twelfth century, if not earlier. Here is a slightly more modern take, to be served cold with meat or fish.

Makes: 500 ml/17 fl oz (2 cups)
Prep time: 15 minutes
{🝆}{🔪}{⌐}{✗}

- 300 g/11 oz herbs (an even mix of parsley, mint, tarragon), finely chopped
- 1 shallot, finely chopped
- 1 clove garlic, finely chopped
- 100 g/3½ oz (½ cup) capers, drained and chopped
- 200 ml/7 fl oz (¾ cup plus 1 tablespoon) rapeseed (canola) oil
- 1 tablespoon mustard
- 1 tablespoon red wine vinegar
- salt and pepper

* Put the herbs, shallot, garlic and capers into a food processor. Pour in the oil and pulse. It's important to maintain texture, so don't over-blend it. You want a loose sauce and not a paste. Add the mustard and vinegar and pulse again quickly to combine. Season to taste with salt and pepper and serve.

UNITED KINGDOM
*

HOLLANDAISE SAUCE

A creamy sauce made from emulsified melted butter and egg yolks, and very much lifted by a little lemon. Typically associated with French cooking, hollandaise has always been adopted into the British kitchen, where it is typically served with fish or poached eggs and tender cooked greens such as asparagus or even sea kale (page 74).

Serves: 4
Prep time: 10 minutes
Cook time: 10–15 minutes
{🥄}{🝆}{⌐}{✗}

- 125 g/4¼ oz (9 tablespoons) butter, diced
- 2 large egg yolks
- juice of ½ lemon
- salt and pepper

* Fill a saucepan about halfway with water and bring it to a simmer.
* Meanwhile, melt the butter in another saucepan slowly over a low heat. Once melted, remove from the heat and leave to cool before skimming the milk solids off the top.
* Put the egg yolks and vinegar into a heatproof bowl that will fit over the saucepan without touching the water, and whisk for about 30 seconds, before setting the bowl on top of the saucepan. Keep whisking, but make sure that you keep the saucepan over a low heat, otherwise the eggs will scramble.
* Slowly add the melted butter, whisking constantly, until it has been completely incorporated. Add a little of the lemon juice at a time (you won't need it all) to loosen up the sauce, then season with salt and pepper and serve.

UNITED KINGDOM
*

ENGLISH MUSTARD

English-style mustard has a distinctive bright yellow colour, and a hot pungent flavour that's equally memorable. Friend to all manner of cold and hot meats, including roasts, pork pies, ham sandwiches and even savoury puddings. When it comes to English mustard, a little goes a long way.

Makes: 4 tablespoons
Prep time: 5 minutes, plus 15 minutes steeping
{🥄}{🍴}{🝆}{🔪}{⌐}{🧂}{✗}

- 2 tablespoons English mustard powder
- 1 tablespoon cider vinegar

* Put the mustard powder into a small bowl, add 1 tablespoon water and the vinegar (or 2 tablespoons water) and whisk the powder into the liquids until combined. Leave to steep for about 15 minutes before tasting and adding more liquid or mustard powder to adjust the strength. It should maintain its pungency.

UNITED KINGDOM
*

TOMATO KETCHUP

A vinegar-based tomato relish that is spiced and sweetened with sugar, the first recipes for British tomato ketchup occur in the early 1800s. The word ketchup comes to English from the word *kêtsiap*, a fermented fish sauce, and, according to *The Oxford Companion to Food* it is also linguistically related to the Malay 'kecap', meaning soy sauce. Some fruity ketchups such as Rhubarb or Damson (page 426) are still made and used similarly, but differ strongly from the thinner Mushroom Ketchup (page 426) – perhaps the earliest of its kind.

Makes: 750 ml/25 fl oz (3 cups)
Prep time: 10 minutes, plus 1 month maturing
Cook time: 2 hours 15 minutes
{🍅}{◊}{🌢}{🔪}{•}

- 2 kg/4½ lb tomatoes, chopped
- 1 stalk celery, diced
- 2 onions, diced
- 1 clove garlic, chopped
- 150 g/5 oz (¾ cup) caster (superfine) sugar
- 1 teaspoon cayenne pepper
- 1 teaspoon ground black pepper
- ½ teaspoon ground allspice
- ½ teaspoon ground cloves
- 15 g/½ oz (1 tablespoon) salt
- 300 ml/10 fl oz (1¼ cups) cider vinegar

* Put all the ingredients into a large saucepan and bring to the boil. Reduce the heat to low and simmer for 1–2 hours, stirring frequently. The mixture will be ready when it is reduced by about half. Leave to cool, then transfer to a food processor and blend until smooth. Press the mixture through a sieve to remove any bits, so it is a uniform consistency.
* Pour the smoothed mixture into the saucepan and heat over a low heat, stirring frequently, until it is reduced and thickened to your desired consistency. When stirring the mixture, it will spit and bubble so take care. Carefully pour into sterilized glass bottles (page 464), leaving a 1 cm/½ inch head space, then cover and seal.
* Keep in a cool, dark place for 1 month before using. Once open, keep in the fridge and use within 2 weeks.

UNITED KINGDOM
*

WALNUT KETCHUP

Walnut ketchup is a concentrated condiment made from the spiced liquor used to pickle walnuts. It is sharp and a touch sweet and provides depth to savoury stews in lieu of Mushroom Ketchup (page 426).

Makes: 800 ml/27 fl oz (3¼ cups)
Prep time: 8 days infusing, plus 3 months maturing
Cook time: 30 minutes
{🌢}{🔪}

- 24 fresh walnuts
- 60 g/2¼ oz (¼ cup) salt
- 500 ml/17 fl oz (2 cups plus 1 tablespoon) cider vinegar, or more
- 500 ml/17 fl oz (2 cups plus 1 tablespoon) port
- 3 blades mace
- 1½ nutmegs, broken up
- 2 teaspoons cloves
- 1 teaspoon ground ginger
- 2 teaspoons black peppercorns
- 2.5 cm/1 inch piece fresh horseradish, sliced
- 2 onions, chopped
- 90 g/3¼ oz salted anchovies

* Sprinkle the walnuts over a work counter and bruise them with a rolling pin, before adding them to a tight-fitting sterilized jar or pot (page 464). Add the salt and vinegar, ensuring that the walnuts are fully covered by the liquid. Seal with a lid and leave to infuse at room temperature for 8 days.
* Strain the walnut liquor into a medium saucepan and add the remaining ingredients. Bring to a simmer and cook for 30 minutes. Leave to cool slightly, then pour back into the re-sterilized jar or pot, cover, seal and leave in a cool, dark space for 2 weeks. Strain the liquor and pour back into the re-sterilized jar, cover and seal.
* Keep in a cool, dark place for 3 months before using. Once open, keep in the fridge and use within 2 months.

ENGLAND: CUMBRIA
*

RHUBARB (OR DAMSON) KETCHUP

This sweet relish can be made with rhubarb or damson plums, and has a similar versatility to Tomato Ketchup (page 425). It works well alongside meat, or in a breakfast roll.

Makes: 1 litre/ 34 fl oz (4¼ cups)
Prep time: 20 minutes, plus 3 months maturing
Cook time: 1½ hours
{♥}{♦}{♨}{♠}{♪}

- 1 tablespoon sunflower oil
- 240 g/ 8½ oz red onions, chopped
- 2 bay leaves
- 2 sprigs of fresh rosemary
- 1 teaspoon black peppercorns
- 1 teaspoon coriander seeds
- 1 star anise
- 2 dried chillies
- 25 g/ 1 oz fresh root ginger, grated
- 2 teaspoons ground ginger
- 1 kg/ 2¼ lb rhubarb or damson plums, trimmed and chopped
- 300 ml/ 10 fl oz (1¼ cups) red wine vinegar
- 300 g/ 11 oz (1½ cups) granulated sugar
- 1 tablespoon salt

* In a stockpot or large saucepan heat the oil over a medium heat and add the onions. Tie the bay leaves and rosemary together with kitchen string and add to the onions. Fry until the onions are translucent, about 10 minutes.
* Tie the spices together in a piece of muslin (cheesecloth) and add to the pan with the remaining ingredients. Turn up the heat and stir until the sugar has dissolved. Reduce the heat and simmer for a further 45 minutes, until everything is very soft and the volume has reduced significantly.
* Allow the mixture to cool slightly, then remove the tied herbs and spices, and process the mixture in a food processor or blender in batches until very smooth. Taste and add more salt if needed – it's best to slightly over season because the salt will be less pronounced once cooled. Pour into sterilized bottles or jars (page 464), leaving a 1 cm/ ½ inch head space, then cover and seal.
* Keep in a cool, dark place for 3 months before using. Once open, keep in the fridge and use within 1 month.

UNITED KINGDOM
*

MUSHROOM KETCHUP

A little goes a long way with this sauce – a thin concentration of mushrooms, spices and sometimes anchovy. Originally devised as a means of pickling mushrooms, over time the liquor itself became the focus. Today it is used to liven up savoury dishes and meaty stews, providing a heady measure of umami.

Makes: 750 ml/ 25 fl oz (3 cups)
Prep time: 15 minutes, plus 4 days resting and 3 months maturing
Cook time: 2 hours
{♥}{♦}{♨}{♠}{♪}

- 750 g/ 1 lb 10 oz mushrooms of choice, sliced
- 100 g/ 3½ oz (⅓ cup plus 4 teaspoons) salt

- Per 1 litre/ 34 fl oz (4¼ cups) liquor:
- ½ teaspoon cayenne pepper
- 2 teaspoons each allspice berries and ground ginger
- 2 blades mace and ½ nutmeg

* Arrange the mushrooms and the salt in layers in a large crock or a lidded plastic container. Cover and leave somewhere cool and dark for 24 hours. Over the following 2 days, stir, squeeze and mash the mushrooms to extrude the juice. Pour the liquor and mushrooms into a measuring jug (pitcher) and note the volume.
* Put the mushrooms and liquor into a large saucepan with the correct amount of spices, cover with a lid and simmer over a low heat for 2 hours. Remove from the heat and leave to cool and steep for 24 hours. Strain the liquor into a clean jug and pour into sterilized bottle/s (page 464), leaving a 1 cm/ ½ inch head space, then cover and seal.
* Keep in a cool, dark place for 3 months before using. Once open, keep in the fridge and use within 1 month.

UNITED KINGDOM
*

BROWN SAUCE

Brown sauce is a spiced tomato and vinegar condiment. It is closely related to Tomato Ketchup (page 425), but much fruitier on account of the dates, tamarind and treacle (blackstrap molasses) included in it. Serve with a Full Breakfast (page 26) or on any breakfast roll.

Makes: 1 litre/ 34 fl oz (4¼ cups)
Prep time: 20 minutes, plus 2 months maturing
Cook time: 1 hour
{♠}{♪}

- For stage 1:
- 140 g/ 5 oz can tomato purée (paste)
- 1 onion, chopped
- 125 ml/ 4¼ fl oz (½ cup) orange juice
- 125 ml/ 4¼ fl oz (½ cup) apple juice
- 60 g/ 2¼ oz (½ cup minus 2 teaspoons) stoned (pitted) dates, chopped
- 150 ml/ 5 fl oz (⅔ cup) tamarind purée
- 2 tart apples, grated
- 40 g/ 1½ oz (3¼ tablespoons) soft dark brown sugar
- 2 tablespoons black treacle (blackstrap molasses)

- For stage 2:
- 1 tablespoon Worcestershire sauce
- 1 tablespoon mustard powder
- ½ teaspoon each cayenne pepper and black pepper
- 1 teaspoon mixed spice
- large pinch of salt
- 175 ml/ 6 fl oz (¾ cup) malt vinegar
- 30 g/ 1 oz (3¾ tablespoons) arrowroot

* Put all the ingredients for stage 1 into a large saucepan and bring to the boil, then reduce the heat to medium-low and simmer for 45 minutes. Leave to cool slightly, then blend and pass through a sieve into a large bowl.
* Add the stage 2 ingredients and whisk or stir through very well. Pour into sterilized jars or bottles (page 464), leaving a 1 cm/ ½ inch head space, then cover and seal.
* Keep in a cool, dark place for 2 months before using. Once open, keep in the fridge and use within 1 month.

UNITED KINGDOM
*
MAYONNAISE

Homemade mayonnaise, made using the best farmhouse eggs, will always outshine the shop-bought variety.

Makes: 350 ml/ 12 fl oz/ 1½ cups:
Prep time: 20 minutes
{👄}{🔥}{🍶}{•••}{✗}

- 3 egg yolks
- 1 tablespoon white wine vinegar
- 1 teaspoon English mustard
- 300 ml/ 10 fl oz (1¼ cups) rapeseed (canola) oil
- ½ teaspoon granulated sugar (optional)
- salt and pepper

* Put the egg yolks, vinegar, mustard and salt and pepper into a large bowl and whisk together to combine. While whisking, add half the oil very slowly, then add the remaining half slightly more liberally, continuing to stir through. Add 1 tablespoon hot water and whisk again. Season with a little salt and pepper, then add the sugar, if desired. Stir through once more before serving.
* The mayonnaise will keep for 10 days in the fridge.

UNITED KINGDOM
*
MUSTARD DRESSING

Use on leafy greens; this dressing is capable of lifting even the simplest watercress salad.

Prep time: 5 minutes
{👄}{♦}{🔥}{🍶}{•••}{✗}

- 1–2 teaspoons mustard, to taste
- generous pinch of salt
- 20 ml/ ¾ fl oz (4 teaspoons) white wine or cider vinegar
- 40 ml/ 1¼ fl oz (¼ cup minus 1½ tablespoons) vegetable oil, such as sunflower or rapeseed (canola)

* Put the mustard, salt and vinegar into a food processor and blend. While blending, slowly pour in the oil until emulsified. Add a small splash of very cold water to help the ingredients combine. Serve.
* The dressing will keep for 1 month in the fridge.

ENGLAND
*
SALAD CREAM

Similar to a mayonnaise, this tangy English condiment is made with the addition of cream, vinegar and lemon juice – as well as a little sugar to balance out the acidity. Use for salads or as a sandwich spread (in lieu of mayonnaise).

Makes: 650 ml/ 22 fl oz:
Prep time: 10 minutes
Cook time: 10 minutes
{👄}{•••}

- 20 g/ ¾ oz (4 teaspoons) plain (all-purpose) flour, sifted
- 40 g/ 1½ oz (3¼ tablespoons) caster (superfine) sugar
- 1 tablespoon English mustard
- ½ teaspoon salt
- 4 eggs
- 200 ml/ 7 fl oz (¾ cup plus 1 tablespoon) cider vinegar
- 300 ml/ 10 fl oz (1¼ cups) double (heavy) cream
- juice of ½ lemon

* Put the flour, sugar, mustard and salt into a large bowl and whisk through.
* Beat in the eggs and vinegar. Tip the mixture into a medium saucepan and heat gently over a medium heat for 5–6 minutes until very thick. Remove from the heat, leave to cool, then beat in the cream and lemon juice. Spoon into sterilized jars or bottles (page 464), leaving a 1 cm/ ½ inch space, then cover and seal.
* The salad cream will keep for 10 days in the fridge.

UNITED KINGDOM
*
BRANDY SAUCE

A creamy pouring sauce for rich Yuletide desserts such as Christmas pudding (page 350).

Serves 6
Prep time: 5 minutes
Cook time: 15 minutes
{👄}{•••}{🍴}

- 50 g/ 2 oz (3½ tablespoons) salted butter
- 50 g/ 2 oz (½ cup minus 2 teaspoons) plain (all-purpose) flour
- 50 g/ 2 oz (¼ cup) caster (superfine) sugar
- 500 ml/ 17 fl oz (2 cups plus 1 tablespoon) full-fat (whole) milk
- 2–3 shots (50–75 ml/ 1¾–2½ fl oz) brandy

* Melt the butter in a medium saucepan over a medium-low heat for 2 minutes, or until foaming. Add the flour and mix it thoroughly with the butter, then cook for another 3 minutes, whisking constantly.
* Slowly whisk in the sugar, followed by the milk. Add brandy to taste and stir through. Remove from the heat and strain through a fine-mesh sieve into a bowl or serving jug (pitcher).

UNITED KINGDOM
*

BUTTERSCOTCH SAUCE

Butterscotch is a sweet caramel-like sauce, which is served like Toffee Sauce (page 358) or Caramel Sauce (see right), over any steamed or baked pudding – from creamy, custardy Bread and Butter Pudding (page 360) to Sticky Ginger Cake (page 323).

Serves 4
Prep time: 10 minutes
Cook time: 10 minutes
{👤}{🛢{⚏}{🍶}{🧈}{⏳}

- 125 g/4¼ oz (½ cup) soft dark brown sugar
- 250 ml/8 fl oz (1 cup) double (heavy) cream
- pinch of salt
- 65 g/2½ oz (4 tablespoons plus 1 teaspoon) salted butter, diced

* Heat the sugar and 1 tablespoon water together in a medium saucepan over a low heat for 10 minutes, or until the sugar has dissolved and turns dark brown. Remove from the heat and slowly add the cream. Once the cream is fully incorporated, add the salt and slowly whisk in the diced butter. Serve.

UNITED KINGDOM
*

CANDIED CITRUS PEEL

A true unsung hero of British baking, a little candied orange peel can spruce up all manner of fruitcake, yeasted buns, sweet pies or steamed puddings. You can find mixed candied peel in most British supermarkets, but the homemade version is a marked improvement in flavour and texture.

Makes: 600 g/1 lb 5 oz
Prep time: 1 hours, plus 12 hours steeping
Cook time: 1 hour 10 minutes
{👤}{♦}{🛢}{🧈}{⚏}{🍶}{🧈}

- 6 oranges or a mix of citrus fruit
- 500 g/1 lb 2 oz (2½ cups) granulated sugar

* Cut the peel from the oranges using a paring knife, then cut the peel into thick matchsticks, about 5 mm/¼ inch wide. Put the peel into a large saucepan, cover with water and bring to the boil. Reduce the heat and simmer for 5 minutes.
* Drain the liquid, reserving the peel, and add 1 litre/34 fl oz (4¼ cups) fresh water to the saucepan, along with the peel again. Once again, bring to the boil, then reduce the heat and simmer for 40 minutes. Add the sugar and stir to dissolve, then cover with a lid and leave the peel to steep for 12 hours in the syrup.
* The next day, bring the orange syrup to the boil, then reduce the heat and simmer for 20 minutes, or until the syrup has almost completely evaporated. Carefully transfer the strips to wire racks and leave to cool.
* When cold, store in airtight containers, either in the fridge or in a cool, dark place, and use within 2 months.

UNITED KINGDOM
*

CARAMEL SAUCE

Recipes for caramel sauce vary, but always use white caster (superfine) or granulated sugar. Serve similarly to Butterscotch Sauce (see left) or Toffee Sauce (page 358): over ice cream, custardy Bread and Butter Pudding (page 360) and sticky sweet steamed ones.

Serves: 4
Prep time: 5 minutes
Cook time: 10 minutes
{👤}{🛢{⚏}{🍶}{🧈}{⏳}

- 200 g/7 oz (1 cup) caster (superfine) sugar
- 50 g/2 oz (3½ tablespoons) unsalted butter, cubed (optional)
- 200 ml/7 fl oz (¾ cup plus 1 tablespoon) double (heavy) cream

* Put the sugar and 20 ml/¾ fl oz (4 teaspoons) water into a medium saucepan and heat over a low heat for 10 minutes to allow the sugar to boil gently until it is completely dissolved. Don't stir.
* When the sugar has turned golden brown, add the butter (if using) and whisk until it is incorporated.
* Remove from the heat and add the cream, stirring until completely incorporated. Serve.

UNITED KINGDOM
*

FAIRY BUTTER

A sweet floral-scented compound butter, especially popular in the eighteenth and nineteenth centuries. Fairy butter can be served in place of jam or Clotted Cream (page 34) at teatime or spread like Brandy Butter (see right) over slices of steamed pudding or ginger loaf.

Serves 4
Prep time: 30 minutes
Cook time: 15 minutes
{👤}{🛢{⚏}{🧈}

- 2 eggs
- 2 teaspoons orange flower water
- 2 teaspoons icing (confectioners') sugar
- 250 g/9 oz (2¼ sticks) unsalted butter, softened

* Bring a small saucepan of water to the boil over a medium heat, carefully add the eggs and cook for 10 minutes, or until hard-boiled. Remove the eggs using a slotted spoon and cool under cold running water.
* Halve the eggs and scoop out the yolks into a small bowl. Add the orange flower water and sugar and beat until smooth using a mini-whisk, fork or stand mixer fitted with a whisk attachment. Add the butter and beat well until smooth and the butter has taken on an even, light orange colour. Serve.
* The fairy butter will keep for 1 week in the fridge.

UNITED KINGDOM
*
BRANDY BUTTER

A sweet and creamy compound butter spiked with brandy, made for spreading over Mince Pies (page 398), Christmas Pudding (page 350) and any other well-spiced wintry cakes. For rum butter, use rum instead of brandy and soft light brown sugar instead of icing (confectioners') sugar.

Serves 6
Prep time: 15 minutes
{ }{ }{ }{ }{ }

- 130 g/4½ oz (9 tablespoons) unsalted butter, softened
- 90 g/3¼ oz (¾ cup) icing (confectioners') sugar
- 2 shots (50 ml/1¾ fl oz) brandy

* Put the butter and sugar into a bowl and whisk until pale and creamy. Add the brandy, 1 teaspoon at a time, and stir until combined. Only add each teaspoon when the last has been fully incorporated into the sauce. Serve.
* The brandy butter will keep for 1 month in the fridge.

ENGLAND
*
VANILLA FUDGE
CLOTTED CREAM FUDGE

Britain and the US both lay claim to this popular confection, which may have originated in 1880s New England as a failed attempt at making caramel – or rather earlier in Britain as a variation of the older Scottish Tablet (see right). In any case, British fudge is dense and has a grainy texture that makes it more reminiscent of Tablet than slabs of creamy American fudge. On both sides of the Atlantic, fudge evokes memories of the seaside, where it is often made and sold. The seaside towns of Cornwall are famous for a rather decadent variety that they make with local clotted cream.

Makes: around 25 pieces
Prep time: 10 minutes
Cook time: 30 minutes
{ }{ }{ }

- about 2 teaspoons sunflower oil, for brushing
- 500 g/1 lb 2 oz (2¼ cups) demerara (turbinado) sugar
- 300 ml/10 fl oz (1¼ cups) double (heavy) cream or Clotted Cream (shop-bought or homemade, page 34)
- 150 g/5 oz (1¼ sticks) unsalted butter
- 1 tablespoon glucose syrup
- ½ teaspoon vanilla extract (optional)

* Line a 20 x 20 cm/8 x 8 inch square cake pan with baking (parchment) paper and brush lightly with the oil.
* Put the remaining ingredients into a large saucepan and stir over a medium heat for 3–4 minutes, until the sugar has dissolved and the butter has melted. When smooth, increase the heat to medium-high and boil hard until the temperature reaches 112°C/234°F on a thermometer.
* Pour the mixture into the prepared pan and leave to cool. While still just warm, cut into small squares and serve.

SCOTLAND
*
TABLET

A Scottish confection popular since the eighteenth century; the earliest mention comes from the household accounts of one Lady Grisell Baillie, which show her family's purchase of 'tablet for the bairns (kids)'. Tremendously sweet, grainy and with a hard crumbly bite, tablet is still recognized across Scotland as a national treat.

Makes: around 25 pieces
Prep time: 5 minutes
Cook time: 40 minutes
{ }{ }{ }

- about 2 teaspoons vegetable oil, for brushing
- 115 g/4 oz (8 tablespoons) unsalted butter
- 150 ml/5 fl oz (⅔ cup) full-fat (whole) milk
- 500 g/1 lb 2 oz (2½ cups) granulated sugar
- 397 g/14 oz can sweetened condensed milk

* Line a 20 x 20 cm/8 x 8 inch square cake pan with baking (parchment) paper and brush lightly with the oil.
* Put the butter and the full-fat (whole) milk into a large saucepan and stir over a medium heat until the butter melts completely. Tip the sugar into the pan, stir until dissolved and bring to the boil. Boil for 1 minute, then reduce the heat to medium.
* Add the condensed milk, stir to combine, then increase the heat to high and boil hard until the temperature reaches 120°C/248°F on a thermometer. Pour the mixture into the cake pan and leave to cool. While still just warm, cut into small squares and serve when cool.

UNITED KINGDOM
*
ROYAL ICING

The traditional icing for British Christmas and wedding cakes, the egg whites and lemon juice in royal icing work to stiffen and harden the mixture. It should be spread evenly using a palette knife or used to form stiff snowy peaks on the cake's top. Royal icing can also be spread over any butter-rich biscuits (cookies).

Makes enough for a 20 cm/8 inch round cake
Prep time: 20 minutes
{ }{ }{ }{ }{ }{ }{ }

- 3 egg whites
- 600 g/1 lb 5 oz (5 cups) icing (confectioners') sugar, sifted
- 1 teaspoon glycerine
- 2 teaspoons lemon juice

* Whisk the egg whites in a large bowl to soft peaks using electric beaters. Fold the sugar into the egg whites, a spoonful at a time. When all the sugar has been incorporated, stir in the glycerine and lemon juice and whisk for 10 minutes, or until the mixture becomes very stiff. The mixture is ready when it starts to hold its shape.

NORTHERN IRELAND
*

YELLOWMAN (HONEYCOMB) SPONGE TOFFEE

A variety of honeycomb toffee, this brittle aerated confection is set in a slab and later, using a hammer, it is broken apart into bite-sized pieces. It is most commonly found at Ould Lammas Fair, a harvest festival held in Northern Ireland at the end of every August.

Serves: 6
Prep time: 5 minutes
Cook time: 15 minutes
{♥}{◆}{▲}{♠}{↗}{🛆}{✕}

- 2 teaspoons sunflower oil, for brushing
- 300 g/11 oz (1½ cups) granulated sugar
- 150 g/5 oz (½ cup minus 1 tablespoon) golden syrup
- 1 level tablespoon bicarbonate of soda (baking soda)

* Line a 20 x 30 cm/8 x 12 inch cake pan with baking (parchment) paper and brush it with the oil.
* Put the sugar and golden syrup into a large saucepan and heat over a medium heat, stirring constantly, for 2 minutes, or until the sugar has dissolved.
* Bring the mixture to the boil over a medium heat and keep cooking for 3–4 minutes until it has turned golden brown. At this point, add the bicarbonate of soda (baking soda), stir once and carefully pour into the prepared cake pan. Leave to cool before breaking into uneven pieces.

WALES / ENGLAND
*

TREACLE TOFFEE

A simple confection made of butter and sugar, toffee was once a special homemade sweet, boiled in copper pots and set to cool in a baking pan or pulled (with greased hands) until aerated and pale in colour. Toffee was frequently made throughout autumn and winter, and in Wales, toffee-pulling often concluded the Christmas celebrations. Welsh cookery writer Bobby Freeman beautifully recalled those scenes, stating 'it resembles nothing so much as a hank of silky platinum hair'.
This recipe involves no pulling, and instead of hard brittle toffee, it produces a softer much chewier sweet (candy).

Serves: 4–6
Prep time: 5 minutes
Cook time: 25 minutes
{♥}{▲}{↗}{🛆}

- 350 g/12 oz (3 sticks) unsalted butter, plus extra for greasing
- 225 g/8 oz (⅔ cup) black treacle (blackstrap molasses)
- 450 g/1 lb (2 cups) soft dark brown sugar
- 397 g/14 oz can condensed milk

* Grease a large rimmed baking sheet with butter and line with baking (parchment) paper. Set aside on a heatproof work counter.
* Put the butter, treacle (blackstrap molasses) and sugar into a large, heavy saucepan and heat over a medium-high heat for 5 minutes until the butter has melted and the sugar has completely dissolved. Once the caramel is boiling, carefully add the condensed milk, then, using a heatproof spatula or wooden spoon and stirring the mixture constantly, reduce the heat to medium and cook until it reaches 120–122°C/248–252°F on a thermometer – though before the toffee reaches 120°C/248°F, reduce the heat again to slow the cooking, ensuring that it does not exceed the temperature.
* Carefully pour the mixture evenly into the prepared baking sheet. Leave to cool slightly before cutting into squares with a knife and leaving to cool completely.

UNITED KINGDOM
*

TOFFEE APPLES

A popular autumnal treat – especially for Bonfire Night in the UK or Halloween – this recipe eschews the classic glossy red colouring for what Dorothy Hartley calls 'that iridescent, luscious gold that crackles'. Serve as is, or roll in chopped nuts, sweets (candies) or hundreds and thousands (sprinkles). **Notes:** Decorated, skewered fruit has deep-running traditions in Wales, where cookery writer Theodora Fitzgibbon suggests it originates in antiquity with the Roman tradition of strena – a New Year's gift.

Makes: 4
Prep time: 5 minutes
Cook time: 10 minutes
{♥}{◆}{▲}{♠}{↗}{🛆}{✕}

- 4 eating apples
- 200 g/7 oz (1 cup) caster (superfine) sugar
- 70 g/2¾ oz (¼ cup minus 2 teaspoons) golden syrup

* Put the apples into a large heatproof bowl and cover with boiling water to reduce any waxy coating that might keep the caramel from sticking. Remove from the water and leave to stand for several minutes before drying thoroughly with a dish towel and removing the stalks. Insert a skewer through to the bottom of the apples to form the handle.
* For the caramel, put the sugar into a medium saucepan with 50 ml/1¾ fl oz (3½ tablespoons) water and cook over a low heat for 2 minutes, or until the sugar has dissolved. Add the golden syrup and cook until it reaches 150°C/300°F on a thermometer.
* When ready, carefully dip the apples into the hot caramel and allow each apple to be completely coated in it. Holding the skewer, tilt the apples and turn them to coat evenly. Take care not to burn yourself. Allow any excess caramel to drain off the apples and put them onto a piece of baking (parchment) paper to cool and harden. The apples can be kept cool for a few days.

Yellowman toffee

ENGLAND

*

LEMON CURD

This thick and creamy lemon spread can be used in place
of jam and has just as many applications – as the fillings in
tarts, such as Lemon Tart (page 392), sweet buns, like Belgian
Buns (page 292) and steamed sponge puddings (page 352),
or just spread on good bread or scones.

Lemon curd has a long history in England dating back to the
1700s. The earliest recipe is for a 'Lemon cream' from Hannah
Glasse's seminal cookbook, *The Art of Cookery Made Plain and Easy*
(1747). Lemon curd has stayed popular since the eighteenth
century and enjoyed a surge in popularity that came with
the advent of tearooms and afternoon tea at the end of the
following century. All lemon curd recipes will involve the same
ingredients – eggs, lemon, butter and sugar – but the exact ratio
and consistency will vary from household to household.

Makes: 700 ml/24 fl oz (3 cups)
Prep time: 5 minutes
Cook time: 15 minutes
{�}{♨}{ॐ}{⚡}

- 6 egg yolks
- 210 g/7¼ oz (1 cup plus 2 teaspoons)
caster (superfine) sugar
- ½ teaspoon salt
- 4 unwaxed lemons, grated zest of 2 lemons
and juice of 4 lemons, about 120 ml/4 fl oz (½ cup)
- 135 g/4¾ oz (9 tablespoons) unsalted butter,
at room temperature, diced

* Fill the saucepan of a double boiler a third of the way
  up with water and heat over a medium-high heat. Once
  boiling, reduce the heat to a simmer, then, add the egg
  yolks, sugar, salt, grated zest and lemon juice to the top
  boiler bowl and, using a wooden spoon, mix together until
  fully incorporated.
* Put the boiler bowl over the heat and cook for 7–10
  minutes, stirring constantly to prevent curdling. The curd
  should be thick and become slightly translucent. If not,
  then stir over the heat for another 2–3 minutes. If you
  don't have a double boiler, use a heatproof bowl set over a
  saucepan of simmering water, making sure the bottom of
  the bowl doesn't touch the water.
* Remove the curd from the heat and begin to slowly whisk
  in the butter to emulsify. Pass the curd through a sieve into
  a bowl, then, using a jam jar funnel, divide the curd evenly
  between sterilized jars (page 464), leaving a 1 cm/½ inch
  head space. Leave to cool.
* The lemon curd will keep for 10 days in the fridge.

UNITED KINGDOM

*

STRAWBERRY JAM

A much-loved summer spread used for spreading on toast
and for baking (see Bakewell Tarts and Victoria Sponge Cake,
pages 378 and 320). Some of the best British strawberries
are found in the southeast of England, where numerous
strawberry farms have existed since the early 1900s.

This jam also works with other fruit – although very soft
fruits like raspberries, blueberries, etc., don't need the
overnight soak in the sugar. Check how much pectin the
fruit has – strawberries hve none, hence why this recipe
uses a proportion of jam sugar; fruits such as blackcurrants
have lots so you can use regular granulated sugar.

Makes: 1.5 litres/50 fl oz (6¼ cups)
Prep time: 20 minutes, plus 8–12 hours soaking
Cook time: 35 minutes
{�}{♦}{♨}{♠}{⚡}{♠}

- 1 kg/2¼ lb strawberries
- 600 g/1 lb 5 oz granulated sugar
- 400 g/14 oz (2 cups) jam sugar (a mixture of sugar
and pectin, although not the same as preserving sugar)
- juice of 1 lemon

* Hull the strawberries and cut them into equal sizes. For
  instance, leave very small ones whole, but quarter the
  larger ones. Tip the berries into a large bowl, toss with
  the granulated sugar, cover with clingfilm (plastic wrap)
  and leave at room temperature overnight.
* The next day, put a saucer into the freezer (you will be
  using it later to test the jam).
* Add the jam sugar and lemon juice to the macerated berries,
  then transfer to a large saucepan and heat over a medium
  heat, stirring until the sugar completely dissolves. Increase
  the heat and boil for about 20 minutes. Remove the frozen
  saucer to test whether the jam has set by spooning a little
  onto it. If it wrinkles when you apply pressure to it, then
  it has set. Alternatively, if you have a thermometer, the
  temperature you are looking out for is 105°C/221°F.
* If the jam is not quite ready, bring it back to the boil for
  10 minutes then test again. When set, leave to stand for
  another 15 minutes, stir away the scum, then ladle into
  sterilized glass jars (page 464), leaving a 1 cm/½ inch
  head space. Cover and seal.
* The jam will keep for 1 month – once opened, keep in
  the fridge.

Lemon curd

SCOTLAND

*

SEVILLE ORANGE MARMALADE

A preserve made from bitter oranges, marmalade also includes thin matchstick slices of orange peel. It originated first as a jelly-like set dessert, before it was adapted into a breakfast spread – first in Scotland in the eighteenth century, and thereafter in England. In Scotland, marmalade has a strong association with the city of Dundee, where the first commercial marmalade brands were produced.

Serve as with any sweet preserve, on buttered toast, teacakes or even Hot Cross Buns (page 288).

Makes: 2 litres/ 68 fl oz (8½ cups)
Prep time: 10 minutes
Cook time: 2½ hours
{👁}{◆}{🛎}{🍴}{↝}{📷}{🏛}

- 1.5 kg/ 3¼ lb Seville oranges, scrubbed
- 3 kg/ 6½ lb (15 cups) granulated sugar

* Put the oranges into a preserving pan or large stockpot with 2.5 litres/ 85 fl oz (10 cups) water. Bring to the boil, then reduce the heat and simmer for 1½ hours, or until the oranges are tender. Put a saucer into the freezer (you will be using it later to test the marmalade).
* Using a slotted spoon, remove the oranges from the pan and leave them to cool. Once cool enough to handle, halve the oranges and scoop out the pulp. Separate the peel and set aside, then spoon the pulp into a 20 x 20 cm/ 8 x 8 inch piece of muslin (cheesecloth). Tie with kitchen string and hang the bag over the pan. Meanwhile, shred the peel as desired (between 1–3mm) and tip it into the pan.
* Once all of the juice has dripped out of the muslin, add the sugar and stir until it has dissolved. Bring the pan to a rolling boil for anywhere between 30–40 minutes, in order to reach the setting point of 105°C/ 221°F. Use a probe or candy thermometer to check. Remove from the heat and spoon some of the marmalade onto the frozen plate. Push the jelly with your fingertip after a minute; if it wrinkles up, the pectin is set. If not, boil the mixture again and retest it after 10 minutes.
* When ready, turn off the heat and leave the marmalade to cool for 15 minutes, then carefully spoon into sterilized glass jars (page 464), leaving a 1 cm/ ½ inch head space. Cover and seal.
* The marmalade will keep for 1 month – once opened, keep in the fridge.

UNITED KINGDOM

*

FRUIT JELLIES

For many Brits, the idea of 'fruit jelly' might bring to mind images of the set gelatine dessert, but jellies, made from fruit juice and strained of all skins and seeds, are also traditional items of the British pantry. Redcurrant and rowan jelly, for example, are among the most common tracklements for game and game birds.

This is a standard recipe template, which you can experiment with as you like, based on what is good and in season.

Makes: 1.5 litres/ 50 fl oz (6¼ cups)
Prep time: 10 minutes, plus 8–12 hours straining
Cook time: 1½ hours
{👁}{◆}{🛎}{🍴}{↝}{🏛}

- 2 kg/ 4½ lb apples, quinces or medlars, chopped, or 1 kg/ 2¼ lb apples and another low-pectin fruit, such as blackberries, redcurrants, rowan berries or pears, chopped
- granulated sugar (see method)

* Put the fruit into a large saucepan, cover with water and bring to the boil, then reduce the heat to low and simmer for 15 minutes, or until very tender.
* Line a colander with a large piece of muslin (cheesecloth) and sit it over a bowl. Pour in the fruit and cooking liquid, then tie the ends of the muslin together and hang it from a handle so that it can drip into the bowl. Leave to strain overnight.
* The next day, put a saucer into the freezer (you will use it to test the jelly). Squeeze the muslin bag to get out any remaining juice and measure the amount of liquid. Pour the juice into a preserving pan and add 500 g/ 1 lb 2 oz (2½ cups) sugar to every 600 ml/ 20 fl oz (2½ cups) juice. Heat over a low heat, stirring until the sugar has dissolved, then increase the heat to high and boil hard for about 20 minutes. Check that setting point has been reached by spooning some jelly onto the plate: it will wrinkle when pushed with a finger. Alternatively, use a thermometer and stop boiling when 105°C/ 221°F has been reached. Turn off the heat and stir the jelly to remove any scum, then pour into sterilized glass jars (page 464), leaving a 1 cm/ ½ inch head space, then cover and seal.
* The jelly will keep for 1 month – once opened, keep in the fridge.

Seville orange marmalade

UNITED KINGDOM

*

FRUIT CHEESES

Fruit cheeses are preserves made from the pulp of puréed and strained fruit, which is boiled down and set in a mould. Slice and eat with Oatcakes (pages 260 and 261) and good British cheese. Fruit cheese will suit everything from a mature Montgomery Cheddar to a creamy Baron Bigod.
This is a basic recipe. When making at home, you can substitute up to 50 per cent of the quince or apple for low-pectin fruit like apricots, pears, blackcurrants, strawberries, etc. – or swap them out entirely for high-pectin fruit like a nice damson plum – however, they will need to be cooked separately and strained if they are seedy soft fruits.

Makes: about 2 litres/68 fl oz (8½ cups)
Prep time: 15 minutes, plus 6 months maturing
Cooking time 2½ hours
{⊙}{♦}{�}{♠}{⌣}{♠}

- 2 kg/4½ lb quinces or apples or a mixture, chopped
- 1 star anise or 1 cinnamon stick (optional)
- caster (superfine) sugar (see method)
- vegetable oil, for brushing

* Put the fruit into a large saucepan, cover with cold water and bring to the boil, adding the spices (if using), then reduce the heat to low and simmer for 30–60 minutes until very tender.
* Strain the cooking liquor into a bowl, then pass the fruit through a fine sieve into a second bowl, then combine the two. Measure the volume of the pulp and pour into a preserving pan with 560 g/1 lb 4 oz (generous 2¾ cups) sugar per 1 litre/34 fl oz (4¼ cups) water. Bring to the boil, stirring until the sugar has dissolved, then reduce the heat and simmer, stirring frequently, until you notice that the paste leaves the side of the pan as you stir.
* Line a baking sheet with baking (parchment) paper and brush with oil. Pour the pulp over the paper, then cover with clingfilm (plastic wrap) and leave to cool. Transfer to sterilized jars (page 464) or an airtight container. Keep in a cool, dark place for 6 months before using. Once open, keep in the fridge and use within 1 month.

UNITED KINGDOM

*

CRYSTALLIZED
STEM GINGER
GINGER PRESERVED IN SYRUP

Stem (preserved) ginger, diced and preserved in syrup, is a friend to numerous spiced cakes, pies and puddings – from a simple Steamed Ginger Sponge (page 352), to a Cumberland Rum Nicky (page 396).

Makes: about 750 g/1 lb 10 oz
Prep time: 20 minutes, plus 8–12 hours freezing
and defrosting and 2 weeks maturing
Cook time: 30 minutes
{⊙}{♦}{☐}{♠}{⌣}{♠}

- 500 g/1 lb 2 oz piece fresh root ginger
- 500 g/1 lb 2 oz (2½ cups) granulated sugar

* Cut the ginger into 2 cm/¾ inch chunks, place on a lined baking sheet and freeze overnight. Freezing will tenderize the ginger.
* The next day, defrost the ginger at room temperature before putting the pieces into a large saucepan and covering with water. Bring to a simmer over a low-medium heat and cook for 15 minutes. Strain, setting aside 350 ml/12 fl oz (1½ cups) of the cooking water.
* Pour the liquor back into the pan and add the sugar. Stir to dissolve, then bring to a simmer and cook for 20 minutes. Remove from the heat and leave the ginger mixture to cool completely in the syrup, then carefully pour into sterilized jars (page 464), leaving a 1 cm/½ inch head space. Cover, seal and leave in a cool, dark place for 2 weeks before using. Once open, keep in the fridge and use within 1 month.

UNITED KINGDOM

*

SPICED PEACHES

Prepare these sweet-pickled peaches in summer, and by late autumn they will provide the antidote to poor, dreary weather. Serve the peaches with a slice of buttery Madeira Cake (page 319), spread with a little extra butter – for good keeping, of course.

Makes: 1.2 litres/40 fl oz (5 cups)
Prep time: 10 minutes, plus 1 month maturing
Cook time: 30 minutes
{⊙}{♦}{☐}{♠}{⌣}

- 1–1.2 kg/2¼ –2½ lb ripe peaches
- 375 ml/13 fl oz (1½ cups) cider vinegar
- 500 g/1 lb 2 oz (2½ cups) granulated sugar
- 30 g/1oz piece fresh root ginger, peeled and thinly sliced
- 1 x 5-cm/2-inch cinnamon stick
- 1 star anise
- 2 dried chillies (optional)

* Have a large bowl of cold water ready nearby. Bring a large saucepan of water to the boil. Carefully lower the peaches into the boiling water and leave for 1 minute. Remove using a slotted spoon and put them into the bowl of cold water. Remove and peel off the skins, which should come away easily. Cut the peaches in half and remove the stones (pits), then set the peaches aside.
* Heat the vinegar, sugar and spices together in a large saucepan over a medium heat, stirring until the sugar has dissolved. When dissolved, bring to the boil for 2 minutes, then reduce the heat to a simmer. Using a slotted spoon, carefully put the peaches into the hot liquor and simmer for just 3 minutes.
* Remove the peaches using a slotted spoon and put them into sterilized jars (page 464). Bring the vinegar syrup back to the boil, then pour through a sieve into a jug (pitcher). Pour the syrup into the jars, leaving a 1 cm/½ inch head space, then cover and seal tightly.
* Keep in a cool, dark place for 1 month before using. Once open, keep in the fridge and use within 2 weeks.

Fruit cheeses

UNITED KINGDOM
*
RED ONION MARMALADE

This jam-like spread is made from thinly sliced red onions which are quickly fried, then softly simmered with sugar and spices, before being cooked down with vinegar. The onions' sticky sweetness makes a very pleasing contrast to slices of hard cheese – preferably mature –with which it makes an excellent sandwich and toastie.

Makes: 1.3 litres/44 fl oz (5¼ cups)
Prep time: 30 minutes, plus 1 month maturing
Cook time: 1 hour 35 minutes
{�}

- 5 tablespoons olive oil
- 2 kg/4½ lb red onions, halved and thinly sliced
- 100 g/3½ oz (½ cup) granulated sugar
- 100 g/3½ oz (½ cup) soft dark brown sugar
- 1 tablespoon chopped thyme leaves
- 4 bay leaves
- 1½ teaspoons salt
- ½ teaspoon ground black pepper
- 250 ml/8 fl oz (1 cup) cider or wine vinegar
- 50 ml/1¾ fl oz (3½ tablespoons) balsamic vinegar

* Heat the olive oil in a large saucepan over a medium-high heat, add the onions, and, using a wooden spoon, coat the onions well in the oil. Add the sugars, thyme, bay leaves, salt and pepper, then reduce the heat to medium and stir through until the sugars have dissolved, about 3–4 minutes.
* Reduce the heat to medium-low and simmer uncovered for at least 50 minutes, or until the onions have turned deep brown. Pour in the vinegars and simmer for another 30 minutes, or until the mixture has become very syrupy and reduced to about one-quarter of its former volume.
* Remove from the heat and leave the marmalade cool for about 10 minutes, then carefully pour into sterilized glass jars (page 464), leaving a 1 cm/½ inch head space, then cover and seal.
* Keep in a cool, dark place for 1 month before using. Once open, keep in the fridge and use within 1 month.

WALES
*
HONEYED PEARS
WITH
MEAD

According to legend, the defeat and slaughter of the Welsh (by the Angles) at the Battle of Catraeth has been attributed to the mead they drank to excess before confronting the enemy. In more recent times, mead was considered to be exempt from the sinfulness of alcohol in Welsh Methodist communities. As a result, many rural families prepared it in time for the harvest. Honeycombs were steeped in cold water, which was then drained off and boiled. Hops and yeast were added during the process, prior to the mead being bottled in stone jars, which were often dug into the ground and left for at least six months before their contents were consumed.

Serves: 3
Prep time: 10 minutes
Cook time: 10 minutes
{☐}{☐}{☐}{☐}{☐}{☐}

- 3 ripe pears
- 75 g/2 ½ oz (¾ stick) unsalted butter
- 1 x 150 ml/5 fl oz mead
- 2 tablespoons runny honey
- pinch of freshly grated nutmeg

* Peel and cut the pears in half, then remove the cores and chop the flesh into 2.5 cm/1 inch chunks.
* Melt the butter in a medium saucepan over a medium heat, add the pears and cook for 7–8 minutes, tossing gently without breaking the fruit to a mash. When the chunks are golden brown, pour in the mead, then arrange the pears in a serving dish, drizzle over the honey, dust with nutmeg and serve hot.

JERSEY
*
JERSEY BLACK BUTTER

Unique to Jersey, in the Channel Islands, this apple 'butter' is traditionally made in spring at the same time that local ciders are being bottled. It is dark burgundy in colour, well-spiced and flavoured with liquorice. Black butter is effectively a thick jam and can be used interchangeably with any strongly flavoured fruit preserve.

Makes: 1.5 litres/50 fl oz (6¼ cups)
Prep time: 10 minutes
Cook time: 6 hours
{☐}{☐}{☐}{☐}{☐}

- 2 litres/68 fl oz (8½ cups) apple juice
- 2 kg/4½ lb Bramley (cooking) apples, peeled, cored and chopped
- 200 g/7 oz dessert apples, peeled, cored and chopped
- 1 whole lemon, chopped
- 2 liquorice sticks, bashed
- 1 teaspoon mixed spice

* Heat the apple juice in a large saucepan over a medium-high heat and cook for 15 minutes, or until it is reduced by half. Add the apples, lemon and liquorice sticks, then cover with a lid, reduce the heat to very low and simmer for 3 hours, stirring occasionally.
* After 3 hours, uncover and simmer for another 3 hours, or until dark and thick. Keep stirring to prevent burning. Remove from the heat and either blend with a hand-held blender or transfer to a food processor and pulse. Stir in the mixed spice. Alternatively, pass the mixture through a sieve. Pour into sterilized pots or glass jars (page 464), leaving a 1 cm/½ inch head space, then cover and seal. Keep in the fridge and use within 1 month.

Red onion marmalade

UNITED KINGDOM
*

ANCHOVY BUTTER

This delicious spread has multitudinous uses but is perhaps most excellent when spread over good bread and topped with rich soft-scrambled eggs, as in the Scotch Woodcock on page 28.

Makes: 275 g/9¾ oz
Prep time: 5 minutes
Cook time: 8 minutes
{⚖}{✐}{✗}

- 250 g/9 oz (2¼ sticks) butter
- 25 g/1 oz anchovy fillets, drained
- cayenne pepper and ground mace, to taste (optional)
- pepper

* Melt 50 g/2 oz (3½ tablespoons) of the butter in a medium saucepan over a medium heat, add the anchovies and fry for 5 minutes, or until they break up. Season with pepper together with the other spices (if using) and cook for 2 minutes. Transfer to a food processor with the remaining butter and pulse into a smooth paste.
* Put the paste into pots or ramekins and cover. Keep in the fridge and use within 2 weeks.

UNITED KINGDOM
*

SMOKED COD'S ROE CREAM

Cod's roe has long featured in the diet of big fishing ports. It was often fried and eaten in slices or smoked and spread on buttered bread. This preparation is a modern take on familiar flavours and is not dissimilar to a British spin on a taramasalata. Spread over good crusty bread with an extra squeeze of lemon.

Serves: 4–6
Prep time: 15 minutes
Cook time: 5–10 minutes
{⚖}{✐}{🍲}{✗}

- 250 g/9 oz smoked cod's roe
- 150 ml/5 fl oz (⅔ cup) double (heavy) cream
- squeeze of lemon juice
- ⅛ teaspoon cayenne pepper (optional)
- pepper (to taste)

* Remove and discard the skin from the cod's roe, then put the roe into a small saucepan. Add the cream and heat over a medium-low heat for 5–10 minutes to slowly warm together and infuse the flavour into the cream.
* Remove from the heat and leave to cool. Add the lemon juice, cayenne (if using) and pepper to taste, then stir through and serve.

UNITED KINGDOM
*

RHUBARB CHUTNEY

This fruity chutney can be served in much the same way as either a Mango Chutney (page 442) or even Red Onion Marmalade (page 438). Excellent with hard cheeses, meats and spread on sandwiches.

Makes: 1.5 litres/50 fl oz (6¼ cups)
Prep time: 15 minutes, plus 1 month maturing
Cook time: 1 hour 40 minutes
{❂}{◆}{⚖}{⬤}{✐}{🍲}

- 1 kg/2¼ lb rhubarb
- 240 g/8½ oz yellow onions (2 medium)
- 240 g/8½ oz (1⅓ cups) sultanas (golden raisins) or raisins
- 1 teaspoon finely chopped rosemary leaves
- grated zest of 1 orange
- 400 g/14 oz (2 cups) granulated sugar
- 300 ml/10 fl oz (1¼ cups) red wine vinegar

* Cut the rhubarb into 2 cm/¾ inch long pieces and set aside.
* Put the remaining ingredients into a large saucepan over a medium heat and stir to dissolve the sugar. Bring to the boil, then reduce the heat to low and simmer for 1½ hours, adding the rhubarb for the final 30 minutes. When thick, spoon into sterilized pots or glass jars (page 464), leaving a 1 cm/½ inch head space, then cover and seal.
* Keep in a cool, dark place for 1 month before using. Once open, keep in the fridge and use within 1 month.

Rhubarb chutney

UNITED KINGDOM
*

TOMATO CHUTNEY

The tomato is not exactly native to Britain or northern climates, but nevertheless there are farms and market gardens from southwest England to east-coast Scotland that still manage to grow them with great success. Serve as other chutneys – with hard cheese and good bread or Oatcakes (pages 260 and 261).

Makes: about 1.5 litres/ 50 fl oz (6¼ cups)
Prep time: 15 minutes, plus 1 month maturing
Cook time: 1½ hours
{♥}{♦}{♠}{♣}{♧}{♨}

- 1 kg/ 2¼ lb tomatoes, quartered
- 200 g/ 7 oz (1 cup) light brown sugar
- 1 large onion, chopped
- 2 apples, peeled, cored and chopped
- 2 cloves garlic, thinly sliced
- 1 fresh red chilli, thinly sliced
- 2 teaspoons mustard seeds
- 1 teaspoon nigella seeds
- 1 piece fresh root ginger,
about 2.5 cm/ 1 inch, peeled and grated
- ½ teaspoon salt
- 2 pinches of ground black pepper
- 500 ml/ 17 fl oz (2 cups plus 1 tablespoon)
malt or cider vinegar

* Put all the ingredients, except 100 ml/ 3½ fl oz (⅓ cup plus 1 tablespoon) of the vinegar, into a large saucepan. Bring to the boil over a medium heat, stirring frequently for 5 minutes, or until the sugar has dissolved. Reduce the heat to low and simmer for at least 1 hour, stirring occasionally, until the mixture has thickened and is starting to become jammy.
* When the mixture is thick and well combined, remove from the heat and stir in the reserved vinegar. Leave to cool slightly, then pour into sterilized glass jars (page 464), leaving a 1 cm/ ½ inch head space. Cover, seal and keep in a cool, dark place for 1 month before using. Once open, keep in the fridge and use within 1 month. .

UNITED KINGDOM
*

MANGO CHUTNEY

This sweet pickle was adapted by British colonialists from the mango *chatni* popular in North India. Chutney is the Anglicization of the Hindi word, which originally described a sort of fresh or pickled relish found all across India, and with many regional variations involving local fruit and spices. Today the British version is typically eaten with cold meat, hard cheeses, pork pies and sandwiches. It is sometimes also added to a fruity homemade curry.

Makes: 1.5 litres/ 50 fl oz (6¼ cups)
Prep time: 20 minutes, plus 3 weeks maturing
Cook time: 1 hour 35 minutes
{♥}{♦}{♠}{♣}{♧}

- 6 medium mangoes, or equivalent
- 450 g/ 1 lb (2¼ cups) granulated sugar
- 450 ml/ 15 fl oz (1⅔ cups plus 2 tablespoons) cider or
wine vinegar
- 1 tablespoon cumin seeds
- 1 tablespoon coriander seeds
- ½ teaspoon cardamom seeds
- 12 cloves
- 2 fresh red chillies, bruised (optional)
- thumb-sized piece fresh root ginger, peeled and grated
- 4 cloves garlic, grated
- ¼ teaspoon chilli powder
- ½ teaspoon ground turmeric

* Peel the mangoes, remove the flesh and cut it into small dice. Set aside.
* Put the sugar and vinegar together into a medium saucepan, stir to dissolve, then simmer over a low heat for 5 minutes.
* Meanwhile, heat a small dry frying pan or skillet over a medium heat, add the cumin, coriander, cardamom seeds and cloves and fry for 2 minutes, or until aromatic. Tip them into the saucepan with the mangoes and remaining ingredients, then bring to the boil. Reduce the heat and simmer for 90 minutes, or until the mixture has gone syrupy.
* Remove from the heat and carefully pour into sterilized glass jars (page 464), leaving a 1 cm/ ½ inch head space, then cover and seal. Keep in a cool, dark place for 3 weeks before using. Once open, keep in the fridge and use within 1 month.

UNITED KINGDOM
*

PICKLED BEETROOT

Slice and serve with winter salads, sandwiches or cold cuts of meat.

Makes: 3 litres/ 101 fl oz (12 cups)
Prep time: 5 minutes, plus 2 weeks pickling
Cook time: 35–75 minutes
{♥}{♦}{♠}{♣}{♧}{♨}

- 1.2 litres/ 40 fl oz (5 cups) cider vinegar
- 15 g/ ½ oz (1 tablespoon) black peppercorns
- 15 g/ ½ oz (1 tablespoon) allspice berries
- 2 kg/ 4½ lb beetroot (beets), trimmed, but unpeeled

* Bring the vinegar and spices to the boil in a large saucepan over a high heat. Reduce the heat and simmer for another 10 minutes, then leave to cool.
* Put the beetroot (beets) into another saucepan, cover with water and simmer over a medium heat for 20–60 minutes until tender.
* When the beetroot are tender, drain and leave to cool, then peel and slice the beetroot to your preferred thickness. Put the beetroot into sterilized pickling jars (page 464) and cover with the strained, cooled vinegar, leaving a 1 cm/ ½ inch head space. Cover and seal.
* Keep in a cool, dark place for 2 weeks before using. Once open, keep in the fridge and use within 2 months.

Mango chutney

UNITED KINGDOM
*

PICKLED RED CABBAGE

Serve as with other British pickles – with hard cheese and roast or cold meats.

Makes: 1 kg/2 lb 3 oz
Prep time: 15 minutes,
plus 24 hours standing and 1 week pickling
Cook time: 5 minutes
{🍅}{♦}{🧂}{🍖}{�™}

- 2 red cabbages, thinly sliced
- 150 g/5 oz (½ cup plus 2 tablespoons) salt
- 1 litre/34 fl oz (4¼ cups) cider vinegar
- 1 teaspoon black peppercorns
- 1 teaspoon allspice berries
- 100 g/3½ oz (½ cup) granulated sugar
- 1 star anise
- 1 teaspoon mustard seeds

* Put the cabbage into a colander set over a bowl and cover with the salt. Cover with aluminium foil or clingfilm (plastic wrap) and leave in the fridge for 24 hours.
* The next day, rinse the cabbage under cold running water to remove the salt, then tip out the liquid from the bowl and spoon the cabbage into sterilized pickling jars (page 464).
* Put the remaining ingredients into a large saucepan and bring to the boil. Reduce the heat and simmer for 5 minutes before removing from the heat and carefully pouring over the cabbage, leaving a 1 cm/½ inch head space. Cover and seal.
* Keep in a cool, dark place for 1 week before using. Once open, keep in the fridge and use within 2 months.

UNITED KINGDOM
*

PICKLED CAPERS
OR NASTURTIUM SEEDS

Once pickled, these unripened flower buds are typically served in a butter sauce with fish – such as the one on page 104. Traditionally, however, there are two further British sauces made with capers: a brown sauce similar to an espagnole, made from a browned roux and meat stock, and a very straightforward white caper sauce made using the basic recipe on page 416. Interestingly, both the white and brown caper sauces are served with lamb and mutton. Nasturtium seeds have been pickled in place of caper buds when they could not be found.

Makes: 120 ml/4 fl oz (½ cup)
Prep time: 20 minutes, plus 24 hours brining
and 2 weeks pickling
{🍅}{♦}{🧂}{🍖}{�™}{🧂}

- 2 teaspoons table salt
- 50 g/2 oz (¼ cup) raw capers or nasturtium seeds
- 100 ml/3½ fl oz (⅓ cup plus 1 tablespoon)
wine or cider vinegar

* Put the salt into a medium bowl, add 100 ml//3½ fl oz (⅓ cup plus 1 tablespoon) water and stir until dissolved. Add the capers or seeds (if using), then cover with clingfilm (plastic wrap) and leave to soak in the fridge or a cool, dark space for 24 hours.
* Drain the capers, discarding the soaking liquid, then spoon the salted capers into sterilized pickling jars (page 464) and fill with the vinegar, leaving a 1 cm/½ inch head space. Cover and seal.
* Keep in a cool, dark place for 2 weeks before using. Once open, keep in the fridge and use within 3 months.

UNITED KINGDOM
*

PICKLED CUCUMBERS

These sweet dill pickles bring balance to a salt beef bagel or sandwich. Slice into thick lengths and don't forget the English Mustard (page 424).

Makes: 2 litres/68 fl oz (8½ cups)
Prep time: 10 minutes, plus 8–12 hours pickling
Cook time: 10 minutes
{🍅}{♦}{🧂}{🍖}{�™}

- 500 ml/17 fl oz (2 cups plus 1 tablespoon)
cider or wine vinegar
- 50–100 g/2–3½ oz (¼–½ cup) caster (superfine) sugar
- 1 kg/2¼ lb cucumbers, halved
- 2 shallots, thinly sliced
- 2 sprigs dill
- 30 g/1 oz (2 tablespoons) salt

* Bring the vinegar and sugar to a simmer in a large saucepan over a medium heat, stirring until the sugar has dissolved, then remove from the heat.
* Put the cucumbers, shallots, dill and salt into a large bowl, making sure that the salt has been evenly spread over the vegetables. Spoon the vegetables into sterilized pickling jars (page 464) and pour over the pickling liquid, leaving a 1 cm/½ inch head space. Cover and seal.
* Keep in a cool, dark place overnight before using. Once open, keep in the fridge and use within 2 months.

UNITED KINGDOM
*
PICKLED ONIONS

A mainstay of the ploughman's lunch and chip shop counters alike, these tiny pickled onions soften and lose their bite as they ferment, picking up a slightly sweet, or even hot and spicy flavour depending on the brine used. This recipe is for the former category.

Makes: 1 kg/ 2 lb 3 oz
Prep time: 10 minutes, plus 8–12 hours standing, and 3–4 weeks pickling
Cook time: 10 minutes
{♨}{◆}{♨}{♨}{☛}

- 1 kg/ 2¼ lb whole small onions, peeled
- 150 g/ 5 oz (½ cup plus 2 tablespoons) salt
- 750 ml/ 25 fl oz (3 cups) malt vinegar
- 100 g/ 3½ oz (½ cup) caster (superfine) sugar
- 1 tablespoon black peppercorns
- 1 bay leaf

* Put the onions into a large bowl and cover with the salt. Leave in the fridge overnight to remove excess water.
* The next day, strain off any water and rinse the onions under cold running water to remove the salt.
* Put the vinegar, sugar and spices into a large saucepan and stir over a medium heat for 5 minutes, or until the sugar has visibly dissolved. Remove from the heat and leave to cool.
* Spoon the onions into sterilized pickling jars (page 464) and pour over the cooled pickling liquid, leaving a 1 cm/½ inch head space. Cover and seal.
* Keep in a cool, dark place for 3–4 weeks before using. Once open, keep in the fridge and use within 3 months.

UNITED KINGDOM
*
PICKLED EGGS

The quintessential pub snack of yore, also found in any self-respecting fish and chip shop. The English cookery writer Dorothy Hartley also imparts some fantastic insight into traditional pickled eggs, sharing that they were 'held in high esteem by all farmhouse epicures'.

Makes: 2 litres/ 68 fl oz (8½ cups)
Prep time: 10 minutes, plus 1 week pickling
Cook time: 20 minutes
{♨}{♨}{♨}{☛}{🍲}

- 12 eggs, at room temperature
- 750 ml/ 25 fl oz (3 cups) cider vinegar
- 2 dried chillies
- 2 cm/ ¾ inch piece fresh root ginger, peeled and sliced
- 1 tablespoon coriander seeds
- 1 tablespoon black peppercorns
- 2 bay leaves

* Fill a large saucepan about two-thirds full with water and bring to the boil. Using a slotted spoon, carefully lower the eggs into the boiling water and cook for 10 minutes,

or until hard-boiled. Cool the eggs quickly by running under cold water at the same time as you carefully tip all the hot water down the drain. Peel the eggs and set aside.
* Put the remaining ingredients into the emptied saucepan and simmer over a medium heat for 5 minutes. Remove from the heat and leave to cool.
* Meanwhile, pack the eggs into large sterilized pickling jars (page 464). Pour in the cooled vinegar, leaving a 1 cm/½ inch head space, then cover and seal.
* Keep in a cool, dark place for 1 week before using. Once open, keep in the fridge and use within 2 months.
* **Notes:** If there's not enough vinegar in the pickling liquid, top up (top off) with some more from the bottle. If there's too much, then set aside to use later in salad dressings.

UNITED KINGDOM
*
BREAD
AND
BUTTER PICKLE

This common household pickle is made using thinly sliced cucumbers and onions, and a slightly sweet brine flecked with mustard (and sometimes celery) seeds. Use on sandwiches – or any occasion that calls for bread and butter.

Makes: 750 ml/ 25 fl oz (3 cups)
Prep time: 10 minutes, plus 1–2 weeks pickling
Cooking: 10 minutes
{♨}{◆}{♨}{♨}{☛}{🍲}

- 3 large pickling cucumbers
- 400 ml/ 14 fl oz (1⅔ cups) cider or white vinegar
- 200 g/ 7 oz (1 cup) caster (superfine) sugar
- 40 g/ 1 ½ oz (3 tablespoons) salt
- 1 tablespoon celery seeds
- 1 tablespoon yellow mustard seeds
- 1 teaspoon ground turmeric
- 2 white onions, sliced

* Cut the cucumber into circles, about 3 mm/⅛ inch thick.
* Heat the vinegar, sugar, salt and spices in a large saucepan over a medium heat, stirring until the sugar has dissolved. Bring to the boil, then remove from the heat and leave to cool to room temperature.
* Put the cucumber and onions into sterilized pickling jars (page 464). Pour over the pickling liquid, leaving a 1 cm/½ inch head space, then cover and seal.
* Keep in a cool, dark place for 1–2 weeks before using. Once open, keep in the fridge and use within 3 months.

UNITED KINGDOM
*

PICKLED WALNUTS

Early every summer unripe walnuts are gathered while soft
and green, and pickled in a sweet, well-spiced brine. The
walnuts, which turn black in the process, are frequently
served with meat (both hot and cold), as well as savoury pies,
casseroles and stews. The walnuts – or even their pickling
brine – can also be used in making a classic British Steak
Sauce (page 418) or they can be served with Cheddar, roast
meat or used to make Walnut Ketchup (page 425).

Makes: 2.25 litres/76 fl oz (9½ cups)
Prep time: 20 minutes, plus 2 weeks brining,
24 hours drying and 2 months pickling
Cook time: 10 minutes
{🖐}{◆}{🏛}{🐟}

- 450 g/16 oz (1¾ cups plus 2 tablespoons) salt
- 1 kg/2¼ lb green walnuts
- 1 litre/34 fl oz (4¼ cups) malt vinegar
- 400 g/14 oz (2 cups) soft brown sugar
- 1 teaspoon black peppercorns
- ½ teaspoon allspice berries
- ½ teaspoon cloves
- 1 small cinnamon stick
- 1 teaspoon grated fresh root ginger

* Pour 1 litre/34 fl oz (4¼ cups) water into a large
  saucepan, add half of the salt and stir to combine. Bring
  to the boil, then remove from the heat and leave to cool.
* Prick the walnuts with a fork and submerge in the brine.
  Cover, and leave for a week in a cool, dark place, then
  drain and refresh the walnuts with a new brine, using
  the remaining salt. Leave for another week. They should
  start to go black. Remove the walnuts from the brine and
  leave to dry on a wire rack for 24 hours. They should
  have turned completely black.
* Put the vinegar, sugar and spices into a medium saucepan,
  stir to combine and bring to the boil. Remove from
  the heat and leave to cool, then remove and discard the
  cinnamon stick. Spoon the walnuts into sterilized pickling
  jars (page 464), then strain the pickling liquid over the top,
  leaving a 1 cm/½ inch head space. Cover and seal.
* Keep in a cool, dark place for 2 months before using. Once
  open, keep in the fridge and use within 3 months.
* **Note:** The walnuts should be picked before they ripen
  and their shells start to harden, around June. To check
  if they are good to use, poke the walnut with a needle.
  If you can feel a hard shell inside the outer flesh of the
  walnut they are too ripe.

UNITED KINGDOM
*

PICCALILLI

This chunky mustard pickle is made from a mix of vegetables
and is tangy and a little sweet. Similar to chutney, piccalilli
is a British adaptation of a traditional Indian style of pickle,
which varies from region to region. Early versions of piccalilli
first start to appear in English cookbooks of the eighteenth
century, including those by Hannah Glasse and Elizabeth
Raffald. Serve with cold meats, hand-raised savoury pies and
hard cheeses.

Makes: 1.5 litres/50 fl oz (6¼ cups)
Prep time: 20 minutes,
plus 24 hours soaking and 1 month pickling
Cook time: 20 minutes
{🖐}{◆}{🏛}{🐟}{🌶}

- 1–1.2 kg/2¼–2½ lb mixed vegetables, such as cauliflower,
  courgettes (zucchini), cucumbers, pickling/button onions,
  runner (string) beans, bell peppers, chillies
- 60 g/2¼ oz (¼ cup) salt
- 1 teaspoon cumin seeds
- 2 teaspoons ground turmeric
- 2 teaspoons English mustard powder
- 1 tablespoon mustard seeds
- 30 g/1 oz (¼ cup) cornflour (cornstarch)
- 500 ml/17 fl oz (2 cups plus 1 tablespoon)
  cider or wine vinegar
- 200 g/7 oz (1 cup) granulated sugar

* Cut the vegetables into coarse 1 cm/½ inch chunks
  and put into a large bowl. Add the salt and stir through
  well. Cover with a dish towel and leave to stand at room
  temperature for 24 hours.
* Put the spices, cornflour (cornstarch) and 3 tablespoons
  of the vinegar into a large heatproof bowl and mix
  together to form a paste. Set aside.
* Pour the remaining vinegar into a small saucepan, stir
  in the sugar and bring to the boil. Remove from the
  heat and beat about 475 ml/16 fl oz (2 cups) of this
  hot liquor into the spice mixture. Whisk well and pour
  the contents back into the pan to rejoin the hot sweet
  vinegar. Simmer for 5 minutes.
* Rinse and drain the vegetables, shaking and squeezing away
  any excess water before folding them through the vinegar
  mixture. Spoon into sterilized pickling jars (page 464),
  leaving a 1 cm/½ inch head space, then cover and seal.
* Keep in a cool, dark place for 1 month before using. Once
  open, keep in the fridge and use within 3 months.

Piccalilli

BIBLIOGRAPHY
AND
INDEX

Acton, Eliza. *Modern Cookery for Private Families.* London: Quadrille Publishing, (1845) 2011.

Allen, Darina. *Irish Traditional Cooking.* London: Kyle Books, 2002.

Armitage, Marian. *Shetland Food and Cooking.* Lerwick: Shetland Times Ltd, 2014.

Bareham, Lindsey. *A Celebration of Soup.* London: Penguin, 2001.

Be-Ro Home Recipes, twentieth edition. Newcastle, Thomas Bell & Sons, 1930.

Beckwith, Lillian. *Lillian Beckwith's Hebridean Cookbook.* London: Arrow Books, 1978.

Beeton, Isabella. *Mrs Beeton's Book of Household Management,* London: Ward Lock, (1861) 1992.

Black, Maggie. *A Heritage of British Cooking.* London: Letts, 1977.

Boxer, Arabella. *Arabella Boxer's Book of English Food: A Rediscovery of British Food From Before the War,* revised and updated edition. London: Fig Tree, 2012.

Brears, Peter. *Traditional Food in Yorkshire.* London: Prospect Books, 2014.

British Cookery. Edited by Lizzie Boyd. Beckenham: Croom Helm Ltd, 1978.

Brown, Catherine. *A Year in a Scots Kitchen.* Glasgow: Neil Wilson Publishing, 1998.

Brown, Catherine. *Broths to Bannocks.* Glasgow: Waverley Books, 2010.

Brown, Catherine. *Scottish Cookery,* new edition. Edinburgh: Mercat Press, 2006.

Brown, Catherine. *Scottish Regional Recipes,* third edition. Edinburgh: Chambers, 1995.

Brown, Pete. *Pie Fidelity: In Defense of British Food.* London: Particular Books, 2019.

Byron, May. *Puddings, Pastries, and Sweet Dishes.* London: Hodder and Stoughton, 1929.

Carter, Charles. *The Complete Practical Cook.* Farmington Hills: Gale ECCO, (1730), 2010.

Cheshire Cookery Book, fifth edition, compiled by members of the Cheshire Federation of Women's Institutes. Whitchurch: The Whitchurch Herald, 1965.

Collingham, Lizzie. *Curry: A Tale of Cooks and Conquerors.* London: Vintage, 2006.

Collingham, Lizzie. *The Biscuit: The History of a Very British Indulgence.* London: The Bodley Head, 2020.

Collingham, Lizzie. *The Hungry Empire: How Britain's Quest for Food Shaped the Modern World.* Rochester: Vintage Digital, 2017.

Collingwood, Francis and John Woollams. *The Universal Cook, and City and Country Housekeeper.* Gale ECCO, (1792), 2018.

Colman, Andrews. *The British Table.* New York: Abrams, 2016.

Conran, Caroline. *British Cooking.* Colchester: Park Lane, 1978.

Cowan, Eleanor. *Traditional Scottish Recipes,* illustrated edition. Glasgow: Waverley Books Ltd, 2009.

Croeso Cymreig, A Welsh Welcome: Recipes for Some Traditional Welsh Dishes, revised edition. Cardiff: Wales Gas Board, 1963.

Croft-Cooke, Rupert. *English Cooking.* London: W.H. Allen, 1960.

Cumberland Women's Institute. *The Cumberland Federation of Women's Institutes Cookery Book,* sixth edition. Carlisle: The Cumberland Federation of Women's Institutes, 1972.

David, Elizabeth. *English Bread and Yeast Cookery.* UK edition. London: Penguin, 2001.

David, Elizabeth. *Spices, Salt and Aromatics in the English Kitchen.* London: Penguin, 1976.

Davidson, Alan. *The Oxford Companion to Food* (Third Edition), edited by Tom Jaine. Oxford: Oxford University Press, 2006.

Davies, Gilli. *Flavours of Wales Collection.* Llanelli: Graffeg, 2016.

Defoe, Daniel. *A Tour Through the Whole Island of Great Britain,* revised edition. London: Penguin, 2005.

Devon Women's Institute. *The Devon Women's Institute Cookery Book.* Wellington: Halsgrove, 1987

Dickson Wright, Clarissa. *A History of English Food.* London: Arrow, 2012.

Digby, Kenelm. *The Closet of the Eminently Learned Sir Kenelme Digbie Opened,* edited by Jane Stevenson & Peter Davidson. London: Prospect Books, (1669) 1997.

Dorset Federation of Women's Institutes. *The Dorset Women's Institute Cookery Book.* Wellington: Halsgrove, 1990.

Drummond, J.C. and Anne Wilbraham. *The Englishman's Food: A History of Five Centuries of English Diet,* revised edition. London: Pimlico, 1994.

Drysdale, Julia. *Classic Game Cookery.* London: Macmillan, 1987.

Duff, Julie. *Cakes Regional & Traditional.* London: Grub Street Publishing, 2015.

Eating For Victory. London: Michael O'Mara Books, 2007.

Edington, Sarah. *Classic British Cooking.* London: National Trust, 2018.

Edington, Sarah. *The National Trust Complete Traditional Recipe Book.* London: National Trust, 2010.

Evans, Hugh. *The Gorse Glen.* Liverpool: Brython Press, 1948.

Farley, John. *The London Art of Cookery, and Housekeeper's Complete Assistant,* seventh edition. Gale ECCO, (1792) 2018.

Farmers Weekly. *Farmhouse Fare.* London: Countrywise Books, 1973.

Fearnley-Whittingstall, Hugh. *The River Cottage Cookbook.* London: Collins, 2011.

Fenton, Alexander. *Scottish Life and Society: The Food of the Scots: A Compendium of Scottish Ethnology Volume 5.* Edinburgh: John Donald Publishers Ltd, 2007.

FitzGibbon, Theodora. *A Taste of Ireland: In Food and Pictures.* London: W&N, 1994.

FitzGibbon, Theodora. *The Art of British Cooking.* London: Dent, 1979.

FitzGibbon, Theodora. *Traditional Scottish Cookery.* London: HarperCollins, 1980.

FitzGibbon, Theodora. *Traditional West Country Cookery.* London: HarperCollins, 1982.

Fletcher, Nichola. *Nichola Fletcher's Ultimate Venison Cookery.* Stroud: Swan Hill Press, 2007.

Fletcher, Nichola. *The Scottish Oats Bible.* Edinburgh: Birlinn, 2016.

Fletcher, Nichola. *The Venison Bible,* illustrated edition. Edinburgh: Birlinn Ltd, 2015.

Floyd, Keith. *Floyd on Britain and Ireland.* London: BBC Books, 1988.

Freeman, Bobby. *First Catch Your Peacock: The Classic Guide to Welsh Food,* rev. edition. Aberystwyth: Y Lolfa, 2006.

Glasgow Queen's College. *The Glasgow Cookery Book: Centenary Edition.* Glasgow: Waverley Books, 2009.

Glasse, Hannah. *The Art of Cookery Made Plain and Easy.* Mineola, New York: Dover Publications Inc, 2018.

Green, Henrietta. *Food Lovers' Guide to Britain.* London: Ebury Publishing, 1993.

Griggs, Annie M. Chambers. *Cookery for Young Housewives.* London: W. & R. Chambers, 1901.

Grigson, Jane. *Good Things.* London: Penguin, 1973.

Grigson, Jane. *Jane Grigson's English Food,* revised edition. London: Penguin Books, 1998.

Grigson, Jane. *Jane Grigson's Fish Book.* London: Penguin Books, 1998.

Grigson, Jane. *Jane Grigson's Vegetable Book.* London: Penguin Books, 1998.

Gwynn, Mary. *The WI Cookbook: The First 100 Years.* London: Ebury Press, 2015.

Hartley, Dorothy. *Food in England.* London: Little, Brown Book, 1954.

Hartley, Dorothy. *Lost Country Life.* London: Random House, 1981.

Heathcote, Paul. *Rhubarb & Black Pudding.* London: Fourth Estate, 1998.

Heaton, Nell. *A Calendar of Country Receipts.* London: Faber and Faber, 1950.

Heaton, Nell. *Home-Made Sweets.* London: Faber and Faber, 1949.

Heaton, Nell. *The Complete Cook.* London: Faber and Faber, 1948.

Heaton, Nell. *Traditional Recipes of the British Isles.* London: Faber and Faber, 1952.

Henderson, Fergus and Trevor Gulliver. *The Book of St John.* London: Ebury Press, 2019.

Henderson, Fergus. *Nose to Tail Eating: A Kind of British Cooking.* London: Bloomsbury, 2004.

Hix, Mark. *British Regional Food: A cook's tour of the best produce in Britain and Ireland with traditional and original recipes.* London: Quadrille Publishing, 2008.

Hix, Mark. *British Seasonal Food.* London: Quadrille, 2008.

Hope, Annette. *A Caledonian Feast.* Edinburgh: Canongate Books, 2002.

Hopkinson, Simon and Lindsey Bareham. *The Prawn Cocktail Years.* London: Penguin, 2008.

Hopkinson, Simon with Lindsey Bareham. *Roast Chicken and Other Stories: A Recipe Book*. London: Ebury Press, 1999.

Hutchins, Sheila. *English Recipes and Others from Scotland, Wales, and Ireland*. London:

Jack, Florence B, *Cookery for Every Household*. Edinburgh: Thomas Nelson and Sons, 1914.

Jaffrey, Madhur. *Madhur Jaffrey's Ultimate Curry Bible*. London: Ebury Press, 2003.

Johnstone, Christian Isobel. *The Cook and Housewife's Manual, by Margaret Dods*. Andesite Press, (1826) 2015.

Lady Clark of Tillypronie. *The Cookery Book of Lady Clark of Tillypronie, with an introduction by Geraldene Holt*. Lewes, Sussex: Southover Press, 1997.

Lady Llanover. *Good Cookery from Wales*. Ludlow: Excellent Press, (1867) 2006.

Lamb, Patrick. *Royal Cookery*. Farmington Hills: Gale ECCO, (1710), 2010.

Lander, William, Daniel Morgenthau and Shaun Searley. *The Quality Chop House*. London: Quadrille Publishing, 2019.

Laudan, Rachel. *Cuisine and Empire: Cooking in World History*, reprint edition. Oakland: University of California Press, 2015.

Lawrence, Sue. *Scottish Baking*. Edinburgh: Birlinn, 2014.

Lawrence, Sue. *The Scottish Soup Bible*. Edinburgh: Birlinn, 2017.

Little, May. *A Year's Dinners, 365 seasonable dinners with instructions for cooking*. London: Harrods, 1900.

Lloyd George's Favourite Dishes Cardiff, edited by Bobby Freeman. Cardiff: John Jones Cardiff Ltd, 1974.

Lockhart, G.W. *The Scots and Their Fish*. Edinburgh: Birlinn, 1997.

Lockhart, G.W. *The Scots and Their Oats*. Edinburgh: Birlinn, 1998.

Lothian, Elizabeth. *Devonshire Flavour: A Cookery Book with a Difference*. Newton Abbot: David & Charles, 1976.

Luard, Elizabeth. *European Peasant Cookery*. London: Grub Street, 2004.

MacMillan, Norma. *The Women's Institutes' Book of 650 Favourite Recipes*. London: Treasure Press, 1992.

Markham, Gervase. *The English Housewife*, edited by Michael R. Best. Montreal: McGill-Queen's University Press, (1615) 1994.

Martin, Martin. *A Description of the Western Islands of Scotland, Circa 1695: A Voyage to St Kilda*. Edinburgh: Birlinn, (1697) 2018.

Mason, Laura with Catherine Brown. *Traditional Foods of Britain: A Regional Inventory* (2nd edition). London: Prospect Books, 2004.

Mason, Laura. *Good Old-Fashioned Roasts*. London: National Trust, 2009.

Mason, Laura. *The National Trust Farmhouse Cookbook*. London: National Trust, 2009.

May, Robert. *The Accomplisht Cook*. Fili-Quarian Classics, (1660) 2010.

McNeill, F. Marian. *The Scots Kitchen: Its Tradition and Lore with Old-time Recipes*. London: HarperCollins, (1929) 1974.

Mennell, Stephen. *All Manners of Food: Eating and Taste in England and France from the Middle Ages to the Present*, 2nd edition. Champaign, Illinois: University of Illinois Press, 1995.

Misson, Henri. *M. Misson's Memoir's and Observations in his Travels over England with some account of Scotland and Ireland*, translated by Mr Ozell. London: D. Browne, A. Bell, J. Darby, A. Bettesworth, J. Pemberton, C. Rivington, J. Hooke, R. Crustenden, T. Cox, J. Batley, F. Clay, and E. Symon, 1719.

Morton, James & Tom. *Shetland: Cooking on the Edge of the World*. London: Quadrille, 2018.

Norwak, Mary. *Best of British Cooking*. London: HarperCollins, 1984.

Norwak, Mary. *English Puddings: Sweet and Savoury*. London: Grub Street, 2015.

Norwak, Mary. *The WI Book of Bread and Buns*. London: Women's Institute, 1984.

Norwak, Mary. *The WI Book of Fish and Seafood*. London: Ebury Press, 1987.

Oliver, Jamie. *Jamie's Great Britain by Jamie Oliver*. London: Penguin Book, 2011.

Outlaw, Nathan. *Nathan Outlaw's British Seafood*. London: Quadrille, 2012.

Patten, Marguerite. *Jams, Preserves, and Chutneys*. London: Grub Street, 2001.

Petty, Florence. *The Pudding Lady's Recipe Book*. London: G. Bell & Sons, 1917.

Rabisha, William. *The Whole Body of Cookery Dissected*. London: Prospect Books, (1682) 2003.

Reader's Digest. *Farmhouse Cookery: Recipes from the Country Kitchen*. London: Reader's Digest, 1991.

Recipes from the Orkney Islands, 2nd edition, edited by Eileen Wolfe. Edinburgh: Steve Savage Publishers Limited, 2005.

Reid, John. *The Scots Gard'ner*. Edinburgh: Mainstream Publishing, (1685) 1988.

Rhodes, Gary. *Rhodes Around Britain*. London: BBC Books, 1994.

Saberi, Helen. *A Pudding Book*. Ludlow: Excellent Press, 2006.

Saberi, Helen. *A Sausage Book*. Ludlow: Excellent Press, 2006.

Scottish Women's Rural Institutes. *Traditional Scottish Recipes*. Edinburgh: Scottish Women's Rural Institutes, 1995.

Simmons, Jenni. *A Shetland Cookbook*. Lerwick: The Shetland Times, 1990.

Smith, Delia. *Complete Cookery Course*. London: BBC Books, 2007.

Smith, Eliza. *The Compleat Housewife*. London: Studio, (1727) 1994.

Smith, Michael. *Fine English Cookery*, 2nd edition. London: Serif, 1998.

Soyer, Alexis. *Soyer's Shilling Cookery for the People*. Whitstable: Pryor Publications, 1999.

Stein, Rick. *English Seafood Cookery*. London: Penguin, 2001.

Steven, Maisie. *The Good Scots Diet*. Edinburgh: Argyll Publishing, 2003.

Stout, Margaret B. *Cookery for Northern Wives*. Lerwick: Shetland Heritage Publications, (1925), 2008.

The Forme of Cury: A Roll of Ancient English Cookery, compiled and translated by Samuel Pegge. London: Forgotten Books, (1390) 2008.

The Gloucester Road Women's Institute. *The Gloucester Road Cookbook*. Bristol: Gloucester Road Women's Institute, 2013.

The Invention of Tradition, edited by Hobsbawm and Ranger. Cambridge: Cambridge University Press, 2012.

The Scottish Women's Rural Institutes Cookery Book: Sixth Edition. Edinburgh: Scottish Women's Rural Institutes, 1946.

The Shropshire Cookery Book, second edition. Shrewsbury: Brown & Brinnand Ltd, 1930.

The Surrey Chicken, compiled and edited by Joan Roulston & Edith Jackman. Kingswood, Surrey: The Surrey Federation of Women's Institutes, 1965.

The W.I. Diamond Jubilee Cookbook, edited by Bee Nilson. Basingstoke: Pan Books, 1977.

The Yorkshire Women's Institute. *Yorkshire Women's Institute Cookery Book*. Skipton: Dalesman Publishing Company, 1996.

Tibbott, S. Minwel. *Welsh Fare*. Cardiff: National Museum of Wales, 1974.

Vogler, Pen. *Scoff: A History of Food and Class in Britain*. London: Atlantic Books, 2020.

Watts, Mary. *The Complete Farmhouse Kitchen Cookbook*. London: HarperCollins, 1993.

Webb, Andrew. *Food Britannia*. London: Random House Books, 2011.

White, Florence. *Good Things in England: A Practical Cookery Book for Everyday Use*, new edition. London: Persephone Books Ltd, 1999.

Whyte, Hamish, and Catherine Brown. *A Scottish Feast: An Anthology of Food and Eating*. Edinburgh: Argyll Publishing, 1996.

Wilson, C. Anne. *Food & Drink in Britain: From the Stone Age to the 19th Century*. Chicago: Academy Chicago Publishers, 1991.

Yates, Annette. *Traditional Welsh Home Cooking: 65 Classics*. Braintree, Essex: Lorenz, 2017.

Ysewijn, Regula. *Oats in the North, Wheat from the South: The History of British Baking, Savoury and Sweet*. London: Murdoch Books, 2020.

The following additional publications were also consulted during the research phase of the book, but lack publishing information or year of publication: *Glamorgan Cookbook* by the Glamorgan Federation of Women's Institutes, *Oxfordshire Federation of Women's Institutes Cook Book*, The Federation of Women's Institutes of Northern Ireland's *The WI Cookbook*, the *North Yorkshire West WI Cookery Book*, and the *Somerset Federation of Women's Institute's Somerset Cookery Book*.

RECIPE NOTES

* Butter is unsalted, unless specified otherwise. Eggs are assumed to be medium (UK)/large (US) and preferably organic and free-range. Herbs are always fresh, unless indicated otherwise. Onions are medium yellow onions, unless specified otherwise.

* Cooking and preparation times are for guidance only, as individual ovens vary. If using a fan (convection) oven, follow the manufacturer's instructions concerning oven temperatures.

* Both metric and imperial measures are used in this book. Follow one set of measurements throughout, not a mixture, as they are not interchangeable.

* All spoon and cup measurements are level, unless otherwise stated. 1 teaspoon = 5 ml; 1 tablespoon = 15 ml. Australian standard tablespoons are 20 ml, so Australian readers are advised to use 3 teaspoons in place of 1 tablespoon when measuring small quantities.

* When no quantity is specified, for example of oils, salts, and herbs used for finishing dishes, quantities are discretionary and flexible.

* Exercise caution when making fermented products, ensuring all equipment is spotlessly clean, and seek expert advice if in any doubt.

* Exercise a high level of caution when following recipes involving any potentially hazardous activity including the use of high temperatures, open flames and when deep-frying. In particular, when deep-frying, add food carefully, wear long sleeves, and never leave the pan unattended.

* All herbs, shoots, flowers and leaves should be picked fresh from a clean source. Do exercise caution when foraging for ingredients, which should only be eaten if an expert has deemed them safe to eat. In particular, do not gather wild mushrooms yourself before seeking the advice of an expert who has confirmed their suitability for human consumption. As some species of mushrooms have been known to cause allergic reaction and illness, do take extra care when cooking and eating mushrooms and do seek immediate medical help if you experience a reaction after preparing or eating them.

* Some recipes include raw or very lightly cooked eggs, meat or fish, and fermented products. These should be avoided by the elderly, infants, pregnant women, convalescents and anyone with an impaired immune system.

* When sterilizing jars, wash the jars in clean, hot water and rinse thoroughly. Heat the oven to 140°C/275°F/Gas Mark 1. Place the jars on a baking sheet and place in the oven to dry.

BEN MERVIS

Ben Mervis is a well-respected food historian, researcher and writer. He has worked at Noma restaurant in Copenhagen, as a contributor and researcher on Netflix's *Chef's Table*, and in 2017 launched the magazine *Fare*, an exploration of city culture through food, history and community. Ben has worked alongside chefs from around the UK to draw together the collection of dishes for *The British Cookbook*.

Phaidon Press Limited
2 Cooperage Yard
London E15 2QR

Phaidon Press Inc.
65 Bleecker Street
New York NY 10012

phaidon.com

First published 2022
Reprinted 2023
© 2022 Phaidon Press Limited

ISBN 978 1 83866 528 9

Ben Mervis has asserted his right under the Copyright, Designs and Patents Act 1988 to be identified as author of this work.

Jeremy Lee has asserted his right under the Copyright, Designs and Patents Act 1988 to be identified as author of the foreword to this work.

A CIP catalogue record for this book is available from the British Library and the Library of Congress.

All rights reserved. No part of this publication may be reproduced, stored in a retrieval system or transmitted, in any form or by any means, electronic, mechanical, photocopying, recording or otherwise, without the written permission of Phaidon Press Limited.

Commissioning Editor: Emilia Terragni
Project Editor: Rachel Malig
Production Controller: Sarah Kramer and Marina Asenjo
Photography: Sam A Harris
Food Stylist: Rosie Mackean
Typesetting: Cantina

Designed by Julia Hasting

Printed in China

The publisher would like to thank Vanessa Bird, James Brown, Lynne Griffin, Sophie Hodgkin, Susan Low, Rosie Mackean, João Mota, May Rosenthal Sloan, Ellie Smith, Caroline Stearns, Kathy Steer and Ana Rita Teodoro for their work on this book.